GENEALOGICAL PERIODICAL ANNUAL INDEX

KEY TO THE GENEALOGICAL LITERATURE

Anna Liisa Fielding, Compiler/Editor
Leslie K. Towle, Editor

VOLUME 34 1995

Copyright 1998
by Heritage Books Inc.

Published 1998 by

HERITAGE BOOKS INC.
1540E Pointer Ridge Place
Bowie, Maryland 20716
800-398-7709

ISBN 0-7884-0947-6

A Complete Catalog Listing Hundreds of Titles on
Genealogy, History, and Americana
Available Free Upon Request

INTRODUCTION

The Genealogical Periodical Annual Index is the only comprehensive surname, locality, topical, and book review index to English-language genealogical periodical literature available today. The current edition covers about 350 publications with approximately 13,000 index citations.

All of the periodicals indexed in GPAI are contributed by their publishers for that purpose. If your periodical was not indexed in this issue of GPAI, you can ensure its inclusion in future editions by contributing a file of back issues (to the extent possible) and a current, ongoing subscription to:

Genealogical Periodical Annual Index
Leslie K. Towle & Anna Liisa Fielding, Editors
1540E Pointer Ridge Place
Bowie, Maryland 20716

All current and back issues received will be indexed and included in the next issue of GPAI.

GPAI is protected by copyright law. No part of GPAI may be reproduced by any means without the express permission of the editors, except brief excerpts, which may be quoted for book review purposes only.

HOW TO USE GPAI

The index is based primarily on surname, locality, and topic categories. As you search for references, bear in mind that names may appear under alternative spellings. Remember also that the names of localities may have been altered or replaced over successive historical periods. As you hunt for references, try to think of alternative categories under which the desired information can be found. For example, if you are searching for information about Native American ancestors who lived in Oklahoma, look under "Native American Genealogy" as well as "Oklahoma." To assist you with this process, a list of topic categories found in GPAI has been provided on page vi.

In preparing the index entries, each article in each periodical is scanned to identify its true content, which is often not revealed adequately by its title. Reviews of genealogical, biographical, and historical books are also cited under the appropriate surname, locality, or topic headings, thus adding greatly to the researcher's ability to locate recently published genealogical material. Articles on heraldry and related subjects are also included. Surname periodicals are listed in a directory at the back of this book but are not indexed in detail. These publications are arranged alphabetically by the principal spellings of the surnames.

Articles dealing with compiled genealogical data, family records, etc., are indexed under the name of the male head of the household or family in most cases.

This is followed by his date of birth, marriage, or death when given, or by the approximate date when he lived and flourished. (When an approximate date is given, it is preceeded by the abbreviation "f," which stands for "flourished.") The names of his spouse(s) are also included in the citation, followed by the geographic areas where he and/or his descendants lived according to the article. In cases where a woman is the principal subject of an article, it is indexed under her name using an analogous format. All spouses are cross-indexed.

Each entry also provides researchers with a brief description of the type and scope of the article indexed. Abbreviations such as "geneal" and "fam rec" are used to summarize the content of articles. For indexing purposes, "geneal" means a compiled genealogical record usually covering three or more generations. "Fam rec" indicates a brief family record that covers one or two generations. "Lineage" usually refers to a multi-generation account of one line of descent. In the interest of brevity, extensive use of these abbreviations have been made. Familiarize yourself with the various abbreviations and terms used in GPAI before beginning your research. A table of abbreviations used in GPAI is provided on page vii.

Articles dealing with source records are indexed under the appropriate geographic headings. For the most part, United States locations are arranged by states. Foreign locations are indexed first by nation, then by state or province as appropriate. The citations include descriptions of the types of records appearing in each article and the time periods covered (when specified).

Book reviews are indexed under surname, locality, or topic headings just like regular articles. Book review citations include the "bk rev" abbreviation to indicate that they are not full articles. Author surnames and dates of publication are listed when provided.

At the end of every citation, there is a three letter code followed by a series of numbers separated by colons. The three letter codes identify the periodicals cited. (A table following this introduction lists the code letters for each periodical along with the addresses of the publishers and the specific issues indexed. Please see page ix.) Codes are followed by numbers that indicate the volume, issue number, and beginning page of the articles indexed, in that order.

GPAI does not index queries, society news, reprinted material, or other items of transient interest, but does index all items of permanent archival value. Because many articles could be indexed under multiple headings, but normally are not, the reader would be well advised to look for possible alternative headings and spend some time browsing through the Index. Lists of topic categories and abbreviations used in GPAI are provided to assist in the research process.

Please note that some entries may appear to be incomplete. For example, a place name or a date may be missing. This is due to the fact that periodical articles do not always supply all of the desired information. For more detail about a particular article, contact the author via the publisher.

The periodicals covered by this index can be found in most large genealogical libraries, and in many smaller libraries as well, depending upon their areas of interest. If your local library does not have the periodicals you are seeking, try to obtain them via inter-library loan. You may also purchase any back issues you need by writing to periodical publishers directly. If you choose the latter approach, send the publisher a self-addressed, stamped envelope and a request for information about availability and cost for the specific issues of interest to you.

If you wish, you may also contact the Prince George's County (Maryland) Genealogical Society, which maintains an archive of materials indexed in GPAI. Photocopies of articles contained in these periodicals are available for a nominal fee. For more information, write to:

The Prince George's County Genealogical Society
P. O. Box 819
Bowie, Maryland 20718-0819

TOPIC CATEGORIES USED IN GPAI

Acadian Genealogy
African American Genealogy
Amish Genealogy
Asian American Genealogy
Caribbean Genealogy
Civil War Genealogy
Computer Genealogy
European Genealogy
French and Indian Wars
Hispanic Genealogy
Huguenot Genealogy
Jewish Genealogy
Latin American Genealogy
Medical Genealogy
Melungeon Genealogy
Mennonite Genealogy
Methodology
Mexican War
Military Genealogy
Native American Genealogy
Orphan Genealogy
Quaker Genealogy
Religious Genealogy
Revolutionary War
Seminole War
Spanish American War
War of 1812
World History
World War I & II

ABBREVIATIONS USED IN GPAI

Please note that GPAI uses standard postal code designations for states. Keep in mind also that some abbreviations can be used to indicate multiple forms of words (i.e. "descr" can stand for "description" or "described," "FR" can stand for "France" or "French," etc.)

AA	Australia	Col	Colonial
abstr	abstract	collect	collection
AC	Alsace Lorraine	comp	compilation
acc	account		
add	addition	d	died
admin	administration	dau	daughter
Am	American	DC	District of Columbia
anc ch	ancestor chart	DK	Denmark
anniv	anniversary	dept	department
appl	application	desc	descendant
assoc	association	descr	description, described
AU	Austria	dict	dictionary
auth	authorized	direct	directory
auto	autobiography	div	divorce
avail	available	doc	document
b	born	emig	emigrant, emigration
BA	Bavaria	EN	England, English
bapt	baptism, baptised	ency	encyclopedia
Bar	Baron, Baroness	Epis	Episcopal
BC	British Columbia	Eur	Europe, European
BE	Belgium	Evang	Evangelical
bibl	bibliography		
biog	biography	f	flourished
bk	book	fam	family
BM	Bermuda	fed	federal, federation
BO	Bohemia	FI	Finland
bro	brother	FR	France, French
bus	business	GR, GE	Germany, German
		geneal	genealogy
c	circa	gov	governor
cat	catalog	govt	government
Capt	Captain	grad	graduates
Cath	Catholic	guard	guardianship
cem	cemetery		
cert	certificate	h	husband
ch	church	hist	history, historical
child	children	HO	Holland
CN	Canada, Canadian	HG	Hungary, Hungarian
Co	county		

vii

		pet	petition
inscr	inscription	photo	photograph
imm	immigrant, immigration	PO	Poland, Polish
inv	inventory	pop	population
IR	Ireland, Irish	Pres	Presbyterian
Isl	Island	Prot	Protestant
IY	Italy, Italian	PU	Prussia, Prussian
		publ	publication
jour	journal		
JP	Japan, Japanese	QB	Quebec
LDS	Latter Day Saints	rec	record
lib	library	recoll	recollections
lic	license	reg	register, regiment
Luth	Lutheran	res	research
LX	Luxembourg	Rev	Revolutionary, Reverend
		rev	review
m	married	RU	Russia, Russian
mag	magazine		
marr	marriage	sch	school
Menn	Mennonite	sched	schedule
Meth	Methodist	soc	society
mil	military	SN	Sweden
misc	miscellaneous	SP	Spain, Spanish
mort	mortality	St	Saint
mss	manuscripts	ST	Scotland
Mtn	Mountain	supp	supplement
MX	Mexico	SW	Switzerland
natu	naturalization	thru	through
NB	New Brunswick	trans	transcription
news	newspaper	twp	township
NF	Newfoundland		
NL	Netherlands	Univ	University
NS	Nova Scotia		
NW	Norway, Norwegian	vol	volume, volunteer
		vr	vital records
ON	Ontario	vet	veteran
obit	obituary		
ofc	office	w	wife
		w/	with
pass	passenger	WE	Wales
PE	Prince Edward Island	wid	widow
period	periodical	WW	World War

PERIODICAL DIRECTORY

AB - Appleland Bulletin, Wenatchee Area Genealogical Society, P O Box 5280, Wenatchee, WA 98807-5280 23:1- -3-4
ACG - American Canadian Genealogist, American Canadian Genealogical Society, P O Box 6478, Manchester, NH 03108-6478 21:1-2- -4 22:1
ACH - Bulletin, Athens County Historical Society & Museum, 65 N Court St, Athens, OH 45701-2506 16:5-6 17:3
AFH - Alabama Family History & Genealogical Newsletter, NC-AL Genealogical Society, P O Box 13, Cullman, AL 35056 16:1-2- -4
AG - American Genealogist, David L. Greene, P O Box 398, Demorest, GA 30535-0398 70:1-2- -4
AGE - Acadian Genealogy Exchange, Janet B. Jehn, 863 Wayman Branch Rd, Covington, KY 41015-2201 24:1-2&3-4
AGM - Magazine, Alabama Genealogical Society, Samford University Library, 800 Lakeshore Dr, P O Box 2296, Birmingham, AL 35229-0001 27:1&2-3&4
AGS - Quarterly, Austin Genealogical Society, P O Box 1507, Austin, TX 78767-1507 36:2-3-4
AH - Ancestor Hunt, Ashtabula County Genealogical Society, 860 Sherman St, Geneva, OH 44041-9101 22:2- -4
AHS - Androscoggin History, Androscoggin Historical Society, Douglas I. Hodgkin, County Building, Auburn, ME 04210 95:14-15-16
AMG - American Genealogy Magazine, Datatrace Systems, P O Box 1587, Stephenville, TX 76401 9:6 10:2&3-4
ANC - Ancestry, Palm Beach County Genealogical Society, P O Box 1746, West Palm Beach, FL 33402-1746 30:1-2-3
ANE - Journal, Aberdeen & Northeast Scotland Family History Society, 164 King St, Aberdeeen, Scotland, AB24 5BD 95:54-55-56-57
APG - Quarterly, Association Of Professional Genealogists, P O Box 40393, Denver, CO 80204 10:1-2-3-4
APR - Appalachian Roots, P O Box 165, Davisville, WV 26142 14:1-2- -4- -6-7- - - -11-12
AQ - Quarterly, Anchorage Genealogical Society, P O Box 212265, Anchorage, AK 99521 6:1- -3-4
ARH - Arkansas Family Historian, Arkansas Genealogical Society, P O Box 908, Hot Springs, AR 71902-0908 33:1-2-3-4
ARN - Arkansas Historical & Genealogical Magazine, Professional Genealogists Of Arkansas Inc., P O Box 1807, Conway, AR 72033 8:1-2-3-4
ASO - Augustan Society Omnibus, Sir Rodney Hartwell, P O Box P, Torrance, CA 90508 25:1
ATE - Ash Tree Echo, Fresno Genealogical Society, P O Box 1429, Fresno, CA 93716 30:1-2
AU - Ancestors Unlimited, Southwest Nebraska Genealogy Society, P O Box 156, Mccook, NE 69001 18:4 19:1-2-3-4
AUQ - Ancestors Unlimited Quarterly, Barry County Genealogical & Historical Society, P O Box 291, Cassville, MO 65625 6:1- - -4
AW - Ancestors West, Santa Barbara County Genealogical Society, P O Box 1303, Goleta, CA 93116-1303 21:2-3 22:1-2

BAT - Vermont Genealogist, Genealogical Society Of Vermont, P O Box 1553, St Albans, VT 05478-1006 24:2
BC - Bethel Courier, Bethel Historical Society, P O Box 12, Bethel, ME 04217-0012 17:2 18:3-4 19:1-2-3-4
BCF - Bennington County Family Searching, RR 1 Box 141A, Shaftsbury, VT 05262 95:FEB-APR/MAY
BCN - Newsletter, Bucks County Genealogical Society, P O Box 1092, Doylestown, PA 18901 14:3 15:1-2-3-4
BCS - Quarterly, Barton County Genealogical Society, P O Box 425, Great Bend, KS 67530 15:1-2-3-4
BG - Berkshire Genealogist, Berkshire Family History Association Inc., P O Box 1437, Pittsfield, MA 01202-1437 16:1-2-3-4
BGG - Newsletter, German Genealogical Society Of America, 2125 Wright Ave #C9, La Verne, CA 91750-5814 3:9
BGN - Newsletter, Blair County Genealogical Society Inc., P O Box 855, Altoona, PA 16603-0855 16:1-2- -4
BGS - Quarterly, Boulder Genealogical Society, P O Box 3246, Boulder, CO 80307-3246 27:2- -4
BHN - Black Hills Nuggets, Rapid City Society For Genealogical Research Inc., P O Box 1495, Rapid City, SD 57709 28:1-2-3-4
BM - Tri-County Searcher, Broken Mountains Genealogical Society, Box 261, Chester, MT 59522 16:1
BT - Buried Treasures, Central Florida Genealogical & Histroical Society, P O Box 177, Orlando, FL 32802-0177 26:4 27:1-2-3-4
BTG - Newsletter, Border Town Genealogical Society, P O Box 1382, 815 Juniper St, Oroville, WA 98844 1:2
BWG - Bulletin, Wautauga Association Of Genealogists, P O Box 117, Johnson City, TN 37605-0117 24:1-2
BYG - Beyond Germanna, John Blankenbaker, P O Box 120, Chadds Ford, PA 19317 7:1- -3- -5-6 8:1
CAA - Heritage Newsletter, California African American Genealogical Society, P O Box 8442, Los Angeles, CA 90008 7:6
CAL - Journal, Caldwell County Genealogical Society, P O Box 2476, Lenoir, NC 28645-2476 14:2- -4
CC - Cracker Crumbs, Manasota Genealogical Society, 1405 4th Ave West, Bradenton, FL 34205-7357 17:2-3-4 18:2
CCG - Carrolltonian, Carroll County Genealogical Society Inc., P O Box 1752, Westminster, MD 21158 14:3-4
CCK - Clark County Kin, Clark County Chapter Ohio Genealogical Society, 102 E Main St #204, Springfield, OH 45502-1314 13:2- -4
CCM - Coweta Courier, Coweta County Genealogical Society Inc., P O Box 1014, Newnan, GA 30264 14:3 15:1-2
CCS - Quarterly, Champaign County Genealogical Society, 201 S Race St, Urbana, IL 61801 16:4 17:1
CDG - Newsletter, Capital District Genealogical Society, P O Box 2175, Empire State Plaza Station, Albany, NY 12220-0175 14:2-3
CGJ - Caribbean Historical & Genealogical Journal, Peter E. Carr, P O Box 15839, San Luis Obispo, CA 93406 3:3-4

CHG - Chicago Genealogist, Chicago Genealogical Society, P O Box 1160, Chicago, IL 60690 27:2-3 28:1
CHI - Quarterly, Concordia Historical Institute, 801 Demun Ave, St. Louis, MO 63105 68:1- -3-4
CI - Quarterly, Central Illinois Genealogical Society, P O Box 1548, Decatur, IL 62525-1548 31:1-2-3-4
CL - County Line, Bay County Genealogical Society, P O Box 662, Panama City, FL 32405 14:1-2
CN - Conestoga Newsletter, Joplin Genealogy Society, P O Box 152, Joplin, MO 64802 4:1-2-3-4
CPN - Newsletter, Centre County Pennsylvania Genealogical Society, P O Box 1135, State College, PA 16804 20:1
CPY - Certified Copy, Greater Cleveland Genealogical Society, P O Box 40254, Cleveland, OH 44140-0254 24:1
CR - Circuit Rider, Sangamon County Genealogical Society, P O Box 1829, Springfield, IL 62705-1829 27:1-2- -4
CRT - Crossroad Trails, Effingham County Genealogical Society, P O Box 1166, Effingham, IL 62401 16:4
CSB - Copper State Journal, Arizona State Genealogical Society Inc., P O Box 42075, Tucson, AZ 85733-2075 30:1- -3-4
CTA - Connecticut Ancestry, Connecticut Ancestry Society Inc., P O Box 249, Stamford, CT 06904-0249 37:3-4 38:2
CTN - Connecticut Nutmegger, Connecticut Society Of Genealogists, P O Box 435, Glastonbury, CT 06033 27:4
CVH - Central Virginia Heritage, Central Virginia Genealogical Association, P O Box 5583, Charlottesville, VA 22905-5583 12:4
DAR - Daughters of the American Revolution Magazine, National Society Daughters Of The American Revolution, 1776 D Street NW, Washington, DC 20006 129:1-2-3- -5-6- -8-9
DCG - Dakota County Genealogist, Dakota County Genealogical Society, P O Box 74, South St Paul, MN 55075 9:2-3
DCH - Last Leaf, Dawson County Historical & Genealogical Society, 1477 Highway 200 South, Glendive, MT 59330-9402 6:2
DFH - Quarterly, Dutch Family Heritage Society, 2463 Ledgewood Dr, W Jordan, UT 84084 8:1-2- -4
DG - Quarterly, Dallas Genealogical Society, P O Box 12648, Dallas, TX 75225 19:2 41:1
DGS - Delaware Genealogist, Delaware County Genealogy Society, P O Box 1126, Delaware, OH 43015 11:4
DM - Magazine, Detroit Society For Genealogical Research, C/O Burton History Collection, Detroit Public Library, 5201 Woodward Ave, Detroit, Mi 48202-4093 58:3-4 59:1
DOG - Trading Path, Durham-Orange Genealogical Society, P O Box 4703, Chapel Hill, NC 27515-4703 6:1
DPL - Die Pommerschen Leute, Myron Gruenwald, 1260 Westhaven Dr, Oshkosh, WI 54904 15:SPRING 17:WINTER-SPRING 18:SPRING-SUMMER
DWC - Quarterly, Dewitt County Genealogical Society Inc., P O Box 632, Clinton, IL 61727-0632 21:1-2- -4

EK - East Kentuckian, P O Box 24202, Lexington, KY 40524-4202 31:1
ETR - East Tennessee Roots, East Tennesee Heritage Foundation, 1345 Oak Ridge Turnpike #318, Oak Ridge, TN 37830 7:3-4
EWA - Bulletin, Eastern Washington Genealogical Society, P O Box 1826, Spokane, WA 99210-1826 32:1-2-3-4
FAH - Flemish American Heritage, Genealogical Society Of Flemish Americans, 18740 13 Mile Rd, Roseville, MI 48066 13:1-2
FAM - Families, Ontario Genealogical Society, P O Box 1231, Lewiston, NY 14092 34:1-2-3-4
FC - Journal, Forsyth County Genealogical Society, P O Box 5715, Winston-Salem, NC 27113-5715 13:2-3-4 14:1
FCM - Frederick Findings, Lineage Search Associates, 7315 Colts Neck Rd, Mechanicsville, VA 23111-4233 7:4 8:2
FCN - Newsletter, Fentress County Tennessee Historical Society, P O Box 1431, Jamestown, TN 38556-1431 6:4 7:3
FCT - Freeborn County Tracer, Freeborn County Genealogical Society, 1033 Bridge Ave, Albert Lea, MN 56007-2205 95:118-119-120- -122-123-124
FGC - Footprints Of Jefferson County, Jefferson County Genealogical Society, P O Box 2215, Pine Bluff, AR 71603 95:28
FHC - Family History Capers, Washtenaw County Genealogical Society, P O Box 7155, Ann Arbor, MI 48107 19:1-2
FIR - Fort Industry Reflections, Lucas County Chapter Ohio Genealogical Society, C/O Toledo-Lucas County Library, 325 N Michigan Ave, Toledo, OH 43624-1614 15:1- - -4
FLG - Florida Genealogist, Florida State Genealogical Society, P O Box 10249, Tallahassee, FL 32302 18:1-2-3-4
FP - Footprints, Fort Worth Genealogical Society, P O Box 9767, Fort Worth, TX 76147-2767 38:1- -3-4
FPG - Newsletter, Florida Parishes Genealogical Society, P O Box 520, Livingston, LA 70754 17:1-2-3-4- -6
FRT - Family Records Today, American Family Records Association, P O Box 15505, Kansas City, MO 64106 16:2-3 17:1
FTC - Fairfield Trace, Fairfield County Chapter Ohio Genealogical Society, P O Box 1470, Lancaster, OH 43130-0570 17:2-3-4
FTP - Footsteps To The Past, Cuyahoga Valley Chapter Ohio Genealogical Society, P O Box 41414, Brecksville, OH 44141 16:3-4
FTR - Family Tree, Howard County Genealogical Society Inc., P O Box 274, Columbia, MD 21045-0274 95:177- -179- -181-182- -184
FWC - Families Of Wyoming County West Virginia, Sally Williams, P O Box 1035, N Highlands, CA 95660 12:2 9:3-4
FYC - Families Of Yancey County North Carolina, Sally Seaman-Williams, P O Box 1035, No. Highlands, CA 95660-1035 12:4
GCH - County Lines, Gibson County Historical Society, P O Box 516, Princeton, IN 47670 7:8- - -12 8:1-2- -4-5-6-7- -9- -11
GEJ - Genealogy Jottings, Jackson County Genealogical Society Inc., 415 1/2 South Poplar St, Brownstown, IN 47220-1939 14:3-4
GEN - Generations, Manitoba Genealogical Society Inc., 885 Notre Dame Ave, Winnipeg, Manitoba, Canada, R3E 0M4 20:1-2-3-4

GF - Gleanings From The West Fields, West Fields Genealogical Society, C/O Westfield Memorial Library, 550 E Broad St, Westfield, NJ 07090 16:1-2-3- -5-6
GFP - Bulletin, Genealogical Forum Of Oregon, 2130 SW 5th Ave Suite 220, Portland, OR 97201-4934 44:3-4 45:2
GG - Greene Genes, Patricia Morrow, P O Box 116, Maplecrest, NY 12454-0116 7:4 8:3
GGD - German Genealogical Digest, P O Box 112054, Salt Lake City, UT 84147 11:2-3-4
GGP - Genealogical Goldmine, Paradise Genealogical Society, P O Box 460, Paradise, CA 95967 28:1
GGS - Quarterly, Georgia Genealogical Society, P O Box 54575, Atlanta, GA 30308-0575 31:1-2
GH - Everton's Genealogical Helper, Everton Publishers, P O Box 368, Logan, UT 84323-0368 49:3-4-5-6
GJ - Genealogical Journal, Utah Genealogical Society, P O Box 1144, Salt Lake City, UT 84110-1144 22:4 23:1-2/3-4
GJB - Gleanings, Beaver County Genealogical Society, C/0 Nancy Lindemann, 3225 Dutch Ridge Rd, Beaver, PA 15009 19:3-4 20:1-2
GL - Gleanings From the Heart of the Cornbelt, McLean County Genealogical Society, P O Box 488, Normal, IL 61761 29:1- - -4
GMN - Genealogical Magazine Of New Jersey, New Jersey Genealogical Society, P O Box 1291, New Brunswick, NJ 08903 70:1- -3
GN - Nova Scotia Genealogist, Nova Scotia Genealogical Association, P O Box 641 Station Central, Halifax, Nova Scotia, Canada, B3J 2T3 13:1-2-3
GR - Genealogical Record, Houston Genealogical Forum, P O Box 271466, Houston, TX 77277 37:1-2-3-4
GRC - Geneline, Renville County Genealogical Society, P O Box 331, Renville, MN 56284 11:2
GRI - GRIVA News & Notes, Genealogical Research Institute Of Virginia, P O Box 29178, Richmond, VA 23242-0178 15:1- -3- -5
GSC - Quarterly, Carlton County Genealogical Society, P O Box 204, Cloquet, MN 55720 17:3-4 18:1
GSM - Goingsnake Messenger, Goingsnake District Heritage Association, Rt 4 Box 6, Colcord, OK 74338 12:1-2
GSN - Newsletter, Genealogical Society of New Jersey, 7 Mercer St, Hopewell, NJ 08525 8:1
GWD - Newsletter, Gateway Genealogical Society Newsletter, C/O Ruth Evans, 618 14th Ave, Comanche, IA 52730 9:1 14:2
GWS - Newsletter, Glasgow & West Of Scotland Family History Society, Unit 5 22 Mansfield St, Glasgow, Scotland, G11 5QP 95:42-43-44
HCG - Newsletter, Hood County Genealogical Society, P O Box 1623, Granbury, TX 76048 12:4 13:2-3
HER - Heraldry, Augustan Society Inc., 1313 Sartori Ave, Torrance, CA 90508 3:3
HGO - Hudson Green, Hudson Chapter Ohio Genealogical Society, Hudson Library & Historical Society, Dept G, 22 Aurora St, Hudson, OH 44236-2947 6:1-2
HH - Hawkeye Heritage, Iowa Genealogical Society, P O Box 7735, Des Moines, IA 50322-7735 30:4

HHH - Newsletter, Hamilton Heritage Hunters Genealogical Society, 943 1st St, Webster City, IA 50595-2001 16:3-4
HJA - Hoosier Journal Of Ancestry, Naomi Keith Sexton, P O Box 33, Little York, IN 47139-0033 18:3 19:1
HNH - Historic New Hampshire, New Hampshire Historical Society, 30 Park St, Concord, NH 03301 49:3-4 50:1/2-3/4
HPF - Holston Pathfinder, Holston Territory Genealogical Society, P O Box 433, Bristol, VA-TN 24203 14:52 95:50
HQ - Heritage Quest Magazine, P O Box 329, Bountiful, UT 84011-0329 95:55-57-58-59-60
HTR - Heart Of Texas Records, Central Texas Genealogical Society Inc., 1717 Austin Avenue, Waco, TX 76701 38:1- -3-4
HY - Hear Ye Hear Ye, Rochester Genealogical Society, P O Box 10501, Rochester, NY 14610 16:1-2
IAN - Newsletter, Iowa Genealogical Society, P O Box 7735, Des Moines, IA 50322 16:1- - - -5
IB - Information Bulletin, Delaware County Historical Society, P O Box 317, Delaware, OH 43015 11:1
IFL - Irish Heritage Links, Irish Heritage Association, C/O Ulster Clans Office, A204 Portview, 310 Newtownards Rd, Belfast, N Ireland, BT4 1Hl 5:8-9-10 6:1
IG - Illiana Genealogist, Illiana Genealogical & Historical Society, P O Box 207, Danville, IL 61834 31:1-2
IGS - Quarterly, Illinois State Genealogical Society, P O Box 10195, Springfield, IL 62791 27:2
IMP - Imprints, Broward County Genealogical Society Inc., P O Box 485, Ft Lauderdale, FL 33302 14:1-3
IS - Septs, Irish Genealogical Society International, P O Box 16069, St Paul, MN 55116 16:1-2-3
ISC - Iowan, Scott County Genealogical Society, P O Box 3132, Davenport, IA 52808-3132 19:1-2- -4
JBC - Journal Of Berks County Genealogical Society, P O Box 305, Kutztown, PA 19530-0305 15:4 16:1
JC - Johnston Journal, Johnston County Genealogical & Historical Society, 305 Market St, Smithfield, NC 27577 21:3
JCG - Johnson County Kansas Genealogist, Johnson County Genealogical Society & Library Inc., P O Box 12666, Shawnee Mission, KS 66282-2666 22:1-2-4
JCL - Jefferson County Lines, Jefferson County Chapter Ohio Genealogical Society, P O Box 4712, Steubenville, OH 43952-8712 9:2-3-4
JL - Judaica Librarianship, Association Of Jewish Libraries, 330 7th Ave 21st Floor, New York City, NY 10001 8:1/2
JTJ - Journeys Through Jackson, Jackson County Genealogical Society, P O Box 2108, Cullowhee, NC 28723 4:9/10
KA - Kentucky Ancestors, Kentucky Historical Society, P O Box 1792, Frankfort, KY 40602-1792 30:3-4 31:1-2
KCG - Kansas City Genealogist, Heart Of America Genealogical Society & Library Inc., C/O Kansas City Public Library, 311 East 12th St, Kansas City, MO 64106-2412 36:1-2

KFR - Kentucky Family Records, 1434 Hickory Lane, Owensboro, KY 42303 95:19

KGF - Knott's Gentlefolk & Flowers Of The Forest, Knott County Historical & Genealogical Society & Library Inc., P O Box 1023, Hindman, KY 41822 1:1/2

KIL - Quarterly, Knox County Genealogical Society, P O Box 13, Galesburg, IL 61402-0013 23:2-3-4

KK - Kansas Kin, Riley County Genealogical Society, 2005 Claflin Road, Manhattan, KS 66502-3415 33:1-2- -4

KR - Kansas Review, Kansas Council Of Genealogical Societies, P O Box 3858, Topeka, KS 66604 20:4 21:1

KSL - Kinfolks, Southwest Louisiana Genealogical Society Inc., P O Box 5652, Lake Charles, LA 70606-5652 19:1-2- -4

KTP - Keys To The Past, Kendall County Genealogical Society, P O Box 623, Boerne, TX 78006 1:1-2-3/4 2:1-2-3-4 3:1-2-3-4 4:1-2-3-4 5:1-2-3-4 6:1-2-3-4 7:1-2-3-4 8:1-2-3-4 9:1-2-3-4 10:1-2-3-4 11:1-2-3-4 12:1-2-3-4 13:1-2-3-4 14:1-2-3-4

KVH - Kalamazoo Valley Heritage, Kalamazoo Valley Genealogical Society, P O Box 405, Comstock, MI 49041 19:6-7- -9-10 20:1/2-3-4- -6

LAB - Lines & By Lines, Louisville Genealogical Society, P O Box 5164, Louisville, KY 40255-0164 10:1- - -4

LC - Quarterly, Lake County Genealogical Society, P O Box 721, Libertyville, IL 60048-0721 16:1

LG - L'estuaire Genealogique, Societe Genealogique De L'est Du Quebec, Case Postale 253, Rimouski, Quebec, Canada, G5l 7C1 95:53-54-55-56

LHS - Newsletter, Lexington Historical Society Inc., P O Box 238, Lexington, IN 47138-0238 95:2

LL - Lifeliner, Riverside Genealogical Society, P O Box 2557, Riverside, CA 92516 30:3 31:1

LLI - JGSLI Lineage, Jewish Genealogical Society Of Long Island, 37 Westcliff Dr, Dix Hills, NY 11746-5627 7:4

LM - Laurel Messenger, Somerset County Historical & Genealogical Society, 10649 Somerset Pike, Somerset, PA 15501 36:1-2-3-4

LOB - A Lot Of Bunkum, Old Buncombe County Genealogical Society, P O Box 2122, Asheville, NC 28802-2122 14:1 16:1-2- -4 17:1

LRT - Livermore Roots Tracer, Livermore-Amador Genealogical Society, P O Box 901, Livermore, CA 94550 14:2 15:1

LWF - Lest We Forget Wyoming County Pioneers, Wyoming County Historical Society, P O Box 309, Tunkhannock, PA 18657-0309 15:2

MAG - Newsletter, Morris Area Genealogy Society, P O Box 105, Convent Station, NJ 07961-0105 8:1-2-3

MCA - Marion County Alabama Tracks, Marion County Genealogical Society, P O Box 360, Winfield, AL 35594 14:1- -3-4

MCG - Herald, Montgomery County Genealogical & Historical Society Inc., P O Box 867, Conroe, TX 77305-0867 18:1/2-3/4

MCI - McHenry County Illinois Connection Quarterly, McHenry County Illinois Genealogical Society, P O Box 184, Crystal Lake, IL 60039-0184 13:1-2- -4

MCQ - Mercer County Genealogical Quarterly, P O Box 1147, Hightstown, NJ 08520 4:1-2-3

MCR - MCGS Reporter, Milwaukee County Genealogical Society Inc., P O Box 27326, Milwaukee, WI 53227-0326 26:1- - -4 27:1
MCS - Stalker, Madison County Genealogical Society, P O Box 631, Edwardsville, IL 62025 15:1-2- -4 16:5
MD - Bulletin, Maryland Genealogical Society, 201 W Monument St, Baltimore, MD 21201-4674 36:1-2- -4
MFH - Mennonite Family History, RR1 Box 20 Mill Road, Morgantown, PA 19543 14:1-2 15:1
MGR - Midwest Genealogical Register, Midwest Historical & Genealogical Society, P O Box 1121, Wichita, KS 67201 29:4 30:3
MGS - Der Kurier, Mid-Atlantic Germanic Society, P O Box 2642, Kensington, MD 20891-9762 13:1- -3-4
MH - Illinois Mennonite Heritage, Illinois Mennonite Historical & Genealogical Society Inc., P O Box 1007, Metamora, IL 61548 22:1- -3-4
MHH - Michigan's Habitant Heritage, French Canadian Heritage Society Of Michigan, P O Box 10028, Lansing, MI 48901-0028 16:1-2- -4
MHP - MHEP Quarterly, Mennonite Historians Of Eastern Pennsylvania, P O Box 82, 565 Yoder Rd, Harleysville, PA 19438 22:1-2-3-4
MI - Michigana, Western Michigan Genealogical Society, Grand Rapids Public Library, 60 Library Plaza NE, Grand Rapids, MI 49503 41:1-2- -4
MIS - Michiana Searcher, Elkhart County Genealogical Society, P O Box 1031, Elkhart, IN 46515-1031 27:2- -4
MM - Mahoning Meanderings, Mahoning County Chapter Ohio Genealogical Society, P O Box 9333, Boardman, OH 44513 19:1-2-3-4-5-6 20:2
MN - Minnesota Genealogist, Minnesota Genealogical Society, P O Box 16069, St Paul, MN 55116-0069 26:2-3-4
MSG - Journal, Missouri State Genealogical Association, P O Box 833, Columbia, MO 65205-0833 15:1- -3-4
MT - Mesquite Tree, Mesquite Historical & Genealogical Society, P O Box 850165, Mesquite, TX 75185-0165 31:3-4
MTG - Middle Tennessee Genealogy, Middle Tennessee Genealogical Society, P O Box 190625, Nashville, TN 37219 8:4 9:2
MTN - Mountain News, Hacker's Creek Pioneer Descendants, RR 1 Box 238, Jane Lew, WV 26378 1:1
NAL - Newfoundland Ancestor, Newfoundland & Labrador Genealogical Society Inc., Colonial Building, Military Road, St John's, Newfoundland, Canada, A1C 2C9 11:1-2-3-4
NC - Family Tree Quarterly, Cobb County Genealogical Society Inc., P O Box 1413, Marietta, GA 30061-1413 5:1-2-3-4
NCC - Newsletter, Cleveland County Genealogical Society, P O Box 6176, Norman, OK 73070 15:1-2
NCG - Newsletter, Nemaha County Genealogical Society, 6th & Nemaha, Seneca, KS 66538 2:3-4 3:1
NCJ - Journal, North Carolina Genealogical Society, P O Box 1492, Raleigh, NC 27602 21:1-2-3-4
NDG - North Central North Dakota Genealogical Record, Mouse River Loop Genealogical Society, P O Box 1391, Minot, ND 58702 95:62-63- -65
NEC - New England Connexion, P O Box 621, Goshen, NY 10924 3:2-3

NEH - Nexus, New England Historic Genealogical Society, 101 Newbury St, Boston, MA 02116 12:1-2/3-4-5-6
NER - New England Historical & Genealogical Register, New England Historic Genealogical Society, 101 Newbury St, Boston, MA 02116 149:593-594-595-596
NFB - Newsletter, Fellowship Of Brethren Genealogists (AKA Brethren Roots), C/O Ron McAdams, 7690 S Peters Rd, Tipp City, OH 45371 27:2-3-4
NGS - Quarterly, National Genealogical Society, 4527 17th St N, Arlington, VA 22207-2399 83:1-2-3-4
NHR - New Hampshire Genealogical Record, New Hampshire Society Of Genealogists, P O Box 2316, Concord, NH 03302 12:1-2-3-4
NPW - Kindred Spirits, Prince William County Genealogical Society, P O Box 2019, Manassas, VA 20108-0812 13:4- -6- - -9-10-11-12
NTT - Natchez Trace Traveler, Natchez Trace Genealogical Society, P O Box 420, Florence, AL 35631-0420 14:3-4 15:1/2 16:3
NW - Wagoner, Northwest Genealogical Society, P O Box 6, Alliance, NE 69301 18:1
NWS - News From The Northwest, Northwest Suburban Council Of Genealogists, P O Box AC, Mount Prospect, IL 60056-9019 15:3-4-5
NYQ - New York State Queries, W 2206 Borden Rd, Spokane, WA 99204 95:11
NYR - New York Genealogical & Biographical Record, New York Genealogical & Biographical Society, 122 East 58th St, New York, NY 10022-1939 126:1-2-3-4
OBN - Ottawa Branch News, Ontario Genealogical Society, P O Box 8346 Station T, Ottawa, Ontario, Canada, K1G 3H8 28:1-2-3-4- -6
OC - Journal, Orange County California Genealogical Society, P O Box 1587, Orange, CA 92856-1587 29:3 31:1-2
OCG - Quarterly, Orange County Genealogical Society, 101 Main St, Goshen, NY 10924-1917 25:1- -3
OCN - Newsletter, Olmsted County Genealogical Society, P O Box 6411, Rochester, MN 55903 18:1-2-3
ODD - Darlington Flag, Old Darlington District Chapter SCGS, P O Box 175, Hartsville, SC 29551 7:1-2- -4
OG - Quarterly, Olympia Genealogical Society, P O Box 1313, Olympia, WA 98507 21:1- - -4
OK - Quarterly, Oklahoma Genealogical Society, P O Box 12986, Oklahoma City, OK 73157 40:1-2
OLR - Old Lawrence Reminiscences, Lawrence County Historical Commission Inc., P O Box 728, Moulton, AL 35650-0728 9:1- -3-4
OPC - Quarterly, Pontotoc County Oklahoma Historical & Genealogical Society, 221 W 16th St, Ada, OK 74820-7603 26:3 27:1
OTC - Origins, Thomasville Genealogical, History & Fine Arts Library, P O Box 1597, Thomasville, GA 31799 4:3
OZ - Ozar'kin, Ozarks Genealogical Society, P O Box 3945, Springfield, MO 65808 17:3-4
PAF - IPAFUG Newsletter, International PAF Users Group, 2463 Ledgewood Dr, W Jordan, UT 84084-5738 7:1- -3
PB - Pioneer Branches, Northeast Washington Genealogical Society, C/O Colville Public Library, 195 South Oak, Colville, WA 99114 10:2-3-4 11:1-2

PCH - Pike County Historical Review, Pike County Society For Historical & Genealogical Research, P O Box 97, Pikeville, KY 41502 1:1-2-3-4
PCI - Newsletter, Poweshiek County Historical & Genealogical Society, P O Box 280, Montezuma, IA 50171 17:3 18:4 19:1-2
PCQ - Quarterly, Polk County Historical Association, P O Box 2749, Bartow, FL 33831 2:3-4 3:1-2-3-4 4:1-2-3-4 5:1-2-3-4 6:1-2-3-4 7:1-2-3-4 8:1-2-3-4-5 9:2-3-4 10:1-2-3-4 11:1-2-3-4 12:1-2-3-4 13:1-2-3-4 14:1-2-3-4 15:1-2-3-4 16:1-2-3-4 17:1-2-3-4 18:1-2-3-4 19:1-2-3-4 20:1- -3-4 21:1-2-3-4 22:1-2-3
PGB - Bulletin, Prince George's County Genealogical Society, P O Box 819, Bowie, MD 20718-0819 26:5-6-7- -9-10 27:2- -4
PM - Pennsylvania Mennonite Heritage, Lancaster Mennonite Historical Society, 2215 Millstream Rd, Lancaster, PA 17602 18:1- - -4 19:1
PR - Prairie Roots, Peoria County Genealogical Society, P O Box 1489, Peoria, IL 61655-1489 22:3-4 23:1-2
PT - Pioneer Trails, Birmingham Genealogical Society Inc., P O Box 2432, Birmingham, AL 35201 37:1- -3/4
PV - Newsletter, Pomona Valley Genealogical Society, P O Box 286, Pomona, CA 91769-0286 23:5-6- -8-9 24:1- -3-4
PW - Pioneer Wagon, Jackson County Genealogical Society, P O Box 2145, Independence, MO 64055 15:1- -3
PWN - Piney Woods Newsletter, Joyce & Dennis Wicks, 5333 7th Ave NE, Seattle, WA 98105 1:1-2-3-4-5 2:1-2-3-4-5-6 3:1-2
QFH - Queensland Family Historian, Queensland Family History Society Inc., P O Box 171, Indooroopilly, Queensland, Australia 4068 16:1-2- -4
QN - Newsletter, Chickasaw County Genealogical Society, P O Box 434, New Hampton, IA 50659-0434 12:3-4
QQ - Quaker Queries, Ruby Simonson McNeill Enterprises, 323 Cedarcrest Court East, P O Box 779, Napavine, WA 98565-0779 95:25
QU - Quest, Florida Chapter Ohio Genealogical Society, C/O RR #3, Box 1720, Madison, FL 32340-9531 12:1-2- -4- -6
QY - Quaker Yeoman, Patti Smith Lamb, 1190 NW 183rd Ave, Beaverton, OR 97006 21:4 22:1- -3
RAG - Rota-Gene, International Genealogy & Heraldry Fellowship Of Rotarians, 10 Fox Tail Lane, Brookfield, CT 06804 16:1-2-3-4 17:1
RCG - Newsletter, Ross County Genealogical Society, P O Box 6352, Chillicothe, OH 45601 22:3-4 23:1
RCP - Root Cellar Preserves, Sacramento Genealogical Society, P O Box 265, Citrus Heights, CA 95611 17:2-3-4 18:1
RCR - Rowan County Register, Jo White Linn, P O Box 1948, Salisbury, NC 28145-1948 10:1-2- -4
RDQ - Root Digger, Solano County Genealogical Society Inc., P O Box 2494, Fairfield, CA 94533-0249 12:1-2-3-4-5-5A
RED - Redwood Researcher, Redwood Genealogical Society Inc., P O Box 645, Fortuna, CA 95540 27:4 28:2
REF - Reflector, Amarillo Genealogical Society Quarterly, Amarillo Public Library, P O Box 2171, Amarillo, TX 79189 37:2- -4
REG - Register, Kentucky Historical Society, P O Box 1792, Frankfort, KY 40602-1792 92:4 93:2-3-4

RES - Researcher, Tacoma-Pierce County Genealogical Society, P O Box 1952, Tacoma, WA 98401 26:3 27:1
RIR - Rhode Island Roots, Rhode Island Genealogical Society, P O Box 433, Greenville, RI 02828 21:1-2-3-4
RL - Rampant Lion, Scottish Historic & Research Society Of The Delaware Valley Inc., 102 St Pauls Rd, Ardmore, PA 19003-2811 30:11 30:2-3- -5-6-7- -9
RM - Regi Magyarorszag, Hungarian American Friendship Society, 2701 Corabel Lane #34, Sacramento, CA 95821 95:8- -10
RSQ - Roots & Shoots Quarterly, Southern Ohio Genealogical Society, P O Box 414, Hillsboro, OH 45133 17:2
RT - Rabbit Tracks, Conejo Valley Genealogical Society Inc., P O Box 1228, Thousand Oaks, CA 91358-0228 13:1-2-3-4
SBA - Quarterly Newsletter, South Bend Area Genealogical Society, P O Box 1222, South Bend, IN 46624-1222 20:1-2-3-4-5- - -8
SCC - Santa Clara County Connections, Santa Clara County Historical & Genealogical Society, 2635 Homestead Road- City Library, Santa Clara, CA 95051 32:1-2
SCG - Journal, Stanly County Genealogical Society, P O Box 31, Albemarle, NC 28002-0031 14:1-2- -4 15:1
SCH - Saline, Saline County History & Heritage Society, P O Box 221, Bryant, AR 72089 10:3-4
SCM - South Carolina Magazine Of Ancestral Research, P O Box 21766, Columbia, SC 29221 23:1-2- -4
SCN - Swenson Center News, Swenson Swedish Immigration Research Center, 639 38th St, Rock Island, IL 61201-2273 95:9-10
SCR - Genealogical Record Of Strafford County NH, Strafford County Genealogical Society, P O Box 322, Dover, NH 03821-0322 18:1-2-3-4-5-6
SCS - Searcher, Southern California Genealogical Society, 417 Irving Dr, Burbank, CA 91504-2408 32:2-3-4-5-6- - - -10-11-12
SD - Quarterly, South Dakota Genealogical Society, P O Box 1101, Pierre, SD 57501-1101 13:2- -4 14:1-2
SE - Southern Echoes, Augusta Genealogical Society, P O Box 3743, Augusta, GA 30914 16:12
SEE - Quarterly, Southern Genealogists Exchange Society, P O Box 2801, Jacksonville, FL 32203-2801 36:153
SEN - SENA, Southeastern Native American Exchange, P O Box 161424, Mobile, AL 36616-2424 1:1-2-3-4 2:1-2-3-4 3:2
SGB - Bulletin, Saskatchewan Genealogical Society, P O Box 1894, Regina, Saskatchewan, Canada, S4P 3E1 26:1-2-3-4
SGS - Bulletin, Seattle Genealogical Society, P O Box 75388, Seattle, WA 98125-0388 44:2-3 45:1
SHI - Shiawassee Steppin' Stones, Shiawassee County Genealogical Society, 224 Curwood Castle Dr, Owosso, MI 48867 24:3
SKC - So-King News, South King County Genealogiccal Society, P O Box 3174, Kent, WA 98032-0203 11:1
SLV - SLVGS News, St. Lawrence Valley Genealogical Society, P O Box 341, Colton, NY 13625-0341 12:1-2-3

SMN - Newsletter, San Mateo County Genealogical Society, P O Box 5083, San Mateo, CA 94402-0083 13:1-2-3-4-5-6-7- -9
SNS - Seeking 'N Searching Ancestors, Peggy Smith Hake, Rt 1 Box 52, St Elizabeth, MO 65075 11:1- -3-4
SQ - Southern Queries, P O Box 23854, Columbia, SC 29224-3854 5:4-5-6 6:1- -3
SSG - Seneca Searchers, Seneca County Genealogical Society, P O Box 157, Tiffin, OH 44883 14:1-2-3-4- -6
STC - Quarterly, St Clair County Genealogical Society, P O Box 431, Belleville, IL 62222 18:1-2-3-4
STK - Stalkin' Kin, San Angelo Genealogical & Historical Society Inc., P O Box 3453, San Angelo, TX 76902 22:4 23:2
STS - Stirpes, Texas State Genealogical Society Quarterly, 204 Glentower, San Antonio, TX 78213 35:1-2-3-4
SUN - Sun Cities Genealogist, Sun Cities Genealogical Society, P O Box 1448, Sun City, AZ 85372-1448 16:2- -4
SVG - Pioneer Pathfinder, Sioux Valley Genealogical Society, 200 W 6th St, Sioux Falls, SD 57104-6001 21:1-2-3
SYH - Seeking Your Heritage, P O Box 2074, N Little Rock, AR 72115 1:1-2-3-4 2:1-2-3-4 3:1-2-3-4
TAC - Ancient City Genealogist, St Augustine Genealogical Society, 1960 Ponce De Leon Blvd, St Augustine, FL 32084 6:1-2-3-4
TAK - The-A-Ki-Ki, Kankakee Valley Genealogical Society, P O Box 442, Bourbonnais, IL 60914 25:1-2
TB - Trail Breakers, Clark County Genealogical Society, P O Box 2728, Vancouver, WA 98668 21:3 22:1
TC - Tree Climber, Smoky Valley Genealogical Society, 211 W Iron #205, Salina, KS 67401-2613 14:1- -3-4
TE - Eaglet, Polish Genealoical Society Of Michigan, Detroit Public Library, 5201 Woodward Ave, Detroit, MI 48202 15:1-2-3
TEG - Essex Genealogist, Essex Society Of Genealogists, P O Box 313, Lynnfield, MA 01940-1313 15:1-2- -4
TEN - Tennessee Queries, 4204 South Conklin St, Spokane, WA 99203 95:16
TF - Franklintonian, Franklin County Genealogical Society, P O Box 44309, Columbus, OH 43204-0309 23:1-2-3
TFG - Trees From The Grove, Cottage Grove Genealogical Society, P O Box 388, Cottage Grove, OR 97424 8:1-2-3/4
TFP - Firelands Pioneer, Firelands Historical Society, 4 Case Ave, Norwalk, OH 44857 95:12
TFT - Family Tree, Ellen Payne Odom Genealogy Library, P O Box 2828, Moultrie, GA 31776-2828 6:2
TG - Genie, Ark-La-Tex Genealogical Association Inc., P O Box 4462, Shreveport, LA 71134 29:1
TGC - German Connection, German Research Association, P O Box 711600, San Diego, CA 92171-1600 19:1-2-3-4
TGO - Genealogist, Australian Institute Of Genealogy, P O Box 339, Blackburn, Victoria, Australia 3130 7:12 8:1
THS - Transactions, Huguenot Society Of South Carolina, 138 Logan St, Charleston, SC 29401 95:100

THT - Thorny Trail, Midland Genealogical Society, 301 W Missouri, Midland, TX 79701 23:2
TJ - Journal, Friends Of Genealogy Inc., P O Box 17835, Shreveport, LA 71138 7:1-2-3
TLL - Licking Lantern, Licking County Genealogical Society, P O Box 4037, Newark, OH 43058-4037 20:2-3-4
TMG - Maine Genealogist, Maine Genealogical Society, P O Box 221, Farmington, ME 04938 17:2- -4
TNC - Nassau Genealogist, Amelia Island Genealogical Society, P O Box 6005, Fernandina Beach, FL 32034 2:2-3-4 3:1
TOP - Quarterly, Topeka Genealogical Society, P O Box 4048, Topeka, KS 66604 25:1-2- -4
TPI - Palatine Immigrant, Palatines To America, Capital University Box 101, Columbus, OH 43209-2394 20:2-3-4 21:1
TR - Report, Ohio Genealogical Society, 713 S Main St, Mansfield, OH 44907 35:12-3-4
TRC - Tri-County Genealogy, Tri-County Genealogical Society, P O Box 580, Marvell, AR 72366 10:1-2
TRI - Newsletter, Tri-City Genealogical Society, P O Box 1410, Richland, WA 99352 35:1-2
TRS - Tree Shaker, Eastern Kentucky Genealogical Society, P O Box 1544, Ashland, KY 41105-1544 19:1-2
TS - Treesearcher, Kansas Genealogical Society, P O Box 103, Dodge City, KS 67801-0103 37:3-4
TSC - Newsletter, Stevens County Genealogical Society, C/O Morris Public Library, 102 E 6th St, Morris, MN 56267 6:1-2-3
TSG - Newsletter, Scott County Genealogical Society, P O Box 258, Lexington, IN 47138-0258 3:2-3-4
TSL - Treasure State Lines, Great Falls Genealogy Society, 1400 1st Ave North, Great Falls, MT 59401 20:1
TTC - Tree Climber, Aberdeen Area Genealogical Society, P O Box 493, Aberdeen, SD 57402-0493 21:1- -3
TTH - Tracer, Hamilton County Chapter Ohio Genealogical Society, P O Box 15851, Cincinnati, OH 45215-0851 16:1- -3-4
TTL - Timbertown Log, Saginaw Genealogical Society, Saginaw Public Library, 505 Janes Ave, Saginaw, MI 48607 23:3 24:1
TTT - Tree Tracers, Southwest Oklahoma Genealogical Society, P O Box 148, Lawton, OK 73502-0148 19:2- -4 20:1
TVF - Tidewater Virginia Families, Virginia Lee Hutcheson Davis, 316 Littletown Quarter, Williamsburg, VA 23185-5519 4:1-2-3
UG - Ulster Genie, Ulster County Genealogical Society, P O Box 536, Hurley, NY 12443 23:1-2-3 24:1
VA - Magazine Of Virginia Genealogy, Virginia Genealogical Society, 5001 W Broad St #115, Richmond, VA 23230-3023 33:2- -4
VAG - Virginia Genealogist, John Frederick Dorman, P O Box 5860, Falmouth, VA 22403-5860 39:1-2-3-4

VCG - Quarterly, Ventura County Genealogical Society, P O Box 24608, Ventura, CA 93002 95:MAR-DEC

VL - Valley Leaves, Tennessee Valley Genealogical Society Inc., P O Box 1568, Huntsville, Al, 35807-0567 29:3 30:1-2

VQ - Virginia/West Virginia Queries, W 1304 Cliffwood Ct, Spokane, WA 99218 94:10

VQS - Valley Quarterly, San Bernadino Valley Genealogical Society, P O Box 2220, San Bernadino, CA 92406 32:1- -3-4

WCG - Newsletter, Whitman County Genealogical Society, P O Box 393, Pullman, WA 99163-0393 11:3-4-5-6-7/8-9/10-11 12:1- -3

WCK - Bulletin, West Central Kentucky Family Research Association, P O Box 1932, Owensboro, KY 42302-1932 28:2-3-4

WCT - Wake Treasures, Wake County Genealogical Society Inc., P O Box 17713, Raleigh, NC 27619-7713 5:2

WI - Wisconsin State Genealogical Newsletter, Wisconsin State Genealogical Society Inc., 131 W Wilson St 1l200, Madison, WI 53703 41:3-4 42:1-2

WMG - Western Maryland Genealogy, Catoctin Press, P O Box 505, New Market, MD 21774-0505 11:1-2-3 12:1

WPG - Quarterly, Western Pennsylvania Genealogical Society, 4400 Forbes Ave, Pittsburgh, PA 15213-4080 21:3-4- - -7 22:1-2

WRB - Waconda Roots & Branches, North Central Kansas Genealogical Society & Library Inc., P O Box 251, Cawker City, KS 67420 17:4 18:1

WT - Windy Times, Liberal Area Genealogical Society, P O Box 1094, Liberal, KS 67905 8:2

WTC - Where The Trails Cross, South Suburban Genealogical & Historical Society, P O Box 96, South Holland, IL 60473-0096 25:3-4 26:1

WTN - Western Trails, Western Trails Genealogical Society, P O Box 70, Altus, OK 73522 8:4 95:SPRING-WINTER

YTD - Yesterdays, Nacogdoches Genealogical Society, P O Box 4634 SFA Station, Nacogdoches, TX 75962-4634 15:1

YV - Bulletin, Yakima Valley Genealogical Society, P O Box 445, Yakima, WA 98907 27:1- - -4

ABBETHERN, Betty Wilhelmine see Friedrick HOLEKAMP
ABBOTT, Jacob fl810, SC, deed ODD 7:1:24
   James Smith bc1860, w Chloe Estella Robison, UT, NV, biog by McIntire/Zolman, bk rev GH 49:3:217
   Moses dc1792, w Christian Stimpson (?), ME, geneal TMG 17:4:99
   Thomas bc1643, w Elizabeth Green, ME, geneal AG 70:2:85
   William Elias, w Mary Jane Leavitt, UT, biog by McIntire et al, bk rev GH 49:3:217
ABELL, George W b1818, w Mary Ann Nalley, VA, jour abstr HPF 95:50:6
ABERDEEN, Countess, CN, biog, repr 1893, bk rev FAM 34:3:180
ABLES, John b1777, w Alice Cochran, OH, IA, corresp abstr TR 35:4:204
   Thomas Jefferson b1835, OH, corresp abstr TR 35:4:204
ABRAHAMS, Isidore see Israel ABRAHAMS
   Israel bc1900, CA, biog sketch LRT 14:2:546
ACADIAN GENEALOGY, CN, archives report 1905, bk rev AGE 24:1:8
   FR origins of Acadians, hist by Prevost, bk rev AGE 24:4:101
   Geneal of misc fam by Lanctot, bk rev AGE 24:1:9
   Geneal of 37 fam by White, bk rev AGE 24:2&3:44
   LA, hist by Braud, bk rev AGE 24:1:9
   QB, hist by Hebert, bk rev AGE 24:2&3:44
ACKER, Fam hist by Elmore, bk rev STS 35:2:74
ACKLEY, Anna fl942, h Edward, IA, news abstr HHH 16:4:7
   Edward see Anna ACKLEY
ADAIR, Robert W, TN, MS, TX, fam hist by Adair, bk rev ARH 33:1:33

ADAM, Conrad fc1890, w Adelbertha Bergmann, TX, fam hist sketch KTP 4:2:26
   Harvey Guenther see Catherine BRANNEN
   Kathinka see Paul TOEPPERWEIN
   Katinka b1857, h Paul Topperwein, TX, obit KTP 5:2:27
ADAMS, Clara A see Adam KEISTER
   George bc1798, w Ann Heywood, EN, CN, geneal by Redhead, bk rev SGB 26:4:iv
   Hannah see Samuel WINKLEY
   Lewis m1788, w Martha Evenswore, MI, Bible rec MI 41:4:126
   Mary b1741, w Clement Skolfield, ME, fam hist TMG 17:4:119
   Robert m1816, w Betsey Vandeburgh, MI, Bible rec KVH 20:4:43
   VA, geneal cont FCM 7:4:213 FCM 8:2:73
ADCOCK, Elizabeth see George STIGGINS
ADDISON, Edwin fl900, w Louva Marie Smith, IN, CA, corresp abstr PR 23:2:56
   Richard bc1859, w Susan Flowers, EN, FL, biog PCQ 22:2:6
ADDY, Sarah Hotchkiss see Gideon STODDARD
ADKINS, Catherine Green see James Knox Polk BEATY
ADLER, David b1834, w Sara Sternweiler, GR, OH, fam hist by Fox, bk rev GH 49:4:224
   Henrietta see Simon FUCHS
   Nannie see Simon FUCHS
AFRICAN AMERICAN GENEALOGY, AL, slave manumission doc from co court rec, 19th cent NGS 83:2:127 NGS 83:3:199
   AR, Desha Co, slave rec from deed bks c1858 ARH 33:3:117
   AR, Marion Co, free black community 1850, hist ARN 8:4:1

1

AFRICAN AMERICAN GENEALOGY (continued)

Army biog 1866-1917 by Schubert, bk rev FCM 7:4:264 GH 49:6:181 HQ 126:3:214

Black Loyalist direct, bk rev NEH 12:6:200

Bureau of Refugees, Freemen & Abandoned Lands rec 1865-1872 by Lawson, bk rev SGS 45:1:30

CA, Santa Clara Valley, settler roster SCC 32:1:21

Civil War vet organizations (little known), geneal res tips HQ 95:57:11

Claiborne Co, slave rec by Terry, bk rev SGS 45:1:32

CT (Greenwich), slave emancipation rec 1776-1838 by Mead, bk rev GFP 44:4:188

FL, Orange Co, deaths 1910-1922 FLG 18:2:50

FL, Polk Co, African Am early hist sketch PCQ 9:4:4

Free Blacks, kidnapping hist 1780-1865 by Wilson, bk rev REG 92:4:418

GA, African population 1870, census abstr by Stewart, bk rev GH 49:3:203

GA, marr rec 1865-1966 by Hancock, bk rev GGS 31:2:122

Gunfighters in Indian territory 1870-1907, hist by Burton, bk rev KTP 11:3:48

IL, early Af-Am residents from 1850 census GL 29:1:28

IN, Orange Co, African Am heritage & hist by Robbins, bk rev GH 49:3:205 SGS 44:2:86

Jewish & African Am relations, res resource guide JL 8:1/2:162

KY, Freedman's Savings & Trust depositor reg 1865-1874 KA 31:1:21

KY, Negro & Mulatto marr decl 1866-1872 KA 30:3:134

LA, Confederate biog sketches KSL 19:2:58

Mil res guide (soldiers & sailors 1526-1900) by Moebs, bk rev BT 27:4:75

AFRICAN AMERICAN GENEALOGY (continued)

MO, Lutheran synod, ch worker training hist, 18th cent CHI 68:3:103

Natl Archives, civilian rec res guide, bk rev CAA 7:6:36

NC, Confederate pensioners, roster NCJ 21:4:343

NC, Gates Co, slave work reg 1847-1861 by Fouts VAG 39:3:228

NC, Morgan Dist, superior court of law & equity slave rec 1788-1806 by Haun, bk rev RCR 10:4:2381

NC, slave work reg 1847-1861 by Fouts, bk rev NCJ 21:3:290

News bibl by Henritze, bk rev ARH 33:1:35 GFP 44:4:187 GH 49:5:185 MN 26:2:89 NCJ 21:2:186 NGS 83:3:218 NYR 126:3:218 VAG 39:1:73 WPG 21:4:55 RCR 10:2:2273 SEE 36:153:23 SGS 44:3:145 TVF 4:2:123

OH, freedom papers abstr from news, early 1800s VAG 39:1:39

OH, news & meeting minutes abstr 1839-1863 TR 35:3:140

PA, Allegheny Co, indentures c1800 WPG 21:3:18

PA, hist & res guide by Blockson, bk rev WPG 22:2:53

Res guide by Byers, bk rev KVH 20:1&2:7

Slave anc res guide by Fears, bk rev GH 49:6:181 SGS 45:1:30

Slave anc, res tips CAA 7:6:31

South, education hist 1865-1900 by Nieman, bk rev REG 92:4:428

TN, Scott Co, slave sched 1850 ETR 7:4:173

Tombstone inscr, res tips FRT 17:1:4

TX, largest slave holders 1860 CAA 7:6:32

VA, Northampton Co, deeds & wills of emancipation 1782-1864 by Latimer, bk rev CHG 28:1:36 SGS 44:2:86

VA, Richmond Co, male free persons of color roster 1850 TVF 4:3:173

AFRICAN AMERICAN GENEALOGY (continued)
Vet res without mil ID numbers, res tips FRT 17:1:4
West Indies, slave trade 1625-1715, hist by Munford, bk rev CGJ 3:3:41
Women in Am, hist ency by Hine, bk rev NGS 83:1:67
Women journalists, hist by Streitmatter, bk rev REG 92:4:439

AGARD, Edward Martin b1830, w Julia E Smith Risley, DK, CT, fam rec THT 23:2:72

AGGES, Tryntje see Jan GUECKE

AGUIRRE, Martin d1987, CA, fam hist VQS 32:4:60

AGUSTINA, LA, fam hist by Jupiter, bk rev NER 149:593:78

AHRENSSEN, Frances Wallace f1995, OK, WA, autobiog, bk rev HQ 95:59:89

ALABAMA, Albert E Casey IR Collect, res tips TFT 6:2:8A
ALABAMA, Atlas of hist co boundaries by Long, bk rev SEE 36:153:53
Bibb Co, Confederate soldier census 1907 AGM 27:1/2:23 AGM 27:3/4:57
Birmingham, Bethlehem cem rec & hist AGM 27:3/4:40
Birmingham, pre-Civil War era hist PT 37:1:3
Birmingham Public Library archives, res guide PT 37:1:23
Blount Co, probate minutes bk index 1852-1856 AFH 16:1:11 AFH 16:2:5
Blount Co, probate minutes bk index 1872-1874 AFH 16:4:7
Chambers Co, Lebanon Pres Ch hist by Spence, bk rev AGM 27:3/4:64
Choctaw Co, census 1850 by Brooks, bk rev VL 29:3:145
Civil War, 28th AL Confederate Infantry Reg roster by Walker/Curren, bk rev PT 37:3/4:73

ALABAMA (continued)
Civil War, Company G, Second Reg Cavalry KY Vol, roster 1862 AFH 16:1:18
Colbert Co, Confederate pensioner & widow rec NTT 15:1/2:13
Colbert Co, marr rec 1874-1887 cont VL 29:3:105 30:1:1 30:2:51
Colbert Co, Mt Pleasant cem rec NTT 15:1/2:17
Colbert Co, probate court minute bk A 1867-1874 NTT 14:3:94 14:4:133 15:1/2:17
Colbert Co, tax sale 1876 NTT 14:3:84
Colonial soldier roster, surnames Lightfoot to Lynn by Gandrud/McLane, bk rev ARH 33:2:82
Confederate reunion roster 1903 NTT 14:3:84
Confederate Roll of Honor cont SEE 36:153:3
Confederate vet census 1907 NTT 14:3:84
Cullman Co, doctors hist 1860-1900 by Morris, bk rev AFH 16:4:3
Cullman Co, probate court rec abstr 1877-1888 AFH 16:1:21
Cullman, news abstr 1920s AFH 16:2:26
Decatur, hist 1861-1865 OLR 9:3:127
Demopolis, Old Springhill Cem rec AGM 27:1/2:30
Div case index, 13th Judicial Circuit Court 1816-1918 by USAA, bk rev NGS 83:1:67 TR 35:4:224
Div rec 1908-1937 cont NTT 14:4:138
Fayette Co, Berea Ch of Christ hist MCA 14:3:74
Fayette Co, deaths from Nick Morris diary 1891-1912 MCA 14:3:78
Fayette Co, map 1917, placenames MCA 14:3:77
Fayette Co, marr & probate rec by Wiltshire, bk rev GH 49:4:205
Fayette Co, marr & probate rec c1851-1871 by Wiltshire, bk rev RAG 16:3:19

ALABAMA (continued)
Fayette Co, marr by Ch of Christ preachers c1860-1910 MCA 14:4:117
Fayette Co, marr rec vol A MCA 14:4:133
Fayette Co, Musgrove Chapel Meth Ch reg 1876 MCA 14:1:5
Fayette Co, Pine Grove Ch reg 1876 MCA 14:1:5
Florence, recoll of, hist sketch NTT 14:3:105
Forbes Trading Company, hist & roster of debtors SEN 3:2:38
Ford's Mtn, Hollingsworth fam cem rec MCA 14:4:119
Franklin Co, Bobo cem rec NTT 15:1/2:24
Franklin Co, div rec 1908-1937 NTT 15:1/2:20
Franklin Co, legal notices from *Belgreen's Franklin News* 1887 cont VL 29:3:109
Franklin Co, news abstr from the *Times* 1899 VL 30:1:6
Greene Co, cem rec by Wiese, bk rev HTR 38:4:103
Greene Co, marr rec (early), 19th cent AGM 27:1/2:8
Greene Co, orphans' court rec index 1824-1829 AGM 27:3/4:1
Hale Co, marr rec (early), 19th cent AGM 27:1/2:8
Hanceville, Wallace State College Library, descr of avail svcs HQ 95:57:71
Henry Co, lighthouse keepers, hist AGM 27:1/2:1
Hist by Rogers et al, bk rev REG 93:2:253
Huntsville, Maple Hill cem rec by Robey et al, bk rev VL 30:2:92
Jackson Co, probate rec 1855-1858 VL 29:3:113 30:1:14 30:2:60
Jackson Mil Road, hist sketch NTT 15:1/2:32
Jefferson Co, ch, school & social life 1870s, hist PT 37:3/4:52

ALABAMA (continued)
Jefferson Co, deeds, wills & admin 1818-1828 PT 37:3/4:33
Jefferson Co, Hicks cem rec PT 37:3/4:23
Jefferson Co, marr rec bk 6 c1870 PT 37:3/4:6
Jefferson Co, marr rec c1869 PT 37:1:16
Jefferson Co, *North Jefferson News* obits 1987-1989 PT 37:3/4:65
Jefferson Co, orphan's court rec 1841-1844 PT 37:3/4:28
Jefferson Co, Reconstruction era hist PT 37:3/4:45
Jefferson, Old Jefferson cem rec AGM 27:1/2:29
Joppa, Joppa Institute hist AFH 16:4:4
Korean War vet direct, 151st Engineer Combat Battalion, Company B, bk rev VL 29:3:145
Land sales 1823-1832 by Reese, bk rev NGS 83:3:229
Lauderdale Co, Canerday cem rec NTT 14:4:146
Lauderdale Co, co court rec 1829-1839 NTT 14:3:84 14:4:151
Lauderdale Co, Creek Indian War vol roster 1895 NTT 14:4:145
Lauderdale Co, deed rec 1822-1828 cont VL 29:3:116 30:1:18 30:2:66
Lauderdale Co, election returns 1856, 1857 & 1858 NTT 14:4:143
Lawrence Co Archives, res tips OLR 9:4:161
Lawrence Co, Aldriudge Grove cem rec OLR 9:3:101
Lawrence Co, cem rec OLR 9:1:12
Lawrence Co, census 1850 AGM 27:1/2:45 27:3/4:25
Lawrence Co, comissioners' court rec 1880 OLR 9:1:23
Lawrence Co, Elams Creek Ch member roster 1869 OLR 9:3:110
Lawrence Co, grand jury report 1865 OLR 9:3:124
Lawrence Co, Hickory Grove Cem rec OLR 9:1:16

ALABAMA (continued)
Lawrence Co, marr rec 1818-1899 OLR 9:4:135
Lawrence Co, marr rec 1820-1829 cont OLR 9:3:93
Lawrence Co, marr rec 1880-1889 OLR 9:1:1
Lawrence Co, marr permission note abstr 1850-1860 cont OLR 9:1:6 9:3:97
Lawrence Co, Milam cem rec OLR 9:4:144
Lawrence Co, motor vehicle reg 1915 OLR 9:4:159
Lawrence Co, orphans court bk 1825 VL 29:3:123 30:1:22 30:2:70
Lawrence Co, permission notes from marr lic & bonds, abstr 1850-1860 OLR 9:4:139
Lawrence Co, tax list 1895 cont OLR 9:1:30
Limestone Co, deeds bk 2 1825 cont VL 29:3:128 30:1:24 30:2:74
Lowndes Co, marr rec 1871, female index AGM 27:1/2:33
Lowndes Co, marr rec add 1840-1842 AGM 27:1/2:43
Lowndes Co, slave owners 1850 AMG 10:2/3:75
Madison Co, probate rec abstr c1850 VL 30:1:28
Madison Co, wills c1848 cont VL 29:3:132
Madison Co, wills c1850 cont VL 30:2:78
Marion Co, *Democrat* news abstr 1904 MCA 14:4:110
Marion Co, news abstr 1890 MCA 14:3:91
Marion Co, news abstr from the *Herald* 1887 MCA 14:1:2
Marion Co, voter reg 1902 MCA 14:3:95
Marshall Co, census 1866 VL 29:3:136 30:1:33 30:2:83
Marshall Co, voter reg list 1867 AFH 16:2:16

ALABAMA (continued)
Mexican War officer rosters 1846-1848 AFH 16:2:10
Milledgeville, news abstr 1835 re:Indian disturbances, bk rev SEN 1:3:21
Mobile, Magnolia Cem, Apache burial rec SEN 2:4:48
Monroe Co, census 1910, Indian population SEN 2:4:24
Morgan Co, death rec 1898-1899 VL 29:3:141 30:1:38 30:2:88
Morgan Co, marr rec 1818-1896 by Minter, bk rev VL 29:3:127
Mountain Home, voter reg c1901-1914 OLR 9:3:114
Mountain People Gazette, collector's set, bk rev NTT 15:1/2:6
Mountain settlers, hist & biog sketches by Wamble, bk rev NTT 15:1/2:6
Mt Hope, voter reg 1901-1914 OLR 9:4:150
News abstr 1823-1869 by Kelsey et al, bk rev SGS 45:1:30
News abstr vol 1 by Kelsey et al, bk rev GH 49:6:185 HTR 38:4:103 KSL 19:4:154 OLR 9:3:126
Nineteenth AL Reg CSA, Company C roll 1904 AFH 16:4:19
North AL, SP-Am War 1898, soldier hist & roster VL 29:3:101
North Fayette Co land rec MCA 14:4:123
Old Spring Hill, Old Lucy cem rec AGM 27:1/2:32
Perry Co, marr rec (early), 19th cent AGM 27:1/2:8
Piper, hist by Walker, bk rev PT 37:3/4:72
Rocky Ford community hist 1818-1952, hist by Brown, bk rev GH 49:3:202
Russell Co, mort sched 1870 AGM 27:1/2:6
Russellville, *Franklin County Times* news abstr 1899 VL 30:2:56
Russellville, Sunday Sch hist NTT 15:1/2:23

ALABAMA (continued)
SC-born AL planters who owned 50 or more slaves, roster 1850 AGM 27:3/4:52
Selma, news abstr from the *Southern Argus* 1869-1870 by Kelsey, bk rev GH 49:3:202
Shoal Creek Bapt Assoc hist & rec NTT 14:4:154 15:1/2:45
Six Mile, hist by Langston, bk rev PT 37:3/4:73
Slave manumission doc from co court rec, 19th cent NGS 83:2:127
SP-Am War 1898, US Vol Infantry, 9th reg, company G, roster AGM 27:1/2:15
St Clair Co, death notices 1873-1910 by Whitten, bk rev GH 49:5:189 NTT 15:1/2:2
Thornhill, hist MCA 14:4:115
Tuscumbia, Our Lady of the Sacred Heart Cath Ch bapt rec 1869-1926 NTT 14:3:89 14:4:126 15:1/2:8
Tutwiler Collect res guide KTP 8:2:19
Union soldiers interred in Natl Cem, roster AFH 16:2:24
Walker Co, marr index 1883-1892 AGM 27:3/4:10
Walker Co, voter reg 1867 cont AFH 16:1:7 16:2:20
Wheeler, voter reg c1901-1914 OLR 9:3:114
Winston Co, death reg 1888-1910 by Nigg, bk rev NC 5:4:178
Women's hist 1819-1990 by Thomas, bk rev REG 93:2:252
ALASKA, Births 1894 AQ 6:1:2
Death notices from the *Alaska Sportsman/Alaska Magazine* 1970-1979 (of people born before 1900) AQ 6:1:14 6:3:47 6:4:65
Fairbanks, Clay Street Cem rec AQ 6:4:53
Homer recording dist, death rec avail list AQ 6:3:35
Juneau, news abstr 1913 AQ 6:1:7 6:3:39 6:4:59
Kenai Peninsula, cem inscr AQ 6:1:6

ALASKA (continued)
Native pop, geneal res guide NGS 83:4:277
Yukon pioneer biog 1850-1950 by Ferrell, bk rev ACG 21:1:24 GEN 20:1:20 NGS 83:4:302 SGS 44:3:143 SLV 12:1:1 TPI 20:2:97 TTL 24:1:23 VQS 32:1:4
ALBERT, Felix b1843, FR, MA, autobiog, bk rev MHH 16:1:31
ALBRIGHT, Frances see Thomas WELLS
Mary see Conrad SLOOP
ALBRITTON, Ray, FL, recoll PCQ 19:3:4
ALDEN, Katheryne see James SAMS
ALEXANDER, Alma Pearl see Rudolph Herbert TOEPPERWEIN
Elizabeth see John ALEXANDER
Frederick Lee b1882, w Ossie May, NC, FL, biog sketch IMP 14:2:58
John fl653, w Elizabeth, EN, VA, fam hist by Pippenger, bk rev CSB 30:4:143
Ossie May see Frederick Lee ALEXANDER
Shelby J L fl995, TN, fam hist by Alexander, bk rev LOB 16:2:41
ALGER, CT, MA, fam hist by Alger, bk rev SGS 44:3:143
Fam data by Alger, bk rev GR 37:1:49
ALLAIRE, FR, NY, geneal cont NYR 126:1:55 126:2:127 126:3:199 126:4:253
ALLARD, Mae see Allen E STRAND
ALLDREDGE, CA, Chico cem rec GGP 28:1:45
ALLEE, Thomas Edward b1840, w Nancy Hill, MO, fam hist SNS 11:4:3
ALLEMANN, Samuel fl844, SW, MO, corresp abstr MSG 15:1:41
ALLEN, Annie Louise, h --- Ward, biog by Shelton, bk rev GH 49:5:236
Barna b1786, w Betsey, VT, Bible rec BAT 24:2:57
Betsey see Barna ALLEN

ALLEN (continued)
  Charles Cabiness fl817, w Martha Ann Carter, VA, MO, Bible by Jasper, bk rev MSG 15:1:56
  Cornelius Milton see Ellen Virginia CAMPBELL
  David m1837, w Catharine Locke, NY, OH, fam rec AH 22:2:186
  Easter see William ALLEN
  Esther see Benjamin THURBER
  Ethan, hist by DePuy, bk rev BCF 95:Apr/May:8
  Ethan, hist by DePuy, bk rev SLV 12:1:14
  Henrietta R see Watson S ALLEN
  Isaac b1797, VT, identity of father BAT 24:2:56
  Martha Keaton (Philpott) see Henry Edward BOTELER
  NC, fam rec by Allen, bk rev LOB 16:1:26
  Watson S b1840, w Rachel C Thompson, w Henrietta R Allen, NY, geneal OCG 25:3:32
  William b1775, w Easter, IR, CN, biog GEN 20:1:11
ALLERTON, Sarah see Degory PRIEST
ALLRED, Savannah see William H EDWARDS
ALSACE, Fortelbach (Fertrupt) Anabaptist burials 1737-1761 MFH 14:1:10
ALSBURY, Charles bc1771, w Jane McElhaney, WV, geneal by Renner, bk rev WPG 22:2:55
ALSUP, Samuel bc1788, TN, geneal by Alsup, bk rev TJ 7:1:38
ALTER, Samuel C m1854, w Nancy J Beale, PA, Bible rec WPG 22:2:47
ALTMAN, Mary see James WHITTON
  Priscilla see Jesse Harris DURRANCE
ALTSCHUL, Joe S d1923, AR, obit FGC 95:28:5
ALVARADO, Mercedes see Cornelius B JENSEN
AMBERGER, Conrad f1728, VA, land patent BYG 7:5:403

AMBROSE, James d1861, IL, biog STC 18:2:104 18:3:145
AMERICAN INDIANS see NATIVE AMERICAN GENEALOGY
AMERICAN REVOLUTION see REVOLUTIONARY WAR
AMISH GENEALOGY see also RELIGIOUS GENEALOGY
  Houses & barns, hist by Scott, bk rev PM 19:1:41
  IL, Amish & Mennonites in southern IL, hist MH 22:4:67
AMMEL, Jean Georges b1796, w Dorothea Goetz, FR, IL, geneal STC 18:3:156
AMMONNETTE, Elizabeth see John GARRETT
AMSBAUGH, Misc fam rec by Seaman-Williams, bk rev HQ 95:58:90
AMSBURY, Jeremiah b1741, RI, anc RIR 21:3:72
ANDERSDOTTER, Brita Lisa see Elizabeth JOHNSON
ANDERSON, G H f1892, KS, diary abstr cont NCG 2:4:2
  James see Elizabeth LIGON
  Joseph b1783, NC, Bible rec RCR 10:1:2187
  Joseph see Melinda KING
  Knud f1864, w Anna Jacobsdotter Eide, NO, IL, KS, fam hist HQ 95:59:56
  KY, Garrard Co, fam cem hist KA 31:1:41
  Mary Adaline see James Abner COX
  Rebecca see Richard MCNATT
  Reuben bc1800, w Lucy Burke, KY, VA, geneal PCH 1:2:27
ANDRES, Rosina see Niklaus BEUTLER
ANDREWS, D f1889, OH, corresp KTP 12:2:21
  Sarah see Alexander T HOLDEN
ANGEL, John F b1821, TN, IL, Bible rec MTG 8:4:171
ANGLEA, E B m1875, s W E Gant, TN, Bible rec MTG 8:4:170

ANKEN, Peter bc1515, w Barbara Durtschi, SW, fam hist by Lehmann, bk rev TPI 21:1:44
APPENTHERN, Betty Wilhelmine see Friedrick HOLEKAMP
ARCHIBALD, Margaret see John DOLEMAN
ARHELGER, Heinrich see Karoline ITZ
ARIAS, Juana see Lorenzo ESPARZA
ARIZONA, Fort Bowie, mil deaths c1871, roster CSB 30:3:89
Gila Bend, cem inscr 1800s & 1900s SUN 16:2:36
Gila Co, Geneal Soc descr AMG 10:2/3:9
Glendale, Old Paths cem rec SUN 16:4:94
Hardyville, census 1880 CSB 30:3:88
Hardyville, hist CSB 30:3:87
Maricopa Co, marr bk 1871-1898 cont SUN 16:4:89
Mineral Park, census abstr 1880 CSB 30:4:134
Mineral Park, hist CSB 30:4:133
Obits c1930-1940 CSB 30:1:9
Pima Co, post ofc & postmaster roster, 19th cent CSB 30:3:117
Res tips GSC 17:3:3
Tiger City, census 1880 abstr CSB 30:1:2
Tiger City, hist CSB 30:1:1
Tucson, hist 1880s from oral hist CSB 30:3:93
Union soldiers buried in AZ territory, roster SUN 16:4:91
ARKANSAS, Alamo, involvement in, hist c1830s SYH 1:4:14
Ancestor Fair Researcher surname direct 1994 by Johnston, bk rev GH 49:4:205
Bauxite Honor Roll, WW2 roster SCH 10:3:86
Bauxite, Mt Olive Bapt Ch cem rec ARH 33:2:71
Benton Co, obits 1884-1898 by Easley/McAnelly, bk rev GH 49:3:202

ARKANSAS (continued)
Benton Co, obits 1899-1904 by Easley/McAnelly, bk rev ARN 8:3:7 MCS 16:5:28
Benton Co, obits 1905-1909 by Easley/McAnelly, bk rev GH 49:6:186 PR 23:1:36 SGS 45:1:30
Benton Co, obits 1910-1913 by Easley/McAnelly, bk rev ARH 33:4:173 SCH 10:4:157
Boone Co, court rec restored after fire, hist sketch & judges 1809-1935 SYH 3:1:18
Boone Co, execution 1913, hist sketch SYH 3:1:16
Boone Co, news abstr from the *Harrison Daily Times* 1936 SYH 2:4:16 3:1:15
Boone Co, news abstr from the *Headlight* 1931 SYH 3:2:22
Brief Case vol 9 1925 SYH 2:2:21
Business res tips ARN 8:2:14
Capps, Garvin Farm, hist sketch SYH 1:1:18
Carroll Co, Crooked Creek, postmaster roster 1838-1934 SYH 3:1:17
Carroll Co, decl of intent c1908 SYH 3:3:14
Census 1850, everyname index by McLane & Allen, bk rev TRC 10:2:74
Chalk Bluff Battle 1863, hist by Ponder, bk rev ARH 33:3:128
Chicot Co, census 1830 surname roster ARH 33:1:17
Chicot Co, tax list 1829 ARH 33:3:101
City & town location guide SYH 2:2:18
Civil War era hist by Weaver et al, bk rev WT 8:2:6
Civil War, 31st AR Infantry Reg roster ARH 33:4:165
Civilian Conservation Corps, hist 1933-1934 by O'Dell, bk rev GH 49:5:189
Clark Co, marr rec 1821-1845 ARH 33:2:65

ARKANSAS (continued)
Cleburne Co, Alexander Cem inscr ARH 33:4:158
Coffee Creek, Yancey cem rec TRC 10:1:27
Commercial Agency reg 1879-1880, bk rev ARN 8:2:15
Confederate surrender & parole rosters 1865 by Ponder, bk rev ARH 33:3:127
Craighead Co, hist, repr 1930, bk rev ARH 33:3:128
Cumberland Pres Ch, geneal abstr from by Eddlemon, bk rev APR 14:6:4
Death notices from the *Arkansas Democrat-Gazette* 1994 by Russell, bk rev ARH 33:2:79
Desha Co, papers of Am statesmen from, hist sketch TRC 10:2:46
Desha Co, slave rec from deed bks c1858 ARH 33:3:117
Dover, cem rec by Boyd, bk rev GH 49:4:205
Drew Co, cem rec by Handley, bk rev GH 49:4:205
Eastern Cos, census 1850 by McLane & Allen, bk rev TRC 10:2:74
Fair Play Masonic Lodge #32 roster 1871 SCH 10:3:81
Family Historian query data 1962-1992 by Roberts, bk rev GH 49:4:205
Fordyce, news abstr from the *Advocate* 1939 ARH 33:3:103
Fountain Co, WW1 war work committee roster 1918 SYH 2:2:23
Garland Co, Blocker-Ellis Cem rec ARH 33:4:159
Gazette obit indexes, res guide ARN 8:1:12
Geneal Soc Resource Direct 1995-1996 by Allen/McLane, bk rev TS 37:4:145
Harrison, *Boone County Headlight* news abstr 1931 SYH 3:4:11
Harrison, hist sketch SYH 1:3:15
Hist by Dougan, bk rev ARN 8:2:10 ARH 33:2:80

ARKANSAS (continued)
Hist Commission co microfilm rec guide SYH 1:2:13 2:2:11 3:2:12
Homesteads, land office hist sketch SYH 3:1:17
Jamestown, teacher roster 1926-1949 ARH 33:2:53
Jefferson Co, marr rec before 1850 FGC 95:28:11
Johnson Co, Union Southern Claims Commission files abstr ARN 8:2:12
Katheren Seals Christensen geneal files, abstr SYH 2:2:17
Laconia, cotton burning by order in Civil War, news abstr TRC 10:2:46
Lee Co, Marianna, marr & death abstr from news 1897-1898 TRC 10:2:48
Lee Co, marr rec 1875-1878 cont TRC 10:1:10 10:2:65
Little Rock, biog sketches of prominent citizens 1921 SYH 1:1:8 1:2:10 1:3:8 1:4:4 2:1:4 2:2:6 2:3:5 2:4:7 3:1:6 3:2:7 3:3:7 3:4:7
Little Rock, high sch class of 1920, roster SYH 1:3:20
Little Rock, high sch faculty of 1920, roster SYH 1:3:26
Little Rock, Little Rock High Sch yearbk abstr 1919 SYH 1:2:20
Logan Co, hist sketch SYH 2:4:22
Logan Co, Paris Academy student roster 1896-1897 ARH 33:4:160
Lonoke Co, cem inscr by Martinet, bk rev ARH 33:4:173
Lonoke Co, marr bks A through U by Shubert, bk rev ARH 33:3:128
Lonoke Co, marr rec index for bks A thru U by Shubert, bk rev ARH 33:4:173
Marion Co, free black community 1850, hist ARN 8:4:1
Marvell, Brickell Funeral Home rec 1926-1929 TRC 10:1:13
Missionary Bapt Ch & assoc, hist 1818-1920 by SAMBCA, bk rev ARH 33:1:33
MO citizens in northwest AR c1850 KCG 36:2:91

ARKANSAS (continued)
  Monroe Co, Cache twp, agriculture census 1850 TRC 10:2:59
  Monroe Co, cem inscr by Turner, bk rev TRC 10:2:74
  Monroe Co, Clarendon 1st Pres Ch minutes abstr 1870 TRC 10:2:47
  Monroe Co, Cotton Plant ch deed abstr 1871 TRC 10:2:45
  Monroe Co, legal voter roster 1917 TRC 10:1:22
  Mountain Meadows, massacre hist sketch SYH 1:3:16
  News abstr c1969 SYH 1:2:17
  News abstr c1973 SYH 2:2:13
  North AR Ancestor Fair Researcher/Surname direct 1995 by Johnston, bk rev ARH 33:1:33
  North Little Rock, 1938 Wildcat yearbk SYH 3:2:20
  Obit & death report index for the *Arkansas Gazette* by Russell, bk rev ARH 33:2:80
  Obits c1915-1955 SYH 3:2:15
  Pea Ridge, Civil War, battle commemoration SYH 2:1:12
  Phillips Co, Court of Common Pleas abstr c1821 cont TPC 10:1:2 10:2:62
  Phillips Co, marr rec 1859-1873 cont TRC 10:1:29 10:2:71
  Phillips Co, probate book 4 abstr 1847-1849 TRC 10:2:43
  Phillips Co, probate rec 1841-1846 cont TRC 10:1:24
  Placenames, hist SYH 1:1:1 1:1:16 1:2:1 1:3:1
  Planters Twp, agriculture census 1850 TRC 10:2:68
  Pope Co, census (reconstructed) 1890 by PLNSDAR, bk rev ARH 33:2:79
  Pope Co, will bk abstr 1860-1910 by PLNSDAR, bk rev ARH 33:2:79
  Rehoboth cem inscr, early 1800s onward TRC 10:2:56
  Res guide by Norris, bk rev ARH 33:2:81
  Rockroe Twp, agricultural census 1850 TRC 10:1:5

ARKANSAS (continued)
  Russellville, AR Polytechnic College student & staff roster 1929 SYH 3:3:15
  Russellville, Cherokee vr from the Dwight Mission 1822-1861 OK 40:2:64
  Salien Co, hist sketch SCH 10:3:96
  Saline Co, Benton Meth Ch members (partial list) 1912 SCH 10:3:95
  Saline Co, land patents before 1902 SCH 10:3:109
  Saline Co, marr rec 1879-1881 SCH 10:4:148
  Saline Co, Mt Olive cem rec SCH 10:4:129
  Saline Co, news abstr from the *Pick & Shovel* c1944 SCH 10:3:85
  Searcy Twp, agricultural census 1850 TRC 10:1:20
  Siloam Springs, Quakers & the Cherokee Nation, hist sketch GSM 12:2:40
  Soldiers buried in Knoxville TN 1862-1863 ARH 33:3:121
  Sons of Confederate Veteran Camps, address list ARN 8:3:15
  Southwestern Trail, hist sketch SYH 1:4:12
  State Name, origins, hist sketch SYH 1:1:14
  Taylor cem rec ARH 33:1:22
  Towns, co location guide SYH 3:2:27 3:3:21 3:3:27
  Tri-County area, funeral notices 1890-1918 TRC 10:1:9
  Twp digest 1820-1990 by Allen, bk rev GH 49:5:190
  Washington Co, cem rec by NAGS, bk rev ARH 33:4:173
  Washington Co, sheriff's census 1865 by Maxwell, bk rev SQ 5:4:43
  Wedding anniv (mainly golden) from news abstr 1969-1973 SYH 1:2:6 2:2:1 3:2:1 3:3:1 3:4:1
  White River steamboats & ferries, hist by Rose et al, bk rev ARN 8:3:12

ARKANSAS (continued)
Wills & admin to 1900, index by Stevenson, bk rev ARH 33:1:35
WW1, pilgrimages for mothers & widows, roster ARN 8:2:4

ARMINGTON, Joseph fl713, MA, fam hist by Armington, bk rev GH 49:5:226

ARMISTEAD, Henry Coles b1848, w Kate Adair Armistead, AL, Bible rec NTT 14:4:124

Kate Adair see Henry Coles ARMISTEAD

ARMSTRONG, IR, clan profile IFL 5:9:3

ARNAUD, Jacques b1781, w Marie Lalonde, FR, LA, MX, desc, bk rev BHN 28:2:20

ARNOLD, AR, fam hist by Kaufman, bk rev ARH 33:4:174

Joseph b1692, w Dorothy Hartwell, w Abigail Newton, MA, geneal & biog NEH 12:4:110

Lucinda W see Stephen A POWER

Susan Brainerd see Henry Fanning NORCROSS

ARROWOOD, NC, burial rec pre-1914 FYC 12:4:360

ARTAXET, Paul fl995, OR, fam hist TFG 8:2:3

ARTHAUD, Emile/Antoine b1806, w Susanna Ebersol, FR, ON, IA, geneal add AG 70:1:27

ARTMAN, Anna Barbara see Nathaniel Banks BUTLER

ASH, John Wesley see Goldie Forrest BEAGHLER

ASHCRAFT, Daniel b1698, w Elizabeth Lewis, CT, PA, geneal by Neal, bk rev HQ 95:57:84 MD 36:1:90 WPG 21:3:46

John bc1644, w Hannah Osborne, EN, CT, fam hist by Neal, bk rev HQ 95:58:90 MD 36:1:90

ASIAN AMERICAN GENEALOGY, Res guide by Byers, bk rev RAG 17:1:14

ASKEW, AL, Choctaw claims for citizenship NTT 15:1/2:27

ASKEY, Thomas fl764, w Betsey Baker, PA, geneal by Askey, bk rev WPG 21:4:55

ASPINWALL, John fl794, NY, travel jour by Collins, bk rev NYR 126:2:153

ATANASOFF, John V fl920, FL, biog PCQ 13:3:4

ATHEY, Henry b1762, MD, SC, fam hist by Athey, bk rev GH 49:4:222

ATKINS, John m1815, w Sally Meeker, NY, OH, fam rec AH 22:2:186

ATKINSON, Anne Eliza see Samuel LAWRENCE

Elizabeth see John CRAIG

Mary see Caleb SHREVE

ATWOOD, Apphia see Isaac SNOW

Rufus B fl929, KY, biog by Smith, bk rev REG 92:4:411

Ruth see James TUTTLE

AUCLAIR, Caroline see Eli AUCLAIR

Eli fl864, w Caroline, CN, ME, biog sketch ACG 21:1:7

AUSTIN, Bryant, GA, Bible rec SCG 15:1:709

Moses fl812, TX, biog sketch GR 37:1:26 PWN 3:2:4

Robert b1870, w Lucy Ann Beauchamp, w Ollie Brown, TN, OK, fam hist by McCornack, bk rev GH 49:4:223

Thomas Homer b1805, MA, geneal by Sikes, bk rev CTN 27:4:586

AUSTRALIA, Actors & actresses 1888, private & professional names, roster TGO 7:12:498

Agriculture, post-harvest, hist 1880-1945, essay QFH 16:2:43

Ballarat riots & Eureka Stockade, hist TGO 7:12:516

Brookfield, Ch of the Good Shepherd 1893-1993, hist by Druve, bk rev QFH 16:2:67

Champion of the Seas pass list TGO 8:1:9

11

AUSTRALIA (continued)
Civil Registration res guide by Smith, bk rev QFH 16:4:140
Colonel Secretary's papers, res tips QFH 16:4:121
Computer geneal res tips QFH 16:1:7
Electoral rolls, res tips QFH 16:2:47
EN & IR anc, res tips QFH 16:1:10
EN (Liverpool) packet & clipper ships, hist TGO 8:1:6
Fam hist res guide by Hall, bk rev NGS 83:1:67 RCR 10:1:2214
Fortitude ship, hist sketch TGO 8:1:16
Gympie One Mile Sch hist by Wegert/Thomson, bk rev QFH 16:4:140
Mount Stewart Elphinstone ship hist 1850 QFH 16:1:11
Paisley, ST vr 1853-1879 GWS 95:43:26
Public Rec Ofc, Ballarat Search Room res guide TGO 7:12:518
Public rec ofc, res tips TGO 8:1:32
Queensland Fam Hist Lib classification scheme, descr QFH 16:1:15
Res guide by Hall, bk rev APG 10:3:89 GH 49:3:194 RAG 16:2:20
ST imm roster, 19th cent ANE 95:57:9
Sydney, Harbour Bridge hist sketch TGO 8:1:28
Sydney, Supreme Court police court rec 1841-1845 by Sheldon, bk rev QFH 16:1:32
Victoria, Gold Rush hist, 1850s TGO 8:1:30
Women anc, res guide by Frost, bk rev QFH 16:1:33
AUSTRIA, Geneal res tips KTP 6:4:53
Salzburg Luth Expulsion, hist, repr 1962, bk rev GR 37:1:50 NCJ 21:1:79 QFH 16:2:66
AUTRY, Giles b1800, w Letitia Miller, SC, KY, IL, brief fam hist KA 30:3:150
AVARY, VA, GA, fam hist by Gelinas, bk rev NC 5:3:125
Yeo, VA, SC, GA, fam hist by Gelinas, bk rev VL 30:2:91

AVILA, Cornelio, w Isabel Urquides, CA, fam hist sketch KTP 7:2:30
BABB, ME, CT, MD, fam hist by Sargent, bk rev DM 59:1:44
Phillip f1652, ME, NH, MA, fam hist by Sargent, bk rev GH 49:5:226
BABINEAU, Hist & geneal 1000-1993 by Babineau, bk rev AGE 24:2&3:45
BACHMAN, Catherine see John ZEHR
BACHMANN, Barbara see Michael ZEHR
BACKENTOSE, Hans Ulrich f1743, SW, PA, fam hist & add by Backensto, bk rev GFP 45:2:91
BACKSENSTOSS, SW, PA, fam hist & add by Backensto, bk rev GFP 45:2:91
BACKUS, Gideon W f1850, w Mary Ann HARDMAN, OR, biog sketch NFB 27:3:41
John b1750, w Magdalena Dockstader, KS, Bible rec TS 37:4:128
BACON, Abigail see Cornelius SHARP
FR, EN, hist of fam origins KTP 14:1:16
BADGET, Adaline see Clavin BRIDGES
BAERG, Johann b1813, w Catrina Newman, PR, MN, fam hist by Janzen, bk rev GFP 44:4:190
BAGENSTROSS, SW, PA, fam hist & add by Backensto, bk rev FRT 16:3:100 GFP 45:2:91
Ulrich b1614, SW, fam hist by Backensto, bk rev FRT 16:3:100
BAGGS, John f1850, w--- Agnes, AR, census rec SYH 2:3:17
BAGLEY, America Jane d1945, h John Curtis, AL, obit PT 37:3/4:26
Huldah see Alvah MALLORY
James Alfred d1938, w Grace Elliott, w Cleo Noe, obit & biog PT 37:3/4:27
John Curtis see America Jane BAGLEY
Lydia see Justin T ROBINSON
BAILEY, Berta see Harvey DAY

BAILEY (continued)
Caleb fl836, w Betsey Hills, OH, fam hist sketch AH 22:4:257
Cecily see Samuel JORDAN
Fam assoc addresses PWN 2:5:23
George W fc1861, FL, abstr from Army manual he owned BT 27:1:6
John W b1830, w Matilda Johnson, NC, geneal PWN 2:5:12
Lucy Mariah see Rufus HARDY MS, fam rec PWN 2:5:24
Temperance see Creed FOSTER TX, fam rec PWN 2:5:6
William Houston b1855, w Emma Francis Burdett, MS, TX, fam rec PWN 2:5:16

BAIN, Jane see Alexander T HOLDEN

BAIRD, Sarah Jane see Porter PHIPPS
Zebulon b1764, w Hannah Erwin, NJ, NC, biog sketch LOB 16:4:83

BAKER, Absalom fl824, IL, Rev War pension appl CR 27:1:4
Betsey see Thomas ASKEY
Betty Jean Cox, MO, biog sketch CN 4:3:42
Daniel H b1815, w Lavina McClay, PA, geneal by Fisher, bk rev GH 49:5:226
Edmund (aka Ebenezer Foote), w Rebecca Phillips, TN, MS, AR, fam hist sketch ARH 33:2:70
Elizabeth see John BAKER
Ezra see Ozro BAKER
John bc1598, w Elizabeth, EN, MA, geneal by Karr, bk rev CI 31:4:150
KY, misc fam rec by Brown, bk rev KA 31:2:46
Louis D fl930, NC, jour abstr FC 14:1:2
Ozro see Caledonia G H MOORE
Peter Philip b1769, w Thorothea Volkner, KS, Bible rec & biog sketch TS 37:4:120

BALDWIN, Elizabeth see Samuel BROWN
Frances J see William T MILLER
William fl808, NC, will abstr QY 22:1:7

BALISON, Joe m1910, w Grace Ward, MT, marr cert DCH 6:2:3

BALL, Agnew see Agnew Ball GRAY
Bartholomew bc1710, fam hist by Ball, bk rev GH 49:4:222
Frank see Sarah Armilda FOREN
Mary Lucille see John William BELLAMY
VA, LA, fam hist by Mills, bk rev RAG 16:1:20

BALLARD, Ephraim see Martha MOORE
Martha see Martha MOORE

BALLOU, Emor S b1798, NY(?), Bible rec AW 21:3:82

BANE, Mary Polly see James BURKE

BANFIELD, Elizabeth fl889, CN, corresp abstr NAL 11:2:83

BANKS, Nathaniel Butler, w Anna Barbara Artman, IL, fam hist by Deever, bk rev CI 31:1:22
William see Elizabeth MCVICKER

BANNON, Patrick fl882, w Annie Mary Ryan, NY, FL, fam hist PCQ 4:1:4

BARBER, Moses W, w Thetis Thomas Caraway, NC, GA, fam hist by Barber, bk rev AGM 27:3/4:64
Nora E see Fredrick RAY
Susan A see Thomas C BEAGHLER
Thomas fl635, CT, fam hist by Barber, bk rev TJ 7:2:73

BARFIELD, Lottie b1900, AA, fam hist sketch TGO 7:12:496

BARKER, Sarah see David MOORE
WA, fam rec cont YV 27:1:19

BARKHIMER, Elizabeth see Isaac VERTREES

BARKLEY, John, IL, MO, KS, TX, fam hist by Fischer, bk rev TJ 7:2:77
John, TN, IL, MO, geneal 1753-1994 by Diacher, bk rev GH 49:3:217

BARLOW, Christopher fl775, KY, Rev War pension appl BYG 7:1:368

BARNES, Daniel M b1809, w Margaret, NC, fam hist by Morley, bk rev HQ 95:58:90

BARNES (continued)
James T m1846, w Mary Ann Potts, MD, Bible rec NGS 83:1:57
Margaret see Daniel M BARNES
Mary see William MEARS
Peter b1744, w Sophia Inman, MD, VA, fam hist by Barnes, bk rev TR 35:1:53
Rebecca see Daniel WILKINS
Rezin m1815, w Catharine Rizer, MD, Bible rec NGS 83:1:57

BARR, Mary see Thomas GILLILAND

BARRETT, Caleb b1785, NJ, PA, fam hist by Sanders, bk rev GSN 8:1:7
Mary see Edmund FISH

BARRON, John f1915, TN, will abstr MTG 9:2:88

BARROW, William f1750, w Olivia Ruffin, LA, fam hist sketch KTP 14:2:23

BARRY, Sally see William INGLE

BARTH, Jonas f1759, SC, fam hist by Burrows, bk rev HQ 95:58:90

BARTH, Josias see Joshua BARTH

BARTLETT, Isabel see John D MERWIN
Joseph see Elizabeth FRENCH
Mehitable see Joseph PARSONS
William b1797, w Betsey Bean, VT, Bible rec GFP 44:4:171

BARTOLF, EN, Am, RU, FR, fam hist by Klieforth, bk rev ANE 95:55:34

BARTRAM, Elijah Gregory b1855, CT, Bible rec CTA 37:4:180
Elizabeth m1672, h William Hammond, h Joseph Fiske, identity NER 149:595:230

BARTTLINGCK, Rudolf f1840, GR, OH, Bibl rec SBA 20:4:10

BASHAM, Arminta Caroline see Luke MCKINNEY

BASQUE GENEALOGY, CA, hist & biog 1860-1890 FRT 17:1:8

BASS, Missouri see Thomas A BASS
Thomas A b1855, w Missouri, GA, FL, biog PCQ 22:3:4
Woodrow R f1988, FL, recoll PCQ 19:3:2

BASSETT, Sarah see Henry HITT

BATCHELLER, David b1807, w Amy Hall, WA, Bible rec SGS 44:3:157

BATCHELOR, Mary Elizabeth b1872, LA, autobiog KSL 19:2:60

BATES, Leven T, w Maggie Johnson, KY, biog sketch LAB 10:1:20
Susan see Charles Edwin JOHNSON
Thomas b1410, EN, geneal by Burt, bk rev RAG 16:2:21 TJ 7:3:111

BATTEREM, Elizabeth see William HAMMON

BAUER, Ida Marie b1886, h Dru W Norman, TX, geneal GR 37:1:40

BAULSTON, Elizabeth f1655, h John Coggeshall, RI, hist of div NER 149:596:361

BAYARD, Dr d1890, TX, obit KTP 1:3/4:22

BAYLAYE, Christopher bc1560, w Elizabeth Berie, EN, geneal TAC 6:4:21

BAYNE, Fannie see D M SIMMS
Mary Ann see R H BAYNE
R H b1827, w Mary Ann, AL, Bible rec OLR 9:1:9

BAYS, Granville b1856, w Sarah Booher, OH, fam reg TR 35:1:26

BEACH, Sarah Platt Beach see Miles MERWIN

BEAGHLER, Goldie Forrest b1882, h John Wesley Ash, David Ira Bevington, OH, Bible rec TR 35:3:155
Thomas C m1881, w Susan A Barber, OH, Bible rec TR 35:3:155

BEAL, EN, fam rec by Strong, bk rev QQ 95:25:21

BEALE, Elizabeth see Andrew MCGINNIS
Nancy J see Samuel C ALTER

BEALL, Margaret Ellen b1840, NC, biog HQ 95:58:58

BEAM, --- see Elizabeth SEAGER

BEAN, Betsey see William BARTLETT
Eva Marion b1895, ME, biog sketch BC 19:1:1

BEAN (continued)
George fl776, TN, *Mathew English vs Bean* testimony abstr ETR 7:4:178
James Mac fl688, DE, PA, fam hist by Alexander, bk rev TR 35:2:107
Roy, w Virginia Chavez, TX, biog sketch KTP 1:3/4:30

BEARD, Rachel see Edward PHAIR
SC, fam hist 1759-1991 by Burrows, bk rev HQ 95:58:90
Susan Margarett see Joshua John ZIMMERMAN
William m1773, w Levinah Gifford, NC, will abstr QY 21:4:6

BEARDEN, AR, GA, LA, MS, fam hist by Clemmons, bk rev GGS 31:1:50
GA, MS, AR, fam hist by Harvey, bk rev ARH 33:1:33

BEASLEY, Jane d1777, SC, estate inv ODD 7:2:24

BEATON, Alexander B b1786, ST, obit ANE 95:55:25

BEATY, Daniel L b1828, w Margaret Rhodes, SC, AR, geneal SCH 10:3:91
Flora see Lewis HALL
James Knox Polk b1842, w Elizabeth Conatser, w Sarah Hill, w Sarah Smith, w Catherine Green Adkins, TN, fam rec FCN 6:4:67
Mary see John R GASTON

BEAUCHAMP, Lucy Ann see Robert AUSTIN

BEAULIEU, Rosalie see Joseph-Germain PELTIER
Simon fl804, QB, fam hist LG 95:56:74

BEAVAN, VA, fam hist corr MD 36:1:81

BEBOUT, Benjamin fl758, Belgium, Am, geneal by Brown, bk rev TPI 20:2:88

BECHTEL, Anna Magdalena see Tobias SCHALL

BECK, George bc1823, w Caroline Rebecca Witt, fam rec LM 36:1:202
Ruth Mabel b1887, AA, biog TGO 7:12:520

BECKFORD, Benjamin b1732, w Elizabeth Wood Herrick, MA, geneal TEG 15:4:227

BECKMAN, Bernard H b1828, w Anna Marie Schonhf, GR, OH, fam hist by Smith, bk rev GH 49:3:217
Bernard Henric b1828, GR, OH, geneal by Smith, bk rev TR 35:2:109

BECKMANN, Emma Mayer, TX, biog by Martinello, bk rev KTP 7:3:43

BECRAFT, MD, fam hist add WMG 11:2:88

BEDDINGFIELD, Joseph b1847, w Elizabeth Dewberry, GA, biog BHN 28:3:19

BEDELL, Abner b1760, w Elizabeth, NJ, PA, fam cem rec WPG 22:2:49
Dorothy see Edward BURWELL
Elizabeth see Abner BEDELL

BEDFORD, William fl621, EN, VA, geneal by Bedford, bk rev MSG 15:3:171

BEDWELL, John D fl831, w Jane Funnel, w Matilda Huehner, EN, NY, OH, geneal by Birdwell, bk rev GH 49:4:223
John D, EN, fam hist by Bidwell, bk rev KK 33:2:38

BEHAIM, Friederich fc1510, GR, fam hist by Ozment, bk rev TGC 19:1:13
Magdalena b1555, h Balthasar Paumgartner, GR, corresp by Ozment, bk rev TGC 19:1:13
Michael fc1510, GR, fam hist by Ozment, bk rev TGC 19:1:13
Stephan Carl fc1510, GR, fam hist by Ozment, bk rev TGC 19:1:13

BEHEATHLAND, Robert fl607, VA, fam hist by Covert, bk rev GH 49:5:229

BELGIUM, Flanders, renaissance musicians, hist FAH 13:1:10
Pittem, emigrant roster c1900-1930 FAH 13:1:15
Poperinge, hist FAH 13:1:18

BELIZE, Mennonites 1765 to today, biog sketches MFH 14:1:40

BELKNAP, Jeremy fl784, NH, biog HNH 49:4:201

BELL, Eliza see Gabriel BELL
Gabriel bc1802, w Mahala White, w Eliza, NC, biog sketch CAL 14:4:80
Harmon b1806, CT, Bible rec CTA 37:4:181
Isaac b1765, CT, Bible rec CTA 38:2:69
John, w Sarah, PA, fam hist by Kinsey, bk rev WPG 21:3:50
Robert b1953, IR, EN, biog sketch IFL 5:9:19
Roger b1768, w Catherine Brockman, VA, fam hist by Bell, bk rev GH 49:4:223
Sarah see John BELL
Walter Lafayette, w Ruth Rankin, fam hist by Willette/Gill, bk rev BWG 24:2:154
William b1685, VA, TN, fam hist by Bell, bk rev GH 49:5:226

BELLAMY, John William b1844, w Mary Lucille Ball, MO, biog sketch KCG 36:1:20

BELLVILLE, Dewitt fl863, OH, corresp TTH 16:1:17

BELTZ, PA, fraktur descr MGS 13:4:51

BENAVIDES, Placido fl836, w Dona Augustina de Leon, TX, biog & geneal KTP 2:1:3

BENDER, Gladys b1902, MI, OH, biog TFP 95:12:81
Hans George b1699, w Kathrina Hostetter, GR, PA, fam hist by Marino, bk rev HQ 95:55:93
Harold S b1897, IN, biog sketch PM 18:1:19

BENJAMIN, Judah P b1811, w Natalie S Martin, British West Indies, LA, biog KSL 19:4:142

BENNETCH, Simon fl732, w Catherine Anna Kolbe, PA, fam hist by Wise, bk rev GH 49:4:223

BENNETT, Anne see Jonas BLACKMAN
Charlie D b1866, w Jocie M Dempsy, MD, Bible rec PGB 27:2:29

BENNETT (continued)
Hiram b1796, w Dosia Dobbs, w Sarah Dougan, GA, SC, AR, TX, biog sketch MT 31:4:163
J W b1834, PA?, Bible rec MGS 13:3:36

BENSON, Bessie see Charles F EMERSON
Ida Irene see Harry HUGHES

BENTLEY, Hannah see Thomas BENTLEY
Thomas bc1725, w Hannah, NC, geneal PCH 1:1:22

BENTON, Robert b1809, LA, biog by Kabel, bk rev FPG 17:3:19

BENTZ, PA, fraktur descr MGS 13:4:51

BERCAW, Ann Mary see William JOHNSTON

BERDAN, Ann see Cornelius R WORTENDYKE

BERGMAN, Rose see William DIETERT

BERGMANN, Adelbertha see Conrad ADAM
Amalia b1844, h Henry Dietert, BO, TX, obit KTP 4:4:51
Johanna b1849, h E A F Toepperwein, BO, TX, obit abstr KTP 6:3:37
Joseph d1882, TX, estate doc KTP 1:3/4:23

BERIE, Elizabeth see Christopher BAYLAYE

BERNARD, Catherine see Leon BERNARD
Leon fl828, w Catherine, FR, OH, fam hist by Bernard, bk rev TR 35:1:53

BERNDHEISEL, Valentine bc1710, PA, fam hist sketch TPI 20:3:135

BERNER, Henry d1877, IL, news abstr re:his murder CHG 27:3:91

BERNHISLE, Valentine see Valentine BERNDHEISEL

BERRINGTON, Agnes/Anne see Robert TINKER

BERRY, Joseph, NH, geneal by Berry, bk rev GH 49:6:206
Rebecca see Joshua D CRANE
Sally see Sally BARRY

BERTOLET, --- see Martin WETZEL
BERTRAND, Laura Julia see Harry J FENNER
BERTRON, Mary b1837, h William Hughes, LA, corresp FPG 17:3:19
Mary f1849, MS, letters FPG 17:2:10
BESAT, Hubert f1864, IL, corresp CI 31:3:100
BESS, Daniel b1765, w Mary Katherine Rhodes (Roth), GR, fam hist by Best, bk rev GH 49:5:227
BEST, Daniel see Daniel BESS
BEUTLER, Niklaus f1851, w Rosina Andres, SW, MO, OH, geneal by Bettcher, bk rev MN 26:2:88
BEVERIDGE, Thomas b1826, w Margaret Kennedy McLeish, ST, CN, geneal by Beveridge, bk rev FRT 16:2:69
BEVILLE, SC, GA, FL, geneal add by Lichliter, bk rev TR 35:4:221
BEVINGTON, David Ira see Goldie Forrest BEAGHLER
BICKEL, Mr d1925, TX, news abstr re:his death KTP 1:3/4:28
BICKHAM, EN, MA, NH, fam hist by Crane, bk rev FP 38:3:141
BIDENBACH, Johann Michael f1752, GR, SC, geneal by Holcomb, bk rev SCM 23:4:211 TPI 21:1:52
BIDWELL, John D see John D BEDWELL
BIEGEL, William Henry f1764, w Mary Magdalena Hoff, PA, biog JBC 15:4:1
BIGBIE, George fc1750, VA, geneal by Bigbie, bk rev OZ 17:4:165
BIGGERS, William fc1671, KY, MO, fam hist by Vaughn, bk rev MSG 15:4:223
BIGGS, Anna see William JAYNE
BIGLO, John b1617, MA, geneal by Bigelow Society, bk rev WPG 21:3:47
BILDERBACK, David f1682, PA, NJ, fam hist WPG 22:1:38
MD, PA, NJ, fam hist WPG 22:1:38
BILLETT, Eliza see Daniel DETER

BILLINGS, Anna see Solomon HAKES
Betsey see Peter LAGUIRE
Lamira Dow f1818, CN corresp abstr OBN 28:6:8
BILYEU, Fam rec vol 2 by Terry, bk rev GH 49:3:217
BINNS, Ethel see John STARR
BIRCHER, Mary see G J DANZEISEN
BIRD, Frances see Moses BIRD
Jeptha fc1790, w Amelia Ann Stuckey, SC, geneal by Da Lee Haidek, bk rev GH 49:4:223
Moses fc1790, w Frances, w Mary Dykes, SC, geneal by Da Lee Haidek, bk rev GH 49:4:223
Stephen fc1790, w Elizabeth Frances Herrin, SC, geneal by Da Lee Haidek, bk rev GH 49:4:223
BISH, David b1804, w Rebecca Confer, PA, geneal by Jesberger, bk rev WPG 22:2:54
BISHOP, Andrew b1764, w Lois, CT, Bible rec CTA 38:2:68
Edwin m1827, w Hannah Palmer, CT, Bible rec CTA 37:3:121
Erastus C b1798, CT, Bible rec CTA 37:4:177
John f1695, CT, books in his lib, add CTA 37:3:123
Lois see Andrew BISHOP
Sarah see Samuel SMITH
BIXBY, George R b1870, w Riley, KS, obit abstr MGR 29:4:106
Riley see George R BIXBY
BIXLER, Mariah see Christian LANDES
BJORKELUND, Carolina see Carl Eric ERICSON
BLACK, Elizabeth see Michael LUNSFORD
Elva b1895, h --- Label, MN, biog sketch LRT 14:2:548
Josiah O, w Elizabeth Ann Rainer, AL, fam tree by Black, bk rev TJ 7:1:38
BLACK GENEALOGY see AFRICAN AMERICAN GENEALOGY
BLACKBURN, Sarah Matilda see Christopher Columbus KALLAM

BLACKMAN, Jonas bc1733, w Anne Bennett, CT, geneal NEH 12:6:204

BLAICH, Christian Frederick b1844, w Amelia Von Kettler Toerkler, fam hist KK 33:4:69
  Edward C f1885, m Ida E Olson, KS, fam hist KK 33:4:69

BLAIR, John, TN, fam hist by Webb, bk rev BWG 24:1:65
  KY, geneal cont EK 31:1:22

BLAISE, Grace see Marvel MOSELEY

BLAKE, Lucy see Warren RUCKER

BLANCHARD, LA, fam hist by Wise, bk rev GH 49:5:234

BLAND, Peyton b1815, LA, biog THT 23:2:80
  Peyton b1815, LA, indenture rec THT 23:2:79

BLANDING, Albert Hazen b1876, w Mildred Hale, IA, FL, biog PCQ 16:3:4
  Fam hist by Blanding, bk rev NCJ 21:3:303 TS 37:3:94
  Noah, fam hist by Blanding, bk rev MI 41:2:58

BLANFORD, VA, fam hist corr MD 36:1:81

BLANKENBAKER, Nicholas f1832, VA, KY, court deposition BYG 8:1:427

BLANKENBECKER, Aron bc1780, w Elizabeth, VA, Bible rec BYG 7:5:408
  Elizabeth see Aron BLANKENBECKER

BLANKNER, Mary Huffaker b1907, FL, recoll PCQ 15:2:2

BLANTINE, William f1639, MA, fam hist by Blanding, bk rev CI 31:2:68

BLANTON, William see William BLANTINE

BLAUVELT, NY, NJ, geneal, revised edition by Moos, bk rev NYR 126:4:283

BLAYLOCK, John b1802, w Hannah Hammer, VA, fam hist by Ordway, bk rev GH 49:4:223

BLAYLOCK (continued)
  William b1789, w Elizabeth Davis, VA, fam hist by Ordway, bk rev GH 49:4:223

BLAZER, SW, fam archives by Blazer, bk rev IGS 27:2:116

BLEDSOE, Elizabeth Ann see William Corwyne BROWN

BLESSING, Jacob bc1728, w Elizabeth Ritschard, GR, PA, geneal by Beiueler, bk rev FP 38:1:13

BLOCKER, Margaretha see Adam STUHR

BLOSSOM, Elizabeth see George Newton BLOSSOM
  George Newton d1885, w Elizabeth, KS, biog KCG 36:2:100

BLOUNT, Ben, FL, recoll PCQ 9:2:2

BLYTHE, William Jefferson b1946, AR, anc, sketch CAL 14:4:80

BOARD, Phillip Schuyler b1760, w Eleanor Thompson, w Mary Polly Castleman, NJ, NY, KY, biog by Neill, bk rev GH 49:5:227 KA 30:3:175 NYR 126:3:215

BOARDMAN, Henry m1842, w Caroline Daniels, MA, Bible rec BG 16:4:136
  Mary see John BULL

BOAZ, Elenor see Thomas BOAZ
  Thomas dc1780, w Elenor, TN, Bible rec ETR 7:3:142

BOBO, Gabriel f1700, FR, VA, SC, geneal THS 95:100:36

BODINE, John fc1750, OH, identity TR 35:1:39

BOERNER, Dorothy see Karl DIENGER

BOGART, William m1891, w Jennie Fast, OH, Bible rec SBA 20:3:7

BOGGS, Andrew M f1821, SC, deed cert abstr SCM 23:1:20

BOHNERT, Wilhelmina see Alexander KAISER

BOILES, Maria B see Alexander MECAY

BOLENDER, Juliana see Philip Jacob SCHENCKEL

BOLIN, KY, fam cem rec KA 31:1:17
Levina May see Ferd J JOHANSEN
Sarah d1896, MO, Bible rec OZ 17:4:104
BONACKER, William B b1834, w Elizabeth King, GR, FL, biog sketch PCQ 14:3:4
BOND, Christy f1990, MI, anc by Bond, bk rev DM 58:4:192
BONEY, John Quincy Adams, w Nancy Mariah Waters, VA, fam hist by Gibb, bk rev NCJ 21:3:303
BONI, Jacob, NC, fam hist by Gibb, bk rev NCJ 21:3:303
BONJOUR, Bertha see Paul Aime JUNOD
BONNET, Margaret see John WAGGONER
Mary see John WETZEL
BONNEY, Ichabod b1762, w Anna Merrill, ME, biog sketch AHS 95:15:1
BOOE, Jacob f1792, NC, plantation slave rec RCR 10:4:2370
BOOHER, Sarah see Granville BAYS
BOON, Hugh b1840, OH, autobiog & biog TR 35:3:129
BOONE, Cynthia Ann, h Moody Grubbs, IL, biog by Parks, bk rev CI 31:4:151
James, w Olly Howell, NC?, desc roster FWC 12:2:256
John see James BOONE
BORING, James f1795, w Sarah, TN, biog sketch BWG 24:2:133
Rachel see Mordecai PRICE
Sarah see James BORING
BORYS, Mary see John GROMEK
BOSCH, Sebastian f1737, w Elizabethia Katherina Heyl, GR, Am, fam hist by Best, bk rev GH 49:5:227
BOST, W L bc1850, NC, oral hist trans KTP 7:2:26
BOSTON, James bc1775, w Nancy Hill, VA, fam hist sketch KA 31:1:18
BOSWELL, William M f1884, w Achsah E Scott, FL, fam hist PCQ 17:2:4

BOTELER, Charles bc1635, w Alice Phillips, EN, MD, geneal AG 70:1:9
Henry Edward bc1755, w Elizabeth Norriss, w Martha Keaton (Philpott) Allen, MD, fam rec WMG 11:1:2 11:3:99
BOUCHER, Marie-Charlotte see Jacques DEVEAU
BOUDREAU, CN, fam hist cont AGE 24:1:11
Joseph b1789, w Marguerite Chaisson, QB, geneal AGE 24:2&3:59
BOUILLON, Francoise fc1763, FR, corresp LG 95:55:61
BOURASSA, Charles see Madeleine DELBEQUE
BOURGEOIS, Jacques, LA, geneal by Bourgeois, bk rev AGE 24:4:101
BOURGET, Edouard Theophile b1870, w Louisa Paradis, QB, MA, biog ACG 21:2:55
BOUTON, Gould bc1731, NY, biog CTA 38:2:49
BOWDEN, Thomas d1911, EN, PA, IA, obit ISC 19:2:30
BOWEN, Abigail see Benjamin FISKE
BOWER, Conrad f1751, w Marie Eva, MD, OH, geneal by Mansfield, bk rev WPG 21:3:50
Marie Eva see Conrad BOWER
BOWERS, Elmer W see Jessie PIERCE
BOWLEGS, Billy b1862, FL, biog PCQ 14:4:1
BOWLES, Josiah f1830, MI, geneal by Powell, bk rev DM 58:4:189
BOWMAN, Ann see Wendel BOWMAN
Daniel dc1812, w Mary, will abstr CAL 14:4:81
Mary see Daniel BOWMAN
Mellissa see Jeter Conley PRITCHARD
Moses f1858, VA, corresp abstr SSG 14:4:53
Wendel d1735, w Ann, PA, geneal PM 18:4:18

BOWSER, John b1774, w Magdelania Byers, MD, OH, fam hist SSG 14:2:28

BOYD, Joseph fl806, AL, citizenship doc & will AFH 16:1:24

BOYDSTUN, John G b1863, w S J Hudson, TX, Bible rec FP 38:3:129
John m1795, w Nancy Gardner, TX, Bible rec FP 38:3:128
Nancy b1775, TX, Bible rec FP 38:3:128

BOYER, Anna Mary see Mary E RIPPLE

BOYLAN, Aaron A b1827, autobiog & fam hist by Sharp, bk rev NGS 83:2:144

BOYLES, James O m1878, w Mary, div rec NTT 14:3:96

BOZARTH, Simon fc1700, w Mary Mason, VA, fam hist by Morley, bk rev HQ 95:58:90

BRACKENRIDGE, George see Isabella Helena MCCULLOCH

BRACY, Alexander m1900, w Samantha Wright, AR, Bible rec & obits SYH 3:3:12

BRADBURY, John fl810, Western travels, autobiog, bk rev STS 35:4:21

BRADFORD, Richard fl653, w Frances Taylor, VA, geneal by Bradford, bk rev AGM 27:3/4:64

BRADHAM, SC, NC, GA, fam hist by Brewster, bk rev AGM 27:3/4:64

BRADLEY, Jefferson C b1802, w Nancy L Hetherington, CA, Bible rec GGP 28:1:46
VA & the South, fam rec by Bradley, bk rev CCS 16:4:138 LOB 16:2:41

BRADSHAW, Susan see R B WHITE

BRADT, Albert Andriessen fl636, NO, NY, fam hist by Christoph, bk rev NYR 126:4:284

BRAINERD, Daniel fl677, w Hannah, CT, brief fam hist PV 24:1:4
Hannah see Daniel BRAINERD

BRANDLINGER, Anna Catharina see Hans Jorg BRANDLINGER

BRANDLINGER (contined)
Hans Jorg bc1660, w Anna Catharina, GR, PA, fam hist 1660-1994 by Brendlinger, bk rev CI 31:4:150 CSB 30:3:105 PGB 27:4:66

BRANDT, Otto J b1879, GR, MI, obit TTL 23:3:56

BRANHAM, David, KY, fam hist by Phillips, bk rev PCH 1:1:38
Milly fc1840, KY, VA, geneal by Salyers, bk rev PCH 1:1:36

BRANNEN, Catherine b1935, h Harvey Guenther Adam, NE, fam tree KTP 12:3:45

BRANSCOMBE, VA, fam hist by Peterson, bk rev APR 14:11:5

BRANSCOME, VA, fam hist by Peterson, bk rev APR 14:11:5

BRASEE, John Trafford fl818, OH, obit abstr FTC 17:3:46

BRASSELL, Mary Polly see Samuel PRUETT

BRASWELL, Jacob bc1750, w Serena, NC, geneal JC 21:3:55
Robert dc1734, w Sarah, VA, NC, biog sketch KTP 14:3:42
Sarah see Robert BRASWELL
Serena see Jacob BRASWELL

BRAY, Dan fl900, AA, biog sketch QFH 16:1:22
David Sutton m1822, w Eliza McLaine, NJ, Bible rec MAG 8:1:5

BRAZEE, Margaret see Henry COLE

BRAZZEALE, Jim b1852, TX, news abstr AFH 16:2:12

BRENDEL, Hans Georg b1713, FR, PA, w Eva Catharina Frey, geneal FC 13:4:3

BRENDLINGER, GR, Am, fam hist 1660-1994 by Brendlinger, bk rev AGS 36:4:119 ARH 33:4:174 CI 31:4:150 CSB 30:3:105 PGB 27:4:66 VQS 32:3:43
Joseph fc1752, GR, PA, fam hist by Brendlinger, bk rev OC 32:2:54

BRENEMAN, Mary see Philip GARMAN

BRENNEMANN, Christian see Melchior BRENNEMANN
Melchior f1671, w Christian, SW, GR, Am, fam hist MFH 15:1:42
BRENT, Mary Elizabeth see Harrison Simpson ROBERTS
VA, fam hist corr MD 36:1:81
BREVARD, Caroline M d1920, FL, obit abstr FLG 18:3:106
BREWER, Electa M see Fitch David CRANDALL
John b1796, w Keziah Johnson, NC, fam hist by Broyhill, bk rev NCJ 21:1:79
NC, fam hist by Broyhill, bk rev NCJ 21:1:79
VA, geneal doc 1626-1776 by Broyhill, bk rev NCJ 21:2:187
BRIANTE, Abigail see William CARPENTER
BRICE, Ruth see Alexander CULBERTSON
BRIDGES, Calvin b1831, w Adaline Badget, IL, Bible rec & fam hist CI 31:4:134
Jonathan b1753, w Prudence, MA, Bible rec BG 16:4:135
Prudence see Jonathan BRIDGES
BRIDGET, Mary see James BROOKSHAW
BRIGGS, Caleb A W b1811, w Ruth Tuell, RI, Bible rec RIR 21:3:80
Hannah see Wolston BROCKWAY
Phoebe see Amos WOOLSEY
BRIGHTMAN, Henry b1839, w Mariah J Salter, MA, Bible rec GN 13:1:5
BRITTAIN, Mrs --- Scruggs b1833, h T F Brittain, AL, TX, recoll PWN 1:2:3
T F see Mrs --- Scruggs BRITTAIN
BRIXEY, John see Rachel MACKIE
BROADWELL, Susannah see Robert MILLER
BROCKENBROUGH, John b1773, w Gabriella Harvie Randolph, slave inv VA 33:2:102
BROCKMAN, Catherine see Roger BELL

BROCKMAN (continued)
Rachel see Robert PAGE
BROCKWAY, Elizabeth see William HARRIS
Wolston f1659, w Hannah Briggs, CT, geneal by Bentley, bk rev GH 49:4:223
BRODHEAD, Ann Elizabeth, h John Cockburn, geneal by Brodhead, bk rev GH 49:3:218
David, w Ann Tye, geneal by Brodhead, bk rev GH 49:3:218
BROOKS, George Washington b1812, w Martha Gibson Smith, SC, biog sketch LOB 16:1:13
James William see Temperance Jane TUCKER
John W b1858, w Barbara Hill, w Nettie Prairie, NY, biog TTT 19:4:161
Nancy see Elijah Vail PITTMAN
Ralph f1596, EN, fam hist sketch HPF 95:50:24
William James b1752, w Nancy Anne Locke, VA, fam hist sketch HPF 95:50:24
Zachariah bc1810, w Sarah Ann (McGill) Cheek, TN, TX, biog HCG 13:3:39
BROOKSHAW, James dc1726, w Mary Bridget, geneal PWN 2:3:3
BROUGHTON, Hester Adamantha, h James Elory Fenner, fam hist by Fenner, bk rev GH 49:6:208
BROUILLARD, Charles bc1667, FR, IL, geneal by Brouillard, bk rev AGE 24:2&3:44
BROUSSARD, Francois, geneal by Conover, bk rev AGE 24:4:101
Nicolas, geneal by Conover, bk rev AGE 24:4:101
BROWDER, Edmund f1693, w Elizabeth, EN, VA, NC, TN, fam hist by Dye, bk rev GH 49:6:206 KSL 19:4:154 SGS 45:1:35
Edward see Edmund BROWDER
Elizabeth see Edmund BROWDER

BROWN, America see Joseph N ELKINS
Anna see Benjamin HARLOW
Charlotte see Meredith E WEBB
Clark dc1817, w Tabitha Moffat, CT, fam hist vol 2 by Young, bk rev MD 36:1:89
D H b1847, w Ella North, GA, biog sketch CCM 15:1:11
Daniel b1800, w Ann McCormick, IR, ON, biog sketch IFL 5:9:16
Elizabeth J see Daniel BRUMLEY
Emma F see Jacob HANSON
Fred T b1853, w Sabra M Hayford, OH, Bible rec TR 35:3:158
Irma Catherine see George Albert OGLE
John b1800, CT, biog HQ 95:58:9
John f1840, WV, hist & biog by Finkelman, bk rev REG 93:3:352
John Martin b1858, w Nannie H Rinshaw, TX, Bible rec GR 37:1:23
John, biog, repr 1929, bk rev REG 92:4:448
Lawrence Bernard f1884, FL, hist of his home PCQ 19:4:1
Lillian see Berton WOLVERTON
Margaret see Robert T HENDERSON
Martha see Isaac GLENNY
Mary b1766, h John Wakefield, h Thomas Washburn, h Joseph Parsons, h Daniel Crosby, h Eliakim Seavey, ME, geneal & data on her husbands TMG 17:4:127
Mary Ann see George Avery WHITE
Mary Ann see William JOHNSTON
Mary Sussie m1904, h Zeffie Morgan Ham, OK, fam hist TTT 20:1:21
Nancy see James MCFATE
Ollie see Mollie ROGERS
Ollie see Robert AUSTIN
Philip, PA, fam hist by Brown Fam reunion, bk rev TPI 21:1:52
Samuel fc1770, w Elizabeth Baldwin, VA, fam hist by Lightburn, bk rev AMG 9:6:5
Sarah see Joshua WHEELER
Sidney see Henry F C JOHNSON

BROWN (continued)
W N f1862, AL, corresp abstr MCA 14:4:120
William b1845, w Mary Etta Stickel, WV, brief geneal & obit AGS 36:2:40
William bc1669, EN, MA, geneal by Brown, bk rev NYR 126:3:217
William Corwyne m1858, w Elizabeth Ann Bledsoe, fam hist by Chanz, bk rev GH 49:3:218
William Douglas b1852, w Mollie Rogers, TN, OK, fam hist by McCornack, bk rev GH 49:4:223
William f1686, EN, MA, geneal by Brown, bk rev TR 35:3:165
William Newton b1807, OH, geneal by Brown, bk rev IGS 27:2:118
BROWNE, Ann see Thomas VARNEY
BROWNELL, Alice see Stephen WILCOX
BROWNING, Meshach, MD, autobiog, repr 1859, bk rev APR 14:2:3
BRUBAKER, Emma J see John H KNEPPER
BRUCE, Andrew fc1880, ST, MD, fam hist by Ellis, bk rev EWA 32:1:27
Norman fc1880, ST, MD, fam hist by Ellis, bk rev EWA 32:1:27
Normand, ST, fam hist by Ellis, bk rev EWA 32:1:27
Selkirk fc1880, ST, MD, fam hist by Ellis, bk rev EWA 32:1:27
BRUMLEY, Daniel b1814, w Elizabeth J Brown, KY, brief fam hist KA 31:2:10
BRUNER, Jacob L b1832, w Lauina Watson Fudge, TX, IL, fam rec KTP 14:3:37
BRUNK, George R f1952, PA, speech abstr PM 19:1:24
BRUNNER, John b1792, w Ann Maria Stickel, MD, Bible rec WMG 11:1:38
BRYAN, Francis, EN, bk 1 of the Bryan scroll by McMurtry, bk rev RCR 10:2:2275

BRYAN (continued)
Morgan b1671, EN, NC, fam hist by McMurtry, bk rev RCR 10:2:2275
Nathaniel Clay b1846, w Martha Jane Howell, FL, fam hist IMP 14:1:22
William b1757, NC, FL, fam hist IMP 14:1:22
BRYANT, Anna see John MILLIMAN
BRYENT, Benjamin Dole fl879, ME, jour abstr AHS 95:14:3
BUCHANAN, Jane see William Hoffman HIGDON
ST, fam hist, repr 1820, bk rev IS 16:1:11
ST, geneal by Buchanan, bk rev GH 49:3:198
BUCK, William b1832, w Esther V Long, PA, biog sketch BGN 16:2:17
BUCKNER, Thomas bc1765, w Hannah Burton, VA, fam hist ARH 33:2:57
BUDD, Joseph D m1878, w Jennie N Spencer, NJ, Bible rec MAG 8:3:9
BUGG, William Emmanuel b1848, VA, NC, jour, bk rev TJ 7:3:109
BUKOVINIAN GENEALOGY, Res tips SGB 26:2:59
BULL, George fl884, w Julia Hartmann, biog sketch KTP 6:1:6
John fl812, w Mary Boardman, EN, biog sketch KTP 6:4:56
BULLACK, Minnie m1902, h Archie MacFarland, OR, biog by Olsen, bk rev GH 49:6:209
BULLOCK, J C fl903, OH, corresp abstr TR 35:3:151
BURBA see BURBEE
BURBEE, Peter bc1729, New England, geneal by Lawrence, bk rev GH 49:4:223
BURBY see BURBEE
BURCHAM, Henry fc1675, w Margaret Haynes, EN, NJ, geneal QY 21:4:5
BURCHSTEAD, John Henry b1719, w Anna Potter, MA, geneal cont TEG 15:4:195
BURDEN, Joseph see Nancy Mahulda BURDEN

BURDEN (continued)
Nancy Mahulda b1831, h Joseph Burden, TN, MO, autobiog MSG 15:3:142
BURDETT, Emma Francis see William Houston BAILEY
BURDIN, Benjamin fc1800, VA, court abstr ETR 7:4:196
BURDINE, Estelle fl898, FL, biog sketch PCQ 3:2:4
BURDYNE, Catherine see Richard BURDYNE
Dorothea see Richard BURDYNE
John fl786, w Elizabeth Dicken, VA, biog sketch BYG 7:6:417
Richard fl739, w Catherine, w Dorothea, VA, SC, biog sketch BYG 7:5:405
BURGE, James Ira b1871, w Janey, LA, Bible rec FPG 17:3:22
Janey see James Ira BURGE
Wilson Williamson bc1866, LA?, Bible rec FPG 17:2:11
BURGER, Henry Edward m1854, w Louisa Myer Smith, CT, Bible rec CTA 37:3:103
BURJES, Annie see Henry BURJES
Henry, w Annie, IL, SD, fam hist by Fitch/O'Neal, bk rev BHN 28:2:19
BURKE, James fc1655, w Mary Polly Bane, IR, fam hist by Alexander, bk rev GH 49:4:227
John fl786, w Mary Stevens, VA, geneal PCH 1:2:26
Lucy see Reuben ANDERSON, Richard, MA, geneal by Boutelle/Burke, bk rev PR 23:2:70
BURKHOLDER, Nora E see Raymond L HARTZLER
BURKS, James Madison b1819, w Narcissa J Holmes, GA, Bible rec YTD 15:1:12
BURLEIGH, Gertrude see Varnum Paine SIMMONS
BURLING, Thomas b1746, w Susanna Carter, NY, biog NYR 126:4:225
BURNETT, John G b1810, TN, autobiog HPF 95:50:33

BURNETT (continued)
VA, fam hist by Peterson, bk rev APR 14:11:5

BURNHAM, Mourning see Silas Smith GLENN

BURNS, Esther see Daniel SWITZER
P fl861, IL, corresp MCS 15:2:83
Rachel see Ferdinand KOEBER

BURR, Ruth Maxine b1911, MI, anc by Burr, bk rev KVH 19:7:80
Washington fl860, MI, geneal by Powell, bk rev DM 58:4:189

BURRELL, Mary see Walter BURRELL
Walter N b1750, w Mary, SC, geneal LOB 16:4:85

BURRESS, Elizabeth see Wilkinson ONEAL

BURRIS, John fc1865, FL, biog sketch BT 27:1:10

BURROW, William Washington d1895, AR, biog sketch SCH 10:3:89

BURT, James, EN, MA, geneal by Burt, bk rev RAG 16:2:18 TJ 7:2:75
Richard, EN, MA, geneal by Burt, bk rev RAG 16:2:18 TJ 7:2:75

BURTIS, Garret fl780, NY, Bible rec NYR 126:2:104

BURTON, Hannah see Thomas BUCKNER
Henry, w Mary Williams, TN, SC, fam hist by Morley, bk rev HQ 95:58:90

BURWELL, Edward fl609, w Dorothy Bedell, VA, geneal by Brown, bk rev GH 49:5:227
Lewis b1710, w Mary Willis, VA, geneal by Brown, bk rev VAG 39:1:77

BUSH, Art b1859, NE, biog AU 19:1:5

BUSS, Elizabeth see Jacob GERHART
Mary Elizabeth see Baltzer YOUNG

BUTCHER, Jennie see George HACKETT

BUTLER, Emma Elizabeth see R B WHITE
Frank see Annie OAKLEY
Hellen Donna see Shirley Burrus SPIVEY

BUTLER (continued)
William see Behethland Foote MOORE

BUTTS, TX, fam hist timeline PWN 2:1:7

BYERLY, Conrad fl789, MD, PA, biog & fam hist PGB 26:5:107 26:6:131

BYERS, Magdelania see John BOWSER
Tillie O fl877, h Jerome Robinson Wilson, PA, autograph bk by Gill, bk rev WPG 22:1:47 21:3:47

BYRAM, Abby bc1765, h Joseph Collins, NJ, biog & fam hist MAG 8:2:7

BYRD, A C b1828, FL, fam cem rec PCQ 12:2:6
Frederick fl834, NY, biog & identity NYR 126:3:167

CABANISS, Scott see Janie GERFERS

CADILLAC, Antoine de Lamothe fl707, MI, biog sketch MHH 16:4:119

CADREAU, Mary see Theodore HAMANN

CADWELL, Mary see Jeremiah DIGGINS

CAINS, Martha see Richard VATCHER,

CAKE, Selina fl889, CN, corresp abstr NAL 11:2:83

CALDWELL, David, w Ann Harris, NC, SC, AR, geneal by Files, bk rev ARH 33:2:82
James d1836, MO, fam hist MSG 15:1:30
Mary see John FINLEY

CALHOUN, John C fl840, SC, biog by Bartlett, bk rev REG 93:3:348
ST, Am, fam hist by Johnson, bk rev GRC 11:2:25 HTR 38:1:8

CALIFORNIA, Agua Mansa, bapt rec 1852 VQS 32:3:35
Agua Mansa, pioneer hist VQS 32:3:37
Agua Mansa-La Placita area, sacramental rec c1851-1893 VQS 32:4:59

CALIFORNIA (continued)
Amador Co, cem rec by Cissna/Church, bk rev GH 49:5:190
Archives addresses PV 23:9:5
Basque population, hist & biog 1860-1890 FRT 17:1:8
Bay Area, museum & geneal search facility address list SMN 13:3:44
Benicia, Benicia Barracks Chapel bapt index RDQ 12:5:101
Benicia, cem rec 1849-1949 by Hayes, bk rev GH 49:5:191
Benicia, St Paul's Epis Ch Rec index 1852-1910 RDQ 12:1:6
Brown's Valley, goldmining news abstr c1865 GGP 28:1:33
Butler Guard hist by Freshour, bk rev FRT 16:2:64
Butte Co, Durham & Nelson cem rec by Corley/Farley, bk rev GH 49:4:206 HQ 95:55:92
Butte Co, Great Voter reg c1878 GGP 28:1:53
Butte Co, natu rec & decl of intention 1843-1929 by Corley/Farley, bk rev HQ 95:59:89
Butte Co, Nelson Cem rec by Corley/Farley, bk rev GH 49:4:206
Butte Co, obits c1897-1940, brief abstr GGP 28:1:17
Butte Co, Oroville, direct 1881 GGP 28:1:59
Camarillo, resident roster 1912-1913 RT 13:2:34
Citrus Heights, State Archives Bldg res tips RCP 17:2:44
Claremont, Rancho Santa Ana Botanical Gardens hist sketch PV 23:5:4
Coloma, pioneer burials by Gold Discovery Park Assoc, bk rev FRT 16:2:66
County census codes, list RT 13:1:7
Dixon, United Meth Ch bapt index, 19th & 20th cent RDQ 12:3:57
Dixon, United Meth Ch deaths, 19th cent RDQ 12:3:66

CALIFORNIA (continued)
Dixon, United Meth Ch marr index, 19th & 20th cent RDQ 12:3:61
Dixon, United Meth Ch minister roster, 19th & 20th cent RDQ 12:3:67
Dows Prairie, precinct reg 1912 RED 27:4:8
Early hist sketch LL 31:1:29
Easton, Washington Union High Sch grads 1913-1925 ATE 30:1:37
Easton, Washington Union High Sch grads 1926-1931 ATE 30:2:43
Emig roster & biog data by Nelson, bk rev GH 49:4:205
Eureka, census 1880 RED 27:4:3
Fairfield, Grace Epis Ch rec c1877-1920 RDQ 12:2:31
Fam Hist Centers, res guide SMN 13:9:154
Fortuna, burial permits 1905-1915 RED 28:2:11
Fresno, early hist & biog sketches ATE 30:2:15
Fresno, women's hist, 19th cent ATE 30:2:2
Fullerton, CA Union high sch & junior college teacher roster 1893-1943 OC 31:1:1
Helena, Holy Cross Cath cem inscr & surname index, bk rev TB 21:3:11
Hispanic builders hist 1769-1850 by Schuetz-Miller, bk rev SCS 32:6:139
Homestead Decl of Marr Persons 1860-1864 RCP 18:1:7
Hueneme Twp, census 1880 RT 13:1:1 13:2:29 13:3:57 13:4:85
Humboldt Co, burial permits 1905-1915 RED 27:4:11
Humboldt Co, men's obits c1966 RED 27:4:21
Humboldt Co, women's obits c1966 RED 27:4:19
Humboldt, census 1880 cont RED 28:2:3
Joaquin Co, cem rec vol 1 by SJGS, bk rev GH 49:5:190
Lake, hist, repr 1873, bk rev GH 49:5:190

CALIFORNIA (continued)
- Livermore-Amador Geneal Soc anc & surnames, bk rev GH 49:3:202
- Marysville, Eugenia Poston Club member roster 1908 OC 32:2:1
- Mendocino Co, hist & biog sketches GGP 28:1:25
- Mendocino Coast, births, deaths & marr 1889-1909 by MCGS, bk rev PR 23:2:64 RT 13:4:101
- Mendocino, hist, repr 1873, bk rev GH 49:5:190
- Monterey Co, mort sched 1860 RCP 17:4:119
- Morgan Hill, hist SCC 32:2:59
- Napa Valley, Memorial Cem inscr by NVGBS, bk rev TB 21:3:12
- Napa Valley, Mercier & Permelee Funeral Home rec 1923-1930, bk rev TB 21:3:14
- Napa Valley, tax assessment rec 1884-1893 by NVGBS, bk rev TB 21:3:12
- Napa, hist, repr 1873, bk rev GH 49:5:190
- Oakland, St Mary's Cem rec NHR 12:4:156
- Orange Co, cem rec up to 1992, alphabetized list OC 32:2:29
- Orange Co, funeral director reg of funerals 1901-1902, cont OC 32:2:35
- Orange Co, street names, hist OC 32:2:4
- Oregon Trail deaths 1852, roster & hist GGP 28:1:15
- Pomona Geneal Soc hist timeline & charter member roster PV 24:4:3
- Pomona, centennial hist 1888-1988 by Lothrop, bk rev PV 23:6:2
- Probate court rec, res tips RCP 17:4:122
- Public rec primer & handbk by Ray, bk rev OC 32:2:55
- Redwood City Public Lib, descr of services avail SMN 13:1:17
- Residents from other states, biog sketches OC 31:1:36 32:2:12
- Riverside Co, Indian reservation data LL 30:3:88

CALIFORNIA (continued)
- Riverside Co, Native American census 1900 LL 30:3:80
- Riverside, current events list 1965 LL 30:3:75
- Riverside, Evergreen cem rec 1933-1935 cont LL 31:1:13
- Sacramento Co, fed pensioner roster 1884 RCP 17:3:86
- Sacramento, fire dept roster 1863 RCP 17:4:133
- Sacramento, natu rec from news 1856-1859 RCP 17:2:61
- Sacramento, probate court lists from news 1862-1873, RCP 17:3:87
- Sacramento, sch graduation rec 1865 RCP 17:4:126
- San Bernardino Co, deaths bk 3 VQS 32:1:5
- San Bernardino Co, deaths c1850-1905 VQS 32:4:57
- San Bernardino Valley, marr cert abstr 1882-1887 VQS 32:4:55
- San Bernardino, death rec bk 3 c1884 VQS 32:3:41
- San Bernardino, marr cert 1882-1887 VQS 32:3:39
- San Francisco, ancestry res guide by Beals, bk rev TB 21:3:14
- San Francisco, earthquake 1906 missing person & casualty rosters cont RCP 17:2:54
- San Francisco, geneal res guide by Beals, bk rev RDQ 12:2:29
- San Francisco, lawyers from OH, roster 1851 TR 35:3:150
- San Francisco, marr returns index 1850-1858 by Beals, bk rev TB 21:3:11
- San Francisco, Minns Normal Sch grads 1861-1862 OC 32:2:3
- San Francisco, res guide by Beals, bk rev GH 49:3:203
- San Salvador Parish, Aqua Mansa Bapt rec c1855 VQS 32:4:53
- Santa Barbara Co, casualty roster 1941-1945 AW 22:2:47

CALIFORNIA (continued)
Santa Barbara Co, imm in census 1850 VCG 95:DEC:17
Santa Barbara High Sch commencement booklet 1903 AW 21:3:76
Santa Barbara High Sch commencement booklet 1904 AW 21:3:77
Santa Barbara High Sch mag abstr 1907 AW 22:1:13
Santa Barbara hist sketch AW 21:2:57
Santa Barbara, 1st United Meth Ch marr rec to 1925 AW 21:3:78
Santa Barbara, High Sch Magazine student roster 1908 AW 22:2:37
Santa Clara Co, decl of intention 1850-1870 by Rose, bk rev RAG 16:2:21
Santa Clara Co, Free Ch of the Holy Saviour hist SCC 32:2:89
Santa Clara Co, Great Reg 1888 cont SCC 32:1:29 32:2:81
Santa Clara Co, Peninsula Funeral & Memorial Soc rec c1900 SCC 32:1:34 32:2:64
Santa Clara Co, probate rec c1878 cont SCC 32:1:12
Santa Clara Co, probate rec c1890 cont SCC 32:2:71
Santa Clara Co, settler roster SCC 32:2:50
Santa Clara Valley, land grant app index SCC 32:1:27
Santa Cruz Cavalry & Butler Guard, hist 1863-1868 by Freshour, bk rev FRT 16:2:64 16:3:99 TJ 7:2:75
SAR centennial reg 1893-1993 by Breithaupt, bk rev NER 149:596:436
Settlers from ME, early hist OC 29:3:93
Solano Co, hist, repr 1879, bk rev RDQ 12:2:29
Solano Co, news abstr from the *Dixon Tribune*, bk rev RDQ 12:5:96
Sonoma, hist, repr 1873, bk rev GH 49:5:190
Spanish naval history 1792 by Cutter, bk rev CGJ 3:4:10

CALIFORNIA (continued)
St Helena, cem inscr vol 1 by NVGBS, bk rev TB 21:3:10
Steamboat explosions, hist & crew rosters RCP 18:1:14
Stockton, birth, death & marr news abstr 1861-1932 by SJGS, bk rev TB 22:1:12
Stockton, misc rec from news 1856-1862 by SJGS, bk rev TB 22:1:12
Sutro Libr, descr of services avail GJ 23:1:28
UCLA Cartographic Info center, res tips OC 32:2:6
Ventura Co, natu petitions & affidavits 1877-1906 RT 13:2:36
Ventura Co, natu rec & decl of intention 1907-1911 RT 13:3:61 13:4:88
Ventura Co, natu rec court orders 1880-1902 RT 13:1:8
Women's obit abstr c1967 RED 28:2:19
Women's repatriation rec c1936 RCP 17:4:136
CALLAHAN, Jacob, geneal by Coffman, bk rev TJ 7:2:73
CALLEY, David b1774, w Dorcas D Shepard, w Mary M Smith, NH, Bible rec NHR 12:3:104
CALLUM, Caleb bc1665, w Elizabeth Dynn, MA, RI, geneal AG 70:2:104
John m1670, w Elizabeth Gutterson, MA, RI, geneal AG 70:1:1
CALNAN, James A f1995, CN, fam hist & autobiog ACG 21:4:169
CALROW, G W f1882, w Mabel King, w Vergil Taylor, TX, biog sketch KTP 5:4:54
CALVERT, George bc1578, EN, Flemish heritage descr FAH 13:1:7
Susan see John Coffee HAYS
CAMBE see CAMBY
CAMBY, Fam hist by Morrison, bk rev OC 31:1:54
Samuel b1762, w Mary Prather, VA, geneal by Morrison, bk rev GFP 44:3:142

CAMBY (continued)
 VA, OH, fam hist by Morrison, bk rev TR 35:1:55
CAMFIELD, Joseph b1743, w Rachel, MA, Bible rec BG 16:4:134
 Rachel see Joseph CAMFIELD
CAMP, Georgia Lizzie see James Thomas WINKLES
 Jackson d1880, OH, SD, biog sketch BHN 28:1:15
 Polly see Pirum R HUNT
CAMPBELL, Ellen Virginia b1853, h Cornelius Milton Allen, TX, recoll FP 38:1:19
 John fl800, w Mary White, ST, TX, fam hist FP 38:1:18
 John fl839, ST, biog sketch GWS 95:44:15
 June see Paul J SHEFFIELD
 Malinda A, MI, fam hist by Northuis, bk rev DM 58:4:190
 Malinda see Jerome TERRILL
CANADA, Acadia, hist chronology ACG 21:4:163
 Acadian hist LG 95:53:3
 Air Mail, first flights, dates SGB 26:3:138
 Anc res guide by Briggs, bk rev GEN 20:2:22
 Archives Report 1905, repr, bk rev ACG 21:1:24 21:2:59 GH 49:5:180 OBN 28:2:71 SGS 44:2:83
 Bathurst Dist, emig locations at the land board 1823-1825, roster OBN 28:1:8
 Battle of Chippawa 1814, hist by Graves, bk rev FAM 34:3:177
 Border entry rec for Great Plains emig 1896-1918, hist MN 26:3:100 NDG 95:62:21
 British Columbia, Courtenay, Civic Cem rec by CVFHRG, bk rev GEN 20:4:24
 Cape Breton, news abstr 1861-1882 by Howard, bk rev GN 13:1:18
 Cape Breton, ST imm hist by Dunn, bk rev GEN 20:1:20

CANADA (continued)
 Carignan Reg 1664-1665, hist sketch ACG 22:1:11
 Census rec, how to trace ethnic origins & fam relationships, res tips GEN 20:2:12
 Census return indexes for 1871, 1881, 1891 & 1901 by BBIS, bk rev GN 13:1:17
 Channel Islanders, hist by Turk, bk rev CHG 28:1:33
 Cole Harbor & Lawrencetown, South-East passage pet 1829 GN 13:1:24
 Computer tips, National Capital Freenet OBN 28:6:4
 Crew agreement collect, res tips ANE 95:56:21
 Criminal Assize Clerk indictment files 1835-1919, res tips FAM 34:1:29
 Des Acadiens sur la Cote-du-Sud, biog sketches LG 95:53:10 95:54:26
 Deschaillons-sur-St Laurent, hist by Carette, bk rev ACG 22:1:22
 Dict of CN fam by Tanguay, bk rev LOB 16:1:27
 Eastern Eur anc geneal res tips GEN 20:3:2
 Epidemics, timeline ACG 22:1:13
 Expeditionary Force, 60th Battery, CN Field Artillery, nominal roll & casualties c1916 SGB 26:4:152
 Fam w/Col Am roots, res guide ANC 30:2:75
 FR language, hist by Halford, bk rev MHH 16:1:30
 FR, CN, misc fam geneal by Lindsay, bk rev SGS 44:3:145
 French-Canadian armorial, guide repr 1915, bk rev GH 49:5:180
 French-Canadian res guide by DuLong, bk rev ACG 21:2:61 SCS 32:6:139
 Geneal ethics, descr GN 13:1:10
 Imm who passed through CN, res tips AMG 10:4:19
 IR imm, landlords & tenants, 19th cent hist by Wilson, bk rev FAM 34:3:176
 IR Palatines in CN, hist by Heald, bk rev FAM 34:1:49

CANADA (continued)
Kenyon Pres Ch hist, repr 1940, bk rev FRT 16:3:102
Land settlement rec, 2nd Dist Land Boards 1819-1825, res tips & rosters FAM 34:3:132
Loyalist geneal res guide AMG 9:6:9
Mail to & from CN, tips SGS 45:1:41
Manitoba, Belmont hist 1889-1989 by BHBC, bk rev FAM 34:1:51
Manitoba, Elizabeth Dafoe Lib res guide GEN 20:2:18
Manitoba, Pipestone Municipality hist by RMPHP, bk rev GEN 20:1:20
Manitoba, Portage la Prairie Home for Incurables hist GEN 20:1:15
Manitoba, St Michael's Anglican Ch hist 1892-1992, bk rev GEN 20:3:32
Martintown, hist by Grant, bk rev FRT 16:3:103
National Archives, res tips AMG 10:2/3:39
National Lib res guide FAM 34:2:81
National Lib res tips AMG 10:2/3:39
Natu rec res tips GEN 20:3:19
New France hist chronology 1760-1798 cont ACG 21:2:74 21:4:174
New France hist chronology 1858-1880 ACG 22:1:37
New France, land rec & geneal, res tips MHH 16:1:21
Newspaper collect res guide FAM 34:4:233
NF, Aircrew Vol roster 1940 NAL 11:2:61
NF and Labrador Geneal Soc founding, hist NAL 11:2:52
NF, Bonne Bay area hist, early 20th cent NAL 11:3:99
NF, Bonne Bay area place names NAL 11:1:16
NF, Bonne Bay, early hist NAL 11:3:94
NF, deaths afar c1990, obit abstr NAL 11:4:148
NF, deaths of citizens abroad, obit abstr NAL 11:3:121

CANADA (continued)
NF, Deep Bight cem rec NAL 11:4:151
NF, Harbour Breton Anglican death rec 1848-1888 NAL 11:3:116
NF, Harbour Breton Anglican rec 1836 NAL 11:4:137
NF, impressment of fishermen by Royal Navy, hist NAL 11:1:11
NF, Maritime Hist Archive, res tips FAM 34:1:5
NF, police marr 1876 NAL 11:4:141
NF post ofc & telegraph staff roster 1914-1918 NAL 11:2:65
NF, res resource addresses NAL 11:1:34
NF, Royal NF Reg hist 1795-1995 NAL 11:2:60
NF, St John's area, WW2 proclamation seeking British Army recruits NAL 11:3:113
NF, St John's, Public Lib Newfoundland Collection, descr NAL 11:1:12
NF, will abstr c1850-1860 NAL 11:1:39 11:2:87 11:3:123 11:4:152
NF, WW2 Roll of Honor casualty roster NAL 11:1:35
NS, Annapolis Co, probate court rec 1763-1938 by Walker, bk rev GN 13:2:89
NS, archives vol 2, repr, bk rev VQS 32:3:43
NS, Argyle Twp rec bks by AMHGS, bk rev AGE 24:1:10 GN 13:1:16
NS, Barrington town rec from 1781 by Terry, bk rev GN 13:1:16 NER 149:594:190
NS, Colchester, women's hist by CHS, bk rev GN 13:2:87
NS, Goodwood area cem rec GN 13:1:27
NS, Halifax, births & marr in the 62nd Reg 1815-1823 GN 13:1:29
NS, Hammonds Plains hist by Evans, bk rev GN 13:1:21
NS, imm connections to Bermuda, 19th cent hist GN 13:2:62

CANADA (continued)
- NS, imm to 1867 vol 2 by Smith, bk rev ACG 21:1:22 AGE 24:1:9 CSB 30:3:106 FAM 34:4:250 GFP 44:3:140 GH 49:5:181 GJ 23:1:41 GN 13:1:15 HQ 95:55:91 KA 31:2:47 NYR 126:2:152 SGS 44:2:91 TR 35:2:109
- NS, pass ships to AA, roster 1852-1853 GN 13:2:100
- NS, patents (inventions)1834-1856 GN 13:2:65
- NS, planter studies, secondary source checklist by Godwin/McNutt, bk rev GN 13:2:86
- NS settler hist by Mission, bk rev NER 149:595:314
- NS, Shelburne Co cem rec vol 5 by SCGS, bk rev GN 13:2:86
- NS, Shelburne Co cem rec vol 7 by SCGS, bk rev GN 13:1:19
- NS, strays, 19th cent GN 13:2:101
- NS, Victoria Co, census 1901 by Morrison, bk rev GN 13:3:138
- NS, Wedgeport, fam hist of misc fam 1767-1900 by CDADW, bk rev AGE 24:1:10
- NS, Yarmouth, hist by Campbell, bk rev GN 13:3:140
- ON, Adjala hist by McDevitt/Munnoch, bk rev FAM 34:3:181
- ON, Am Loyalist geneal, repr 1973, bk rev GJ 22:4:129
- ON, Carleton Co cem rec OBN 28:6:10
- ON, Cornwall, hist 1784-1984 by Senior, bk rev FRT 16:3:101
- ON, eastern land reg, list & phone numbers OBN 28:6:9
- ON, eastern twp, list of OBN 28:6:9
- ON, Fergus, town hist by Mestern, bk rev FAM 34:4:248
- ON, geneal misc 1858-1872 abstr from Meth news by McKenzie, bk rev FAM 34:2:118
- ON, Halladay Burial Ground cem rec GEN 20:4:24

CANADA (continued)
- ON, Hamilton, criminal roster 1829 FAM 34:3:175
- ON, land registry rec res guide by OGS, bk rev GH 49:4:201
- ON, land settlement rec, res guide OBN 28:1:4
- ON, Lib & Archives geneal collect direct by Taylor, bk rev FAM 34:1:47 NER 149:593:82
- ON, Manotick, Watson's Mill hist OBN 28:3:75
- ON, Mara, town hist by CTM, bk rev FAM 34:4:249
- ON, Newcastle Dist land board rec 1819-1825, alphabetical roster FAM 34:3:138 34:4:208
- ON, Newcastle, location of town descr FAM 34:1:41
- ON, Ottawa Branch Geneal Soc hist OBN 28:6:7
- ON, PA Germans, settler hist 1776-1812 by Reaman, bk rev CHG 28:1:33
- ON, Waterloo Co, annotated bibl of regional hist to 1972 by Bloomfield et al, bk rev FAM 34:1:49
- ON, Wesleyan Meth bapt rec cont OBN 28:1:36
- ON, Wilno Parish PO marr rec 1897-1899 TE 15:2:81
- ON, Woodstock, Old St Paul's Ch hist sketch FAM 34:2:99
- Ottawa East Dist, census 1871 index by Samuelsen, bk rev GH 49:5:181
- Ottawa, Bathurst Dist land locations 1840-1842, roster OBN 28:3:81
- Ottawa, cem hist OBN 28:6:10
- Ottawa, hist, CD-ROM rev OBN 28:4:130
- Ottawa, imm 1870 (names) & res tips OBN 28:3:77
- Ottawa, land board dist rec of emig locations c1825 OBN 28:2:40
- Ottawa, Ottawa Branch Geneal Soc guest speaker roster 1984-1995 OBN 28:6:17

CANADA (continued)
- Ottawa, strays who died c1990-1991 OBN 28:4:128
- Ottawa, working class grocery list 1870 OBN 28:3:80
- Pass lists, res tips TE 15:3:121
- Pass/emig reg compilation by Ptak, bk rev TVF 4:2:122
- Pass/emig reg, res guide GH 49:5:14
- Post ofc res tips SGB 26:4:166
- Prairie provinces, bibl & index to 1853 by Peel, bk rev GEN 20:1:14
- QB & Am Rev, hist by Coffin, repr, bk rev RCP 17:3:82
- QB, Argenteuil Co, census index 1871 by Samuelsen, bk rev GH 49:4:201
- QB, foremothers hist sketch MHH 16:2:35
- QB, garrison life 1748-1759, hist by Proulx, bk rev MHH 16:4:129
- QB, Ottawa Centre Dist census index 1871 by Samuelsen, bk rev GH 49:4:201
- Quebec, Jette Biog & geneal dict, descr MHH 16:1:6
- Quebec, migration patterns to New England, hist ACG 22:1:7
- Quebec, Revolutionary War era hist, repr 1896, bk rev AMG 10:2/3:8
- Railroads, importance of, hist FAM 34:2:67
- Railway archives sources for fam historians, guide by Richards, bk rev SGB 26:4:iv
- Railway links res tips SGB 26:4:166
- Railway rec res guide by Douglas, bk rev FAM 34:1:46 NER 149:593:82
- Res guide by Baxter, bk rev APG 10:3:90 GFP 44:3:139 GH 49:5:180 LC 16:1:15 MN 26:4:185 SCS 32:5:113 SGS 44:2:91
- Res resource address list OBN 28:3:98
- Riviere-Ouelle, hist sketch LG 95:54:33
- Royal Canadian Air Force burials in EN (Evesham), roster FAM 34:4:237
- Saskatchewan Geneal Soc, hist by SGS, bk rev SGB 26:1:iv

CANADA (continued)
- Saskatchewan, Air Ambulance Svc formation hist SGB 26:3:118
- Saskatchewan, Edam hist by EHS, bk rev GEN 20:1:20
- Saskatchewan, Ivermay's first cem, hist SGB 26:3:124
- Saskatchewan, land claims c1883 SGB 26:2:81
- Saskatchewan, North West Mounted Police, D Division, officer roster 1885 SGB 26:3:136
- Saskatchewan, obit cards referring to Manitobans, abstr GEN 20:4:17
- Saskatchewan, Regina, St Paul's Cathedral hist by Powell, bk rev SGB 26:2:iv
- Saskatchewan, res indexes avail, descr SGB 26:3:108
- Sault Ste Marie, Cath pet to Rev A McDonald & John Colborne 1834 MHH 16:4:125
- Township council minutes & poor relief, hist & roster OBN 28:3:90
- Troupes de la Marine officer roster cont MHH 16:4:109
- Upper CN, pet & grant abstr c1823 OBN 28:1:21
- WW2 victory, hist NAL 11:2:58
- Yukon, pioneers 1850-1950, biog by Ferrell, bk rev SLV 12:1:1 TPI 20:2:97

CANFIELD, Eleanor see Elias Smith CANFIELD
- Elias Smith bc1808, w Eleanor, NY, PA, geneal LWF 15:2:98

CANNADY, --- see Warren RUCKER

CANTER, Arthur Benjamin b1860, w Frances Margaret Roberts, MO, FL, biog PCQ 18:3:6

CANTERBURY, Beatrix see Francis PLUMMER

CAPLINGER, Marshall fl1898, w Anna, KY, KS, fam hist by Caplinger, bk rev KA 31:1:43

CAPP, ST, GR, fam hist sketch LL 30:3:99

CAPPS, Jessie Paul b1905, w Sarah Hortense Wilkins, NC, Bible rec JC 21:3:57

CARAWAY, Thetis Thomas see Moses W BARBER

William b1796, w Harriet Musgrave, FL, fam rec BT 27:2:33

CARDEN, Beulah see John Gilbert SANDERSON

CAREY, Charles b1743, PA, fam hist by Carey, bk rev MD 36:1:92 TJ 7:3:108

John, EN, fam hist by Carey, bk rev TJ 7:3:108

KY, OH, PA, fam hist by Carey, bk rev EWA 32:2:81

CARGILL, Ithiel b1775, w Lucy Grosvenor, VT, fam hist by Stevens, bk rev RAG 16:1:18 SCS 32:4:88 SEE 36:153:50

CARIBBEAN GENEALOGY, Cuba & US policy, hist by Schulz, bk rev CGJ 3:4:9

Danish West Indies, slave society hist by Hall, bk rev CGJ 3:4:10

Democracy, hist by Edie, bk rev CGJ 3:3:41

FR pass lists index 1749-1778 CGJ 3:3:10 3:4:18

Haiti, Cath Ch, hist by Greene, bk rev CGJ 3:3:41

Hist & geneal bibl CGJ 3:3:14

Hist & geneal bibl for res cont CGJ 3:4:5

Hist timeline 1773-1797 CGJ 3:3:8 3:4:23

Jews, hist & geneal resources avail, descr CGJ 3:4:14

West Indies, English presence, hist by Froude, bk rev CGJ 3:4:9

CARLILE, James fc1755, w Ann Irvin, IR, SC, GA, geneal NC 5:2:49

CARLTON, George Washington b1843, w Nancy Rogers, TN, AR, TX, biog notes HCG 13:2:21

Lydia see Lydia Carlton Hendry MOODY

CARLTON (continued)
Martha Jane see Jeremiah Madison HAYMAN

CARMICAL, W W b1833, w Elizabeth Robinson, SC, GA, biog sketch CCM 15:1:12

Hugh b1827, NC, geneal by Steele, bk rev RES 26:3:162

John, w Isabella Pomeroy, TN, fam hist by Webb, bk rev BWG 24:1:65

PA, TN, fam hist by Bell et al, bk rev BWG 24:2:154

Patrick b1819, w Mary A W Speer, GA, biog sketch CCM 15:1:12

CARNAGHAN, John see John CARNAHAN

John b1765, w Mary Sara Simpson, w Martha McKissick, PA, geneal by Nichols, bk rev WPG 22:2:56

CARNAL, John, w Sarah Hipkins Clark(e), VA, KY, fam hist by Christian, bk rev KA 30:3:175

CARNALLE, Millie see Douglas OLIVER

CARNEAL, Josiah b1810, w Catherine Galbreath, w Nancy Jo Rice Harris, w Lucy Jane McQuary, VA, fam hist by Christian, bk rev GH 49:5:228 KA 30:3:175

CARPENTER, Ann see James T MARTIN

Elizabeth see Nathaniel ROGERS

Lillian b1890, FL, biog PCQ 9:4:1

Liz bc1920, TX, autobiog, bk rev STS 35:2:72

William m1625, w Abigail Briante, EN, MA, fam hist AG 70:4:193

CARR, James R bc1808, w Margaret Royston, TN, geneal BWG 24:2:134

Margaret Ann see Jonas Austin LATHROP

MO, group sheets by Smith, bk rev MSG 15:4:225

Susannah see William CARR

Thomas b1678, VA, identity TVF 4:2:80

William d1760, w Susannah, VA, identity TVF 4:2:80

CARRICO, Mary see Benjamin Harrison KERRICK
CARROLL, IR, surname hist NAL 11:4:132
  Minnie see W J LEADINGHAM
  Nathaniel see Mary PEASE
CARSON, Nettie S see Clinton W NUGENT
CARTER, Charles Waters m1850, w Martha Lucinda Story, GA, Bible rec CCM 15:1:8
  Fam hist supp by Weyher, bk rev GGS 31:2:119
  H B f1900, w Lucy, FL, fam hist PCQ 11:4:1
  Isaac d1834, MS, geneal STK 23:2:92
  Jimmy b1924, campaign 1976 hist by Anderson, bk rev REG 93:2:248
  John W m1868, w Elizabeth B Wright, CT, Bible rec CTA 38:2:64
  Lucy see H B CARTER
  Martha Ann see Charles CABINESS
  Susanna see Thomas BURLING
  VA, KY, fam hist by Carter, bk rev PR 22:4:49
  William J b1858, NC, FL, fam hist PCQ 11:4:1
CARVER, Susanna see William PERRY
CARVEY, Emily J see Thomas W SMITH
CARY, Lura M see Jacob A SCHWA
CASE, Ann see Aaron MILLIMAN
  Henry d1916, OH, obit TLL 20:4:80
  John d1675, w Martha Philbrick, NH, geneal by Berry, bk rev GH 49:6:206
  Stephen b1818, NY, NJ, Bapt funeral rec OCG 25:1:11 25:3:35
CASEY, James McCager b1862, w Emma Salilla Walding, AL, TX, fam hist MCG 18:1/2:75
CASS, John see John CASE
CASSEL, Frances Eugenia see Leander W TURNER
  Mary Harley b1828, PA, h Abram L Moyer, Samuel K Harley, diary abstr MHP 22:3:3 22:4:3

CASSEL (continued)
  Sarah Elizabeth f1910, KS, biog sketch KK 33:2:33
CASTLE, Michael see Michael KASLER
CASTLEMAN, Mary Polly see Phillip Schuyler BOARD
CASTRO, Henry f1842, TX, biog STS 35:2:34
CATE, William f1742, w Elizabeth Cotton, NH, biog & will SCR 18:3:37
CATHEY, Sarah see Samuel GIVENS
CATRON, see Mary Elizabeth TAYLOR
CAUSER, Mary Ann see John STEIGER
CAVATA, F F f1863, VA, jour re:Libby prison life, repr 1863, bk rev BTG 1:2:6 GH 49:5:224
CAVNES, Charles see Charles CABINESS
CECIL, Betty see Erwin Frank CHELL
  Louisa see John M DARNELL
CHADBOURNE, Abigail bc1781, h Benjamin Grant, ME, fam hist NER 149:593:49
CHAISSON, Marguerite see Joseph BOUDREAU
CHALKER, Elizabeth m1727, h Jonathan Ingham, CT, biog & identity AG 70:1:49
CHAMBERS, ST, IR, VA, fam hist by Chambers, bk rev NPW 13:10:57
CHAMLEE, Tilmon b1809, GA, fam cem rec GGS 31:1:43
CHAMP, John bc1670, w Elizabeth Washington, VA, geneal NPW 14:6:34
CHANDLER, Jane see Robert JEFFERS
CHANDLER, John b1599, EN, fam charts by Reeves, bk rev THT 23:2:90
  Joseph Lecompte m1900, w Hallie Moore, KY, Bibl rec KA 30:4:182
CHANDONE, Marie-Anne see Francois ONEL

CHANEY, Milkah see William GARDNER
CHAPMAN, Elijah b1826, w Sarah, CA, Bible rec GGP 28:1:47
   James Appleton fl882, AL, FL, biog PCQ 9:2:6
   Samuel H b1845, w Nancy Penelope Dodson, TX, fam rec FP 38:3:126
   Sarah see Elijah CHAPMAN
   Sarah see W M HUMPHEYS
CHARLEBOIS, Fam hist by Hanrahan, bk rev ACG 21:4:161
CHARLEBOIS-WOOD, Eusebe see Marie RIEL
CHASE, Aquila fl635, EN, NH, geneal by Chase/Chamberlain, bk rev CTN 27:4:587 MD 36:1:89 TMG 17:2:44
   Horace Asa b1852, NY, geneal LAB 10:4:117
   Salmon P fl829, jour by Niven, bk rev REG 92:4:420
   Thomas fl635, NH, geneal by Chase/Chamberlain, bk rev CTN 27:4:587 MD 36:1:89
CHAVEZ, Virginia see Roy BEAN
CHELL, Erwin Frank fl995, w Betty Cecil, CO, autobiog, bk rev GH 49:5:228
CHENEVERS DIT LEMARBRE, Fam bapt & burial rec 1800-1850 MHH 16:2:47
CHENEY, Agnes m1580, h William Heath, EN, anc NER 149:594:173
CHERRY, Francis R see Joseph Alexander HAMILTON
   TN, fam hist by Stone, bk rev MN 26:3:137
   WA, NC, KY, fam hist by Stone, bk rev TJ 7:2:77
CHESTER, Joseph Lemuel b1821, CT, biog GH 49:4:14
   TN, fam hist & doc BWG 24:2:118
CHILES, Frances see Enoch GRIGSBY
CHILTON, IL, fam hist cont MCS 15:2:60
   James bc1730, VA, fam rec MCS 15:1:23

CHRISTENSON, Brynhil see Ole J STORDAHL
CHRISTIAN, James, HO, KY, fam hist sketch FWC 9:3:240
CHURCHILL, Winston b1874, EN, relationship w/Franklin Delano Roosevelt, hist by Sainsbury, bk rev REG 93:3:365
CIVIL WAR GENEALOGY,
   Albemarle ship, hist by Elliott, bk rev RAG 16:1:21
   Andersonville prison, hist by Marvel, bk rev REG 93:2:226
   AR, Confederate surrender & parole rosters 1865 by Ponder, bk rev ARH 33:3:127
   AR, Laconia, cotton burned by mil order, news abstr TRC 10:2:46
   Army life, descr hist by Billings, bk rev REG 92:4:450
   Battle name variants FTP 16:4:6
   Battle of Fredericksburg, hist by Finfrock, bk rev GH 49:6:182
   Battle of the Wilderness, hist 1864 by Priest, bk rev RAG 16:4:18
   Brazil, Fraternidade Descendencia Americana, hist sketch VCG 95:DEC:16
   British Foreign Service involvement, hist by Berwanger, bk rev REG 93:2:230
   Chattanooga battle, hist by Cozzens, bk rev REG 93:4:486
   Civil War Soldiers System, res aid FTR :182:6
   Cold Harbor battle, hist 1864 by Maney, bk rev RAG 16:2:20
   Confederacy, Adjutant & Inspector General's ofc act 1862 GR 37:1:10
   Confederacy, hist sketch & res tips AB 23:1:3
   Confederacy, women in the war, biog data, bk rev GGS 31:2:99
   Confederate anc res guide by Segars, bk rev CSB 30:4:143 SE 16:12:117
   Confederate anc res guide KSL 19:2:54

CIVIL WAR GENEALOGY
(continued)
Confederate animals & mascots, hist KSL 19:4:138
Confederate army compendium by Sifakis, bk rev NTT 15:1/2:3
Confederate exiles in Brazil, hist by Dawsey, bk rev REG 93:3:356
Confederate flags, hist HQ 95:59:66
Confederate Republic, hist by Rable, bk rev REG 93:2:228
Confederate soldiers, recoll 1861-WW1 by SCDUDC, bk rev TR 35:3:164
Confederates, archive collect res guide by Neagles, bk rev CR 27:2:38
Confederates, boy soldiers, biog info by Hall, bk rev GGS 31:2:99
Federal dead, rec of, repr 1866, bk rev ANC 30:3:124
GA, Andersonville prison, hist KSL 19:2:50
Gettysburg hist by Brown, bk rev REG 92:4:425
Great battles, hist by Macdonald, bk rev CSB 30:3:107
Hist & corresp by Vandiver, bk rev REG 93:2:251
Libby prison, Union prisoner hist, repr 1864, bk rev TB 21:3:12
Maple Leaf escape hist by Witt, bk rev BTG 1:2:6
MD, monument guide by Soderberg, bk rev RAG 16:4:21
MS River campaign, hist by Miles, bk rev RAG 16:1:19
Natl Archives, res tips RT 13:1:22
New York Times news abstr c1862 TAC 6:1:13
Northerners & the South, hist 1865-1900 by Silber, bk rev REG 93:2:231
Photo bks vol 2, repr 1912-1913, bk rev KCG 36:2:106
Photographic hist by Elson, bk rev
Photographic hist, repr 1912-1913, bk rev BTG 1:2:6 CN 4:4:65 GH 49:5:188 MGR 29:4:123
Prison list LL 30:3:95

CIVIL WAR GENEALOGY
(continued)
Prisoner of War camps, list & hist GRI 15:1:81 NCC 15:2:13 PGB 26:10:223
Prisoner of War experiences of Lt Colonel F F Cavada by Cavada, bk rev BTG 1:2:6
Res guide by Schweitzer, bk rev TTC 21:1:6
Seceded states, hist essays by McDonald, bk rev REG 92:4:449
Soldier burial guide by Hughes, bk rev GH 49:6:180
Soldier diaries 1861-1865 by McPherson, bk rev REG 92:4:422
Southern Loyalists Claims Commission rec & index by Mills, bk rev APG 10:2:62 FLG 18:2:72 GH 49:3:201
Southern Loyalists, case file direct 1870-1880, repr, bk rev SEE 36:153:22
Southerner's guide to Civil War res HQ 95:58:54
Swedish imm in the war, hist SCN 96:10:5
Terms, glossary GWD 9:1:2
U S Quartermaster's Union Roll of Honor, repr, bk rev PB 11:1:12
Union draft, hist sketch PGB 27:2:18
Union Roll of Honor 1865-1871, index by Reamy, bk rev SGS 45:1:38
Union Roll of Honor 1869-1871, repr, bk rev CSB 30:3:106 GH 49:3:199 GJ 23:1:42 NYR 126:1:86 TR 35:1:53
Union vet biog by DUVCW, bk rev GH 49:5:187
VA, Fredericksburg campaign hist by Gallagher, bk rev REG 93:4:485
VA, Jeff Davis Artillery hist by Laboda, bk rev RAG 16:4:21
Vet organizations (little known), geneal res tips HQ 95:57:11
Women soldiers, hist sketch CHG 27:2:53
CLAIBORNE, John Herbert b1828, VA, autobiog, bk rev GH 49:4:221

CLAIBORNE (continued)
William f1621, VA, geneal by Dorman/Smith, bk rev VAG 39:4:316

CLAIRBORNE, John Herbert b1828, VA, autobiog, bk rev SGS 44:2:86

CLARK, Arthur Samuel b1855, TX, Bible rec FP 38:1:10
Carey see Desire THOMAS
David b1756, w Aseneth Fisher, NS, Bible rec GN 13:2:61
David b1788, w Betsey Woodruff Price, NJ, fam rec GMN 70:1:23
David Howe b1827, w Emily Frances Holly, CT, Bible rec CTA 37:3:109
Jacob, w Temperance, NJ, geneal cont GF 16:3:19
LaRena d1991, ON, biog by Fowke/Rahn, bk rev FAM 34:4:247
Martha A f1850, IL, corresp MCS 15:1:8
Sarah Hipkins see Sarah Hipkins CLARKE
Sarah see James TUTTLE
Temperance see Jacob CLARK

CLARKE, Alfred b1844, w Matilda Zink, CA, geneal & biog sketches GGP 28:1:11
Sarah Hipkins see John CARNAL
Thomas fc1600, EN, Am, fam hist by Clarke, bk rev GH 49:4:223 FRT 16:3:110

CLAUS, C Hugo f1855, TX, recoll KTP 1:2:14

CLAYTON, George b1723, w Sarah, VA, NC, geneal by Green, bk rev LOB 17:1:24 RCR 10:2:2277
Lambert b1755, w Sarah Davidson, DE, NC, biog LOB 17:1:16
Sarah see George CLAYTON
William W f1835, TN, biog BWG 24:2:145

CLEERE, George D f1883, AL, court rec cont NTT 14:4:141 15:1/2:25
Lawrence P f1883, AL, chancery rec NTT 14:3:100 14:4:141 15:1/2:25

CLELLAND, ST, fam hist by Schnegelberger, bk rev FRT 16:3:109 GH 49:5:228

CLEMENTS, Adam Quincy b1830, w Sarah Lane, TX, fam hist STS 35:1:29

CLINE, Arnold H d1944, IL, biog MCS 15:1:36
Conrad, OH, identity, bk rev TR 35:1:53

CLINTON, William see William Jefferson BLYTHE

CLORE, Hanna see Elias WEAVER

CLOSE, Sarah b1830, h Nathan Brisco Palmer, OH, biog TFP 95:12:17

CLOUGH, Nathaniel, w Susannah, MD, geneal by Surles/Phillippe, bk rev TR 35:3:168
Susannah see Nathaniel CLOUGH

CLOWES, Samuel b1674, NY, fam hist by Witherspoon, bk rev DM 58:3:143

COALTER, Mary see John GLASSELL

COBB, Asa b1817, w Marion Samuel, KY, IN, biog sketch LL 30:3:94

COBLE, Mary Malinda see Joshua HUDSON

COBURN, Charles b1877, w Ivah Wills, GA, anc ACG 21:4:167
Jean see William Croscomb COBURN
William Croscomb b1833, w Jean, CN, IL, biog sketch CHG 28:1:29

COCHAMY, Ward f1848, AL, biog add SEN 2:4:46
Ward f1848, AL, corresp SEN 1:2:4

COCHRAN, Alice see John ABLES
James A m1860, w Ann M Davis, IL, Bible rec CI 31:2:48
William Westley see Susan Alice KENNEDY

COCKBURN, John see Ann Elizabeth BRODHEAD
Pierre de Thomas f1292, EN, fam hist KTP 7:4:56

COCKERHAM, William Westley see William Westley COCHRAN

COE, Lucy Mae see George STULL

COFFMAN, Andrew m1790, w Betsy Ramsey, TX, Bible rec & fam hist GR 37:4:27
Jacob, geneal by Coffman, bk rev TJ 7:2:73
COGGESHALL, John see Elizabeth BAULSTON
COKER, Martha Ann Francis see Stephen Collins MCMICHAEL
COLBERT, James Logan f1783, NY, NC, biog NCJ 21:1:25
COLBORNE, Edward b1618, w Hannah, MA, geneal by Bosworth, bk rev GH 49:3:218
Hannah see Edward COLBORNE
John f1835, CN, pet abstr MHH 16:4:126
COLE, David Rodney b1931, w Margaret Ann Davis, NY, anc by Cole, bk rev GH 49:3:218
George A f1863, NH, corresp SCR 18:3:38
Henry b1805, w Margaret Brazee, CA, Bible rec GGP 28:1:47
COLEMAN, John G b1814, w Sally Knepper, Bible rec LM 36:1:201
COLES, Icey see Isaac COLES
Isaac fc1847, w Icey, VA, manumission doc TR 35:1:41
James Albert b1859, w Frances Margaret Hindes, MI, Bible rec MI 41:1:31
COLIJN, Helen f1995, HO, autobiog & regional tour guide, bk rev DFH 8:2:48
COLLEY, Richard bc1802, w Sarah Hitchcock, MD, fam hist & corresp MD 36:4:626
COLLIER, John f1863, AL, corresp abstr OLR 9:4:149
COLLINGS, Thomas b1848, w Delitha (Workman) Martindale Bartley, w Sarah Jane (Cunningham) Brazell, IN, TX, fam hist HCG 13:3:38
COLLINS, Amos, NY, fam hist by Collins, bk rev RAG 16:2:30
Geneal 3rd ed by Collins, bk rev TPI 20:2:90

COLLINS (continued)
Joseph see Abby BYRAM
Rachel see John Riley HUNT
William E f1910, FL, biog PCQ 22:1:5
COLLUM, MA, RI, see John CALLUM see also CALLUM
COLLY, Nancy see Lewis HALL
COLMAN, Sally f1677, MA, CN, biog sketch ACG 21:2:64
COLORADO, Boulder Co, natu rec 1904-1920 BGS 27:2:48 27:4:122
Boulder Co, news abstr 1875 BGS 27:2:61
Boulder Co, news abstr from the *Boulder County News* c1875 BGS 27:4:133
Boulder Co, St Vrain Ch of the Brethren cem rec OC 29:3:98
Boulder, City Assoc stock certs 1859 BGS 27:4:129
Boulder, land rec 1859-1861 BGS 27:2:56
Boulder, land transfer rec 1859-1861 cont BGS 27:4:128
Logan Co, hist 1887-1987 by Wells, bk rev TB 22:1:13
Ouray, hist by Gregory, bk rev NER 149:596:434
COLQUHOUN see also CALHOUN
ST, fam hist by Johnson, bk rev GRC 11:2:25
COMBS, Fanny see Seth N COMBS
Seth N b1838, w Fanny, OH, biog TR 35:3:124
COMPERE, Thomas H b1827, AR, corresp abstr ARH 33:4:156
COMPUTER GENEALOGY, America Online, geneal forum, descr & res tips SCS 32:2:32
America Online, geneal res tips HQ 95:59:78
Ancestral Quest, software rev PAF 7:1:15
Ancestral Timelines database, software rev GGP 28:1:24
Ancillary geneal software, guide GH 49:6:220

COMPUTER GENEALOGY
(continued)
AniMap, software rev LRT 14:2:551 OK 40:1:10
AniMap Plus, software rev BT 27:3:56
Backups & upgrades, res tips MTG 8:4:156
Beginner's guide IMP 14:2:37
Beginner's guide by Hawgood, bk rev SGB 26:3:iv
Beginner's guide by Publ Soc of Genealogists, bk rev GWS 95:42:37 QFH 16:2:66
Beginner's tips GCH 8:11:202 IAN 16:5:7 QFH 16:4:123
Biography Maker software rev TEN 95:16:25
Black Oak Mapper 6.0 software rev CPN 20:1:7
Brother's Keeper 4.5, software rev SMN 13:3:50
Brother's Keeper, software rev (in French) LG 95:56:87
Bulletin boards & geneal problem solving techniques, tips NC 5:2:64
Bulletin boards, geneal res guide by Dunn, bk rev QFH 16:2:67
CD-ROM beginner's guide SMN 13:4:67
CD-ROM geneal res tips GH 49:4:240
Citations made quick & easy, tips PAF 7:3:55
Computer aided research, beginner's guide HQ 95:55:81
Computer classes helpful to genealogists, list QU 12:1:9
DeedMapper, software rev BYG 7:1:366
DosBar, software rev PAF 7:1:16
E-mail, reading & sending tips GRI 15:5:128
Electronic data, responsible use of, guide HQ 95:60:83
Exercise Break, software rev TE 15:3:125
Family Atlas for Windows, software rev FCM 8:2:135 FRT 17:1:17 KVH 20:6:65

COMPUTER GENEALOGY
(continued)
Family History System, software rev PWN 1:3:7 SMN 13:3:50
Family Origins 3.2 for DOS, software rev FCM 8:2:134
Family Origins 4.0 for Windows, software rev ACG 22:1:19
Family Origins 4.0, software rev CSB 30:4:148
Family Origins 4.1 for Windows, software rev FRT 17:1:17
Family Reunion 4.0, software rev SMN 13:5:87
Family Search guide by Nichols, bk rev GSC 18:1:8 TJ 7:2:74
Family Search, res guide MCR 26:4:130
Family searches on computers, beginner's guide QFH 16:4:125
Family Ties 1.17, software rev SMN 13:3:50
Family Tree Etc, program rev SMN 13:2:32
Family Tree Journal 8.0, software rev SMN 13:2:32
Family Tree Maker 2.0 for Windows, software rev SQ 5:5:48
Family Tree Maker 3.0, software rev CSB 30:4:148
Family Tree Maker 3.1, software rev SMN 13:5:87
Family Tree Maker, custom reports, how to create HQ 95:58:76
Family Tree Maker for Windows CD-ROM by Banner Blue, software rev QQ 95:25:17
Family Tree Maker for Windows, software rev QFH 16:2:49
Family Tree Maker V Deluxe Edition, software rev SMN 13:5:88
Filing & organization tips MTG 8:4:156
GEDCOM hints MAG 8:3:4
GEDCOM Server System, descr PWN 3:1:20
GEDCOM version 1.0, software rev RCP 17:2:52

COMPUTER GENEALOGY
(continued)
Geneal res guide by Crowe, bk rev NGS 83:3:217
Geneal software direct 1993 by Archer, bk rev FAM 34:1:45
Geneal software guide by GPC, bk rev SEE 36:153:24
Geneal software guide by Prezecha/Lowrey, bk rev FAM 34:1:50
Geneal uses of computers, descr IS 16:1:7
Genealogy (Getting Started) program, software rev SMN 13:2:32
Hard disks, what to do when they are full, tips IB 11:1:3
Historian's Guide to Computing by Greenstein, bk rev REG 93:3:382
Images, publication tips MTG 8:4:157
Index program by Picton Press, software rev TMG 17:2:45
Internet & geneal, beginner's guide APG 10:2:44
Internet beginner's guide RES 27:1:23
Internet descr & res tips FAM 34:1:33
Internet geneal res tips RAG 17:1:17
Internet navigation guide by Gibbs/Smith, bk rev APG 10:1:28
KINPUBLISH program, rev HQ 95:57:73
KINWRITE program, rev HQ 95:57:73
Lib of Congress, access through Internet, tips OK 40:2:49
Libraries; classification, cataloging & computer guide by Mann, bk rev APG 10:2:61
Macintosh computers & BBS, geneal res tips RES 26:3:121
Map programs, tips BT 26:4:84
Master Genealogist program, rev PGB 26:7:147
Medieval geneal on-line, guide ASO 25:1:18
Millenium, software rev OK 40:1:10
Modem beginner's tips HGO 6:1:5

COMPUTER GENEALOGY
(continued)
My Family Ancestry 1.0, software rev GH 49:4:252
Names, PAF, & computerized databases, essay PAF 7:3:60
On-line geneal, beginner's guide JCG 23:2:47
PAF & Windows 95, guide PAF 7:3:50
PAF 2.3 advanced features for the IBM PC, guide by Parker, bk rev TJ 7:3:108
PAF 2.3, software rev SCS 32:5:118
PAF 2.31, rev SCS 32:3:70
PAF 2.31, tips SCS 32:4:94
PAF, beginners' hints PAF 7:1:12
PAF, IMPORT.EXE utility, rev SMN 13:1:14
PAF, LOWCASE utility, rev SMN 13:1:14
PAF, MOVNAM11.EXE utility, rev SMN 13:1:14
PAF, NAMCLEAN utility, rev SMN 13:1:14
PAF, NOTECLEN.EXE utility, rev SMN 13:1:14
PAF, notes & documentation explained PAF 7:1:2
PAF, notes enhanced using Windows, guide PAF 7:1:8
PAF tips SCS 32:10:238 SGB 26:2:90
PageMaker 5 for Windows, software rev APG 10:2:61
Parent's Geneal Version 4.5 for Windows, software rev GH 49:4:252
Personal Ancestral File 2.3, user guide CTA 37:3:149
Personal Ancestral File data entry solutions CTA 37:4:189
Phone bk res tips WCG 11:7/8:52
Photographs, reproducing with computers, tips MN 26:3:118
Power Translator, software rev FAM 34:2:91
Printers, guide GRI 15:3:104
Progenitors V 1.2, software rev SMN 13:2:32

COMPUTER GENEALOGY
(continued)
Programs used in geneal, descr KTP 10:2:32
RDF 2.2/2.3 for IBM, guide by Harris, bk rev TJ 7:3:111
Relatively Yours 5.0 program, rev TGO 8:1:3
Research Data Filer, indexing tips PAF 7:3:63
Roots IV, guide by Willard, bk rev ACG 21:1:23
ROOTS-L Internet bulletin board, tips LL 31:1:27
Scanners, guide by Ledden, bk rev FAM 34:4:249
Scanning & printing for your fam hist, guide MN 26:4:162
Selecting a computer for geneal use, tips GRI 15:5:129
Selecting a geneal program, tips IAN 16:1:8
SiteFinder, software rev BT 27:3:56
SKY Index 4.0 for Windows, software rev FCM 7:4:263
Social Security Death Index to 1993 by AGLL, CD-ROM rev QQ 95:25:18
Software guide by Przecha/Lowrey, bk rev TTL 24:1:23
Street Atlas USA CD by DeLorme Mapping, software rev, SMN 13:7:122
Telephone bk geneal, res tips GH 49:5:2
Visual Roots for Windows, software rev FCM 7:4:269
Visual Roots, software rev BT 27:3:56
Windows 95 & PAF, tips SCS 32:12:286
WordPerfect & geneal, beginner's tips HY 16:1:4
World Fam Tree CD-ROM, descr SGB 26:3:135
World Wide Web sites list SMN 13:6:103
COMSTOCK, Gertrude see Robert Sturgeon MUSSER
CONATSER, Elizabeth see James Knox Polk BEATY
CONDOR, Sarah M see Joseph Alexander HAMILTON
CONFER, Rebecca see David BISH
CONGDON, John fc1730, WE, VA, fam hist by Crandall, bk rev RIR 21:4:123
CONLEE, Isaac bc1745, w Mary, NC, TN, KY, geneal by Morgan, bk rev GFP 45:2:92
Mary see Isaac CONLEE
CONNECTICUT, Atlas of hist co boundaries by Long, bk rev CTA 37:4:185 FRT 16:3:104 GH 49:4:206 NER 149:594:188 RAG 16:2:30 RAG 16:4:25 REG 93:4:511 SEE 36:153:53
Barbour Collect of CT Town Rec by White, bk rev ACG 21:2:60 HQ 95:58:87 SGS 44:3:144 WPG 21:4:49
Barkhamsted, Barbour Collect of rec 1779-1854 by White, bk rev GFP 44:4:188 STS 35:3:69 TR 35:4:220
Berlin, Barbour Collect of rec 1785-1850 by White, bk rev GFP 44:4:188 STS 35:3:69 TR 35:4:220
Bethany, Barbour Collect of rec 1832-1853 by White, bk rev GFP 44:4:188 STS 35:3:69 TR 35:4:220
Bethlehem, Barbour Collect of rec 1787-1851 by White, bk rev GFP 44:4:188 STS 35:3:69 TR 35:4:220
Bloomfield, Barbour Collect of rec 1835-1853 by White, bk rev GFP 44:4:188 STS 35:3:69 TR 35:4:220
Bozrah, Barbour Collect of rec 1786-1850 by White, bk rev GFP 44:4:188 STS 35:3:69 TR 35:4:220
Branford, Barbour Collect of rec 1644-1850 by White, bk rev GN 13:3:139 HQ 95:59:87 TR 35:4:220
Branford, cem rec by Griswold, bk rev BG 16:1:32
Bridgeport Lib holdings, res guide CTA 37:3:134

CONNECTICUT (continued)
- Bridgeport, Barbour Collect of rec 1821-1854 by White, bk rev GN 13:3:139 HQ 95:59:87 TR 35:4:220
- Canton, settler geneal & hist, repr 1856, bk rev AW 21:2:62 CTA 37:4:183
- Colchester, deaths from the Barbour Collect through 1850 cont CTN 27:4:593
- Co boundary atlas 1630-1990 by DenBoer, bk rev TMG 17:2:46
- Fairfield Co & adjacent NY communities, mil pensioners 1840 CTA 37:4:157
- French & Indian War rolls 1755-1762 by CT Hist Soc, bk rev GRI 15:1:78 GSM 12:2:47
- French & Indian War rolls 1758-1764 by CT Hist Soc, bk rev GSM 12:2:47
- Geneal & fam hist, repr 1911, bk rev BT 27:3:47
- Hartford Dist, probates (pre-1750) by Manwaring, bk rev AG 70:2:122
- Hartford, births to 1850 cont CTN 27:4:607
- Hartford, city direct 1799 by Andrews, bk rev RT 13:1:16
- Hartford, Rev. Thomas Hooker's followers in census 1635, roster VCG 95:DEC:19
- Hebron, hist 1708-1958 by Sibun, bk rev TJ 7:2:76
- Litchfield Co, mil pensioners in 1840, roster CTA 38:2:72
- Marlboro, Ch & Soc rec c1800 RAG 16:3:12
- Middletown, births c1730-1850 CTN 27:4:614
- New Britain, geneal & ecclesiastical hist, repr 1867, bk rev CN 4:4:65 SGS 45:1:31
- New Haven Co, cem inscr by Griswold, bk rev GGP 28:1:23
- New Haven, hist, repr 1902, bk rev SGS 44:2:88
- New Haven, vr from news c1879-1888 CTN 27:4:566

CONNECTICUT (continued)
- Norwalk, 250th anniv, hist, repr 1901, bk rev BG 16:3:104
- ON, land grant pet 1793 FAM 34:4:244
- Probate rec digest 1635-1750 by Manwaring, bk rev GJ 23:2/3:144
- Probate rec digest to 1750, repr 1904-1906, bk rev NYR 126:4:280
- Probate rec digest to 1750, repr 1949, bk rev HQ 95:58:87
- Residents who migrated 1700-1800, hist by Knox/Ferris, bk rev PB 10:2:47
- Saybrook Colony, res tips HQ 95:55:61
- Settlers in Chautauqua Co NY, biog sketches CTN 27:4:542
- Suffield, Bapt Ch centennial hist 1905 CTN 27:4:564
- Waterbury, marr rec to 1850 cont CTN 27:4:626
- West Simsbury, settler geneal & hist, repr 1856, bk rev AW 21:2:62 CTA 37:4:183
- West Suffield, Oath of Fidelity 1771-1779, roster CTA 37:3:138

CONNELLY, Mary Catherine see David Charles HUGHES

CONNER, John Milton b1814, w Bridget Rogers, w Sarah Ann Mobley Estes, NC, geneal by Baxter, bk rev NCJ 21:1:80
- NC, fam hist by Herring, bk rev NCJ 21:3:304

CONRAD, Eliabeth see Daniel F STEIN

CONRADT, Casper bc1771, BA, NY, fam hist by Rowe, bk rev IGS 27:2:118

CONSOLATI, MA, fam hist by Consolati, bk rev RAG 17:1:14

CONSTANCE OF PROVENCE, FR, Egyptian anc TPI 21:1:22

CONSTANT, Elizabeth see Ralph MORGAN

CONVERSE, Mary S see C C DUNLAP

CONWAY, Charles b1874, FL, fam cem rec FLG 18:1:30
COODEY, William Shorey f1840, OK, corresp GSM 12:1:1
COOK, Andrew, w Anna, PA, CN, fam hist by Cook, bk rev CHG 28:1:35
Anna see Andrew COOK
Burrell Hamilton b1887, WV, brief geneal FWC 9:3:268
Ellen see Robert VICKERS
William, TN, KY, geneal by Bruner, bk rev WCK 28:4:44
WV, fam cem inscr FWC 9:4:305
COOKE, John b1752, w Nellie Goodall Pemberton, EN, WV, biog sketch FWC 9:3:259
Maria see Truman SMITH
William see Catherine STEWART
COOMES, M F f1909, KY, FL, hist of his home PCQ 2:4:4
COON, Elizabeth see William COON
William m1839, w Elizabeth, CA, Bible rec GGP 28:1:51
COONROD, Casper see Casper CONRADT
COOPER, Gabriel bc1763, PA, NJ, fam hist by Sanders, bk rev GSN 8:1:7
John Sherman f1901, KY, biog REG 93:2:133
COOTER, Philip C m1873, w Frances P Daugherty, MO, geneal sketch MSG 15:3:133
COPE, John see Charity JEFFERIES
COPPEDGE, Jane Rowe see David MILLS
CORBIN, William b1720, w Sally Ann Jenkins, PA, MD, fam hist 1620-1993 by Helwig, bk rev KCG 36:1:47
CORDOUNER, Jonet see Thomas PETER
CORMACK, William Eppes b1796, NF, biog NAL 11:1:7
CORMIERE, Robert f1644, w Marie Piraude, FR, Acadia, contract AGE 24:2&3:73
CORN, WA, fam rec cont YV 27:1:19
CORTES, Fam hist sketch TFT 6:2:17B

CORTNER, Peter see Peter COTNER
CORY, RI, MA, NY, Am, fam hist by Cory, bk rev GH 49:5:228 NYR 126:3:215
COSBEY, Adam Lee b1816, w Mary P Ferris, OH, Bible rec TR 35:2:99
COST, Francis b1814, GR, PA, fam hist by Ward, bk rev WPG 21:3:48
COTNER, Peter see also Peter GORTNER
Peter b1704, SW, NC, MO, AR, fam hist by Cotner, bk rev ARH 33:3:127 MSG 15:4:224 NCJ 21:3:304
COTTON, Elizabeth see William CATE
COVERT, Janssen f1651, VA, fam hist by Covert, bk rev GH 49:5:229
COVINGTON, Mary Hamilton f1905, OH, fam hist & autobiog, bk rev GH 49:4:218
COWAN, Leo f1940, NC, recoll re:great flood cont JTJ 4:9/10:101
COWARD, Samuel b1815, w Lucretia Edwards, NC, Bible rec GR 37:2:12
COWART, Eleazor fc1900, MS, fam hist by Turner, bk rev HQ 95:58:89
COWGILL, Ellin b1682, PA, geneal by Stuebing, bk rev KCG 36:1:49
COWLIN, Matthew b1840, w Maria E Loomis, EN, NY, OH, biog NGS 83:4:245
COX, --- see Elizabeth SEAGER
Elizabeth Josephine see Samuel Boone MUIR
James Abner b1837, w Mary Adaline Anderson, MS, FL, biog sketch PCQ 16:3:5
Prior m1851, w Isabella Frances Maize, OH, Bible rec IB 11:1:6
VA, fam hist by Peterson, bk rev APR 14:11:5
CRAFTS, Granger Cushman f1862, ME, diary abstr AHS 95:16:3
CRAIG, John bc1755, w Elizabeth Atkinson, PA, OH, fam hist by Williams, bk rev WPG 22:1:48
CRAIGHEAD, William d1827, ST, fam hist sketch ANE 95:56:22

CRAIN, Fam hist by Pelcher, bk rev AGS 36:3:100

CRAMER, John fl800, w Mary Davis, PA, fam hist by Morley, bk rev HQ 95:58:90

CRANDALL, Fitch David m1879, w Electa M Brewer, MI, Bible rec MI 41:2:56

CRANE, Joshua D m1815, w Rebecca Berry, OR, Bible rec GFP 44:3:122

CRANSTON, James fl811, NY, OH, fam hist ACH 16:6:51

CRAVENS, William see Ellen T ELDER

CRAWFORD, Phebe M see E D PAYNE

CRAWFORD, William A fl862, AR, corresp SCH 10:4:158

CREGO, Stephen fl682, NY, hist by Crego, bk rev AG 70:1:60

CREQUI, Medard b1802, MI, biog sketch MHH 16:1:18

CRESSON, Pierre fc1651, VA, fam hist by Covert, bk rev GH 49:5:229

CREVIER, Adolphe b1824, w Domitlde Mathilda Baudreau Graveline, CN, fam hist ACG 21:2:87

CRIGLAR, Mary A see James Wesly HARSH

CRIPPS, John fl844, OH, mil pension appl TR 35:2:72

CROCKER, Alice see William CROCKER

Jane see John CROCKER

John fl634, w Jane, EN, MA, geneal by Leonard, bk rev EWA 32:3:134

William fl634, w Alice, EN, MA, geneal by Leonard, bk rev BG 16:3:102 RAG 16:4:19 SLV 12:3:9

CROCKETT, Davy fl836, Alamo hist STS 35:1:22

Emaline see James Martin REID

LA, fam hist by Wise, bk rev GH 49:5:234

CROFFORD, Elizabeth see Thomas R FREE

CROOKER, Charlotty see Jesse SEGOINE

CROSBY, Daniel see Mary BROWN

George fl842, TN, jour abstr 1842-1846 & biog ETR 7:3:101

CROSS, Isabelle K d1934, NH, will BAT 24:2:59

Walter B b1855, w Carrie J Ricker, VT, fam hist sketch BAT 24:2:59

CROSSER, George see Minnie Hale GORTON

CROSSLEY, Dianna Lee see Raymond Clyde LANTZ

Geneal by Lantz, bk rev SGS 44:3:142

CROUCH, Laurena see Thomas J CURL

CROW, Jessie Wilson fl898, TX, biog sketch KTP 3:4:49

CROWNOVER, Mary see John RABB

CRUM, James B fl859, w Ann Caroline Phelps, FL, biog PCQ 15:4:4

CRUMP, Adam m1734, w Anna Barbara McCarty Fitzhugh, w Hannah Bushrod Heale, biog GR 37:2:3

Eva b1777, h Dudley Forrest, NC, geneal SCG 14:1:658

James Bushrod bc1750, w Isabelle Monroe, VA, geneal GR 37:3:23

William Newton fc1841, AL, hist of his home AFH 16:4:16

CRUTCHER, James Beard fl855, w Susan Ramey, KY, farm acct bk abstr by Simmons, bk rev GH 49:6:207

James Beard fl860, KY, farm acct bk abstr by Elliot, bk rev KA 31:1:43

CUBA, Am Consulate passport reg 1857 CGJ 3:4:13

Cronicas de Santiago de Cuba, death abstr 1870-1896 CGJ 3:4:26

Havana, US Citizen's Reg index 1869-1935 CGJ 3:4:20

Independence & war w/SP, hist sketch CGJ 3:4:30

US policy & Cuba, hist by Schulz, bk rev CGJ 3:4:9

CUBLEY, Emma f1875, h George J Gervais, NE, WA, biog sketch YV 27:1:12

CUDMORE, William f1835, MO, citizenship doc 1840 CR 27:4:104

CULBERTSON, Alexander bc1760, w Ruth Brice, PA, OH, fam hist by Fish, bk rev WPG 21:4:52
 John f1712, DE, PA, fam hist by Fish, bk rev WPG 21:4:52

CULLINAN, Mary b1842, h Richard Hegarty, IR, AA, biog sketch QFH 16:4:118

CULP, C W f1869, KS, brief autobiog WRB 18:1:6

CULVER, Sheryl Furbish f1995, FL, recoll BT 27:3:53

CUMMINS, Nettie see Washington Lafayette SANDERS

CUNDALL, Isaac b1768, RI, geneal RIR 21:3:77

CUNNINGHAM, Martha see Thomas DARNALL
 Sarah Jane see Thomas COLLINGS
 William Everhart f1908, GA, jour abstr NC 5:3:113 5:4:165
 William, w Nancy Ann Green, VA, SC, geneal by Paget, bk rev GH 49:6:207

CURL, John see Tilithia SELF
 Thomas J b1808, w Laurena Crouch, TX, Bible rec YTD 15:1:14

CURTIS, Rebecca Folwell f1855, PA, MS, diary abstr MCG 18:3/4:174

CURTISS, Carroll Coburn bc1885, CA, biog sketch GGP 28:1:5
 Olive see Gideon STODDARD

CURTSI, Samuel Ryan f1846, OH, jour by Chance, bk rev REG 93:3:382

CUSHING, Alonzo Hereford b1841, NY, biog by Brown, bk rev REG 92:4:425

CUSICK, James M f1844, NY, CA, corresp abstr SEE 36:153:12 36:153:63
 Morris f1865, NY, corresp abstr SEE 36:153:63

CUSTER, Sarah see Charles FULK

CYLLIN bc99, EN, fam hist by Hansen, bk rev GH 49:3:218

CZECHOSLOVAKIA, SD, Czech fam hist by Petrik, bk rev TJ 7:3:111

D'AMOURS, Mathieu fc1618, FR, biog LG 95:55:47

DAGGERLINCKX, John m1841, w Susannah Haight, BE, PA, MI, Bible rec SBA 20:5:5

DAGUE, John f1753, w Barbara Waltner, geneal by Schetter, bk rev TPI 21:1:49

DAILEY, Wilhelmina Elmira see Carl Arthur STROM

DAKIN, Lydia E see Charles K JONES

DALRYMPLE, James Isaac, w Elizabeth Hazen, fam hist by Langley, bk rev TS 37:4:147

DANBY, Jane Carr see Japer FORBES

DANCY, Florida Fosyth b1818, h Francis L, GA, obit TAC 6:3:21
 Francis L see Florida Forsyth DANCY

DANIEL, James bc1700, w Jean Kelso, PA, VA, fam hist by Dillard, bk rev SEE 36:153:49
 John f1862, IL, corresp CI 31:4:152
 Thomas f1789, VA, KY, geneal by Daniel, bk rev GH 49:6:207 SGS 45:1:35
 Wilma Sue b1942, h Donald Clare McKinnon, TN, fam rec BWG 24:2:133

DANIELS, Caroline see Henry BOARDMAN

DANNENBERGER, Mary see Orville Merritt KELLY

DANZEISEN, G J b1834, w Mary Bircher, GR, IL, obit CI 31:2:72

DARBY, Columbus T b1876, w Jimmie Gilmer, TX, biog sketch MCG 18:1/2:88

DARE, William bc1653, EN, geneal by Dare, bk rev GH 49:6:207

DARNALL, Thomas m1794, w Martha Cunningham, KY, Bible rec KA 30:3:127

DARNELL, John M b1840, w Louisa Cecil, KY, biog by Darnell, bk rev LAB 10:1:30

DAUGHERTY, Frances P see Philip C COOTER

Hill Carter m1827, w Catherine McCustian, w Cynthia Miller, CA, fam rec GGP 28:1:48

DAVENPORT, Ambrose R b1771, w Elizabeth, VA, MI, biog sketch DM 59:1:41

Ambrose see Susan Des Carreaux DAVENPORT

Elizabeth see Ambrose R DAVENPORT

Susan Des Carreaux bc1804, h Ambrose Davenport, MN, MI, biog sketch DM 59:1:41

DAVEY, Mary see Isaac THOMAS

DAVIDSON, Estelle see Theodore Roosevelt WHITNEY

Odus f1913, AR, last legal execution SYH 3:1:16

Sarah see Lambert CLAYTON

DAVIES, Mary see Isaac THOMAS

DAVILA, Maria see Lorenzo ESPARZA

SP, fam name hist sketch KTP 8:1:9

DAVIS, Andrew Jackson b1841, AR, biog FGC 95:28:22

Ann M see James A COCHRAN

Anna see William MARTIN

Aquilla f1818, IL, Rev War pension appl CR 27:1:6

Edd Doug b1827, NC, autobiog JTJ 4:9/10:99

Elender d1822, h William Davis, WA, fam rec YV 27:1:14

Elizabeth see William BLAYLOCK

Isabell see John ROUPE

Jefferson f1862, papers by Crist et al, bk rev REG 93:4:483

John b1789, w Nancy Patterson, EN, NC, GA, fam hist by Davis, bk rev NTT 15:1/2:7

Laura E see John Henry ROUPE

DAVIS (continued)

Leslie E f1933, ME, autobiog & fam hist BC 17:2:11 18:3:9 18:4:7 19:2:2 19:4:10 19:3:9

Lloyd b1861, FL, biog PCQ 17:4:4

Margaret Ann see David Rodney COLE

Mary Cloeta see Garner Eulas HUTCHINS

Mary see John CRAMER

Mary see Levi WAGNER

Rebecca see Daniel PITCHFORD

Samuel bc1610, NC, LA, TX, geneal by Dietz, bk rev RAG 16:2:21

William b1803, w Sarah Smith, ME, Bible rec SCR 18:5:74

William R f1865, KY, corresp PCH 1:1:32

DAVISON, John f1778, ST, IR, VA, biog LOB 16:2:37

John see Maria GUNDY

DAWES, W J d1887, OH, WI, biog sketch MCR 26:1:21

DAY, George W see Florinda MCCULLOCH

Harvey b1882, w Berta Bailey, TX, fam rec PWN 2:5:17

John, NJ, WI, geneal by Stafford, bk rev FRT 16:3:102 TR 35:4:221

DE LEON, Dona Augustina see Placido BENAVIDES

DEALY, James b1819, w Matilda York, NC, MO, CA, biog & fam hist PW 15:3:123

DEARBORN, Henry b1751, NH, jour by Peckham, bk rev GH 49:6:207

Henry b1751, jour abstr by Smith, bk rev GGP 28:1:21

Henry b1751, Rev War jour 1775-1783 by Brown, bk rev TSC 6:2:5

DEARING, John f1745, VA, fam hist by Dearing, bk rev KCG 36:2:103

William f1745, VA, geneal by Dearing, bk rev GH 49:5:229

DEATON, Rufus A see Caledonia G H MOORE

DEBLONDIN, Baron fc1480, FR, EN, fam hist by Blanding, bk rev CI 31:2:68

DECOOPMAN, Kathy f1995, BE, fam hist & res FAH 13:1:3

DEGENARO, Rosalina f1951, IY, NY, biog sketch HQ 95:58:37

DEGGE, William m1758, w Judith Haley, VA, marr rec abstr QY 22:3:2

DEGODOI, Luceros, fam hist by Buxton, bk rev TB 21:3:10

DEGREINVILLE, Joan see John ENGAYNE

DEKALB, Esther b1821, h Jonathan, MA, diary abstr & fam hist sketch BAT 24:2:58
 Jonathan m1844, w Ester, NY, fam rec CDG 14:2:13

DELAFONTAINE, John bc1500, FR, fam hist by Maury, bk rev GH 49:4:224

DELASHMUTT, Elias bc1710, w Elizabeth Nelson, MD, geneal by Close, bk rev WMG 11:1:43

DELAWARE, Bible rec late 1700s vol 4 by Hehir, bk rev GH 49:6:186 NCJ 21:3:298 OK 40:2:45 TR 35:2:107
 Christiana Meth Epis Ch hist by White, bk rev DWC 21:2:58 PV 23:6:2 SGS 44:3:141
 Gazetteer, repr 1904, bk rev GH 49:3:210
 Geneal & fam hist bibl by Hehir, bk rev MD 36:1:87
 New Castle Co, archives inv by DHRS, bk rev MGS 13:3:44
 New Castle Co, ch rec (early) by Wright, bk rev MD 36:1:85
 Soldier & sailor hist 1638-1776 by Peden, bk rev HQ 95:59:88 MD 36:2:313
 Sussex Co, land rec 1769-1782 by Wright, bk rev MD 36:1:85
 Sussex Co, rec by Turner, bk rev PR 22:4:48
 Tax assessment & census lists 1782 by Nelson, bk rev DM 58:3:141

DELAWARE (continued)
 Trivia guide by Shalk, bk rev AW 22:2:32
 Wills & estates to 1800, index by Virdin, bk rev BHN 28:1:20 CL 14:2:9 GH 49:5:191 SGS 44:2:89

DELBEQUE, Madeleine m1742, h Charles Bourassa, identity solved AGE 24:2&3:52

DELLINGER, Jacob f1733, w Maria Barbara, GR, PA, fam hist by Billet/Dellinger, bk rev EWA 32:3:134
 Maria Barbara see Jacob DELLINGER

DEMARANVILLE, Diadema see Ambrose CHAPMAN

DEMPSY, Jocie M see Charlie D BENNETT

DENHAM, William Thomas, w Louisa Adella Fudge, FL, fam hist PCQ 15:4:2

DENISON, George b1618, MA, biog & fam hist PW 15:3:117

DENISSEN, MI, fam hist corr & add MHH 16:1:25

DENNEY, Allison James, fam hist by Graves, bk rev ARH 33:3:128

DENNIS, NC, TN, see TENNISON

DENNISON, Edmund d1889, VA, WV, biog by Priest, bk rev VAG 39:4:319

DENTON, Hiram King b1820, TN, fam hist by Hereford, bk rev NTT 15:1/2:3

DEPINON, Maria Fernandez see Domingo de LUACES

DEPUY, Nicholas bc1634, w Catherine Renard, New Netherlands, FR, fam hist by Heidgerd/Smith, bk rev GH 49:4:224

DERAPALJIE, Janssen f1623, NY, fam hist by Covert, bk rev GH 49:5:229

DEROSETTE, James Matthew b1849, w Temperance J McAllister, KY, fam hist sketch TRS 19:1:6

DESCARREAUX, Francois bc1775, FR, MN, fam hist MHH 16:1:2

DESROSIERS, Jeannia see Walter YOUNG

DETER, Daniel b1840, w Eliza Billett, PA, biog sketch BGN 16:1:18

DEVEAU, Jacques fl740, w Marie-Charlotte Boucher, w Angelique Mignier, FR, geneal LG 95:54:36
Jacques fl740, geneal cont LG 95:55:53

DEVEREAUX, Rachael Fanny see Rachael Fanny MARTIN

DEVORE, Fam hist 1500-1992 by Mann, bk rev TOP 25:1:5

DEVOST, Jacques see Jacques DEVEAU

DEVOT, Jacques see Jacques DEVEAU

DEWBERRY, Elizabeth see Joseph BEDDINGFIELD

DEWEY, Elizabeth see Thomas INGERSOLL

DIANARD, Dominique see Domenico ZENNARO

DIBBLE, Ambrose Chapman d1899, w Diadema De Maranville, w Ellen M Fuller, NY, OH, obit GG 7:4:176

DICKASON, Susannah E dc1836, TX, memorials MT 31:4:144

DICKEN, Elizabeth see John BURDYNE
Isaac H m1825, w Elizabeth Jones, KY, brief fam hist KA 31:2:10

DICKENSON, Joseph Rives b1828, w Mary Williams Shelby, VA, WA, fam hist RES 26:3:144
Margaret A see George Houston GODDARD

DICKEY, Clara fc1868, KS, memoirs WRB 18:1:7

DICKINSON, Jonathan m1792, w Crocia Sizer, VA, geneal VAG 39:1:57
Thomas bc1750, w Nancy Ann Woolfolk, VA, geneal VAG 39:2:143

DIEHL, Ludwig fl853, OH, corresp abstr cont SSG 14:1:6 14:2:22

DIENGER, Karl b1824, w Dorothy Boerner, GR, TX, fam hist sketch KTP 4:3:38

DIERSTEIN, Barbara see Samuel DIERSTEIN
Samuel dc1731, w Barbara, PA, fam rec MHP 22:3:8

DIETERT, Henry see Amalia BERGMANN
William b1830, w Rose Bergman, GR, TX, biog sketch KTP 6:2:31
William fl854, TX, biog KTP 3:3:29

DIGGINS, Jeremiah bc1650, w Mary Cadwell, CT, geneal AG 70:1:18

DILLARD, George fl650, VA, fam hist by Dillard, bk rev SEE 36:153:49
Martha Ann Elender see George Washington WALDREP

DILLEY, Elizabeth see Henry DOCKSTADER

DILLINGER, John fl934, IL, biog by Girardin/Helmer, bk rev REG 93:2:240

DISHNER, Robert E b1894, TN, fam cem rec HPF 95:50:11

DIXON, Jane see Daniel IBBOTSON
Nancy Ann see Daniel Marion FOSTER
Thomas b1777, w Lydia Kay, EN, fam hist sketch TLL 20:2:34

DOBBS, Dosia see Hiram BENNETT

DOCKSTADER, Henry b1791, w Elizabeth Dilley, MI, Bible rec DM 58:4:165
Magdalena see John BACKUS

DODD, David fl864, AR, biog sketch SYH 1:4:19

DODSON, Nancy Penelope see Samuel H CHAPMAN

DOHERTY, Paul fl992, NH, autobiog, bk rev BC 17:2:5
Rosa see Robert Walton WHITWORTH

DOHMEIER, Caroline Dorothy see Andreas Frederick HERMS

DOLEMAN, John b1759, w Margaret Archibald, ST, fam hist GWS 95:44:12

DONAHUE, James fc1845, IR, NY, DC, geneal by Donahue, bk rev GH 49:5:229

DONGAN, Thomas fl685, NY, misc rec by Christoph, bk rev AG 70:1:59

DOOLEY, Elizabeth see Thomas DOOLEY

DOOLEY, Thomas fl756, w Elizabeth, VA, NC, geneal CAL 14:2:44

DORMAN, Ellen see Thomas DORMAN

George see Katherine DORMAN

Katherine b1820, h George, NY, obit GG 7:4:176

Thomas b1600, w Ellen, EN, MA, geneal by Dorman, bk rev AG 70:2:123 GH 49:6:207 MN 26:2:89 NER 149:596:433 SGS 44:3:143 STK 22:4:199 VL 30:1:42

DORNER, Jacob fl746, w Anna Maria Barbara Sturm, GR, PA, geneal by Kiddoo, bk rev WMG 12:1:43

DORSEY, Augustus b1841, w Frances Minerva Shultz, w Ersula Frye, PA, KS, geneal by Alvis, bk rev WPG 22:1:48

DORSEY, Mary Ann see Peter VANCLIEF

DOUB, John b1742, w Mary Eve Spainhour, GR, NC, fam hist FC 14:1:48

DOUGAN, Sarah see Hiram BENNETT

DOUGLAS, William A see Hattie MAY

DOVES, Lloyd see Lloyd DAVIS

DOWNER, William fl808, VA, will abstr TVF 4:2:120

DOWNING, Susana see George EDWARDS

William fl805, w Eliza Simmons, OH, fam hist by Harrison, bk rev GH 49:6:208

DOWNS, Joshua fc1850, AL, biog sketch MCA 14:3:102

DOYLE, William Jacob b1878, TN, TX, biog PWN 2:6:29

DRAKE, Asahel b1722, CT, PA, anc NGS 83:3:180

DRAKEFORD, Ann see Richard DRAKEFORD

Richard fl690, w Ann, VA, geneal VAG 39:2:135

DRAKELEY, Lydia see Azariah ROOD

DRAPEAU, Marguerite see Domenico ZENNARO

DRAPER, Lyman Copeland b1815, NY, biog & descr of hist collect KTP 8:3:37

DRAUGHN, J D b1845, NC, fam hist by Kallam, bk rev NCJ 21:2:189

DREW, Frances d1774, h John Simpson, NS, biog sketch GN 13:1:11

DRINKWATER, Sumner fl859, w Alice Gray, ME, jour & memorabilia, repr 1981, bk rev GH 49:3:209

DRIVER, FR, IR, ON, fam hist by Kapas, bk rev GEN 20:3:32

DRUCKER, Olga Levy fl939, GR, EN, recoll JL 8:1/2:95

DRUSHAL, Mary see William MCDONALD

DRYER, William Wilbert b1886, w Margaret Frances Robson, PA, geneal by Dryer, bk rev WPG 22:1:48

DUBBS, Joseph S b1796, PA, burial rec JBC 15:4:3

DUBOIS, Elisabeth see Jacques RITCHOT

Harrison fl863, KS, biog sketch KK 33:2:31

NY, fam hist notes NYR 126:3:175

DUCHESNE, Susanna see Philippe DU TRIEUX

DUDLEY, Elizabeth see Abraham FORREST

DULANEY, Daniel fl703, IR, MD, biog sketch FTR 95:179:6

DUNCAN, Thomas, ST, PA, geneal by Smith, bk rev TEN 95:16:23

William C b1820, w Emma Jane Hanmer, Sarah E Heath, MI, biog sketch DM 58:3:144

DUNKIN, SC, GA, AL, fam hist by Cress, bk rev NC 5:4:180

DUNLAP, C C m1876, w Mary S Converse, OH, Bible rec IB 11:1:7

DUNN, Ellen see Alexander GOODWIN

DUNN (continued)
Henry Allen b1851, w Rebecca Jane Hill, TN, geneal BWG 24:2:135
John f1852, TX, fam hist KTP 4:1:13
John Henry f1852, TX, fam hist KTP 4:1:13
Patrick f1852, TX, fam hist KTP 4:1:13
DURANT, Benjamin f1801, w Sophia, GA, will SEN 1:2:15
DURBIN, Thomas f1638, MD, fam hist by Carson, bk rev DM 59:1:46
DURET, Marie f1847, FR, geneal LG 95:53:13
DURRANCE, Jesse Harris b1818, w Priscilla Altman, GA, FL, biog & geneal PCQ 12:2:2
DURRE, William Joseph b1822, w Caroline Turner, CT, Bible rec CTA 38:2:64
DURTSCHI, Barbara see Peter ANKEN
DUTCH GENEALOGY, Art & society yearbk 1995-1996 by FNF, bk rev DFH 8:4:92
  Beginner's guide, cont DFH 8:2:26
  Beginner's res tips DFH 8:1:2
  Computer resource guide DFH 8:4:85
  HO, Colchester bapt reg 1645-1728, repr 1905, bk rev GH 49:3:196
  Imm court rec, 17th cent, by Currer-Briggs, bk rev PR 22:3:8
  Name adoption, hist & res tips DFH 8:2:44
  Naming conventions UG 23:1:3
  New Netherland res guide by Epperson, bk rev AG 70:1:59
  NY, Clymer, Dutch settlement, hist DFH 8:4:80
  PA, Quaker migration hist by Hull, bk rev OK 40:2:46
  Source citations, tips DFH 8:4:87
  Vr, Dutch terminology, trans FAH 13:2:26
  Zeeland, res tips DFH 8:4:75

DUTRIEUX, Philippe m1615, w Jaquemyne Noiret, w Susanna Du Chesne, NL, NY, fam hist sketch SGS 44:3:120
DVORAK, Frank f1876, w Frances Jukl, GR, NE, fam hist by Billingsley/Davis, bk rev TOP 25:4:130
DWIGHT, Sarah see Benjamin MILLS
DYAR, Joseph Daniel bc1885, AL, news abstr AFH 16:2:13
DYCKMAN, Johannes, NY, CT, geneal vol 2 by Chamberlain NYR 126:2:153
DYE, George Washington b1859, w Mary Louise Spillman, TX, Bible rec KTP 7:3:37
DYER, Pleasant b1818, MO, Bible rec OZ 17:4:150
DYESS, SC, fam hist by Trammell, bk rev TG 29:1:47
DYKES, Mary see Moses BIRD
DYNN, Elizabeth see Caleb CALLUM
EADS, William b1797, w Rebecca Robinson, KY, MO, IA, brief fam hist KA 30:3:150
EAGAN, Rachel see Joshua TIPTON
EAGLESON, Sarah Ann see James B RAINEY
EARP, Wyatt Berry Stapp b1848, IL, CO, NV, fam hist by Jones, bk rev HQ 95:58:90
EASTON, Rebecca see William JAMES
EATON, Andrew Boyd b1860, TN, obit abstr ETR 7:4:170
EBERSOL, Barbara b1846, PA, biog by Luthy, bk rev PM 19:1:39
  Susanna see Emile/Antoine ARTHAUD
EBY, Benjamin f1841, PA, biog sketch & religious views descr PM 19:1:2
EDDS, William see William EADS
EDDY, Sarah Hotchkiss see Sarah Hotchkiss ADDY
EDGAR, Isaac f1861, w Mary L Zimmerman, PA, biog sketch HQ 95:55:65

EDMONDSON, John m1830, w Amanda S Randolph, TN, Bible rec MTG 8:4:169
EDMONDSTON, Catherine Ann Devereux fl860, NC, jour by Crabtree/Paton, bk rev RAG 16:4:25
EDUWARTZ, Jan see Marritje GONSALUS
EDWARD III, EN, fam hist by Stuart, bk rev KA 31:2:47
EDWARDS, Daniel fl846, FL, fam hist FLG 18:1:32
EDWARDS, George b1772, w Susana Downing, IL, fam hist IG 31:2:39
Hannah bc1644, h Joseph Hills, CT, fam hist NER 149:593:41
James C m1890, w Julia Holstein, MO, Bible rec OZ 17:3:101
John Edgar see Susan Alice KENNEDY
Lucretia see Samuel COWARD
William b1741, w Chloe Stokes, FL, fam hist FLG 18:1:32
William H m1896, w Savannah Allred, AL, Bible rec AFH 16:2:23
EGNOR, James Harvey mc1903, w Salina Susan Willis, WV, fam rec FWC 9:4:78
EGYPT, Tomb of Ramesses II's sons, descr ASO 25:1:14
EIDE, Anna Jacobsdotter see Knud ANDERSON
EIGSTI, Alma fl940, IL, biog sketch MH 22:1:1
EKLEBERRY, Jacob b1775, w Abigail Rose Prior, PA, OH, biog sketch IB 11:1:14
ELDER, Ellen T b1821, h William Cravens, KY, biog LAB 10:4:111
ELDER, Nettie see Charles HARRIS
ELGIN, Lionel b1750, w Elizabeth Hooper, EN, PA, fam hist by Rosen, bk rev GH 49:5:229
ELKINS, Joseph N m1865, w America Brown, AL, Bible rec OLR 9:4:142
ELLINGTON, W D d1923, TX, obit PWN 3:2:8

ELLIOTT, Abraham m1835, w Mary Runyan, WA, Bible rec TB 21:3:38
Elizabeth see Edmund LUSH
Grace see James Alfred BAGLEY
ELLIS, Abram b1825, w Annice, AL, fam hist NTT 14:4:137
Annice see Abram ELLIS
James b1758, w Sarah Riggs, NY, TN, geneal by Ericson, bk rev ACG 21:4:160 GG 8:3:112 SGS 45:1:35
Samuel b1712, w Anne Evans, WE, NY, biog sketch IMP 14:1:10
WE, MD, KY, OH, fam hist by Boles, bk rev GH 49:4:224
ELLISON, Betty see Daniel SHUMATE
ELLOT, Elizabeth see Edmund LUSH
ELMORE, Cathern see Nathaniel WILDS
ELSWICK, G Ed b1921, KY, autobiog sketch PCH 1:3:19
Jacob see Ona/Onnica SANDERS
ELTING, Jessie see Charles A FIELD
ELVIDGE, Joseph b1827, EN, IL, biog sketch MCS 15:2:78
ELY, Susan Childers, TX, biog sketch KTP 7:1:13
EMBREE, Margaret see Margaret EMORY
Misc fam data by Williams, bk rev GH 49:4:224
EMERSON, Charles F, w Bessie Benson, fam hist by Swigart, bk rev NER 149:595:315
John (Samuel) b1773, w Lydia Webster, NH, geneal NHR 12:1:24
Moses b1775, w Tabitha Foss, NH, geneal NHR 12:1:24
EMONEAU, Elizabeth see Samuel EMONEAU
Samuel b1702, w Elizabeth, NS, fam hist NEH 12:5:146
EMORY, Margaret see John McDonald
ENDERS, Geneal & add 1740-1990 by Enders Fam Assoc, bk rev TPI 21:1:49
ENDICOTT, Donald d1994, VA, anc ANC 30:2:62

ENDICOTT (continued)
  John b1588, EN, MA, fam hist by Harrison, bk rev GH 49:6:208
ENGAYNE, John dc1296, w Joan de Greinville, EN, fam hist, AG 70:2:96
ENGELBRECHT, Jacob f1820, MD, marr ledger abstr by Long/Eader, bk rev GH 49:3:218 RCR 10:4:2377 TJ 7:3:108 TR 35:3:166
ENGELKING, Sigismund b1875, w Annie Laura James, TX, obit KTP 10:1:8
ENGEN, Johanna see Ole Jacobsen HAGEN
ENGLAND, Administrative areas, terminology, glossary GGP 28:1:40
  Ancestor origin res guide by Camp, bk rev FAM 34:3:181
  Ancestry res guide by Chapman, bk rev GWS 95:43:34
  Ancestry res guide by Irvine, bk rev KVH 20:1&2:8 MAG 8:2:4 MD 36:1:95 NGS 83:1:60
  Anglo-Norman fam geneal, repr 1951, bk rev PR 22:3:8
  Army pensioners abroad, pension rec 1772-1899 by Crowder, bk rev ACG 21:2:61 GN 13:2:90 HQ 95:58:87 NYR 126:3:218 OBN 28:3:111 SGB 26:2:iv SGS 44:3:144 TR 35:4:220
  Bellmakers & bellringers, hist TGO 7:12:515
  Bristol, servants sent to foreign plantations, reg 1654-1686 by Coldham, bk rev TVF 4:1:54
  British anc, res guide by Chapman, bk rev ACG 22:1:21
  British Isles directories, res guide FRT 16:2:58
  Burke's fam rec, geneal of cadet houses, repr 1897, bk rev GH 49:5:227
  Calendar reform 1752, brief hist NTT 16:3:15
  Carlisle Castle, res tips & hist SGB 26:1:13
  Cem & crematoria, res guide by Wolfston, bk rev TGO 8:1:40

ENGLAND (continued)
  Census returns 1841-1891, microfilm guide by Gibson, bk rev SGB 26:2:iv
  Cheshire, geneal bibl by Raymond, bk rev SGB 26:4:iv
  Clan system, brief descr HQ 95:59:54
  CN, apprentices imm to CN 1869-1924 by Parr, bk rev FAM 34:2:116
  Co York, Allerton Mauleverer & Askham Richard parish ch reg 1557-1812, repr 1908, bk rev ACG 21:4:160 GH 49:6:178 SGS 45:1:29
  Colchester, Dutch Ch bapt rec 1645-1728, repr 1905, bk rev DFH 8:4:91 SGS 44:2:90
  Company & Business rec, res guide by Gibson/Hunter, bk rev FAM 34:3:178
  Congregationalists, hist & res guide by Clifford, bk rev RT 13:1:16
  Cornish Mining Index, res tips SKC 11:1:12
  Cornwall Mining Index, res tips NAL 11:4:140
  Cornwall, census 1881, LDS transcr edition, res tips SCS 32:12:284
  Domesday Bk, property rec descr CC 17:2:12
  Dorchester, life in 17th cent, hist by Undertown, bk rev GH 49:5:181
  Emigration, 19th cent, hist by Erickson, bk rev REG 93:3:344
  Falaise Roll, companions of William the Conquerer, repr 1938, bk rev PR 22:3:8
  Farms, locating anc property, res tips HQ 95:57:47
  Feudal era, hist & geneal, repr 1895, bk rev GR 37:1:49
  Feudal hist studies, 11th & 12th cent, repr 1909, bk rev GH 49:3:196
  Gamekeeper's Reg & manorial rec, res tips CSB 30:4:169
  Geneal res tips OC 32:2:8
  General Reg Ofc index of one-name lists in Lib of Soc of Geneal, bk rev QFH 16:4:140

ENGLAND (continued)
Gulval, parish reg 1598-1812, repr 1893, bk rev SGS 45:1:29
Handwriting samples 1600s GWD 9:1:3
Hulks, shipboard confinement 1776-1857 hist by Campbell, bk rev CGJ 3:4:12 TSC 6:1:4
Immigrant court rec, 17th cent, by Currer-Briggs, bk rev PR 22:3:8
Jacobite soldiers & sympathizers, roster 1715 RAG 16:2:26
Jacobites of 1715, hist by Dobson, bk rev FAM 34:4:249
Lanisley, parish reg 1598-1812, repr 1893, bk rev SGS 45:1:29
Lathes of Kent, hist QFH 16:4:144
Liverpool, Champion of the Seas pass list TGO 8:1:9
Liverpool, packet & clipper ships to AA, hist TGO 8:1:6
Lloyd's shipping, hist, bk rev TGO 8:1:10
Lloyd's shipping, res tips TGO 8:1:11
London area, cem & crematoria guide by Wolfston, bk rev FAM 34:3:179
London, cem & crematoria guide by Webb, bk rev GJ 22:4:130
London, marr (irregular) before 1754, hist by Benton, bk rev QFH 16:2:67
London, marr lic & allegations 1821-1869, repr 1887, microfiche rev GH 49:4:228
London, port hist sketch TGO 8:1:25
London, *Times* news, res tips TGO 8:1:22
Manorial tenants, res guide by Park, bk rev GJ 22:4:131
Marske, shipwreck 1808, crew roster & hist ANE 95:56:20
Military rec res guide SMN 13:1:11
Naming patterns, descr KTP 8:4:60
Old Jordans, Mayflower barn hist sketch BT 27:1:15
Ordnance survey maps, res guide by Oliver, bk rev ANE 95:57:21
Pedigrees & geneal vol 3 & 4, repr 1895-1896, bk rev GR 37:4:5

ENGLAND (continued)
Peers of the realm, titles & rights descr HQ 95:55:39
Pensioners abroad 1772-1899, index by Crowder, bk rev GFP 44:4:188
Petworth, imm to ON, hist sketch FAM 34:2:85
Poor laws & paupers, hist TGO 7:12:494
Public Rec Ofc, res guide GH 49:4:10
Public Rec Ofc, res guide by Colwell, bk rev GJ 22:4:134
Public Rec Ofc, res trip tips NAL 11:2:84
Quarter sessions rec for fam historians, guide by Gibson, bk rev SGB 26:4:iv
Register Ofcs, guide to finding civil reg certs by Christensen, bk rev GH 49:6:178
Repository res guide by Moulton, bk rev MAG 8:2:3
Res guide by Baxter, bk rev APG 10:4:128 ARH 33:1:34 GFP 44:3:139 GWS 95:42:39
Res guide by Irvine, bk rev
Res tips CC 17:3:22
Rev War, prison ship convict lists, repr, bk rev FRT 16:3:106
Shropshire, hist, gazetteer & direct, repr 1851, bk rev SGS 45:1:29
Surname dict by Reaney, bk rev AG 70:4:255
Surnames, res tips AMG 10:2/3:37
Transportation of criminals to the colonies, hist by Coldham, bk rev NHR 12:4:193
Victorian era, women & domestic service, hist IMP 14:2:49
Victuallers' Lic, res guide by Gibson/Hunter, bk rev FAM 34:3:178
Visitation of EN & Wales vol 1-4, repr, bk rev SGS 45:1:29
William the Conqueror's desc by Moore, bk rev AG 70:4:255
Wiltshire, Gloucestershire, biog hist by Badeni, bk rev FAM 34:1:52

ENGLAND (continued)
 Yorkshire, fam hist res guide by Litton, bk rev SGB 26:4:iii
ENGLEBRECHT, Jacob fl820, MD, marr ledger abstr by Long/Eader, bk rev MD 36:1:90
ENGLISH, Mathew f1776, TN, *English vs George Bean* testimony abstr ETR 7:4:178
ENSMINGER, Charles E d1953, PA, Bible rec NGS 83:4:301
ERBACH, Jacob b1756, w Esther Funk, PA, fam hist MFH 14:2:84
ERFURT, Anna Gertraud see Ludwig SHMITT
ERICSON, Carl Eric m1860, w Carolina Bjorkelund, SN, KS, geneal by Streeter, bk rev TJ 7:1:38
ERION, IL, fam corresp by O'Day, bk rev PR 23:2:69
ERWIN, Hannah see Zebulon BAIRD
ESPARZA, Lorenzo b1745, w Maria Davila, w Juana Arias, MX, CA, fam hist sketch KTP 8:3:46
ESSEX, Hannah Fuller see Henry OUGHTON
 Henry f1885, OH, legal notice TLL 20:3:56
ESTES, Eliuah A J b1836, w Mary Jane, SD, biog SVG 21:1:10
 Elizabeth see John RHODES
 Mary Jane see Eliuah A J ESTES
 Sarah Ann Mobley see John Milton CONNER
ETHELBERTSON, Edward f1057, EN, biog SGS 44:2:75
ETHERIDGE, Henrietta f1863, h John Kelso, AR, corresp ARH 33:2:55
EUBANK, Alfred see Eliza Ann EUBANK
 Eliza Ann f1836, h Alfred Eubank, VA, div doc TVF 4:1:44
EUROPEAN GENEALOGY, Eastern Eur geneal res guide by FEEFHS, bk rev GGD 11:3:68
 Eastern Eur geneal res tips SGB 26:4:171

EUROPEAN GENEALOGY (continued)
 Eastern Eur, LDS Lib microfilm res tips RM 95:8:3
 Eastern Eur, travel & res tips RM 95:8:5
 Galician geneal organizations, hist & addresses SGB 26:1:23
 Hamburg pass lists, res tips GH 49:6:35
 Knighthood & chivalry descr ASO 25:1:22
 Res guide by Baxter, bk rev AGE 24:1:9 GFP 44:3:138 GH 49:3:196 LC 16:1:15 MN 26:3:137
 Viking hist TFG 8:1:3
 Wends, hist & descr KTP 10:2:31
EVANS, Anne see Samuel ELLIS
 Anthony, VA, fam hist, bk rev TJ 7:3:109
EVENSWORE, Martha see Lewis ADAMS
EWER, Mary Wallen see John JENKINS
EWING, Margaret Ann see Alexander TOWNSLEY
 ST, IR, MD, PA, WV, fam hist by Carson/Wooley, bk rev GJB 20:2:32
EXON, Mary see Celestin MERCIER
EYER, Elizabeth f1816, PA, sch doc TGC 19:4:79
FAGAN, James fc1671, KY, MO, fam hist by Vaughn, bk rev MSG 15:4:223
FAIRBANKS, Frederick C f1906, w Helen C Scott, OH, news abstr re:marr JCL 9:3:26
FAKES, Clara I see William Edward MARCONNET
 Thorton P, EN, Bible rec TS 37:4:125
FANCHER, Martha see Richard FANCHER
 Richard b1700, w Martha, NJ, fam hist by Fancher, bk rev FRT 16:2:66
FANNING, David bc1755, VA, SC, biog CI 31:2:69
FARABEE, Eleanor L f1930, MS, FL, recoll BT 27:4:68

FARE, Edmund bc1762, w Priscilla (Preshy) Lovelace, VA, biog NPW 13:12:64

FARMER, John b1789, New England, anc NEH 12:1:22

FARNHAM, EN, Am, fam hist by Stepanek, bk rev GH 49:6:207

FARNI, Christian f1858, IL, biog cont MH 22:4:65

FARRINGTON, NC, fam hist by Jagmin, bk rev RCR 10:1:2217

FAST, Jennie see William BOGART

FAUBION, John b1735, w Dianna Rector, TN, fam hist by Harrison, bk rev GH 49:6:208

FAULCONER, Thomas f1622, VA, geneal by Faulconer/West, bk rev GH 49:5:230 TVF 4:2:121

FAUST, Anna see Peter FREESE

FAWCETT, John b1739, NH, biog DAR 129:5:499

FAWKES, Mary Elizabeth f1995, CN, father's biog by Fawkes, bk rev FAM 34:3:177

FAWLEY, Jacob b1802, w Sarah Minnick, VA, geneal by Ritchie, bk rev GH 49:4:224

FEAY, George b1829, PA, Bible rec BGN 16:4:13

FEAZEL, Elizabeth see Michael FEAZEL
  John O, LA, fam hist by Gritzbaugh, bk rev TG 29:1:47
  Michael fc1749, w Elizabeth, GR, VA, fam hist by Gritzbaugh, bk rev TG 29:1:47

FEIPEL, Peter m1874, w Barbara Reiff, IL, fam hist by Stiens et al, bk rev FRT 16:3:111

FELCH, Hannah see Samuel PARKER

FENNER, Arthur, RI, fam hist by Fenner, bk rev GH 49:6:208
  George b1757, NY, fam hist by Fenner, bk rev GH 49:6:208
  Harry J m1920, w Laura Julia Bertrand, MA, fam hist sketch ACG 21:2:62

FENNER (continued)
  James Elroy b1844, w Hester Adamantha Broughton, PA, fam hist by Fenner, bk rev AH 22:4:245

FEODOROVNA, Alexandra d1918, RU, biog ASO 25:1:20

FERGUSON, James f1800, w Elizabeth Fleming, NC, TN, geneal by Ferguson, bk rev TR 35:3:169
  John b1839, ON, fam hist sketch IFL 5:8:9

FERNALD, Elizabeth Hunking see Samuel WINKLEY

FERNANDEZ, Mariana see Francisco RENCUREL

FERRALL, William b1794, w Jane Hays, OH, Bible rec TR 35:3:153

FERRELL, Elizabeth see Alsey STRICKLAND

FERRIS, Mary P see Adam Lee COSBEY

FESSENDEN, Benjamin bc1700, w Rebecca Smith, MA, geneal NER 149:596:381

FETTERS, William b1794, w Mary B Leech, PA, OH, geneal by Fetters, bk rev MGS 13:3:46

FICK, H W f1869, AR, biog sketch SYH 3:1:19

FIELD, Charles A, w Jessie Elting, NY, fam rec UG 23:2:16
  Martha fc1758, CT, identity VCG 95:DEC:4
  NY, fam rec 1800s UG 23:1:5 23:3:29

FILLER, Margaret see Zachariah HARSHBARGER

FILLINGER, Andrew Louis d1917, IL, obit IG 31:1:12

FINK, Johannes b1797, IL, fam hist RCR 10:1:2165

FINLEY, George f1902, WA, biog sketch TRI 35:1:15
  John f1740, w --- Thompson, w Mary Caldwell, VA, geneal VAG 39:1:3 39:2:94 39:3:202
  John, VA, identity of more children, cont VAG 39:4:282

FINNISH GENEALOGY, MI, Finnish Am Heritage Center, res guide HQ 95:58:65
  MN, Iron Range Finns in early 1900s, hist sketch & roster MN 26:2:74
  Res guide by Vincent/Tapio, bk rev GGP 28:1:23 HQ 95:55:91 SGS 44:3:146
FISCHER, Ella d1935, IL, obit abstr MCS 15:1:13
FISH, Charles fl853, CA, jour abstr KTP 14:2:28 14:3:46
  Edmund b1824, w Mary Barrett, MI, biog KTP 13:4:67
  Elijah Stanton b1791, w Fanny Spencer, MA, biog KTP 13:4:64
  Fam rec vol 7 by Logsdon, bk rev TR 35:3:168
  Josiah fl795, NY, misc doc KTP 13:2:31
  Josiah Ward fl849, CA, corresp KTP 14:1:12
  Lafayette fl848, TX, jour abstr KTP 14:4:63
  Lafayette Irving m1881, w Frances Lillian Webster, CA, fam hist sketch KTP 14:3:48
  Libbeus b1781, w Polly Holcomb, NY, fam rec & fam hist KTP 14:1:5
  Mary see Stephen FISH
  Philotheta b1783, VT, TX, autobiog KTP 13:3:50
  Sophia b1779, h Frederick Hosmer, VT, fam rec KTP 14:1:5
  Stephen fl687, w Mary, MA, TX, fam rec KTP 13:2:27
  TX, fam rec cont KTP 13:3:41 13:4:62
  VT, TX, fam rec KTP 14:1:5
FISHBACK, Alice see John FISHBACK
  John fl779, w Alice, VA, Bible rec BYG 8:1:428
FISHER, Aseneth see David CLARK
  Emily fl808, h Robin, KY, KS, biog sketch KCG 36:2:76
  Robin see Emily FISHER

FISKE, Benjamin d1765, w Abigail Bowen, RI, parentage NER 149:595:239
  Joseph see Elizabeth BARTRAM
FITCH, James b1622, EN, CT, biog by Fitch, bk rev CTN 27:4:588 NER 149:595:313
FITZHUGH, Anna Barbara see Adam CRUMP
FITZPATRICK, Levisa see Robert SPRADLIN
FLEENOR, Jacob William, w Mary Susannah Hope, fam hist by Hanson, bk rev BWG 24:1:67
  Michael fl777, w Sally, PA, MD, VA, Rev War pension appl HPF 14:52:38
  Sally fl844, h Michael, VA, Rev War widow's pension appl HPF 14:52:40
FLEGG, Mary see Thomas FLEGG
  Thomas b1615, w Mary, EN, MA, geneal AGS 36:2:60
FLEMING, Elizabeth see James FERGUSON
  Robert bc1730, SC, lineage by Linn, bk rev SCM 23:2:120
FLEMISH GENEALOGY, Artists, famous, biog sketches FAH 13:2:27
  Pittem, emig roster c1900-1930 cont FAH 13:2:32
  Poperinge, hist FAH 13:2:34
  Roeselare, hist FAH 13:2:36
FLETCHER, Lydia Bates fl632, MA, corresp AW 22:1:14
FLINT, Mary fl775, h Samuel Hartwell, MA, biog DAR 129:5:480
FLORA, David fl812, IN, hist of his fort GCH 8:7:122
FLORIDA, Acton, hist PCQ 8:4:4
  Alachua Co, muster roll of Capt William Cason 1837-1838 TAC 6:1:2
  Alachua Co, Old Fort White hist & cem rec TAC 6:1:1
  Alafia River hist PCQ 18:2:1
  Auburndale, hist PCQ 3:3:2
  Babson Park, Christmas hist sketch PCQ 5:3:2

FLORIDA (continued)
Bartow, Associate Reformed Pres Ch hist 1895 PCQ 16:4:7
Bartow, Bartow High Sch hist sketch PCQ 14:1:4
Bartow, First Providence Missionary Bapt Ch hist PCQ 20:1:6
Bartow, first school hist PCQ 4:4:5
Bartow, hist PCQ 8:5:2
Bartow, Homeland Heritage Park hist PCQ 17:4:1
Bartow, post ofc hist PCQ 19:1:6
Bartow, Summerlin Inst hist PCQ 8:56
Bartow, Summerlin Institute hist sketch PCQ 14:1:4
Bartow, Union Academy hist PCQ 17:2:6
Bartow, Wonder House hist PCQ 22:3:1
Bay Co, Brake Funeral Home rec c1910-1930 cont CL 14:2:12
Big Freeze 1894-1895, hist sketch PCQ 10:4:6
Black Creek, rations roster 1837 FLG 18:4:123
Bok Tower hist PCQ 19:3:1
Brewster hist PCQ 7:4:4 8:3:4
Carl A Bailey memorial cem rec by CCGS, bk rev TJ 7:2:74
Cattle drives, hist PCQ 20:1:4
Census 1885 index by Martin, bk rev NTT 15:1/2:7
Charlotte Co, Charlotte Harbor cem rec by CCGS, bk rev TJ 7:2:73
Chicora fence cutting hist PCQ 19:1:4
Chicora, hist PCQ 20:4:4
Citrus Exchange hist sketch PCQ 7:4:6
Citrus growing techniques of the past, descr PCQ 21:2:1
Citrus industry hist facts PCQ 10:3:7
Civil War, Bowlegs Creek Battle hist 1864 PCQ 11:4:4
Civilian Pilot Training Program hist PCQ 16:4:1
Clay Co, Beulah cem rec FLG 18:1:23
Clay Co, Blue Pond cem rec FLG 18:1:30

FLORIDA (continued)
Clay Co, Conway cem rec FLG 18:1:30
Clay Co, Lee cem rec FLG 18:1:29
Company D roster PCQ 20:1:7
Confederate POWs buried in Columbus, OH, roster FLG 18:3:107
Cypress Gardens, hist PCQ 20:1:4
Davenport, Holly Hill Fruit Products Inc hist PCQ 4:1:3
Deaths & marr from the *Florida Mirror*, bk rev TNC 3:1:19
Detroit Tigers move to Lakeland 1934, hist PCQ 21:1:1
Dundee, early hist sketch PCQ 5:1:6
Eagle Lake, tent city hist sketch PCQ 3:3:4
Evergreen, Higginbotham cem rec TNC 2:4:98
Execution roster 1827-1904 FLG 18:3:104
Fernandina Beach, Bethel Primitive Bapt Ch cem rec TNC 2:3:56
Fernandina Beach, St Michael's Cath Ch bapt rec 1869 TNC 3:1:21
Fernandina Beach, St Peter's Epis Ch rec 1858-1900 TNC 2:3:67 2:4:89
Fernandina, commercial importance descr 1874 TAC 6:1:14
Fernandina, deaths 1877 during yellow fever epidemic TNC 2:2:42
Fernandina, first auto accident, news abstr 1912 TNC 2:4:82
Fernandina, letters at post ofc 1882 TNC 2:4:85
Fernandina, newspaper roster TNC 2:3:75
Flagler, first fam hist by Holland, bk rev TAC 6:3:30
Florida Southern College hist PCQ 8:3:1 11:3:4
Food industry & freezes, hist PCQ 17:3:1
Fort Arbuckle, hist PCQ 11:4:6
Fort Meade area, Lake Hendry Pavilion PCQ 13:4:4
Fort Meade, band roster 1926 PCQ 10:4:4

FLORIDA (continued)
  Fort Meade, Christ Epis Ch hist PCQ 8:2:6
  Fort Meade, hist PCQ 12:1:1
  Fort Meade, hist (early) PCQ 3:1:12 3:2:2
  Fort Meade, hist sketch PCQ 2:3:2
  Fort Meade, parties 1880s, hist PCQ 5:1:5
  Fort Ogden, cem rec by CCGS, bk rev TJ 7:2:74
  Fort Ogden, cem rec by Youmans, bk rev FRT 16:3:112 GH 49:5:191
  Forts, hist sketch PCQ 7:3:1
  Frostproof, Am Women's League roster 1910 PCQ 4:1:6
  Frostproof, early schools, hist PCQ 3:1:4
  Frostproof, hist homes, hist PCQ 16:4:4
  Governors, biog sketches FLG 18:1:21
  Haines City, first canning plant hist sketch PCQ 3:3:7
  Haines City, hist sketch PCQ 8:2:2
  Haskell hist sketch PCQ 13:4:6
  Hickory Bluff cem rec by CCGS, bk rev TJ 7:2:74
  Highland City hist sketch PCQ 13:4:6
  Hillsborough Co, biog census 1850, bk rev PCQ 18:3:7
  Hog hist PCQ 21:4:6
  Jacksonville, destitute persons roll 1842 TAC 6:2:24
  Jacksonville, Duval High Sch class of 1915 reunion (1950), roster SEE 36:153:35
  Jacksonville, Old Duval cem rec SEE 36:153:14
  Kissengen Springs, hist sketch PCQ 11:2:1
  Kissimmee River steamboats, hist PCQ 17:1:1
  Lake Alfred, hist PCQ 3:4:3
  Lake Morton sch roster 1923 PCQ 3:1:9
  Lake Wales, Christmas 1912 hist PCQ 5:3:7
  Lake Wales, hist PCQ 16:1:1

FLORIDA (continued)
  Lake Wales, Plantation Inn hist PCQ 3:4:1
  Lakeland hist PCQ 11:3:1
  Lakeland hist 1883 PCQ 4:4:2
  Lakeland Sch hist sketch PCQ 4:3:5
  Lakeland Tourist Club 1923 PCQ 3:4:5
  Lakeland, Carpenter's Court rec PCQ 15:3:6
  Lakeland, fire dept hist PCQ 18:3:1
  Lakeland, High Sch class of 1919, roster PCQ 15:2:6
  Lakeland, hist PCQ 10:4:2
  Levy Co, cem rec by Lindsey, bk rev FLG 18:2:73
  Lodwick Sch of Aeronautics, bk rev PCQ 21:1:7
  Lucerne Park, hist PCQ 20:4:2
  Maitland cem rec BT 27:2:26
  Manatee Co, birth cert (delayed) cont CC 17:2:20 17:3:30 18:2:12
  Mayport, folk hist by Floyd, bk rev FLG 18:2:72 SEE 36:153:47
  Melbourne, cem rec by GSSB, bk rev RAG 17:1:15
  Miami, Metropolis news abstr c1915 IMP 14:2:60
  Miami, news abstr from the *Metropolis* c1900 IMP 14:1:26
  Mulberry Public Sch hist PCQ 22:1:4
  Mulberry, Civilian Public Svc camp hist, WW2 era PCQ 22:3:2
  Nassau Co, co officials, roster 1880 TNC 2:3:74
  Nassau Co, election results 1828 TNC 3:1:3
  Nassau Co, letters at two co post ofcs 1881, 1899 TNC 2:4:89
  Nassau Co, St Peter's Epis Ch bapt rec cont TNC 3:1:4
  Native American hist PCQ 22:2:1
  Newnansville Land Ofc, land rec 1825-1892 by Davidson, bk rev PCQ 16:3:7
  Okaloosa Co, cem rec vol 2 by GSOC, bk rev GH 49:6:186 HQ 95:58:88

FLORIDA (continued)
  Palm Beach Co Geneal Soc CD holdings, list ANC 30:2:71
  Palm Beach Co, census 1910 ANC 30:1:11 30:2:46 30:3:90
  Palm Beach Co, Lakeview cem hist ANC 30:1:4
  Peace River hist PCQ 14:1:1
  Peace River region, settlement hist PCQ 18:1:1
  Peas Creek Camp Ground & Meth hist PCQ 15:3:1
  Pembroke, hist PCQ 21:3:1
  Pembroke, post ofc hist & postmaster roster 1911-1983 PCQ 10:3:1
  Pioneer activities, salt mullet hist PCQ 20:1:6
  Pioneer activitiess, water witching, hist PCQ 21:2:6
  Pioneer children's toys & games, hist sketch PCQ 21:1:6
  Polk City Drug Store hist 1928 PCQ 4:4:4
  Polk City hist PCQ 8:4:2
  Polk Co, abandoned & ghost towns, list PCQ 7:4:2
  Polk Co, African Am early hist sketch PCQ 9:4:4
  Polk Co, agriculture hist 1927 PCQ 10:3:4
  Polk Co, Black Hills Passion Play 1939, hist PCQ 3:2:5
  Polk Co, Brown home hist PCQ 19:4:1
  Polk Co, CCC camp hist PCQ 16:2:1
  Polk Co, Christmas decorating traditions PCQ 5:3:1
  Polk Co, Christmas traditions, hist PCQ 19:3:7
  Polk Co, city roster PCQ 20:3:2
  Polk Co, co commission rec abstr 1886-1933 PCQ 9:4:3
  Polk Co, co motto hist PCQ 20:3:1
  Polk Co, Cooperative Extension Home Economics hist PCQ 14:2:1
  Polk Co, courthouse construction hist 1909 PCQ 14:1:3
  Polk Co, courthouse hist PCQ 13:3:1

FLORIDA (continued)
  Polk Co, Crystal Ice Works & other ice plants, hist PCQ 12:2:4
  Polk Co, early cattle industry hist PCQ 13:2:2
  Polk Co, early grocery stores, hist PCQ 19:2:1
  Polk Co, early roads, hist sketch PCQ 9:4:4
  Polk Co, early tourist accomodations, hist sketch PCQ 11:2:2
  Polk Co, early transportation hist sketch PCQ 5:2:2
  Polk Co, Ebenezer Lodge hist sketch PCQ 3:1:3
  Polk Co, education hist PCQ 4:1:7 15:2:1
  Polk Co, first consolidated sch, hist 1905 PCQ 10:2:6
  Polk Co, first court house hist sketch PCQ 3:1:13 14:1:2
  Polk Co, first poor farm, hist PCQ 8:4:5
  Polk Co, first schools, hist PCQ 20:3:4
  Polk Co, first youth fair 1947, hist PCQ 8:4:6
  Polk Co, fishing lure hist PCQ 18:2:6
  Polk Co, Green Swamp hist PCQ 16:3:1
  Polk Co, Greenwood Community hist 1881-1887 PCQ 8:3:6
  Polk Co, Greenwood hist PCQ 21:2:4
  Polk Co, Grits Mill hist PCQ 13:2:6
  Polk Co, Haven Hotel hist PCQ 7:4:3
  Polk Co, Highland Park hist PCQ 3:2:6
  Polk Co, historical markers, location guide PCQ 9:3:1
  Polk Co, Homelands sch roster 1935-1936 PCQ 3:1:14
  Polk Co, Indian trails, hist PCQ 16:1:4
  Polk Co, Land Pebble Community hist 1880-1898 PCQ 8:4:3
  Polk Co, logos & seals PCQ 20:3:2
  Polk Co, marr rec 1869-1873 PCQ 11:4:7
  Polk Co, marr rec 1870-1877 PCQ 14:3:7

FLORIDA (continued)
  Polk Co, marr rec 1873-1874 PCQ 12:1:7
  Polk Co, marr rec c1862-1876 PCQ 13:4:5
  Polk Co, marr rec c1866-1878 PCQ 13:1:7
  Polk Co, marr rec c1876-1880 PCQ 12:4:6
  Polk Co, Medical Association hist 1910 PCQ 10:2:2
  Polk Co, mil forts & camps, hist PCQ 11:1:2 11:2:7
  Polk Co, news abstr re:Christmas celebration 1924 PCQ 6:3:3
  Polk Co, news abstr re:murder & lynching 1886 PCQ 17:1:5
  Polk Co, orange culture hist PCQ 10:3:2
  Polk Co, Pebble Heights hist PCQ 21:2:4
  Polk Co, Phosphate company villages, hist PCQ 7:4:5
  Polk Co, phosphate mining hist PCQ 13:4:1
  Polk Co, pioneer merchants, hist sketch PCQ 7:2:6
  Polk Co, pioneer oral hist excerpts PCQ 20:1:2
  Polk Co, pioneer recoll PCQ 18:2:4 19:2:4
  Polk Co, pioneer recoll of sch days PCQ 15:2:4
  Polk Co, pioneer rocking chair hist PCQ 17:2:1
  Polk Co, Polk Canning Plant hist 1915-1951 PCQ 10:2:7 10:3:8
  Polk Co, Polk General Hospital hist PCQ 15:1:1
  Polk Co, Polk Lake sch roster c1910 PCQ 3:1:15
  Polk Co, Polk Theater hist PCQ 18:4:1
  Polk Co, post ofc location guide PCQ 8:2:3
  Polk Co, products & lands, hist PCQ 7:3:4
  Polk Co, Sand Mountain hist sketch PCQ 8:1:2

FLORIDA (continued)
  Polk Co, schools (now extinct), hist sketch PCQ 2:4:6
  Polk Co, Scott Lake, hist PCQ 6:4:2
  Polk Co, South Prong fishing, hist PCQ 20:3:6
  Polk Co, State Militia hist PCQ 20:3:8
  Polk Co, strawberry schools, hist PCQ 6:4:6
  Polk Co, Summerlin Institute grads 1909, biog sketches PCQ 21:3:6
  Polk Co, swimming holes, hist PCQ 20:1:1
  Polk Co, Tillis Farm Indian attack hist 1856 PCQ 6:4:4
  Polk Co, towns 1885, hist PCQ 10:1:4
  Polk Co, Watson Mine Washer hist 1938-1989 PCQ 16:2:6
  Polk Co, weddings, hist PCQ 13:1:1
  Polk Co, WW2 hist PCQ 12:3:1
  Polk Co, WW2 pilot training programs, hist PCQ 12:3:4
  Punta Gorda, Indian Springs cem rec by CCGS, bk rev FP 38:1:12
  Railroad hist PCQ 5:4:1 6:1:1
  Real estate brokers active 20 years or more as of 1939, roster FLG 18:4:134
  Roads, early hist sketch PCQ 15:3:7
  Rome City hist 1883 PCQ 4:4:2
  Sainte Anne des Lacs shrine, hist PCQ 6:2:1
  Santa Rosa Co, marr rec 1869-1906 by Lembeck, bk rev GH 49:6:187
  Santa Rosa, marr rec 1869-1906 by GSOC, bk rev HQ 95:58:88
  Seminole Indians 1850-1874 by Lantz, bk rev GH 49:3:203
  Sesquicentennial hist PCQ 22:1:1
  Socrum region hist PCQ 12:1:3
  South FL Railroad hist PCQ 12:4:1
  Spanish moss hist PCQ 14:3:1
  Spanish West FL, WPA trans, res tips AMG 10:4:38
  St Augustine sch census 1892 TAC 6:1:15
  St Augustine, city direct of colored residents 1885-1886 TAC 6:3:23

FLORIDA (continued)
St Augustine, death rec from Health Dept 1904 TAC 6:1:4
St Augustine, death rec from Health Dept 1907-1908 TAC 6:2:9
St Augustine, Evergreen Cem burials cont TAC 6:2:1 6:3:1 6:4:1
St Augustine, Free Sch monthly return Sept 1846 TAC 6:3:19
St Augustine, Huguenot Cem rec TAC 6:1:6
St Augustine, pupils w/perfect attendance 1904-1905 TAC 6:2:12
St John's Co, public sch rec (non-residents) 1904-1905 TAC 6:1:26
St John's Co, public sch rec (non-residents) 1905-1906 TAC 6:2:25
St John's Co, public sch rec (non-residents) 1907-1908 TAC 6:2:26
St Joseph, Constitutional Convention State Museum Dedication descr FLG 18:2:44
St Mary's River area, mounted militia reports 1793 TNC 2:2:45
St Mary's River, King's Ferry hist sketch TNC 2:4:84
State College for Women, grad roster 1917 FLG 18:2:45
Strawberry Culture, hist PCQ 10:1:2
Swamp cabbage cutting procedures PCQ 19:2:7
Syrup making hist PCQ 18:4:4
Tallahassee Land Ofc, land rec 1825-1892 by Davidson, bk rev PCQ 16:3:7
Tampa, mortuary statement 1889 FLG 18:3:84
Walton Co, voting rec abstr 1828-1836 FLG 18:3:109 18:4:151
Wild's Landing cem rec TNC 2:2:30
Winston & Bone Valley Railroad hist PCQ 18:3:4
Winter Haven, hist PCQ 3:3:5
WW2 victory gardens, hist PCQ 19:3:6
Yellow fever epidemic 1877, hist TNC 2:2:37
FLOWERS, Susan see Richard ADDISON

FOERSTER, Erlwin fl910, CN, corresp SGB 26:4:167
FOGLE, Grayson H b1853, w Anna Mary Boyer, w Mary E Ripple, MD, Bible rec WMG 11:2:86
FOGLER, Christian, OH, identity, bk rev TR 35:1:53
FOLCK, Martha see James TULEY
FOLEY, Malachy fc1650, w Rosie O'Neill, IR, geneal by Foley, bk rev GH 49:5:230
Spencer, w Nancy Rector, KY, fam hist by Foley, bk rev PCH 1:4:24
FOLK, Frederick Arnst fl786, PA, fam hist by Lowe, bk rev KCG 36:1:47
FOLSOM, Needham Bryant d1836, w Malinda Hooks, NC, FL, fam hist sketch QU 12:4:42
FONTAINE, James fc1715, jour & fam hist by Maury, bk rev GH 49:4:224
John fl714, IR, PA, jour abstr BYG 7:3:386
FOOTE, Ebenezer see Edmund BAKER
Gilson b1802, Bible rec NTT 14:3:102
Nancy Lenora see Gabriel Pickens PHILLIPS
FORBES, Jasper b1796, m Polly Shepherd, w Jane Carr Danby, MA, OH, biog & fam hist TR 35:4:188
FORD, Charity see Abraham KITCHEL
John Perley b1794, w Cynthia Moore, w Susannah Gallman, NY, MS, biog by Ford, bk rev NGS 83:2:145
FOREN, Sarah Armilda b1882, h Frank Ball, CA, Bible rec GFP 44:3:123
William C b1828, w Sarah A Prine, CA, Bible rec RCP 17:3:97
FOREST, CN, Am, fam hist 1091-1769 vol 1 by Forest, bk rev AGE 24:4:101
Michel, w Marie Hebert, FR, KY, geneal by Jehn, bk rev ACG 21:1:21
FORIST, Abraham see Abraham FORREST
FORMAN, John m1793, w Sarah Morton, wedding witness roster WPG 21:3:31

FORREST, N B fl864, hist of his raid through AL & TN OLR 9:3:127
Abraham bc1740, w Elizabeth Dudley(?), VA, NC, geneal SCG 14:2:672
Dudley see Eva CRUMP
FORRESTER, William fc1880, CN, fam hist GEN 20:3:22
FORTNER, Benjamin Mitchell b1885, w Cenetta L Hancock, w Zannie Sumner, FL, biog PCQ 12:1:5
FOSS, Tabitha see Moses EMERSON
FOSTER, Creed fl824, w Temperance Bailey, VA, geneal by Elton, bk rev TPI 20:2:88
Daniel Marion fl887, w Nancy Ann Dixon, WA, fam hist SGS 44:3:115
FOTHERINGHAM, Joan Walker see William RICHARDSON
FOURRIER, Jeanne see Fracois-Noel VENARD-VANASSE
FOWLER, Littleton see Missouri M LOCKWOOD
W S m1846, w Elizabeth Hatfield, IN, biog sketch HJA 18:3:252
FOX, Ebenezer fl770, RI, autobiog, repr 1838, bk rev GH 49:6:208 SGS 45:1:35
FOY, Sarah Jane see William FOY
William b1803, w Sarah Jane, IL, Bible rec GL 29:1:2
FOYE, William see William FOY
FRANK, Sarah A see James NICHOLSON
FRANKLIN, Mary A see Charles RHODES
FRAZIER, David, w Margaret Kathryn Hursh, fam hist by Frazier, bk rev NGS 83:2:143
Ian fl994, fam hist by Frazier, bk rev NGS 83:2:143
FREE, Thomas R bc1819, w Susan Rucker, w Icy Callahan Woodruff, w Elizabeth Crofford, SC, biog sketch OLR 9:3:100
FREEMAN, Benjamin bc1740, w Nancy, PA, WV, fam hist by Freeland, bk rev WPG 21:3:47

FREEMAN (continued)
Hannah see John FREEMAN
John fl673, w Hannah, VA, NC, geneal by Mosher, bk rev CN 4:2:31 GH 49:6:208 IMP 14:2:61 NCJ 21:3:304 RCR 10:2:2273 SCM 23:2:119 SGS 44:3:142 TVF 4:3:194 VAG 39:1:78
Nancy see Benjamin FREEMAN
FREESE, Peter b1800, w Anna Faust, PA, OH, fam rec TR 35:2:82
FREEZE, Mary see Abraham SECHLER
FREEZE, Polly see Mary FREEZE
FRENCH, Alcey see Richard SPELLMAN
Elizabeth b1877, h Joseph Gardner Bartlett, New England, anc NEH 12:1:22
Ruth Moorhead b1896, CA, autobiog RED 27:4:14
FRENCH & INDIAN WAR, CT soldiers 1755-1762, roster by CT Hist Soc, bk rev GSM 12:2:47
Hist 1754-1763 by Schwartz, bk rev WPG 22:2:55
VA, Capt Orme's seaman's detachment, roster 1755 NHR 12:3:100
FRENCH CANADIAN GENEALOGY, Anc vol 20 by LaForest, bk rev AGE 24:2&3:44
Fam hist, misc fam, by Moore, bk rev GSC 18:1:7
Les Voyageurs (fur traders), hist ACG 21:4:186
New Frances, hist & res tips MHH 16:4:107
Res guide by DuLong, bk rev ACG 21:2:61 AGE 24:2&3:45 SCS 32:6:139
FRENCH GENEALOGY, Alsace emig bk I c1817-1869 by Schrader-Muggenthaler, bk rev APR 14:12:4
Alsace emig bk II (19th cent) by Schrader-Muggenthaler, bk rev APR 14:12:4
Am, hist of FR population, repr 1906, bk rev GH 49:5:185

FRENCH GENEALOGY (continued)
Aquitaine hist & geneal by Maxson, bk rev ACG 21:1:21 GH 49:5:182
Caribbean colonies, pass lists index 1749-1778 CGJ 3:4:18
Colonists & exiles in Am, hist by Rosengarten, bk rev SE 16:12:117
French CN geneal res guide by DuLong, bk rev ACG 21:2:61 SCS 32:6:139
Isle of Re hist & geneal by Maxson, bk rev GH 49:5:182
Migration to North Am, hist 1600-1900 by Houde, bk rev ACG 21:1:23
Nantes, Acadian exiles 1775-1785, hist by Robichaux, bk rev KSL 19:2:73
New Rochelle, hist by Maxson, bk rev ACG 21:1:25
Poitou, imm to CN by Larin, bk rev AGE 24:4:100
Republican calendar dates KTP 4:3:37
St Nicolas de la Grave, hist sketch MHH 16:1:1

FREY, Eva Catharina see Hans Georg BRENDEL
Ida see Samuel W LOWER

FRIAR, Civility see John Baggs RAULERSON

FRIEDLINE, Adam m1870, w Lucinda Horner, PA, Bible rec LM 36:4:231

FRIEND, Embry E f1803, VA, oath doc BWG 24:1:50

FRIER, Ryan b1800, w Sarah Peacock, FL, fam hist PCQ 12:1:4

FRITTS, John Henry b1770, GR, NC, geneal by Fritts, bk rev TPI 20:2:88

FROEBE, Elizabeth see John V FROEBE
John V f1871, w Elizabeth, GR, PA, fam rec WPG 21:7:57

FROST, Emma, fam hist by Graves, bk rev ARH 33:3:128
Jim f1903, MO, news abstr CN 4:1:15

FRYE, Ersula see Augustus DORSEY

FUCHS, Simon b1863, w Henrietta Adler, w Nannnie Adler, GR, NY, OH, fam hist by Fox, bk rev GH 49:4:224

FUDGE, John b1801, w Barbara Tool, VA, fam rec KTP 14:3:38
Lauina Watson see Jacob L BRUNER
Louisa Adella see William Thomas DENHAM

FUGATE, KY, fam cem rec KA 31:1:20

FULGHUM, DK, EN, Am, fam hist by Fulghum, bk rev THT 23:2:90
Fam hist by Fulghum, bk rev KK 33:2:38

FULK, Charles, w Sarah Custer, VA, fam hist by Ritchie, bk rev GH 49:4:224

FULKERSON, Catherine see Shapley Prince ROSS

FULL, EN, ME, OR, fam hist by Harris, bk rev TB 21:3:11
Richard m1756, w Mary Tapper, EN, geneal by Harris, bk rev GH 49:3:218

FULLARTON, see FULLERTON

FULLER, Ellen M see Ambrose CHAPMAN
Mary Ann bc1825, h Pertillar Fuller, TX, biog sketch STS 35:3:58
Melville W f1880, biog by Ely, bk rev REG 93:4:492
Pertillar see Mary Ann FULLER

FULLERTON, North Am, fam hist by Fullerton, bk rev GEN 20:4:24

FULLINGTON, see FULLERTON

FUNK, Esther see Jacob ERBACH

FUNNEL, Jane see John D BEDWELL

FURBISH, Philip G f1965, NH, recoll BT 27:4:80

GABLER, Clyde W f1945, autobiog by Gabler, bk rev EWA 32:2:81
Johan Michael f1850, w Margaretha Nau, BA, NY, fam hist by Gabler, bk rev CI 31:2:69 EWA 32:2:82 TR 35:4:222
Margaretha see Michael GABLER

GAGE, Ruth see Samuel STRONG

GAINES, Sarah Frances see Joseph Addison KING

GALARNEAU, Charles m1721, CN, identity of mother NGS 83:1:32

GALBRAITH, Alexander bc1720, w Nancy Agnes Miller, ST, PA, fam corresp & hist ETR 7:4:190

GALBREATH, Catherine see Josiah CARNEAL

GALLAHER, James dc1791, TN, will abstr BWG 24:2:117

GALLEMORE, Roy T fl920, FL, biog PCQ 4:1:2
Roy T f1921, FL, WW1 submarine logbk abstr PCQ 19:1:1
Virginia Holland f1979, FL, recoll PCQ 6:3:7

GALLMAN, Susannah see John Perley FORD

GAMBLE, James see Clarissa LEGGE
John d1814, GA, estate rec abstr BT 27:1:14

GAMEWELL, Whatcoat Asbury f1866, SC, corresp ODD 7:4:25

GANT, W E see E B ANGLEA

GARBER, Samuel H f1785, w Marian Stoner, MD, TN, biog sketch NFB 27:3:44

GARDNER, Frances see Joseph ROGERS
Nancy see John BOYDSTUN
William b1736, w Milkah Chaney, geneal by Vry/Gardner, bk rev MD 36:1:91

GARINET, Constance see Pierre LAURENT

GARLAND, Gutridge, w Bridget Hampton, geneal by Garland, bk rev BWG 24:1:67

GARMAN, Philip b1841, w Mary Breneman, PA, biog sketch BGN 16:4:18

GARNER, Lila Niemann f1995, NE, anc HQ 95:59:23
Paralee see Franklin L LOWRY

GARRARD, VA, PA, OH, IN, fam group sheets 1720-1980 by Murphy, bk rev WPG 21:4:53

GARRET, Eva Mary b1883, TX, heirship affidavit PWN 3:2:10
Elizabeth see John JACK

GARRET (continued)
John m1778, w Elizabeth Ammonnette, VA, fam rec LOB 14:1:2

GARRISON, Martha Lee f1920, SD, autobiog, bk rev KCG 36:1:47

GARVIN, AR, death notices SYH 1:2:26
Isaac Castleberry f1912, AR, hist of his farm SYH 1:2:24

GASCOIGNE, Edward see Edward GASKILL

GASKILL, Edward f1635, EN, MA, geneal by Koleda, bk rev WPG 22:2:57

GASKIN, Edward see Edward GASKILL

GASTON, John R b1770, w Mary Beaty, PA, OH, fam corresp ETR 7:4:190

GATES, Thomas b1833, AZ, biog by Sorensen, bk rev GH 49:5:230

GATEWOOD, Adaline see Jordan B LUCK

GATZ, Joseph f1844, w Elisabetha Graff, FR, marr contract TTL 23:3:45

GAUDET, Laura C b1902, CT, CN, biog ACG 22:1:25

GAUNT, John f1340, EN, fam hist by Jones, bk rev GH 49:5:230

GAUTHIER, Renee see Louis THIBAULT

GAYLORD, Naomi see Thomas TOPPING

GEDDES, Alice b1876, h Arthur Lloyd, MA, KY, biog REG 93:2:180

GEER, Daniel f1715, w Hannah, CT, identity of wife AG 70:4:240
Hannah see Daniel GEER

GEESEY, Henry b1807, w Elizabeth Koofer, PA, Bible rec BGN 16:2:13

GEFELLERS, Abraham d1870, TN, biog sketch ETR 7:4:172

GEHMAN, Henry, MI, fam hist sketch PM 18:4:29

GEIGER, GR, MO, fam hist by Geiger, bk rev TPI 20:4:192

GEIGER (continued)
W L f1878, KY, diary abstr TRS 19:1:14 19:2:33
GELDING, Elizabeth see Jerom GRIFFITH
GENTRY, Elizabeth see Neil THOMPSON
Martin Luther b1872, w Dora Hadley, MO, biog sketch AUQ 6:4:86
GEORGE, Joseph Forbes b1842, w Mahala E Jeffries, MO, biog SNS 11:4:9
Thomas f1825, NF, fam hist NAL 11:2:59
GEORGIA, African population 1870, census abstr by Stewart, bk rev GH 49:3:204
Atlanta area, WW1 draft reg by Cook/Geiger, bk rev GGS 31:1:49
Atlanta Athletic Club, hist by Neill, bk rev NC 5:4:181
Atlanta, congressional testimony 1872 re:Ku Klux Klan GGS 31:2:90
Austell, Shady grove cem rec NC 5:1:16
Baldwin Co, news abstr from the *Union Recorder* 1830-1833 by Evans, bk rev GGS 31:1:51
Baldwin Co, news abstr from the *Union Recorder* 1834-1836 by Evans, bk rev GGS 31:2:124
Ball Ground, Bapt Ch cem rec GGS 31:1:2
Bapt ministers & Bapt settlers, biog sketches cont SEE 36:153:31
Bay Co Public Lib, geneal res guide NC 5:4:176
Bibl of fam hist bks by Hehir, bk rev PB 10:2:47
Brooks Co, news abstr vol 1 1866-1889 by Evans, bk rev GGS 31:2:124
Burials in 600 cem alphabetized by Austin, bk rev GH 49:5:191 HQ 95:57:84 KA 31:1:45 NCJ 21:2:185 SEE 36:153:22 STS 35:3:70
Campbell Co, inferior court rec 1833-1872 CCM 15:2:20

GEORGIA (continued)
Campbell Co, news abstr from the *News* 1898 CCM 14:3:21
Campbell Co, obits from news c1899 CCM 15:1:25
Catoosa Co, census 1860 by CCHSCC, bk rev BWG 24:1:68
Census 1820-1900, locations of alternative copies, descr GGS 31:2:105
Census 1870, CD-ROM rev TEN 95:16:22
Cherokee Co, Chamlee fam cem rec GGS 31:1:43
Cherokee Co, land lottery rec 1838, repr 1969, bk rev GH 49:5:187
Cherokee Co, land rec 1840-1841 by Taylor, bk rev GGS 31:1:51
Cherokee Co, land rec vol 5 by Taylor, bk rev GH 49:4:206
Cherokee Co, land rec vol 6 by Taylor, bk rev HQ 95:59:89
Cherokee Co, Little River Mills site hist sketch NC 5:3:122
Citizens in Austin TX convention, roster 1861 NC 5:2:74
Citizens in Rusk Co TX voter reg 1867 cont NC 5:2:73
Civil War, 7th Calvary POW roster 1864 NC 5:4:169
Civil War, Newnan guard casualty roster 1866 CCM 15:2:2
Civil War, Phillips Legion infantry battalion paroled at Appomattox 1865, roster NC 5:3:99
Civil war, Sherman's march, hist by Kennett, bk rev REG 93:4:488
Co population rec 1890 CCM 15:1:9
Co rec microfilm guide KTP 7:3:38
Cobb Co, deed bk A, 19th cent NC 5:3:121
Cobb Co, marr (white & black) 1865-1966 by Hancock, bk rev GGS 31:2:122
Cobb Co, marr affidavits, 20th cent NC 5:1:11
Cobb Co, news abstr 1889 cont NC 5:2:58 5:3:106

GEORGIA (continued)
- Cobb Co, tax digest 1848 cont NC 5:1:7 5:2:54 5:3:102
- Cobb Co, trivia facts NC 5:3:123
- Coweta Co, Confederate pension rec 1898 CCM 14:3:10
- Coweta Co, Confederate widows named in the *Newnan Herald* 1894 CCM 15:2:17
- Coweta Co, country estate distributions c1844 CCM 14:3:19
- Coweta Co, estate index c1830-1850 CCM 14:3:12 15:1:13 15:2:12
- Coweta Co, Mount Lebanon Bapt Ch hist CCM 14:3:3
- Coweta Co, *Newnan Herald* news abstr 1865 CCM 15:2:14
- Coweta Co, *Newnan Herald & Advertiser* abstr 1887-1902 CCM 15:1:6
- Coweta Co, *Newnan Herald & Advertiser* abstr 1898 CCM 15:2:7
- Coweta Co, obit abstr from the *Newnan Herald & Advertiser* 1890 CCM 15:1:10
- Coweta Co, road overseers roster 1897 CCM 14:3:18
- Cullman, Bowdenites reunion 1925, news abstr AFH 16:4:14
- Decatur Co, agricultural census 1860 cont OTC 4:3:21
- Dublin, Northview Cem rec 1902-1992 by Adams, bk rev NC 5:4:179
- Fayette Co, probate rec 1824-1874 by Austin, bk rev HQ 95:59:88
- Forsyth Co, Strickland cem rec GGS 31:2:101
- Friendsborough, Quaker rec 1776-1777 by Davis, bk rev TJ 7:1:39
- General Assembly of GA acts passed 1830, abstr GGS 31:1:31
- Gwinnett Co, WW1 draft reg by Cook/Geiger, bk rev GGS 31:1:49
- Hancock Co, Darien Bapt Ch rec 1794-1862 by Lawrence, bk rev GGS 31:2:123
- Hapeville, hist by Milton, bk rev NC 5:4:180

GEORGIA (continued)
- Henry Co, census 1870 by Turner, bk rev GGS 31:2:123
- Henry Co, obits 1900-1907 FRT 16:2:65
- Henry Co, obits 1900-1907 by Bowen, bk rev GGS 31:1:51 GH 49:5:192 SCM 23:2:119
- Hist doc 1730-1790 by GA Dept of Archives, bk rev GGS 31:1:47
- Huxford Lib book & source material guide by HGS, bk rev GGS 31:2:121
- Jackson Co, superior court rec 1796-1803 by Dunn/Walls, bk rev GGS 31:2:122
- John E Ladson Hist & Geneal Foundation Lib, fam hist avail, guide by Hartz, bk rev GGS 31:1:50
- Knights Templar, misc biog, lib holdings GGS 31:2:113
- Land distribution hist by Baker, bk rev TPI 20:4:198
- Land grant & lottery res tips SE 16:12:111
- Land lotteries, res guide SCS 32:10:224
- Long Pond, biog sketches of early residents by Johnson, bk rev NC 5:4:179
- Macon Co, marr rec 1879-1901 vol 2 by Hay/Stewart, bk rev GGS 31:2:121
- Macon, Washington Memorial Lib res guide SQ 5:6:45
- Marietta, news abstr c1889 NC 5:1:17
- Meriwether Co, hist 1827-1974 by Pinkston/Freeman, bk rev NC 5:3:125
- Meth preachers 1783-1900, supp by Lawrence, bk rev GGS 31:2:123
- Milledgeville, *Georgia Journal* news abstr 1809-1840 by Hartz et al, bk rev GGS 31:1:51 GGS 31:2:124
- Montgomery Co, hist to 1918 by Davis, bk rev NC 5:4:181
- Moultrie, Ellen Payne Odom Geneal Libr, descr of svcs avail GJ 23:4:186

GEORGIA (continued) Newnan, news abstr from the *Semi-Weekly News* 1912 CCM 14:3:8

Newton Co, Hopewell Associate Reformed Pres Ch rec 1830-1917 by Richardson, bk rev GGS 31:1:49 GH 49:4:206

Oglethorpe Co, marr rec 1792-1852 AMG 9:6:22 10:2/3:59 10:4:29

Paulding Co, census 1870 by Richter, bk rev VL 30:1:43

Pickens Co, cem rec by Teague/Reece, bk rev GGS 31:2:123 NC 5:2:72

Salt List 1862, hist KTP 14:2:25

Thomas Co, news abstr 1857-1881 by Evans, bk rev NGS 83:4:311

Thomas Co, tax digest 1890 cont OTC 4:3:1

Thomasville, marr & death notices from the *Southern Enterprise* c1873-1874 OTC 4:3:13

Union Co, census 1860 by Casada, bk rev GH 49:3:204

Upson Co, census 1850 supp GGS 31:2:74

Upson Co, taxpayers omitted from census 1850, roster GGS 31:2:80

War of 1812, widow & orphan roster GGS 31:1:28

Washington Co, census 1890 pop sched by Henry, bk rev GGS 31:2:121

Wrightsboro, Quaker rec 1772-1793 by Davis, bk rev TJ 7:1:39

GERFERS, Janie f1900, h Scott Cabaniss, TX, corresp KTP 2:3:28

GERHART, Jacob mc1743, w Elizabeth Buss, PA, geneal JBC 16:1:4

GERLOFF, Joachim f1895, IL, hist of his farm MCI 13:2:43

GERMAN GENEALOGY,
Achievements in Am, hist, repr 1916, bk rev KGF 1:1/2:88

Address & telephone bk, bk rev TSC 6:3:6

Addressbk by Thode, bk rev BHN 28:2:20

GERMAN GENEALOGY (continued)
Addressbk for geneal by GGS, bk rev STS 35:4:20

Ahnenlistenumlaufs (ancestor charts), res guide GGD 11:3:70

Alardus ship to AA, hist TGO 8:1:15

Alsace emig bk I c1817-1869 by Schrader-Muggenthaler, bk rev APR 14:12:4

Alsace emig bk II (19th cent) by Schrader-Muggenthaler, bk rev APR 14:12:4

Am from GR, hist & bibl, repr 1976, bk rev TPI 21:1:38

Am-GR names, res guide by Jones, bk rev HQ 95:60:93

Am Rev, GR troops, res guide, repr 1904, bk rev NFB 27:3:54

Amish Mennonite hist by Guth, bk rev NFB 27:4:74

Ancestry res guide by Palen, bk rev TPI 21:1:37

Baden, village lineage bks, res tips GGD 11:2:34

Baden-Wurttemberg, geneal queries & res reports by Oertel, bk rev TTL 23:3:48

Baumholder, Prot & Cath Ch rec 1679-1798 by Jung, bk rev TPI 21:1:51

Beginner's res guide by Smith, bk rev TPI 20:4:198

Bibl of GR-Americana by Tolzmann, bk rev GH 49:6:185 GRC 11:2:28 TPI 20:4:194

Brandenburg, rec in print, res guide GGD 11:2:56 11:3:82

Bukovinian res tips SGB 26:2:59

Chicago GR Aid Soc 1883, hist add TGC 19:4:82

Colonial GR, bibl by Meynen, bk rev CSB 30:4:143

Correspondence tips SGS 44:3:123

Customs & lifeways, hist by Rippley, bk rev TGC 19:3:66

Deutschen Familienarchiv surname list KTP 13:4:56

GERMAN GENEALOGY (continued)

Die Borfahren cont DPL 17:WINTER:4 17:SPRING:4 18:SPRING:4 18:SUMMER:4

Die Vorfahren cont DPL 15:SPRING:4 17:WINTER:11 17:SPRING:4 18:SPRING:11 18:SUMMER:6

Early hist cont TGC 19:3:55

Eastern Eur, GR settlement hist RM 95:10:1

Eichstetten, hist TGC 19:1:6

Fraktur geneal res guide by Hoch, bk rev GGP 28:1:22

Fraktur guide TGC 19:4:75

Geneal corresp to clergymen, sample format TGC 19:3:61

Glossary of common GR terms found in geneal rec, KTP 10:1:12 10:2:28

Gothic-Roman alphabet comparison charts TGC 19:3:60

GR element in Am, bibl by Tolzmann, bk rev TPI 20:2:96

GR hist timeline TPI 20:4:176

GR in America, hist, repr 1916, bk rev TPI 20:4:194

GR Reformed Ch news abstr 1840-1843 by Manning, bk rev GJB 20:1:14 MGS 13:3:43 TGC 19:4:90 TPI 20:3:160 WPG 22:1:43

GR speaking parts of Eur, fam hist res guide TPI 20:3:124

GR-Am biog by Haller, bk rev TGC 19:4:90

GR-Am fam rec in fraktur vol 2 by Earnest/Hoch, bk rev SGS 44:2:91

GR-Am hist by Adams, bk rev OC 32:2:54

GR-Am surnames, reference guide to meanings by Jones, bk rev AW 22:2:32 GGD 11:2:37 GN 13:3:140 KA 31:2:47 NYR 126:4:280 TGC 19:4:90 TPI 20:4:195 TS 37:4:147 WPG 22:1:46

GR-Americana, bibl, repr 1975, bk rev SGS 44:3:142

GR-Americans of note, biog hist by Haller, bk rev GGD 11:2:36 TPI 20:4:193

GERMAN GENEALOGY (continued)

Hamburg, marr abstr, res tips GGD 11:2:34

Hamburg, pass lists, res tips GH 49:6:35

Hamburg, pass lists 1850-1934, res guide GJ 22:4:100

Hesse-Homburg area, descr & hist TGC 19:3:51

Hessian hist outline AW 21:3:95

Hist of GR in Am, repr 1909, bk rev TGC 19:4:91

Hist outline cont TGC 19:1:9

Hungary, Fejer Co, GR in land census 1828 by Connor, bk rev GH 49:5:182

IA, settler geneal dict by Palen, bk rev GH 49:3:205 LL 31:1:10

Imm corresp home by Vogel et al, bk rev DPL 15:SPRING:1

Imm to Am 1865-1870 by Glazier & Filby, bk rev NTT 14:3:83

Imm to Am, hist BYG 7:5:409

IR Palatines in CN, hist by Heald, bk rev FAM 34:1:49

Kammonsham Roy ship, pass list 1843 TTL 24:1:6

Kreis Lingen emig to Am, roster c1845-1864 TTH 16:3:73 16:4:110

KY, GR Evang ch rec, res tips LAB 10:4:126

LA, GR heritage & hist, repr 1927, bk rev GH 49:3:209

LA, GR heritage & hist, repr 1927, bk rev MGS 13:1:7

Leipzig Center, res guide MI 41:2:63

Luth Parish Buer emig lists 1855-1864 by Poetker, bk rev TR 35:3:133

MD, GR heritage, geneal hist by Tolzmann, bk rev AB 23:4:12 GR 37:1:50 GSM 12:2:47 NFB 27:2:34 TGC 19:2:43 TPI 20:2:97

MI, imm vr by Podall, bk rev TTL 24:1:23

Mid-Atlantic Germanic Soc Locality Index for researchers, descr MGS 13:1:1

Mid-Atlantic Germanic Soc surname exchange index, descr MGS 13:1:1

GERMAN GENEALOGY (continued)
Migration pattern hist & geneal res guide by Brandt, bk rev FCT 96:124:3 GGD 11:2:36 MN 26:4:183 TPI 20:3:169 TS 37:4:145
Mil rec res guide GGD 11:2:38
Minden, emig 1814-1900, roster by SGFRW, bk rev TPI 20:4:196
Modern hist of GR by Fisher, bk rev AW 22:2:33
Name dict by Bahlow, bk rev TPI 20:2:93
Naming conventions, guide UG 23:2:15
Naming patterns in Am, descr KTP 8:4:60
Naming patterns, res tips UG 23:3:24
NC, GR speaking people west of the Catawba River 1750-1800 by Eaker, bk rev NCJ 21:2:183 TPI 20:2:97
Newspaper res tips TGC 19:2:29 19:4:80
Nuremberg State Archive, emig rec res tips TTL 23:3:49
Occupation glossary GRI 15:5:133
OH, Cincinnati, GR heritage, hist by Tolzmann, bk rev MGS 13:1:7
Ostfriesland, village lineage bks, res tips GGD 11:2:34
PA, GR Reformed Ch rec, 18th cent, by Wright, bk rev GH 49:5:213
PA, MD, teamsters, roster & hist sketch JBC 16:1:9
PA, Philadelphia, imm servant contracts 1817-1831 by Grubb, bk rev GFP 44:3:142 GH 49:5:182 IS 16:3:78 MGS 13:1:10 MN 26:2:90 NYR 126:1:86 RCR 10:1:2213 TGC 19:2:43 TR 35:2:109 WMG 11:1:44 WPG 21:3:45
Palatinate, imm to EN 1709, rosters by Tribbeko/Ruperti, bk rev GH 49:5:182
Palatinate, Irish Palatinate Heritage Ctr, res aid TPI 20:2:85
Palatines in colonial Am, hist by Cobb, bk rev NFB 27:3:54

GERMAN GENEALOGY (continued)
Parish rec in print, res bibl by AGLL, bk rev HQ 95:55:55
Peasants' achievements, 9th-20th centuries, hist sketch TPI 20:2:64
Permission papers for travel, hist TGC 19:2:31
Place names, hard to locate, res tips TGC 19:3:52
PO, Galicia, GR hist sketch SGB 26:4:176
Pomerania, Lauenburg Dist, gazetteer & res sources GGD 11:4:114
Pomerania, marr abstr, res tips GGD 11:2:34
Pomerania, marr rec from Stettin Civil reg 1877 GGD 11:3:89
Printing & handwriting guide, character chart KTP 9:4:60
Prussian provinces, early hist cont TGC 19:3:55
Queries in GR Geneal publications, tips TGC 19:2:39
Query letter to a newspaper, example format TGC 19:2:38
Questions & answers, res tips HQ 95:57:36
Reformed Church news geneal abstr 1840-1843 by Manning, bk rev GGD 11:2:37
Res bibl, res aid KTP 9:2:22
Res guide BGS 27:2:65
Res guide by Baxter, bk rev APG 10:3:90 GFP 44:3:139 GH 49:3:195 LC 16:1:15 MGS 13:1:11 TGC 19:1:19
Res guide by Palen, bk rev MGS 13:4:60 NFB 27:4:74 SGS 45:1:30
Res guide by Schweitzer, bk rev TTC 21:1:8
Res guide by SLCFHL, bk rev LRT 14:2:556
Res guide on migration patterns by Brandt, GGD 11:2:36
Res outline by FHLCJCLDS, bk rev GH 49:3:195 TGC 19:1:19
Res tips SGS 44:3:123

GERMAN GENEALOGY (continued)
  Rheinland, village lineage bks, res tips GGD 11:2:34
  RU, pass arriving in NY 1875-1886 by Glazier, bk rev GGD 11:2:36
  RU-GR hist GL 29:1:20
  Rufnamens explained JBC 16:1:8
  Saxony, archives addresses TGC 19:2:37
  Saxony, hist & maps by Hall, bk rev GGD 11:3:68
  St Hedwig, res tips MCR 27:1:56
  Ste Marie Aux Mines, GR Reformed Reg 1687-1694 by Wollmershauser, bk rev TPI 21:1:43
  Study Group of GR Geneal Soc, direct 1994 by Zwinger, bk rev GJ 22:4:126
  Telephone direct 1994 on CD-ROM, rev DPL 17:WINTER:12
  Thuringia, archives addresses TGC 19:2:37
  Thuringia, hist & maps by Hall, bk rev GGD 11:3:68
  Tips & techniques, guide by Ostwald, bk rev NFB 27:4:74
  TX, imm hist 1847-1861, repr 1970, bk rev GH 49:5:216
  TX, settler hist KTP 4:4:56
  Type & handwriting guide PCI 19:2:10
  Vr from Vorwaerts 1912 notices by Goertman, bk rev GH 49:6:179
  Waldeck, village lineage bks, res tips GGD 11:2:34
  Wars of the Unification, mil rec, hist & res tips, GGD 11:2:38
  Wurttemberg, emigration to RU, PO, AU, HG, Am, roster & hist GGD 11:4:102
GERONIMO, bc1829, AZ, FL, biog SEN 2:4:20
GERRARD, VA, PA, OH, IN, fam group sheets 1720-1980 by Murphy, bk rev WPG 21:4:53
GERRY, Elbridge f1812, MA, biog sketch HQ 95:57:13
GERVAIS, George J f1875, w Emma Cubley, NE, WA, biog sketch YV 27:1:12
GIBBONS, Peter b1821, NY, biog sketch IFL 5:8:14
GIBSON, William, VA, desc & related fam before 1759 by Linder, bk rev APR 14:6:3
GIDDENS, FL, fam cem rec FLG 18:3:82
GIDDINGS, Edwin b1818, w Laura M Sweet, OH, biog KTP 13:3:51
GIFFORD, Levinah see William BEARD
  William f1640, EN, MA, surname booklet by Gifford, bk rev NYQ 95:11:20
GIGER, Christian f1737, GR, PA, IL, geneal by Schwarz, bk rev CR 27:1:7
GIGNAC, Francois f1688, w Marie-Ann Richard, QB, geneal LG 95:53:18
GILBERT, Barnhart d1809, MD, fam hist sketch MD 36:4:605
  Elizabeth see Hiram B SCOTT
  George b1779, PA, fam hist sketch MD 36:4:605
  Hans Georg b1698, w Anna Elisabetha Gruber, GR, PA, fam hist, MD 36:4:605
  Leland R f1918, OR, corresp GFP 45:2:79
  William f1893, PA, biog sketch LM 36:3:227
GILILAND, David R m1864, w Lucy J Seaman, PA, biog sketch BGN 16:4:17
GILLHAM, Robert f1879, NY, MO, biog PW 15:1:5
GILLIAM, Fortune see James MACLEMORE
GILLILAND, Henry C f1875, OK, autobiog WTN 95:SPRING:3
  Thomas b1791, w Mary Barr, NC, IL, fam rec cont MCS 15:4:154
GILMER, Jimmie see Columbus T DARBY
GIRARD, Delia see Henry Joseph TETREAULT

GIRTY, Simon fc1775, w Catherine Malott, PA, MD, VA, fam hist by Malott, bk rev DM 58:3:142

GISH, Lillian Diana b1893, OH, birth certif CCK 13:4:7

GIVENS, Samuel f1739, w Sarah Cathey, IR, TX, fam hist STS 35:3:18

GLARDON, FR, OH, geneal by English, bk rev GH 49:4:226

GLASS, George Davis b1859, w Kate Stephenson, NE, biog sketch NW 18:1:22

GLASSELL, John, w Mary Coalter, ST, fam hist by Hayden, bk rev GH 49:4:224

GLATFELTER, Daniel f1878, PA, corresp RT 13:1:19

GLAZE, James M b1845, w Mary Etta, AL, obit PT 37:1:14

Mary Etta see James M GLAZE

GLEASON, Manley L m1898, Hattie L Miller, AK, marr rec AQ 6:1:13

GLEN, Hannah see James GLEN

James dc1762, w Hannah, VA, geneal, repr 1975, bk rev AGM 27:1/2:58 GGS 31:1:48 GH 49:4:225 NCJ 21:2:188

GLENN, Anne Coskey see Simon MCCARROLL

James dc1763, SC, equity suit SCM 23:2:82

Silas Smith bc1811, w Mourning Burnham, KY, MO, TX, fam hist VQS 32:3:44

GLENNY, Isaac b1697, w Martha Brown, w Elizabeth Livingston, IR, geneal IFL 5:10:16

GLICK, Aaron S b1903, PA, autobiog, bk rev PM 18:1:29

Elam b1914, w Thelma A Stoltzfus, PA, fam hist MFH 14:2:86

GLIMP, Francis E see Thomas J WILLIAMS

GLUCH, Julian f1893, PU, CN, geneal by Collins, bk rev GEN 20:1:19

Martin f1893, PU, CN, geneal by Collins, bk rev GEN 20:1:19

GNAGEY, Moses b1823, w Susanna Wiltrout, PA, fam rec LM 36:1:196

GOAD, Abraham d1771, w Katherine Williams, MO, fam hist CN 4:3:44

GODDARD, George Houston b1861, w Margaret A Dickenson, AL, biog sketch MCA 14:3:82

GOEBBELS, Joseph f1927, GR, hist of his publication *Der Angriff*, bk rev REG 92:4:454

GOERLITZ, Otto b1862, w Selma Von Wedel, PU, MI, biog sketch DM 58:4:172

GOFF, Harold Alvin, w Grace Irene Zeller, KS, fam hist by Goff, bk rev KK 33:1:16

Hiram d1882, w Charlotte M Watkins, NY, obit GG 7:4:174

GOHN, Adam f1738, GR, PA, OH, fam hist by McTeer, bk rev GRI 15:1:78 TR 35:1:52

Johannes f1738, GR, PA, OH, fam hist by McTeer, bk rev TR 35:1:52

John f1738, GR, PA, OH, fam hist by McTeer, bk rev GRI 15:1:78

Philip f1738, GR, PA, OH, fam hist by McTeer, bk rev GRI 15:1:78 TR 35:1:52

GONSALUS, Marritje, s Jan Eduwartz, fam rec vol 3 by Johnson, bk rev GH 49:3:218

GOOD, Peter, fam hist by Weber, bk rev HQ 95:58:90

GOODENOW, Edmond f1638, EN, MA, fam hist by Banvard, bk rev FP 38:1:12

John f1638, EN, MA, fam hist by Banvard, bk rev FP 38:1:12

MA, NY, fam hist by Banvard, bk rev NYR 126:2:151

Thomas f1638, EN, MA, fam hist by Banvard, bk rev FP 38:1:12

Ursula f1638, EN, MA, fam hist by Banvard, bk rev FP 38:1:12

GOODMAN, Clothida see George Washington WALDREP

Robert Hans f1857, w Mary Ann Holtermann, IL, biog CCS 16:4:127

GOODSON, William fc1814, SC, deed abstr ODD 7:2:29

GOODSPEED, Caroline m1837, h Aaron Haskins, VT, fam hist HQ 95:60:68

GOODWIN, Alexander b1767, w Ellen Dunn, w Ann Hutchinson, ST, CN, geneal by Pontifex, bk rev GEN 20:4:25

James fl648, VA, fam hist, repr 1897, bk rev EWA 32:3:135 FP 38:3:143 GEN 20:3:32 HTR 38:3:70 VL 30:1:44

GOODWYN, Frank fl993, TX, autobiog, bk rev STS 35:2:72

GORDON, Annie fc1860, h Frank Whithall, biog MCR 27:1:50

Ralph bc1880, w Netta Haasis Mills, ST, PA, biog HQ 95:55:13

William Ary b1858, IL, fam hist by Lord, bk rev IGS 27:2:118

William see Mary Moore HIGGINSON

GORMLEY, Bernard fl852, IR, CN, fam hist by Spear, bk rev IFL 5:9:5

GORTNER, Peter see also Peter COTNER

Peter b1704, VA, NC, MO, AR, fam hist by Cotner, bk rev MSG 15:4:224 NCJ 21:3:304

GORTON, Minnie Hale b1885, h --- Hight, h --- Slaughter, h George Crosser, MA, MI, NY, fam hist by Volpe, bk rev AG 70:2:127 KCG 36:1:48 NYR 126:2:152 SGS 45:1:38

GOURDIN, Louis bc1666, FR, SC, geneal by Gourdin, bk rev GFP 45:2:92

GOURLEY, Rebecca see Alexander KERR

TX, news abstr re:reunion c1945, roster KTP 4:3:45

GOWER, Mary see John ROBERTSON

GRABILL, Mary see Peter GRABILL

Peter dc1811, w Mary, MD, fam hist 4th ed by Grable, bk rev WPG 21:3:49

GRAFF, Elisabetha see Joseph GATZ

Fam hist by Byler, bk rev TPI 21:1:48

William George b1788, w Anna Elizabeth Schramm, GR, PA, geneal by Schultz, bk rev WPG 21:3:47

GRAGG, Robert fc1740, VA, TN, geneal by Gragg, bk rev FRT 16:3:105

GRAHAM, John b1742, NC, KY, biog RCR 10:1:2182

Ruth Ann see Henry STEPHENSON

GRAMLY, H Jurg see H Jurg RAMLY

GRAN, Lilly Edahl b1901, NW, IL, biog CHG 27:3:118

GRANDLIENARD, Charles Augustus fl852, w Marienna Emilene Guardian, SW, OH, fam hist FTC 17:2:22

GRANT, Benjamin see Abigail CHADBOURNE

Elizabeth see William GRANT

Ulysses S b1822, papers 1868-1870 by Simon, bk rev REG 93:3:358

William bc1670, w Elizabeth, ST, VA, geneal by Hirschi, bk rev GH 49:4:225

GRANTHAM, Henry fl851, SC, estate abstr ODD 7:2:30

GRAVELINE, Domitilde Mathilda Baudreau see Adolphe CREVIER

GRAVES, AZ, fam hist by Mattson, bk rev MSG 15:1:57

GRAY, Alice see Sumner DRINKWATER

Benajah m1856, w Mary Ann Williams, TN, Bible rec MTG 8:4:167

Helen M fl925, FL, corresp TAC 6:4:14

Mrs Agnew Ball d1971, h Alfred F, obit SYH 2:1:15

PU, PA, fam hist sketch KTP 14:4:60

GREAR, Willie b1871, IL, biog sketch FRT 17:1:4

GREBENSTCHIKOFF, George b1883, w Tatiana, RU, FL, biog PCQ 21:4:1

GREBENSTCHIKOFF (continued)
Tatiana see George
GREBENSTCHIKOFF
GREEK GENEALOGY, Imm pass lists 1885-1910 by Voultsos, bk rev GH 49:4:12
GREEN, Abigail fl732, h Joseph Park, RI, anc NER 149:596:399
Elizabeth see Thomas ABBOTT
Fam hist supp by Weyher, bk rev GGS 31:2:119
Malinda see John M HAYES
Mary Fran see Joseph HUTSON
Mary Hoxsie see William Browning GREENE
Mary see Charles HARRIS
Mary see Nathan LONGFELLOW
Nancy Ann see William CUNNINGHAM
GREENE, William Browning, w Mary Hoxsie Green, fam hist by Wright, bk rev STS 35:2:67
GREENO, Jacob see Jacob GREENOUGH
GREENOUGH, Jacob bc1760, w Jane, w Magdalena (?), OH, fam hist sketch FTC 17:2:20
Jacob bc1760, w Jane, w Magdalena (?), OH, biog sketch & update FTC 17:3:35
Jane see Jacob GREENOUGH
Magdalena see Jacob GREENOUGH
GREGORY, Henry, CT, court doc RAG 16:1:13
GREIBIL, Eve see Christian WENGER
GRESHAM, Edward fc1400, EN, VA, fam hist by Gritzbaugh, bk rev TG 29:1:48
GREY, Nancy see Joseph STIGGINS
GRIEG, Edvard b1843, ST, anc ANE 95:55:16
GRIFFIN, John b1878, GA, FL, biog PCQ 11:3:6
GRIFFITH, Jerom bc1639, w Elizabeth Gelding, VA, fam hist by Griffin, bk rev NCJ 21:3:305
GRIFFITH, Victor S fl920, AZ, news abstr re:wedding anniv CSB 30:1:6

GRIGGS, Leaverett Stearns fl870, w Cornelia, MI, diary abstr MI 41:2:43
GRIGSBY, Enoch m1818, w Frances Chiles, LA, Bible rec TJ 7:2:45
GRIMES, Josiah fl875, w Lydia Wheatcraft, OH, fam hist TR 35:4:200
Sarah see Joseph STILLGESS
GRISET, Francis b1911, CA, autobiog & fam hist OC 31:1:15
GRISWOLD, Abigail b1746, h Roger Mills, CT, identity NER 149:596:390
Abigail see Noah GRISWOLD
Noah b1722, w Abigail Griswold, w Mindwell Phelps, CT, geneal NER 149:596:390
GROGAN, E K see William GROGAN
William fl886, w E K, EN, TX, biog sketch KTP 5:3:33
GROMEK, John fl920, w Mary Borys, PO, NJ, brief fam hist TE 15:1:12
GROOM, Samuel Dabney, w Lucinda Thompson, IL, KS, fam hist by Krehbiel, bk rev TS 37:3:95
GROSVENOR, Chauncey F fl861, diary, bk rev TSC 6:1:5
Lucy see Ithiel CARGILL
GRUBBS, Moody see Cynthia Ann BOONE
GRUBER, Anna Elisabetha see Hans Georg GILBERT
GRUMBLES, Benjamin fl855, w Isabella O'Conner, TX, marr rec GR 37:1:28
GRZECHOWIAK, Wojciech Albert, w Marianna Jarecka, PO, geneal by Wangerow, bk rev MI 41:1:2
GUARDIAN, Mariennna Emilene see Charles Augustus GRANDLIENARD
GUAY, Charles, CN, biog sketch LG 95:53:7
GUECKE, Jan fl636, w Tryntje Agges, NY, fam rec NYR 126:4:239
GUENARD, Dominique see Domenico ZENNARO
GUILLAUME, Marie Benard see Pierre LEMIEUX

GUINN, Mordecai see Mordecai GWIN
  William Riley b1832, w Mary Martha Harris, MO, TX, geneal STS 35:3:11
GUMM, Julia Ann see James Riley WISEMAN
GUNDY, Maria b1835, h John Davison, IL, obit IG 31:1:17
GUNZELMAN, Katie see Peter HANSEN
GUSCOTT, Jane Davy b1833, h John Guscott, EN, AA, diary abstr QFH 16:2:51
  John see Jane Davy GUSCOTT
GUTHRIE, Henry f1800, w Nancy Ann Shackelford, TN, fam hist PT 37:3/4:13
  Mary F see E O THOMPSON
GUTMANN, Robert Hans see Robert Hans GOODMANN
GUTT, Andreas bc1530, SW, fam hist by Weber, bk rev HQ 95:58:90
GUTTERSON, Elizabeth see John CALLUM
GWIN, Elizabeth see Mordecai GWIN
  Mordecai mc1748, w Elizabeth, NC, TX, fam rec STS 35:1:51
HACHE, Marie f1812, h Francois Sevin, LA, hist of their separation KSL 19:4:144
HACKETT, George b1829, w Jennie Butcher, SD, MN, fam hist SVG 21:2:42
  Julia Catherine see Joseph F SONNANSTINE
HACKLEMAN, WA, Bible rec cont YV 27:1:13
HADDEN, Samuel f1749, KY, UT, geneal by Hadden, bk rev GH 49:5:231
HADLEY, Dora see Martin Luther GENTRY
HADLY, Joshuway fc1788, TN, papers BWG 24:1:42
HAGA, NO, fam hist by Haga, bk rev GH 49:3:218
HAGAR, Nathaniel b1794, w Olive Lynch, MA, Bible rec BG 16:4:138
HAGEL, Anna see Peter SCHINDLER

HAGEMANN, Maria Margaretha see Philipp Peter NEU
HAGEN, Ole Jacobsen b1860, w Johanna Engen, NO, MN, biog & hist of his ch MN 26:3:108
HAHN, Valentine f1844, OH, corresp MFH 14:2:64
HAIGHT, Susannah see John DAGGERLINCKX
HAIMS, OH, fam hist by Hutchinson, bk rev TR 35:4:223
HAINES, Calvert b1867, w Gitta K, IA, Bible rec HH 30:4:224
  Gitta K see Calvert HAINES
HAISE, Wilhelmine see Christian RASCH
HAKES, Solomon bc1688, w Anna Billings, geneal by Williams, bk rev ANC 30:1:25
HALE, Mildred see Albert Hazen BLANDING
  Philo f1838, IL, biog sketch CI 31:4:132
  Sarah Josepha f1827, PA, biog DAR 129:9:816
HALEY, Judith see William DEGGE
HALL, Amy see David BATCHELLER
  Delilah see Henry F C JOHNSON
  George b1808, w Elizabeth Knight, EN, OH, MO, fam hist by Shaw, bk rev CSB 30:1:7
  John d1814, GA, estate abstr BT 27:2:27
  Laban b1856, w Susi Elizabeth Pointer, MS, TN, KY, AR, fam rec TRC 10:2:50
  Lewis b1753, w Flora Beaty, w Nancy Colly, NC, GA, biog & geneal SEE 36:153:27
  Thomas f1747, VA, KY, fam hist PCH 1:3:32
  William D f1890, PA, burial rec he kept BGN 16:1:9 16:4:9
HALLETT, Andrew fc1635, MA, geneal by Smith, bk rev HQ 95:57:84
HALLMAN, Martha Dean see Thomas Leroy SIMS

HALLMAN (continued) PA, NC, GA, fam hist by Linn, bk rev RCR 10:2:2279

HALLMARK, George b1742, w Leannah Mynatt, EN, VA, geneal by Henderson, bk rev FP 38:4:214

HALLOCK, Geneal add by Hallock Fam Assoc, bk rev NYR 126:1:85

HALSEY, Elizabeth see Thomas HALSEY
Martha Victoria see William H H STEWART
Thomas f1638, w Elizabeth, MA, NY, fam hist by Halsey, bk rev SGS 45:1:35 YV 27:4:103

HALVERSON, Mary Kaja see Anton JENSEN

HAM, Betsey see Hiram RANDALL
Betty see Betsey HAM
Zeffie Morgan see Mary Sussie BROWN

HAMANN, Dorothea Christina see Heinrich Friedrich THIER
Theodore b1852, w Mary Cadreau, GR, MI, biog sketch DM 59:1:41

HAMBLETON, George f1881, w Mary Knight, FL, biog PCQ 13:2:4

HAMILTON, George see George HAMBLETON
Jonathan Newman b1797, diary by Williams, bk rev GH 49:4:225
Joseph Alexander b1833, w Francis R Cherry, w Sarah M Condor, w Elizabeth Helena Morrison, NC, FL, biog sketch TAC 6:2:8
Sarah see John MCCREIGHT

HAMITER, Thomas f1752, GR, SC, fam hist SCM 23:1:3

HAMM, Jacob bc1843, w Catherine Schantz, NY, CA, fam rec OC 31:1:14

HAMMER, Hannah see John BLAYLOCK

HAMMON, TN, TX, AR, OK, fam hist by Hammons, bk rev GH 49:4:225
William f1668, w Elizabeth Batterem, MA, identity NER 149:595:211

HAMMOND, William see Elizabeth BARTRAM

HAMOR, Ralph bc1588, EN, biog sketch VAG 39:2:93

HAMPSTON, Elizabeth see Charles SPALDING

HAMPTON, Bridget see Gutridge GARLAND
Charles Chester Colson f1769, VA, fam hist TVF 4:1:3
John, ST, NJ, VA, NC, AL, geneal by Belcher, bk rev OLR 9:1:39

HANCE, Fam hist by Mattson, bk rev MSG 15:1:57

HANCHEY, Elizabeth see William E NICHOLS

HANCOCK, Cenetta L see Benjamin Mitchell FORTNER
EN, Am, fam hist by Hancock, bk rev MD 36:1:94
Leon f1995, PA, fam hist by Hancock, bk rev WPG 22:1:48
Vera H b1895, WA, Bible rec GFP 44:4:170

HANEY, Catherine see John PHIPPS

HANGER, Frederich f1740, VA, fam hist by Joyner, bk rev APR 14:12:3
Peter f1740, VA, fam hist by Joyner, bk rev APR 14:12:3

HANMER, Emma Jane see William C DUNCAN

HANN, John f1791, NJ, deed rec GMN 70:1:36
William f1791, NJ, deed rec GMN 70:1:36

HANNA, Albert f1844, CN, fam hist sketch IFL 5:8:10

HANNAH, James see Mary Elizabeth HANNAH
Mary Elizabeth b1872, h James Hannah, TX, biog TTT 19:2:91

HANNAMAN, Geneal supplement 1728-1989 by Hannaman, bk rev TPI 20:2:90

HANSEL, John Washington fc1840, KS, fam hist PR 23:2:51

HANSEN, EN, fam hist by Hansen, bk rev GH 49:3:218

HANSEN (continued)
 H M m1878, w Mary Kesilka, AR, surname rec SYH 2:3:20
 Peter b1859, w Katie Gunzelman, DK, KS, fam hist sketch KK 33:2:26

HANSON, AR, CA, IL, early fam rec by Miner, bk rev APR 14:6:3 KGF 1:1/2:88 MN 26:2:87 SQ 6:3:54
 DE, DC, MD, VA, WV, misc fam rec by Miner, bk rev WPG 22:1:44
 Jacob f1865, w Wilhelmina D Nutter, w Emma F Brown, NH, corresp SCR 18:2:19
 Olaf fc1880, WI, ND, fam hist by Schwinkendorf, bk rev GH 49:4:202
 Phineas Butler b1827, w Sarah J Hobbs, ME, corresp abstr SCR 18:6:100

HARDEMAN, Thomas f1660, EN?, WE?, VA, geneal REF 37:2:24

HARDESTY, George f1652, MD, fam hist by Wesley, bk rev GH 49:5:231
 Thomas, w Isabell Winder, EN, fam hist by Wesley, bk rev GH 49:5:231

HARDISTY, Fam hist by Mattson, bk rev MSG 15:1:57

HARDMAN, Mary Ann see Gideon W BACKUS

HARDY, Rufus m1846, w Lucy Mariah Bailey, GA, fam rec CCM 14:3:7

HARJU, Jerry f1938, MI, memoirs, bk rev KVH 20:4:39

HARLAN, Fam hist 1687-1987 by Tally, bk rev IFL 5:10:5

HARLEY, Samuel K see Mary Harley CASSEL

HARLOW, Benjamin F d1916, w Anna Brown, w Mary Stevens Hastings, OK, MI, biog sketch WTN 95:SPRING:7

HARNESS, Walter b1912, w Doreen Mary Jacques, CN, fam hist by McCutcheon, bk rev GEN 20:1:19

HARNSBERGER, Anna Barbara see John HARNSBERGER
 Elizabeth see John HARNSBERGER
 John bc1690, w Anna Barbara, GR, PA, geneal BYG 7:1:361

HARNSBERGER (continued)
 John bc1742, w Elizabeth, VA, fam hist BYG 7:6:415 8:1:426

HARPST, George b1799, w Christena Stambaugh, PA, OH, fam hist TR 35:1:42

HARRINGTON, Lydia see James NICHOLS

HARRIS, Ann see David CALDWELL
 C C f1865, AL, corresp abstr OLR 9:4:149
 Charles b fc1730, MD, OH, KY, fam hist by Stevens, bk rev TR 35:1:54
 Charles b1864, w Nettie Elder, IL, obit CCS 16:4:121
 Charles f1767, w Mary Green, w Hannah Noble, MD, OH, KY, geneal by Stevens, bk rev GH 49:3:219
 Eudora Virginia see Thomas Jefferson WHITTON
 John, MD, OH, KY, fam hist by Stevens, bk rev SGS 44:2:84
 Mary Martha see William Riley GUINN
 MD, OH, KY, fam hist by Stevens, bk rev CI 31:1:21
 Minyard b1846, VA, NC, TX, fam hist by Carter, bk rev SCM 23:2:118
 Nancy Jo Rice see Josiah CARNEAL
 William b1675, w Elizabeth Brockway, CT, fam hist AG 70:4:233
 William, MD, OH, KY, fam hist by Stevens, bk rev SGS 44:2:84

HARRISON, Basil b1771, w Martha Stillwell, MD, MI, biog by Crose, bk rev KVH 19:7:79
 Mary see Abraham VANGILDER
 Samuel b1730, fam hist by Harrison, bk rev GH 49:6:208
 Sarah Gignilliat f1857, FL, corresp abstr TNC 2:2:44
 William D fc1835, w Jane Patton, TX, fam hist by Farley, bk rev TJ 7:3:110
 William Henry b1869, TN, fam rec ARH 33:1:9

HARSH, James Wesly m1880, w Mary A Criglar, OH, Bible rec IB 11:1:6

HARSHBARGER, Zachariah b1824, w Margaret Filler, w Margaret Hetton, PA, TN, fam rec BWG 24:1:52

HART, James fl839, FL, biog PCQ 9:4:6

HARTMAN, Matilda see Richard HUMPHREYS

HARTMANN, Julia see George BULL

HARTWELL, Dorothy see Joseph ARNOLD

Samuel see Mary FLINT

HARTZLER, Raymond L b1893, w Nora E Burkholder, IN, IL, geneal MH 22:4:71

HARVEY, AR, GA, LA, MS, fam hist by Clemmons, bk rev GGS 31:1:50

GA, MS, AR, fam hist by Harvey, bk rev ARH 33:1:33

HASKINS, Aaron see Caroline GOODSPEED

Jonas b1788, w Rhoda Pennock, NY, OH, geneal by Lowry, bk rev TJ 7:1:37

HASLAM, Thomas b1783, w Elizabeth Moore, IR, CN, geneal by Haslam et al, bk rev GH 49:3:219

HASSETT, John Robert fl890, AA, biog sketch TGO 7:12:499

HASTINGS, Mary Stevens see Benjamin HARLOW

HATCHER, Dorty see John HATCHER

John b1790, w Rittie Landon, TN, NC, biog sketch KTP 4:1:14

John fl765, w Dorty, NC, biog sketch KTP 4:1:14

Lida Edna see Ralph Augustus HELLIER

HATFIELD, Charles (aka Mountain Charley) fl859, CO, biog sketch KCG 36:1:17

Elizabeth see W S FOWLER

George Goff b1715, VA, WV, KY, TN, fam hist by Sellards, bk rev GH 49:6:208

John b1717, VA, WV, KY, TN, fam hist by Sellards, bk rev GH 49:6:208 PCH 1:1:38

HATTON, John m1842, w Adaline Wynkoop, biog sketch TR 35:2:88

HAUTZIG, Esther fl995, recoll re:Holocaust JL 8:1/2:87

HAWAII, Women missionaries, 19th cent, hist by Zwiep, bk rev NER 149:594:187

HAWES, Bethyah see Obadiah SEWARD

Richard Simrall, w Marie Christy Johnson, MA, SC, VA, geneal by Bond, bk rev GJ 23:1:46 NYR 126:4:283 VAG 39:3:228

Susan Elizabeth b1816, KY, biog sketch KA 31:1:14

HAWKINS, John b1766, TX, Bible rec FP 38:1:6

HAWORTH, Fam hist vol 1 by Boone/Morgan, bk rev QQ 95:25:25

HAY, Alfred fl916, CN, biog by Sinclair, bk rev GEN 20:2:22

Andrew fl917, CN, biog by Sinclair, bk rev GEN 20:2:22

HAYDON, Thomas fl657, EN, VA, biogby Haydon, bk rev KA 31:1:43

HAYES, David b1781, w Barbara Hendrix, GA, desc by Hayes, bk rev GGS 31:2:121

Isaac S fl857, w Judea Varner, GA, Bible rec GGS 31:2:112

John M m1867, w Malinda Green, GA, Bible rec GGS 31:2:109

Mary B see Samuel J JONES

Thomas T b1817, w Frances M Hedges, KY, notebks KA 30:4:195

HAYFORD, Sabra M see Fred T BROWN

HAYMAN, Henry fl835, GA, pension appl BT 26:4:82

Jeremiah Madison b1822, w Martha Jane Carlton, GA, FL, biog PCQ 21:4:4

HAYNES, Margaret see Henry BURCHAM

Raleigh Rutherford b1851, NC, biog by Crow, bk rev RCR 10:2:2272

HAYS, Jack fl836, TX, CA, biog by Greer, bk rev STS 35:2:72

HAYS (continued)
Jack see John Coffee HAYS
Jane see William FERRALL
John Coffee b1817, w Susan Calvert, TN, CA, biog sketch KTP 12:1:5
William S d1907, KY, biog REG 93:3:286

HAZEN, Elizabeth see James Isaac DALRYMPLE

HEAD, Ann see William HEAD
William f1658, w Ann, MD, KY, geneal WMG 12:1:2

HEADY, IN, fam hist 1820-1900 by Martin, bk rev OC 32:2:53

HEALE, Hannah Bushrod see Adam CRUMP

HEARD, Periodical compendium by Zarnowitz, bk rev BWG 24:1:67 GH 49:4:225

HEATH, Bartholomew bc1615, w Hannah Moyce, EN, MA, geneal by Giorgi, bk rev BAT 24:2:43 GH 49:5:231 HQ 95:57:84 NYR 126:3:217
Henry b1795, w Nancy, PA, Bible rec WPG 21:3:38
Nancy see Henry HEATH
Sarah E see William C DUNCAN
Susannah see William HEATH
William d1799, w Susannah, SC, geneal by Richey, bk rev ODD 7:2:39
William see Agnes CHENEY

HEBERT, Jean Baptiste, FR, MA, fam hist by Hebert, bk rev ACG 21:1:24
Marie see Michel FOREST

HEDGES, Frances M see Thomas T HAYES

HEDRICK, Mary Jane see John Winn RICHARDSON

HEGARTY, Richard see Mary CULLINAN

HEIL, Louis, w Elizabeth Susan Steves, GR, KS, TX, CA, fam hist by Heil, bk rev OC 32:2:56

HEIMBAUGH, PA, fam rec 1820-1842 LM 36:1:203

HEISKELL, J N d1972, w Wilhelmina Mann, AR, obit SYH 2:1:15

HELGOY, NO, fam hist by Haga, bk rev GH 49:3:218

HELLIER, Ralph Augustus b1871, w Lida Edna Hatcher, KY, biog sketch PCH 1:1:6

HEMMANT, Susanna see Robert B HUGMAN

HENABERGER, Martha see Christian MYERS

HENDERSON, Belle Elizabeth b1895, h John Wesley Roberts, KS, Bible rec TOP 25:2:51
Elizabeth see James Madison HENDERSON
James Madison bc1812, w Elizabeth, TX, Bible rec GR 37:3:15
Lorrie Foster f1933, TX, recoll AGS 36:3:98
Marzaime J f1861, AR, news abstr SCH 10:4:145
Robert T b1779, w Margaret Brown, MD, Bible rec MD 36:2:272
SC, fam hist 1850-1870 by Henderson, bk rev GH 49:5:232 NCJ 21:2:188 TFT 6:2:23B

HENDRICKS, George Walter b1871, AR, biog sketch SYH 2:2:21

HENDRIX, Barbara see David HAYES

HENDRY, James E see Lydia Carlton Hendry MOODY
Lydia Carlton see Benjamin MOODY

HENGERER, Frederich see Frederick HANGER
Peter see Peter HANGER

HENNESSEY, David d1890, LA, biog sketch KSL 19:1:17

HENNEY, Josephine Esther see Charles Wesley WILCOX

HENNING, Marion Alice Seibert b1910, MN, recoll IMP 14:1:8

HENNIS, Rebecca see Preston Hill ROPER

HENRY, Frances see Robert MORRISON
GA, MS, AR, fam hist by Harvey, bk rev ARH 33:1:33

HENRY (continued)
  Marvin b1794, w Elizabeth Sutton, NY, MI, IN, fam hist by Lodoen, bk rev GH 49:6:208
  Mary see Singleton RHEA
  Spencer b1805, w Elizabeth Mayze, TN, biog ETR 7:4:169
HENSON, AR, CA, IL, fam hist by Miner, bk rev APR 14:6:3 KGF 1:1/2:88 MN 26:2:87
  C F f1896, w Nellie Henson, KS, marr resolution doc THT 23:2:76
  DE, DC, MD, VA, WV, misc fam rec by Miner, bk rev WPG 22:1:44
  Jerry d1905, AL, fam cem rec NTT 14:4:131
  Misc fam rec by Miner, bk rev SQ 6:3:54
  Nellie see C F HENSON
HERALDRY, Augustan color bk, folio II by the Augustan Soc, bk rev HQ 95:59:90
  Basic guide, heraldry beginner's tips RAG 17:1:9
  Coats of arms, hist ANC 30:3:127
  Fam historians & heraldry, guidebk by Swinnerton, bk rev SGB 26:3:iv
  Feudal coats of arms from heraldic rolls 1298-1418, repr 1902, bk rev GH 49:3:194
  Gaelic Heraldry hist HER 3:3:4
  Goldenhorn steinbock hist HER 3:3:12
  Res guide by Von Volbroth, bk rev HQ 95:59:90
  Role of Arms of Crusaders by Augustan Society, bk rev HQ 95:59:90
  Scottish heraldry hist & res aid, repr 1956, bk rev GH 49:3:197
  SP, Arms of Mantegna of Calascibetta & Mendola of Cammarata, hist HER 3:3:30
  ST, ordinary of arms in the public reg 1672-1901, repr 1903, bk rev GH 49:3:198
  Steinbocks, hist HER 3:3:12
  Westminster Abbey armorial shields, hist RAG 16:2:15

HERALDRY (continued)
  Westminster Abbey, descr of coats of arms RAG 16:4:15
HERD see HEARD
HERMAN, Christian f1752, w Christina Magdalena Lenhard, GR, PA, fam hist TPI 21:1:11
HERMS, Andreas Frederick fc1862, w Caroline Dorothy Dohmeier, GR, TX, fam hist sketch KTP 4:2:24 4:3:38
HERNDON, Joel J b1829, w Elizabeth Kempson, GA, biog sketch CCM 15:1:11
  Lewis fc1775, VA, KY, geneal by Herndon, bk rev GH 49:4:225
HERR, Hans b1639, PA, geneal, repr 1908, bk rev GH 49:5:232 TPI 20:2:91
  Hans b1639, PA, index to geneal by Olde Springfield Shoppe, bk rev CC 17:4:37 GH 49:4:225 MGS 13:3:45 TR 35:2:110
HERRICK, Diana see David MOORE
  Elizabeth Wood see Benjamin BECKFORD
HERRIN, Eli R f1923, biog & tribute SCG 14:1:656
  Elizabeth Frances see Stephen BIRD
HERSHEY, Benjamin f1775, PA, biog sketch & religious views PM 19:1:2
HESTER, Sallie bc1837, CA, diary abstr AFH 16:4:12
HESTON, Joseph T b1839, w Sarah E. Keith, OH, KS, biog sketch RAG 16:3:9
  Zebulon f1684, w Dorothy Hutchinson, MA, PA, biog sketch RAG 16:2:12
HETHERINGTON, Nancy L see Jefferson C BRADLEY
HETTON, Margaret see Zachariah HARSHBARGER
HEUSON, Eliza see Orville Merritt KELLY
HEYING, MO, fam hist by Fabula, bk rev MSG 15:1:55
HEYL, Elizabethia Katherina see Sebastian BOSCH

HEYWOOD, Ann see George ADAMS
HIATT, Fam hist by Mattson, bk rev MSG 15:1:57
HICKMAN, Jesse m1828, w Martha A B Temple, AL, Bible rec NGS 83:2:124
  Robert f1790, w Mary Magdalena Livengood, PA, geneal by Hickman, bk rev WPG 21:3:48
HICKOK, Herman f1846, w Lucinda, will rec AH 22:2:189
  Lucinda see Herman HICKOK
HICKS, Robert dc1765, SC, estate inv ODD 7:4:17
HIGDON, Rose Musacchio f1995, IY, anc by Higdon, bk rev FRT 16:3:103
  William Hoffman b1816, w Jane Buchanan, NC, biog & siblings LOB 16:1:14
HIGGINS, Elizabeth see Christopher THOMAS
HIGGINSON, Jane see John Barton TAYLOR
  Mary Moore b1852, h William Gordon, IR, AA, biog QFH 16:2:63
HIGGS, William see Caledonia G H MOORE
HIGHT, --- see Minnie Hale GORTON
HILDERBRAND, John Christopher f1754, HO, SC, fam hist & geneal ARH 33:4:148
HILGEN, Frederick f1844, GR, SC, WI, geneal by Wendt, bk rev HQ 95:58:90
HILL, Barbara see John W BROOKS
  Nancy see James BOSTON
  Nancy see Thomas Edward ALLEE
  Rebecca Jane see Henry Allen DUNN
  Sarah see James Knox Polk BEATY
HILLS, Betsey see Caleb BAILEY
  Joseph see Hannah EDWARDS
HINDES, Frances Margaret see James Albert COLES
HINDMAN, Alexander f1797, w Margaret Ann Walker, VA, KY, fam hist sketch KGF 1:1/2:2

HINES, John William bc1600, IR, NC, VA, fam hist by Hurley, bk rev APR 14:6:4 RT 13:3:73
HINESLEY, John Jefferson b1822, geneal by Doris/Hinesley, bk rev ARH 33:4:174
HINNANT, William m1861, w Sarah Eveline Williamson, NC, Bible rec JC 21:3:58
HINSON, AR, CA, IL, Am, early fam rec by Miner, bk rev APR 14:6:3 KGF 1:1/2:88 MN 26:2:87 SQ 6:3:54
  Bushrod H b1826, w Sarah Ellen Miller, VA, fam hist KCG 36:2:87
  DE, DC, MD, VA, WV, misc fam rec by Miner, bk rev WPG 22:1:44
HINTON, Eleanor Ann see Charles Glen JOHNSON
HIRD, See HEARD
HIRDLER, Carl b1854, w Marie Regina Margaretta Wagenknecht, GR, MO, geneal AGS 36:2:72
HIRST, Bessie Randolph b1873, IL, IA, CA, autobiog & recoll RT 13:3:77 13:4:102
HISPANIC GENEALOGY, Basques in CA, hist & biog 1860-1890 FRT 17:1:8
  Beginner's res tips FP 38:3:131
  Mex-Am hist by Hoobler, bk rev AMG 9:6:5
  Res guide for beginners by Flores/Ludwig, bk rev MAG 8:2:3
  Res tips FRT 16:3:96
  Sourcebk by Nyers, bk rev RAG 16:3:21
  TX, Catholic Archives, descr FRT 16:2:60
HITCHCOCK, Sarah see Richard COLLEY
HITT, Henry f1665, w Sarah Bassett, NJ, CT, geneal by Hitt, bk rev CTN 27:4:589
HOAG, Mary see Thomas T WEEKS
HOAGLAND, John Collins, w Patricia Ann Hoagland McEwen, OH, fam hist by McEwen, bk rev TR 35:4:218

HOBART, Deborah see Robert PARKER
Edmund bc1570, EN, MA, geneal by Hobart/Griffith, bk rev FRT 16:2:67

HOBBS, Sarah J see Phineas Butler HANSON

HOBGOOD, Preston d1869, AL, obit NTT 14:4:137

HOBSON, Elizabeth see George HOBSON
George, w Elizabeth, EN, PA, VA, lineage by Hobson, bk rev GH 49:4:225 TJ 7:3:110

HOCHSTETLER, OH, fam members in 1860 census TR 35:3:137

HOCKER, Willie K f1936, AR, autobiog sketch SYH 1:2:14

HOCKMAN, Jacob F, PA, fam hist by Hockman, bk rev TPI 21:1:47

HODGES, Erastus b1781, CT, biog & rec by Hodges, bk rev NER 149:593:79
John b1802, TN, fam hist by Morley, bk rev HQ 95:58:90
Lavina see William INGLE

HODGKINS, J E f1862, MA, Civil War Diary by Turino, bk rev TEG 15:1:37

HODGMAN, Samuel C f1887, MI, FL, biog sketch & corresp abstr PCQ 12:1:8

HOFF, Mary Magdalena see William Henry BIEGEL

HOFFELBAUER, Georg Balthasar b1724, AU, GR, PA, geneal by Rohrbach, bk rev AG 70:2:122
GR, Am, geneal by Rohrbach, bk rev TB 21:3:11
Philipp Jacob b1718, AU, GR, PA, geneal by Rohrbach, bk rev AG 70:2:122

HOFFMAN, Lydia see Clark J PERKINS

HOFFPAUIR, Thomas bc1735, w Marie Charlotte Perrillard, GR, LA, fam hist sketch KSL 19:2:48

HOGG, James Stephen b1851, w Sallie Stinson, TX, biog PWN 1:5:10

HOGG (continued)
NH, fam name changes, roster NHR 12:4:147
Sarah see Joseph P VANN

HOLBROOK, KY, geneal cont EK 31:1:28

HOLCOMB, Polly see Libbeus FISH

HOLDEN, Alexander T b1823, w Jane Bain, w Sarah Andrews, IN, biog IG 31:1:16
Anna Jane b1893, ID, anc & geneal by Newcomb, bk rev GH 49:5:232
Margaret see William PARISH

HOLEKAMP, Betty Wilhelmina d1902, h Fred Holekamp, TX, obit KTP 9:1:10
Friedrick b1812, w Betty Wilhelmine Appenthern, TX, fam hist KTP 5:4:55 6:1:3

HOLLCROFT, John b1741, w Sarah Mesherool, fam hist by Hollcroft, bk rev WPG 22:2:57

HOLLINGSWORTH, AL, fam cem rec MCA 14:4:119

HOLLOWAY, Marshall G f1996, FL, biog PCQ 13:3:5

HOLLY, Emily Frances see David Howe CLARK

HOLMAN, Mary Campbell Lovering b1868, New England, anc NEH 12:1:22

HOLMES, James f1848, OH, biog sketch HQ 95:55:18
Narcissa J see James Madison BURKS
Noah Dortch b1833, AR, obit & biog FGC 95:28:20

HOLSAPPLE, W D f1919, w Henrietta Smith, IA, wedding aniv news notice ISC 19:2:29

HOLSTEIN, Julia see James C EDWARDS

HOLTERMANN, Mary Ann see Robert Hans GOODMAN

HOLTON, Sarah see John KING

HOLZHAUSER, William f1880, w Gertrude Schorr, MI, WA, geneal by Montgomery, bk rev GH 49:4:225

HOLZWARTH, Karl Jacob (Charles), GR, TX, fam hist by Vaughan, bk rev STS 35:2:71

HOLZWORTH, GR, TX, fam hist by Vaughan, bk rev STS 35:2:71

HOME, George see George HUME

HOOGHTEELING, Mathys Coenratsen bc1639, w Maria Hendricks Marselis, NY, geneal by Kassak, bk rev NYR 126:4:283

HOOKER, Joseph b1814, New England anc NEH 12:2/3:64

HOOKS, John McCullough fc1822, AL, Bible rec NTT 15:1/2:40
Malinda see Needham Bryant FOLSOM

HOOPER, Elizabeth see Lionel ELGIN

HOOSIER, Harry bc1750, IN, biog sketch GCH 8:7:120

HOOVER, Dorothea B b1896, MO, biog sketch CN 4:3:43
Herbert b1874, CA, biog sketch SCC 32:1:19
Levi G b1832, w Eliza Shaffer, w Harriet M Justice, PA, biog sketch BGN 16:1:18

HOPE, Mary Susannah see Jacob William FLEENOR

HOPKINS, Francis see Mary JOSLIN
Giles f1620, MA, fam hist by Allen, bk rev TJ 7:1:37
Stephen f1620, MA, fam hist by Allen, bk rev TJ 7:1:37

HOPPE, Henry see Mary Elizabeth STILES

HOPPER, Anne see Charles HOPPER
Charles f1683, w Anne, MD, geneal MD 36:1:22

HOPPOCK, John bc1726, NJ, fam hist by Sanders, bk rev GSN 8:1:7

HORN, Elizabeth see E G SMALLIN

HORNBECK, Warnaar bc1645, NL, NY, geneal by Hornbeck, bk rev GH 49:4:226 IGS 27:2:115

HORNER, Lucinda see Adam FRIEDLINE

HORTON, J W f1862, TX, corresp STS 35:2:23

HORTON (continued)
John see Elizabeth MCCULLOCH

HOSMER, Frederick see Sophia FISH

HOSTETLER, Harold, anc LM 36:3:227
OH, fam members in 1860 census TR 35:3:137

HOSTETTER, Kathrina see Hans George BENDER

HOTCHKIN, Francis b1799, w Nancy Matoon, MA, Bible rec BG 16:4:136

HOUGH, CT, VT, fam hist by Hough, bk rev KGF 1:1/2:88

HOUPT, Sebastian f1779, w Catherine Wright, NC, geneal by Houpe, bk rev NCJ 21:1:81

HOUSTON, M F b1840, w --- Snyder, IL, news abstr re:wedding anniv CI 31:3:81
Sam, TX, biog by Williams, bk rev REG 92:4:448

HOW, Margreat see John SLUTS

HOWARD, Andrew f1843, NH, hist of his execution SCR 18:4:55

HOWE, John see Edith Berry KIMBALL

HOWELL, Hugh fc1700, w Margaret, NJ, VA, OH, geneal by Wallace et al, bk rev BTG 1:2:7 GH 49:5:232 QQ 95:25:25 SGS 44:2:85 VL 29:3:145
John Gilson f1865, WA, biog & fam hist EWA 32:4:166
Margaret see Hugh HOWELL
Martha Jane see Nathaniel Clay BRYAN
Olly see James/John BOONE

HOWLAND, John see Elizabeth TILLEY

HOWLE, Epaphroditus, SC, fam hist ency by Howle, bk rev ODD 7:4:7

HOYT, Dorothy see Zerubbabel HOYT
Harriet H see Samuel B HOYT
Samuel B f1867, w Harriet H, CT, bapt rec of daughter CTA 38:2:66
Zerubbabel f1737, w Dorothy, CT, identity of wife CTA 38:2:52

HUBBARD, Charles fl795, w Jemima, KY, MO, geneal by Foster, bk rev GH 49:4:226
Israel b1797, NY, obit GG 7:4:178
James Henry b1857, w Lousina Catherine Stirewalt, IL, Bible rec GL 29:1:8
Jemima see Charles HUBBARD
Nathaniel b1772, w Mary Mackay, CT, Bible rec CTA 38:2:70 37:3:117
HUDSON, Joshua b1828, w Mary Malinda Coble, NC, biog sketch SCG 14:4:692
S J see John G BOYDSTUN
HUEHNER, Matilda see John D BEDWELL
HUFF, Engelbert d1765, w Maria Willemsze, NY, geneal by Trigg, bk rev CTA 37:3:146
HUGHES, Charles Evans b1862, NY, fam hist GH 49:6:208 NYR 126:1:85
David Charles fl855, w Mary Catherine Connelly, fam hist by Johnson, bk rev GH 49:6:208
Gerard H fl995, EN, recoll KTP 8:4:61
Harry b1877, w Ida Irene Benson, IA, WA, biog sketch TRI 35:1:15
Mary Bertron fl850, LA, corresp FPG 17:4:25
NC, deed rec, 18th & 19th cent FYC 12:4:367
Robert b1841, w Elizabeth Roberts, WE, EN, biog sketch RAG 16:1:11
William George fl878, EN, TX, biog KTP 5:3:44
William see Mary BERTRON
Robert B b1826, w Susanna Hemmant, w Martha Lowe, EN, TX, geneal KTP 6:3:40
HUGUENOT GENEALOGY, Am, hist, repr 1906, bk rev GH 49:5:185
EN, Huguenot imm & settlement 1550-1700 by Cottret, bk rev THS 95:100:59
EN, IR, hist by Smiles, bk rev IS 16:3:79
Hist by Reaman, bk rev FP 38:3:140

HUGUENOT GENEALOGY (continued)
Hist, repr 1843, bk rev GH 49:5:181
IR, hist 1685-1850 by St Leger, bk rev GN 13:3:140
MD, hist by HSM, bk rev MD 36:1:89
Natl Huguenot Soc Reg of qualified anc by Finnell, bk rev MN 26:2:87
NY, births, marr & deaths 1688-1804 by Wittmeyer, bk rev GN 13:2:96
NY, French Ch of NY, vr 1688-1804, repr 1886, bk rev GH 49:5:204
HULICK, Rachel see Jared YOUNG
HULL, George bc1590, w Thamzen Michell, EN, MA, CT, fam hist by Hull, bk rev GH 49:4:226 KVH 19:9:102
HUMBLE, John fl836, VA?, indenture rec GFP 45:2:83
HUME, George fl715, w Elizabeth Proctor, ST, VA, biog BYG 7:1:363
HUMPHEYS, W M b1842, w Sarah Chapman, TN, TX, biog sketch MT 31:4:160
HUMPHREYS, Richard fl813, w Rebecca Miller, w Matilda Hartman, TN, biog sketch BWG 24:2:131
HUNGARIAN GENEALOGY, China, HG roots in, hist RM 95:8:7
Fejer Co, Hungarians & GR in land census 1828 by Connor, bk rev GH 49:5:182
Magyar origins, hist RM 95:8:1
Vital statistics & geneal, tips RM 95:8:1
HUNT, Abigail see Josiah SNELLING
Betty see John Winn RICHARDSON
John Riley b1835, KY, MO, w Rachel Collins, fam hist BWG 24:1:54
Mary see Caleb SHREVE
Pirum R m1814, w Polly Camp, NY, OH, Bible rec FHC 19:2:28
Samuel H b1814, NJ, Bible rec MAG 8:3:8
William dc1677, w Ann, VA, inv VAG 39:1:48
HUNTER, William see William H SEWARD

HURLEY, Amos bc1755, NC, TN, KY, geneal by Hurley, bk rev OLR 9:4:165 SGS 45:1:35
Cornelius bc1795, NC, TN, KY, geneal by Hurley, bk rev OLR 9:4:165 SGS 45:1:35
Daniel b1658, MD, DE, NC, VA, geneal by Hurley, bk rev FCM 8:2:138 SGS 45:1:35
Moses bc1750, NC, TN, KY, fam hist by Hurley, bk rev OLR 9:4:165 SGS 45:1:35
Nehemiah bc1755, NC, TN, KY, geneal by Hurley, bk rev OLR 9:4:165 SGS 45:1:35
HURSH, Henry, w Susanna Rudisill, PA, fam hist by Hursh, bk rev PM 18:1:28
Margaret Kathryn see David FRAZIER
HURT, Jean fc1935, OK, recoll GSM 12:1:5
HUSTON, Archibald dc1774, w Mary Stephenson, VA, brief geneal KA 31:2:37
HUTCHINS, Fam hist by Mattson, bk rev MSG 15:1:57
Garner Eulas, w Mary Cloeta Davis, NC, fam hist by Sprinkle, bk rev LOB 16:1:26
HUTCHINSON, Ann see Alexander GOODWIN
Anne Marbury fl634, MA, major hist figures desc from her NEH 12:6:210
Dorothy see Zebulon HESTON
HUTSON, Joseph b1830, w Mary Fran Green, IL, Bible rec CI 31:1:1
HYARD, Jean, FR, fam hist LG 95:55:56
HYER, Anna E see John S WARD
John b1810, w Mary Ann, PA, MO, obit MSG 15:1:4
Mary Ann see John HYER
HYLTON, VA, fam hist by Peterson, bk rev APR 14:11:5
HYNSON, AR, CA, IL, fam hist by Miner, bk rev APR 14:6:3 KGF 1:1/2:88 MN 26:2:87 SQ 6:3:54

HYNSON (continued) DE, DC, MD, VA, WV, misc fam rec by Miner, bk rev WPG 22:1:44
IBBOTSON, Daniel b1809, w Isabella Jackson, w Jane Dixon, EN, MI, biog sketch DM 58:4:172
ICELAND, Imm hist HQ 95:57:50
IDAHO, Coeur D' Alene Indian reservation cem rec EWA 32:4:171
Washington Co, marr rec 1879-1902 by Samuelsen, bk rev GH 49:5:192
IDDINGS, Hiram fl864, IN, corresp IMP 14:1:13
IKENBERRY, John b1763, w Elizabeth Rush, PA, biog sketch NFB 27:4:79
ILLINOIS, Adjutant General annual report 1861-1862, repr, bk rev GH 49:6:187 SGS 45:1:31
Algonquin, St John's Evang Luth Ch centennial booklet name index 1876-1976 MCI 13:2:45
Amish & Mennonites in southern IL, hist MH 22:4:67
Amish distillery & economic network hist MH 22:3:45 22:4:65
Aroma Twp, Aroma Cem rec TAK 25:2:17
Auburn Citizen news abstr 1894 CR 27:1:8
Barnett Twp, census 1880 DWC 21:4:91
Bloomington Co, early Af-Am residents from 1850 census GL 29:1:28
Bloomington High Sch alumni 1918-1922 GL 29:1:15
Bond Co, census 1910 by Hawley, bk rev GH 49:6:187
Boone Co, pioneers before 1841, hist by Rowland, bk rev HQ 95:58:89
Bremen Twp, batchelor Grove cem hist & rec WTC 26:1:1
Bremen, Batchelor Grove burial rec from the *Blue Island Sun Standard* c1930 WTC 26:1:44
Brethren Hist Lib, res tips LC 16:1:12
Brookfield, hist by BHBC, bk rev GH 49:4:207

ILLINOIS (continued)
  Burton Twp, WW1 draft reg 1918 MCI 13:4:103
  Carlinville, obits abstr from the *Free Democrat* 1862-1864 by McKenzie/Leonard, bk rev FRT 16:2:68 GH 49:6:189 IGS 27:2:115
  Carpentersville, news abstr from the *Fox Valley Mirror* 1932 MCI 13:1:5
  Champaign Co, delinquent tax list 1873 cont CCS 16:4:117
  Champaign Co, map 1873, name index cont CCS 16:4:112 17:1:3
  Champaign Co, marr lic 1903 CCS 16:4:122
  Champaign Co, news abstr from the *Herald* 1884 CCS 16:4:128 17:1:23
  Champaign-Urbana, city direct 1906 CCS 16:4:111
  Chicago, Czech Old Settlers Club anniv 1898, hist CHG 28:1:27
  Chicago, Municipal Court feeblemindedness rec 1915-1936, res guide CHG 27:2:57
  Chicago, news abstr from the *Tribune* 1877 CHG 27:3:89
  Chicago, oldest saloon, hist sketch CHG 27:2:55
  Chicago Press Club hist by William H Freeman, abstr 1894 CHG 27:3:97
  Civil War, 39th Reg, IL Vol Vet Infantry hist 1861-1865 by Clark, bk rev IG 31:2:58
  Civil War, mil units 1861-1865, microfiche rev ATE 30:1:2
  Cook Co, natu rec res tips LC 16:1:11
  Cook Co, news abstr c1909 NWS 15:3:21
  Cook Co, news abstr from the *Herald* c1909 NWS 15:4:29
  Cook Co, obits from the *Herald* 1909 NWS 15:5:37
  Cook Co, probate court rec 1871-1872 by McClure/Szucs, bk rev GH 49:4:206
  Crittenden Twp, St Mary cem rec CCS 17:1:14

ILLINOIS (continued)
  Cumberland Pres Ch, geneal abstr from by Eddlemon, bk rev APR 14:6:4
  Danville area, Mater & Salladay funeral home rec c1926-1927 IG 31:2:57
  Danville, coroner's rec 1920 IG 31:1:19
  Danville, Elk Lodge # 332, roster of dead honored in 1920 IG 31:1:14
  Danville, obits c1917-1934 IG 31:1:21
  Decatur, census 1870 by DGS, bk rev GH 49:4:207
  Decatur, deaths at state soldier home 1904 CI 31:4:133
  Decatur, Greenwood cem rec by DGS, bk rev IGS 27:2:114
  Decatur, hist sketch CI 31:4:132
  Decatur, letters at post ofc 1865 CI 31:3:81
  Decatur, Millikin Academy grads 1919 CI 31:2:71
  Decatur, news abstr from the *Review* 1891 CI 31:2:47
  Decatur, news abstr from the *Review* 1899 CI 31:2:43
  Decatur, obits 1937 CI 31:2:49
  Decatur, railroad hist 1854-1954 by Aldrich, bk rev CI 31:1:24
  Decatur, settler deaths from news 1900 CI 31:4:152
  Decatur, subscription rec from the *Daily Republican* 1878 CI 31:2:42
  Deerfield twp, census 1900 by Dolph, bk rev GH 49:3:204
  DeWitt Co, soldier reg 1898 DWC 21:2:59
  Division of property laws, guide RT 13:2:52
  Doctors (early), biog sketches CI 31:1:9
  Dunham, letters at post ofc 1854, roster of names MCI 13:4:106
  Du Page Co, hist cont OC 29:3:114
  Edwards Co, census 1865 by ECHS, bk rev GH 49:5:193 IGS 27:2:115
  Edwardsville Spectator news abstr 1819 MCS 15:1:6

ILLINOIS (continued)
Edwardsville, Eden Evang Ch German Sch student roster 1910-1911 MCS 15:4:153
Edwardsville, GR Evang Ch bapt reg 1880-1886 MCS 15:1:14 15:2:54
Edwardsville, Wheeler Sch hist MCS 15:2:92
Effingham, Centenary Meth Ch hist CRT 16:4:23
Effingham, Jewel Cook Book surname roster & abstr CRT 16:4:5
Effingham Co, orphan train hist CRT 16:4:21
Effingham Co, tax rec 1852 by ECGS, bk rev IGS 27:2:116
Egypt Sch Dist 98 reg 1905-1908 KIL 23:3:76
Egypt Sch Dist 98 reg 1917-1922 KIL 23:4:109
Fancy Creek Twp, cem rec by SCGS, bk rev GH 49:4:208
Franklin Co, will bk 1845-1879 by FCGS, bk rev GH 49:6:188
Franklin Grove, Emmert meeting house cem rec NFB 27:3:46
Freeport, Mennonite Ch hist MH 22:3:45
Freeport, Mennonite Ch MCC meat canning project hist MH 22:3:47
Freeport City, cem inscr by SCGS, bk rev HQ 95:57:84
Galesburg public sch, high sch alumni roster, early 20th cent KIL 23:4:92
Galesburg, high sch alumni 1861-1911 KIL 23:3:63
Galesburg, Pres Ch bapt rec 1837-1865 KIL 23:4:104
Gallatin Co, census 1870 by Gildehaus, bk rev GH 49:5:193
Gallatin Co, marr rec 1859-1870 by Gildehaus, bk rev GH 49:5:193
Gallatin Co, news abstr 1841-1843 by Shewmake, bk rev GH 49:4:207
Geneal Soc anc chart compendiun by GSSI, bk rev IGS 27:2:116
Geneal Soc of Southern IL anc charts vol 1 by GSSI, bk rev GH 49:5:192

ILLINOIS (continued)
GR Cath clergy in IL 1892, roster STC 18:1:46
Grundy Co, coal mining hist c1870-1880 by WGCGS, bk rev IGS 27:2:117
Harristown Dist, draft reg 1864 CI 31:1:2
Harvard, property title abstr c1921 MCI 13:1:23
Huntingdon Normal Sch roster 1877 NFB 27:4:68
Iroquois Co, marr rec 1851-1878 by ICGS, bk rev GH 49:5:193 IGS 27:2:115
Jasper Co, deaths 1850 CRT 16:4:30
Jersey Co, census 1850 by French, bk rev GH 49:4:207
Kankakee Co, births 1879 TAK 25:1:8
Kankakee Co, co court rec from the *Gazette* 1879 TAK 25:1:9
Kankakee Co, deaths 1879 TAK 25:1:8
Kankakee Co, geneal misc 1879 from the *Kankakee Gazette* TAK 25:2:6
Kankakee Co, hist TAK 25:2:20
Kankakee Co, hist bk abstr cont TAK 25:1:20
Kankakee Co, marr rec 1879 TAK 25:1:7
Kaskaskia, settler hist by Olles, bk rev TJ 7:2:77
Knox Co, birth index 1878-1916 KIL 23:2:35 23:3:71 23:4:87
Knox Co, ch list KIL 23:2:30
Knox Co, Civil War rec KIL 23:2:50
Knox Co, Civil War soldier biog sketches KIL 23:4:100
Knox Co, Egypt Sch dist 98 roster 1894-1899 KIL 23:2:46
Knox Co, State Hist Lib news holdings, list KIL 23:3:60
Lake Co, census 1900 by Dolph, bk rev GH 49:3:204
Local hist collect guide WTC 25:3:129
Logan Co, coal mine casualties 1925 CR 27:4:101

ILLINOIS (continued)
Macoa, Caplinger Funeral Home rec 1931-1950 by DGS, bk rev GH 49:4:208
Macon Co, census 1870 cont CI 31:1:11 31:4:122
Macon Co, census 1870 vol 1 by DGS, bk rev GH 49:4:207
Macon Co, census 1870 vol 2 by DGS, bk rev GH 49:4:207
Macon Co, lost towns, hist sketches CI 31:2:53
Macon Co, stillbirth rec 1877-1902 by DGS, bk rev GH 49:4:207 IGS 27:2:114
Madison Co, Civil War vet reunion roster 1893 MCS 15:2:75
Madison Co, deaths from news c1840-1880 MCS 15:2:79
Marengo, land title abstr index MCI 13:4:107
Marengo, letters at post ofc 1854, roster of names MCI 13:4:106
Marengo Republican news abstr 1935 MCI 13:4:99
Maroa, unclaimed letters at post ofc, roster 1930 CI 31:3:99
Marr rec from the *Primitive Christian* 1880 NFB 27:4:69
McDonough Co, Blandinsville-Glade City cem add by MCGS, bk rev GH 49:4:208
McDonough Co, cem rec by MCGS, bk rev HQ 95:55:92
McDonough Co, Larkin cem rec by Worthington, bk rev GH 49:4:208
McHenry Co, Geneal Soc anniv index 1981-1991, bk rev MCI 13:4:105
McHenry Co, mil census 1862-1863 MCI 13:1:11
McHenry Co, residents who died in Smith Co KS c1896 MCI 13:2:39
McHenry Co, settler biog sketches MCI 13:1:17 13:2:33 13:4:93
McHenry Co, SP-Am War vol roster 1898-1899 MCI 13:2:47

ILLINOIS (continued)
McLean Co, Civil War news abstr from the *Weekly Pantagraph* 1862 GL 29:4:146
McLean Co, early Af-Am residents from 1850 census GL 29:1:28
McLean Co, map index (19th cent) by LaBounty, bk rev HQ 95:59:89
McLean Co, marr from the *Weekly Pantagraph* 1862 GL 29:4:124
McLean Co, natu rec 1834-1900 GL 29:4:131
McLean Co, WW1 servicemen corresp abstr GL 29:4:134
Modern Woodmen of America Benefit Assessment No.5 1894 MCI 13:1:15
Momence Twp, Shrontz cem rec TAK 25:1:17
Morgan Co, coal mine casualties 1925 CR 27:4:101
Moro, St John's Evang & Reformed Ch cem inscr MCS 15:2:82
Moro, St John's Evang & Reformed Ch hist sketch 1948 MCS 15:2:81
Mt Gilead, burial rec 1880-1974 CI 31:3:104 31:4:142
Mt Olive, cem rec by MCGS, bk rev IGS 27:2:115
Mt Olive, cem rec vol 2 by MCGS, bk rev GH 49:5:193
Mt Zion, census 1870 CI 31:3:85
Normal, news abstr from the *Daily Pantagraph* 1896 GL 29:1:5
Normal, news abstr from the *Weekly Pantagraph* 1862 GL 29:1:13
Normal, news abstr re:jail break 1862 GL 29:1:18
Normal, Soldiers' Orphan Home rec 1869 GL 29:1:10
Oakley Dist, draft reg 1864 CI 31:1:2
Oakley, census 1870 CI 31:2:55
Oakley, Evang Luth Brethren ch hist 1946-1968 CI 31:2:63
Oakley, United Brethren in Christ ch hist 1884-1946 CI 31:2:63
Oakley, United Methodist Ch hist 1946-1968 CI 31:2:63

ILLINOIS (continued)
Obits 1880-1882 from the *Daily Pantagraph* GL 29:1:31 29:4:149
Peoria Co, census 1888, cont PR 22:3:1
Peoria Journal news abstr 1895 PR 23:2:44
Peoria Star news abstr 1902 PR 23:2:48
Peoria, Catholicism, hist 1673-1889 PR 22:3:21
Peoria, census 1888 cont PR 22:4:1
Peoria, centenarian roster c1890 PR 22:3:29
Peoria, Easton Mansion, hist PR 22:3:11
Peoria, Farrell Mansion, hist PR 22:3:13
Peoria, First Memorial Day, hist 1868 PR 22:4:38
Peoria, Ford Home, hist PR 22:3:15
Peoria, GAR Jubilee Anniv 1916, hist & member roster PR 22:4:29
Peoria, King Mansion hist PR 22:4:8
Peoria, McKinney Mansion hist PR 22:4:10
Peoria, Morrill Mansion hist PR 23:1:2
Peoria, Morron Mansion hist PR 23:1:4
Peoria, news abstr from misc news 1895 PR 23:1:32
Peoria, obit abstr of people buried in Springdale Cem PR 23:1:17 23:2:55
Peoria, Presbyterianism, hist PR 22:3:41
Peoria, public lib hist & committee roster 1892 PR 23:1:24
Peoria, public lib visitor reg 1994 PR 22:3:30
Peoria, Purple Mansion hist PR 23:1:6
Peoria, Robert Ingersoll Mansion hist PR 22:4:6
Peoria, Springdale Cem Assoc hist PR 22:3:36 22:4:17
Peoria, Van Buskirk home hist PR 23:1:8
Pioneer roster IGS 27:2:95

ILLINOIS (continued)
Pope Co, census rec 1818-1850 by Allen, bk rev GH 49:6:188
Pope Co, obits vol 2 by Foss/Lee, bk rev RCR 10:1:2210
Pope Co, pioneer cem inscr by McNerney/Meyer, bk rev KA 30:3:176 RCR 10:1:2211
Probate rec res guide IGS 27:2:104
Pulaski Co, Swan Lake sch dist commencement exercises 1908, rosters TS 37:3:105
Quincy, St Rose of Lima Ch hist 1892-1992 by Ullmen, bk rev TR 35:4:218
Res tips KTP 7:4:64 OC 31:1:11
Richmond Twp, WW1 draft reg 1918 MCI 13:4:103
Rock Island, AR Confederate dead reg FGC 95:28:26
Rock Island Co, vr from news 1876 IGS 27:2:108
Rockville, news abstr from the *Kankakee Gazette* 1879 TAK 25:1:11
Saline Co, probates vol 6 by Shewmake, bk rev GH 49:3:204
Sangamon Co, almshouse inmate rec 1888-1897 by SCGS, bk rev GH 49:4:208
Sangamon Co, coal mine casualties 1925 CR 27:4:101
Sangamon Co, guardians case files index 1825-1901, 1910-1911 by SCGS, bk rev GH 49:5:194
Sangamon Co, poor farm inmate rec 1897-1905 by SCGS, bk rev GH 49:5:194
Sangamon Co, Rev War, burials of heroes CR 27:2:32
Santa Anna Twp, census 1880 DWC 21:1:1 21:2:31
Scott Co, coal mine casualties 1925 CR 27:4:101
Senators, biog sketches CR 27:4:100
South Suburban Geneal Soc, 25 year anniv periodical index WTC 25:4:143

ILLINOIS (continued)
South Suburban Geneal Soc, mil rec index WTC 25:4:143
Springfield, settlers, biog data CR 27:4:105
St Clair Co, Co Farm Board rec 1875-1879 IGS 27:2:66
St Clair Co, probate index 1771-1964 STC 18:1:5 18:2:65 18:3:121 18:4:173
St Libory, St Liborius Cath cem rec add STC 18:2:114
Staunton, miner roster from news 1908 IGS 27:2:111
Stephenson Co, cem inscr by SCGS, bk rev GH 49:5:194 IGS 27:2:114
Sugar Creek Dist, pet roster 1830 CR 27:2:39
Union Co, hist 1818-1865 by Dexter, bk rev GH 49:4:208 RCR 10:1:2215
Vermilion Co, death rec abstr 1879 IG 31:1:8
Wabash Co, hist & geneal by WCHS, bk rev GH 49:6:188
Waldron, news abstr from the *Kankakee Gazette* 1879 TAK 25:1:13
Waukegan Twp, census 1900 by LCGS, bk rev GH 49:6:188
Will Co, Bohemian National cem rec by Skuban, bk rev IGS 27:2:117
Will Co, coal mining hist c1870-1880 by WGCGS, bk rev IGS 27:2:117
Will Co, pioneer necrology 1902-1907 by Bale, bk rev IGS 27:2:117
Wilmington, Old Cath cem rec by Bale, bk rev IGS 27:2:117
Winnebago Co, pioneers before 1841, hist by Rowland, bk rev HQ 95:58:89
Woodstock, letters at post ofc 1853, roster of names MCI 13:4:106
WW1, soldier news abstr & corresp 1918 MCI 13:4:103
INDIANA, Allen Co Public Lib, res tips MSG 15:3:166
Atlas of hist co boundaries by Long, bk rev SEE 36:153:53

INDIANA (continued)
Brown Co, settler biog sketches HJA 18:3:189
Clark Co, civil order bk 1824-1826 HJA 19:1:7
Columbia Twp, hist sites descr GCH 7:8:145
Crawford Co, hist cont HJA 18:3:191
Crawford Co, marr bk A 1818-1845 cont HJA 18:3:197 19:1:12
Crawford Co, probate bk 2 1829-1848 cont HJA 18:3:195
Dearborn Co, Gore area, early settlers by Mikesell, bk rev APR 14:6:4
Dearborn Co, marr bk 1833-1836 HJA 18:3:201 19:1:16
Dearborn Co, marr bk 1833-1836 brides index HJA 18:3:204
Dearborn Co, probate order bk 1826-1834 HJA 18:3:206
Eel River Twp, census 1870 HJA 19:1:30
Elkhart Co, marr lic 1889 MIS 27:4:77
Evansville, hist sketch GCH 8:7:132
Evansville, settler geneal by Kleymeyer, bk rev CTN 27:4:590
Evansville, settler geneal supp by Kleymeyer, bk rev CTN 27:4:590
Fountain Co, settler biog sketches IG 31:2:55
Francisco, coal mine demolition descr & hist GCH 8:6:102
Francisco, hist sketch GCH 8:7:127
Gibson Co, Barton Twp hist GCH 8:1:3
Gibson Co, Center Twp, resident roster c1901 GCH 8:5:97
Gibson Co, courthouse architecture descr GCH 8:9:171
Gibson Co, hist GCH 8:4:62 8:6:107
Gibson Co, Indian occupation, hist GCH 8:11:203
Gibson Co, Killpatrick cem rec GCH 8:1:8
Gibson Co, marr 1813-1850 GCH 8:2:23
Gibson Co, McGregor cem rec GCH 8:1:7

INDIANA (continued)
Gibson Co, Morris cem rec GCH 8:1:6
Gibson Co, news abstr from the *Democrat-Clarion* 1847 GCH 8:2:35
Gibson Co, Rev War soldier & patriot burials, roster GCH 8:2:33
Gibson Co, Salem United Meth Ch hist GCH 8:1:14
Gibson Co, St Paul's United Ch of Christ hist GCH 8:1:11
Gibson Co, Washington Twp, hist sketch GCH 8:5:82
Gibson Co, White River Twp, resident roster c1901 GCH 8:5:96
Gibson Co, will & probate rec c1815 GCH 8:1:15
Gore area (Dearborn Co), settler hist 1803-1820 by Mikesell, bk rev GEJ 14:3:32 GH 49:6:189
GR language press bibl by Ziegler, bk rev TPI 20:3:162
Hamilton Twp, land rec, 19th cent HJA 19:1:35
Hancock Co, tombstone inscr 1833-1933 by Baker, bk rev TTL 24:1:23
Harrison Co, deed bk A 1809-1817 cont HJA 18:3:210
Harrison Co, probate rec 1817-1829 HJA 18:3:212
Hazleton, Thorn cem rec GCH 8:4:73
Henry Co, atlas 1857, repr, bk rev GH 49:4:208
Hoosier nickname, origins & hist AW 21:3:86
Indianapolis, Athenaeum Turners Collect index by McDougal, bk rev TPI 21:1:49
Jackson Co, cem rec, unmarked burials GEJ 14:3:27
Jackson Co, Cooperative Christian Missionary Assoc roster 1904 GEJ 14:4:45
Jackson Co, delinquent tax list 1885 GEJ 14:3:33 14:4:42
Jackson Co, marr rec 1854 GEJ 14:3:28 14:4:39

INDIANA (continued)
Jackson Co, obits 1854-1885 by Johnson, bk rev GH 49:3:204 GSM 12:2:47 LHS 95:2:8 TSG 3:2:9
Jackson Co, obits 1854-1885 by Johnson, bk rev TSG 3:2:9
Jackson Co, probate court fee bk 2 index cont GEJ 14:3:29 14:4:40
Jefferson Co, news abstr from the *Indiana Republican* 1817-1818 HJA 19:1:47
Jefferson Co, order bk 1810-1819 HJA 19:1:40
Kosciusko Co, location & description of Brethren cem NFB 27:2:26
Lake Co, natu rec 1854-1932 by LMNIGS, bk rev TB 22:1:12
Lake Co, sch enumerations 1890 & 1896, bk rev TB 22:1:13
Lawrence Co, probates 1818-1835 HJA 18:3:214 19:1:51
Lexington, dog reg 1847 LHS 95:2:9
Lexington, news abstr from the *Chronicle* 1880 cont TSG 3:3:2
Liverpool, Ft Washington hist GCH 8:7:122
Marion College students & staff 1925 SYH 3:3:22
Martin Co, marr bk 1 1846-1859 HJA 18:3:221 19:1:56
Martin Co, marr bk 1 1846-1859 brides index HJA 18:3:225
Martin Co, probate rec A 1821-1838 HJA 18:3:218
Millersburg, hist sketch GCH 8:7:130
Mishawaka, news abstr from the *Enterprise* 1892 SBA 20:1:5
Monroe Co, probate order bk 1818-1831 HJA 19:1:64
Monroe Co, will rec 1836-1851 HJA 18:3:227 19:1:60
Morgan Co, census 1830 cont HJA 18:3:231 19:1:68
National Road, hist GCH 7:12:222
Northern Wabash Co, Brethren cem list NFB 27:3:45
Oakland City, hist dist descr GCH 7:8:145

INDIANA (continued)

Oakland City, hist sketch GCH 8:7:127
Orange Co, African Am hist by Robbins, bk rev SGS 44:2:86
Orange Co, marr bk 1826-1849 HJA 19:1:79
Orange Co, probate order bk 1829-1842 HJA 19:1:73
Oswego & CA Mining & Operating Company 1849, hist by Lamoree, bk rev GH 49:4:209
Owen Co, hist by OCHGS, bk rev GH 49:5:194
Owensville, hist district descr GCH 7:8:142
Patoka, Milburn cem rec GCH 8:4:71
Patoka, pioneer roster 1901 GCH 8:4:77
Porter Co, natu rec index 1849-1955 by LMNIGS, bk rev TB 22:1:13
Porter Twp, sch rec 1895-1920 by Crook et al, bk rev TB 22:1:13
Posey Co, DAR Rev War anc biog sketches by Roberts, bk rev GH 49:5:195
Putnam Co, biog & hist rec, repr 1887, bk rev HH 30:4:196
Railroad hist GCH 7:8:152
Railway stops, hist GCH 8:7:135
Randolph Co, hist 1818-1990 by RCHS, bk rev GH 49:4:209
Rev War soldier & patriot burials by O'Byrne, bk rev GH 49:5:194
Salt Creek Twp, census 1860 HJA 19:1:21
Scott Co, deaths 1886-1950 TSG 95:2:2
Scott Co, news abstr c1880 TSG 3:4:3
Scott Co, news abstr from the *Chronicle* c1880 TSG 3:2:2
Soc of IN Pioneers, yearbk, bk rev TS 37:3:94
South Bend, Cedar Grove cem rec by Szymarek, bk rev GEJ 14:3:32
St Joseph Co, court rec c1918-1936 SBA 20:8:10

INDIANA (continued)

St Joseph Co, emig to CA from *South Bend Register* news 1850 SBA 20:8:15
St Joseph Co, firearms permits, roster SBA 20:8:12
St Joseph Co, hospital rec 1850-1920 SBA 20:8:3
St Joseph Co, insanity rec c1900-1915 SBA 20:2:11
St Joseph Co, marr abstr 1882 cont SBA 20:2:4 20:3:9 20:4:2
St Joseph Co, probate & marr rec through 1920, res tips SBA 20:4:15
St Joseph Co, residents in IN hospitals 1850-1920 SBA 20:4:10
St Joseph Co, sch officials & teachers 1919-1920 SBA 20:3:2
St Joseph Co, teacher & school official roster 1920-1921 SBA 20:4:13 20:5:10
St Joseph Co, vr from news c1900-1910 SBA 20:2:9
St Joseph Co, Walkerton, vr 1904-1910 SBA 20:5:7
State hospitals, patient index to 1920 SBA 20:5:3
Switzerland Co, marr bk A 1829-1837 HJA 18:3:233
Tippecanoe Co, alien reg & natu rec 1826-1906 by McCoy, bk rev GH 49:3:205
Union Co, land entry bk by Dean, bk rev TR 35:1:51
Valparaiso, Porter Co Public Lib, descr of avail svcs HQ 95:57:70
Walkerton, vr from news c1900-1915 SBA 20:3:3 20:4:7 20:1:6
Warren Co, Armstrong Chapel hist IG 31:1:5
Washington, fort 1812, hist GCH 8:7:122
Wayne Co, census 1910 by Dean, bk rev TR 35:1:51
Wayne Co, census 1910, index by Dean, bk rev GH 49:3:205
Wayne Co, stock marks 1823-1835 AMG 10:2/3:57

INDIANA (continued)
Westfield Quaker cem rec cont QY 21:4:1
White River Twp, hist, GCH 8:4:62
White River, Cunnigham cem rec GCH 8:4:72
White River, Old Hazleton cem rec GCH 8:4:72
Women journalists, hist 1876-1976 GCH 7:8:149
WW1, draft cards, use of TSC 6:2:9

INGERSOL, George Goldthwait fl822, VT, rec of bapt, marr & burials he performed, repr, bk rev FRT 16:3:110

Robert, IL, hist of his home PR 22:4:6

Thomas fl820, w Elizabeth Dewey, w Mercy Smith, w Sarah Whiting, MA, biog & hist BG 16:3:75

INGHAM, Jonathan see Elizabeth CHALKER

INGLE, William b1805, w Sally Barry, w Lavina Hodges, w Margaret O'Neal, AL, geneal & fam hist MCA 14:1:18

INGLISH, Mathew see Mathew ENGLISH

INGRAM, John, VA, MO, KY, fam hist by Ingram, bk rev TJ 7:2:75

INMAN, Sophia see Peter BARNES

INSALL, Caroline fl923, TX, news abstr KTP 4:3:34 4:4:49

IOWA, Blairsburg Twp, tax list 1873 HHH 16:3:3
Buffalo, Rose Hill & St Peters cem rec ISC 19:4:61
Burlington, natu rec 1853-1887 HH 30:4:200
Census 1925, misc rec ISC 19:1:9
Centenarians 1987, biog sketches HH 30:4:207
Chickasaw Co, census 1860 surname roster QN 12:4:26
Clinton Co, draft hist & rosters 1864 GWD 14:2:3
Davenport, bus owner roster 1858 ISC 19:4:68

IOWA (continued)
Davenport, shinplaster pledge roster 1858 ISC 19:4:67
Des Moines, natu rec abstr HH 30:4:206
Geneal Soc direct IAN 16:1:9
GR settler geneal dict by Palen, bk rev GH 49:3:205 LL 31:1:10 MGS 13:1:7
Hamilton Co, voter roster abstr 1900 HHH 16:4:8
Keokuk, natu rec 1853-1887 HH 30:4:200
Le Claire, Glendale cem, war vet burials as of 1973 ISC 19:2:24
National Guard, Battery B roster, c1916 ISC 19:2:22
New Hampton, news marr rec index 1897 QN 12:3:19
New Hampton, news marr rec index 1898 QN 12:4:27
Pioneers, biog sketches HH 30:4:211
Poweshiek Co, marr bk B c1870-1871 cont PCI 17:3:2 18:4:9
Poweshiek Co, poor farm roster 1902 PCI 17:3:6
Poweshiek Co, settler biog sketches PCI 19:2:3
Residents relocated to MN (Kandiyohi Co) 1915 HH 30:4:221
Scott Co, Buffalo, Rose Hill & St Petersburg cem inscr ISC 19:1:1
Scott Co, Davenport, pioneers' reunion 1870 ISC 19:1:14
Scott Co, Davenport, unclaimed letters at post ofc 1871 ISC 19:1:7
Scott Co, Summit Ch member roster, Civil War to WW2 ISC 19:2:21
SP-Am War deaths, Adjutant Generals' report 1900 HH 30:4:190
SP-Am War, res bibl HH 30:4:195
Statewide indexes for geneal res, tips IAN 16:1:3
Tama Co, census 1885 index by Samuelsen, bk rev GH 49:5:195
Wayne Co, marr from the *Ottawa Courier* 1899 HH 30:4:223

IOWA (continued)
Webster City, news abstr from the *Tribune* 1896 cont HHH 16:3:7 16:4:4
West Union, news abstr 1895 by Hoover, bk rev GH 49:4:209
WW1, draft cards, use of TSC 6:2:9

IRESON, Alice see Edward IRESON
Edward bc1603, w Elizabeth, w Alice, EN, MA, geneal TEG 15:1:10
Elizabeth see Edward IRESON
James C b1823, w Eleanor Lynch, TN, fam hist sketch BWG 24:1:51

IRICK, KY, fam hist by Clark, bk rev PCH 1:1:36

IRISH GENEALOGY, Adoption res tips IS 16:1:10
Am, Irish hist by O'Brien, bk rev GH 49:5:182
Beginner's guide to res by Davis, bk rev SGB 26:2:iv
Belfast, freeholder roster 1784 IFL 5:8:3
Birth, marr & death civil rec, res tips IFL 6:1:1
Census substitutes, 18th cent, res tips IFL 5:10:13
Ch rec res guide by Ryan, bk rev MAG 8:2:3
Clan profiles, cont IFL 5:10:20
Clan system, brief descr IFL 5:9:27
CN, IR imm, landlords & tenants, 19th cent hist by Wilson, bk rev FAM 34:3:176
Co & grand jury rec, res tips IFL 5:9:2
Co Cork, Casey Collect, guide IS 16:3:90
Co Cork, census rec 1851 by Masterson, bk rev GH 49:5:184 GN 13:2:95 IS 16:2:45
Co Cork, hist IS 16:3:61
Co Donegal, ch reg list PGB 27:2:34
Co Kerry, biog hist by IR Geneal Foundation, bk rev RAG 16:2:18
Co Kerry, biog of misc early fam by O'Laughlin, bk rev GH 49:4:201
Co Kerry, gardens, hist IS 16:2:39
Co Kerry, hist IS 16:2:33

IRISH GENEALOGY (continued)
Co Tipperary, magistrate roster 1804-1839 TTH 16:4:109
Common words & their translations, brief glossary KTP 8:1:16
Computer resource guide IS 16:3:84
Cork, Huguenot hist 1685-1850 by St Leger, bk rev GN 13:3:140
Drinks, hist by Booth, bk rev IFL 6:1:5
Dublin area, subscribers to an IR bk 1819, roster SGS 45:1:23
Dublin, Geneal Ofc consolidated index vol 1 by McAnnis, bk rev GH 49:5:184
Emig hist 1735-1743 by McDonnell, bk rev PGB 27:4:65
English rebellions, hist, repr 1802, bk rev TR 35:3:166
Estate rec, res guide CTA 37:4:173
Fam Hist Lib Cat guide by Hjelm, bk rev GSC 17:4:6
Famine 1850 & imm, hist ARH 33:4:151
Famine imm anc, res tips STS 35:4:23
Famine years c1845-1851, hist sketch SGS 45:1:28
Gaelic Heraldry hist HER 3:3:4
Geneal Collections, res guide CTA 37:4:164
Geneal Ofc Consultancy Svc on Anc Tracing, addresses AB 23:4:8
High Kingship of IR, hist ASO 25:1:8
Hist & geneal soc address list BGN 16:2:22
Hist sketch GRI 15:3:106
IFHF member centers, res aid PGB 26:10:214
IR Archives fam data by IGF, bk rev RAG 16:4:20
IR Geneal Database disks, software rev IS 16:2:51
IR Heritage Assoc, descr TAC 6:3:27
Kingdom of Desmond hist HER 3:3:4
Kingdom of Munster, hist essays by Ellis, bk rev GH 49:3:197 RAG 16:1:21
Lib of Congress, Natl Lib of Dublin mss films, res tips TTH 16:4:109

IRISH GENEALOGY (continued)
Limerick, co hist IS 16:1:1
Lyon conjunctural tree showing ST & IR clans cont IFL 6:1:22
MA, Boston, imm ads for missing friends in the Boston Pilot vol 3 by Harris/O'Keefe, bk rev AG 70:1:61 NEH 12:2/3:49
MA, deaths 1859-1860 NEH 12:2/3:56
Norse heritage links, pedigree chart IFL 5:10:22
NY, Flatbush, Cem of the Holy Cross, IR cem rec by Silinonte, bk rev SGS 44:3:141
NY, res guide IS 16:2:40
Parish reg, guidebk by IFHS, bk rev RAG 16:1:18
Pass lists 1803-1806 by Mitchell, bk rev GH 49:5:183 GN 13:2:94 HQ 95:57:83 KA 31:1:44 NGS 83:3:227 NYR 126:3:218 SCM 23:1:59
Pass lists 1811-1816 by Hackett/Early, bk rev GH 49:5:183
Pass lists 1847-1871 by Mitchell, bk rev GN 13:2:94
Place name masterbk & atlas by O'Laughlin, bk rev FRT 16:3:108 GH 49:5:183 RAG 16:2:28 SCS 32:3:64
Poor Law rec, res tips IFL 5:9:26
Protestation returns 1641-1642 by Gibson/Dell, bk rev GEN 20:4:25 SGB 26:4:iv
Quakers in PA, imm hist 1682-1750 by Myers, bk rev IS 16:1:11
Rathkeale, Castle Matrix hist sketch HQ 95:55:41
Rebellion of 1798, hist, repr c1800, bk rev FAM 34:4:247 NAL 11:4:135
Registrar general of Shipping & Seamen rec 1786-1854 IFL 5:8:15
Res guide FRT 16:3:93
Res guide by Baxter, bk rev APG 10:4:128 ARH 33:1:34 GFP 44:3:139 IS 16:3:78
Res guide by Begley, bk rev NTT 15:1/2:2

IRISH GENEALOGY (continued)
Res guide for North Americans by Betit/Radford, bk rev GEN 20:2:22 HQ 95:58:87 IS 16:3:80 KVH 20:1&2:7 SGB 26:2:iii
Res resource address list BT 27:4:69
Res sites in IR FTR :182:3
Res tips CC 17:2:13 GWS 95:43:4
Septs, affiliations & origins IFL 6:1:18
Sligo, Markree Castle, hist sketch IFL 6:1:10
South Leitrim, hist & rec by Farrell, bk rev GN 13:2:93
Surname atlas by Osborne, bk rev HQ 95:58:87 IS 16:3:81
Surname origin guide by O'Laughlin, bk rev AMG 10:2/3:7 APG 10:3:92 GSC 17:3:9 SCS 32:2:39
Surnames, variations & synonyms, guide repr 1901, bk rev RT 13:4:102
Tartan guide by Smith, bk rev IS 16:3:80 GN 13:2:90 GSC 17:4:5 RL 30:3:5 SGS 45:1:30
Tiree, emig to CN, res tips GWS 95:43:16
Tuam, Roman Cath marr 1820-1829 by Murphy/Reilly, bk rev CTN 27:4:592 LRT 14:2:556
Will index, pre-1922 by Clare, bk rev OK 40:2:46
IRVIN, Ann see James CARLILE
Charles m1877, w Minnie Kuykendall, NY, Bible rec UG 24:1:11
ISKENIUS, Gorg Thomas fl726, GR, NY, fam corresp by Sypher, bk rev MGS 13:1:10
ISLAUB, Johann Friedrich b1809, GR, fam hist by McClenathen, bk rev MSG 15:1:57
ITALIAN GENEALOGY, 20th cent geneal res tips HQ 95:60:42
Civil, ecclesiastical, & other rec, res guide by Cole, bk rev AGM 27:3/4:64 WPG 22:1:44
Pass arrival lists in Am vol 5 (New York 1890-1891) by Glazier/Filby, bk rev GH 49:6:179

ITALIAN GENEALOGY (continued)
Professional geneal res guide APG 10:1:9
Res guide by Cole, bk rev DM 59:1:45 HQ 95:59:87 NYR 126:4:281 RAG 16:4:20 RCP 17:3:82 SKC 11:1:5 TR 35:3:166
Res guide for Americans by Colletta, bk rev CHG 28:1:34
Res tips KTP 7:4:69 TSL 20:1:5
Roman Forum, Arch of Augustus, hist ASO 25:1:2
Sicily, Alia, births, marr & deaths 1851-1861 by Robichaux, bk rev KSL 19:2:74

ITZ, Karoline b1834, h Heinrich Arhelger, h Christian Reeh, TX, biog sketch KTP 7:1:10

JACK, John bc1788, w Elizabeth Garrett, TX, TN, fam rec LOB 14:1:1

JACKSON, Frank m1944, w Ela Walker, VA, Bible rec NPW 13:11:59
Isabella see Daniel IBBOTSON
Olive S see Steadman S JACKSON
Richard Roland m1854, w Martha Elizabeth Smith, IN, Bible rec HJA 19:1:1
Steadman S f1907, w Olive S, FL, biog sketch PCQ 8:1:1
Thomas J, biog by Farwell, bk rev REG 92:4:423
Thomas Jonathan (Stonewall) b1824, biog sketch, PCQ 2:3:2 2:4:2

JACOBS, Belitje see Theunis Thomaszen QUICK

JACOBUS, Donald Lines b1887, CT, anc NEH 12:1:26

JACQUES, Doreen Mary see Walter HARNESS
FR, OH, geneal by English, bk rev GH 49:4:226

JAMES, Annie Laura see Sigismund ENGELKING
Jesse, MO, news abstr re:his burial 1902 KCG 36:1:51

JAMES (continued)
William dc1730, w Rebecca Easton, RI, geneal NER 149:594:122

JAMESON, Sally see Jefferson F JONES

JANECK, L O f1894, WA, acc bk YV 27:1:15

JANS, Anneke, NY, fam feud hist NYR 126:2:105

JARECKA, Marianna see Wojciech GRZECHOWIAK

JARVIS, Margaret see Patrich Floyd JARVIS
Patrich Floyd d1852, w Margaret, AL, geneal LL 30:3:79

JAY, John b1789, w Sarah Van Brugh, NJ, fam hist DAR 129:2:126

JAYNE, William m1675, w Anna Biggs, NY, fam hist corr OCG 25:1:10

JEFFERIES, Charity, h John Cope, PA?, TX?, anc STS 35:3:62

JEFFERIS, Robert see Robert JEFFERS

JEFFERS, Robert fc1681, w Jane Chandler, PA, fam hist STS 35:2:53

JEFFERSON, Thomas b1743, VA, biog of his nephews ARN 8:1:8

JEFFRIES, Mahala E see Joseph Forbes GEORGE

JENKINS, Charles f1759, NC, fam hist by Dozier, bk rev NCJ 21:1:81
George W f1925, GA, FL, biog PCQ 7:1:1
Hannah f1995, OR, fam hist TFG 8:1:3
Jo f1858, IN, news abstr TSG 3:4:6
John bc1609, w Mary Wallen Ewer, EN, MA, geneal NER 149:596:339
John d1681, NC, fam hist by Dozier, bk rev NCJ 21:1:81
Sally Ann see William CORBIN

JENKS, Mary b1789, MA, Bible rec BG 16:3:99

JENNINGS, Carlton W, w Violet Leavitt, fam hist by Zeavin, bk rev FRT 16:2:68
Clark W f1995, MO, anc by Jennings, bk rev NCJ 21:2:189

JENNINGS (continued)
Fam hist by Zeavin, bk rev TJ 7:2:73
JENSEN, Anton f1873, w Mary Kaja Halverson, NO, TX, fam hist AGS 36:2:68
Cornelius B b1814, w Mercedes Alvarado, CA, biog sketch VQS 32:1:9
Hans f1873, w Julia, NO, TX, fam hist AGS 36:2:68
Julia see Hans JENSEN
JESS, Ann see Caleb SHREVE
JEWISH GENEALOGY, African Am & Jewish relations, res resource guide JL 8:1/2:162
Caribbean, hist & geneal resources avail CGJ 3:3:4 3:4:14
Communal hist, res tips TFT 6:2:9B
GR, Jewish Archival holdings, inv project descr JL 8:1/2:17
Israel, reference works 1992-1993, bibl JL 8:1/2:166
Israel, Yeshivat Har Etzion Lib, guide JL 8:1/2:132
Lib of Congress classification changes for Jewish Studies, res guide JL 8:1/2:73
Lib of Congress classification changes for Judaica, res guide JL 8:1/2:68
Memoirs, misc, bk rev HQ 95:57:54
MT, Jewish communities, biog hist by Coleman, bk rev GH 49:4:213
Names, Romanized, hist & theory JL 8:1/2:45
NH, Manchester, Jewish community hist HNH 50:3/4:147
NY, Albany area, synagogue vr res guide HQ 95:59:9
PO Judaica, bibl by Pilarczyk, bk rev JL 8:1/2:12
PO, Jewish Hist Inst, descr LLI 7:4:13
Res guide by Rottenberg, bk rev GFP 45:2:89 TS 37:4:147
Res guide, repr 1977, bk rev SGS 45:1:37
Res tips HQ 95:60:47
RLIN Hebraica rec, modifications, descr JL 8:1/2:25

JEWISH GENEALOGY (continued)
RU, Minsk, res tips HQ 95:58:49
RU, Moscow, Baron Guenzburg Collect of Hebrew mss, descr JL 8:1/2:142
Shetl finder, gazetteer by Cohen, bk rev MN 26:3:137
SP & Portuguese Jewry, bibl by Singerman, bk rev JL 8:1/2:12
Telephone bks & geneal, res tips FRT 17:1:6
Ukraine, anc towns, res tips HQ 95:55:56
JININGS, Charles Lawson, MD, NC, geneal by Weber, bk rev TJ 7:2:76
JOB, Andrew b1620, w Elizabeth, WE, PA, geneal BWG 24:2:149
Elizabeth see Andrew JOB
JOHANSEN, Ferd J b1876, w Levina May Bolin, NE, biog sketch NW 18:1:21
JOHN OF GAUNT, EN, fam hist by Stuart, bk rev KA 31:2:47
JOHNS, Susan Docia see Abram TRIGG
JOHNSON, Charles Edwin b1824, w Susan Bates, RI, Bible rec RIR 21:2:49
Charles Glen b1948, w Eleanor Ann Hinton, NM, TX, anc by Johnson, bk rev GH 49:6:209
Charles Wendell f1945, w Mary Allen Mathis, NM, fam hist by Johnson, bk rev GH 49:6:209
Elizabeth b1841, aka Brita Lisa Andersdotter, h Erland Persson, h Nils Johan Jonsson, SN, KS, fam hist KK 33:2:24
Gloria Roupe, h Thurman, KS, recoll KCG 36:2:86
Henry b1800, w Martha Wood, IL, Bible rec OZ 17:3:103
Henry F C f1855, w Sidney Brown, w Delilah Hall, KY, IN, TX, biog & corresp DG 41:1:71
Keziah see John BREWER
Maggie see Leven T BATES

JOHNSON (continued)
Marie Christy see Richard Simrall HAWES
Martha Ann see Washington MOORE
Matilda see John W BAILEY
Nilla see August LARSON
Samuel f1857, KY, corresp PCH 1:4:20
Sarah see Christopher LANCE
Thurman see Gloria Roupe JOHNSON
Tilmon/Tillman b1804, NC, AR, news abstr ARH 33:2:56
William b1732, w Elizabeth Ellis, WE, NC, geneal FC 13:3:2
William Hampton b1843, GA, FL, biog PCQ 4:2:4

JOHNSTON, C S f1916, AL, corresp NTT 14:4:132
William m1835, w Ann Mary Bercaw, w Mary Ann Brown, KS, Bible rec TOP 25:4:134

JOINER, Fam hist by Griner, bk rev PR 22:4:48
see also JOYNER

JONES, Annie f1865, PA, biog sketch LM 36:4:232
Charles K m1867, w Lydia E Dakin, OH, Bible rec TR 35:4:212
Daniella see Joseph WHEELER
Elizabeth see Isaac H DICKEN
Elizabeth see Jesse JONES
Emmett f1892, TX, corresp KTP 2:2:14
Jefferson F b1817, w Sally Jameson, KY, MO, biog by Jones, bk rev EWA 32:3:135
Jesse d1845, w Elizabeth, NC, fam rec LOB 16:1:22
Joshua b1771, WE, AL, GA, geneal by Billingsley, bk rev GH 49:4:226
LA, fam hist by Wise, bk rev GH 49:5:234
Lewis b1603, w Anna Stone, MA, geneal by Harrison, bk rev GH 49:6:209 SGS 45:1:35 SLV 12:3:9
Mary Ann Elizabeth see John Henry TAYLOR

JONES (continued)
Rees b1800, w Elizabeth Hunt Strode, MI, Bible rec KVH 19:9:103
Samuel J b1838, w Mary B Hayes, GA, Bible rec OTC 4:3:19
Shandy Wesley bc1816, w Evalina Love, AL, geneal by Pinkard/Clark, bk rev TJ 7:2:74

JONSSON, Martein b1855, w Bertha Sigertson, Iceland, WA, biog HQ 95:57:51
Nils Johan see Elizabeth JOHNSON

JOOSTEN, Jan fc1662, HO, NY, fam hist sketch YV 27:1:19

JORDAN, Gadsia Lillian see James Frank JORDAN
James Frank b1888, w Gadsia Lillian, AL, Bible rec PT 37:3/4:70
Margaret see Samuel LAMB
Mary Bell see Emery LASSETER
Samuel b1572, w Cecily Bailey, VA, fam hist ARH 33:1:7
Samuel d1623, VA, hist sketch of his plantation GRI 15:5:127

JOSLIN, Mary m1743, h Francis Hopkins, RI, fam hist by Phillips, bk rev GH 49:6:206

JOURDAIN, Nicolas b1742, CN, biog sketch ACG 21:4:166

JOWERS, Nancy see Gillum KING

JOY, Elizabeth see John POUND

JOYNER, Charlotte f1835, FL, govt doc re:payment for soldier care TAC 6:2:19
Thomas b1619, EN, VA, NC, fam hist by Griner, bk rev CAL 14:2:28 NCJ 21:3:305

JOYNES, Hely Bagnell b1858, w Margaret Lickiss, VA, fam rec AMG 9:6:44

JUKL, Frances see Frank DVORAK

JUNE, Caroline L see Charles E STUDWELL

JUNEAU, Narcisse f1862, w Madeline Yott, KS, fam hist by Hrenchir, bk rev TOP 25:2:46

JUNEAU (continued)
Solomon, w Josette Vieux, WI, KS, fam hist by Hrenchir, bk rev TOP 25:2:46

JUNOD, Paul Aime b1846, w Bertha Bonjour, SW, KS, biog sketch NCG 2:3:6

JUSTICE, Fam hist by Parris, bk rev SQ 5:4:43
Harriet M see Levi G HOOVER

JUSTIS, Fam hist by Parris, bk rev SQ 5:4:43
John b1741, fam hist by Parris, bk rev SQ 5:4:43

JUSTUS, Fam hist by Parris, bk rev SQ 5:4:43

KABELMACHER, Heinrich bc1858, TX, fam cem rec KTP 3:4:51 4:1:12

KAEMPFER, Fam hist by Byler, bk rev TPI 21:1:48

KAISER, Alexander, w Wilhelmina Bohnert, TX, biog sketch KTP 4:3:40
Mary Ann see Mary Ann CAUSER

KALLAM, Christopher Columbus b1848, w Sarah Matilda Blackburn, NC, fam hist by Kallam, bk rev NCJ 21:2:189

KAMM, Pearl Griggs, New England, anc by Jones, bk rev NEC 3:2:22

KANE, Henry B b1855, IL, biog sketch CR 27:4:92

KANSAS, Anderson Co, will bk index 1869-1919 by Samuelsen, bk rev GH 49:5:195
Atchison Co, hist & biog rec index 1900 by Ostertag, bk rev GH 49:3:206
Barton Co, birth reg 1892 BCS 15:2:5 15:3:1 15:4:1
Barton Co, Civil War vet biog sketches BCS 15:1:10 15:2:10
Barton Co, vr abstr from the *Barton Beacon* 1900-1901 cont BCS 15:1:1 15:2:1
Beattie, news abstr from the *Star* 1885 TOP 25:2:65
Beloit, hist TS 37:4:131

KANSAS (continued)
Big Creek Twp, commissioners 1859 KCG 36:2:75
Biog Index by Smith, bk rev GH 49:3:206
Bourbon Co, will bk index 1867-1925 by Samuelsen, bk rev GH 49:5:195
Brown Co, census 1860 by Ostertag, bk rev GH 49:6:189
Brown Co, hist & biog rec index 1900 by Ostertag, bk rev GH 49:3:206
Brown Co, settler roster 1855 TOP 25:1:12
CA obits of KS natives 1988-1989 cont TOP 25:2:71 25:4:157
Camp Doniphan, Company G 3rd KS Infantry Reg roster 1917 WRB 18:1:28
Cass Co, pet for new roads 1861 KCG 36:2:75
Chautauqua Co, marr & death rec 1894-1895 MGR 29:4:103
Chautauqua Co, news abstr from the *Sedan Times Journal* 1885 TOP 25:1:19 25:2:58 25:4:139
Cimarron, death rec 1931-1936 TS 37:3:100
Civil War & border w/MO, hist AW 22:1:4
Civil War, Vol Reg enlistment doc 1861-1865, index cont JCG 23:4:142
Clay Co, births 1885-1887 KK 33:2:27 33:4:64
Clay Co, pet 1878, roster KCG 36:2:69
Clear Creek, news abstr 1900 cont NCG 2:4:7
Corning, deaths from the *Gazette* 1899 TOP 25:1:26
Death rec cont TS 37:4:141
Dickinson Co, Chapman's Creek settler hist sketch TC 14:3:61
Dickinson Co, Elmo & Banner twp settler roster 1800s TC 14:1:11
Dodge City, Dunsford Funeral Home rec 1926-1935 TS 37:3:89 37:4:133
Doniphan Co, hist & biog rec index 1900 by Ostertag, bk rev GH 49:3:206

KANSAS (continued)
Doniphan Co, will bk index 1867-1925 by Samuelsen, bk rev GH 49:5:195
Douglas Co, fam hist 1991-1992 vol 1 by DCKGS, bk rev GH 49:6:190
El Dorado, sch teacher roster 1873-1874 MGR 29:4:100
Ellsworth Co, pet list 1876 TC 14:1:7
Elm Creek Twp, sch dist 7 teacher list 1905-1906 TC 14:3:48
Enlistment paper index 1861-1865 JCG 23:2:64
Eureka, news abstr from the *Herald* re:distribution of orphans TOP 25:4:143
Fort Osage, hist sketch KCG 36:2:94
Franklin Co, hist by FCGS, bk rev TS 37:4:146
Geary Co, will bk index 1898-1923 by Samuelsen, bk rev GH 49:5:196
Golden census guide by Pierce, bk rev TS 37:3:93
Great Bend, city business list 1903 BCS 15:1:8
Great Bend, Civil war vets, autobiog sketches BCS 15:3:10 15:4:9
Great Bend, news abstr from the *Tribune* re:saloons BCS 15:4:11
Grenola Elk Co, Green Lawn cem rec cont TOP 25:1:15 25:2:56
Heritage server, Internet res tips KR 20:4:85
Hutchinson, obits from the *News* 1994 (of persons age 97 & over) TS 37:3:107
Ionia, hist WRB 18:1:11
Iuka cem rec CN 4:3:46
Jamestown, high sch alumni roster 1896-1980 OC 31:1:20
Jewell Center, agricultural meeting roster 1874 WRB 17:4:12
Johnson Co, news abstr from the *Olathe Mirror* 1861 JCG 23:2:70
Johnson Co, news in KS State Hist Soc Archives, descr of holdings JCG 22:1:30
Johnson Co, will bk 5 c1905-1908 cont JCG 22:1:7 23:2:45 23:4:122

KANSAS (continued)
Kansas City, Blossom House hist 1882-1915 KCG 36:2:95
Kansas City, Diamond Building & 9th St hist KCG 36:2:70
Kechi, Kechi Sch rec 1894 MGR 30:3:90
Kingman Co, vr from the *Kingman Mercury* 1878-1880 KR 21:1:15
Ladies of the Grand Army of the Republic roster KR 21:1:21
Lane Co, hist to 1884 by Stanley, bk rev TR 35:1:55
Lawrence, hist to 1865, repr 1895, bk rev TOP 25:1:4
Leavenworth Co, alien reg 1917 KR 20:4:97 21:1:5
Legislative Direct 1933 WRB 18:1:30
Linn Co, marr rec 1855-1884 by Samuelsen, bk rev GH 49:4:209
Manhattan, Ch of Christ hist 1923-1973 by Keen, bk rev KK 33:2:38
Manhattan, trolley line hist KK 33:4:74
Marshall Co, news abstr from early papers 1885 TOP 25:2:61
Marshall Co, news abstr from the *Axtell Anchor* 1885 TOP 25:1:21
Marshall Co, news abstr from the *Frankfort Bee* 1881 TOP 25:2:64
Marshall Co, news abstr from the *Frankfort Record* 1879 TOP 25:4:153
Marshall Co, news abstr from the *Star* 1886 TOP 25:4:150
Marshall Co, news abstr from the *Visitor* 1884 TOP 25:4:144
McPherson Co, Lindsborg, Bethany Academy school rec 1883-1884, roster w/birthplaces TC 14:1:15
Meade Co, early biog list TOP 25:4:156
Mitchell Co, militia rolls 1895-1896 WRB 17:4:3
Morton Co, census 1895 KR 21:1:11
Morton Co, tax reg 1886-1888 TOP 25:4:162

KANSAS (continued)
  Mt Hope, birth rec c1913-1930 MGR 29:4:111
  Nemaha Co, census 1857 NCG 2:3:4
  Nemaha Co, decl of intention abstr 1906 NCG 3:1:4
  Nemaha Co, hist & biog rec index 1900 by Ostertag, bk rev GH 49:3:206
  Nemaha Co, hist by Tennal 1916, everyname index by Ostertag, bk rev GH 49:3:206
  Nemaha Co, natu rec 1871-1878 cont NCG 2:3:4
  Nemaha Co, natu rec c1903-1906 NCG 2:4:4
  Nemaha Co, news abstr from the *Corning Gazette* 1898-1902 by Ostertag, bk rev HQ 95:59:89
  Nemaha Co, news abstr from the *Goffs Weekly* 1891 TOP 25:2:68
  Nemaha Co, obstetrics cases 1886-1897 cont NCG 2:3:2
  Nemaha Co, obstretrics cases from diary of G H Anderson c1892, cont NCG 2:4:2
  Nemaha Co, servicemen roster 1920 NCG 3:1:8
  Nemaha Co, settler roster NCG 2:4:6
  Nemaha Co, slavery issue, *Courier* news abstr 1938 NCG 3:1:9
  News abstr from the *Courier Democrat* 1900 NCG 2:3:8
  News abstr from the *Weekly Kansas Chief* vol 7 1890-1891 by Ostertag, bk rev GH 49:6:189
  Newton, death & marr abstr from the *Journal* 1884 MGR 30:3:75
  Newton, death & marr abstr from the *Journal* c1902 MGR 29:4:101
  Obit abstr of people age 97 & over 1995 TS 37:4:151
  OR obits of KS natives 1988 TOP 25:2:73 25:4:160
  Osage City, marr & death abstr from the *Free Press* 1911 KK 33:1:17
  Osborne Co, dist sch staff rosters c1926-1927 WRB 18:1:21

KANSAS (continued)
  Osborne Co, funeral rec & coffin sales 1889-1896 WRB 17:4:6
  Ottawa Co, Civil War roll of Captain A H Boss 1864 TC 14:3:41
  Pawnee Rock Leader news vr abstr c1886-1887 BCS 15:3:7 15:4:6
  Residents at picnic in Long Beach, CA 1939 KK 33:4:75
  Residents mentioned in *Fretz Family History* 1890, roster MGR 29:4:113
  Richmond Twp, *Courier* news abstr 1879 NCG 3:1:7
  Salina, purchase rec of land for a new college 1883 TC 14:4:74
  Saline Co Farm residents 1900-1918 cont TC 14:4:69
  Saline Co, Brookville Meth Epis Ch bapt list TC 14:1:3
  Saline Co, Civil War, discharges 1860 in deed & mortgage bk A TC 14:1:5
  Saline Co, Dist #7 Lockard sch rec & roster 1868-1869 TC 14:1:13
  Saline Co, farm residents 1900-1918, roster cont TC 14:3:57
  Saline Co, marr rec 1917 TC 14:1:9 14:3:53 14:4:75
  Saline Co, mort sched 1880 TC 14:1:1 14:3:49 14:4:78
  Saline Co, personal property tax roll 1871 cont TC 14:3:44 14:4:65
  Saline Co, Salina sch rec & roster 1868-1869 TC 14:1:13
  Santa Fe line towns, origins of names KR 20:4:89
  Sedgwick Co, death certs 1905 MGR 29:4:105
  Sedgwick Co, marr rec 1896-1897 MGR 29:4:107 30:3:69
  Seneca, obstetrics cases c1895 cont NCG 3:1:2
  Shawnee Co, news abstr from the *Kansas Children's Home Finder* 1898-1901 TOP 25:1:28
  Shawnee Co, probate index bk TOP 25:4:136
  Shawnee Mission, Johnson Co Lib, descr of avail svcs HQ 95:57:70

KANSAS (continued)
  Smith Co, *Kansas Free Press* news abstr 1879-1881 cont WRB 17:4:16 18:1:14
  Swiss RU Mennonite fam before 1874, hist by Krehbiel, bk rev TS 37:4:146
  Topeka, obit abstr from the *Daily Capital* 1879-1880 TOP 25:2:70
  Topeka, obit abstr from the *Daily Capital* 1994 (of persons age 97 & over) TS 37:3:107
  Valley Center, Lodge #364 membership & obit roster MGR 29:4:119
  Wabaunsee Co Sch souvenir 1904-1905 TOP 25:2:52
  Wabaunsee Co, Harveyville High Sch grads 1928 TOP 25:4:161
  Waconda, hist WRB 18:1:3
  Wakefield, birth & death rec from the *Advertiser* 1897-1898 KK 33:1:13
  Washington Co, hist atlas 1882, index of landholders cont TOP 25:1:31 25:2:75 25:4:163
  White Rock Valley hist sketch WRB 17:4:10
  Wichita, Gill funeral home rec 1890-1980 MGR 29:4:109
  Wichita, marr & death abstr from the *Times* 1881-1882 MGR 29:4:116
  Wichita, news abstr from the *Daily Beacon* 1885 MGR 30:3:78
  Wichita, settler death notices c1885 MGR 29:4:114
  Women's Relief Corp roster 1894 KR 20:4:95 21:1:19
  WW2 draft reg rec KK 33:4:71
  Wyandotte Co, Maple Hill cem rec vol 1 by Scott, bk rev GH 49:5:196
KARR, John C fl775, fam rec supp by Karr, bk rev IGS 27:2:115
KASDORF, Julia Spicher fl995, PA, fam hist sketch PM 19:1:28
KASLER, Michael fc1775, w Susan Minkler, VT, biog sketch ACH 16:5:56

KAUFFMAN, Samuel Jared b1911, w Margaret C Renninger, PA, biog MFH 14:1:37
KAUFMAN, Anne bc1765, PA, geneal by Kaufman, bk rev GFP 44:4:191
  Henry, KY, biog sketch LAB 10:1:30
  Peter, w Susie Sanderson, biog sketch LAB 10:1:30
KAY, Lydia see Thomas DIXON
KEEBLE, Amanda S see Amanda S RANDOLPH
KEEFER, FR, GR, PA, fam hist by Keefer, bk rev WPG 21:3:48
KEELING, James H m1821, w Laura A Waring, NY, Bible rec CDG 14:2:12
KEENEY, Sarah Marcia see Henry Fanning NORCROSS
KEIM, John b1792, w Barbara Livengood, PA, obit LM 36:4:238
  Susan b1809, h Stephen Yoder, OH, IN, biog sketch MFH 14:1:28
KEISTER, Adam b1795, w Clara A Adams, PA(?), Bible rec TR 35:1:24
KEITH, Fam & clan hist NC 5:1:20
  Sarah E see Joseph T HESTON
KELLAM, Cora Fanny Hopkins b1860, PA, NY, biog sketch SEN 2:4:6
KELLER, NO, fam hist by Haga, bk rev GH 49:3:218
KELLEY, Eunice Ann see William G MARTINI
  Holland Andrew f1949, FL, biog sketch PCQ 5:2:2
KELLY, AL, Autauga Co, marr rec c1844 SEN 2:3:13
  AL, Coosa Co, deeds, warrants & patents c1834 SEN 2:3:10
  Caroline d1914, PA, obit BGN 16:2:4
  Judge John Alexander f1821, w Martha Matilda Peck, fam hist by Kelly, bk rev GH 49:4:226
  Moses f1835, w Sara, deed abstr SEN 2:3:12
  Orville Merritt b1851, w Eliza Heuson, w Mary Dannenberger, IL, fam hist by Bates, bk rev CI 31:1:24 GH 49:6:209
  Sara see Moses KELLY

KELLY (continued)
SC, GA, fam hist by Kelly, bk rev BT 26:4:74
Shipwreck f1927, KS, biog sketch KCG 36:2:74

KELSO, Jean see James DANIEL
John see Henrietta ETHERIDGE
Margaret see David MORROW

KEMP, Joseph see Euphemia SIMSON
PA, misc fam data LM 36:2:208

KEMPSON, Elizabeth see Joel J HERNDON

KENDRICK, James b1733, w Susannah Roberson, VA, geneal PWN 2:4:25

KENNARD, M Shelby b1833, w Mary E Saunders, AL, LA, MS, AR, biog sketch SYH 2:1:10

KENNEDY, Daniel d1802, TN, fam hist sketch BWG 24:2:124
John F b1917, hist of new frontier diplomacy 1961-1963 by Maga, bk rev REG 93:2:247
Susan Alice b1860, h John Edgar Edwards, h William Westley Cochran/Cockerham, MS, OK, fam hist by Stubbs, bk rev GH 49:3:219

KENTON, Simon, KY, biog by Clark, bk rev REG 92:4:443

KENTUCKY, Atlas of hist co boundaries by Long, bk rev SEE 36:153:53
Augusta, letters at post ofc 1820, roster KA 31:2:7
Ballard Co, Confederate pension appl abstr by BCHGS, bk rev GH 49:4:210 KA 31:1:43
Bardstown, involvemnt in Vietnam War, hist by Wilson, bk rev REG 93:4:465
Barren Co, Civil War hist, repr from *Glasgow Republican* 1961 LAB 10:4:124
Barren Co, taxpayer roster 1799 by TLC Geneal, bk rev KA 30:3:176
Bath Co, marr bonds 1811-1850 & returns 1811-1852 by McClure, bk rev CHG 28:1:36

KENTUCKY (continued)
Bath Co, tax assessor's list 1823, cont EK 31:1:18
Beda, Beulah Cumberland Pres Ch cem rec KFR 95:19:69
Beda, Mt Hermon Meth Ch cem rec KFR 95:19:79
Berea Cem rec 1870-1872 by Dimitrov, bk rev GH 49:5:197
Bibl of fam hist bks by Hehir, bk rev WCK 28:3:33
Black Patch area, violence, hist by Marshall, bk rev REG 93:3:340
Boone Co, court orders 1789-1815 by Worrel/Fitzgerald, bk rev GH 49:5:196
Boone Co, Hopeful Cem hist sketch BYG 7:6:416
Boyd Co, ordinary suit abstr c1860 TRS 19:1:1
Breathitt Co, marr rec (reconstructed) 1839-1877 by Hayes, bk rev CR 27:4:91 GH 49:3:207 LHS 95:2:8 SGS 44:2:86 TEN 95:16:25 TSG 3:2:9
Bullitt Co, women's hist by Darnell/French, bk rev KA 30:3:175 LAB 10:1:29
Caldwell Co, deaths c1852-1910 by Jerome, bk rev GH 49:5:196 KA 30:3:176
Calhoun, early homes, hist KFR 95:19:45
Calhoun, maps 1903 KFR 95:19:59
Calhoun, River Rise 1937 hist sketch KFR 95:19:65
Calloway Co, census 1850 by Stilley, bk rev GH 49:6:190
Calloway Co, deed bks 1823-1830 by Simmons, bk rev GH 49:4:210
Calloway Co, news abstr vol 4 by Simmons, bk rev GH 49:4:210
Calloway Co, wills & admin vol 1 1836-1840 by Willis, bk rev GH 49:6:190
Carlisle Co, Confederate pension appl by BCHGS, bk rev GH 49:3:207 KA 31:1:43

KENTUCKY (continued)
Carson cem rec KFR 95:19:86
Carter Co, death rec abstr 1852-1862 TRS 19:1:13
Carter Co, marr rec abstr c1860-1861 TRS 19:1:8 19:2:29
Carter Co, pictorial hist by Wolfford, bk rev TR 35:1:51
Cem preservation tips WCK 28:3:27
Census 1810, index by Wagstaff, bk rev GH 49:3:206 49:5:217
Census 1850 (multi vol set) by Sistler, bk rev NTT 15:1/2:6
Census 1890, res tips PCH 1:4:13
Census index 1850 by AA, CD-ROM rev TEN 95:16:24
Christian Co, contributors to foreign missions, roster 1850 KA 31:2:11
Christian Co, deed bk 1816-1817 by TLC Geneal, bk rev GH 49:3:207
Christian Co, hist & biog, repr 1884, bk rev TSG 3:2:9
Christian Co, will bk A index KFR 95:19:40
Civil War era corresp abstr TRS 19:2:31
Clark Co, deaths & abstr from news by Elliston, bk rev KA 30:3:176
Clark Co, Ellis-Shipp cem rec KA 31:1:19
Cold Spring, St Joseph Roman Cath cem rec by Adams, bk rev GH 49:5:197
Columbus, hist by Anthony, bk rev REG 93:2:213
Confederate burials in Atlanta GA, Oakland cem rec KA 30:3:145
Confederate burials in MD KA 30:4:188
Confederate soldiers buried in GA, roster KA 31:1:3
Crittenden Co, census 1860 by CCGS, bk rev GH 49:3:207
Crittenden Co, court order bk 1842-1852 by Jerome, bk rev KA 31:1:43
Cumberland Pres Ch, geneal abstr by Eddlemon, bk rev APR 14:6:4

KENTUCKY (continued)
D-Day, KY participants in, hist REG 93:3:333
Eastern KY, feuds, hist by Pearce, bk rev REG 93:2:209
Eastern region, hist & res tips PCH 1:4:6
Entertainment figures from KY, trivia bk by Harrison, bk rev REG 93:3:380
Estill Co, census 1920 by Wise, bk rev KA 30:3:177
Fam hist bibl, bk rev SEE 36:153:24
Fictional works about KY, bibl by Foley, bk rev PCH 1:4:24
Fleming Co, deed bk 1797-1801 EK 31:1:7
Fleming Co, folk hist by Rolph, bk rev REG 93:2:214
Freedman's Savings & Trust Company depositor reg 1865-1874 KA 31:1:21
Freedman's Savings & Trust Company depositor reg 1865-1874, index KA 31:2:17
Fulton Co, census 1870 by FCGS, bk rev GH 49:3:208
Fulton, Lucus & Lowe Undertaking Company funeral rec 1926-1929 by FCGS, bk rev GH 49:3:208
Garner, Pratt cem rec KGF 1:1/2:23
Grant Co, taxpayer roster 1820 KA 30:3:140
Grant Co, Union soldier discharge rec from deeds 1863 KA 31:1:46
Grapevine, misc fam hist by Bevins, bk rev PCH 1:1:36
Graves Co, Bryn Funeral Home rec 1962-1964 by Dublin, bk rev GH 49:4:210
Graves Co, news abstr 1914 by Simmons, bk rev GH 49:6:191
Graves Co, news abstr vol 44 & 45 by SHS, bk rev GH 49:4:210
Graves Co, news abstr vol 50 & 51 by Simmons, bk rev KA 31:1:45
Greenup Co, lunacy inquests 1804-1902 by Phillips, bk rev SGS 45:1:31 WCK 28:3:33

KENTUCKY (continued)
Greenup Co, misc rec 1804-1902 by Phillips, bk rev GH 49:6:191
Greenup Co, natu rec 1804-1902 by Phillips, bk rev SGS 45:1:31 WCK 28:3:33
Greenup Co, Rev War pensions 1804-1902 by Phillips, bk rev SGS 45:1:31 WCK 28:3:33
Greenup Co, tax list (delinquent) 1888 cont TRS 19:1:11
Harlan Co, class & ethnographic hist by Scott, bk rev REG 93:4:468
Hickman Co, deeds vol 2 1832-1833 by Willis, bk rev GH 49:6:191
Hickman Co, will bks vol 2 1834-1838 by Willis, bk rev GH 49:6:191
Hist Society Bible collect, surname index KA 30:4:185
Honor Roll of Ancestors, pioneers by WCKFRA, bk rev WCK 28:2:19
Irish American news abstr 1899 LAB 10:1:18
Jefferson Co, births 1856 LAB 10:1:8 10:4:113
Knott Co, birth rec 1902-1903 KGF 1:1/2:4
Knott Co, Cody cem rec KGF 1:1/2:28
Knott Co, deaths 1902-1910 KGF 1:1/2:17
Knott Co, deed bk 1 c1884 KGF 1:1/2:43
Knott Co, fiscal court minutes 1888 KGF 1:1/2:36
Knott Co, Hindman Meth itinerant minister roster 1886-1958 KGF 1:1/2:76
Knott Co, Jasper Byrd Stewart & Marion Stamper cem rec KGF 1:1/2:30
Knott Co, last wills & testaments c1890 KGF 1:1/2:32
Knott Co, marr bonds & certs 1891-1895 KGF 1:1/2:8
Knott Co, marr rec 1884-1898 by Smith, bk rev APR 14:6:5
Knott Co, mil hist KGF 1:1/2:77
Knott Co, obits KGF 1:1/2:20

KENTUCKY (continued)
Knott Co, Old Johnson cem rec KGF 1:1/2:26
Knott Co, sch dist #22 enrollment census 1907-1910 KGF 1:1/2:72
Knott Co, surveys c1884 KGF 1:1/2:41
Knott Co, tax assessments 1889 KGF 1:1/2:45
Knox Co, hist & geneal 1799-1994 by Mitchell, bk rev KA 31:2:46
KY Iron, Coal & Manufacturing Co stockholder roster 1854 TRS 19:1:5
Land warrants after French & Indian War by Taylor, bk rev APR 14:6:3
Lawrence Co, deeds c1825 TRS 19:1:12
Letcher Co, census 1860 by Horn, bk rev APR 14:7:2
Lewis Co, sch census rec 1879 TRS 19:1:17
Lexington, Chamber of Commerce member roster 1897 KA 30:3:133
Littel's Laws Of KY, index, repr 1931, bk rev GH 49:3:206
Little Sandy Salt Works employee rosters c1808 cont TRS 19:2:26
Livingston Co, marr rec 1799-1808 TJ 7:1:28
Livingston Co, Smith Funeral Chapel rec 1950-1967 by Birchfield, bk rev KA 30:4:201
Logan Co, contributors to foreign missions, roster 1850 KA 31:2:11
Louisa, news abstr from misc papers 1908 TRS 19:2:37
Louisville Anzeiger death notices 1863 LAB 10:1:21
Louisville, Cave Hill cem rec, Confederates & civilians KA 30:3:147
Louisville, cultural hist, repr from the *Anzeiger* 1914 LAB 10:4:128
Louisville, death abstr from the *Record* 1883 LAB 10:1:15
Louisville, Free Public Lib racial segregation hist 1905-1935 REG 93:2:159

KENTUCKY (continued)
Louisville, obits from the *Public Advertiser* 1837 KA 31:2:8
Louisville, Portland cem rec LAB 10:1:4
Lyon Co, census abstr 1860 by Jones, bk rev KA 30:4:200
Lyon Co, *Land Between the Lakes* reunion bk vol 2 by Ladd, bk rev KA 30:4:203
Madison Co, marr rec 1852-1876 by Vockery, bk rev KA 30:4:201
Mammoth Cave National Park, African Am participation, hist REG 93:4:446
Marr rec 1801-1825 by KRI, bk rev TEN 95:16:21
Mason Co, marr rec abstr c1791-1792 TRS 19:1:3 19:2:24
May House hist by Perry, bk rev REG 92:4:443
McLean Co, Civil War soldiers & hist by Bennett/Eaton, bk rev WCK 28:2:19
Morgan Co, marr reg 1867-1891, cont EK 31:1:15
Nelson Co, inquest rec c1855 KA 31:1:8
Nelson Co, lunacy rec abstr, 19th cent KA 31:1:11
Nelson Co, Negro & Mulatto marr decl 1866-1872 KA 30:3:134
Nelson Co, pet for divisions of land c1870 KA 31:2:40
News abstr c1929 TRS 19:2:28
News abstr from the *Irish American* 1899 LAB 10:4:121
Owen Co, cem rec by OCHS, bk rev GH 49:5:197 TJ 7:3:111
Owsley Co, census 1880, annotated by Hayes, bk rev BHN 28:1:20 GH 49:5:197 MGR 29:4:123 NCJ 21:2:185 SGS 44:2:87
Paducah, Maplelawn Park cem rec by Birchfield, bk rev KA 30:4:201
Pendleton Co, natu rec 1847-1899 by Nagle/Ford, bk rev KA 30:4:200
Pension roll 1835, repr, bk rev GH 49:5:196

KENTUCKY (continued)
Perry Co, census 1850 by Riley, bk rev APR 14:7:2
Perry Co, vr 1852-1859 by Riley, bk rev APR 14:7:2
Pike Co Seminary hist PCH 1:2:9
Pike Co, Clevinger fam cem rec PCH 1:2:31
Pike Co, hist by Justice, bk rev KGF 1:1/2:87
Pike Co, hist essays 1822-1972, bk rev APR 14:4:2
Pike Co, hist papers 1822-1987 vol 2-6, bk rev APR 14:4:2
Pike Co, news abstr from the *Record* 1945 PCH 1:1:2
Pike Co, Salem United Meth Ch hist PCH 1:3:15
Pike Co, sch census bk 1 1895 PCH 1:2:18 1:3:7 1:4:10
Pike Co, Union vet & widow census 1890 PCH 1:1:15 1:2:13 1:3:1
Pike Co, writers native to the co, roster & biog sketches PCH 1:2:5
Pikesville, Day & Night Natl Bank, hist PCH 1:4:2
Pikeville, Mountain Water Company hist PCH 1:1:7
Pioneer fam hist by Kozee, bk rev LRT 14:2:555
Post ofc hist vol 2 by Rennick, bk rev KA 30:4:201
Postcard hist by Hall, bk rev REG 93:2:210
Quilts & their makers, hist & biog by Clarke, bk rev REG 92:4:444
Radio & TV hist by Nash, bk rev REG 93:4:511
Residents who colonized TX, biog sketches & hist by Connor, bk rev GH 49:3:206
Russell Co, Bolin fam cem rec KA 31:1:17
Salem Meth Epis Ch Sunday sch class-bk 1889 PCH 1:3:22
Settler roster, cont KA 30:3:151
Spencer Co, cem rec by Burgin, bk rev KA 31:2:47

KENTUCKY (continued)
Springfield Pres Ch hist TRS 19:2:35
Synagogues, hist & architecture by Weissbach, bk rev REG 93:4:470
Third Constitution, politics of the elective judiciary 1850-1891, hist REG 93:4:387
Todd Co, contributors to foreign missions, roster 1850 KA 31:2:11
Trigg Co, Bible rec by Taylor, bk rev GH 49:6:192
Trigg Co, geneal abstr from the *Cadiz Record* 1939 by Simmons, bk rev KA 30:4:202
Trigg Co, hist rec vol 5 by Simmons, bk rev GH 49:4:210
Trigg Co, hist, repr 1884, bk rev GH 49:6:191 GR 37:1:50 LAB 10:1:29 RES 26:3:161 SGS 44:2:87
Trigg Co, land surveys 1825-1827 by Simmons/Smith, bk rev KA 30:4:203
Trigg Co, news abstr vol 16 by Simmons, bk rev GH 49:4:210
Trigg Co, news abstr vol 23 by Taylor, bk rev KA 31:1:45
Union Co, deed bk 1811-1819 by Heady, bk rev KA 31:2:47 WCK 28:4:43
Univ of KY, banning of women's sports 1902-1924, hist REG 93:4:422
Univ of KY, College of Education hist 1917-1927 REG 93:3:307
Washington Co, marr rec 1792-1825 by Sanders, bk rev KA 30:4:201
Webster Co, news abstr from the *Dixon Journal* vol 1 by McBroom, bk rev GH 49:6:192 KA 31:1:45
Whitley Co, hist & geneal 1818-1993 by WCHBC, bk rev KA 30:4:202
Wilderness Road & settlement hist VCG 95:MAR:15
Wills & inv, repr 1933, bk rev GH 49:4:209

KERN, Martin bc1777, w Rahel Waibel, SW, TX, geneal GR 37:4:5 KTP 14:3:39

KERR, Alexander bc1757, w Rebecca Gourley, VA, NC, Bible rec RCR 10:2:2241
C R fl910, IL, corresp GL 29:4:136
William Stewart b1803, w Jane/t Vail, DE, NJ, PA, fam hist by Manfrina, bk rev KA 31:1:45 TR 35:4:219

KERRICK, Benjamin Harrison b1812, w Mary Carrico, w Catherine Jett Newman, MD, KY, Bible rec KA 30:3:122

KERSEY, AR, GA, LA, MS, fam hist by Clemmons, bk rev GGS 31:1:50
William b1791, w Nancy Thomas, GA, Bible rec CCM 14:3:4

KESILKA, Mary see H M HANSEN

KESSEL, Michael b1750, WV, geneal by Ross, bk rev GH 49:5:233

KETTLE, Cornelius d1808, NJ, funeral cost list GMN 70:1:12

KIDD, Anne Nancy see Henry MCCARTNEY
William E d1902, ND, biog TTC 21:3:60

KIEL, Marvin, w Louise Ringer, SD, autobiog, bk rev BHN 28:2:19

KIFER, Jacob b1845, w Elizabeth Loy, PA, biog sketch BGN 16:2:17

KILLPATRICK, Josiah b1810, IN, fam cem rec GCH 8:1:8

KIMBALL, Edith Berry b1894, h John Howe, ME, biog sketch BC 18:4:5
Helen Jane see Robert S LOWRY

KIMBROUGH, MD, NC, misc fam doc abstr RCR 10:4:2365
R S fl888, TX, biog sketch MT 31:3:107

KING, Deliverance see John TUTHILL
Edmund fl875, TX, biog sketch KTP 6:3:38
Elizabeth see William B BONACKER
Florence Ann see Murray MOLESWORTH
Frank d1885, CN, fam hist sketch IFL 5:8:11
Gillum b1783, w Nancy Jowers, w Margaret Outlaw, SC, geneal by Lyles, bk rev ODD 7:4:36

KING (continued)
John f1645, w Sarah Holton, EN, CT, fam hist by Cooper, bk rev AGM 27:3/4:64
Joseph Addison b1837, w Sarah Frances Gaines, NC, TX, Bible rec FP 38:1:8
Josephine see Manuel KING
Mabel see G W CALROW
Manuel f1854, w Josephine, Portugal, CA, biog sketch RCP 17:3:104
Martin Luther b1929, papers 1951-1955 by Carson et al, bk rev REG 93:3:369
Melinda d1908, h Joseph Anderson, TN, obit abstr ETR 7:4:171
Richard H, TN, fam hist corr & add ETR 7:3:139
Roswell, GA, fam hist by Cooper, bk rev AFH 16:4:3
Solomon, NC, geneal by Billingsley, bk rev GH 49:4:226
Thomas J f1950, AL, autobiog, bk rev VL 30:2:91
William dc1840, w Demaris, AR, will & deed rec SYH 3:1:20

KINNEY, Hannah b1840, h James, MO, biog sketch SYH 1:3:14

KINTNER, Edward, w Glada Snyder, VA, geneal by Kintner, bk rev MGS 13:3:45

KIPLINGER, Catherine see Peter LAMB

KIRBY, Elizabeth see Abraham STREET
Jemima see Joseph KIRBY
Joseph m1837, w Jemima, NF, geneal NAL 11:4:156

KIRK, John Patrick b1841, w Mary E, TX, Bible rec REF 37:2:37
Mary E see John Patrick KIRK
SC, misc fam, geneal corr SCM 23:2:74

KIRKHAM, Lucy Dean see George Washington PEAIRS

KISTLER, Johan George bc1748, w Eva Rosina Ritter, NC, geneal TPI 20:2:102

KITCHEL, Abraham b1736, w Charity Ford, NJ, Bible rec MAG 8:2:11

KITCHEN, Hannah see Johannes Eberhart PENCE

KLINGEL, Clara m1972, h Arthur J Schneider, IL, marr notice MCS 15:4:175

KLINGELHOEFFER, Mathilde see Ferdinand VONHERFF

KLOPFENSTEIN, Susan Hochstetler b1870, OH, fam hist TR 35:3:135

KLOTZ, Jacob F m1878, w Elizabeth Titus, IL, Bible rec HH 30:4:228

KLUCKHOHN, Charles Louis, MN, geneal by Luckhohn, bk rev TB 21:3:10

KLUVER, Christian f1863, w Mary Romanda, GR, AA, fam hist QFH 16:1:29

KNAPP, Elizabeth see Samuel SCRIPTURE
Ellen see Franklin KNAPP
Franklin m1872, w Ellen, MI, Bible rec KVH 19:6:71
Hannah see James SKELDING
Hariette see Samuel WATERBURY
Silvanus m1767, w Abigail Weed, CT, Bible rec CTA 37:3:112

KNEPPER, John H b1849, w Emma J Brubaker, PA, biog sketch LM 36:2:206
Sally see Joseph G COLEMAN

KNIBBE, Augusta f1892, TX, corresp KTP 2:2:14
Clara b1884, TX, recoll KTP 3:2:23 3:3:36

KNIGHT, Eleanora Bauer Knight b1893, TX, fam hist GR 37:1:40
Elizabeth see George HALL
Keziah see Sherod E ROBERTS
Mary E see Benjamin MOODY
Mary see George HAMBLETON

KNORR, Lynne Jaques f1995, FL, fam hist recoll BT 27:2:23

KNOWLES, Charles, OH, desc of in Ashtabula Co AH 22:2:186

KNOX, Sally see Samuel RICKER

KOCH, Mary Ann see Daniel F STEIN

KOCHENDOERFER, Violet f1943, IA, autobiog, bk rev REG 92:4:431

KOEBER, Ferdinand b1824, w Rachel Burns, GR, PA, biog sketch BGN 16:2:18

KOLASINSKI, Dominic f1884, MI, abstr from a hist he wrote TE 15:2:50

KOLBE, Anna Maria see Catherine Anna KOLBE
 Catherine Anna see Simon BENNETCH

KOLLMAN, John b1777, w Elizabeth Maurer, Bible rec LM 36:1:200

KOLP, David see David KULP

KOOFER, Elizabeth see Henry GEESEY

KOOSER, Johannes b1717, w Sybilla, GR, PA, geneal LM 36:3:224
 Sybilla see Johannes KOOSER

KOST, Francis see Francis COST

KOTT, Ernst d1900, TX, obit KTP 7:1:8

KOUKAL, John m1887, w Mary Svobada, NB, fam hist by Wheeler, bk rev GH 49:4:226

KRAMER, John see John CRAMER
 Peter C see Rhoda Thomas PITCHFORD

KRAMM, Johanna see August PIEPER

KRATTLI, Georg b1819, w Dorthea Philipp, SW, MO, corresp abstr MSG 15:1:41
 Georg b1819, w Dorthea Philipp, SW, MO, fam hist MSG 15:4:198
 George f1700, w Elsbeth Perrina, MO, geneal MSG 15:1:44

KREHBIEL, Peter bc1630, SW, GR, biog & fam hist by Krehbiel, bk rev GH 49:4:202 TR 35:4:221

KREIDER, Jonathan Pearse b1968, PA, anc PM 19:1:32

KREISER, Casper f1753, PA, fam hist TPI 21:1:4

KREMAN, Henry b1859, GR, NE, biog sketch NW 18:1:24

KRICK, NO, fam hist by Haga, bk rev GH 49:3:218

KRIMPHOFF, GR, fam hist by Baty, bk rev GH 49:4:227

KRIST, Daniel O b1852, w Sarah Stover, MD, Bible rec WMG 11:1:39

KROUS, Anna b1822, TN, diary abstr BWG 24:1:26 24:2:111

KUBLINGER, Catherine see Catherine KIPLINGER

KULP, David b1777, PA, biog & misc doc MHP 22:1:4

KUNKEL, Sarah Elizabeth see William REEP

KUNTZ, Matthias f1710, GR, NY, geneal by James, bk rev UG 24:1:3

KUYKENDALL, Elizabeth see Jesse KUYKENDALL
 Jesse f1840, w Elizabeth, NC, misc rec LOB 16:4:79
 Minnie see Charles IRWIN

LABEL, --- see Elva BLACK

LABUDA, Frank bc1855, PO, fam hist sketch TE 15:2:77

LACKEY, William b1754, w Elizabeth White, AL, geneal by Lackey, bk rev OLR 9:1:39

LACORNE, Luc de, QB, fam hist by Burnham/Martin, bk rev GH 49:5:233

LACOUNT, Eugene Delion b1844, MA, fam hist DAR 129:9:824

LACY, Eva M see Eva Mary GARRET

LADD, George A b1853, CT, MN, biog sketch DCG 9:2:9

LAFFERTY, AR, NC, VA, geneal by Wilson/Redman, bk rev ARH 33:4:174 GH 49:6:209
 Sarah b1741, NC, VA, fam hist by Wilson/Redman, bk rev GH 49:6:209

LAGUIRE, Peter bc1822, w Betsey Billings, CN, geneal by LaGuire, bk rev GH 49:3:219

LAIN, Matilda A G see Miles LAIN
 Miles m1851, w Matilda A G Lain, TX, Bible rec YTD 15:1:9

LAKE, John fc1645, NY, fam hist by Mullane/Johnson, bk rev NYR 126:2:154

LALANDE, Calude, FR, fam hist LG 95:55:56

LALONDE, Marie see Jacques ARNAUD

LAMAR, Dorcas Ann see John RHODES

LAMARR, Paul E fl910, IL, corresp GL 29:4:134

LAMB, AR, GA, LA, MS, fam hist by Clemmons, bk rev GGS 31:1:50
 GA, MS, AR, fam hist by Harvey, bk rev ARH 33:1:33
 Peter bc1747, w Catherine Kiplinger, OH, fam hist FTC 17:3:35
 Samuel bc1745, w Margaret Jordan, IR, PA, geneal by Lamb, bk rev KCG 36:2:104 WPG 21:3:49

LAMONT, Benjamin b1824, w Maria T Niles, ME, WI, Bible rec WI 41:4:205
 CA, fam hist by Spurgeon, bk rev OC 29:3:130

LANCASTER, Ely John d1914, IA, obit ISC 19:2:30

LANCE, Christopher fl795, w Sarah Johnson, OH, biog sketch TR 35:2:85
 OH, first fam reunion descr & roster 1899 TR 35:2:86

LAND, Polly Ann see Jonas SHOOK

LANDES, Christian bc1728, w Barbara Strickler, w Mariah Bixler, PA, geneal MFH 14:1:36 14:2:52

LANDIS, Hans d1614, SW, fam hist PM 18:4:9
 SW, misc Anabaptist fam of same name, hist PM 18:1:13

LANDON, Rittie see John HATCHER

LANE, Sarah see Adam Quincy CLEMENTS
 Simeon J m1874, w Lucinda Ramey, WV, OH, fam rec FWC 9:4:294

LANG, Wilhemina b1839, IL, anc & fam hist STC 18:4:205

LANGBEIN, Emma Agnes b1860, h Charles Offer, TX, obit KTP 7:3:45
 Emma see Charles OFFER

LANGE, Bertha Friederike Anna b1861, h Wilhelm Heinrich Mann, GR, fam hist sketch TGC 19:2:33

LANGESAE, Knud b1836, w Ane Mathiasen, DK, KS, fam hist sketch KK 33:2:25

LANGFORD, Matthew fl811, w Peggy Nelson, TX, biog KTP 11:2:29

LANGLEY, John b1651, IR, CN, will abstr GEN 20:1:15

LANGSTON, Nathan J fl889, AR, fam hist ARH 33:1:11

LANGWORTHY, John E fl862, NH, corresp SCR 18:5:75

LANTERMAN, Peter fl821, IL, will & testament CR 27:1:5

LANTZ, Christopher see Christopher LANCE
 Geneal by Lantz, bk rev SGS 44:3:142
 Raymond Clyde fl995, w Dianna Lee Crossley, MI, MD, PA, anc by Lantz, bk rev DM 58:3:143 DOG 6:1:8 GH 49:6:209

LAPHAM, William B b1828, ME, obit BC 19:2:7

LAPLACE, Ernest, St.Kitt's Island, NY, identity CGJ 3:4:27

LARD, Mary Lucy m1846, h Riley Septimus Moultrie, CA, biog sketch SCC 32:2:77

LARICK, Henry b1844, w Sarah Elizabeth Humiston, OH, IA, hist sketch NFB 27:2:21

LARIMORE, Philemon bc1736, MD, NC, geneal vol 8 by Ziegler, bk rev CCS 16:4:138

LARMOUR, Elizabeth see John LARMOUR
 John b1783, w Elizabeth, IR, biog sketch IFL 5:9:8

LARSON, August b1857, w Nilla Johnson, SN, MN, geneal by Kitts, bk rev GFP 44:4:191

LASSETER, Emery b1778, w Mary Bell Jordan, GA, geneal FLG 18:4:135

LATCH, Will Z b1877, w Amanda Peeples, GA, TX, fam hist by Lloyd, bk rev STS 35:2:67

LATHAM, Elizabeth see Rotheas LATHAM

LATHAM, Rotheas b1725, w Elizabeth, MA, fam hist by Topping, bk rev GH 49:5:235

LATHROP, Jonas Austin m1829, w Margaret Ann Carr, VT, brief fam hist BAT 24:2:69

LATIN AMERICAN GENEALOGY, Urbanization, hist by Greenfield, bk rev CGJ 3:3:42

LAUER, Philip b1754, PA, Bible rec KTP 8:3:43

Sophia see Peter RUTH

LAURENT, Pierre f1699, w Constance Garinet, FR, geneal LG 95:54:39

LAW, Mary C see James MACLAUGHLIN

William f1840, ST, daybk by Beverly, bk rev RAG 16:1:21

LAWRENCE, Joseph bc1800, NC, TX, biog sketch KTP 14:2:21

Samuel b1815, w Anne Eliza Atkinson, SC, biog & obit NC 5:2:62

LAWTON, Thomas b1614, fam hist by Shurtleff, bk rev GH 49:4:228

LAXTON, Joseph Lavender f1864, VA, NC, treasury bk by Momier, bk rev NCJ 21:1:69

LEA, NC, fam hist by Rose, bk rev NCJ 21:4:423

LEA, William dc1771, NC, fam rec KTP 14:2:22

LEACHMAN, Abraham see Virginia Robards LEACHMAN

Jennie d1946, KY, obit KFR 95:19:53

Virginia Robards b1860, h Abraham Leachman, KY, fam hist KFR 95:19:54

LEADINGHAM, W J b1877, w Minnie Carroll, KY, obit abstr TRS 19:1:7

LEATHERS, Edward, NH, fam hist & misc doc SCR 18:6:98

LEAVITT, Fam hist by Zeavin, bk rev TJ 7:2:73

LEAVITT (continued)

Mary Jane see William Elias ABBOTT

Violet see Carlton W JENNINGS

LECLAIRE, Antoine f1836, w Margaret, IA, land rec & fam land rec ISC 19:4:70

Margaret see Antoine LECLAIRE

LEDBETTER, Alford see Temperance Jane TUCKER

LEE, Gasham f1846, w Delilah, TN, MO, AR, fam rec SYH 1:4:8

Jamin C b1814, FL, fam cem rec FLG 18:1:29

Jason, OR, biog, repr 1907, bk rev GGS 31:1:48

John see Augusta Christine NEWMAN

Mary see Robert TURNER

O A f1900, KS, court case abstr MGR 30:3:94

Richard H f1785, letter from Indian agents SEN 1:4:20

LEECH, Mary B see William FETTERS

LEESCH, TX, fam cem rec KTP 3:1:11

LEFTON, Gwen f1995, CN, fam hist by Lefton, bk rev GH 49:4:200

LEGATT, Margaret see Samuel YOUNGLOVE

LEGGART, Margaret see Margaret LEGATT

LEGGE, Clarissa b1821, h James Gamble, OH, biog TLL 20:4:75

LEGRAND, Nicole see Francois NOEL

LEIDNER, GR, fam hist by Leidner, bk rev IGS 27:2:118

Harold C f1995, IL, autobiog, bk rev IGS 27:2:118

LELAND, Margaret Sloan b1876, h Willard C Leland, TN, biog sketch RAG 17:1:8

LEMASTER, KY, geneal cont EK 31:1:3

LEMASTERS, Abraham fc1660, FR, MD, fam hist by Hardway, bk rev KCG 36:2:104

Benjamin f1776, w Rebecca Martin, VA, fam hist by Hardaway, bk rev GH 49:3:219

LEMIEUX, Pierre f1648, w Marie Benard Guillaume, CN, geneal ACG 22:1:15

LENHARD, Christina Magdalena see Christian HERMAN

LENOIR, William f1795, NC, biog & misc papers cont CAL 14:2:31

LENTZ, Henry Jackson b1819, MS, Bailey fam rec from his diary PWN 2:5:24

LEONARD, Nancy see John SMITH

LEPPO, Jacob d1801, w Mary, MD, geneal CCG 14:4:51
Mary see Jacob LEPPO

LERNOUT, Daniel bc1525, FR, fam hist cont NYR 126:3:185

LEROY, Fam rec by Yelle, bk rev ACG 21:1:23

LESLIE, EN, Am, RU, FR, fam hist by Klieforth, bk rev ANE 95:55:34
Mary T see B J Littleberry NIX

LEVESQUE, Caroline see Felix LEVESQUE
Felix b1847, w Caroline, CN, WY, geneal & fam hist ACG 21:4:149
Jean fc1763, FR, corresp LG 95:55:61

LEVIS, Mary see Joseph PENNOCK

LEWIS, Ann M see Z L NEVILL
Daphne Valerie see Milton D WILSON
Edward f1766, w Mary, VA, fam hist sketch SCH 10:3:88
Elizabeth see Daniel ASHCRAFT
Fam hist by Anderson, bk rev VAG 39:3:235
Francis Wesley b1815, w Jane Thompson, fam hist sketch SCH 10:3:88
James K Polk f1865, jour by Nettles, bk rev GH 49:3:219
Mary Ann see Alfred Washington LUNN
Mary see Edward LEWIS
Robert fc1640, WE, VA, fam hist TVF 4:3:150
VA, fam hist by Anderson, bk rev HQ 95:60:93

LEWIS (continued)
VA, fam hist by Lewis, bk rev KA 31:2:46

LEX, Peter b1849, TX, fam cem rec KTP 3:2:19

LEYH, John Henry f1850, GR, MN, brief fam hist DCG 9:2:8

LIBBY, Charles Thornton f1882, geneal vol 2 by Rodgers/Trafton, bk rev NHR 12:1:48

LICHTENFELD, Auguste Dorothee see Franz Gustav LINDEMANN
Catherine Elizabeth see Peter LINDEMAN
Marie Katherine Elizabeth see Johann Peter LINDEMANN

LICKISS, Margaret see Hely Bagnell JOYNES

LIDE, David R 1842, w Francis Cornelia Lide, SC, corresp ODD 7:4:19
Francis Cornelia see David R LIDE

LIGGET, Henry Bell f1880, IA, corresp abstr HH 30:4:222

LIGHTSEY, Ulysses A b1860, GA, FL, fam hist PCQ 17:1:6

LIGON, Elizabeth b1701, h James Anderson, VA, identity of husband VAG 39:3:163

LILLIE, Gordon W b1860, IL, West region, biog by Shirley, bk rev RAG 16:3:19

LINCOLN, Abraham b1809, assassination hist by Mills, bk rev GH 49:6:178
Abraham b1809, KY, biog by Burlingame, bk rev REG 93:4:482
Abraham b1809, KY, essays on leadership by Williams et al, bk rev REG 93:3:341
Abraham b1809, KY, hist of his presidency by Paludan, bk rev REG 93:2:222

LINDEMAN, Peter b1816, w Catherine Elizabeth Lichtenfeld, PU, TX, fam rec KTP 11:3:43

LINDEMANN, Franz Gustav b1848, w Auguste Dorothee Lichtenfeld, PU, TX, biog sketch KTP 12:3:40
Johann Peter b1816, w Marie Katherine Elizabeth Lichtenfeld, PU, TX, fam rec KTP 12:2:28
LINDSEY, PA, NC, GA, fam hist by McMichael, bk rev NC 5:3:125
LINK, Elizabeth see Lewis WAYLAND
LINN, Mary Ann see James SOMERVILLE
LINNEL, Joshua P b1809, w Hannah B Samson, OH, Bible rec TR 35:2:100
LITHUANIA, Jewish geneal res tips LLI 7:4:11
Mennonite hist MFH 14:2:79
LITTELL, John, IR, fam hist by Littell Fam of Am, bk rev GH 49:4:227
LITTLE, Daniel fl1753, NC, biog & hist by Shook/Roberts, bk rev NCJ 21:1:74 RCR 10:1:2210
LIVENGOOD, Barbara see John KEIM
Mary Magdalena see Robert HICKMAN
Peter fl1775, SW, PA, biog MFH 14:2:68
LIVINGSTON, Elizabeth d1862, CT, Bible rec CTA 38:2:66
Elizabeth see Isaac GLENNY
Mary fl1995, TX, recoll STS 35:3:51
LIZOTTE, CN, fam hist & photos, bk rev ACG 21:4:159
LLOYD, Arthur see Alice GEDDES
LOCKE, Catharine see David ALLEN
Elizabeth see Sebastian J TREFETHEN
Nancy Anne see William James BROOKS
LOCKHART, E R fl1869, AL, corresp abstr BT 27:4:71
LOCKWOOD, Edmund fl1769, w Hannah, CT, Bible rec CTA 37:3:105
Hannah see Edmund LOCKWOOD
Missouri M fl1835, h John James Porter, h Littleton Fowler, h John C Woolam, TX, desc PWN 2:2:10

LOGAN, Andrew bc1705, w Alida Pruyn, IR, NY, VA, SC, geneal by Logan, bk rev GH 49:3:219 SGS 44:2:85
Deborah see John LOGAN
James fl1798, w Deborah Steele, IR, SC, geneal by Bales/Medd, bk rev FRT 16:3:99
James L b1798, w Elizabeth Mann, geneal by Bales/Medd, bk rev TJ 7:3:108
John fl1798, w Deborah, IR, SC, fam hist by Bales/Medd, bk rev EWA 32:1:27
O T m1867, s N J Ward, IL, Bible rec CI 31:3:83
LOGSDON, MD, fam hist by Carson, bk rev DM 59:1:46
LOKER, Sarah see Benjamin MILLS
LOMBARD, Edward bc1880, MN, biog MN 26:3:104
LONG, Bloomfield fl1770, VA, geneal VAG 39:1:27
Esther V see William BUCK
Jane fl1820, TX, biog sketch KTP 9:3:49
PA, misc fam data, corr LM 36:2:213
Robert see Susanna UPDIKE
Stephen fl1820, biog by Nichols/Halley, bk rev RAG 16:4:18
LONGFELLOW, Isabel see William LONGFELLOW
Nathan b1690, w Mary Green, MA, NH, geneal TEG 15:2:104
Samuel b1754, w Mary Perkins, MA, fam hist cont TEG 15:4:220
Stephen b1685, w Abigail Thompson, MA, geneal TEG 15:1:24
William bc1475, w Isabel, EN, geneal TEG 15:1:18 15:4:220
LONGSTREET, John d1923, IL, obits CI 31:1:30
LOOMIS, Maria E see Matthew COWLIN
LOONEY, Meredith b1889, w Sarah Wright, w Winnie Wright, KY, geneal PCH 1:2:29

LOOP, NY, PA, fam hist by Bennison, bk rev NYR 126:3:216

LORD, Margaret f1852, h David Varnum, ME, jour abtr TMG 17:4:122

LOTHROP, Hannah see John LOTHROP
John f1600, w Hannah, MA, fam rec AG 70:4:250

LOTT, Henry see Mary LOTT
Mary f1826, h Henry Lott, PA, NY, OH, corresp by Bachar, bk rev GH 49:3:220 NER 149:596:441 TR 35:4:223 WPG 22:1:49

LOUCKS, Catarina see Peter P WAGNER

LOUDEN, TN, fam hist by Alexander, bk rev LOB 16:2:41

LOUIS, Frank see Franz Ludwig SCHMID

LOUISIANA, Acadian exiles in Nantes FR 1775-1785, hist by Robichaux, bk rev KSL 19:2:73
Acadian weddings, hist KSL 19:4:134
Allen Parish, Durio cem rec KSL 19:1:8
Army generals & Reconstruction 1862-1877, hist by Dawson, bk rev REG 93:3:383
Baton Rouge, geneal abstr 1831 & 1840-1841 from news FPG 17:2:12
Baton Rouge, news abstr from the *Gazette* c1830-1870 FPG 17:6:44 17:1:7
Bible rec vol 5 by LGHS, bk rev EWA 32:2:82 RCP 17:2:51
Caddo Parish, succession abstr c1841-1846 TJ 7:2:40 7:3:97
Caddo Parish, WW1 discharge rec bk cont TJ 7:1:16 7:2:58
Census & militia lists 1770-1789 by Robichaux, bk rev KSL 19:2:73
Civil War, Confederate States Rangers roster KSL 19:2:59
Colonial LA geneal res tips AMG 10:2/3:72
Dutch Colonial res tips KSL 19:4:149

LOUISIANA (continued)
East Feliciana Parish, notarial rec bk A, abstr 1828 THT 23:2:78
FL parishes, Bapt & Meth rec vol 6 1800s by Adams, bk rev FPG 17:2:9
Florida Parishes, marr news abstr c1862 FPG 17:3:23
Florida Parishes, railroad related news abstr c1850-1900 FPG 17:1:6
Florida Parishes, women in news abstr c1831 FPG 17:6:45
Fountainbleau, heads of households 1704 VCG 95:DEC:20
FR colonists, marr rec 1720-1733 by De Ville, bk rev GH 49:4:211
Genealogical Register vol 4 by Boersma, bk rev TS 37:3:96
Genealogical Register vol 39, repr 1992, bk rev EWA 32:2:82
GR heritage & hist, repr 1927, bk rev GH 49:3:209 MGS 13:1:7
GR settlers, 18th cent, hist TPI 20:3:147
GR settlers, hist by Blume, bk rev TPI 21:1:42
Grant Parish, marr rec 1878-1916 cont TJ 7:1:9 7:2:53 7:3:101
Italian population, hist KSL 19:1:11
Lafourche Interior Parish, land owners & census 1810 by Westerman, bk rev AGE 24:4:101
Lake Charles, early hist cont KSL 19:2:68 19:4:147
Lake Charles, news abstr from the *American* 1896 cont KSL 19:1:27
Mansura, St Paul the Epistle Ch bapt bks 1796-1872 by APC, bk rev AGE 24:4:101
Militia & census lists 1770-1789 by Robichaux, bk rev KSL 19:2:73
Morehouse Parish, conveyance & mortgage rec (spouses in) 1845-1870 TJ 7:1:14
Morehouse Parish, Mound Chapel cem rec TG 29:1:17
Morehouse Parish, spouses in conveyance/mortgage rec 1845-1870 TJ 7:2:64

LOUISIANA (continued)
New Orleans, Roman Cath Ch sacramental rec 1807-1809 by Nolan, bk rev AGE 24:1:8
News on microfilm at LA State Univ, list TJ 7:3:112
Pilgrimage for mothers & widows of AR soldiers, roster 1929 TJ 7:1:1
Shreveport, First Pres Ch marr rec 1905-1907 TJ 7:3:84
Shreveport, news abstr from the *Times* 1880s-1890s, bk rev TJ 7:2:69
Shreveport, Oakland Cem burials 1899-1904 TJ 7:3:86
Shreveport, Osborn Funeral Home rec index TJ 7:3:87
Shreveport, Shreve Memorial Lib vertical file topic list TJ 7:3:104
Slaves & slaveowners, misc news abstr c1830 FPG 17:3:17
St Helena Parish courthouse estate papers c1821 FPG 17:4:27
Succession laws & estates, descr TJ 7:3:82
Tensas parish, Elder Shade Plantation cem rec TJ 7:3:107
Toledo Bend, cem relocation guide TJ 7:3:86
Troops 1720-1770 by DeVille, bk rev GH 49:4:210
LOUNSBERRY, Elizabeth see Richard LOUSBERRY
Richard m1670, w Elizabeth, NY, CT, fam hist cont CTA 38:2:78
LOUNSBURY, CT, fam hist cont CTA 38:2:78
Deborah see Robert TOWNSEND
LOVE, Evalina see Shandy Wesley JONES
LOVELACE, Priscilla (Preshy) see Edmund FARE
LOVELESS, Priscilla see Priscilla (Preshy) LOVELACE
LOWE, Martha see Robert B HUGMAN
Thomas f1900, Dept of Interior testimony trans SEN 3:2:34
LOWER, Samuel W b1854, w Ida Frey, OH, Bible rec TR 35:1:25
LOWRY, Franklin L b1848, w Paralee Garner, MI, AR, geneal SCH 10:4:156
Robert S b1880, w Helen Jane Kimball, FL, biog sketch IMP 14:2:57
LOY, Elizabeth see Jacob KIFER
LOYD, Bessie f1898, OH, legal notice TLL 20:3:59
LUACES, Domingo de mc1688, w Maria Fernandez de Pinon, SP, Cuba, Am, fam rec CGJ 3:3:18
LUCE, Hannah see Elder Albert MERRY
Henry f1670, MA, geneal by McCourt et al, bk rev NGS 83:4:311
Matthew Roger b1820, TX, Bible rec MCG 18:1/2:67
LUCK, Jordan B b1791, w Adaline Gatewood, VA, Bible rec VA 33:2:115
LUCKEN, Johann bc1595, w Beatrix ter Meer, GR, geneal QY 22:3:1
LUCKENBACH, Bertha see Louis P VOLLBRECHT
LUCKHOO, Lionel, Guyana, coat of arms & pedigree AMG 10:2/3:11
LUCY, --- f1826, KY, freedom paper for her & her children CR 27:2:39
LUEDERS, Harry f1967, TX, recoll STS 35:1:9
LUMNEY, William H b1862, w Frances Potter, TX, biog sketch MT 31:4:162
LUNDY, C E, VA, autobiog, bk rev BWG 24:1:66
LUNN, Alfred Washington bc1845, w Julia McClelland, w Mary Ann Lewis, FL, biog PCQ 13:1:4
LUNSFORD, Bascom Lamar f1949, NC, speech abstr LOB 17:1:3
Michael f1845, w Elizabeth Black, NC, geneal LOB 16:4:91
LUPP, Anthony dc1646, NY, PA, fam hist by Bennison, bk rev NYR 126:3:216

LUSH, Edmund bc1675, w Elizabeth Ellot/Elliott, EN, geneal by Hull, bk rev KCG 36:1:49

LYBARGER, GR, PA, fam hist by Lybarger, bk rev TPI 21:1:38
OH, fam hist by Hutchinson, bk rev TR 35:4:223

LYLE, John fl801, KA, diary abstr (geneal gleanings) KA 31:2:2
William Brownlow fl885, FL, hist of his home PCQ 9:2:1

LYMAN, Theodore fl863, corresp by Lyman, bk rev REG 92:4:451

LYNCH, Catherine fl900, KS, court case abstr MGR 30:3:69
Charles, VA, biog sketch PCQ 6:2:6
Eleanor see James C IRESON
Olive see Nathaniel HAGAR

LYON, IR, clan pedigree chart IFL 5:9:24
Lewis Salmon b1840, w Charlotte Weisel, OH, biog sketch TR 35:2:94

MABILLE, Michelle see Guillaume PELLETIER

MACARTHUR, Arthur fl896, WI, biog by Young, bk rev REG 93:3:364

MACCALLUM, John see John CALLUM

MACDONALD, Lewis b1778, ST, biog ANE 95:55:16
Marion A fl995, MA, fam hist & autobiog TEG 15:4:229

MACDOUGALL, J Munroe b1895, w Edith May MacEwen, CN, fam hist by Lefton, bk rev GH 49:4:200

MACEWEN, Edith May see J Munroe MACDOUGALL

MACGREGOR, Gregor Willox bc1750, biog by McGregor, bk rev ANE 95:55:33 RAG 16:3:21
James b1759, w Ann MacKay, NS, biog GN 13:3:134
William H b1815, w Eunice B Starboard, CT, Bible rec CTA 38:2:66

MACKAY, Ann see James MACGREGOR

MACKAY (continued)
Mary see Nathaniel HUBBARD

MACKIE, Rachel fl760, h John Brixey, h Barnabas Strickland, NC, GA, MO, biog MSG 15:1:33
Rachel, MO, geneal corr & add MSG 15:4:222

MACLAUGHLIN, James b1789, w Mary C Law, NC, TN, Bible rec MTG 8:4:168

MACLEMORE, James bc1680, w Fortune Gilliam, ST, VA, fam hist SEN 2:4:2

MACLEOD, Norman d1873, ST, memoirs, bk rev GEN 20:1:19

MACMILLAN, John fc1840, w Margaret, MI, fam hist by CRC, bk rev MI 41:2:57
Margaret see John MACMILLAN

MACNAUGHTON, Dougald fl841, w Catherine McFarlan, MI, fam hist by CRC, bk rev MI 41:2:57

MACPHERSON, ST, IR, fam hist sketch GWS 95:42:25

MADDEN, Sarah b1758, VA, fam hist by Madden, bk rev NTT 15:1/2:2

MADDOX, MD, fam hist in southern MD since 1600s by Hurley, bk rev GRC 11:2:28 NFB 27:2:34
PA, NC, GA, fam hist by McMichael, bk rev NC 5:3:125
Samuel bc1640, WE, MD, geneal by Hurley, bk rev EWA 32:2:81

MADISON, James b1751, ency of hist essays by Rutland, bk rev REG 93:3:380

MAFFIT, Samuel d1907, IL, obit CI 31:2:52

MAGEE, Felix W fl896, TX, corresp GR 37:1:20

MAGNET, FR, OH, geneal by English, bk rev GH 49:4:226

MAHAN, William Templeton b1822, GA, fam cem rec GGS 31:1:44

MAHAR, Margaret see Edward D MORRIS

MAINE, Atlas of hist co boundaries
1630-1990 by Long, bk rev CTA
37:4:185 FRT 16:3:104 GH 49:4:206
NER 149:594:188 RAG 16:2:30
RAG 16:4:25 REG 93:4:511 SEE
36:153:53 TMG 17:2:46
- Bethel, Bridge & Cross St hist BC
17:2:1
- Bethel, Elm, Summer & Winter streets, hist BC 19:4:1
- Bethel, hist by True, bk rev BT
27:3:54
- Bethel, Meth Ch hist cont BC 19:1:1
- Bethel, Old Grover Hill Road hist & biog sketches BC 18:3:1
- Bethel, soldiers of 1861, hist cont BC
18:3:7 18:4:7 19:1:11 19:2:4 19:3:6
19:4:7
- Camp Brockton, hist BC 18:4:1
- Census 1790, annotated & indexed by ME Geneal Soc, bk rev AG 70:2:126 NGS 83:2:149 TMG 17:2:43
- Census 1790, duplicate names explained TMG 17:2:7
- Cumberland Co, hist & biog sketches, repr, bk rev BC 19:1:10
- Cumberland Co, warnings out 1762-1774, list & explanation TMG
17:2:25
- Fam collect 1790 vol 4 by Anderson, bk rev TMG 17:2:43
- Gotts Island, hist 1880-1992 by Kenway, bk rev NER 149:596:435
- Hist by Judd et al, bk rev BC 19:4:9
- Hist, repr 1795, bk rev GH 49:3:209
- Hist, repr 1975, bk rev SGS 44:2:88
- Lewiston, buildings built by T D Thorne AHS 95:15:2
- Lewiston, hist sketch AHS 95:16:1
- Lewiston, oldest homes, hist sketch AHS 95:14:4
- Minot, Center Cong Ch rec, hist AHS 95:14:1
- Name changes of residents 1803-1892 TMG 17:4:114
- Newfield, early fam (misc rec) by Ayers, bk rev RAG 16:3:20

MAINE (continued)
- Oxford Co, Greenback Movement hist BC 19:3:1
- Oxford Co, marr returns prior to 1892 by McAllister/Naas, bk rev AG
70:2:126
- Paris, hist 1893-1993 by PCHS, bk rev BC 18:3:6
- Penobscot, pioneer fam, hist vol 3&4 by Gray, bk rev NHR 12:3:146 TMG
17:4:139
- Portland, news index 1785-1835 by Jordan, bk rev BC 19:1:10 SGS
44:3:142
- Sanford-Springvale, biog of misc fam by Boyle, bk rev ACG 22:1:20 TMG
17:4:137
- Settlers of northern CA, hist OC
29:3:93
- St Albans, hist by Bigelow/Knowles, bk rev SGS 45:1:31
- State Grange, hist by Howe, bk rev BC
19:2:3
- Washington Co, marr returns prior to 1892 by Long, bk rev AG 70:2:126
- White Mtns, hist by Bennett, bk rev
BC 19:3:9
- Winthrop, hist by Stackpole w/geneal notes by Young, bk rev BC 19:1:10
CR 27:4:91 GH 49:3:209 OCN
18:1:3 SGS 44:2:88
- Women in cotton mills, hist sketch AHS 95:16:1

MAIZE, Isabella Frances see Prior COX

MAJOR, Marie see Antoine ROY-DESJARDINS

MALLINCKRODT, GR, MO, fam hist by Mallinckrodt, bk rev NGS
83:2:145 TGC 19:3:65

MALLORY, Alvah b1799, w Huldah Bagley, NY, obit GG 7:4:175
- Daniel fl1832, w Fanny, VT, OH, fam hist sketch TFP 95:12:87
- Fanny see Daniel MALLORY
- Mary see Stephen MALLORY
- Stephen b1694, w Mary, CT, biog NEH 12:6:203

MALONE, Christine Crawford, TN, diary abstr by Zimmerman, bk rev RCR 10:2:2278

MALOTT, Catherine see Simon GIRTY
Peter bc1727, NJ, fam hist by Malott, bk rev WMG 11:2:91

MANN, Daniel f1794, MD, free paper NGS 83:1:59
Elizabeth see James L LOGAN
Richard f1644, EN, MA, possible EN origins descr AG 70:4:220
Wilhelm Heinrich b1857, GR, PO, fam hist sketch TGC 19:2:33
Wilhelmina see J N HEISKELL

MANNING, Fam hist by Pelcher, bk rev AGS 36:3:100
George b1765, GA, fam rec NC 5:3:108

MANRY, Henry bc1688, VA, fam hist by Shephard, bk rev NC 5:4:178

MAPEL, Stephen b1759, NJ, geneal by Maples, bk rev AG 70:1:62

MAPLE, Benjamin d1727, NJ, geneal by Maples, bk rev AG 70:1:62
William b1755, NJ, geneal by Maples, bk rev AG 70:1:62

MARCONNET, William Edward b1880, w Clara I Fakes, KS, Bible rec TS 37:4:122

MARCY, Zebulon f1790, PA, town rec bk cont LWF 15:2:104

MARES, William f1806, w Elizabeth Stephenson, TN, marr doc BWG 24:1:53

MARK, Magdalena see Jacob SALA

MAROTZ, Caroline see Johann Friedrich Ferdinand RUFF

MARR, Daniel see Daniel MANN

MARSDEN, James Edward b1846, w Mary Ellen Sisk, TX, fam rec AMG 9:6:45

MARSELIS, Maria Hendricks see Mathys Coenratsen HOOGHTEELING

MARSH, Elizabeth see Henry MARSH
Henry f1783, w Elizabeth, MI, Bible rec DM 58:3:130

MARSHALL, F M f1878, NE, autobiog AU 19:3:5
John m1797, w Anna Rickerson, PA, NS, Bible rec GN 13:1:6
NF, fam hist & misc doc NAL 11:2:54
Thomas Charles b1854, EN, KS, recoll KK 33:1:7

MARSHAM, VA, fam hist corr MD 36:1:81

MARTIN, Agnes see Andrew RUSSELL
AR, fam hist by Kaufman, bk rev ARH 33:4:174
Elizabeth b1811, h Isaac Whitehead, NJ, OH, biog sketch TLL 20:4:79
Henry Anderson b1811, GA, geneal by Steele, bk rev RES 26:3:162
James T b1818, w Ann Carpenter, VA, fam hist by Ratcliffe, bk rev FRT 16:3:108
John Joseph b1691, GR, VA, geneal by Martin, bk rev DM 59:1:45 MGR 30:3:67 MGS 13:3:44 VAG 39:3:229
John T f1863, KY, corresp PCH 1:1:31
John, VA, fam hist by Kaufman, bk rev VAG 39:3:235
Natalie S see Judah P BENJAMIN
Polly see Robert WHATLEY
Rachael Fanny f1850, AL, FL, biog & identity AG 70:1:37
Rebecca see Benjamin LEMASTERS
Shirley Stephens f1995, TX, anc STS 35:1:17
W E E f1830, GA, biog sketch CCM 15:2:5
William b1816, w Anna Davis, KY, geneal PCH 1:1:28
William fc1780, w Mary Stuart, ME, surname correction TMG 17:2:6

MARTINI, William G b1830, w Mary Ann Pischel, w Eunice Ann Kelley, PA, IA, obit ISC 19:2:28

MARX, Emilie see Freidrich Wilhelm ZIEGENFUSS

MARYLAND, Anne Arundel Co, founder hist, repr, bk rev NFB 27:3:54

MARYLAND (continued)
- Anne Arundel Co, residents in Talbot & Dorchester Co land rec before 1710, bk rev MD 36:2:259
- Anne Arundel Co, settler geneal, repr 1905, bk rev GH 49:6:193 SGS 45:1:31
- Annual Valuations, res tips MD 36:2:296
- Baltimore City & co jail rec 1831-1853 MD 36:1:68
- Baltimore Co, natu rec abstr 1794-1851 by Oszakiewski, bk rev HQ 95:60:91
- Baltimore, Fell's Point hist TAC 6:3:17
- Baltimore, Meth rec 1799-1839 by Peden, bk rev GH 49:5:200 WMG 11:2:89
- Baltimore, obit & marr index to the *Baltimore Sun* 1871-1875 by O'Neill, bk rev MD 36:4:675
- Bibl of bks & articles on MD fam MD 36:4:648
- Calendar of wills 1772-1774 by Wright, bk rev WMG 11:2:89
- Calendar of wills 1774-1777 by Wright, bk rev HQ 95:60:91
- Calendar of wills, 17th cent, corr MD 36:1:47
- Camp David & presidents, hist by Nelson, bk rev REG 93:4:502
- Caroline Co, hist, repr 1920, bk rev GH 49:3:210
- Carroll Co, cem rec corr & add CCG 14:4:50
- Carroll Co, chancery bks 1837-1873 by Stanley, bk rev GH 49:5:199 WMG 11:2:90
- Carroll Co, Jerusalem Luth Ch cem rec CCG 14:3:35 14:4:55
- Carroll Co, outdoor pensioner roster 1837-1852 cont WMG 12:1:24
- Carroll Co, pension papers 1837-1841 WMG 11:2:50
- Cecil Co, settler hist doc 1649-1774 by Peden, bk rev MD 36:1:93
- Census index 1850, CD-ROM rev APR 14:6:4

MARYLAND (continued)
- Charles Co, circuit court & land rec 1694-1722 by Jourdan, bk rev GH 49:5:199
- Charles Co, hist, repr 1958, bk rev RDQ 12:4A:92
- Charles Co, land rec 1765-1775 by TLC Geneal, bk rev VAG 39:2:156
- Colonial Dames of Am anc biog sketches by NSCDA, bk rev MD 36:1:94
- Convicts 1671-1680 from land patents, hist & roster NGS 83:1:44
- Damascus, cem inscr MD 36:2:268
- Early fam hist, repr 1903, bk rev HQ 95:58:88
- Eastern Shore, news abstr 1790-1805 by Wright, bk rev TPI 20:2:92
- Eastern Shore, obits 1835-1850 abstr from news by Harper, bk rev FTR :182:4
- Eastern Shore, obits 1850-1900 abstr from news by Harper, bk rev FTR :182:4
- Eastern Shore, Rev War soldier & sailor hist by Nottingham, bk rev VAG 39:3:233
- First provinces & ch, hist 1692, repr 1923, bk rev GH 49:5:198
- Frances Day Collect, descr of holdings FTR 95:179:4
- Frederick Co, fam hist by Gilland, bk rev HQ 95:59:88 WPG 22:1:45
- Frederick Co, hist by Williams/McKinsey, add & corr by Schildknecht, bk rev GH 49:5:199 WMG 11:1:42
- Frederick Co, indentures 1808-1815 WMG 11:2:75 11:3:117 12:1:30
- Frederick Co, land rec abstr 1748-1752 by Anderson, bk rev PGB 26:9:195 RAG 17:1:15 WMG 11:3:140
- Frederick Co, land rec abstr 1752-1756 by Andersen, bk rev PGB 27:2:24 WMG 12:1:43
- Frederick Co, marr & death rec 1849 from *The Examiner* WMG 11:1:9 11:2:60

MARYLAND (continued)
Frederick Co, marr ledger of J Englebrecht 1820-1890 by Long/Eader, bk rev GH 49:3:218 HQ 95:57:83 MD 36:1:90 RCR 10:4:2377 TJ 7:3:108 TR 35:3:166 WMG 11:1:42
Frederick Co, militia hist 1812 MD 36:2:286
Frederick Co, misc fam rec, repr c1935, bk rev WMG 11:3:141
Frederick Co, Taney Town & Piney Creek Hundreds assessment 1798 WMG 11:1:16
Frederick Co, tax assessment 1798 WMG 11:2:66 11:3:128
Frederick Co, Upper Catoctin & Tom's Creek Hundred tax assessment 1798 WMG 11:1:18
Frederick, St John the Evang Ch bapt rec 1811-1822 WMG 12:1:11
Gazetteer, repr 1904, bk rev GH 49:3:210
Geneal & fam hist bibl by Hehir, bk rev MD 36:1:87
Geneal of misc fam, repr 1913, bk rev ARH 33:2:81 SGS 44:3:145 TR 35:4:219
Goshen, hist by Gunderman, bk rev ANC 30:2:74
GR heritage & hist, repr 1914, bk rev AB 23:4:12 GH 49:5:198 GR 37:1:50 GSC 17:3:9 GSM 12:2:47 NFB 27:2:34 SGS 44:2:84 TGC 19:2:43 TPI 20:2:97
Harford Co, land commission rec 1799-1824 MD 36:1:26
Harford Co, marr lic 1777-1865 by Livezey/Davis, bk rev MD 36:2:312
Hist fam geneal, repr 1913, bk rev WPG 21:4:49
Howard Co, settler biog, repr 1905, bk rev GH 49:6:193 NFB 27:3:54 SGS 45:1:31
Howard Co, Trinity of Howard Co maps, res hints FTR 95:181:4
Huguenot hist by HSM, bk rev MD 36:1:89

MARYLAND (continued)
Kent Co, hist 1630-1916, repr 1916, bk rev GH 49:3:210 GSM 12:1:17 TRC 10:1:32
Kent Co, Rev War patriot biog sketches by Peden, bk rev GH 49:5:199 MD 36:4:676
Kent Co, settler rec & hist by Peden, bk rev MD 36:1:87
Laws & acts 1867 MD 36:1:62
Linganore Meth Circuit bapt rec 1872-1889 WMG 11:1:31 11:2:54
Middletown, Christ Reformed Ch, United Ch of Christ hist by Fogle, bk rev MGS 13:3:43 TPI 21:1:43
Montgomery Co, tax assessment 1793 WMG 12:1:17
Mt Airy, cem inscr MD 36:2:268
Natives imm to NC & SC prior to 1800 by Peden, bk rev WMG 11:1:41
New Market, Grace Epis Ch rec 1872-1899, WMG 11:3:106
News abstr from the *Examiner* 1849 WMG 11:3:123
Prerogative court balance bk abstr c1751-1777 by Moxey et al, bk rev HQ 95:59:88 WMG 11:3:141 12:1:44 WPG 22:1:45
Prerogative court rec abstr 1691-1706, supp by Skinner, bk rev GH 49:6:192
Prerogative court rec abstr 1712-1718 by Skinner, bk rev GH 49:6:193 MD 36:1:91 WMG 11:2:90
Prince George's Co, bibl of geneal source rec by Sargent, bk rev PGB 26:7:140
Prince George's Co, cem rec by Sargent, bk rev PGB 26:7:142
Prince George's Co, census 1850 by Wilcox, bk rev PGB 26:7:142
Prince George's Co, hist PGB 27:2:20
Prince George's Co, land rec 1696-1702 by Wilcox, bk rev PGB 26:7:142
Prince George's Co, land rec 1726-1733 by Jourdan, bk rev HQ 95:59:88 MD 36:4:675

MARYLAND (continued)
  Prince George's Co, marr & death rec in 19th cent news by Baltz, bk rev FCM 8:2:137 MD 36:4:676 PGB 27:4:65 SGS 45:1:31 WPG 22:2:51
  Prince George's Co, natu rec from circuit court 1799-1850 PGB 27:2:35
  Prince George's Co, natu rec from circuit court 1861-1920 PGB 27:4:59
  Prince George's Co, probate rec index 1696-1900 by PGCGS, bk rev PGB 26:7:141
  Prince George's Co, sheriffs 1696-1995 PGB 26:6:125
  Prince George's Co, tax list 1828 by Wilcox, bk rev PGB 26:7:141
  Provincial Court rec 1637-1683, sons & daughters MD 36:1:33
  Quaker rec (early) & hist MD 36:1:3
  Queen Anne's Co, cem rec vol 1 by USGS, bk rev GH 49:4:211 MD 36:1:86
  Queen Anne's Co, news obits 1851-1853 by Surles, bk rev TR 35:3:169
  Queen Anne's Co, news obits 1898-1899 by Surles, bk rev TR 35:3:169
  Queen Anne's Co, news obits 1920-1921 by Surles, bk rev TR 35:3:169
  Queen Anne's Co, Rev War patriot biog sketches by Peden, bk rev GH 49:5:199 MD 36:4:676
  Residents in PA wills, 18th cent MD 36:4:663
  Residents mentioned in PA (Centre Co) marr bk 1800-1885 MD 36:2:257
  Residents who moved to NC & SC prior to 1800, geneal by Peden, bk rev MD 36:1:93
  Rev War soldiers in Accomack Co VA, brief roster MD 36:1:61
  Rev War, land grants 1787 in Allegany Co to soldiers by Meyer, bk rev WMG 11:1:41
  Rev War, muster rolls & other rec 1775-1783 by MHS, bk rev FTR 95:177:3

MARYLAND (continued)
  Settler hist 1679-1700 by Coldham, bk rev FTR :182:4 HQ 95:59:88 KA 31:1:44 MD 36:4:677 PGB 27:2:24 TR 35:4:220 WCK 28:2:20 WPG 22:1:46
  Settler hist by Skordas, bk rev PGB 27:2:24
  Somerset Co, geneal (misc fam) 1700-1776 by Batchelder, bk rev GFP 44:4:190
  Somerset Co, judgment abstr 1709-1716 MD 36:4:645
  Southern region & Eastern Shore, early fam geneal by Jourdan, bk rev GH 49:5:198 MD 36:1:88
  St Mary's Co, administrative acc 1674-1720 by TLC Geneal, bk rev MD 36:1:86
  St Mary's Co, deaths & burials by Cryer, bk rev MD 36:4:678 WCK 28:2:20
  Talbot Co, hist, repr 1915, bk rev AW 21:2:63 GH 49:3:210 GSM 12:1:17
  Washington Co, Civil War hist by Keller, bk rev RAG 16:2:28
  Washington Co, Hancock, Riverview Cem inscr WMG 11:1:36
  Washington Co, Rev War militia roster 1778 MFH 15:1:41
  Washington Co, will bk A2 1790s WMG 11:1:23 11:2:80 11:3:136 12:1:34
  Will calendar 1772-1774 vol 15 by Wright, bk rev GH 49:5:198
  Will calendar 1774-1777 by Wright, bk rev WMG 12:1:44
MASON, Emma b1864, TX, Bible rec FP 38:1:10
  Mary see Simon BOZARTH
  Rebecca see Charles PORTER
  Richard b1422, EN, CN, fam hist by Mason, bk rev FAM 34:4:250
MASSACHUSETTS, Abington, vr to 1850 by NEHGS, microfiche rev ATE 30:1:2
  Andover, hist sketches, repr 1880, bk rev GH 49:6:194

MASSACHUSETTS (continued)

Atlas of hist co boundaries by Long, bk rev CTA 37:4:185 FRT 16:3:104 GH 49:4:206 NER 149:594:188 RAG 16:2:30 16:4:25 REG 93:4:511 SEE 36:153:53 TMG 17:2:46

Barnstable area, cem inscr 1600-1900 by Bunnell, bk rev BG 16:3:102

Barnstable Co, hist & geneal atlas by Gibson, bk rev CTA 37:3:142 NER 149:593:80

Barrington, town rec c1737 NER 149:593:46

Becket, map 1876, landholder index BG 16:4:123

Berkshire Athenaeum, geneal resource guide BG 16:2:39

Boston, births 1700-1800, repr 1883, bk rev GH 49:4:211

Boston, births, bapt, marr & deaths 1630-1699, repr 1883, bk rev GH 49:4:211

Boston, GR imm arrival abstr 1835 TPI 21:1:30

Boston, Harvard St Bapt Ch marr & deaths c1892-1893 GN 13:2:97

Boston, New North Ch rec 1714-1799, repr 1867, bk rev SGS 45:1:37

Boston Pilot ads for missing imm 1857-1860 by Harris/O'Keefe, bk rev TTT 20:1:20

Boston, taxpayers 1821 by Rohrbach, bk rev AW 21:3:92 TB 21:3:10

Charlestown, vr vol 2 by Joslyn, bk rev NEH 12:2/3:49

Chatham, hist by Smith, bk rev TB 22:1:12

Chelsea, deaths 1800s TEG 15:2:69

Chelsea area, deaths c1802 cont TEG 15:4:187

Cheshire, landowner map & index 1760s BG 16:1:22

Colonial & Indian hist by BFHA, bk rev RAG 16:2:25

Dennis, vr 1793-1900 by Bratti et al, bk rev CTN 27:4:587

Essex Co, deed reg, hist TEG 15:4:183

MASSACHUSETTS (continued)

Geneal misc vol 1 (1899) by Mayflower Soc, bk rev GSM 12:2:48

Geneal misc vol 2 (1900) by Mayflower Soc, bk rev GSM 12:2:48

Geneal misc vol 3 (1901) by Mayflower Soc, bk rev OK 40:2:44

Geneal misc vol 4 (1902) by Mayflower Soc, bk rev OK 40:2:45

Gloucester, mariner hist by McIntosh, bk rev AW 22:2:33

Gloucester, natu rec, res tips TEG 15:4:228

Gloucester, suffrage before 1920, hist & voter reg roster TEG 15:4:192

Hancock, land ownership rec 1876 BG 16:3:84

Hardwick, hist & geneal reg, repr 1883, bk rev BG 16:1:31 GH 49:6:194

Hardwick, hist repr 1883, bk rev FC 13:2:28

Hist collect, repr 1844, bk rev GFP 45:2:90

Lee, census 1855 cont BG 16:1:28 16:2:68 16:3:86 16:4:130

Lee, religious certs, 19th cent BG 16:2:44

Lenox & Berkshire Highlands, hist, repr 1902, bk rev BG 16:3:103

Linebrook parish, ch rec 1747-1819 by Perley, bk rev SCS 32:4:87

Linebrook Parish, ch rec 1747-1819 by Townsend, bk rev GGP 28:1:22

Malden area, deaths c1802 cont TEG 15:4:187

Malden area, deaths late 1800s listed TEG 15:2:69

Mayflower see also UNITED STATES

Mayflower Descendant vol 1 & 2, repr 1899-1900, bk rev BG 16:1:31

Medway, birth, marr & death rec 1850-1900 by Donovan, bk rev GH 49:6:194 SGS 45:1:32

Merrimac Valley, gravestone carvings & carvers, hist TEG 15:1:3

Monterey, land owner roster & map 1876 BG 16:2:42

MASSACHUSETTS (continued)
Nantucket, Civil War hist by Miller/Mooney, bk rev NER 149:593:80
New Salem, hist RAG 16:1:9
Newbury, proprietors rec 1720-1768 by Hale/Townsend, bk rev GFP 44:4:189
Newburyport, births to 1849 by Essex Institute, bk rev RT 13:1:16
NS residents in census 1855, abstr GN 13:3:143
Oxford Co, settler roster BG 16:3:76
Photographer direct 1839-1900 by Polito, bk rev NER 149:594:190
Pilgrims, geneal & hist vol 1 by Mayflower Soc, bk rev VAG 39:1:72
Pilgrims, geneal & hist vol 2 by Mayflower Soc, bk rev VAG 39:1:72
Pioneers who went west, esp MI, rosters, repr 1915, bk rev GH 49:4:211
Pittsfield, St Stephen's Epis Ch bapt reg 1883-1899 BG 16:2:61 16:3:95 16:4:111
Pittsfield, Zion's Evang Luth Ch births & bapt 1860-1923 BG 16:1:24 16:2:55 16:3:90 16:4:124
Plymouth, Burial Hill cem inscr, repr 1894, bk rev GH 49:5:200
Plymouth, Burial Hill epitaphs, repr 1892, bk rev GH 49:5:200
Plymouth, Pilgrim fathers chronicles 1602-1625 by Young, bk rev SGS 45:1:37
Prescott, hist by Coolidge, bk rev BG 16:3:103
Reading, geneal hist, repr 1874, bk rev GH 49:4:212 TR 35:1:51
Reading, geneal hist, repr 1901, bk rev SGS 44:2:88
Roxbury, hist, repr 1878, bk rev ACG 21:2:61 BG 16:3:102
Savin Hill, fam hist sketches NER 149:593:28
Suffolk Co, Boston, King's Chapel Cem hist sketch TEG 15:2:67

MASSACHUSETTS (continued)
Tisbury, vr to 1850 by NEHGS, bk rev OC 29:3:131
Western border, colonial & Indian hist, repr 1886, bk rev GH 49:4:211
Williamstown, hist by Perry, bk rev BCF 95:Apr/May:9
Women's repatriations from US Dist Court in Boston, res guide NEH 12:1:19
Worcester, Notre-Dame-des-Canadiens Parish hist 1869-1995 by Gagnon, bk rev ACG 21:4:162

MASSENGILL, Elizabeth Isabella see Isaac THOMAS

MASTON, OH, fam hist by Hutchinson, bk rev TR 35:4:223

MATHIASEN, Ane see Knud LANGESAE

MATHIS, Mary Ann see Charles Wendell JOHNSON

MATOON, Nancy see Francis HOTCHKIN

MATTHEWSON, Mary E see Thomas N O'SHIELDS

MAUDLIN, James T b1842, w Louvisa Terrell, IN, biog sketch IG 31:2:45

MAURER, Adolph see Birdie (Claraman) PEASLEY
Elizabeth see John KOLLMAN

MAY, Caleb bc1780, w Margaretta Patrick, NC, KY, geneal by May, bk rev GH 49:6:209
Carey b1849, AL, TX, Bible rec REF 37:4:67
Hattie fl899, h William A Douglas, ON, NY, news abstr FAM 34:4:243
Samuel fl817, KY, hist of his house by Perry, bk rev REG 92:4:443
William fl803, EN, geneal KFR 95:19:31
William fl881, KY, wills & other fam doc KFR 95:19:34
William S m1849, w Margaret A McGill, TX, Bible rec REF 37:4:67

MAYER, Eve see Ulrick MAYER
Ulrick bc1675, w Eve, GR, PA, fam hist MFH 14:1:22

MAYFIELD, Shoto Martin bc1848, w Liza Stanley, OK, TX, geneal PWN 3:1:8

MAYHEW, Susannah see John ROBERTS

MAYZE, Elizabeth see Spencer HENRY

MAZER, John Gottlieb b1832, w Anna Margaret Peter, MD, PA, geneal LM 36:4:236

MCALLISTER, Temperance J see James Matthew DEROSETTE

MCBRAYER, Rebecah see William MCBRAYER
William b1696, w Rebecah, ST, PA, geneal PCH 1:1:27

MCCALL, Thomas f1917, IA, anniv news notice ISC 19:2:28

MCCARROLL, Simon bc1775, w Anne Coskey Glenn, IR, biog sketch CTN 27:4:591

MCCARTNEY, Henry bc1745, w Mary Watts, w Anne Nancy Kidd, IR, OH, fam hist SSG 14:2:28

MCCARTY, Anna Barbara see Anna Barbara FITZHUGH
Eleanor see William REMY
Fayette Asbury f1866, WA, biog & fam hist EWA 32:4:166

MCCLARAN, Clem d1849, TN, will abstr MTG 8:4:158

MCCLAY, Lavina see Daniel H BAKER

MCCLELLAN, George Brinton b1826, New England anc NEH 12:2/3:64

MCCLELLAND, Julia see Alfred Washington LUNN
Silas b1795, FL, biog PCQ 7:3:3

MCCLINTIC, Nancy Agnes see James STRAIN

MCCLURE, Emeline f1880, h Joseph Grice McClure, MI, fam hist FHC 19:2:29

VA, KY, fam hist sketch BT 27:4:78

MCCONNELL, James bc1715, w Mary McGarth, IR, PA, geneal by Eagan, bk rev GH 49:4:227 TR 35:2:110

MCCORMICK, Ann see Daniel BROWN

MCCRAY, ST, IR, Am, fam hist by McCray, bk rev PB 11:2:41

MCCREIGHT, John m1791, w Sarah Hamilton, SC, Bible rec SCM 23:4:205

MCCUBBIN, G W f1862, IL, corresp MCS 15:2:84

MCCULLA, Elizabeth see Elizabeth MCCULLOCH
Florinda see Florinda MCCULLOCH
Isabella Helena see Isabella Helena MCCULLOCH
William Ann see William Ann MCCULLOCH

MCCULLOCH, Elizabeth f 1860, h John Horton, TX, fam hist STS 35:4:4
Florinda f1850, h George W Day, h Claiborne West, TX, fam hist STS 35:4:4
Isabella Helena f1855, h George Brackenridge, TX, fam hist STS 35:4:4
William Ann see James J THORNTON

MCCULLOUGH, William b1821, w Nancy Whidden, KY, OH, FL, biog PCQ 20:4:6

MCCURRY, Amos, w Rachel Webb, VA, NC, GA, geneal add & corr by Williams, bk rev LOB 16:4:93 VL 30:1:43

MCCUSTIAN, Catherine see Hill Carter DAUGHERTY

MCDONALD, Alexander f1834, CN, pet abstr MHH 16:4:125
Anita Schwarz b1919, h Oren Edgar McDonald, TX, biog sketch KTP 13:1:8
Caroline see Meredith E WEBB
John b1792, w Margaret Emory/Embree/Emmory, TN, AL, fam hist by McDonald, bk rev NTT 15:1/2:4
Oren Edgar see Anita Schwarz MCDONALD

MCDONALD (continued)
William H b1833, w Mary Drushal, OH, fam hist NFB 27:4:63

MCDOUGALL, Walter b1789, w Clarissa Stark, VA, NJ, fam hist sketch HQ 95:59:33

MCDOWELL, John fl783, w Margaret Patterson, w Jane Reed, PA, geneal by Murphy, bk rev WPG 21:4:49

MCELHANEY, Jane see Charles ALSBURY

MCELVAIN, Andrew mc1774, w Margaret Workman, PA, IL, fam rec CR 27:2:47

MCEWEN, Patricia Ann Hoagland see John Collins HOAGLAND

MCFARLAN, Catherine see Dougald MACNAUGHTON

MCFARLAND, Archie see Minnie BULLACK
J C b1823, IL, obit GL 29:4:144

MCFARLANE, Alexander dc1755, Jamaica, will CGJ 3:3:37
James fl789, PA, apprenticeship doc WPG 22:1:14

MCFATE, James b1837, w Nancy Brown, PA, IA, obit ISC 19:2:29

MCFATRECH, Androw b1775, IL, fam rec GL 29:4:129

MCGARTH, Mary see James MCCONNELL

MCGAUGHEY, Margaret see William MCGAUGHEY
William fc1740, w Margaret, PA, geneal by Sutton, bk rev OLR 9:3:128

MCGILL, Margaret A see William S MAY
Sarah Ann see Zachariah BROOKS

MCGINNIS, Andrew m1824, w Elizabeth Beale, PA, Bible rec WPG 22:2:48

MCGRATH, J W b1848, PA, MN, biog sketch DCG 9:2:9

MCGREGOR, Andrew b1776, IN, fam cem rec GCH 8:1:7

MCGUIRE, Hugh fl818, SC, will ODD 7:2:11

MCHUGO, William d1773, SC, estate inv rec ODD 7:1:22

MCINTIRE, Lucretia see Joshua SNOW

MCINTOSH, Alexander fl759, SC, muster roll ODD 7:1:29

MCINTURFF, PA, VA, NC, fam hist by Kringer, bk rev TJ 7:1:38

MCINTYRE, Robb see Jennie YUILL

MCIVER, Mary Polly see John NICHOLSON

MCKARAHER, Charles b1793, PA, diary by Blizard, bk rev CR 27:4:92 FLG 18:2:73 GG 7:4:156 GH 49:5:233 GJB 19:3:70

MCKASKILL, John m1859, w Mary Morrison, ST, CN, geneal SGB 26:1:36

MCKAY, Carroll Frances b1913, h George C Seward, VA, NY, biog & fam hist by Seward, bk rev GH 49:6:210

MCKENZIE, William Alexandre, w Henriette Ouellette, CN, MA, geneal by McKenzie, bk rev ACG 22:1:18

MCKILLOP, Hart fc1900, FL, recoll PCQ 12:3:7

MCKINNEY, Abraham, IL, hist of his home PR 22:4:10
Luke fl877, w Arminta Caroline Basham, WV, fam rec FWC 9:4:280

MCKINNON, Donald Clare see Wilma Sue DANIEL
Donald fl772, QB, biog LG 95:56:70
MCKINNON, Sarah bc1846, IR, CN, FL, news abstr FLG 18:4:133

MCKISSICK, Martha see John CARNAHAN

MCLAINE, Eliza see David Sutton BRAY

MCLAUGHLANE, Archibald dc1763, ST, biog sketch GWS 95:44:10

MCLEAN, George fl831, WV, diary abstr by ARFHS, bk rev GH 49:4:227

MCLEISH, Margaret Kennedy see Thomas BEVERIDGE

MCLELEN, Bailey George fc1860, autobiog by Rouke, bk rev RAG 16:3:21

MCMICHAEL, PA, NC, GA, fam hist by McMichael, bk rev NC 5:3:125
  ST, IR, CN, fam hist by Kapas, bk rev GEN 20:3:32
  Stephen Collins b1858, w Martha Ann Francis Coker, GA, Bible rec GGS 31:2:109

MCMILLAN, Susannah see Norman MCRAE

MCMULLEN, James R f1940, FL, WW2 mission notes BT 27:1:9

MCNATT, Richard f1734, w Rebecca Anderson, PA, fam hist by McCornack, bk rev GH 49:5:234

MCQUARY, Lucy Jane see Josiah CARNEAL

MCRAE, Norman b1799, w Susannah McMillan, GA, Bible rec CCM 15:2:11

MCVICKER, Elizabeth b1822, h William Banks, OH, obit TLL 20:4:80

MEACHAM, Aseneath see Elder Albert MERRY

MEADOR, Thomas d1840, SC, estate rec ODD 7:1:32

MEARS, William b1780, w Mary Barnes, w Elizabeth Stevens, VA, fam hist BWG 24:2:142

MEASELL, Julia A S see John Nicholas ZIMMERMAN

MEASHAM, George Herbert f1910, CN, Manitoba, biog GEN 20:4:13

MECAY, Alexander m1829, w Maria B Boiles, OH, Bible rec DGS 11:4:70

MEDICAL GENEALOGY, 19th cent medical terms, glossary MCS 15:1:10
  Diseases, old names & modern definitions AB 23:4:17
  Fam health hist & medical fam trees, res guide by Krause, bk rev KA 31:2:49
  Fam health hist, beginner's tips TSL 20:1:4

MEDICAL GENEALOGY (continued)
  Fam health hist res guide by Nelson-Anderson et al, bk rev GH 49:5:180
  Fam health hist, res guide by NGS, bk rev LRT 14:2:556
  Fam medical & behavioral hist, res guide by Krause, bk rev SGS 44:3:145
  FL, yellow fever epidemic 1877, hist TNC 2:2:37
  Genes & geneal, essay IMP 14:1:11
  Genetic heritage, descr & guide SD 14:1:12
  Genetics & fam health, resource list SD 14:1:20
  Glossary of medical terms FCT 95:122:5
  Illness, disease & death certs, res guide by Briggs, bk rev FAM 34:1:45
  Medical fam tree, descr CRT 16:4:25
  Medical fam tree, res aid by Krause, bk rev SCS 32:11:255
  Medical hist chart SD 14:1:17
  Medical hist, diseases & geneal, res tips MCR 27:1:48
  Medical hist, res tips FAH 13:2:45
  Medical organization address list SD 14:1:21
  Medical pedigree, symbols used SD 14:1:18
  Milk sickness, descr AW 21:3:89
  Opium, descr c1896 MCR 27:1:53
  Terminology, 18th cent, glossary RT 13:3:76
  Yellow fever hist TNC 2:2:36

MEEKER, IN, geneal cont HJA 19:1:5
  Sally see John ATKINS
  William H, IN, geneal cont HJA 18:3:183

MEEKS, John bc1815, w Polly, TN, IL, fam hist CI 31:1:3
  Mary see William MEEKS
  Polly see John MEEKS
  William bc1805, w Mary, NC, TN, fam hist CI 31:1:3

MEERS, A J f1887, OK, corresp abstr WTN 95:WINTER:9

MELTON, Nancy see Harvey MURDOCK

MELUNGEON GENEALOGY, Hist SEE 36:153:16 STS 35:3:64
  TN, NC, VA, hist by Kennedy, bk rev BWG 24:1:65 NCJ 21:1:77 NTT 15:1/2:5 SEE 36:153:15

MEMMINGER, Christopher Gustavus b1865, FL, biog PCQ 18:4:6

MENDENHALL, Sarah Ann see Matthias MOUNT

MENGEL, Catharine see Johann Wilhelm MENGEL
  Johann Wilhelm f1753, w Catharine, GR, PA, biog BGS 27:4:137

MENGES, Jefse b1827, w Louisa, PA, Bible rec MGS 13:3:39

MENNONITE GENEALOGY see also RELIGIOUS GENEALOGY
  GR, PA, Pike Mennonite Ch imm fam hist MFH 14:1:4
  IL, Amish & Mennonites in southern IL, hist MH 22:4:67
  Swiss RU Mennonite fam in SD & KS before 1874, hist by Krehbiel, bk rev TS 37:4:146

MERCER, Christopher, w Mary Simson, geneal by Richey, bk rev ODD 7:1:36
  Red f1905, FL, recoll PCQ 15:4:6

MERCIER, Celestin m1872, w Mary Exon, CN, lineage MHH 16:4:129

MEREDITH, TX, fam hist add by Mitchell, bk rev STS 35:2:67

MERIWETHER, VA, fam hist by Anderson, bk rev HQ 95:60:93 VAG 39:3:235
  VA, fam hist by Lewis, bk rev KA 31:2:46

MERO, Dennis f1675, w Jane Penley, ME, MA, CT, geneal NER 149:594:155

MERRIAM, Athelred see John RHODES

MERRILL, Anna see Ichabod BONNEY
  Julius C b1840, ME, jour by Merrill, bk rev CTA 37:4:184

MERRIMAN, Lulu see William G SCHRAM

MERRY, Elder Albert b1807, w Hannah Luce, w Aseneath Meacham, MA, Bible rec BG 16:4:137

MERTEN, Johann Jost see John Joseph MARTIN

MERWIN, John D bc1490, w Isabel Bartlett, EN, geneal NER 149:595:295
  Mary see Robert TINKER
  Miles bc1623, w Elizabeth Powell, w Sarah Platt Beach, w Sarah Youngs Scofield, CT, anc NER 149:595:295

MESHEROOL, Sarah see John HOLLCROFT

MESSENGER, Andrew bc1588, EN, res aid APR 14:6:5

METHODOLOGY, Abbreviations frequently encountered in geneal, glossary LL 31:1:9
  Adoption & geneal, essay exploring the issues involved TE 15:3:118
  Adoption res tips GH 49:3:16
  Aerial photos of fam cem or houses, tips ARN 8:4:4
  Age estimating guide OG 21:1:27
  Ahnentafel numbers, guide MSG 15:1:52
  Ahnentafels, how to read PCH 1:4:15
  Alphabetization tips SGS 44:2:63
  Am religion ency by Gale Research, bk rev ARN 8:2:11
  Amer Geneal Biog Index, res tips AGS 36:4:138
  Ancestor problem-resolution worksheet TS 37:3:85
  Ancestor res guide by Tregillis, bk rev BC 19:1:10
  Ancestral heritage scholarships, addresses STS 35:4:30
  Antique clothes, how to make padded hangers SMN 13:4:63
  Antique clothes, storage tips SMN 13:4:63
  Antiques & geneal, res tips OC 32:2:7
  Approximate dates of basic rec in many countries, guide HQ 95:55:76

METHODOLOGY (continued)
Archival res basics for beginners (microfilm) WPG 21:7:53
Arrival rec of imm anc, res guide by Colletta, bk rev APG 10:2:62
Assets, tips on finding lost fam funds by Folsom, bk rev GH 49:3:194
Assoc of Professional Geneal Direct 1995-1996by Kerstens, bk rev FCM 7:4:270 NGS 83:3:229
Assoc of Professional Geneal, hist sketch APG 10:3:100
Autobiog & preserving your personal hist, guide by Polk, bk rev GGP 28:1:20
Autobiog writing guide by Penna-Oakes, bk rev GSC 18:1:8
Autobiog writing tips PB 10:3:65
Baptismal sponsors, questions & answers JBC 16:1:14
Barn styles, res guide PCI 18:4:2
Basic geneal reference bks, res tips ATE 30:1:43
Basic res tips KTP 8:1:17
Bastardy, explanation of rate of occurance HGO 6:2:1
Beginner's guide by Cooper, bk rev GH 49:3:194
Beginner's guide by Dieterle, bk rev GFP 45:2:89 TR 35:4:219
Beginner's guide by Johnson, bk rev TPI 20:4:197
Beginner's guide to geneal fundamentals by Jaussi, bk rev GH 49:4:200 GJ 23:1:36
Beginner's guides, bibl essay GJ 23:1:12
Beginner's res guide by Latham, bk rev TR 35:4:222
Beginner's tips APR 14:2:1 KSL 19:1:30 KTP 6:1:16 11:1:11 LRT 15:1:593 RAG 17:1:18 SQ 6:3:7 SVG 21:3:74 TJ 7:2:61
Beginners' kit by Dollarhide, bk rev FAM 34:2:117
Biog & Geneal Master Index by Gale Research, bk rev ARN 8:2:11
Birth rec, address list KTP 10:2:24

METHODOLOGY (continued)
Birth rec, tips on obtaining KTP 11:1:13
Birthdates, determine from tombstone inscr, res aid TNC 3:1:2
Board for Certification of Geneal roster 1995 by Hatten, bk rev NGS 83:3:229
Book repair tips FCT 95:122:3 KTP 11:3:35
Bounty land rec, res tips SCS 32:2:29
Burned courthouses, res tips HTR 38:4:104
Business rec for fam hist, res tips GWS 95:42:12
Calendar changes over time, hist sketch WRB 17:4:14
Calendar for 225 years, res aid MI 41:1:34
Calendar systems, geneal dates, guide by Smith, bk rev KVH 20:6:67
Calendar, perpetual HTR 38:3:77
Calendars, hist QFH 16:1:5
Calendars, res guide SMN 13:9:151
Case studies in the unusual by Wright, bk rev GH 49:5:180 HQ 95:60:93 RCR 10:1:2215 TR 35:2:109
Cem address & res guide by Burek, bk rev LRT 14:2:556 NER 149:596:438 NGS 83:3:220 RAG 16:2:25
Cem address bk 1995 by Kot, bk rev GH 49:3:200
Cem & gravestone designs, hist videos, rev ARN 8:2:8
Cem guide by Gale Research, bk rev ARN 8:2:11
Cem inscr, religious symbol guide CHG 27:2:52
Cem preservation tips MSG 15:1:1
Cem rec res tips PGB 26:5:104
Cem res guide GEN 20:3:13 HQ 95:55:29 MN 26:4:171
Cem transcriptions, res tips MN 26:3:134
Census (state) rec, res guide by Lainhart, bk rev LL 30:3:80
Census 1790-1830, using to establish birth dates, tips KTP 7:3:46

METHODOLOGY (continued)
- Census 1790-1980, items included, list KTP 10:1:14
- Census 1910, res hints DG 19:2:38
- Census 1920, res tips KTP 10:1:2
- Census 1920, Soundex, use of GRI 15:3:100
- Census hist sketch KTP 10:1:2
- Census population & housing questions, guidebk by USDC, bk rev BHN 28:2:19
- Census problem solving techniques SGS 44:3:121
- Census rec res guide GH 49:6:6
- Census rec, res guide on cassette by Parker, bk rev NGS 83:4:304
- Census rec, res tips OC 31:1:28
- Census res (pre-1841) guide by Chapman, bk rev ACG 22:1:21
- Census res tips FRT 16:3:128 KIL 23:3:75
- Census, using to find approximate birthdates, tips GGP 28:1:10
- Censuses, colonial & federal, list & guide UG 23:3:27
- Censuses, items included, yearly chart PT 37:1:12
- Censuses, social hist by Anderson, bk rev APG 10:1:30
- Certification, descr & requirements MCR 26:1:22
- Challenges of 21st cent geneal, descr TTC 21:1:12
- Chamber of Commerce res tips SCS 32:4:78
- Children & heritage, teaching tips MN 26:2:56
- Ch rec res tips JCG 23:2:57 PGB 26:7:146
- Citations, res handbk by Hay, bk rev APG 10:4:126
- Citizenship doc, res tips KTP 8:1:13
- City directories, res guide IMP 14:2:52 SQ 6:1:42
- Civil registration rec, res guide by Wood, bk rev SGB 26:3:iv
- Classroom guide to geneal by Tregillis, bk rev CN 4:2:31

METHODOLOGY (continued)
- Client files, organization tips APG 10:4:116
- Clients, how to gain new ones, guide by Connor/Davidson, bk rev APG 10:4:127
- CN, railway rec, res guide by Douglas, bk rev FAM 34:1:46
- Co courthouse res guide by Bentley, bk rev ACG 22:1:19 MN 26:4:184 NGS 83:4:309 STS 35:4:18
- Collateral kin, res tips LOB 17:1:20
- Collateral relatives, importance of searching, descr CSB 30:3:97
- Collateral relatives, res guide RES 26:3:122
- Company & bus rec for fam hist, res guide by Probert, bk rev SGB 26:1:iv
- Common reference bks descr HQ 95:58:72
- Common terms in geneal defined PV 24:3:4
- Computing birthdates, tips KTP 9:1:7
- Contracts & geneal res business, tips APG 10:2:51
- Copyright law explained BYG 7:1:369 SUN 16:2:34
- Copyright reference guide for geneal by Hay, bk rev APG 10:3:90
- Copyrights descr HQ 95:59:80
- Coroner's inquest rec, res guide RCP 17:2:53
- Correspondence tips KIL 23:3:61 PGB 26:9:187 SGB 26:3:121
- Courthouse rec res tips KTP 11:2:19
- Courthouse rec, legal term glossary MCG 18:1/2:90
- Courthouse res etiquette tips KTP 7:1:7
- Cousin chart KTP 1:3/4:21
- Cousins, calculating using algorithms, descr TGO 7:12:493
- Credential guidelines NGS 83:3:215
- Credentials & postnomials, usage guide APG 10:3:96
- DAR Lib, res tips GH 49:6:12
- DAR res guide AU 19:2:2
- DAR res tips SCS 32:6:126

METHODOLOGY (continued)
- Dates & calendars explained LRT 14:2:549
- Dates & calendars, res guide by Smith, bk rev AG 70:1:60 DM 58:4:190 HQ 95:58:91 MGS 13:1:10 NGS 83:2:148
- Dates & calendars, res guide by Webb, bk rev FAM 34:3:179
- Days of the week, how to determine from specific dates FAM 34:1:32
- Death certs, causes of death, glossary SGB 26:3:140
- Death rec, address list KTP 10:2:24
- Death rec, tips on obtaining KTP 11:1:13
- Deed rec terms, glossary CC 17:4:34
- Deed res tips TMG 17:2:31
- Deeds to prove marr & parentage, res tips NGS 83:3:192
- Descendancy numbering, tips AGS 36:2:83
- Dewey Decimal System guide EWA 32:2:63 SMN 13:6:96
- Dict of common words for genealogists GWD 9:1:6
- Dict of hist terms for geneal by Drake, bk rev BC 19:1:10 JTJ 4:9/10:107 KVH 20:6:67
- Direct of Professional Geneal 1995 by Kerstens, bk rev TTT 19:4:169
- Direct of Professional Geneal by Allen, bk rev MN 26:2:89
- Direct Tax of 1798, res tips GH 49:6:16
- Disabilities & geneal res business, tips APG 10:2:51
- Doc preservation tips PCI 19:2:11
- Documentation, ethics of HQ 95:60:20
- Documentation tips CC 18:2:9 DFH 8:1:15 HQ 95:55:32 OC 31:1:34 SQ 6:1:7
- Dowsing or divining for graves, descr MSG 15:1:25
- Draft rec, res tips KTP 6:4:59
- Editing tips GR 37:3:27
- Eight disciplines of geneal descr APR 14:11:1

METHODOLOGY (continued)
- EN, handwriting samples 1600s GWD 9:1:3
- EN, ordnance survey maps, res guide by Oliver, bk rev ANE 95:57:21
- English naming patterns, descr KTP 8:4:60
- Envelopes, postal guidelines for addressing OCN 18:2:4
- Estate inv, res tips FP 38:4:190
- Evaluating the reliability of misc geneal sources, res guide WMG 11:3:112
- Everyday geneal, essay KTP 10:3:43
- Evidence, descr WCT 5:2:3
- Evidence, res tips HH 30:4:199
- Fam assoc direct 1993-1994 by Bentley, bk rev APG 10:4:129
- Fam assoc organization & management guide by Rose, bk rev AG 70:4:256 DM 59:1:44 VAG 39:3:230
- Fam bk writing & publishing guide by GPS, bk rev TS 37:4:145 VL 30:1:43
- Fam chart workbk by McHugh, bk rev STS 35:3:67
- Fam doc preservation techniques IGS 27:2:112 LOB 16:2:36
- Fam fortunes, fraud & geneal, essay HQ 95:59:20
- Fam heirlooms, identification tips APR 14:6:9
- Fam hist & memoirs, writing guide by Polking, bk rev APG 10:4:127
- Fam hist beginner's guide by Drake, bk rev RCR 10:1:2217
- Fam hist beginner's guide by Pelling, bk rev SGB 26:3:iv
- Fam hist beginner's guide by Rodgers, bk rev QFH 16:1:32
- Fam hist beginner's tips KTP 10:1:10
- Fam Hist Center res handbk by Austin, bk rev HQ 95:59:90
- Fam hist compilation techniques KTP 4:2:18
- Fam hist in the home, source ideas, res guide by Swinnerton, bk rev SGB 26:4:iii
- Fam Hist Lib, beginner's tips LLI 7:4:7

METHODOLOGY (continued)
  Fam Hist News & Digest 1977-1982 microfiche rev SGB 26:2:iv
  Fam hist publication & marketing guide by Boyer, bk rev FRT 16:3:105
  Fam hist res, beginner's guide by Allen/Billingsley, bk rev GH 49:4:200
  Fam hist res guide by Vandagriff, bk rev MAG 8:2:3
  Fam Hist Res Manager by Num et al, bk rev QFH 16:1:32
  Fam hist, tips on making it fun, cassette rev APG 10:4:129
  Fam hist videotaping guide by Bannister, bk rev RCR 10:1:2216
  Fam hist writing & publishing guide by GPS, bk rev NCJ 21:3:301
  Fam hist writing tips PB 10:2:33
  Fam historian, how to become one FAM 34:4:223
  Fam historians & heraldry, guidebk by Swinnerton, bk rev SGB 26:3:iv
  Fam rec organization guide by Swinnerton, bk rev SGB 26:4:iii
  Fam narrative workbk by Gouldrup, bk rev MAG 8:2:3
  Fam jour by Heun, bk rev GH 49:6:178
  Fam newsletters, business management tips APG 10:4:109
  Fam newsletters, publishing guide STS 35:4:24
  Fam rec organization guide by Swinnerton, bk rev SGB 26:4:iii
  Fam relationship guide KIL 23:3:78
  Fam reunion planning guide by Anthenat, bk rev APR 14:6:5
  Fam stories, guide to collecting APG 10:1:29
  Fam tree guide by Dollarhide, bk rev AMG 10:2/3:7 GR 37:4:5 RAG 17:1:15 TTT 20:1:20
  Fam trees, publishing tips HQ 95:58:13
  Fam writing activity bk by Stillman, bk rev RAG 16:1:18
  Faxes, money saving tips ARN 8:2:8
  FBI rec res guide HQ 95:58:15

METHODOLOGY (continued)
  Federal censuses (odd), res tips HQ 95:55:17
  Feminist biography, essays by Alpern et al, bk rev REG 92:4:452
  Filing guide by Dorff, bk rev APG 10:2:60
  Filing methods, descr RCP 17:4:123
  Finding a lost researcher, tips SGS 44:3:159
  Forgery & deception in geneal, descr of past incidents FAM 34:1:15
  French Republic Calendar, hist CSB 30:1:29
  Funeral home rec, res tips PW 15:1:10
  Funeral rec res tips PGB 26:5:104
  Geneal & hist soc address list BHN 28:3:26 28:4:21
  Geneal addressbk by Bentley, bk rev ACG 21:1:25 ARH 33:1:35 DM 58:4:191 GFP 44:4:187 GGS 31:2:120 GN 13:2:89 HQ 95:57:85 KA 30:3:177 MN 26:2:88 NCJ 21:2:187 NHR 12:2:98 NYR 126:3:219 RCR 10:2:2273 SGS 44:3:144 SQ 5:4:42 STS 35:3:67 TGC 19:3:67 TR 35:2:107 TVF 4:2:123 VAG 39:1:74 WPG 21:4:55
  Geneal by mail, writing & res tips RAG 17:1:7
  Geneal classes, teaching tips APG 10:4:123
  Geneal companion & sourcebk by Croom, bk rev MAG 8:1:3 NGS 83:1:62 TTT 19:2:72
  Geneal dict by Ancestry, bk rev TNC 3:1:18
  Geneal formats, descr & examples BT 27:4:76
  Geneal fundamentals, res guide by Jaussi, bk rev GJ 22:4:123
  Geneal grammar tips ARN 8:4:3
  Geneal handbk by Schweitzer, bk rev TTC 21:3:57
  Geneal handbk by Wright, bk rev NGS 83:4:305
  Geneal hobby kit by Everton Publishers, rev STS 35:4:21

METHODOLOGY (continued)
Geneal Lib Direct 1995 GH 49:3:32
Geneal lib, purpose & protocol, essay HQ 95:59:73
Geneal motivation, descr FAM 34:3:149
Geneal of the future, essay CSB 30:1:11
Geneal organization & enhancement guide by Whitaker, bk rev MD 36:4:680
Geneal reference bk bibl 1990-1992 GJ 22:4:109
Geneal refresher course by Jacobsen, bk rev HQ 95:59:90
Geneal Research Direct 1995 by Johnson/Sainty, bk rev SGB 26:3:iii
Geneal scams, tips on avoidance AW 22:2:28
Geneal services, marketing tips APG 10:3:83
Geneal Soc Direct 1994 by Meyer, bk rev GH 49:3:200 TB 21:3:12
Geneal Soc Direct 1995 GH 49:4:29
Geneal Soc, tips on joining SMN 13:1:7
Geneal sourcebk & res guides by Croom, bk rev KVH 19:9:102
Geneal teaching guide by Tregillis, bk rev SGS 44:3:143
Geneal terms in 5 languages, translations MCS 15:4:170
Geneal workbk by McBride, bk rev GH 49:3:194
Geneal, geography & railroads, res tips FAM 34:3:161
Geneal, making your geneal a part of local hist, tips HQ 95:59:28
Genealogical Advertiser by Southwick, bk rev SGB 26:2:iii
General res guide by Dieterle, bk rev RAG 16:4:21
General res tips RCR 10:2:2269 WTN 8:4:1
Generations, essay on common generational themes SQ 5:4:45
GR naming patterns in Am, descr KTP 8:4:60

METHODOLOGY (continued)
Grammar guide SGS 44:3:133
Grand aunts & uncles, terminology descr GEN 20:3:30
Grave rubbings, tips GJB 19:4:94
Gravestone art, meanings of symbols descr STK 23:2:90 TTL 24:1:25
Graveyard preservation primer by Strangstad, bk rev CTA 37:3:143
Gregorian Calendar descr KTP 11:3:49 WRB 17:4:14
Guardianship rec, beginner's tips SCS 32:3:55
Handwriting & symbols of colonial Am, list GWD 9:1:4
Handwriting chart, 17th cent characters PB 11:1:20
Handwriting, interpreting old documents, tips DG 19:2:34
Handybk for geneal by Everton, bk rev KTP 1:2:15
Heirloom res guide by Earnest, bk rev KVH 19:6:67
Heritage societies, res tips KTP 14:4:61
Hints & tips by Heisey, bk rev GGD 11:4:101
Hist assoc & soc list AH 22:2:178
Hist dict by Drake, bk rev MAG 8:1:3 NGS 83:3:223
Historians, their role in contemporary soc, essay REG 92:4:400
Homestead & fed land rec res guide by Barsi, bk rev AMG 9:6:5 GH 49:4:202 HQ 95:55:93
Houses, establishing past ownership, res guide GJB 20:1:2
IGI, res cautions ANE 95:54:19
Illness, disease & death certs, res guide by Briggs, bk rev FAM 34:1:45
Imm & US passport appl, res guide GH 49:3:6
Incorporation, business guide by McQown, bk rev APG 10:4:127
Indentured servants, descr KTP 7:1:5 STS 35:2:10
Independent Scholar's Handbook by Gross, bk rev ARN 8:1:16

METHODOLOGY (continued)
Indexes, legal ethics descr SQ 6:1:47
Indexes, pros & cons SGB 26:3:108
Indexing geneal publications, guide by Reeder/Earnest, bk rev IGS 27:2:117 RAG 16:2:27
Indexing tips BT 27:3:46
Information management tips PCI 19:1:5
Insolvency files, geneal res tips TR 35:2:88
Interviewing fam members, tips SQ 6:3:50
Interviewing tips AU 18:4:4 MSG 15:3:169
Julian Calendar descr KTP 11:3:49
Kindred, names & definitions OC 29:3:126
Kinship & relationship reference guide by Arnold, bk rev CTN 27:4:586 GFP 44:3:138 GJ 22:4:127 LC 16:1:15 NYR 126:1:87 RAG 16:2:19
Kinship reference guide AGE 24:1:9
Land measurement terminology FAM 34:2:109
Land measures, diagram, res aid IG 31:2:48
Land patents, how to obtain copies MCA 14:1:21
Land patents, res tips SMN 13:3:47
Land rec beginner's res tips & glossary SMN 13:7:115
Land rec glossary AW 22:2:34 CC 17:4:34 PT 37:3/4:19
Land rec res tips APR 14:7:1 CPN 20:1:3 GCH 8:6:115 MN 26:2:84 OC 32:2:21
Latin for fam historians, res guide by Gandy, bk rev SGB 26:4:iii
Latin trade & occupation terms, translations TGO 8:1:15
LDS Library, res trip tips LAB 10:1:12
Lecture tapes, sharing, ethical discussion APG 10:4:111
Legal definitions GWD 9:1:5
Legal terms & abbreviations, glossary KTP 14:4:54

METHODOLOGY (continued)
Letter writing tips AU 19:1:3 KTP 6:4:61
Lib of Congress access through internet, guide OK 40:2:49
Lib of Congress cataloging system, guide SGS 45:1:17
Lib of Congress geneal catalog by LOC, bk rev RT 13:1:17
Lib of Congress on-line cat, news search techniques MSG 15:1:21
Libraries; classification, cataloging & computer guide by Mann, bk rev APG 10:2:61
Life hist writing guide by Neubauer, bk rev TR 35:1:51
Light boxes for project layout, tips TB 21:3:4
Living persons, how to locate, guide by Tillman bk rev NGS 83:3:221
Living relatives, tips on finding ACG 21:2:85
Local newspapers, how to locate MSG 15:1:16
Local newspapers, res tips GR 37:1:24
Long distance res tips JTJ 4:9/10:112
Maiden names, res tips GSC 17:3:6
Mail, techniques for addressing properly CR 27:4:93
Mailing tips WPG 21:3:20
Manners & res tips IMP 14:1:5
Maps, geneal res guide TR 35:1:2
Maps, res techniques AU 19:1:3 OC 32:2:5 SGS 44:2:80
Marketing for consulting & professional svcs, guide by Connor/Davidson, bk rev APG 10:2:60
Marr licenses, descr AW 22:2:39
Marr, div, & coverture, common-law concepts descr NGS 83:3:165
Measurements, guide to past systems LOB 16:4:83
Measurements, res tips SGS 44:2:82
Medical pedigree, symbols used SD 14:1:18

METHODOLOGY (continued)
- Memorabilia & memories, preservation ideas by Bosley/Healey, bk rev GH 49:6:178 MGR 30:3:93
- Microfilm beginner's res tips GFP 44:3:131
- Microfilm data storage, descr FCT 96:124:8
- Migration patterns, Ravenstein's laws of migration PGB 26:5:111
- Mil rec see also MILITARY GENEALOGY
- Mil rec, guide to federal & state sources by Neagles, bk rev AH 22:2:184 VL 29:3:145
- Mil rec, res guide on cassette by Parker, bk rev NGS 83:4:304
- Mil rec res tips PW 15:1:11
- Militia lists & musters 1757-1876 by Gibson/Medlycott, bk rev SGB 26:2:iv
- Missing data, res ideas & tips FRT 16:2:62
- Missing marr rec, res tips KTP 8:1:8
- Modern Woodmen of America, res guide HQ 95:55:8
- Mortuary rec res tips PGB 26:5:104
- Multilingual geneal trans guide by Hoffman, bk rev DPL 15:SPRING:5
- Names & spelling, res tips HQ 95:59:22
- Names, EN, meanings of common surnames HQ 95:57:21
- Naming conventions descr PAF 7:3:60
- National Archives res tips NCC 15:2:9 PGB 26:6:134
- National Archives, beginner's guide to non-microfilm rec GFP 44:4:185
- National Archives, geneal res guide MN 26:2:52
- National Archives, Southwest Branch, res guide FP 38:1:1
- National Archives, where & who to write for misc rec, guide QU 12:4:46
- National cem, address list GGP 28:1:28

METHODOLOGY (continued)
- Natu rec, beginner's res tips SMN 13:4:62
- Newspaper archives, res tips KTP 11:3:47
- Newspaper obits, res guide FP 38:4:192
- Newspaper res tips OC 32:2:22 SGB 26:1:29 TTC 21:3:57
- Nicknames, res guide by Rose, bk rev DM 59:1:44 VAG 39:3:230
- Nonpopulation census schedules, res tips GFP 45:2:67
- Numbering systems in geneal, overview JCG 23:4:139 SMN 13:6:98
- Numbering systems, tips on dealing with special cases (adoptions, step relationships, name changes, etc) NGS 83:2:85
- NY, imm rec res strategies GJ 23:2/3:117
- Obits & copyrights descr HQ 95:60:85
- Obits, use of, res tips WPG 21:7:59
- Occupational terms of the past, glossary KTP 9:2:19
- Oral hist guide by Penna-Oakes, bk rev GSC 18:1:8
- Oral hist beginner's tips KTP 7:2:32
- Oral hist interviews, res tips LC 16:1:5
- Oral hist res guide APG 10:3:72
- Oral hist res tips OBN 28:3:93
- Ordnance survey maps, res guide for geneal by Oliver, bk rev GWS 95:42:39
- Organization & enhancement guide by Whitaker, bk rev APG 10:1:30 GJ 22:4:132 NGS 83:3:219 SGS 44:2:83
- Organization tips ARN 8:3:14 AU 19:1:2 CPN 19:5:34 HQ 95:57:18
- Orphan anc, tips on finding parentage SKC 11:1:14
- Paper & photo preservation guide by Tuttle, bk rev FTR :182:4 SGS 45:1:38
- Paper preservation guide by Sagraves, bk rev MN 26:4:183

METHODOLOGY (continued)
  Paper preservation tips SMN 13:1:8 13:2:26
  Parish reg, res tips GEN 20:1:9
  Pass arrival rec res tips GJ 23:2/3:139
  Pass/emig reg, res guide GH 49:5:14
  Pass list res guide by Colletta, bk rev GSC 17:4:5
  Passports, res tips HQ 95:57:9
  Pedigree charts, guidebk by Whitaker, bk rev MAG 8:2:3
  Peerage titles, guide STS 35:3:39
  People Finders, res tips NGS 83:2:96
  Periodical annual index by Clegg & Witcher, bk rev NTT 14:3:82
  Perpetual calendar KTP 9:1:9
  PERSI 1993, bk rev MAG 8:2:4
  Personal hist preservation tips MTG 9:2:75
  Personal hist writing tips KTP 6:2:21 VCG 95:MAR:20
  Personal story workbk by Zeigler, bk rev HQ 95:59:90
  Personalized geneal forms, tips on creating GH 49:3:30
  Photograph albums, how they damage photos, descr TRI 35:2:44
  Photograph & paper preservation guide by Tuttle, bk rev FTR :182:4 GJ 23:1:44
  Photograph copyright questions, answers & tips HQ 95:57:76
  Photograph copyright tips (personal use) HQ 95:55:83
  Photograph dating & identification tips AU 19:3:2 TEG 15:1:9
  Photograph dating techniques AW 22:2:45 KTP 7:3:49
  Photograph dating techniques, guide by Pols, bk rev SGB 26:4:iii
  Photograph identification guide by Nickel, bk rev NGS 83:3:219
  Photograph identification methods, tips PWN 2:2:4
  Photograph labeling hints NPW 13:9:52
  Photograph preservation tips MHP 22:1:2 SGB 26:2:80

METHODOLOGY (continued)
  Photographs, reproducing with computers, tips MN 26:3:118
  Photographs, techniques for tracing roots HQ 95:59:61
  Pioneers prior to 1850, res tips SGB 26:3:122
  Place location hints WPG 21:7:61
  Poor law doc before 1834, res guide by Cole, bk rev GEN 20:2:22
  Poor Law Records, res guide by Cole, bk rev GEN 20:1:20
  Post ofc site location reports, tips on how to obtain them NCC 15:1:10
  Postage meters, leasing tips ARN 8:4:2
  Postnomial guidelines NGS 83:3:215
  Pre-1900 rec, res tips RES 26:3:129
  Preponderance of evidence, descr & res tips NGS 83:1:5
  Preservation guide by Sagraves, bk rev CSB 30:4:144 MSG 15:4:225
  Preservation of fam doc & fam hist, tips MN 26:2:72
  Preserving fam keepsakes, guide by Miller, bk rev PB 11:2:41
  Price index for use as a deflator of money values in the US economy by McCusker, bk rev REG 92:4:447
  Probate rec & wills, res guide IMP 14:1:14
  Probate rec res guide CTA 38:2:91
  Problem-solving guide by McDowell, bk rev ACG 21:4:160 ARH 33:4:173 GFP 45:2:89 MN 26:4:184 NHR 12:4:193 SGB 26:4:iv SGS 45:1:37 STS 35:3:66 WCK 28:4:43
  Problem solving strategies TS 37:3:81
  Problem solving tips PCI 19:1:10
  Professional Geneal Researchers Direct 1995 GH 49:5:30
  Professionalization, tips APG 10:4:121
  Proper Name Master Index by Abate, bk rev RAG 16:1:19
  Psychic geneal & superstition, anecdotal evidence, essay HGO 6:1:1
  Publishing cem rec, guide FP 38:4:194
  Query writing tips BG 16:1:back cover ISC 19:1:19 TB 21:3:40

METHODOLOGY (continued)
- Railroad employee rec explained SCS 32:5:102
- Record-keeping tips VCG 95:DEC:11
- Refunds for unsatisfactory geneal products, tips RDQ 12:5A:110
- Regional hist bk, writing with a committee, manual by Torrance, bk rev APR 14:6:5 BC 19:1:9 GH 49:3:194
- Relationship & kin res guide by Everton Publishers, bk rev APR 14:2:2
- Relationships explained, guide by Arnold, bk rev FAM 34:2:116
- Relative search agencies, addresses VCG 95:DEC:2
- Reliability of misc sources descr LOB 16:2:46
- Reliable, time-tested geneal techniques, res tips GH 49:5:6
- Religious periodicals as a resource, res guide MFH 14:1:35
- Relocating, tips on how to re-establish your geneal business APG 10:2:40
- Res business tips, cassette rev APG 10:3:93
- Res experience, hunting for anc GSM 12:2:26
- Res guide SYH 2:3:19
- Res guide by Bremer, bk rev GH 49:3:199
- Res guide by Croom, bk rev MAG 8:1:2
- Res guide by Dieterle, bk rev GR 37:4:5
- Res guide by Goerlich, bk rev CTN 27:4:589
- Res guide by Greenwood, bk rev FTP 16:3:4
- Res guide by Vandagriff, bk rev PW 15:3:146
- Res guide on cassette by Meyerink, bk rev NGS 83:4:304
- Res hints GWD 9:1:2
- Res tip bk by McDowell, bk rev WCK 28:4:43
- Res tips PWN 3:1:5

METHODOLOGY (continued)
- Res tips, articles by Heisey, bk rev MGR 30:3:86
- Res tips (general) APR 14:12:2 RT 13:1:10
- Reunion planning guide by Bauer, bk rev HQ 95:60:93
- Reunion planning tips ACG 21:2:57
- Rev War, pension rec, use of FHC 19:1:5
- Royal anc res tips AB 23:3:11
- Salt Lake City, res guide by Carlberg, bk rev KTP 7:2:21
- Salt Lake City, res guide by Carlyle, bk rev MAG 8:2:3
- Salt Lake City, res tips TF 23:3:70
- Scams, tips to avoid FTP 16:3:3
- Scrapbk preservation guide KSL 19:1:7
- Secret society rec, res tips & address list SVG 21:3:69
- Sharing of geneal data, tips HQ 95:55:26
- Ship pass lists, brief hist TTL 24:1:3
- Short Cuts in Fam Hist, res guide by Gandy, bk rev FAM 34:1:48
- Skeletons in the closet, techniques for dealing with SQ 5:6:7
- Small business advocacy groups, address list APG 10:3:84
- Social hist, descr ARN 8:2:1
- Social register, use of FTR :182:5
- Social Security number guide EWA 32:1:5
- Social Security numbers, states indicated, list OCN 18:1:5
- Social Security numbers, tips on determining states of origin KTP 8:3:49
- Social Security res tips TS 37:3:84
- Soundex cards, abbreviation list FGC 95:28:20
- Soundex cards, abbreviations used, list SCS 32:2:34
- Soundex guide PWN 3:2:11
- Speaker's Direct 1994 by Geneal Speakers Guild, bk rev APG 10:3:89 RAG 16:2:18

METHODOLOGY (continued)
  Speech giving guide APG 10:1:20
  Standard time system descr GGP 28:1:69
  State Archives referral list LL 30:3:90
  State guidebk, writing guide by Lenzen, bk rev APG 10:4:107
  State postal abbreviations CR 27:2:54 KTP 8:3:51
  State public rec restrictions guide SMN 13:2:28
  State tourism ofc addresses OC 31:1:11
  State vr, res address list SMN 13:2:30
  Surname bks, how to make your own, tips ARN 8:3:3
  Surname hist bks, purchasing tips NCC 15:2:7
  Surname product alert, consumer tips FCT 95:120:4
  Surnames, 50 most common in Am, list MCS 15:4:171
  Surnames in the USA, statistics SKC 11:1:4
  Surnames, res hints for common surnames APR 14:6:1
  Surnames, study of by Gratz, bk rev MGR 30:3:86
  Telephone search for fam, guide by MCI, bk rev RDQ 12:1:4
  Time management tips, cassette rev APG 10:3:93
  Tombstone protection & imaging tips MSG 15:1:3
  Tombstone reading tips AW 22:2:35
  Tracing Your Ancestors: The A-Z Guide by Saul, bk rev SGB 26:3:iv
  Trades & occupations of the past, glossary KIL 23:2:28
  Transcription & abstraction techniques APG 10:3:87
  Twenty way to avoid geneal grief, tips RAG 17:1:12
  Unusual geneal sources, res tips, cassette rev APG 10:4:130
  Updating your research, tips MSG 15:1:29
  Verification of facts, tips HQ 95:57:22

METHODOLOGY (continued)
  Verifying data, res tips GH 49:5:10
  Veteran search hints WPG 21:7:61
  Victualler's licenses, res guide by Gibson/Hunter, bk rev SGB 26:2:iv
  Video res guide by Casper, rev FAM 34:3:176 GJ 23:1:48 NGS 83:2:147
  Video res guide by Video Knowledge, rev OC 31:1:53
  Videotaping your fam hist, guide by Bannister, bk rev GH 49:5:180 HQ 95:59:90 TR 35:3:164
  Videotaping your fam hist, video guide by Peterson, bk rev TTT 19:2:72
  Vr, intl handbk by Kemp, bk rev ARH 33:1:34 FRT 16:2:68 16:3:98 GFP 44:3:138 GN 13:1:20 IS 16:1:11 NCJ 21:1:77 NYR 126:1:86 OC 31:1:53 RCR 10:1:2211 SGS 44:2:90
  Vr res tips AU 18:4:3 SMN 13:2:27
  Weekdays & months in misc languages, guide RT 13:2:49
  Weights, money & measures, guide by Chapman, bk rev ACG 22:1:21
  Western (Christian) Calendar, hist CSB 30:1:29
  Western Am, guide to mss collect at Univ of OK by DeWitt, bk rev GSM 12:2:46
  Women ancestors, res tips WCT 5:2:96
  Women in museums, essays by Glaser/Zenetou, bk rev HNH 50:3/4:231
  Writing & publishing guide by Akens, bk rev VL 30:1:43
  Writing & publishing guide by GPS, bk rev RCP 17:2:51
  Writing & punctuation tips RCR 10:2:2271
  Writing guide for geneal by Eardley, bk rev BC 19:1:9 GH 49:6:178 IMP 14:2:61 RCP 17:2:49 SEE 36:153:51 VAG 39:1:74
  Writing tips, topics to get you started on a personal hist PB 10:4:91
  WW1 draft reg, res tips GH 49:6:20
METHOT, Fam hist by Methot, bk rev ACG 22:1:18

METIS GENEALOGY, Beginner's tips MN 26:2:62

MEXICAN WAR, AL, officer roster 1846-1848 AFH 16:2:10

MEXICO, Colonial era, bigamists & fam, hist by Boyer, bk rev CGJ 3:4:11

MEYERS, B A fl910, TX, obit KTP 7:4:62

MICHAELS, Rose Ersig see Frank Dora WILLARD

MICHEL, Franz Ludwig fl707, EN, biog sketch BYG 7:6:413

MICHELL, Thamzen see George HULL

MICHIGAN, Atlas & plat map collect at Western MI Univ, list KVH 20:1&2:5 20:3:24 20:4:40
Berrien Co, census 1860, bk rev TB 21:3:10
Bible Christian Ch, hist by Ebbott, bk rev GH 49:6:194
Bowne cem rec cont MI 41:2:65
Charleston, women elector reg 1917-1936 KVH 20:1&2:11 20:3:28 20:4:45 20:6:73
Coldwater Twp, Justice of the Peace docket & acc bk abstr 1838-1840 KVH 20:1&2:13 20:3:30 20:4:42
Courtland Twp, early rec 1848 MI 41:4:151
Detroit, Christ Ch bapt rec 1849-1860 DM 58:3:120
Detroit, Civil War bounty payments 1864-1865 cont DM 58:3:107 58:4:155 59:1:11
Detroit, Elmwood Cem interments 1854-1857 DM 58:3:99 58:4:147 59:1:3
Detroit, Female Seminary roster 1867 DM 58:4:173
Detroit, hist by Hivert-Carthew, bk rev ACG 21:2:59
Detroit, Mariner's Ch burial rec 1849-1915 DM 58:3:111 58:4:159 59:1:15
Detroit, natu rec from recorder's court c1896 cont DM 58:3:125 58:4:168 59:1:28

MICHIGAN (continued)
Detroit, New City cem rec DM 58:3:139
Detroit, PO minister biog sketches 1907 TE 15:3:108
Detroit, PO natu pet abstr 1929 TE 15:2:84 15:3:112
Detroit, PO settlers, early hist c1884 TE 15:2:50
Detroit River region, hist & biog sketches by Jacobson, bk rev GH 49:3:201
Detroit, Sacred Heart of Jesus Polish Natl Cath Ch founders 1942 TE 15:3:103
Detroit, St Anne of Detroit parish, marr rec index 1842-1874 MHH 16:1:13 16:2:52 16:4:121
Detroit, St Mary's Hospital patient roster 1855-1873 cont DM 58:3:131 58:4:180 59:1:32
Ecorse Twp, census 1884 cont DM 58:3:135 59:1:36
Ecorse, St Francis Xavier cem rec cont DM 58:3:115
Elkhart Co, marr lic 1889 cont MIS 27:2:32
Fifth Reg of Infantry, Company C roster 1844 DM 59:1:43
Fork Twp, Brown cem rec DM 59:1:19
Freedom Twp, Union vets & widows census 1890 FHC 19:2:30
Frenchtown, battle of 1812, hist by Clift, bk rev HQ 95:58:89
Genesee Co, Old Flint City cem rec by Ladd, bk rev GH 49:3:211
GR heritage & hist, repr 1927, bk rev SGS 44:3:140 TPI 20:3:161
Grand Rapids, vr from the *Eagle* 1880-1881 MI 41:4:144
Grandville, high sch grad roster 1882-1922 MI 41:2:60
Grosse Pointe, hist by Woodford, bk rev MHH 16:1:30
Hancock, Finnish Am Heritage Center, res guide HQ 95:58:65
Justices of the peace, descr of hist duties KVH 20:4:42

MICHIGAN (continued)
 Kalamazoo, Central High Sch reunion news abstr 1940 KVH 20:1&2:11
 Kalamazoo, directories 1860-1896, res guide KVH 19:7:78
 Kalamazoo, news abstr from the *Gazette* 1895 MI 41:4:137
 Kent Co area, marr performed by H E Wylie 1902-1924 by Wylie, bk rev GH 49:3:211
 Kent Co, Bowne Cem rec MI 41:1:17
 Kent Co, cem rec descr MI 41:1:3
 Lima Twp, Congregational Ch rec 1830-1868 DM 59:1:23
 Lima Twp, Union vets & widows census 1890 FHC 19:2:27
 Logging Wheels, hist TTL 24:1:1
 Manchester Village, taxpayers 1869 FHC 19:2:23
 Mecosta Twp, Fairview cem rec DM 58:4:163
 Michiana area, memorial cards c1966 cont MIS 27:2:38
 Michilimackinac, voter reg 1821 DM 58:3:140
 Monroe, battle at Frenchtown (War of 1812), hist by Clift, bk rev HQ 95:58:89
 Oakland Co, census 1890 by OCGS, bk rev DM 58:3:141
 Oakland Co, census 1890, Union vets & widows by Pate, bk rev GH 49:4:212 TR 35:2:111
 Owosso, High Sch alumni 1925 SHI 24:3:16
 Owosso, hist poem SHI 24:3:3
 Presque Isle Co, cem rec by Pines, bk rev GH 49:4:212
 Quaker death rec 1861-1862, MI 41:2:64
 Saginaw, city direct, hist & res tips TTL 23:3:53
 Saginaw Co, deaths, 19th cent, cont TTL 24:1:18
 Saginaw Courier Herald news abstr 1893 TTL 23:3:60
 Saginaw Courier news abstr 1888 TTL 23:3:47

MICHIGAN (continued)
 Saginaw Herald news abstr 1881 TTL 23:3:59
 Saginaw, Hoyt Lib, descr of svcs avail TTL 24:1:11
 Saginaw, news abstr from the *Evening News* 1901 TTL 24:1:8
 Saginaw, State Labor Bureau data, leading diversified industries 1900 TTL 23:3:58
 Saginaw, unemployment bureau roster 1931 TTL 24:1:22
 Scio Twp, mort sched 1860 FHC 19:1:17
 Settlers prior to 1900, biog sketches DM 58:3:129
 Seweba, West Seweba Cem rec MI 41:4:129
 Shiawassee Co, sch teachers (rural) 1893-1934 by Han, bk rev GH 49:4:212
 St Albertus Parish hist sketch 1872-1973 TE 15:2:47
 St Albertus Parish, marr rec 1873-1875 showing anc villages TE 15:2:54
 Sturgis, hist to 1930 by Hair, bk rev KVH 19:7:79
 Union vet & widow census 1890 by Pate, bk rev MI 41:1:35
 Vergennes Twp, voter reg 1882-c1900 MI 41:1:4
 Wakeshma, burial permit abstr (citizens who died elsewhere) c1900-1940 KVH 20:6:72
 War of 1812, muster rolls index MHH 16:2:38
 Washtenaw Co, Manchester Twp, mort sched 1860 FHC 19:1:6
 Washtenaw Co, natu rec 1887-1896 FHC 19:1:13
 Washtenaw Co, Northfield Twp, Civil War vet census 1890 FHC 19:1:7
 Washtenaw Co, poorhouse inmate roster 1847-1850 FHC 19:2:33
 Wayne Co, census 1884 cont DM 58:4:184
 Wayne Co, landowners 1876, index by Huntington, bk rev HQ 95:60:92

MICHIGAN (continued)
Wayne Co, physicians reports 1860-1869 by Ibbotson, bk rev DM 58:4:191
Western area, marr jour by Herbert E Wylie 1915-1924, bk rev STS 35:2:66
Woodhull Twp, hist rec 1837-1962 by Han, bk rev GH 49:4:212

MIGNIER, Angelique see Jacques DEVEAU

MILAM, Benjamin Rush b1788, KY, TX, biog sketch SYH 2:1:16

MILES, James fl779, EN, NF, biog sketch NAL 11:1:10

MILITARY GENEALOGY, Army manual abstr on rifle & light infantry tactics BT 27:1:6
Army, hist reg & dict, repr 1903, bk rev GJ 23:1:43
Army, Western region, uniforms, weapons & equipment guide 1870-1880 by McChristian, bk rev REG 93:4:509
Beginner's res tips HQ 95:60:13
Civil War Army life, descr hist by Billings, bk rev REG 92:4:450
Confederate anc res guide by Segars, bk rev CSB 30:4:143
Fed & state agencies & organizations, res addresses MCI 13:4:89
Glossary of common terms in mil rec FRT 16:3:114
Mil rec res tips PW 15:1:11
Res guide MTG 8:4:149
Res guide by Neagles, fed & state mil resources, Colonial Am to the present, bk rev ARH 33:1:34 AW 21:2:62 FRT 16:3:111 GGS 31:1:47 GH 49:3:200 IGS 27:2:116 MN 26:3:136 NCJ 21:1:79 NTT 15:1/2:5 PGB 26:5:99 RAG 16:1:19 STS 35:3:68 TMG 17:4:135 VL 29:3:145
Res guide on cassette by Parker, bk rev NGS 83:4:304
Res tips AB 23:1:15 MAG 8:1:13

MILITARY GENEALOGY (continued)
Rev War, bounty land warrant appl files, fed sources, res guide SCH 10:3:83
Sources, queries & rev vol 2 by Terry, bk rev GH 49:5:188 HQ 95:57:85

MILLAR, Mary Drummond see William M'LAREN

MILLER, Abraham fl885, OH, legal notice TLL 20:3:56
Catherine bc1817, h Jean Verly, FR, corresp abstr & fam hist PM 18:1:2
Gayen fc1675, geneal by Miller, bk rev corr QQ 95:25:24
Harvey J fl994, NC, compilation of columns from the *North Carolina News Journal*, bk rev GH 49:5:231
Hattie L see Manley L GLEASON
Jacob Milton m1865, w Susan Virginia Sloneker, TX, Bible rec FP 38:4:174
John dc1857, IL, probate rec DWC 21:1:28
John M fl838, OH, diary abstr, bk rev TR 35:1:52
Lena see Bernhard Dietrich THIER
Nancy Agnes see Alexander GALBRAITH
Nancy dc1865, IL, estate rec DWC 21:1:29
OH, Greenlawn fam cem rec up to 1981 TF 23:3:60
Rebecca see Richard HUMPHREYS
Robert, w Susannah Broadwell, GA, AL, MS, TX, fam hist by Benoit, bk rev AFH 16:4:3
Sarah Ellen see Bushrod H HINSON
William D m1891, w Anna M Gilbert, Bible rec SBA 20:5:6
William T fl873, w Frances J Baldwin, TN, TX, biog sketch MT 31:4:160

MILLIGAN, OH, fam hist by Hutchinson, bk rev TR 35:4:223

MILLIKAN, Sarah see John MILLS

MILLIMAN, Aaron fl701, w Ann Case, RI, geneal by Austin, bk rev NER 149:596:440

MILLIMAN (continued)
John d1739, w Anna Bryant, RI, geneal by Austin, bk rev NER 149:596:440
MILLS, Ambrose, NC, fam hist by Styles, bk rev LOB 17:1:24
Benjamin m1774, w Sarah Dwight, w Sarah Loker, ME, anc TMG 17:2:12
David b1791, w Jane Rowe Coppedge, AR, Bible rec ARH 33:3:99
John bc1740, w Sarah Millikan, TN, geneal abstr QY 22:3:3
John Henry f1944, FL, biog PCQ 19:4:6
Netta Haasis see Ralph GORDON
Roger see Abigail GRISWOLD
MILTON, Catherine d1930, FL, obit FLG 18:2:71
MINER, Charles fc1845, PA, corresp, repr 1845, bk rev NFB 27:4:74
William fc1845, PA, corresp, repr 1845, bk rev NFB 27:4:74
MINKLER, Susan see Michael KASLER
MINNESOTA, Adoption & name changes 1855-1881 by Green, bk rev GH 49:4:213 HQ 95:55:92 MN 26:2:90
Albert Lea, natu & citizenship news abstr c1891 FCT 96:124:5
Albert Lea, natu & citizenship news abstr 1900 FCT 95:123:5
Albert Lea, news abstr from the *Times* Enterprise c1895 FCT 95:122:7
Allen Co Libr, descr MN 26:4:180
Bk conservation service providers, address list FCT 95:123:7
Carlston, plat map 1895 FCT 95:118:8
Carlton Co, marr rec 1899 GSC 17:3:7
Carlton Co, res resource direct MN 26:4:160
Clear Creek Twp, plat map c1927 GSC 18:1:4
Computer res sources TSC 6:2:3
County seats & info phone numbers, res aid OCN 18:1:7
Ethnic hist MN 26:4:148

MINNESOTA (continued)
Freeborn Co, geneal gleanings from the *Standard* c1880 FCT 95:119:5
Freeborn Co, geneal gleanings from the *Standard* c1906 FCT 95:120:7
Freeborn Co, plat bk index 1895 by Hiedemann, bk rev MN 26:4:183
Freeborn Co, surname index to the *Times* 1889-1894 FCT 95:118:5
Freeborn Co, twp & village settlement data FCT 95:118:7 95:119:8 95:120:12
Geneal reference guide by Warren, bk rev GH 49:4:212
Grant Co, atlas 1900 every name index by Swartz, bk rev MN 26:4:183
Hartland Twp, map 1895 FCT 95:122:6
Houston Co, res resource direct MN 26:4:166
Itsaca Co, pre-1909 residents, where living in 1958 MN 26:3:120
Land owner maps & direct by Bateman, bk rev GH 49:4:213 HQ 95:55:92 NGS 83:3:224
Melville Twp, GR Evang Luth Ch cem rec GRC 11:2:24
Mil pensioners roll 1883 by PGB, bk rev MN 26:3:136
Minneapolis, firefighter hist & roster 1898 MN 26:3:128 26:4:172
Moose Lake Twp plat map c1927 GSC 17:4:7
Murray Co, Hadley Luth Ch rec 1895-1906 MN 26:3:108
Nininger, early fam origins, list DCG 9:3:12
Nininger, endorsement roster 1858 DCG 9:3:10
Nininger, firsts in hist, list DCG 9:3:8
Nininger, hist news abstr c1932 DCG 9:3:4
Nininger, map & hist of twp borders DCG 9:3:7
Nininger, obit abstr c1920 DCG 9:3:11
Northeast MN Hist Center, descr of svcs avail MN 26:4:156

MINNESOTA (continued)
Olmsted Co, Cutshall photo collect index (Hist Center Lib) OCN 18:3:6
Pensioners (mil) 1883 w/every name index by PGB, bk rev MN 26:4:185
Project for Automated Lib Systems, automated searching guide MN 26:2:58
Renville Co Union news name index 1882-1888, cont GRC 11:2:27
Residents in Roseland Twp ND, census 1910 MN 26:2:80
Rochester, city officers 1938-1963 OCN 18:1:8
Rock Co, Rose Dell (Trefoldighed) Cem rec MN 26:2:76
Sauk Centre, resident roster 1855-1905 MN 26:4:155
Silver Twp, plat map c1927 GSC 17:3:11
St Louis Co, courthouse res guide MN 26:4:158
St Louis Co, res resource direct MN 26:4:160
St Michael's parish hist DCG 9:2:10
St Paul, city election judges by ward, roster 1894 MN 26:2:70
State Fair premium winners 1888 MN 26:3:141
Stevens Co, marr rec 1884-1886 TSC 6:1:8 6:2:8 6:3:7
Stockholm, cem rec by DAHS, bk rev HQ 95:58:89 MN 26:2:87
Virginia, PO ch hist sketch & roster 1955 MN 26:2:86
Vr registrars, address list FCT 95:120:9
West St. Paul hist DCG 9:2:3 9:2:7
West St. Paul, postmaster appointments, roster DCG 9:2:7
West St. Paul, Riverview Bapt Ch hist sketch DCG 9:2:10
West St. Paul, Salem Luth Ch hist sketch DCG 9:2:10
West St. Paul Times news abstr c1906 DCG 9:2:4
Windom, First Meth Ch hist MN 26:3:132

MINNESOTA (continued)
Winona Co, Moravian Ch reg c1882-1900 MN 26:4:167
WW2, Army dead roster by PGB, bk rev MN 26:3:136
WW2, Army dead roster by US War Dept, bk rev MN 26:4:184
MINNICK, Sarah see Jacob FAWLEY
MINTON, Jessie Mack b1922, TX, biog sketch KTP 3:4:49
MISSISSIPPI, Atlas of hist co boundaries by Long, bk rev NER 149:594:188 SEE 36:153:53
Choctaw Co, misc rec c1835-1845 by Wiltshire, bk rev RAG 16:3:19
Civil Rights struggles, hist by Dittmer, bk rev REG 93:3:367
Claiborne Co, slave data abstr from court rec 1804-1833 & property rec 1846-1858 by Terry, bk rev FPG 17:6:42 SGS 45:1:32 WRB 18:1:35
Court rec 1799-1835, repr 1936, bk rev GH 49:5:200 49:5:217
Court rec, repr 1958, bk rev GH 49:5:200
Cumberland Pres Ch, geneal abstr by Eddlemon, bk rev APR 14:6:4
Dept of Archives & Hist res guide HQ 95:60:65
Evangelicalism 1773-1876, hist by Sparks REG 93:3:345
Geneal res guide by Lipscomb/Hutchison, bk rev NGS 83:1:63
Greene Co, agricultural census 1850, 1860, 1870, 1880 by Strickland/Edwards, bk rev GH 49:3:211
Greene Co, tax rolls 1822-1847 by Strickland/Edwards, bk rev GH 49:3:211
Jones Co, cem rec bks 1-3 by Strickland et al, bk rev GH 49:5:201 SQ 5:5:43
Lauderdale Co, marr rec 1839-1864 by Henry, bk rev OLR 9:4:165
Masonic rec 1819-1849 by Henry, bk rev OLR 9:4:166

MISSISSIPPI (continued)
 Monroe Co, Pickle cem rec MCA 14:1:22
 Oktibbeha Co, Confederate soldier & widow enumeration 1907 SYH 3:3:19
 Oktibbeha Co, Confederate soldier & sailor roster SYH 3:4:17
 Panola Co, cem rec by PHGS, bk rev PT 37:1:18
 Petitioners to Congress, roster 1800 AMG 9:6:30
 Woodville, news abstr from the *Republican* 1878-1880 by Wiese, bk rev GH 49:3:211

MISSOURI, 2nd Battalion headquarters company 1939 MSG 15:3:168
 Arlington Junction, Argentine, Maple Hill cem rec by Scott, bk rev GH 49:5:202
 Barry Co, cyclone 1880, hist AUQ 6:4:74
 Barry Co, early hist by Mathews, bk rev AUQ 6:1:11
 Barry Co, hist bk abstr re:pioneer hist AUQ 6:1:19
 Barry Co, hist by England, bk rev AUQ 6:1:10
 Barry Co, hist locations, hist by Mills, bk rev AUQ 6:1:10
 Barry Co, marr bk 1837-1877 cont AUQ 6:1:20 6:4:78
 Barry Co, marr bk index 1837-1876 by Lamp, bk rev OZ 17:4:166
 Barry Co, Mt Pleasant cem rec cont AUQ 6:1:21 6:4:89
 Barry Co, news abstr 1908 AUQ 6:4:87
 Barry Co, pensioners 1883 OZ 17:4:156
 Barry Co, sch officers & teachers roster 1917-1918 AUQ 6:4:84
 Barry Co, sch rec abstr, 19th cent AUQ 6:1:4
 Bates Co area, deaths & obits 1868-1888 by Fritts, bk rev KCG 36:1:51
 Bates Co, probate rec 1850-1923 by Kusek, bk rev FRT 16:2:68 16:3:98

MISSOURI (continued)
 Battle of Wilson's Creek, hist news abstr CN 4:3:36
 Battlefield, domestic money orders at post ofc 1915-1917 OZ 17:4:105 17:4:153
 Benton Co, pensioners 1883 OZ 17:4:155
 Benton Co, St Paul's Evang Luth Ch bapt rec 1890-1900 MSG 15:3:150
 Biog sketches from misc co, repr 1888, bk rev MT 31:3:113
 Blue Springs, news abstr from the *Sni-a-Bar Voice* c1903 PW 15:1:19
 Boone Co, Reserve Army Officers residing in co, roster 1938 MSG 15:3:167
 Boulware Twp, voter reg 1896, 1898, 1900 & 1910 by O'Dell, bk rev GH 49:3:212
 Buckner, Henthorn Funeral Home rec & hist PW 15:3:99
 Cape Girardeau Co, birth reg c1852-1874 MSG 15:3:170
 Cassville, Barry Co courthouse hist AUQ 6:1:2
 Cassville, draft roster 1917 AUQ 6:4:75
 Cem inscr sources, print & microfilm, guide by Kot/Thomson, bk rev NGS 83:4:310
 Chalk Bluff Battle 1863, hist by Ponder, bk rev ARH 33:3:128
 Civil War & border w/KS, hist AW 22:1:4
 Civil War hist vol 3 by DUVCW, bk rev MSG 15:1:56
 Civil War vet & widow census 1890 vol 1-3 by DeGood, bk rev MSG 15:3:172
 Crawford Co, hist & biog by Goodspeed Publishing, bk rev KA 30:3:177 SNS 11:4:2
 Crawford Co, hist, repr 1888, bk rev GH 49:6:196 SGS 44:3:142
 Crawford Co, hist, repr part 2, bk rev TFG 8:2:11

MISSOURI (continued)
Cumberland Pres Ch, geneal abstr by Eddlemon, bk rev APR 14:6:4
Dade Co, div rec abstr c1845-1859 OZ 17:3:96
Deaths out-of-state of SW Missourians 1993-1995 OZ 17:4:159
Delaware Dist, marr lic (unclaimed) c1870-1890 CN 4:1:7
Div, separation, & annulments 1769-1850 by Blattner, bk rev NTT 15:1/2:5
Douglas Co, res tips OZ 17:4:163
Douglas Co, Union companies, hist OZ 17:4:123
Franklin Co, hist & biog by Goodspeed Publishing, bk rev KA 30:3:177 SNS 11:4:2
Franklin Co, hist, repr 1888, bk rev GH 49:6:196 SGS 44:3:142
Franklin Co, hist, repr part 2, bk rev TFG 8:2:11
Gasconade Co, hist & biog by Goodspeed Publishing, bk rev KA 30:3:177 SNS 11:4:2
Gasconade Co, hist, repr 1888, bk rev GH 49:6:196 SGS 44:3:142
Gasconade Co, hist, repr part 2, bk rev TFG 8:2:11
Gasconade Co, marr rec 1821-1873 by Blattner, bk rev CN 4:3:41 KCG 36:2:105 SNS 11:3:8
Gasconade Co, news abstr from the *Owensville Argus* 1904 OZ 17:4:115
Geneal gleanings c1840-1886 vol 1 by Eddlemon, bk rev ARN 8:3:8 GEJ 14:3:32 GH 49:3:212 SGS 45:1:32 WCK 28:4:43
Geneal gleanings 1840 & beyond vol 2 by Eddlemon, bk rev GH 49:6:195 SQ 6:1:45
Grape Grove Twp, cem rec by McKenney, bk rev GH 49:5:202
Greene Co, probate rec 1833-1871 by Rising, bk rev GH 49:5:201
Harrison Co, Baker marr rec CN 4:3:50

MISSOURI (continued)
Henry Co, justice of the peace rec abstr 1849-1858 MSG 15:4:189
Howard Co, birth rec 1883-1889 by Boggs, bk rev MSG 15:1:54
Howard Co, death reg 1883-1892 by Boggs, bk rev MSG 15:1:54
Independence, cem rec by NCGS, bk rev GH 49:5:202
Independence, First United Meth Ch rec hist PW 15:3:129
Independence, news abstr from the *Chronicle* 1840 PW 15:1:13
Independence, news abstr from the *Examiner* 1909 PW 15:1:27
Independence, probate docket 1895 PW 15:1:46
Independence, United SP-Am war vets, Independence camp #31, roster 1898 PW 15:1:31
Jackson Co, cem (lost), res tips PW 15:1:39
Jackson Co, Grand Army of the Republic roster 1895 KCG 36:1:34
Jackson Co, high sch grads 1908 KCG 36:1:43
Jackson Co, marr rec by Meador, bk rev PW 15:3:147
Jasper Co, assessment list 1861 MSG 15:3:134 15:4:181
Jasper Co, probate court rec index CN 4:2:25
Jasper Co, probate court rec index by JGS, bk rev CN 4:3:41
Jefferson Co, hist & biog by Goodspeed Publishing, bk rev KA 30:3:177 SNS 11:4:2
Jefferson Co, hist, repr 1888, bk rev GH 49:6:196 SGS 44:3:142
Jefferson Co, hist, repr part 2, bk rev TFG 8:2:11
Joplin Daily Globe obits 1899 CN 4:2:28
Joplin, letters at post ofc 1887 CN 4:1:14
Kansas City, news abstr from the *Catholic Register* 1902 PW 15:1:17

MISSOURI (continued)
Kansas City, street names (discarded), news abstr 1889 PW 15:1:29
LaClede Co, hist 1820-1926, repr 1926, bk rev GH 49:5:201
Lawrence Co, delinquent tax list 1818 MSG 15:1:2
Lawrence Co, first co court, hist OZ 17:4:160
Lewis Co, circuit court rec index 1833-1851 by Eddlemon, bk rev GH 49:3:212 NCJ 21:1:77 VQS 32:1:4
Lexington, P O W list 1862 KCG 36:2:102
Linn Creek, Moulder House hotel arrival roster 1906 OZ 17:4:118
Lutheran synod, African Am ch worker training hist, 18th cent CHI 68:3:103
Lutheran synod, hist of director of Christian education position CHI 68:3:133
Maries Co, fam hist (misc) vol 2 by HSMC, bk rev GH 49:6:196
Maries Co, marr bk index 1881-1890 by Schwegler, bk rev GH 49:6:196
Maries Co, pos ofc & postmaster hist by Hutchison, bk rev GH 49:6:196
Marr rec 1826-1850 by KRI, bk rev TEN 95:16:21
Miller Co, mark & brand bk 1837-1856 cont SNS 11:3:4 11:4:4
Miller Co, marr rec c1840, cont SNS 11:3:5
Miller Co, marr rec 1837-1861 cont SNS 11:4:5
Miller Co, news abstr from the *Autogram* 1903 SNS 11:1:4
Montgomery Co, deaths & marr from news 1880-1899 by Wheeler, bk rev KCG 36:1:50
Montgomery Co, natu rec c1900-1920 MSG 15:3:165
Mountain Grove Academy teacher roster 1888 OZ 17:4:112
New Madrid, pioneer hist & geneal by Anton et al, bk rev MSG 15:1:55
News abstr (misc) 1940-1945 OZ 17:4:161

MISSOURI (continued)
Newton Co, Jolly Mill hist CN 4:2:19
Newton Co, marr data from news abstr c1930-1950 CN 4:4:61
Newton Co, marr data from obits, 20th cent CN 4:2:21
Newton Co, pioneer hist vol 6 by James, bk rev GH 49:5:201
Oak Grove Banner news abstr 1899 cont KCG 36:1:25
Osage County Republican news abstr 1903 OZ 17:4:157
Ozark Co, census 1860 by Looney, bk rev GH 49:5:202
Ozark Co, census 1880 by Looney, bk rev GH 49:6:197
Palmyra Massacre hist sketch CN 4:1:2
Phelps Co, Hale sch resident tax payers 1887-c1897 MSG 15:3:130
Polk Co, Mexican War vets, biog data OZ 17:3:97
Postmasters in Northeast MO, roster 1905 MSG 15:4:217
Pulaski Co, news abstr 1903 OZ 17:4:109
Purdy High Sch hist 1930 AUQ 6:1:13
Randolph Co, death rec 1800s from the *Clark Chronicle* MSG 15:3:149
Ripley Co, div rec 1885-1888 OZ 17:4:145
Rolla, probate rec abstr from the Weekly *Herald* 1895 MSG 15:3:144
Salem, masquerade ball participants roster 1884 OZ 17:4:147
Sch commissioner election results 1903 AUQ 6:1:16
Schuyler Co, census 1860 by Buckley, bk rev GH 49:6:197
Sedalia, Pacific Railway Shop Employees Seniority & job lists 1937-1939 by O'Dell, bk rev GH 49:5:201
Shamrock, Augusta Pres Ch misc rec 1846-1953 by Dale, bk rev GH 49:6:195
Shannon Co, *Current Wave* news abstr 1887 OZ 17:4:144

MISSOURI (continued)
Springfield, geneal gleanings from scrapbk c1930s-1950s OZ 17:4:125
St Louis area, geneal resource guide MSG 15:3:161
St Louis Co, marr rec of out-of-state persons c1910 MSG 15:4:192
St Louis, death abstr from the *Globe-Democrat* 1895 MSG 15:4:202
St Louis, fur trade papers 1752-1925 by UPA, bk rev NGS 83:2:150
St Louis, letters at post ofc 1870 MSG 15:3:121
St Louis, marr lic from the *Globe-Democrat* 1895 MSG 15:4:219
St Louis, news abstr from the *Globe-Democrat* 1895 MSG 15:4:210
Taney Co, census 1850 by Looney, bk rev GH 49:4:213 49:5:202
Texas Co, fed census 1900 by Melton/Bryant, bk rev OZ 17:4:165
Texas Co, settler's reunion 1906, news abstr OZ 17:4:113
Vernon Co, Sheldon Meth Ch hist OZ 17:3:99
Washington Co, hist & biog by Goodspeed Publishing, bk rev KA 30:3:177 SNS 11:4:2
Washington Co, hist, repr 1888, bk rev GH 49:6:196 SGS 44:3:142
Washington Co, hist, repr part 2, bk rev TFG 8:2:11
Washington Co, Rock Springs Sch roster 1890-1898 MSG 15:1:5
MITCHELL, George see Eva WILSON
Thomas, NY, geneal cont NYR 126:1:67 126:2:122
MIZELL, Morgan Bonaparte b1862, FL, biog by Tinsley, bk rev BT 27:1:2
M'LAREN, William m1859, w Mary Drummond Millar, ST, Bible rec GWS 95:42:24
MOBLEY, John Henry b1885, GA, fam cem rec GGS 31:1:45
MOFFAT, Tabitha see Clark BROWN
MOGNETT, F M fl876, w Sarah E, OR, AZ, hist sketch SUN 16:2:31
MOLESWORTH, Murray m1885, w Florence Ann King, TX, biog sketch KTP 6:1:8
MONDEY, Joan see Robert NOYES
MONJAR, James, OH, biog sketch BT 27:1:4
MONKS, Z C fl862, Civil War letters CPY 24:1:21
MONNETT, Susan Beatty fl882, OH, diary abstr TFP 95:12:91
MONROE, Isabelle see James Bushrod CRUMP
ST, New England, fam hist by Guilford, bk rev AG 70:1:64
MONTAGU, Ruth Mabel see Ruth Mabel BECK
MONTANA, Chester, city & co govt hist & early rec BM 16:1:22
Chester, court house hist & early rec BM 16:1:8
Chouteau Co & Liberty Co, hist & early rec BM 16:1:2
Chouteau Co, marr rec c1880-1930 BM 16:1:28
Dawson Co, sch census, dist #43, 1910 DCH 6:2:8
Great Falls, birth reg 1901 TSL 20:1:9
Great Falls, WW1 selective svc reg 1917 TSL 20:1:11
Jewish communities, biog hist by Coleman, bk rev GH 49:4:213
MONTGOMERY, Alexander, VA, NC, geneal by Ledgerwood, bk rev ARH 33:2:79
Charles W, IR, OH, fam hist news abstr TLL 20:3:57
Elizabeth see John WEBB
MOODY, Benjamin b1811, w Nancy Eugene Wilson, w Mary E Knight, w Lydia Carlton Hendry, GA, FL, fam hist PCQ 18:1:4
Deborah b1586, NY, biog by Cooper, bk rev ACG 22:1:21
Elizabeth see John SEGAR
Lydia Carlton Hendry d1898, h James E Hendry, h Benjamin Moody, GA, FL, biog sketch PCQ 2:3:7

MOODY (continued)
  Martha Priscilla Galbreath b1853, AL, biog AFH 16:4:25
  Nancy Eugenia Wilson b1862, FL, fam hist sketch PCQ 20:1:7
MOORE, Baylis bc1812, w Sarah Stroud, NC, geneal LOB 16:1:21
  Behethland Foote fc1775, h William Butler, SC, biog sketch DAR 129:2:166
  Caledonia G H bc1825, h James A Spears, h William Higgs, h Ozro Baker, h Rufus A Deaton, MS, biog & fam hist ARH 33:2:70
  CN, Ottawa, fam hist add OBN 28:3:97
  Cynthia see John Perley FORD
  David b1819, w Susan Varce, w Sarah Barker, w Diana Herrick, CN, corresp & jour abstr OBN 28:2:50
  Elizabeth see Thomas HASLAM
  Frank M f1854, TN, TX, obit abstr KTP 9:3:47
  Georgia Lewis f1995, AR, autobiog essays, bk rev ARN 8:3:5
  Hallie see Joseph Lecompte CHANDLER
  Hugh d1908, IL, news abstr re:his death CRT 16:4:36
  James bc1712, IR, SC, lineage by Linn, bk rev SCM 23:2:120
  Martha b1735, h Ephraim Ballard, MA, ME, diary by McCausland, bk rev CTN 27:4:592
  Nancy Agnes see John PRICE
  Sarah see Samuel B NELSON
  SC, MS, fam hist by Linn, bk rev RCR 10:2:2279
  Sharpless, w Rachel Roberts, anc, repr 1937, bk rev QY 22:1:7
  Washington m1876, w Martha Ann Johnson, AL, TX, biog by Dietrich, bk rev VL 29:3:146
  William bc1767, NC, geneal LOB 16:1:21
  William Walker b1841, w Julia Hathaway Rowan, NY, NJ, MD, fam hist by Linn, bk rev NCJ 21:3:306

MOORES, Mary Pearl f1923, FL, biog PCQ 19:4:3
MOORMAN, Andrew bc1730, w Catherine Robinson, GA, geneal QY 22:3:7
  Elizabeth see William MOORMAN
  NC, fam rec abstr & biog sketches QY 22:3:5
  William, w Elizabeth, EN, NY, OH, MI, fam hist 1822-1994 by Brummel, bk rev MI 41:2:58
MORGAN, John Hunt f1863, IN, biog & hist by Taylor, bk rev REG 92:4:451
  Margaret see Thomas Benjamin THOMAS
  Mary D see Morris OTYSON
  Meleta Ann see B J Littleberry NIX
  Ralph b1789, w Elizabeth Constant, IL, fam hist by Collins/Tuohy, bk rev CR 27:4:91
  VA, NC, fam hist by Morgan, bk rev APR 14:11:5
MORIARTY, George Andrews b1883, New England, anc NEH 12:1:26
MORRELL, Thomas f1666, NY, fam hist by Mullenneix, bk rev NYR 126:3:220
MORRIS, Betty Jane d1928, FL, obit FLG 18:2:43
  Edward D, w Margaret Mahar, fam hist by Haizlip, bk rev ARN 8:2:16
  John T b1838, IN, fam cem rec GCH 8:1:6
  Mary Frances see Samuel Leonadeth Chester MORRIS
  Melissa f1995, TX, anc KTP 4:1:14
  Nick f1891, FL, diary abstr MCA 14:3:78
  Samuel Leonadeth Chester, w Mary Frances, TX, CA, fam hist ATE 30:1:14
MORRISON, Elizabeth Helena see Joseph Alexander HAMILTON
  Mary see John MCKASKILL
  Robert f1875, w Frances Henry, Jamaica, geneal TNC 2:3:65

MORROW, David m1783, w Margaret Kelso, SC, AL, geneal by Tomback, bk rev AGM 27:1/2:58

MORSE, Charles Copeland f1892, CA, biog SCC 32:2:91

James M d1877, FL, obit TNC 2:2:40

Jane Rebecca d1898, FL, obit TNC 2:2:41

MORTON, Sarah see John FORMAN

Solomon G d1859, TN, obit abstr MTG 8:4:178

MOSBY, Daniel fc1775, w Sarah, TX, fam hist add GR 37:1:23

Edward b1655, fam hist by Harrison, bk rev GH 49:6:208

Elizabeth see Hezekiah MOSBY

Francis Powell see Abraham WILHOIT

Hezekiah fc1775, w Elizabeth, TX, fam hist add GR 37:1:23

Martha Ann (Patsy) see Abraham WILHOIT

Sarah see Daniel MOSBY

MOSELEY, Marvel f1677, w Grace Blaise, w Sarah, VA, geneal TVF 4:3:163

Sarah see Marvel MOSELEY

MOSER, Claude Rankin b1898, GR, PA, anc by Beddingfield, bk rev NCJ 21:3:306

Leonard b1718, GR, PA, fam hist by Beddingfield, bk rev NCJ 21:3:306

MOSES, Annie see Annie OAKLEY

MOSEY, Phoebe Ann see Annie OAKLEY

MOSIER, Wilma Jo see Clyde Wendell RHODES

MOTHERAL, NC, OR, fam hist by Clan Motheral, bk rev ARH 33:3:128

MOTTERN, William bc1768, GR, TN, fam hist BWG 24:1:48

MOUGEY, FR, OH, geneal by English, bk rev GH 49:4:226

MOULTON, Angelina see Jonathan L PEIRCE

MOULTRIE, Riley Septimus see Mary Lucy LARD

MOUNT, Matthias, w Sarah Ann Mendenhall, VA, NC, fam hist by Pohl, bk rev PGB 26:6:123

MOUTON, Jean Jacques Alexandre Alfred f1755, Acadia, LA, biog KSL 19:4:135

MOYCE, Hannah see Bartholomew HEATH

MOYER, Abram L see Mary Harley CASSEL

MUHLENBERG, Henry Melchior f1742, GR, PA, jour by Tappert/Doberstein, bk rev DM 58:3:144 GH 49:3:219 HQ 95:57:84

Henry Melchior f1742, GR, PA, jour vol 2 by Tappert/Doberstein, bk rev WPG 21:4:55

MUIR, Robert b1827, ST, AA, biog QFH 16:4:128

Samuel Boone b1860, w Elizabeth Josephine Cox, KY, fam hist by Vallentine, bk rev NGS 83:1:61

MULDOON, Michael f1821, TX, biog YTD 15:1:37

MULLER, Elisabeth see Johannes WETZLER

MULLINS, Mary Elizabeth Trumbull see Jerome TERRILL

MUNGER, Elizabeth see Cornelius SHARP

MURDOCK, Hamilton f1768, w Mary, IR, SC, GA, fam hist NC 5:1:3

Harvey m1827, w Nancy Melton, VA, IN, NY, fam rec SYH 2:3:18

Mary see Hamilton MURDOCK

Seth f1890, OH, pension appl TR 35:2:74

MURFREE, William f1768, NC, tax receipt bk by Fouts, bk rev RCR 10:1:2217

MURLIN, William f1778, PA, geneal add by Wurster, bk rev GH 49:4:227

MURPHY, Maggie see Frank Dora WILLARD

Martha Ann see Peter J SMART

MURRAY, Alta Palmer f1907, CO, recoll AU 18:4:5

MUSCHAMP, Anne see Drew PICKAYES

MUSGRAVE, Harriet see William CARAWAY

Richard f1798, IR, memoirs of IR Rebellion, repr 1802, bk rev HQ 95:59:87

MUSGROVE, Cuthbert, EN, FR, MD, VA, fam hist by Musgrove, bk rev GR 37:3:25

EN, VA, fam hist by Musgrove, bk rev STS 35:2:69

MUSSER, Robert Sturgeon b1842, w Gertrude Comstock, PA, MO, anc by Musser, bk rev WPG 22:1:48

MYERS, Christian b1796, w Martha Henaberger, PA, biog WPG 21:3:32

Henry fc1880, w Mattie, TX, biog sketch MCG 18:1/2:57

Mattie see Henry MYERS

MYNATT, Leannah see George HALLMARK

NAESMYTH, Elizabeth see Michael NAESMYTH

GA, fam rec by NesSmith, bk rev OLR 9:1:39

Michael m1544, w Elizabeth, ST, fam hist by NesSmith, bk rev TJ 7:1:38

NAHNYBIDA, CN, fam hist by Findlay, bk rev GEN 20:2:23

NALLEY, Mary Ann see George W ABELL

NAPIER, KY, fam hist KA 31:2:34

NASH, Harvey m1833, w Emily Wilmot, CT, Bible rec CTA 38:2:64

Simpson J b1844, w Hettie Martha Palmer, NC, TX, biog SCG 15:1:710

NATION, NC, fam rec JTJ 4:9/10:108

NATIVE AMERICAN GENEALOGY, AK, native pop, geneal res guide NGS 83:4:277

AL, Coosa Co, deed abstr c1836 SEN 2:3:5

AL, FL, Friendly Creek Indians Reg, full name index by Snider, bk rev SEN 1:4:12

AL, Mobile, Apache cem inscr in Magnolia Cem SEN 2:4:48

NATIVE AMERICAN GENEALOGY (continued)

AL, Monroe Co, census 1910, Indian population SEN 2:4:24

Ancient site guide by Durham, bk rev RAG 16:2:27

Atlas of the North Am Indian by Waldman, bk rev NTT 15:1/2:2

Beginner's tips HQ 95:58:67 MN 26:2:62 SEN 1:3:24

Bibl of geneal rec by Kirkham, bk rev LL 30:3:85

Black Dutch hist SEN 3:2:28

Buffalo Ridge Cherokee hist by Rice, bk rev GEJ 14:4:47

CA, Riverside Co, Native American census 1900 LL 30:3:80

Caddo tribe, OK, migration hist TTT 20:1:38

Cherokee, anc rec in U S Court of Claims 1906-1910 vol 3 by Jordan, bk rev HTR 38:1:8

Cherokee Drennen Roll 1851 by Chase, bk rev OK 40:1:8

Cherokee geneal res guide AMG 9:6:6

Cherokee geneal res guide by Gormley, bk rev ARN 8:2:15 SQ 5:5:42

Cherokee geneal res guide by Mooney, bk rev GGS 31:2:120

Cherokee, Guion-Miller appl to the Drennen Roll 1851 vol 4-5 by Garrett, bk rev BWG 24:1:68

Cherokee Guion Miller Roll 1909 by Blankenship, bk rev TTL 23:3:48

Cherokee Old Settler Roll index 1851 SEN 1:3:9 1:4:2 2:1:2 2:2:2

Cherokee rolls, Delaware Dist 1851 by Garrett, bk rev GSM 12:1:16 NCJ 21:3:301 TG 29:1:49

Cherokee rolls, Goingsnake & Delaware Dist, by Garrett, bk rev FP 38:1:13 NTT 15:1/2:4 OK 40:2:45

Cherokee rolls, Goingsnake Dist roll 1906-1910 by Garrett, bk rev ARH 33:2:81 NCJ 21:3:301 TG 29:1:49

Cherokee roots, anc res guide by Blankenship, bk rev GEJ 14:3:32

NATIVE AMERICAN GENEALOGY
(continued)

Cherokee, Saline Dist & Cherokee Orphanage rec vol 3 by Garrett, bk rev NCJ 21:1:78

Cherokee tribe roster 1817-1924 by Blankenship, bk rev BWG 24:1:69

Cherokee War vol soldiers 1836-1839, roster by Mountain Press, bk rev MTG 9:2:70

Cherokee-White intermmarr rec, abstr c1850 cont AMG 10:2/3:21 10:4:11

Cheyenne, Sioux War hist by Greene, bk rev RAG 16:2:19

Chicasaw leaders, biog sketches, repr 1891, bk rev NGS 83:3:228

Chickasaw Annuity Rolls 1857-1860 by Armstrong/Curry, bk rev SEN 3:2:49

Chickasaw Dist Roll 1856 by Armstrong/Curry, bk rev SEN 3:2:49

Chickasaw Nation hist FRT 16:2:56

Choctaw emig to the West, reg 1831-1832 by Wiltshire, bk rev RAG 16:4:19

Choctaw leaders, biog sketches, repr 1891, bk rev NGS 83:3:228

Choctaw Reg 1831 SEN 1:2:2

Choctaw Roll, Citizens by Blood 1907-1914 SEN 2:2:30 2:3:21 2:4:12 3:2:2

Citizens & Freedmen of the Five Civilized Tribes final roll, res tips OK 40:1:34

Correspondence concerning Indian affairs (misc) 1831 SEN 2:1:11

Creek & Sam Menac Indians, relief payment rec c1816 SEN 2:2:19

Creek Indians, AL, wills c1834-1842 SEN 2:3:2

Creek Nation, chiefs 1830 SEN 1:2:11

Creek Nation, permit fees & accts 1884-1887 OK 40:1:20

Delaware Nation, res tips FRT 17:1:2

Diplomats, hist by Viola, bk rev CN 4:3:40

Dunn Roll abstr cont SEN 3:2:45

Early hist sketch FRT 16:3:90

NATIVE AMERICAN GENEALOGY
(continued)

FL, Polk Co, Indian trails, hist PCQ 16:1:4

FL, Seminoles 1850-1874, annuity & per capita rolls by Lantz, bk rev BTG 1:2:7 GH 49:3:203 NTT 14:3:83 SEN 1:4:12 SQ 5:4:43

FL, Seminoles 1875-1879, annuity & per capita rolls by Lantz, bk rev SEN 3:2:49

FL, settlement hist PCQ 22:2:1

Formula to calculate degree of Indian blood SEN 3:2:50

FR contacts in North Am, archaeology hist by Walthall/Emerson, bk rev MHH 16:1:30

Geronimo bc1829, AZ, FL, biog SEN 2:4:20

Gunfighters in Indian territory 1870-1907, hist by Burton, bk rev KTP 11:3:48

Indian territory, leaders, biog hist, repr 1891, bk rev ARN 8:1:8

Lakota, Sioux War hist by Greene, bk rev RAG 16:2:19

Loan words used in English, hist by Cutler, bk rev REG 93:2:216

Maps, geneal res aid SEN 2:3:inside cover

Mesquakie & Fox Wars, hist by Edmunds/Peyser, bk rev MHH 16:1:32

Misconceptions, hist essays by Hauptman, bk rev REG 93:4:496

MN, Sioux, hist of uprising 1862 by Tolzmann, bk rev TPI 20:2:98

Natl Archives res guide, bk rev CAA 7:6:36

NE, Crazy Horse Surrender Ledger by NHS, bk rev NW 18:1:6

NY Indians in ON & QB, geneal reference by Prevost, bk rev GH 49:6:199 TPI 21:1:37 VQS 32:4:50

NY Indians in WI & elsewhere, geneal reference by Prevost, bk rev GH 49:6:199

NATIVE AMERICAN GENEALOGY
(continued)
OK & Southwest Am, U of OK rec guide by DeWitt, bk rev TRC 10:2:74
OK, Cherokee Nation, marr lic 1867-1874 CN 4:1:11
OK, Cherokee Nation, marr pet abstr 1868-1891 CN 4:1:5
OK, fam traditions, abstr from US Court of Claims rec c1905 OK 40:1:25
OK, WW2 death rec 1945 TTT 19:2:84
Omaha death rites CN 4:1:9
PA, hist by Heckwelder, bk rev BTG 1:2:7
Pocahontas, h John Rolfe, VA, biog by Woodward, bk rev CN 4:4:65
Res guide SEN 2:2:9
Res guide by Alton, bk rev GH 49:3:200
Res guide by Gormley, bk rev RCR 10:2:2278
Res hints, personal experiences descr GSM 12:2:26
Ridge fam hist 1790-1840 by Wilkins, bk rev CN 4:4:64
Sam Menac & Creek Indians, relief payment rec c1816 SEN 2:2:19
SD reservations, res guide BHN 28:4:15
Seminole enrollment papers 1900 SEN 3:2:34
Seminole Roll, Indians by Blood 1898 SEN 1:3:2 1:4:13 2:1:24 2:2:20 2:3:34 2:4:36 3:2:10
Southeastern tribes, oral hist by Perdue, bk rev CN 4:4:64
Tecumseh, biog FAM 34:4:194
WA, Kittitas Indians, hist sketch YV 27:1:6
WI, marr rec direct for Ashland Co 1874-1907 by Munnell, bk rev KVH 19:7:80
Words & terminology, res guide by Waldman, bk rev WPG 21:4:50

NAU, Henry d1956, MO, biog & tribute CHI 68:4:166
Margaretha see Johan Michael GABLER
NAYLOR, Mary Ann fl849, KY, MS, biog sketch HQ 95:58:61
NEBRASKA, Butte Co, cem list NW 18:1:5
Guide Rock, hist of name WRB 18:1:12
Lancaster Co, plat bk 1903 index by LLCGS, bk rev TB 21:3:11
Lincoln Nebraska State Journal News surname index 1900 by LLCGS, bk rev TB 21:3:14
Lincoln-Lancaster Co, geneal soc lib cat 1994 by LLCGS, bk rev GH 49:6:197
Red Willow Co, servicemen roster, Am Rev to WW2 AU 19:2:11
Southwest NE Geneal Soc hist AU 19:4:2
Western NE Compendium name roster 1909 NW 18:1:25
NEEL, Asberry b1841, w Elly, OH, Bible rec TR 35:2:103
Asbury see Asberry NEEL
Elly see Asberry NEEL
NEFF, Esther see Gabriel SCHWEINHARDT
Frederike see Baldus Frederick SEIBOLD
Jacob d1887, PA, obit LM 36:4:237
NEIKIRK, Thomas fl893, VA, news abstr SSG 14:4:53
NELSON, Elizabeth see Elias DELASHMUTT
Knute fl860, MN, biog by Gieske, bk rev MN 26:3:138
Martin b1796, NC, AR, geneal by Gilbert, bk rev GH 49:3:217
Peggy see Matthew LANGFORD
Samuel B m1845, w Sarah Moore, TN, Bible rec MTG 8:4:168
Thomas fl704, EN, VA, fam hist sketch KTP 13:3:53
NEMECEK, Marie D fl913, IL, jour abstr CHG 28:1:19

NEU, Philipp Peter b1825, w Maria Margaretha Hagemann, BA, IL, biog STC 18:4:196

NEUHEUSEL, Andreas fl1867, GR, IN, fam hist by Kennedy, bk rev TPI 20:4:192

NEVILL, Z L b1833, w Ann M Lewis, TX, Bible rec STK 22:4:153

NEVILLE, Thomas fc1650, EN, fam hist by Mapes, bk rev RDQ 12:4A:92 SGS 45:1:36

NEW, Ambrose C b1814, w Elizabeth Ring, TX, biog sketch MT 31:4:161

NEW ENGLAND see UNITED STATES

NEW HAMPSHIRE, Atkinson, fam rec from town rec c1768 NHR 12:1:28
 Atlas of hist co boundaries by Long, bk rev AG 70:1:63 NER 149:594:188 NGS 83:3:225 SEE 36:153:53
 Broadcasting hist by Brouder, bk rev HNH 49:3:190
 Dartmouth College catalog & grads 1769-1925 by Rodda, bk rev TB 21:3:11
 Dover, Cocheco Manufacturing Corporation employee roster (women) 1838 SCR 18:6:102
 Dover, marr & death rec from the *Gazette* c1826 cont NHR 12:1:30
 Dover, vr 1686-1850, repr, bk rev BG 16:4:144 SCR 18:6:106 SGS 45:1:32
 Dover, vr from *Foster's Daily Democrat* c1874 cont SCR 18:1:8 18:2:21
 Dover, vr from news 1790-1829 by NHSG, bk rev SCR 18:1:17
 Estate list 1742 PR 22:4:49 SCR 18:3:51
 Estate list 1742 by Oesterlin, bk rev SCS 32:11:255 SGS 44:3:141
 Fam rec (misc) 1800-1900 by Copeley, bk rev ACG 21:2:59 BG 16:2:53 CN 4:2:30 DM 58:4:190 GH 49:6:197 JCG 23:4:138 NCJ 21:3:298 SGS 44:3:144
 Fam hist repository direct by Green, bk rev NHR 12:1:47

NEW HAMPSHIRE (continued)
 Geneal misc, surname index 1800s by Copeley, bk rev OK 40:2:45
 Hingham, settler hist 1623-1655 by Gilman, bk rev GH 49:6:198
 Inhabitants 1776 by Wilson, bk rev FAM 34:2:117
 Kingston, early fam geneal by Hosier, bk rev NGS 83:1:64
 Lee, town rec, 19th cent SCR
 Lee, town rec c1821-1866 cont SCR 18:1:1 18:2:27 18:3:39 18:4:65 18:5:78
 Lempster, Free Public Lib hist & rec, HNH 49:3:157
 Londonderry, vr 1719-1910, repr 1914, bk rev ACG 21:1:22 GFP 44:3:141 GH 49:5:203 GJ 23:4:189 GN 13:1:15 HQ 95:55:91 SGS 44:2:91 TR 35:2:108
 Manchester, Guide Canadien-Francais 1894-1895 by Dubois, bk rev ACG 22:1:18
 Manchester, Jewish community hist HNH 50:3/4:147
 Militia officers 1820-1850 by Lanzendorf, bk rev SCR 18:6:107
 Moultonborough, marr by Jeremiah Shaw 1779-1810 SCR 18:4:60 18:5:85
 Mount Washington Expedition, hist 1870-1871, repr 1871, bk rev NHR 12:2:96
 Natives in the MA censuses 1855 & 1865 cont NHR 12:2:66 12:3:116 12:4:157
 New Durham, vr c1820-1831 cont NHR 12:1:9 12:2:84 12:3:135 12:4:176
 Peace Movement hist c1900 HNH 50:3/4:185
 Peterborough, Easy Hill cem inscr by Aceto Bookmen, bk rev RAG 16:2:21 SCS 32:10:232
 Peterborough, cem inscr, repr 1908, bk rev FRT 16:3:107 GFP 44:4:189 GH 49:5:203

NEW HAMPSHIRE (continued)
- Portsmouth, news abstr from the New Hampshire Spy 1786-1793 by Scobie, bk rev BG 16:4:144 SGS 45:1:32
- Randolph, hist HNH 49:3:133
- Scotch-IR settlers 1719-1776, hist & roster HNH 50:3/4:213
- Stamp Act hist 1765 HNH 49:4:229
- Strafford, marr & death rec from the *Advertiser* c1826 cont NHR 12:1:30
- Strafford, marr rec 1827-1866 SCR 18:6:91
- Strafford Co, marr rec 1630-1860 by Canney, bk rev RES 27:1:40
- Taverns, 18th & 19th cent, hist HNH 50:1&2:23
- Warren, hist, repr 1870, bk rev CTA 37:3:145
- White Mtn resort hotels, decline, hist HNH 50:1&2:125
- White Mtns, artists c1850-1925, hist HNH 50:1&2:81
- White Mtns, hist by Bennett, bk rev BC 19:3:9
- White Mtns, resort hotel hist HNH 50:1&2:51
- White Mtns, resort hotel iconography, 19th cent, hist HNH 50:1&2:67
- White Mtns, resort hotel marketing strategies, hist HNH 50:1&2:95
- White Mtns, tourism c1900, hist HNH 50:1&2:109
- White Mtns, transportation hist HNH 50:1&2:39

NEW JERSEY, Archives general index by Ricord, bk rev CTN 27:4:593
- Atlantic Co, early ch rec by Wright, bk rev HQ 95:60:91
- Bergen Co, deed rec 1689-1801 by Davis, bk rev DFH 8:4:90 LWF 15:2:67
- Burlington Co, census mort sched 1860 cont GMN 70:1:13
- Burlington Co, ch rec (early) by Meldrum, bk rev GH 49:5:203 QQ 95:25:20

NEW JERSEY (continued)
- Cape May Co, early ch rec by Wright, bk rev HQ 95:60:91
- Census mort sched 1860 cont GMN 70:1:13
- Chester Co, will abstr 1748-1766 by Martin, bk rev HQ 95:59:88
- Colonial life 1704-1770, hist from news abstr by Marrin, bk rev FC 13:2:40 GH 49:5:203 GSN 8:1:6 IMP 14:1:29 QQ 95:25:21 SGS 44:2:88
- Court of Oyer & Terminer rec 1749-1762 cont GMN 70:1:37 70:3:130
- Cumberland Co, census res tips 1759 GMN 70:3:109
- Cumberland Co, hist & biog, repr 1883, bk rev GH 49:6:198 SGS 45:1:32 WPG 22:2:51
- Egg Harbour Twp, overseer of the poor rec 1839-1903 cont GMN 70:1:25
- Genesis index 1953-1971 by Nissen, bk rev TB 21:3:11
- Glendora & Gloucester Twp, Ashbrook's Burial Ground hist & names by Leap, bk rev TPI 21:1:51
- Gloucester Co, hist & biog, repr 1883, bk rev GH 49:6:198 SGS 45:1:32 WPG 22:2:51
- Gouldtown, hist, repr 1913, bk rev GSN 8:1:8
- Hunterdon Co, marr rec of Benjamin Smith 1789-1792 GMN 70:3:136
- Labor hist MAG 8:3:13
- Mercer Co, acct bk of James Smith c1818-1826 MCQ 4:1:1
- Mercer Co, admin & guard letters1840s MCQ 4:2:31 4:3:51
- Mercer Co, natu rec bk A res tips MCQ 4:1:12
- Mercer Co, probation appl 1880s MCQ 4:2:21 4:3:41
- Mercer Co, wills 1840s MCQ 4:2:36 4:3:55
- Monmouth Co, hist, repr 1887, bk rev GH 49:3:212

NEW JERSEY (continued)
- Monmouth Co, Yellow Meeting House Ch cem rec GMN 70:1:3 70:3:118
- Morris Co, graveyard & gravestone inscr locators by Raser, bk rev AG 70:1:62
- Morris Co, marr rec bk D c1840 cont MAG 8:1:5 8:2:5 8:3:5
- Morristown, hist sketch MAG 8:2:10
- Mt Salem, Bapt funeral rec of Rev Stephen Case 1884-1887 OCG 25:1:11
- Mt Salem, Bapt funeral rec 1892-1893 OCG 25:3:35
- Passaic Co, census mort sched 1860 cont GMN 70:3:99
- Plainfield Pres Ch cem rec cont GF 16:2:11 16:3:22 16:5:35 16:6:41
- Res tips, misc OC 31:1:8
- Residents in VA, corr & add GMN 70:1:35
- Rev War bibl by Sinclair, bk rev GSN 8:1:7
- Salem Co, hist & biog, repr 1883, bk rev GH 49:6:198 SGS 45:1:32 WPG 22:2:51
- Sussex Co, census mort sched 1860 cont GMN 70:1:13
- Trenton, GR Evang Luth Trinity Ch marr rec 1851-1870 GMN 70:3:138
- Union Co, sheriff biog sketches 1857-1993 by Dutcher, bk rev CTN 27:4:588
- Upsala College, hist sketch SCN 96:10:2
- West Jersey Society tract dwellers 1782-1788, hist & roster GMN 70:3:126
- Westfield, fam geneal collect GF 16:1:3
- Westfield, Plainfield Pres Ch Cem rec GF 16:1:6
- Wills & admin 1670-1730, repr 1901, bk rev GH 49:3:212 SGS 44:2:88
- Wills & admin 1730-1750, repr 1918, bk rev DM 58:3:141 GH 49:5:203 OK 40:1:6 QQ 95:25:19 SGS 44:2:88

NEW JERSEY (continued)
- Wills & admin 1751-1760, repr 1924, bk rev GSN 8:1:6 SGS 44:3:140
- Wills & inv before 1901, index by Stryker-Rodda, bk rev GH 49:3:212

NEW MEXICO, Albuquerque, bapt rec 1706-1850 by NMGS, bk rev TB 21:3:10
- Albuquerque, Ch of the Immaculate Conception burials 1876-1924 by Taylor, bk rev TB 21:3:10
- Albuquerque, news surname index to the *Daily Citizen* 1888 by Drew/Henry, bk rev GH 49:4:213
- Bernalillo Co, census 1850 by Windham, bk rev TB 21:3:13
- Bernalillo Co, Mt Calvary Cem rec by Brewer, bk rev TB 21:3:13
- Censuses (Col SP & Am) 1750-1830 by Olmsted, bk rev TB 21:3:14
- Censuses (Col SP & Am) 1790, 1823, & 1845 by Olmsted, bk rev TB 21:3:13
- Immaculate Conception of Tome Ch marr rec by Windham, bk rev TB 21:3:13
- La Junta Precinct & surrounding areas, census 1860, 1870, & 1880 by Myers, bk rev TB 21:3:12
- *New Mexico Genealogist* Index 1962-1994 by Brylinski/Mossman, bk rev GH 49:6:199
- Our Lady of Belen Ch marr rec by Windham, bk rev TB 21:3:13
- Rio Abajo region, Socorro, census 1833 & 1845, bk rev TB 21:3:13
- Rio Arriba Co, census 1850 by Windham, bk rev TB 21:3:12
- San Antonio de Sandia Ch marr rec 1771-1864 by Windham, bk rev TB 21:3:13
- San Miguel Co, census 1850 by Windham, bk rev TB 21:3:12
- Santa Ana Co, census 1850 by Windham, bk rev TB 21:3:12
- Santa Cruz de la Canada Ch bapt 1710-1794 by Windham/Baca, bk rev TB 21:3:13

NEW MEXICO (continued)
- Santa Fe Co, census 1850 by Windham, bk rev TB 21:3:13
- Santa Fe Parish, census 1821 by Esterly, bk rev TB 21:3:13
- Taos Co, census 1850 by Windham, bk rev TB 21:3:12
- Taos Co, *NM Genealogist* abstr by Hayes, bk rev TB 21:3:14
- Union Co, marr rec 1893-1940 by Windham, bk rev TB 21:3:13
- Valencia Co, cem rec by NMGS, bk rev TB 21:3:13
- Valencia Co, census 1850 by Windham, bk rev TB 21:3:12

NEW YORK, Albany area, ch vr res guide HQ 95:59:9
- Albany area, synagogue vr res guide HQ 95:59:9
- Albany, res tips HQ 95:60:53
- Albany, St Peter's Epis Ch rec 1785-1831 cont CDG 14:2:14 14:3:22 14:4:30 15:1:5
- Alfred, First Alfred Seventh Day Bapt Ch membership rec 1816-1886 by Sanford, bk rev NYR 126:4:282
- Allegany Co, will bk index 1836-1906 by Samuelsen, bk rev GH 49:5:205
- Ashland, Mountain Valley cem rec & hist GG 8:3:84
- Atlas of hist co boundaries by Long, bk rev NER 149:594:188 SEE 36:153:53
- Beekman Patent, settler geneal & hist by Doherty, bk rev AG 70:4:254 AW 22:2:32 IG 31:2:58 RCP 17:4:118 TR 35:4:221 VQS 32:3:43
- Brooklyn, hist, repr 1867-1870, bk rev CTA 37:3:147
- Brooklyn, Roman Cath parishes 1822-1872, res address list SMN 13:1:13
- Castle Garden imm receiving station hist 1855-1890 FCT 95:119:3
- Catskill, Goodwin cem rec GG 8:3:82
- Cattaraugus Co, will bk index 1830-1888 by Samuelsen, bk rev GH 49:5:205

NEW YORK (continued)
- Cayuga Co, direct 1868, repr 1963, bk rev GH 49:5:205
- Cayuga Co, hist, repr 1963, bk rev FRT 16:3:109 GH 49:5:205 RAG 16:2:25
- Central region, geneal & fam hist, repr 1912, bk rev GH 49:5:205
- Chautauqua Co, cem inscr & co hist, repr 1931, bk rev GH 49:5:205 RAG 16:2:28
- Chautauqua Co, RI residents in census 1855 RIR 21:1:11
- Civil War, 144th Reg Vol Infantry hist, repr 1903, bk rev BTG 1:2:6 MGR 29:4:123 NYQ 95:11:21 OK 40:1:7
- Clymer, Dutch settlement, hist DFH 8:4:80
- Denization rec, natu rec, & oaths of allegiance, colonial era, repr 1975, bk rev GH 49:3:212
- Documentary hist on CD-ROM, rev TPI 21:1:45
- Durham, Morrison Road cem rec GG 8:3:96
- Ellis Isl, hist & ship manifests GJ 23:2/3:51
- Ellis Isl, res bibl GJ 23:4:147
- Ellis Isl, res tips GJ 23:4:176
- Ellis Isl myths & misconceptions, hist & res tips GJ 23:2/3:65
- Erie Co, centennial hist, repr 1876, bk rev ACG 21:4:159 SGS 45:1:32
- Flatbush, Cem of the Holy Cross, IR cem rec by Silinonte, bk rev GSC 17:4:6 SGS 44:3:141 YV 27:1:11
- Franklin Co, *Franklin Historic Review* abstr 1968-1985 SLV 12:3:4
- Franklin Co, will bk index 1809-1916 by Samuelsen, bk rev GH 49:5:206
- French Ch of NY, vr 1688-1804, repr 1886, bk rev GH 49:5:204
- Gazetteer, repr 1860, bk rev GFP 44:4:189 GH 49:5:204 HQ 95:57:83 NYR 126:3:218 SGS 44:3:145
- Geneal & Biog Rec, founding, hist NYR 126:1:3

NEW YORK (continued)
  Geneal notes of misc fam, repr 1883, bk rev GH 49:5:204
  Goshen, Meth Epis Ch bapt & marr rec 1851-1912 OCG 25:1:10 25:3:34
  Goshen, Pres Ch rec c1796-1800 OCG 25:1:12
  Goshen, Pres Ch rec 1817 OCG 25:3:35
  GR settlement 1710, hist by Dixon, bk rev NYR 126:3:214
  Greene Co, news & biog rev abstr on misc people, 19th cent GG 7:4:158
  Greene Co, supervisors proceedings 1898 GG 8:3:98
  Greenville, Bapt funeral rec of Rev Stephen Case 1884-1887 OCG 25:1:11
  Greenville, Bapt funeral rec 1892-1893 OCG 25:3:35
  Hempstead, ear marks 1785-1861 cont NYR 126:2:132 126:3:201 126:4:250
  Hempstead Town, hist essays by Naylor, bk rev NYR 126:3:217
  Herkimer Co, census index 1835 by Samuelsen, bk rev GH 49:4:214
  Holland Purchase, pioneer hist, repr 1849, bk rev NYQ 95:11:21
  Holland Society yearbk, repr 1906, bk rev CN 4:4:65 DFH 8:4:90 YV 27:4:105
  Hudson River hist & paintings, repr 1866, bk rev CTA 37:3:147
  Huguenot births, marr & deaths 1688-1804 by Wittmeyer, bk rev GN 13:2:96
  Imm rec res strategies GJ 23:2/3:117
  Indians from NY in ON & QB, geneal res guide by Prevost, bk rev TPI 21:1:37
  Jefferson Co, geneal hist abstr 1905 cont SLV 12:2:12
  Kerhonkson, Federated Ch marr rec c1874 cont UG 23:2:12
  Kings Co, settler reg to 1700, repr 1881, bk rev GH 49:5:206

NEW YORK (continued)
  Kingsbury, cem rec by Moore, bk rev GH 49:5:207
  Kinship Valley, source rec & publications on CD-ROM, rev TTL 23:3:48
  Macomb, Civil War soldier biog sketches SLV 12:1:4 12:2:5 12:3:6
  Manhattan, hist 1614-1987 by Allgeyer, bk rev ARH 33:4:173 ARN 8:4:13
  Marr rec from the rec of Ashbel Parmalee c1831 SLV 12:3:5
  Monroe Co, news abstr from the *Christian Leader* 1873-1878 HY 16:1:5
  Montgomery, Pledge of Association of Hanover Precinct 1775 OCG 25:1:9
  New Netherland Reg 1624-1674 by O'Callaghan, bk rev HQ 95:58:88
  New Netherland res guide by Epperson, bk rev AG 70:1:59
  New Netherland, council minutes 1655-1656 by Gehring, bk rev GJ 23:4:189 NYR 126:3:215 RAG 16:3:19
  New Netherland, naming systems & customs, hist NYR 126:1:35
  New Rochelle, wills 1784-1830, microfiche rev ATE 30:1:2
  New York City, admiralty court & other rec of T Dongan by Christoph, bk rev AG 70:1:59
  New York City, census 1870, CD-ROM rev APG 10:3:90
  New York City, GR Reformed Ch rec 1759-1776 NYR 126:2:97 126:3:179 126:4:261
  New York City, GR section hist sketch SCS 32:5:114
  New York City, hist atlas by Homberger, bk rev NYR 126:2:152
  New York City, Loyalist inhabitants 1774-1776 by Wilson, bk rev GN 13:2:92
  New York City, Meth marr 1785-1893, brides & grooms index by Scott, bk rev MGS 13:3:45

NEW YORK (continued)
- New York City, Meth marr 1785-1893 w/brides index by Fisher, bk rev GH 49:5:207
- New York City, pass lists 1715-1844, index by Samuelsen, bk rev GH 49:5:204
- Orange Co, biog hist, repr 1895, bk rev BT 27:2:32 DWC 21:2:58 NYR 126:3:214.
- Orange Co, post ofc hist OCG 25:3:33
- Orange Co, wills c1810 OCG 25:3:31
- Orange Co, wills c1813 OCG 25:1:8
- Orphans who emig to Great Plains regions, res address list TC 14:1:16
- Otsego Co, biog sketches of leading citizens, repr 1893, bk rev GG 8:3:111 LWF 15:2:65 SGS 45:1:33 SLV 12:3:10
- Owego, Tioga Co Hist Soc, descr KTP 9:3:39
- Palenville, Gloria Dei Epis Ch burials c1910 cont UG 23:2:18
- Parishville, census enumerator's blotter 1892 SLV 12:2:10
- Pitcairn, news abstr from the *Gouverneur Herald* c1875 SLV 12:3:11
- Pompey, reunion & hist 1875, name index, repr 1960, bk rev FRT 16:3:109 GH 49:5:206
- Queensbury, gazetteer & bus direct 1871 by Child, bk rev HQ 95:60:91
- Rensselaer Co, First Reformed Ch hist 1793-1993 by Bowman/Hintermaier, bk rev GH 49:5:206
- Rensselaer Co, surrogate rec surnames 1794-1873 by Wells, bk rev TJ 7:2:75
- Saratoga Co, early hist by VanDerwerker, bk rev HQ 95:58:88
- Saratoga Co, gazetteer & bus direct 1871 by Child, bk rev HQ 95:60:91
- Saratoga Co, hist, repr 1928-1938, bk rev GH 49:5:206
- Saratoga, will bk index 1799-1921 by Samuelsen, bk rev GH 49:4:214

NEW YORK (continued)
- Saugerties, news abstr from the *Telegraph* 1861-1870 by Klinkenberg, bk rev SGS 44:2:89
- Saugerties, obits & death notices from the *Telegraph* 1861-1870 by Klinkenberg, bk rev BT 27:4:70 GH 49:5:207 NYR 126:2:155
- Schoharie Co, hist 1713-1882, repr 1882, bk rev CTA 37:3:143 GH 49:4:214 NYQ 95:11:21 RAG 16:2:29 SCS 32:3:63 SGS 44:2:89 YV 27:1:11
- Sennett, First Bapt Ch rec, repr 1963, bk rev FRT 16:3:109 GH 49:5:205 RAG 16:2:25
- Seventh Day Bapt rec (central NY area) 1797-1940s by Sanford, bk rev GH 49:3:212 SGS 44:2:89
- Shawangunk Mtns, berry picker oral hist by Fried, bk rev NYR 126:4:280
- St Lawrence Co, Parishville, census 1892 SLV 12:1:11
- St Lawrence Co, residents listed in Jefferson Co NY 1800s SLV 12:1:8
- Ulster Co, Geneal Soc Lib descr DFH 8:4:74
- Ulster Co, Kerhonkson, Federated Ch marr rec 1869-1873 UG 23:1:6
- Ulster Co, Olive Bridge Meth Ch members c1890s UG 23:3:25
- Ulster Co, will bk 1804 UG 24:1:10
- Vr res tips GSC 17:3:6
- War of 1812 claim awards index, repr 1860, bk rev GH 49:5:186
- Washington Co, marr news abstr 1799-1880 by Jackson, bk rev LWF 15:2:67
- West Point, grads who died in the Civil War, roster OCG 25:3:34
- Westchester Co, census name indexes 1790-1840 by Fuller, bk rev GH 49:4:214
- Westchester Co, marr notices in the *Eastern State Journal* 1845-1875 by Fuller, bk rev GH 49:4:214

NEW YORK (continued)
 Westchester Co, obits & death notices in *Eastern State Journal* 1845-1875 by Fuller, bk rev GH 49:4:214
 Westchester Co, wills 1664-1784 by Pelletreau, bk rev GH 49:3:213 RAG 17:1:16
 Woodside, Calvary Cem internments by surname, cont IS 16:1:17 16:2:51 16:3:82
NEW ZEALAND, African War soldier rolls & casualties 1901-1903 by NZSG, bk rev GH 49:4:202
 Civil Registration res guide by Smith, bk rev QFH 16:4:140
 Electoral roll 1893 (women) by NZSG, bk rev GH 49:3:197
NEWCOMBE, Eliza see Joseph TURNER
NEWELL, Jeffrey b1780, VT, biog sketch BAT 24:2:69
NEWHALL, Nathaniel b1660, w Elizabeth Symonds, fam rec TEG 15:2:93
 Thomas bc1595, EN, MA, geneal TEG 15:1:38 15:4:210
NEWMAN, Augusta Christine b1852, h John Lee, IL, IA, obit HH 30:4:197
 Catherine Jett see Benjamin Harrison NEWMAN
 Catrina see Johann BAERG
 Leslea f1995, MA, recoll JL 8:1/2:121
NEWTON, Abigail see Joseph ARNOLD
 Prudence see Rufus WELLS
 Wilberforce f1883, MA, ch bapt reg BG 16:4:111
NEY, Philip see Philipp Peter NEU
NEYER, OH, fam rec TTH 16:3:78
NICHOLLS, EN, TX, fam hist KTP 7:4:56
NICHOLS, James b1755, w Lydia Harrington, CT, biog sketch BCF 95:FEB:2
 Jesse Clyde, MO, geneal by Curran, bk rev NGS 83:2:146
 Kathleen Lipsmeyer f1995, AR, autobiog, bk rev ARH 33:3:127

NICHOLS (continued)
 Robert bc1764, w Sarah Robertson, MD, fam hist MD 36:1:56
 Sarah see Solomon Johnson NICHOLS
 Solomon Johnson b1824, w Sarah, KY, biog sketch KA 31:2:36
 William E bc1810, w Elizabeth Hanchey, SC, AL, fam hist FLG 18:3:87
NICHOLSON, James m1857, w Sarah A Frank, IN, biog sketch MIS 27:4:83
 John b1804, w Mary Polly McIver, TX, geneal PWN 2:4:21
NICKOLS, Frances Elizabeth see Robert Walton WHITWORH
NICODEMUS, Johann Heinrich, GR, OH, fam hist & corr by Nicodemus, bk rev TR 35:3:167
NICOLLE, Amy f1939, NF, recoll NAL 11:3:99
NIFONG, Harvey b1828, w Rebecca Jane Spangler, IL, AR, fam hist ARH 33:1:18
NILES, Maria T see Benjamin LAMONT
NIMMONS, Anna Thomas see John Stephen POWELL
NISSLY, Feronica f1833, PA, fam fraktur MGS 13:3:35
NIX, B J Littleberry b1820, w Meleta Ann Morgan, w Mary T Leslie, GA, TX, fam rec PWN 2:5:17
NIXON, Richard b1913, biog by Friedman/Levantrosser, bk rev REG 93:3:384
 Richard b1913, biog by Hoff, bk rev REG 93:3:371
NOBLE, Hannah see Charles HARRIS
NOBLES, Laura Francis bc1875, h Hubert Shands, TX, biog & fam hist MCG18:1/2:45
NOE, Cleo see James Alfred BAGLEY
NOEL, Francois f1669, w Nicole Le Grand, QB, geneal LG 95:54:38
NOIRET, Jaquemyne see Philippe DU TRIEUX

NORCROSS, Henry Fanning f1857, w Sarah Marcia Keeney, w Susan Brainerd Arnold, CT, diary abstr CTA 37:3:127

NORMAN, Dewey f1945, FL, recoll of WW2 PCQ 12:3:5

Dru W see Ida Marie BAUER

Hetty Elizabeth Wilhelm f1956, autobiog, bk rev STK 23:2:95

NORRIS, EN, LA, fam hist by Wise, bk rev GH 49:5:234

Henry DeButts f1869, LA, pet FPG 17:2:9

James M b1819, w Sophronia, SC, TN, TX, biog & corresp abstr GR 37:4:19

Sophronia see James M NORRIS

NORRISS, Elizabeth see Henry Edward BOTELER

NORTH, Ella see D H BROWN

Murtella Harper f1879, MI, diary abstr cont DM 59:1:7 58:3:103 58:4:151

NORTH CAROLINA, Albemarle, Old Albemarle Cem rec SCG 14:2:675

Anson Co, mort sched 1860 SCG 15:1:706

Archival & mss repositories, direct by Hofmann, bk rev RCR 10:1:2212

Archival & mss repositories, direct by SNCA, bk rev SEE 36:153:22

Arden, Christ Sch cem survey LOB 16:1:12

Artisans, hist by Lewis, bk rev REG 93:4:472

Bertie Co, deeds 1785-1794 by Bradley, bk rev GH 49:3:213 NCJ 21:1:66

Bertie Co, estates 1734-1788 by Gammon, bk rev GH 49:4:215

Bibl of bks on NC & SC fam by Hehir, bk rev AW 21:3:93 CSB 30:4:143 GH 49:4:214 RCR 10:1:2210 SGS 44:2:85

Brunswick Co, board of co commissioners minutes 1868-1872 by Thompson, bk rev NCJ 21:1:67

Brunswick Co, court of pleas & quarter sessions minutes 1805-1813 by Butler, bk rev NCJ 21:1:66

NORTH CAROLINA (continued)

Brunswick Co, voter reg rec 1902, 1904, 1906 & 1908 by Haskett, bk rev NCJ 21:1:67

Buncombe Co, biog sketches of first fam LOB 17:1:1

Buncombe Co, court minutes 1794-1795 LOB 16:1:1 16:2:34 16:4:76

Buncombe Co, Tabernacle Cem rec & hist 1837-1994 by Goodson et al, bk rev NCJ 21:3:288

Buncombe Co, will abstr 1831 cont LOB 14:1:3

Buncombe Co, will abstr 1890-1900 cont LOB 16:2:31 16:4:94 17:1:22

Burke Co, treasury bk of J L Laxton by Momier, bk rev NCJ 21:1:69

Cabarrus Co, court of pleas & quarter sessions rec 1805-1817 by Bost et al, bk rev RCR 10:4:2376

Caldwell Co, deed bk c1840 CAL 14:4:88

Caldwell Co, entry takers bk 2 c1854, cont CAL 14:2:35 14:4:82

Caldwell Co, Yadkin Bapt Ch minutes 1787-1839 CAL 14:2:40

Cape Fear (lower), cem inscr vol 1 & 3 by Kellam, bk rev NCJ 21:1:71

Catawba Co, will bk 1817-1867 by Sherrill, bk rev GH 49:6:200 RCR 10:1:2214

Census 1870, CD-ROM rev TEN 95:16:22

Census index 1850 CD-ROM rev APR 14:6:4

Census res guide by Pierce, bk rev NCJ 21:4:422

Civil War soldier biog sketches 1861-1865 vol 1 by Sheppard, bk rev NCJ 21:3:291

Civil War soldier biog sketches by MCGS, bk rev HQ 95:58:88

Civil War troop roster 1861-1865 by Jordan/Manarin, bk rev LOB 16:1:26

Clay Co, hist by HBCCC, bk rev GH 49:4:215

NORTH CAROLINA (continued)
Cleveland Co, court of pleas & quarter sessions rec 1844-1845 by Caldwell, bk rev NCJ 21:3:288
Cleveland Co, superior court minutes 1841-1848 by Thompson, bk rev NCJ 21:3:289
Co maps 1663-1943 LOB 17:1:7
Colonial land entries 1758-1768 by Pruitt, bk rev NCJ 21:3:295
Colonial rec of the executive council 1755-1775 by Cain, bk rev NCJ 21:2:183 RCR 10:2:2272 TR 35:3:167
Company A, NC Volunteers 1847, biog sketches NCJ 21:3:245
Concord, hist 1796-1860 by Horton, bk rev NCJ 21:2:177
Confederate Militia & Home Guard letters & rec 1862-1865 by Bradley, bk rev NCJ 21:3:296 VAG 39:2:152 39:4:319 NCJ 21:4:421
Council rec 1755-1775 (exec council) by Cain, bk rev VAG 39:1:73
Co level rec, res aids by Hofmann, bk rev NCJ 21:3:302
Court rec 1697-1701 (higher court) by Parker, bk rev VAG 39:1:72
Craven Co, census 1860 by Beauchamp, bk rev NCJ 21:1:69
Craven Precinct, tithables 1720 NCJ 21:1:16
Cumberland Co, deed abstr 1754-1770 by Fields, bk rev GH 49:4:216 NCJ 21:2:177
Currituck Co, cem rec by AGS, bk rev NCJ 21:3:289
Currituck Co, tax & militia rec from 18th cent by Bennett, bk rev GH 49:5:208
Death notices from the *North Carolina Presbyterian* 1860 NCJ 21:4:375
Div & separation pet to the General Assembly c1779 cont NCJ 21:1:49 21:3:254
Dobbs Co, grantor/grantee index 1746-1773 NCJ 21:1:3 21:2:139 21:3:268 21:4:399

NORTH CAROLINA (continued)
Duplin Co, court of pleas & quarter sessions minutes abstr 1814-1816 by Franks, bk rev NCJ 21:3:289
Duplin Co, gravestone rec vol 1 & 2 by Kellam/Brown, bk rev NCJ 21:1:69
Eden, Ch of the Epiphany hist 1844-1944 by Atkins, bk rev RCR 10:1:2213
Edenton Dist, loose estate papers 1756-1806 by Bradley, bk rev NCJ 21:4:421 VAG 39:3:232 39:4:319
Edgecombe Co, will abstr 1824-1857 by Gammon, bk rev GH 49:4:216
Edgecombe Co, will abstr 1858-1910 by Gammon, bk rev GH 49:4:216 NCJ 21:2:178
Executive Council rec 1755-1775 by Owens/Trimble, bk rev RAG 16:2:29
Fayetteville, marr & death notices from the *North Carolina Presbyterian* 1859 NCJ 21:2:115
Forsyth Co, Blacksmith Nathaniel F Sullivan's jour c1846 cont FC 13:3:34
Forsyth Co, court of pleas & quarter sessions rec 1858 FC 13:2:26 13:3:20 14:1:37
Forsyth Co, Nazareth Evang Luth Ch hist FC 13:2:6
Forsyth Co, *Twin City Daily Sentinel* news abstr 1901 FC 14:1:17
Fourth Creek Congregation, Sharpe's 1773 map, index of names RCR 10:1:2201
Gates Co, census 1900 by Powell, bk rev NCJ 21:2:179
Gates Co, court of pleas & quarter sessions minutes 1779-1786 by Fouts, bk rev NCJ 21:2:178 RCR 10:1:2217 VAG 39:1:71
Gates Co, slave work reg for Great Dismal Swamp 1847-1861 by Fouts, bk rev RCR 10:4:2378 VAG 39:3:228
Geneal of GR west of Catawba River NC 1750-1800 by Eaker, bk rev TPI 20:2:97

NORTH CAROLINA (continued)
Germanton, blacksmith acc c1847 FC 13:4:37
Globe Valley, hist CAL 14:2:29
GR speaking people west of the Catwaba River in NC & MO 1750-1800 by Eaker, bk rev GH 49:4:215 NCJ 21:2:183
Graylyn Estate, jour abstr & hist FC 14:1:2
Greensboro, Buffalo Pres Ch hist & cem rec by Donnell, bk rev NCJ 21:1:70
Guilford Co, fam burying grounds & abandoned ch cem guide by Smith, bk rev NCJ 21:2:179
Guilford Co, fam cem rec, repr 1978, bk rev GH 49:5:208
Guilford Co, hist, repr 1902, bk rev GH 49:3:213
Guilford Co, population sched 1860, annotated by Browning/Normandy, bk rev NCJ 21:3:290
Halifax Co, deed abstr 1807-1817 by Bradley, bk rev GH 49:4:216 NCJ 21:2:179 21:3:291 VAG 39:2:152
Halifax, news abstr from the *North Carolina Journal* 1806-1810 by Fouts, bk rev RCR 10:1:2216
Harnett Co, hist & heritage by HHBC, bk rev NCJ 21:1:71
Haywood Co, deeds 1809-1815 AMG 9:6:16 10:2/3:41 10:4:21
Haywood Co, hist & heritage by HCGS, bk rev GH 49:4:216 LOB 16:2:41 NCJ 21:3:291
Hertford Co, tax receipt bk of W Murfree 1768-1770 by Fouts, bk rev RCR 10:1:2217
Hillsboro, census 1920 index DOG 6:1:9
Hillsborough Dist, equity bond docket 1789-1817 cont NCJ 21:2:160
Hist 1776, repr 1854-1856, bk rev GH 49:5:208 NCJ 21:2:184
Hist bks, annotated bibl by Jones, bk rev NCJ 21:3:297

NORTH CAROLINA (continued)
Jackson Co, mort sched 1870 JTJ 4:9/10:105
Johnston Co, deed abstr by Haun, bk rev RCR 10:4:2381
Johnston Co, early settlers, hist & biog JC 21:3:54
Johnston Co, estate division rec 1818-1850 cont JC 21:3:44
Johnston Co, grantor/grantee index 1746-1773 NCJ 21:1:3 21:2:139 21:3:268 21:4:399
Johnston Co, marr 1764-1867 by Meldrum, bk rev TVF 4:2:121
Johnston Co, taxpayer roster 1815 JC 21:3:47
Jonesboro Heights Bapt Ch hist 1869-1994, video by JHBCHC, bk rev NCJ 21:3:309
Kendall Bapt Ch cem rec SCG 15:1:713
Land entries 1753-1756 by Pruitt, bk rev NCJ 21:1:76
Land patent abstr 1663-1729 by Hofmann, bk rev APR 14:2:2 BWG 24:1:67 RCR 10:1:2212
Landowners (early), maps & roster by Kluttz, bk rev RCR 10:2:2274
Lenoir Co, grantor/grantee index 1746-1773 NCJ 21:1:3 21:2:139 21:3:268 21:4:399
Lincoln Co, state docket 1779-1780 by Crow et al, bk rev NCJ 21:1:75 RCR 10:2:2272
Littleton, hist by Dozier, bk rev NCJ 21:1:71
Madison Co, apprentice bonds 1874-1914 LOB 16:1:6
Madison Co, estate list 1833 & 1851-1943 FWC 12:2:259 12:4:361
Madison Co, geneal hist by MCHBC, bk rev GH 49:4:217
Marr notices from the *North Carolina Presbyterian* 1860 NCJ 21:4:375
Marr statute abstr 1669, 1741 & 1766 NCJ 21:1:90

NORTH CAROLINA (continued)
McDowell Co, marr rec 1870-1894 by Williams, bk rev LOB 16:4:93 VL 30:1:43
Mecklenburg Co, census 1850 by Schmidt, bk rev NCJ 21:3:292
Mecklenburg Co, court of common pleas & quarter sessions rec 1780-1800 by Ferguson, bk rev ARH 33:2:81 MTG 8:4:165 NCJ 21:3:292 RCR 10:2:2276 SCM 23:2:118 TR 35:3:169
Mecklenburg Co, tax list 1810 NCJ 21:3:227
Mecklenburg Decl of Independence, hist HQ 95:60:60
Mero Dist, Superior Court minutes c1795 MTG 9:2:78
Moore Co, misc rec 1754-1850 by Wicker, bk rev NTT 14:3:82
Morgan Dist, superior court of law & equity slave rec 1788-1806 by Haun, bk rev RCR 10:4:2381
Morristown, biog sketches & land rec from 1922 LOB 16:4:75
Murphy, Harshaw Meth Ch cem rec LOB 16:2:42
Nantucket land rec & owner hist, repr 1901-1913, bk rev RCR 10:4:2379
Nash Co, court minutes 1801-1804 by Rackley, bk rev NCJ 21:2:181 21:3:293
Nash Co, voter reg 1902-1908 by Rackley, bk rev NCJ 21:3:293
National Intelligencer news abstr 1813 FC 14:1:35
New Bern Dist, loose estate papers 1755-1810 by Bradley, bk rev GH 49:4:215 NCJ 21:2:184
New Hanover Co, Confederate troop roster by St Armand, bk rev NCJ 21:1:73
New Hanover Co, marr contracts 1728-1855 by Kellam, bk rev NCJ 21:1:72
North Carolina Standard-Weekly news abstr c1865 WCT 5:2:53

NORTH CAROLINA (continued)
Oakdale, cem rec vol 4 1950-1969 by Haskett, bk rev NCJ 21:1:73
Oakdale, cem rec vol 5 1970-1988 by Haskett, bk rev NCJ 21:1:73
Old New Hanover Geneal Soc newsletter index 1989-1992 by Reaves, bk rev NCJ 21:2:181
Onslow Co, hist by Watson, bk rev RAG 16:4:25 VAG 39:4:318 WCT 5:2:59
Orange Co, deed bks 10 & 11 by Bennett, bk rev NCJ 21:1:74
Orange Co, deed rec 1805-1807 by Bennett, bk rev NCJ 21:4:416
Orange Co, deeds vol 14 by Bennett, bk rev RCR 10:1:2212
Orange Co, equity bond docket 1789-1817 cont NCJ 21:2:160
Person Co, deed bk abstr 1792-1825 by Kendall, bk rev GH 49:5:209 NCJ 21:2:181
Pigeon Roost, biog sketches by Miller, bk rev HQ 95:57:84
Raleigh, biog sketches of early residents WCT 5:2:22
Raleigh, Death Reg 1887-1904 WCT 5:2:64
Raleigh, hist WCT 5:2:9
Raleigh, land ownership map & roster c1792 WCT 5:2:16
Raleigh, vr abstr from news 1830-1839 by Neal, bk rev NCJ 21:4:419
Rev Army acc 1781-1783 by Kellam, bk rev NCJ 21:1:76
Rev Army acc vol 2 by Haun, bk rev RCR 10:1:2213
Rev Army acc vol 7 by Haun, bk rev SCM 23:1:60
Rev War Loyalists, hist, repr 1940, bk rev GH 49:3:213
Rev War soldiers pensioned in other states, pension abstr NCJ 21:4:353
Robeson Co, cem rec by Townsend, bk rev RAG 16:2:26
Rockingham Co, cem rec by NSDAR, bk rev NCJ 21:4:416

NORTH CAROLINA (continued)
  Rowan Co, cem rec vol 5 by GSRC, bk rev NCJ 21:4:417
  Rowan Co, cem rec vol 6 by GSRC, bk rev NCJ 21:4:418
  Rowan Co, census 1870 by GSRC, bk rev NCJ 21:4:417
  Rowan Co, census 1880 by GSRC, bk rev NCJ 21:4:417
  Rowan Co, court of pleas & quarter sessions rec 1792 cont RCR 10:1:2189
  Rowan Co, loose estate papers 1753-1850 cont RCR 10:4:2352
  Rowan Co, pet 1773 to governor RCR 10:1:2203
  Rowan Co, powers of attorney in Mecklenburg Co court of pleas & quarter sessions 1859 RCR 10:1:2206
  Rowan Co, tax lists 1830s RCR 10:4:2345
  Rowan Co, wills c1810 cont RCR 10:2:2255
  Salisbury, biog hist by Shook, bk rev NCJ 21:1:74
  Salibury Dist, superior court minutes 1783 cont RCR 10:2:2243
  Smithfield, Elizabeth Meth Ch hist sketch JC 21:3:43
  South Regiment, jour c1830s-1840s cont FC 13:2:2
  Stanly Co, Mason Family Cem hist SCG 14:1:657
  Stanly Co, news abstr from the *Southern Vidette* 1891 SCG 14:4:703
  Stanly Co, tax list 1845 SCG 14:1:660 14:2:668
  Statesville, marr & death notices from the *Landmark* 1885-1899 vol 2 by Black, bk rev NCJ 21:2:180
  Stokes Co, cem rec vol 2 by NSDAR, bk rev NCJ 21:4:416
  Stokes Co, South Reg jour c1846 cont FC 13:3:9
  Stokes Co, South Reg jour c1854-1910 cont FC 13:4:17 14:1:23

NORTH CAROLINA (continued)
  Sumner Co, census 1870 by SCA, bk rev MTG 8:4:166
  Surry Co, cem bk 29 by Kallam, bk rev NCJ 21:3:294
  Surry Co, court of pleas & quarter sessions rec 1815-1819 by Harvey/Wells, bk rev NCJ 21:3:293
  Surry Co, deed abstr 1795-1800 by Snow, bk rev NCJ 21:4:419
  Surry Co, heritage & hist vol 2 by SCGA, bk rev RCR 10:1:2218
  Surry Co, heritage vol 1-2 by Jackson, bk rev GH 49:5:209
  Surry Co, population sched 1900 by Barrett, bk rev NCJ 21:4:418
  Surry Co, state road inn ledger 1854 HPF 95:50:42
  Surry Co, tax lists 1820 by Harvey, bk rev NCJ 21:3:294 RCR 10:1:2219
  Toe River Valley, geneal hist by Bailey, bk rev GH 49:4:215 LOB 16:2:41
  Tryon Co, crown docket 1769-1776 by Crow et al, bk rev NCJ 21:1:75 RCR 10:2:2272 LOB 16:1:27
  Tryon Co, state docket 1777-1779 by Crow et al, bk rev NCJ 21:1:75 RCR 10:2:2272
  Tuckasiege Bapt Assoc minutes 1829 LOB 17:1:14
  Tyrell Co, wills 1812-1900 by Bradley, bk rev GH 49:3:213
  Tyrrell cem rec 1732-1984, bk rev SEE 36:153:24
  Tyrrell cem rec 1732-1984, res guide by Everton, bk rev NCJ 21:3:294
  Tyrrell Co, wills 1812-1900 by Bradley, bk rev NCJ 21:1:75
  Valdese, Waldesian Pres Ch hist 1893-1993 by WPCHC, bk rev NCJ 21:1:68
  Valdese, Waldesian settler hist 1893-1900 by HCWPC, bk rev NCJ 21:1:68
  Wake Co, apprentice bonds & rec 1770-1860, 1872-1903 WCT 5:2:24

NORTH CAROLINA (continued)
Wake Co, bastardy bonds & rec cont WCT 5:2:31
Wake Co, court minutes 1808-1811 by Haun, bk rev RCR 10:4:2382
Wake Co, div rec 1831-1952 cont WCT 5:2:44
Wake Co, General Assembly members 1777-1850 WCT 5:2:6
Wake Co, hist WCT 5:2:4
Wake Co, Reg of Deaths 1887-1904, descr of cem mentioned WCT 5:2:60
Warren Co, estates 1833-1851 by Gammon, bk rev GH 49:4:217
Warren Co, estates 1852-1868 by Gammon, bk rev NCJ 21:2:182
Warren Co, tax lists 1779-1790 by Gammon, bk rev GH 49:4:217 NCJ 21:2:182
Warrenton, settlements 1786, rec by Haun, bk rev SCM 23:1:60
Washington Co, court of pleas & quarter sessions minutes 1778-1779 BWG 24:1:14 24:2:88
Western NC, fam hist rec by Parris, bk rev LOB 16:1:27 NCJ 21:2:183
Western NC, hist 1730-1913 LOB 17:1:12
Wilkes Co, land entry abstr 1796-1810 by Pruitt, bk rev NCJ 21:3:295
Wills & inv, repr 1912, bk rev GH 49:5:208
Wilmington, marr & death notices from news 1797-1842 by Kellam, bk rev NCJ 21:1:72
Wilson Co, cem rec vol 3 by Howell, bk rev NCJ 21:3:295
Winston Twp, tax list abstr 1890 FC 13:2:10 13:3:13 13:4:20 14:1:25
Winston, news abstr from the *Republican* 1898 FC 14:1:60
Yancey Co, marr 1850-1920 cont FYC 12:4:363

NORTH DAKOTA, Aberdeen & Brown Co, news res tips TTC 21:3:66
Aberdeen, obit index for the *Daily News* 1895 TTC 21:3:69

NORTH DAKOTA (continued)
Anna Twp Cem rec 1906-1917 NDG 95:63:29
Burke Co, twps in SE area, twp organization pet index c1900 NDG 95:62:4
Deering, geneal gleanings from news abstr 1963 NDG 95:65:5
Denbigh area, geneal gleanings from news c1905 NDG 95:65:21
First ND Vol Infantry Reg roster index 1898-1899 NDG 95:63:14
Larson, news abstr from the *Larson Paper* 1908 NDG 95:62:8
Norma Gazette news abstr c1914 NDG 95:63:8
Renville Co, sch census 1910 NDG 95:63:3
Roseland Twp, census 1910 NDG 95:62:13
Towner area, geneal gleanings from news c1905 NDG 95:65:21
Vr, res tips NDG 95:65:19
Ward Co, cem inscr bk corr NDG 95:63:29

NORTON, David mc1794, w Sarah Shelton, PA, NC, desc LOB 17:1:4
Martha see Mercer NORTON
Mercer (Messer) dc1800, w Martha, VA, NC, KY, geneal by Dulaney, bk rev HTR 38:1:7

NORWEGIAN GENEALOGY, Imm to Am, hist speech trans SGS 44:2:65
MO, Lutheran Synod hist CHI 68:4:151

NORWOOD, William d1703, VA, geneal by McSwain, bk rev AG 70:2:124

NOVAK, Anna Frances, IL, biog CHG 28:1:24
Jan b1835, w Marie, CZ, fam hist CHG 27:3:84
Marie see Jan NOVAK

NOYES, Elisabeth see Fletcher RANSOM
Lula May see Charles Franklin RHODES

NOYES (continued)
 Robert bc1465, w Joan Mondey (?), EN, geneal NER 149:594:105
NUGENT, Clinton W b1865, w Nettie S Carson, TX, biog sketch MCG 18:1/2:86
NUTTER, Wilhelmina D see Jacob HANSON
OAKLEY, Annie b1860, h Frank Butler, OH, biog by Riley, bk rev RAG 16:1:20 REG 93:2:235
OBANNON, Presley Neville b1776, VA, biog & geneal by Sundberg/Gott, bk rev CN 4:2:30 FGC 95:28:24 LHS 95:2:8 SGS 44:3:141 TSG 3:2:9
OBERHOLTZER, Henrich fl1810, VA, notebk, bk rev MHP 22:2:7
 Marcus bc1664, GR, PA, fam hist MFH 14:2:76
OBERN, GR, CA, fam hist by Obern, bk rev TPI 20:4:193
OCONNER, Isabella see Benjamin GRUMBLES
OCONNOR, John b1883, CT, Bible rec CTN 27:4:585
ODELL, Gracie P fl1920, AL, autobiog, bk rev RAG 16:4:19
 TN, Civil War soldier biog sketches HPF 95:50:38
OFFER, Charles d1940, w Emma Agnes Langbein, TX, obit KTP 7:1:9
OGLE, George Albert m1910, w Irma Catherine Brown, IL, Bible rec GL 29:4:127
 Joseph d1821, VA, IL, fam hist STC 18:1:44
OGLESBY, John fl1911, MO, FL, biog PCQ 10:2:1
OHIO, Adams Twp, elector roster 1849 SSG 14:4:54
 Ashland, Centennial Homecoming Week 1815-1915 souvenir & index by Duff, bk rev TR 35:2:109
 Ashtabula Co, childrens' home inmates census 1920 AH 22:2:180

OHIO (continued)
 Ashtabula Co, Jefferson, Maple Grove Public School, student roster 1907 AH 22:2:185
 Ashtabula Co, migration patterns of imm into co descr AH 22:2:191
 Athens Co, census 1830 by Whiteman, bk rev GH 49:6:200
 Athens Co, census 1850 everyname index by Whiteman, bk rev GH 49:6:200
 Athens Co, entrymen on lands, roster by Kocher, bk rev TR 35:2:105
 Athens Co, everyname index to Harris Hist by Whiteman, bk rev GH 49:6:200
 Athens Co, news abstr from the *Gazette* 1900 ACH 16:6:57 17:3:31
 Athens, Woman Suffrage Centennial hist ACH 16:5:53
 Auburndale, biog hist cont FIR 15:1:2
 Auglaize Co, birth rec 1867-1877 by SCCOGS, bk rev TPI 20:4:191
 Auglaize Co, probate court birth rec by ACCOGS, bk rev TPI 20:4:191
 Auglaize Co, probate court birth rec vol 2 1877-1887 by ACCOGS, bk rev TR 35:2:110
 Bibl of bks on OH fam by Hehir, bk rev PR 22:3:9
 Bloom Twp, Mennonite community & cem rec SSG 14:3:37
 Bloom Twp, St John Evang Luth Ch rec 1853-1920 by FCCOGS, bk rev TR 35:3:168
 Brown Co, Arnheim, Luth ch parish reg by Nishimoto, bk rev TPI 20:2:94
 Brown Co, GR Ch rec 1863-1895 Nishimoto, bk rev TPI 20:2:94
 Brown Co, hist, repr 1883, bk rev SGS 45:1:33
 Census (agricultural), list of years documented in archives QU 12:6:66
 Chappelle Creek, hist & news abstr c1850 TFP 95:12:102
 Chief Inspector of Mines reports, res tips TR 35:4:183

OHIO (continued)
  Chillicothe, Greenlawn cem inscr by RCGS, bk rev TPI 21:1:50
  Cincinnati, Barrere Funeral Home rec 1927-1953 by Thomas, bk rev TR 35:2:110
  Cincinnati Daily Times death notice index 1840-1879 by Herbert, bk rev GH 49:5:209 GJB 19:3:70 GSM 12:2:48 OC 31:1:55 QU 12:2:21 TR 35:2:110
  Cincinnati, First GR Reformed Ch microfilm, rev corr TTH 16:1:16
  Cincinnati, GR heritage & hist by Tolzmann, bk rev GH 49:4:218 MGS 13:1:7 SGS 44:2:86 TOP 25:1:4
  Cincinnati, St Johannes Gemeinde membership roster 1919 TTH 16:3:79
  Circleville, news abstr from the *Democratic Guard* 1845 TR 35:3:147
  Civil War, Company A, 115th OH Vol Infantry, cabin assignment rosters in TN TR 35:4:182
  Civil War, mil & personal sketches of vets, name index TR 35:2:93
  Civil War, Sherman Brigade hist & roster TR 35:1:15
  Clark Co, news abstr from the Sun 1900 CCK 13:4:8
  Clark Co, will bk 4 abstr c1869 CCK 13:4:3
  Clark Co, will bk 5 cont c1873 CCK 13:2:7
  Cleveland, news abstr from the *Herald* 1866-1867 MM 19:1:5 19:2:18 19:4:43
  Cleveland, St Thomas Aquinas School, 8th grade grads 1934 CPY 24:1:20
  Cleveland, Swedish Lodge reg CPY 24:1:12
  Colored Teachers' Assoc hist 1860-1863 TR 35:4:186
  Columbiana Co, cem inscr vol 20 by CCOGS, bk rev TR 35:4:223
  Columbiana Co, settler hist vol 4 by Fetters, bk rev TPI 20:4:192

OHIO (continued)
  Columbus, geneal resource guide IB 11:1:11
  Connaut, Masonic Direct 1910 cont AH 22:4:263
  Crawford Co, census 1860 by CCCOGS, bk rev TR 35:3:163
  Crosby Twp, death rec 1717-1911 cont TTH 16:1:20 16:3:74 16:4:111
  Courthouse fires, dates QU 12:6:66
  Dayton Twp, taxable property list 1798 TR 35:1:19
  Delaware Co, draft rec 1940 DGS 11:4:79
  Delaware Co, hist 1880 IB 11:1:8
  Delaware Co, hist 1880 cont DGS 11:4:72
  Delaware Co, marr rec abstr 1866 DGS 11:4:74
  Delaware Co, marr rec abstr 1866 IB 11:1:12
  Delaware Co, news abstr from the Semi-Weekly *Gazette* 1901 IB 11:1:4 11:4:69
  Delaware Co, property tax duplicate rec 1890 DGS 11:4:76
  Dentist direct 1901 by Page, bk rev TR 35:3:165
  Dunham Twp cem rec by Sams, bk rev TR 35:3:163
  Epworth, Literary Social Club minutes abstr 1883-1885 TR 35:2:97
  Erie Canal hist by Halackna, bk rev GJB 19:3:70
  Fairfield Co, entrymen on lands, roster by Kocher, bk rev TR 35:2:106
  Fairfield Co, indentures 1824-1880 by FCCOGS, bk rev TR 35:3:167
  Fairfield Co, infirmary rec 1848 & deaths 1911-1980 by OCOGS, bk rev TR 35:2:108
  Fairfield Co, section maps & entrymen on lands, roster by Kocher, bk rev TR 35:2:106
  Fairfield Co, St Peter's GR Reformed Ch rec cont FTC 17:4:49
  Firelands Hist Soc, past president roster 1857-1987 TFP 95:12:60

OHIO (continued)
Firelands, hist TFP 95:12:97
First fam, roster TR 35:2:56 35:4:174
Franklin Co, direct 1893, abstr TF 23:3:55
Franklin Co, land patent grantor index, 19th cent TF 23:1:17 23:2:38
Frontier advance & retreat on the Upper OH 1778-1779, hist by Kellogg, bk rev GR 37:1:48 SGS 44:2:84
Geauga Co, geneal hist, repr 1880, bk rev AW 22:1:7 GGS 31:2:119 GH 49:6:200 KCG 36:2:106 RES 26:3:161 SGS 44:3:142
Geneal Soc chapters, address list AW 21:2:59
Geneal Soc Lib hist by OGS, bk rev TR 35:3:163
Germano, Zion Luth Ch parish rec 1805-1945 by Ruff, bk rev TR 35:3:168
Gibraltar Isl summer home hist TFP 95:12:55
GR imm biog sketches TTH 16:1:14
GR population, hist before 1850 by Thode, bk rev TPI 20:4:198
Granville, obits from the *News* 1917 TLL 20:3:55
Greene Co, women's hist by Trolander, bk rev TR 35:2:111
Greenwich Twp, enumeration of householders 1826 TFP 95:12:96
Hamilton Co, burial rec vol 5 by HCOGS, bk rev SGS 44:2:84
Hamilton Co, burial rec vol 8 by HCOGS, bk rev GJB 19:3:70
Hamilton Co, census 1920 enumeration districts, res guide TTH 16:1:10
Hamilton Co, census 1920, institution roster TTH 16:1:11
Hamilton Co, Colerain Twp, burial rec vol 6 by Remler, bk rev TR 35:2:110
Hamilton Co, marr (restored) 1870-1884 by Herbert, bk rev GJB 20:1:14 GRC 11:2:28 NGS 83:1:68 TR 35:2:104

OHIO (continued)
Hamilton Co, Sycamore Twp burial rec by HCOGS, bk rev SCS 32:4:88
Harrison Co, hist collect, repr 1900, bk rev GH 49:5:209
Harrison Twp, cem rec bk A & B by MCCOGS, bk rev GH 49:6:201
Harrison Twp, Shiloh Park & Westmont cem rec by MCCOGS, bk rev TR 35:4:224
Hocking Co, entrymen on lands, roster by Kocher, bk rev TR 35:2:105
Hocking Twp, cem rec by FCOGS, bk rev TR 35:2:108
Holmes Co, 67th OH Volunteers, hist TR 35:3:115
Holmes Co, census 1830 index (revised) by HCGS, bk rev TR 35:1:54
Holmes Co, maps, descr TR 35:1:4
Huron Co, vr abstr 1874 TFP 95:12:72
Jefferson Co, first fam roster JCL 9:2:2
Jefferson Co, news abstr from the *Ohio Press* 1888 JCL 9:2:7
Jefferson Co, Rev War pension rec JCL 9:4:47
Jefferson Co, Second Pres Ch semi-centennial hist 1838 JCL 9:2:5
Johnson's Isl, Confederate burials LOB 17:1:9
Johnson's Isl, Confederate prison hist KTP 3:1:8
Land divisions, hist CCK 13:4:5
Lawrence Co, Cath cem rec by Slimp, bk rev TR 35:4:224
Lawrenceville, High Sch grads 1945 CCK 13:2:10
Leesburg, pioneer reunion roster 1875 RSQ 17:2:24
Legislative acts abstr 1803-1821 by Bowman, bk rev TR 35:1:51
Liberty Twp, cem inscr by PCGS, bk rev TR 35:4:223
Licking Co, deaths & obits c1897 TLL 20:2:38
Licking Co, First Family roster TLL 20:2:27

OHIO (continued)
- Licking Co, legal notice abstr c1870 TLL 20:3:51
- Licking Co, obits c1897 TLL 20:3:63
- Licking Co, street name changes, list TLL 20:4:76
- Lucas Co, births, deaths, marr & lawsuit rec c1909-1940 by LCCOGS, bk rev TR 35:3:163
- Lucas Co, Civil War hist cont FIR 15:4:53
- Lucas Co, probate court rec 1855 FIR 15:1:5
- Lucas Co, Toledo Poor Farm home infirmary reg 1855-1882 by LCCOGS, bk rev TR 35:3:163
- Madison Co, news abstr from the *Democrat* 1896 CCK 13:4:10
- Mahoning Co, Chaney High Sch grads 1944 MM 19:5:64
- Mahoning Co, div rec supp 1846-1887 MM 19:2:25
- Mahoning Co, geneal abstr 1866 from the *Cleveland Herald* MM 19:3:37
- Mahoning Co, homeowners at Loveland Farm 1919, roster MM 19:3:33
- Mahoning Co, Old Stone House at Meander Creek, hist cont MM 20:2:3
- Mahoning Co, res tips MM 19:6:76
- Mahoning Co, South High Sch grads 1945 MM 19:2:26
- Marion Twp, cem inscr by HCCOGS, bk rev TR 35:3:165
- Marr notices from the *Ohio Observer* series 1827-1855 by Caccamo, bk rev TR 35:4:218
- Martinsburg Pres Ch supporter roster 1835 TLL 20:2:33
- Miami Valley, index to *Beside the Stillwater* by Brentlinger, index by Keister TR 35:4:224
- Miami Valley, rec on computer databases, res guide NFB 27:2:39
- Mines & geologic survey abstr 1908 TR 35:2:95
- Monroeville, news abstr c1874 TFP 95:12:75

OHIO (continued)
- Monroeville, St Joseph's cem inscr & hist TFP 95:12:61
- Montgomery Co, index to *Beside the Stillwater* by Brentlinger, index by Keister TR 35:4:224
- Morgan Co, census 1820 & 1830 by MCCOGS, bk rev TR 35:4:222
- Morgan Co, entrymen on lands, roster by Kocher, bk rev TR 35:2:105
- Muskingum Co, probate index 1 by Klaiber/Blackstone, bk rev GH 49:5:210
- New London, Cath cem hist TFP 95:12:25
- New London, vet list 1882 TFP 95:12:37
- New Richmond, Cranston Memorial Pres Ch hist 1821-1993 by Whitt, bk rev TR 35:4:222
- Newark, first locomotive, news abstr 1902 TLL 20:4:81
- Newark, legal notices from the *Weekly Advocate* c1883-1889 TLL 20:4:83
- Newark, letters (unclaimed) at post ofc 1897 TLL 20:2:31
- Newark, marr notices from the *Newark Advocate* 1860 TLL 20:4:73
- Newark, news abstr from the *Advocate* 1871 TLL 20:3:52
- News abstr from the *Ohio Press* 1885 JCL 9:4:51
- News abstr from the *Pickaway & Fayette Pilot* 1845 TR 35:3:147
- Newton Twp, misc rec abstr 1897-1902 TLL 20:2:29
- North Fairfield, high sch alumni in WW2, roster TFP 95:12:99
- Norwalk area, obits 1980s-1990s TFP TFP 95:12:107
- Norwalk, people over age 70 listed in news 1891 TFP 95:12:94
- Norwalk, senior citizen roster 1895 TFP 95:12:72
- Norwalk, St Peter's Evang Luth Ch financial rec 1929 TFP 95:12:85
- Norwalk, taxpayer holdings 1891, roster TFP 95:12:16

OHIO (continued)
- Obit abstr from co news 1987-1994, index & abstr by CCOGS, bk rev TR 35:4:219
- OH River, towboat hist by Casto, bk rev REG 93:4:503
- OH Valley geneal by Hanna, bk rev KTP 9:3:48
- Ohioans in US Official Reg 1820-1829, roster TR 35:2:77
- Ohioans in US Official Reg 1833-1838, roster TR 35:4:194
- Ohioans who died in IY, Protestant Cem of Rome rec TR 35:4:181
- Owsley Co, marr rec 1843-1929 by Smith, bk rev KA 30:4:200
- Palmer Twp, cem inscr by PCGS, bk rev TR 35:4:223
- Pataskala, sch reunion, news abstr 1906 TLL 20:3:60
- Pavonia, Literary Social Club minutes abstr 1883-1885 TR 35:2:97
- Physician direct 1901 by Page, bk rev TR 35:3:164
- Pickaway Co, marr rec 1810-1862 by PCHS, bk rev TR 35:3:168
- Pickaway Co, pictorial hist by PCHS, bk rev TR 35:3:168
- Pleasant Twp, cem rec by FCCOGS, bk rev TR 35:3:167
- Pleasant Twp, Floral Hills Memory Gardens cem rec by FCCOGS, bk rev TR 35:3:164
- Pleasant Twp, St Peter's GR Reformed Ch rec, 19th cent FTC 17:2:24 17:3:44
- Political culture 1787-1861, hist by Brown/Cayton, bk rev REG 93:4:508
- Preble Co, cem inscr, repr 1969, bk rev GH 49:5:217
- Preble Co, land rec 1839-1848 by Gilbert, bk rev TR 35:4:218
- Preble Co, marr rec 1808-1840, repr 1966, bk rev GH 49:5:218
- Reading Twp, cem rec vol 4 by PCCOGS, bk rev TPI 20:4:191
- Res guide by Schweitzer, bk rev SGS 45:1:38 TTC 21:3:56

OHIO (continued)
- Res tips, how to overcome problems TR 35:1:8
- Res tips, misc OC 31:1:10
- Rev War soldiers 1859 TR 35:4:178
- Rev War, frontier advance hist 1778-1779, repr 1916, bk rev GH 49:4:217
- Richland Co, Shelby Oakland & Most Pure Heart of Mary Cath cem burials to 1988 by RCSCOGS, bk rev TR 35:2:104
- Roman Catholic sacramental rec, res tips TR 35:3:160
- Ross Co, census 1840 by RCGS, bk rev TR 35:4:225
- Ross Co, Civil War soldier burial rec RCG 22:4:47
- Ross Co, entrymen on lands, roster by Kocher, bk rev TR 35:2:105
- Ross Co, Geneal Soc member anc charts by RCGS, bk rev TR 35:4:225
- Ross Co, marr rec 1798-1849 by Casari, bk rev GH 49:5:210 SSG 14:1:3 TR 35:2:110
- Ross Co, obit abstr prior to 1940 in Geneal Soc files, list RCG 23:1:10 22:3:32
- Rushcreek Twp/Marion Twp, St Jacobus/St James Evang Luth Ch rec 1834-1891 by FCOGS, bk rev TR 35:2:108
- Rutherford B Hayes Presidential Center Lib, geneal res guide HQ 95:57:63
- Sandusky, Norwalk, Mansfield electric railroad hist TFP 95:12:43
- Scienceville, high sch grads 1942 MM 19:6:72
- Scioto Co, gold seekers in the 1850 census RCP 17:3:98
- Seneca Co, Civil War soldier roster SSG 14:2:26 14:4:59 14:6:90
- Seneca Co, high sch grads 1915 SSG 14:6:87
- Seneca Co, hist cont SSG 14:2:26

OHIO (continued)

Seneca Co, hist, repr 1886, bk rev AW 21:3:93 CHG 27:3:121 GH 49:5:210 JCL 9:2:4 PB 10:2:47 RCP 17:2:50 SGS 44:2:84 TR 35:2:108

Seneca Co, legal notices from the *Advertiser* 1885 SSG 14:1:12

Seneca Co, marr rec 1841-1899 by Seigley, bk rev GH 49:5:210 SSG 14:1:1 TR 35:2:104

Springfield Twp, burial rec by HCCOGS, bk rev TR 35:3:168

Springfield Twp, burial rec vol 7 by HCOGS, bk rev BTG 1:2:7 GSM 12:1:17

Springfield Twp, cem & death rec by MCCOGS, bk rev WPG 22:2:54

Springfield Twp, cem & death rec by Simon, bk rev TR 35:4:219

Springfield Twp, cem rec by HCOGS, bk rev GH 49:4:218

Statehood trivia & data QU 12:4:44

Steubenville, High Sch commencement 1897, roster & news abstr JCL 9:3:27

Summit Co, centennial hist, repr 1908, bk rev GH 49:5:211

Sycamore Twp, burial rec vol 8 by HCOGS, bk rev GSM 12:2:47

Sycamore Twp, cem rec by HCOGS, bk rev MSG 15:1:56 SGS 44:3:143

Sylvania, election results 1833, roster FIR 15:1:3

Sylvania, sch dist #3 report abstr 1840-1878 FIR 15:4:52

Tax rec & index to 1838 by Powell, bk rev TR 35:4:220

Tiffin citizens, OH Veterans Home death rec SSG 14:3:39

Tiffin, early hist from news abstr SSG 14:3:43

Tiffin, Old Tiffin Burying Ground & Modern Greenlawn Cem hist SSG 14:1:9

Toledo, deaths from the City Direct cont FIR 15:4:50

Toledo, foreign aliens abstr from news 1862 TR 35:3:159

OHIO (continued)

Toledo, Holland High Sch alumni 1898-1941 cont FIR 15:4:48

Twin Twp, Board of Trustees Minutes & rec 1810-1844, children mentioned in TR 35:4:176

Twin Valley, news abstr & hist by Gilbert, bk rev TR 35:4:218

Underground Railroad hist sketch TFP 95:12:17

Vets from misc wars buried in Indiana (Delaware Co) TR 35:4:184

War of 1812 soldier roster, repr 1916, bk rev ANC 30:3:124 TOP 25:4:130 TR 35:3:164

Warren Co, Caesar Creek Pioneer Friends & Quakers cem rec by Pruitt, bk rev QQ 95:25:18

Warren Co, hist, repr 1994, bk rev BT 26:4:81

Washington Co, Geneal Soc newsletter compendium, bk rev TR 35:4:219

Waterville, Columbian House hist sketch FIR 15:4:52

Wayne Co Company roster c1850 TR 35:1:10

Wayne Co, hist, repr 1878, bk rev AW 21:2:63 CI 31:1:23 GH 49:3:213 GR 37:1:50

Wayne Co, tavern lic reg 1834 TR 35:3:149

Williams Co, marr rec 1881-1889 by Sprow/Lash, bk rev GH 49:4:218

Wood Co, biog sketches (misc fam), bk rev TR 35:1:52

Worthington Female Seminary roster 1841 TF 23:1:14

Worthington, landmarks, hist & photos by McCormick, bk rev TR 35:3:163

Worthington, Scioto Company desc, biog hist by McCormick, bk rev TR 35:3:163

Worthington, Worthington Male Academy catalogue 1840 TF 23:2:43

Wyandot Co, hist vol 1, repr 1884, bk rev GH 49:5:211 GRI 15:1:78 LAB 10:1:29 NCJ 21:3:299 SGS 44:2:84

OHIO (continued)
  Wyandot Co, hist vol 2, repr 1885, bk rev GJB 19:4:110
  Youngstown, news abstr from the *Sheet & Tube Bulletin* 1919 cont MM 19:2:21 19:4:44 19:6:79
  Youngstown, sch building construction dates MM 19:6:72
  Youngstown Telegram news abstr 1904 MM 19:1:4
  Youngstown Vindicator news abstr 1904 MM 19:1:6
OKLAHOMA, Ada, news abstr from the *Evening News* 1925 OPC 27:1:9
  Ada, police chief biog sketches OPC 27:1:4
  Asbury, mission sale & auction purhcaser list 1888 OK 40:1:16
  Caddo Co, Anadarko, lot purchaser roster 1901 OK 40:2:51
  Cherokee Nation, marr lic 1867-1874 CN 4:1:11
  Cherokee Nation, marr pet abstr 1868-1891 CN 4:1:5
  Cherokee rolls, Delaware dist, cross-linked by Garrett, bk rev OK 40:2:45
  Cherokee rolls, Goingsnake district, cross-linked by Garrett, bk rev OK 40:2:45
  Comanche Co, div index 1901-1928 TTT 20:1:41
  Congress & Five Tribes, paving the way to statehood, hist by Burton, bk rev CN 4:3:40
  Cotton Co, birth rec 1912-1918 cont TTT 19:2:81
  Custer Co, marr rec c1892-1907 TTT 19:2:76 19:4:181 20:1:33
  Delaware Co, cem lists vol 1 by Cemeteries, bk rev OK 40:2:46
  Delaware Co, real property ownership plat map c1930 by Davis/Hart, bk rev GSM 12:1:16
  Delaware Dist, Guion Miller roll names, vol 5 by Garrett, bk rev GGS 31:2:120
  Duke Co, census 1900 cont WTN 95:WINTER:4 95:SPRING:4

OKLAHOMA (continued)
  Elk City, obits from the *News-Democrat* 1916-1918 TTT 19:4:177
  Goingsnake Dist, Guion Miller roll names, vol 4 by Garrett, bk rev GGS 31:2:120
  Goingsnake Messenger index 1984-1993 by Talbot, bk rev GH 49:6:201
  Greer Co, Chilton Sch hist WTN 95:SPRING:5
  Greer Co, letters advertised in the *Sun Monitor* 1902-1906, roster WTN 8:4:5
  Greer Co, letters at post ofc 1902-1906 WTN 95:SPRING:9
  Greer Co, Liberty Sch dist # 38 roster 1898 WTN 95:WINTER:6
  Greer Co, sch dist #97 enumeration report 1912 OK 40:1:31
  Greer Co, sch dist #166 Jester-Valley View, enumeration report 1913 OK 40:2:72
  Harmon Co, Civil War vet roster WTN 95:WINTER:2
  Harper Co, marr rec 1907-1929 by Samuelsen, bk rev GH 49:5:212
  Hughes Co, marr rec 1909-1922, grooms names starting with A & B by Young, bk rev GH 49:5:212
  Jackson Co, sch dist roster 1908 WTN 95:SPRING:8
  Keota, Iron Bridge cem rec by McCannon, bk rev GH 49:4:218
  Keota, Old Cache cem rec by McCannon, bk rev GH 49:4:219
  Kiowa Co, news abstr from the *Mountain Parker Newspaper* 1935-1943 by Garrison, bk rev TTT 19:4:169
  Kiowa Co, obits & death notices from the *Mountain Parker* c1936 cont TTT 19:4:185 20:1:25
  Kiowa Co, pioneer hist by KCHS, bk rev GH 49:5:212
  Kiowa Co, Union Dale Sch hist & rosters TTT 20:1:23
  Lawton News Republican news abstr 1906 TTT 20:1:29

OKLAHOMA (continued)
Lawton Public Lib, descr of avail svcs HQ 95:57:72
Lawton Public Lib, Indian-Pioneer Hist Collect, res guide TTT 19:4:163
Lawton, 50th wedding anniv index to the *Lawton Constitution* cont TTT 19:2:89
Lawton, First Congregational Ch marr rec 1924-1933 TTT 19:4:191
Lawton, letters at post ofc 1905 TTT 19:2:93
Lawton, news abstr from the *News-Republican* 1905 TTT 19:2:66 19:4:173
Locust Grove Sch Twp #41, Meers map 1890 & census 1898 abstr WTN 8:4:3
Loveland, Loveland cem rec TTT 20:1:37
Marr & death notices from the *Indian Missionary* 1884 OK 40:1:11
Mayes Co, census 1910 vol 1 by MCGS, bk rev GSM 12:1:16
McIntosh Co, marr rec 1907-1908 by Young, bk rev GH 49:5:212
Mingo, death abstr index 1893-1923 by Hayes, bk rev GH 49:4:218
News abstr from the *Blair Progress* 1936 WTN 95:WINTER:7
Pontotoc Co, news abstr (misc) 1918 OPC 26:3:9
Pontotoc Co, Red Cross chapter hist OPC 26:3:5
Post Oak M.B. Ch hist 1895-1995 by CHBC, bk rev TTT 20:1:19
Quaker rec by Hinshaw & Hubbard, bk rev GSM 12:2:42
Quaker res sources GSM 12:2:42
Rock Creek cem rec cont TTT 19:2:86
Roger Mills Co, Cheyenne Sch hist TTT 19:4:170
Sequoyah Co, census 1920 vol 1 by MGS, bk rev GH 49:5:212
Sequoyah Co, Muldrew Grade Sch rec 1921-1962 by MGS, bk rev GH 49:5:213

OKLAHOMA (continued)
Statehood hist 1866-1906 by Burton, bk rev RAG 17:1:16
Talequah, Cherokee Seminaries alumni list 1961 GSM 12:1:12
Talihina, city payment warrants 1921-1934 by Young, bk rev GH 49:4:219
Talihina, Drake Funeral Home Rec 1938-1950 by Young, bk rev GH 49:5:212
Univ of OK, Western Hist Collect mss guide by DeWitt, bk rev GSM 12:2:46 KCG 36:2:106 SGS 44:3:140 SQ 6:1:45
Vet census abstr 1890 WTN 95:WINTER:3
Whites working in Indian nation, roster 1889 CN 4:1:13
WW2 Native Am death rec 1945 TTT 19:2:84

OLIVER, Douglas b1753, w Millie Carnalle, VA, biog sketch KTP 3:4:50

OLSON, Donald fl945, WA, recoll RES 27:1:18
Ida E see Edward C BLAICH

OMALLEY, Grace b1530, IR, biog HER 3:3:22

ONEAL, Margaret see William INGLE Wilkinson m1833, w Elizabeth Burress, KY, IA, Bible rec KA 31:2:38

ONEIL, CN, see ONEL

ONEILL, IR, pedigree chert IFL 5:10:8
Rosie see Malachy FOLEY

ONEL, Francois m1751, w Marie-Anne Chandone, CN, geneal ACG 21:4:166

OPPER, Louisa see Louis SIMMEN

ORBEN, GR, CA, fam hist by Obern, bk rev TPI 20:4:193

ORECKOVSKY, Abraham bc1815, w Hylech, RU, MN, fam hist by Traubman, bk rev GH 49:5:234 GSC 17:3:4 HQ 95:57:84
Hykeh/Hylech see Abraham ORECKOVSKY

OREGON, Civil War vets, roster GFP 44:3:133
Clatsop Co, voter roster (immigrant) 1914 GFP 44:4:172
Columbia Co, marr rec 1855-1900 by Viles, bk rev GH 49:3:213
Comstock cem rec TFG 8:3/4:15
Death rec res tips GSC 17:3:3
Emig roster & biog data by Nelson, bk rev GH 49:4:205
Hist sketches, repr 1907, bk rev GGS 31:1:48
Linn Co, Lebanon Pioneer cem rec by Dunn/Gentry, bk rev HQ 95:60:92
Mahler Co, marr rec 1887-1911 by Hill, bk rev GH 49:3:213
Malheur Co, census 1900 index by OGS, bk rev GH 49:3:213
Malheur Co, census 1910 by Bartlett et al, bk rev GH 49:3:213
Multnomah Co, tax rolls, res tips GFP 44:3:113
National Guard, First Reg Army hist & roster GFP 45:2:68
Natu rec & decl of intention 1906-1925 by Samuelsen, bk rev GH 49:4:219
News clipping index by Herzberg, bk rev TB 22:1:13
Nyssa, news abstr from the *Gate City Journal* 1904-1933 by Hill/Chamberlin, bk rev GH 49:3:213
Oregon City, letters at post ofc 1854 GFP 45:2:82
Oregon Trail deaths 1852, roster & hist GGP 28:1:15
Oregon Trail sources, queries & rev vol 4 by Terry, bk rev HQ 95:55:92
Pacific Fur Company employee roster 1813-1814 TRI 35:2:52
Pioneer hist by Lockley, bk rev TB 22:1:14
Pioneer necrology 1925-1926 GFP 44:3:124
Portland State Lib res guide GFP 44:4:166
Portland, building improvements 1890, list GFP 45:2:87

OREGON (continued)
Portland, Lone Fir cem rec 1846-1880 cont GFP 44:4:164 45:2:84
Res tips ARN 8:1:14
Settlement hist sketches, repr 1907, bk rev GH 49:5:213
State Penitentiary rec c1865-1870 GFP 45:2:75
Women of the West, hist by Steber, bk rev TB 21:3:14
ORME, Peggy Marie see John Douglas (Jack) ROBERTS
ORPHAN GENEALOGY, Adoption res aid GH 49:3:16 WPG 21:4:30
Adoption res, pros & cons descr HQ 95:60:76
Adoption search techniques, res guide by Rillera, bk rev TTL 24:1:23
Birth mothers, tips for finding HQ 95:59:72
Children's Aid Soc, hist by Holt, bk rev CHG 27:2:78
NY, orphans who emig to Great Plains regions, res address list TC 14:1:16
Orphan Train Riders, hist HQ 95:60:81
OSHIELDS, Thomas N b1839, w Mary E Matthewson, AR, Bible rec TRC 10:1:16
OTEY, James Harvey fl850, TN, diary abstr by Otey, bk rev BWG 24:2:153
OTIS, Susan see John WINKLEY
OTT, Robert G fl945, recoll of CZ, autobiog ISC 19:2:31
OTYSON, Morris m1872, w Mary D Morgan, GA, Bible rec GGS 31:2:111
OUELLET, Ida see Frank WOOD
OUELLETTE, Henriette see William Alexandre MCKENZIE
Archange see Archange Chevalier WILLMETTE
OUGHTON, Henry m1863, w Hannah Fuller Essex, EN, TX, biog sketch KTP 5:4:53
OUTLAW, Margaret see Gillum KING
OVERHOLT, Joseph G b1832, PA, fraktur decorated acct bk, bk rev MHP 22:2:7

OWEN, David b1713, w Sarah, MO?, Bible rec OZ 17:4:149
Lewis fc1546, w Margaret Puleston, WE, fam hist OZ 17:4:139
Sarah see David OWEN
OWSLEY, John see Dorothea POYNTZ
PABST, GR, RU, fam hist by Schnegelberger, bk rev FRT 16:3:108
PACE, EN, VA, NC, fam hist 1607-1750 by Turner/Pace, bk rev NC 5:3:125 SEE 36:153:48
VA, SC, GA, fam hist essays by Turner, bk rev HQ 95:59:90 SCM 23:2:118
PAGE, Anthony fl799, w Milley Pate, TN, power of attorney doc MTG 9:2:88
Joseph d1813, EN, NJ, PA, fam hist by Wyld, bk rev CHG 28:1:37
Robert m1773, w Rachel Brockman, VA, NC, SC, geneal by Page, bk rev TJ 7:2:77
PAINE, Tom fl776, EN, Am, biog by Keane, bk rev REG 93:4:474
PALMATARY, Robert, DE, geneal by Nelson, bk rev ANC 30:2:74
PALMER, Ann see Francis PLUMMER
Gershom b1722, w Ruth Randall, CT, Bible rec NGS 83:1:54
Hannah see Edwin BISHOP
Hettie Martha see Simpson J NASH
James V b1818, w Deborah Skeiks, NY, MI, Bible rec AW 21:2:45
Lefayre Heslehurst fl995, AA, anc QFH 16:1:13
Nathan Brisco see Sarah CLOSE
PANAMA, Am deaths recorded by US Consul 1850-1851 CGJ 3:4:34
PANCOAST, Fam hist 1840-1990s by Pancoast, bk rev TR 35:2:106
John fl680, EN, geneal vol 2 by Pancoast, bk rev GH 49:6:209
PANNILL, Edmund see Elizabeth A PANNILL
Elizabeth A fl836, h Edmund Pannill, VA, div case pet TVF 4:3:187

PAPINEAU, Samuel fl688, w Catherine Quevillon, FR, geneal by LeBlanc, bk rev AGE 24:2&3:44
PAPUA NEW GUINEA, Civil Registration res guide by Smith, bk rev QFH 16:4:140
PARADIS, Louisa see Edouard Theophile BOURGET
PARISH, William b1801, w Margaret Holden, LA, fam hist KSL 19:1:20
PARK, Joseph see Abigail GREEN
NC, misc rec by Park, bk rev RCR 10:2:2275
PARKE, Robert b1580, EN, MA, fam hist by Parke, bk rev FRT 16:3:106 NTT 15:1/2:2 WPG 21:4:53
PARKER, Amy see Thomas PARKER
Benjamin fc1765, NY, biog by Mullane/Johnson, bk rev NYR 126:2:154
Clara F fl995, NC, recoll cont JC 21:3:41
Parkers in America (1910) index by Lee, bk rev FRT 16:2:67
Robert b1720, w Deborah Hobart, MA, geneal AG 70:2:112
Samuel b1670, w Hannah Felch, MA TEG 15:2:75
Thomas bc1605, w Amy, EN, MA, geneal TEG 15:1:48 15:4:205
PARKES, Hannah see William PARSONS
PARMALEE, Ashbel fl831, NY, abstr of marr performed by him SLV 12:3:5
PARMER, Charles Augustus fl933, CN, biog SGB 26:1:35
PARRIGIN, Caroline see John W PARRIGIN
John W b1845, w Caroline, TN, geneal FCN 7:3:44
PARRISH, Fam hist by Boyd, bk rev TB 21:3:14
PARROTT, Fam hist supp by Weyher, bk rev GGS 31:2:119
PARRY, Edward fl792, NH, biog NHR 12:3:99

PARSLEY, Walter d1920, w Theresia Schlerth, ID, WA, fam hist sketch WCG 11:7/8:54

PARSONS, Joseph bc1635, w Mehitable Bartlett, EN, CT, geneal NER 149:593:58
Joseph fl836, NC, deed abstr SCG 14:1:659
Joseph see Mary BROWN
William bc1630, w Hannah Parkes, CT, geneal NER 149:593:53

PASCO, Hugh see Mary PEASE

PATE, Bacchus dc1858, VA, execution for murder FWC 12:2:281
Milley see Anthony PAGE

PATRICK, Margaretta see Caleb MAY

PATTEN, Matthew fl754, NH, diary & acct abstr, repr 1903, bk rev HNH 49:3:193 NER 149:595:314

PATTERSON, E B fl858, KY, memoirs REG 92:4:347
Margaret see John MCDOWELL
Nancy see John DAVIS
Patterson Post newsletter index 1985-1989 by Patterson, bk rev HQ 95:58:90
Sarah see John THOMSPON

PATTISON, George Oliver b1834, CT, fam hist sketch IFL 5:8:12

PATTON, Ann see Joseph PATTON
Jane see William D HARRISON
John fl790, geneal by Dallas/Patton, bk rev CHG 28:1:33
Joseph b1810, w Ann, PA, Bible rec BGN 16:4:13

PAUMGARTNER, Balthasar see Magdalena BEHAIM

PAXSON, Henry fl682, EN, PA, geneal corr NGS 83:1:39
Thomas fl682, EN, PA, geneal corr NGS 83:1:39
William fl682, EN, PA, geneal corr NGS 83:1:39
Fam hist by Mattson, bk rev MSG 15:1:57

PAYNE, E D m1849, w Phebe M Crawford, OH, Bible rec TR 35:2:101

PAYNE (continued)
Eli fl925, NF, autobiog NAL 11:1:17
LA, fam hist by Wise, bk rev GH 49:5:234

PEACOCK, Sarah see Ryan FRIER

PEAIRS, George Washington bc1785, w Lucy Dean Kirkham, PA, TN, MO, fam hist by Renner, bk rev GH 49:3:220 WPG 22:2:55

PEARSON, EN, fam hist sketch HQ 95:58:39

PEASE, Mary b1667, h Electious/Alexius Reynolds, MA, fam hist AG 70:4:205
Mary bc1640, h Nathaniel Carroll, MA, fam hist AG 70:4:205
Mary m1678, h Hugh Pasco, MA, fam hist AG 70:4:205

PEASLEY, Birdie (Claraman) fl895, h Adolph Maurer, KS, recoll WRB 17:4:4

PECK, Martha Matilda see Judge John Alexander KELLY

PEDDIE, Agnes bc1841, ST, biog sketch TGO 7:12:502

PEEPLES, Amanda see Will Z LATCH

PEIRCE, Jonathan L b1799, w Angelina Moulton, NH, Bible rec NHR 12:4:153

PELLETIER, Guillaume fl619, w Michelle Mabille, fam rec LG 95:53:19

PELTIER, Joseph-Germain fl767, w Rosalie Beaulieu, FR, fam hist LG 95:54:23

PEMBERTON, EN, fam hist sketch FWC 9:3:260
Nettie Goodall see John COOKE

PENCE, Johannes Eberhart m1764, w Hannah Kitchen, GR, NJ, fam hist by Heer, bk rev AG 70:1:58

PENLEY, Jane see Dennis MERO

PENNINGTON, Ephraim, NC, geneal by Jones, bk rev NCJ 21:3:306

PENNOCK, Joseph fl738, w Mary Levis, SC, hist of his home RAG 16:2:7
Rhoda see Jonas HASKINS

PENNSYLVANIA, Adams Co, wall map 1858, repr, bk rev GH 49:4:219
Air Twp, non-resident roster 1780-1781 WPG 21:3:19
Allegheny area, map 1899, bk rev WPG 21:4:53
Allegheny Co, Bethany Pres Ch cem rec WPG 22:1:16
Allegheny Co, Black indentures c1800 WPG 21:3:18
Allegheny Co, cem inscr vol 1-3 by Kraynek, bk rev TPI 20:2:94
Allegheny Co, North Zion Luth Ch cem rec WPG 22:2:28
Allegheny Co, soldiers' orphans schools, roster 1896 BGN 16:4:3
Altoona, news abstr from the *Morning Tribune* 1874 BGN 16:1:16
Ambridge, direct 1905 cont GJB 19:3:58
Antis Twp, laborer roster cont BGN 16:2:19
Antis Twp, Salem Luth Ch hist & roster c1806-1814 BGN 16:1:3
Armstrong Democrat & Sentinel news abstr 1892-1894 by Hidinger, bk rev TR 35:4:222
Atlas of hist co boundaries by Long, bk rev SEE 36:153:53
Beaver, prominent fam roster 1915 GJB 20:1:20
Beaver Co, Am Legion cem data 1936 GJB 19:4:96
Beaver Co, funeral director roster 1936 GJB 19:4:98
Beaver Co, list of causes 1830 WPG 21:3:36
Beaver Co, Meth Epis Ch of West Bridgewater Missionary Soc members 1853-1860 WPG 22:2:39
Beaver Co, poor farm resident roster 1870 GJB 19:3:80
Beaver Co, poor farm resident roster 1880 cont GJB 19:4:101
Beaver Co, poor farm resident roster 1900 GJB 20:1:5
Beaver Co, tax rec 1841-1850 by Clear/Winne, bk rev WPG 21:4:50

PENNSYLVANIA (continued)
Beaver Co, vr registrars, address list 1936 GJB 19:4:99
Beaver Co, WPA cem project 1936 cont GJB 19:3:76
Bedford Co, cem rec comp NFB 27:2:34
Bedford Co, delinquent tax list 1772-1789 WPG 22:2:6
Berks Co, bapt & confirmation rec bk of D Schumacher, edited by Weiser, bk rev AG 70:1:58
Berks Co, ch rec vol 4, 18th cent by Wright, bk rev GH 49:5:213 TPI 20:2:91 WMG 11:2:89
Berks Co, Hist Soc annuals 1905-1909, repr 1910, bk rev GJB 20:2:32 LWF 15:2:66 SGS 45:1:33
Berks Co, Lehigh Co, burial rec of Joseph S Dubbs c1800-1830 JBC 15:4:3
Berks Co, res guide JBC 16:1:8
Blair Co, Civil War draftees cont BGN 16:1:19
Blair Co, deaths from court rec 1897 BGN 16:1:5 16:2:5 16:4:5
Blair Co, natu rec c1875-1886 BGN 16:1:6 16:2:7 16:4:7
Blair Co, news abstr from the *Hollidaysburg Register* 1843 BGN 16:4:19
Blair Co, news abstr from the *Huntingdon Inquirer* 1843 BGN 16:4:19
Blair Co, Union soldier burial rec c1880-1899 BGN 16:1:9
Blair Co, Union soldier burial rec by W D Hall c1864-1894 BGN 16:2:9
Blair Co, Union soldier burial roster BGN 16:4:9
Blair, Juniata, laborer roster cont BGN 16:2:20
Boundary changes, res tips SSG 14:6:83
Bowmansville, hist sketch PM 18:1:23
Branford, Quaker monthly meeting rec 1737 onward by Reamy, bk rev HQ 95:59:88

PENNSYLVANIA (continued)
Brethren preachers, distribution in 20 counties 1912 NFB 27:2:22
Bucks Co, constable rosters 1804 & 1808 BCN 15:1:4
Bucks Co, Danube Swabs/Donau Schwabs, hist & roster BCN 15:1:1
Bucks Co, geneal & personal hist, repr 1905, bk rev GH 49:5:214
Bucks Co, GR-HG hist & roster BCN 15:1:1
Bucks Co, lic granted by the court 1859 BCN 14:3:32
Bucks Co, marr & death abstr from the *Newtown Enterprise* 1868 BCN 15:1:6
Bucks Co, mechanics liens c1836-1837 BCN 14:3:27
Bucks Co, natu rec abstr 1859 BCN 14:3:30
Bucks Co, tavern lic 1860 BCN 14:3:33
Bucks Co, will abstr 1685-1785 by Wright, bk rev HQ 95:60:91
Burgenland geneal res tips HQ 95:60:57
Cambria Co, St Joseph's Cath Ch rec abstr c1830-1850 WPG 21:3:26
Carnegie, centennial hist 1894-1994 by Agostino, bk rev WPG 21:4:50
Cath fam, early settler hist by Adams/O'Keefe, bk rev KTP 9:3:48
Centre Co, misc rec by Rice, bk rev TR 35:3:167
Centre Co, orphans court docket index CPN 20:1:5
Chester Co, births 1682-1800 by Humphrey, bk rev GH 49:4:219
Chester Co, Bradford Monthly Meeting Ch rec by Reamy, bk rev WPG 22:1:45
Chester Co, hist & geneal, repr 1881, bk rev OLR 9:3:126 RT 13:2:48 WCK 28:3:34
Chester Co, wills 1748-1766 by Martin/Wright, bk rev WPG 22:1:45

PENNSYLVANIA (continued)
Civil War vets, Roundheads 100th Reg, PA Vol Infantry, roster 1877 WPG 22:1:34
Civil War, 2nd Reg PA Reserve Volunteers, hist by Zamonski, bk rev RAG 16:3:18
Civil War, 78th Vol Infantry hist by Gancas, bk rev WPG 21:4:53
Clarion Co, iron furnaces, list WPG 21:3:34
Clarion Co, Mt Zion Evang Luth Ch rec 1867-1929 by Mcnamara, bk rev WPG 22:2:52
Clearfield Co, *Raftsman's Journal* news abstr 1857-1858 WPG 22:2:23
Clinton Co, birth, marr & death rec by Rice, bk rev GH 49:4:219
Clinton Co, misc rec by Rice, bk rev TR 35:3:166
Co Lieutenants accts 1777-1789 by Egle, bk rev GG 7:4:157
Colonial & Rev War era fam geneal by Jordan, bk rev QQ 95:25:23
Courthouse res, Russell Index System, res guide WPG 21:3:27
Cumberland Co, cem rec by Zeamer/McElwain, bk rev BHN 28:1:20 GH 49:5:214 OLR 9:1:40 SGS 44:2:89 WPG 21:4:48
Cumberland Co, direct tax lists 1798 by McElwain, bk rev CCS 16:4:138 TR 35:2:107
Cumberland Co, div rec 1789-1860 by Throop, bk rev GH 49:3:214 LHS 95:2:8 TSG 3:2:9 WPG 21:4:49
Cumberland Co, tax lists 1798 by McElwain, bk rev OC 31:1:56 SGS 44:3:143
Delaware Co, births 1682-1800 by Humphrey, bk rev TPI 21:1:39
Delaware Co, hist, repr 1914, bk rev GG 7:4:156 GH 49:6:202 SGS 44:2:89
Dunlap Creek Academy Bulletin & rosters 1939 WPG 21:4:19
Dutch Quaker migration to PA by Hull, bk rev OK 40:2:46

PENNSYLVANIA (continued)
Erie Canal hist by Halackna, bk rev GJB 19:3:70
Erie, Mercyhurst College Archives, res guide WPG 22:1:8
Executions 1794-1830 WPG 21:3:17
Fallston, city direct 1869 GJB 20:1:8
Fawn Grove, Quaker rec MD 36:2:197
Fayette Co, GR Ch bapt 1783-1806 index by Ruff, bk rev TPI 20:2:93
Fayette Co, I O O F Odd Fellows cem rec by Burchinal/Robinson, bk rev WPG 22:1:47
Fayette Co, Mt Moriah Bapt Ch cem rec by Burchinal/Robinson, bk rev WPG 22:1:47
Franklin Co, Waynesboro, Antietam Ch ministers before 1820 NFB 27:2:21
Franklin Twp, Camp Run U P Ch cem inscr by Copper, bk rev GJB 20:2:32
Freedom, resident direct 1869 GJB 20:2:38
Geneal & local hist guide, bk rev BHN 28:2:20
Geneal & personal hist of northern PA, repr 1913, bk rev SGS 45:1:33 WCK 28:4:44
Geneal guide to rec by Woodroofe, bk rev HQ 95:60:91 TPI 20:3:165
General Loan Ofc mortgage guide 1724-1756 by Duffin, bk rev GH 49:6:201 WPG 22:2:53
GR-Am Bible subscribers 1819, roster WPG 22:1:6
GR geneal by Egle, bk rev GH 49:4:219
Germanna, Hebron Ch, women in the congregation c1776, biog sketches BYG 7:3:381
Germantown Reformed Ch rec 1753-1800 by Wright, bk rev GH 49:5:213 WMG 11:2:91 WPG 21:3:45
Germantown Reformed Ch of PA rec, 18th cent by FLP, bk rev NFB 27:3:54

PENNSYLVANIA (continued)
Gettysburg, 140th Reg soldiers on Civil War monument, roster WPG 22:1:21
Green Twp cem inscr by Lyon, bk rev GJB 19:4:110
Hanna's Town, archaeology hist by Smith, bk rev WPG 21:4:51
Hanover, St Matthew's Evang Luth Ch rec 1741-1831 by Weiser, bk rev AG 70:1:58 WMG 11:1:43
Harlansburg, letters at post ofc, roster 1836 WPG 21:3:21
Harrisburg, annals, repr 1883, bk rev GRC 11:2:28
Harrisonburg annals, repr 1858, bk rev MD 36:1:92
Haverford, Welsh population hist, repr 1896 GH 49:3:214
Hist & geneal, repr 1913, bk rev WCK 28:4:44
Hist Collect, repr 1843, bk rev GJB 20:2:32 LWF 15:2:65 MD 36:4:680 NFB 27:4:74 WPG 22:2:51
Hoenstine Rental Libr, guide to services avail KVH 20:6:71
Huntingdon Co, will bk index 1787-1908 by Samuelsen, bk rev GH 49:5:214
Imm rec 1786-1808 by Egle, bk rev GH 49:4:219
Indiana Twp, hist vol 2 by ITHC, bk rev WPG 22:1:47
Indiana Twp, Pine Creek Pres Ch communicants 1839 WPG 21:3:22
Jenner Twp, Beams GR Reformed Ch rec by Palmer, bk rev WPG 22:2:52
Johnstown, Welsh people who died in flood 1889, hist WPG 21:3:30
Lackawanna Co, hist, repr 1880, bk rev LWF 15:2:68
Lancaster Co, ch rec 1700s by Wright, bk rev TPI 20:2:92
Lancaster Co, New Holland Charge hist, repr 1877, bk rev WPG 21:4:54
Laurel Messenger bound vol 1960-1970, bk rev LM 36:2:207

PENNSYLVANIA (continued)
Lawrence Co, Mount Prospect Seceder (Pres) Ch cem rec WPG 22:1:28
Lawrence Co, Valley View cem rec by Copper, bk rev WPG 21:4:53
Lawrenceville, St John's Luth Ch rec 1859 WPG 21:3:24
Lebanon Valley Standard marr & death notices by Heilman, bk rev RT 13:2:47
Lehigh Co, bapt & confirmation rec bk of D.Schumacher, edited by Weiser, bk rev AG 70:1:58
Lib res guide MFH 14:2:69
Little Beaver Twp, tax list 1815 GJB 20:2:44
Logan Twp, laborer roster cont BGN 16:2:20
Luzerne Co, hist, repr 1880, bk rev LWF 15:2:68
Main Line Canal drawings & hist 1826-1857, repr, bk rev WPG 21:4:54
Markle Norma Academy roster 1933 & teacher biog sketches WPG 21:4:8
Marr prior to 1790, repr 1890, bk rev LRT 14:2:555
Mercer, letters at post ofc, roster 1808 WPG 21:3:15
Mercer Co, Meth Ch list & hist WPG 21:3:39
Mercer Co, Mount Prospect Seceder (Pres) Ch cem rec WPG 22:1:28
Merion, Welsh population hist, repr 1896 GH 49:3:214
Morrison's Cove, tax rec 1789 MFH 14:2:74
Mount Pleasant, Mount Pleasant Pres Ch marr rec 1794-1804 WPG 22:1:32
New Brighton, direct of inhabitants 1869 GJB 19:3:64 19:4:88
New Brighton, teachers & students of early private sch up to 1910, biog sketches GJB 19:3:71
New Brighton, private sch early hist cont GJB 19:4:104

PENNSYLVANIA (continued)
New Hanover Twp, Falckner Swamp Reformed Ch rec JBC 16:1:1
News abstr 1785-1890 by Wright, bk rev TPI 20:2:92
News abstr from the *Gazette* 1726-1769, CD-ROM rev RES 27:1:30
News abstr from the *Pittsburg Leader* 1876-1888 GJB 19:4:83
Nicholson Twp, census 1840 LWF 15:2:71
North Sewickley Twp, students from census 1870, roster WPG 22:1:27
Northampton Co, bapt & confirmation rec bk of D.Schumacher, edited by Weiser, bk rev AG 70:1:58
Northern PA, geneal hist by Jordan, bk rev RCR 10:4:2380
Oaths of allegiance rec 1727-1775 by Egle, bk rev GH 49:4:219
OH Valley geneal by Hanna, bk rev KTP 9:3:48
Old Dansbury (aka Stroudsburg), resident diaries 1748-1755 by Schwarze/Hillman, bk rev DM 58:3:143
PA Dutch, possible Swiss origins, res tips TGC 19:1:3
PA German religion, hist 1700-1850 by Longenecker, bk rev PM 18:1:28
Penn Twp, hist 1844-1994 by PTSC, bk rev WPG 21:4:50
Perry Twp, Camp Run Covenanter Cem inscr by Copper, bk rev GJB 20:2:32
Philadelphia, geneal res guide by Luecke, bk rev WPG 21:4:54
Philadelphia, GR imm servant contracts 1817-1831 by Grubb, bk rev GFP 44:3:142 GH 49:5:182 HQ 95:55:91 MGS 13:1:10 MN 26:2:90 NYR 126:1:86 RCR 10:1:2213 TGC 19:2:43 TR 35:2:109 WPG 21:3:45
Philadelphia, Pres Hist Soc res guide SCS 32:11:252
Philadelphia, *Restitution* obit & marr announcement abstr 1874-1900 by Williams, bk rev THT 23:2:89

PENNSYLVANIA (continued)
- Philadelphia, seamen's protection cert index 1824-1861 by Dixon, bk rev GH 49:4:219 NER 149:596:437
- Philadelphia Wagon Road, hist HQ 95:57:59
- Philadelphia Co, births 1644-1765 by Humphrey, bk rev GH 49:3:214
- Philadelphia Co, births 1766-1780 by Humphrey, bk rev TPI 21:1:39
- Pittsburgh & Allegheny City Protestant Orphans Home inmates 1870 WPG 21:3:37
- Pittsburgh, Christ Epis Ch Lonsdale cem hist & rec WPG 21:4:34
- Pittsburgh, news abstr from the *Leader* & other news 1876-1888 cont GJB 20:1:15 20:2:27
- Pittsburgh, St Cyprian's Mission rec 1896-1903 WPG 22:1:30
- Pittsburgh, Univ of Pittsburgh dentistry grads 1913, roster WPG 22:1:20
- Pleasant Union, Pleasant Valley, hist sketch LM 36:3:219
- Polk Run Academy catalogue 1920 WPG 21:4:26
- Polk Run Academy students 1914 WPG 21:4:22
- Pres colleges & academies, list WPG 21:4:5
- Radnor, Welsh population hist, repr 1896 GH 49:3:214
- Reading, hist sketch 1863 JBC 16:1:4
- Res guide by Woodroofe, bk rev HQ 95:57:83 NGS 83:3:226 WPG 21:4:51
- Res tips, misc OC 31:1:9
- Rev War, co lieutenants & treasury rec 1777-1789 by Egle, bk rev GJB 19:4:110
- Rev War era treasury rec 1777-1789 WPG 22:1:42
- Rochester, educator roster 1910 GJB 20:2:37
- Rochester, Evang Luth Orphans Home inmates 1880 WPG 21:3:29
- Rochester, prominent fam roster 1915 GJB 20:2:33

PENNSYLVANIA (continued)
- Rose Point, Reformed Pres Ch reg 1834-1894 WPG 21:3:5
- SAR Patriot Index 1893-1993, bk rev WPG 22:1:47
- Schuyhill Co, bapt & confirmation rec bk of D.Schumacher, edited by Weiser, bk rev AG 70:1:58
- Scotch-Irish colonial hist, repr 1944, bk rev WMG 12:1:45
- Scotch-Irish geneal by Egle, bk rev GH 49:4:219
- Scotch-Irish population, hist by Dunaway, bk rev DM 59:1:45
- Seamen's protection cert appl 1796-1823 by Dixon/Eberly, bk rev SGS 45:1:37
- Slippery Rock, Reformed Pres Ch reg 1834-1894 WPG 21:3:5
- Somerset Borough finances 1890 LM 36:2:213
- Somerset Co, atlas, repr 1876, bk rev LM 36:2:207
- Somerset Co, Brothersvalley Twp, Pine Hill Ch confirmations 1789 & 1791 LM 36:1:197
- Somerset Co, centennial celebration article, repr 1895 LM 36:2:210
- Somerset Co, Johnsburg Cem inscr LM 36:1:203
- Somerset Co, mapmakers hist LM 36:4:229
- Somerset Co, Paint Twp, hist sketch NFB 27:2:24
- Somerset Co, place names of the past LM 36:4:233
- Somerset Co, Samuel's Ch rec cont LM 36:2:214
- Somerset Co, Shade Twp, census 1820 LM 36:1:198
- Somerset, courthouse hist sketch LM 36:1:195
- Somerset, news abstr re:storm 1910 LM 36:3:217
- Spotsylvania Co, St Mark's Parish vestry minutes c1730-1752 BYG 7:1:365

PENNSYLVANIA (continued)
- Sunbury, news vr alphabetical guide, vol. 3 by Eisley, bk rev TJ 7:1:38
- Sunbury, news vr alphabetical guide, vol 19 (1890) by Eisley, bk rev GH 49:4:219
- Sunbury, news vr alphabetical guide, vol 20 (1891) by Eisley, bk rev GH 49:4:220
- Sunbury, news vr alphabetical guide, vol 21 (1892) by Eisley, bk rev GH 49:5:214
- Sunbury, news vr alphabetical guide, vol 22 (1893) by Eisley, bk rev GH 49:5:214
- Tunhannock Post Ofc, hist LWF 15:2:107
- Tyrone Boro, Snyder Twp, laborer roster cont BGN 16:2:20
- Venango Co area, scrapbk abstr by Romig, bk rev WPG 22:2:53
- Venango Co, cem rec & ch hist by VCHS, bk rev TR 35:3:165
- Venango Co, marr rec 1795-1885, 1886-1921 by Hanson, bk rev WPG 21:4:50
- War of 1812, muster rolls of PA Vol, repr 1890, bk rev GH 49:5:218
- Washington Co hist by Crumrine, bk rev APR 14:6:3
- Washington Co, GR Ch bapt 1783-1806 index by Ruff, bk rev TPI 20:2:93
- Washington Co, hist & biog sketches, repr 1882, bk rev GH 49:5:215 NCJ 21:3:299
- Westmoreland Co, deeds 1773-1784 by TLC Genealogy WPG 22:2:52
- Westmoreland Co, oaths of allegiance 1777-1778 WPG 21:4:45
- Wyoming Co, div rec 1842-1900 cont LWF 15:2:87
- Wyoming Co, hist, repr 1880, bk rev LWF 15:2:68
- Wyoming Co, marr & deaths from *North Branch Democrat* c1858 cont LWF 15:2:75

PENNSYLVANIA (continued)
- Wyoming Co, marr docket of Asa Stevens 1819-1828 cont LWF 15:2:74
- Wyoming Co, marr rec 1885 cont LWF 15:2:84
- Wyoming Co, orphans court rec c1863 cont LWF 15:2:79
- Wyoming Co, wills c1897 LWF 15:2:81
- Wyoming Valley hist through corresp of Charles & William Miner, repr 1845, bk rev NFB 27:4:74
- York Co, early fam geneal by Dull, bk rev HQ 95:60:91 WPG 22:1:45
- York Co, will abstr 1749-1819 by Wright, bk rev HQ 95:60:92

PERCIVAL, Benjamin fl777, MA, jour by Barrow, bk rev STS 35:2:74

PERCY, Walker, fam hist by Wyatt-Brown, bk rev REG 93:3:373

PERKINS, Clark J fl833, w Lydia Hoffman, NY, biog sketch HQ 95:58:11
- Jabez, AL, fam hist by Wells, bk rev VL 30:2:91
- John b1733, NC, biog CAL 14:2:26 14:4:75
- Mary see Samuel LONGFELLOW
- Solomon b1775, NC, biog sketch TG 29:1:23

PERRILLARD, Marie Charlotte see Thomas HOFFPAUIR

PERRINA, Elsbeth see George KRATTLI

PERRY, Oliver Hazard fl1813, biog & hist of Battle of Lake Erie by Altoff, bk rev WPG 21:3:51
- Oliver Hazard fl1836, OH, diaries by Howard, bk rev TR 35:2:107
- William fl644, w Susanna Carver, MA, geneal AG 70:1:42
- William, MA, geneal corr AG 70:2:84

PERSSON, Erland see Elizabeth JOHNSON

PETER, Anna Margaret see John Gottlieb MAZER

PETER (continued)
  Thomas f1666, w Jonet Cordouner, ST, geneal GWS 95:44:4
PETERMAN, Frank f1887, w Josephine, TX, fam hist STS 35:2:58
  Josephine see Frank PETERMAN
  Rudolph f1887, w Romilda Usener, TX, fam hist STS 35:2:58
PETERS, Barbara see Charles PORTER
PETERSON, Allen Dean, ahnentafel, bk rev TAC 6:3:30
  EN, fam hist by Hansen, bk rev GH 49:3:218
PETTIJOHN, Isaac f1847, MO, OR, jour abstr TOP 25:1:36 25:2:79
PHAIR, Edward b1720, w Rachel Beard, IR, VA, NC, fam hist GR 37:1:8
PHELPS, Ann Caroline see James B CRUM
  Asa Gray b1892, NC, geneal by Phelps, bk rev NCJ 21:4:423
  James bc1735, NC, biog by Heinbuch, bk rev NCJ 21:4:424
  Mindwell see Noah GRISWOLD
PHILBRICK, Martha see John CASE
PHILEN, Fereby see Peter PHILEN
  Peter bc1760, w Fereby, SC, geneal by Philen, bk rev ODD 7:2:39
PHILIPP, Dorthea see Georg KRATTLI
PHILLIP, J V f1870, TX, will KTP 2:4:46
PHILLIPS, Alice see Charles BOTELER
  Asaph b1764, w Esther Whipple, RI, geneal by Faig, bk rev THT 23:2:88
  Charles Duval b1835, w Sarah Evalina Smith, GA, fam hist NC 5:4:146
  Dutch see Elijah Jackson PHILLIPS
  Elijah Jackson bc1860, w Mini Phillips, GA, biog sketch MCA 14:3:83
  Elizabeth see Stephen PHILLIPS
  Gabriel Pickens, w Nancy Lenora Foote, AL, Bible rec NTT 14:3:102
  Gordon Leigh b1918, KY, biog & fam hist by London, bk rev GFP 45:2:93

PHILLIPS (continued)
  Jesse b1804, w Mary Robinson, NY, obit GG 7:4:178
  John f1826, NY, OH, corresp by Bachar, bk rev GH 49:3:220
  Joseph b1716, w Mary, WE, PA, geneal by Philips, bk rev WPG 22:1:49
  Mary see Joseph PHILLIPS
  Mini see Elijah Jackson PHILLIPS
  Rebecca see Edmund BAKER
  Reuben f1833, w Lavenia Runnion, NC, fam rec FWC 12:2:264
  Rhoda f1862, NY, corresp by Phillips/Paresegian, bk rev GH 49:3:220 NER 149:593:80
  Richard f1862, NY, corresp by Phillips/Paresegian, bk rev GH 49:3:220 NER 149:593:80
  Stephen f1790, w Elizabeth, KY, fam hist by London, bk rev GFP 45:2:93
  William b1824, w Catharine Anna Mongin Smith, w Mary Ann Olin Waterman, NC, GA, biog NC 5:3:93
PHIPPS, John b1765, w Catherine Haney, PA, fam doc, bk rev WPG 21:4:52
  Porter b1842, w Sarah Jane Baird, PA, journals, bk rev WPG 21:4:52
PICKAYES, Drew b1564, w Anne Muschamp, EN, fam hist cont AG 70:4:223
PIEPER, August f1845, w Johanna Kramm, GR, TX, fam hist KTP 2:4:38
  Thomas fc1670, EN, CT, geneal by Pierre, bk rev CN 4:3:41 EWA 32:4:177 FP 38:4:177 GH 49:6:209
  Delos fc1860, NY, identity AW 22:1:10
  George, fc1860, NY, identity AW 22:1:10
  Jessie b1891, h Elmer W Bowers, KS, OK, biog by Shacklee, bk rev GH 49:5:234
PIERESONE, Wautier f1298, EN, fam hist sketch HQ 95:58:39

PIERPONT, Eliza see James Lord PIERPONT
  James Lord f1893, w Eliza, FL, biog PCQ 17:4:6
PINE, NY, CT, geneal cont NYR 126:1:60 126:2:117
PIPKIN, Beulah Mary b1896, FL, autobiog PCQ 3:1:2 6:3:7 6:4:2
  Beulah Mary b1896, FL, biog PCQ 22:1:7
  FL, fam reunion 1902, roster PCQ 14:1:6
  FL, geneal sketch PCQ 14:4:7
  Sarah Moore f1931, FL, recoll PCQ 2:4:5
PIRAUDE, Marie see Robert CORMIER
PISCHEL, Mary Ann see William G MARTINI
PITCHFORD, Daniel f1761, w Rebecca Davis, VA, fam hist by Morley, bk rev HQ 95:58:90
  Rhoda Thomas, h Peter C Kramer, fam hist by Morley, bk rev HQ 95:58:90
PITTMAN, Elijah Vail, w Nancy Brooks, NC, Bible rec GR 37:2:12
PLACE, Thomas f1779, RI, biog & identity RIR 21:3:69
PLANK, Samuel L b1821, w Catherine Yoder, PA, geneal MFH 14:2:88
PLANO, Ellen see Jack C PLANO
  Jack C f1995, w Ellen, MI, autobiog, bk rev DPL 15:SPRING:6
PLOWMAN, Jonathan f1794, MD, fam cem rec CCG 14:4:50
PLUMB, John, CT, ancestry AG 70:2:65
PLUMER, William m1833, w Pamelia M Waldron, NH, Bible rec SCR 18:5:73
PLUMMER, Francis bc1594, w Ruth, w Ann Palmer, w Beatrix Canterbury, EN, MA, biog NGS 83:2:112
  Ruth see Francis PLUMMER
POCAHONTAS, bc1595, h John Rolfe, VA, EN, biog by Woodward, bk rev CN 4:4:65

POCAHONTAS (continued)
  bc1595, h John Rolfe, VA, EN, how to prove descent AW 22:2:31
  bc1595, h John Rolfe, VA, EN, info on her desc SCS 32:10:234
POGUE, Robert f1820, w Lucinda Snow, IL, biog sketch MCS 15:1:4
POINTER, Susi Elizabeth see Laban HALL
POIRIER, Geneal & documentary 1626-1992 by Poirrier, bk rev AGE 24:2&3:45
POITVIN, Jean f1677, CN, biog sketch ACG 21:2:64
POLISH GENEALOGY, Archives addresses TGC 19:2:38
  Church direct res tips TE 15:2:82
  CN, Ontario, St Mary's Roman Cath Ch marr rec 1885-1896 TE 15:1:28
  Czermno Parish, bapt rec 1872 TE 15:1:20
  Czermno Parish, bapt rec 1873 TE 15:2:78
  Czermno Parish, bapt rec 1874 TE 15:3:104
  Galicia, geneal gazetteer by Lenius, bk rev TE 15:3:125
  Galicia, GR hist sketch SGB 26:4:176
  Geneal soc address list TE 15:3:123
  Geneal soc list TE 15:1:25
  Imm to Am, res guide HQ 95:55:71
  Konin, hist by Richmond, bk rev LLI 7:4:7
  Kosiska, ch hist TGC 19:2:48
  Legowo/Wagrowiec Par, surname roster 1593-1690 TE 15:1:27
  Leszno, Holy Cross Ch hist sketch MCR 27:1:58
  MI, Detroit, PO natu pet abstr 1929 TE 15:1:4 15:2:84
  MI, Detroit, PO publications 1903-1953 TE 15:1:18
  MI, Detroit, PO settler hist c1884 TE 15:2:50
  Natu rec, res tips TE 15:3:126
  Puck Parish, births 1850-1858 TE 15:2:66
  Res tips JBC 16:1:6 TE 15:1:12

POLISH GENEALOGY (continued)
RU doc translation tips TE 15:1:30
St Albertus Parish, marr rec 1873-1875 TE 15:3:100
Surnames, tips on tracing to specific locations TE 15:1:26
TX, imm hist by Hill, bk rev STS 35:2:73

POLK, James K b1795, NC, biog DAR 129:8:763

POLTHRESS, Jane see John ROLFE

POMEROY, Isabella see John CARMICHAEL

POND, Thomas f1635, EN, New England, fam hist by Pounds, bk rev HQ 95:58:90 MN 26:2:87

PONTBRIAND, Benoit b1914, QB, biog LG 95:55:60

PORTER, Charles b1729, w Rebecca Mason, w Barbara Peters, PA, geneal WPG 21:3:16
James see Missouri M LOCKWOOD
Robert f1795, diary abstr of the Whiskey Rebellion WPG 21:7:52
WI, fam cem rec WI 42:1:22

POSEY, Nehemiah m1767, w Anna Trantham, NC, marr rec abstr NCJ 21:4:398

POTTER, Andrew Jackson b1830, MO, TX, biog KTP 2:2:15
Anna see John Henry BURCHSTEAD
Fam Civil War letters by Dooley, bk rev BTG 1:2:6
Frances see William H LUMNEY

POTTS, Mary Ann see James T BARNES

POUND, John f1635, EN, VA, fam hist by Pounds, bk rev HQ 95:58:90
John m1683, w Elizabeth Joy, VA, fam hist by Pounds, bk rev MN 26:2:87 SGS 44:3:140
John see also John POWND
Thomas f1635, EN, New England, fam hist by Pounds, bk rev HQ 95:58:90
Thomas see Thomas POND

POWELL, Elizabeth see Miles MERWIN

POWELL (continued)
John Stephen b1857, w Anna Thomas Nimmons, GA, biog sketch CCM 15:2:9
Robert f1799, w Charity York, NC, geneal by Powell, bk rev GH 49:3:220

POWER, James f1794, PA, marr rec of his congregation WPG 22:1:32
Leathy A f1890, GA, fam rec NC 5:3:108
Stephen A b1809, w Lucinda W Arnold, OH, Bible rec TFP 95:12:105

POWND, John f1635, EN, VA, fam hist by Pounds, bk rev HQ 95:58:90 MN 26:2:87

POYNTER, Robert Harrison b1844, TN, KY, AR, PA, diary abstr TRC 10:1:17 10:2:52

POYNTZ, Dorothea, h John Owsley, VA, maternal anc by Bodine/Spalding, bk rev AG 70:4:254

POYTHRESS, James Edward f1828, w Catherine Speed Preston, VA, fam rec VA 33:2:111

PRAIRIE, Nettie see John W BROOKS

PRATER, Fam hist by Prather, bk rev CI 31:1:23
Thomas f1622, w Mary, EN, VA, geneal vol 2 by Prather, bk rev WMG 11:1:40

PRATHER, Fam hist by Prather, bk rev CI 31:1:23
Mary see Samuel CAMBY
Robert Alexander b1882, AR, biog sketch SCH 10:3:94
Thomas b1604, KY, IN, geneal by Prather, bk rev KA 30:4:200 PCH 1:1:37

PRATOR, Fam hist by Prather, bk rev CI 31:1:23

PRATT, Anc direct 1995 by Ancestor House, bk rev RAG 16:4:26
John bc1607, CT, origins descr NER 149:596:374
Rosa see Joshua SCHECTER

PRATT (continued)
William f1636, CT, origins descr NER 149:596:374
William Lapp b1847, w Marietta Augusta Randolph, EN, MO, KS, Bible rec TS 37:3:104

PRECHTEL, Johann Ernst b1737, GR, diary abstr by Burgoyne, bk rev GH 49:6:185
John f1777, NY, PA, diary by Burgoyne, bk rev TGC 19:4:90

PREE, Martin J f1910, IL, corresp GL 29:4:135

PRESCOTT, Moses C b1820, NH, Bible rec NHR 12:1:23

PRESTON, Catherine Speed see James Edward POYTHRESS
William b1816, KY, biog REG 93:3:257

PREVATT, Valentine Rowell b1809, w Huldah Ward, GA, FL, biog FLG 18:2:47

PRICE, Betsey Woodruff see David CLARK
Hannah see John PRICE
Isabella see William SAMUELS
John b1763, w Nancy Agnes Moore, PA, OH, geneal by Griffiths, bk rev RAG 16:4:20 TS 37:3:95 WPG 22:1:49
John, w Hannah, NC, fam hist vol 1 by Sheppard, bk rev HQ 95:58:90
M S see John B WISE
Mordecai b1749, w Rachel Boring, TN, geneal BWG 24:2:134

PRIEST, Degory b1569, w Sarah Allerton, HO, MA, geneal by Wakefield, bk rev AG 70:2:128 DM 59:1:44

PRIME, Desire see Azariah ROOD

PRINE, Sarah A see William C FOREN

PRINGLE, Alexander, ST, CT, fam hist by Wallace, bk rev PR 23:2:67

PRIOR, Abigail Rose see Jacob EKLEBERRY

PRITCHARD, Jeter Conley b1857, w Augusta Ray, w Mellissa Bowman, w Lillian Saum, TN, biog sketch BWG 24:2:137

PROCTOR, Elizabeth see George HUME
Zeke f1872, OK, news abstr re:fight GSM 12:2:38

PRUETT, James Albert f1995, TX, anc PWN 2:6:26
Samuel b1806, w Mary Polly Brassell, TX, geneal PWN 2:6:26

PRUSSIA, Hualco ship, pass list 1843 TTL 24:1:4
Luth imm to NY 1843, hist by Camann, bk rev GH 49:3:197
MI, imm vr by Podall, bk rev TTL 24:1:23
Parishes, how to locate town of origin, res tips QFH 16:4:142
RU, emig hist by Anuta, bk rev GH 49:4:202
St Hedwig, res tips MCR 27:1:56

PRUYN, Alida see Andrew LOGAN
Lydia see Andrew LOGAN

PULESTON, Margaret see Lewis OWEN

PULSIFER, Josiah D b1820, w Helen A Woodbury, PO, ME, CA, biog sketch AHS 95:15:1
Josiah D b1820, w Helen A Woodbury, PO, ME, CA, corresp abstr AHS 95:14:1 95:15:3

QUAKER GENEALOGY see also RELIGIOUS GENEALOGY
MI, death rec 1861-1862 MI 41:2:64
VA, Quaker geneal ency vol 6, repr 1950, bk rev QQ 95:25:16

QUANTA, Santa f1882, FL, news abstr TNC 2:4:87

QUEVILLON, Catherine see Samuel PAPINEAU

QUICK, Theunis Thomaszen m1625, w Belitje Jacobs, NL, fam hist UG 24:1:8

RABB, Andrew bc1740, w Mary Scott, PA, geneal by Wegenhoft, bk rev WPG 21:3:49 22:2:55

RABB (continued)
John b1798, w Mary Crownover, PA, TX, biog STS 35:3:4
William b1770, w Mary Smalley PA, TX, biog STS 35:4:13

RABURN, W M b1856, w Elizabeth, w Mary Ellen, TX, Bible rec KTP 4:4:55

RACKETT, Anna see John RACKETT
John bc1650, w Anna, NY, geneal NYR 126:4:232

RAE, Thomas f1770, geneal by Dallas/Patton, bk rev CHG 28:1:33

RAINER, Elizabeth Ann see Josiah O BLACK

RAINEY, James b1812, w Sarah Ann Eagleson, IR, fam hist by Clary, bk rev IGS 27:2:118

RAISON, Nellie f1898, OH, legal notice TLL 20:3:59

RAMEY, Lucinda see Simeon J LANE
Susan see James BEARD

RAMLY, H Jurg bc1728, GR, PA, fam hist by Remaley, bk rev WPG 21:3:48

RAMSEY, Betsy see Andrew COFFMAN

RAMSEYER, Elisabeth see Michael ZEHR

RANDALL, Hiram b1810, w Betsey Hamm, NH, Bible rec NHR 12:3:102
Ruth see Gershom PALMER

RANDLES, OH, fam hist by Hutchinson, bk rev TR 35:4:223

RANDOLPH, Amanda S see John EDMONDSON
Lydia see Richard RANDOLPH
Marietta Augusta see William Lapp PRATT
Richard b1769, w Lydia, DE, PA, OH, fam rec TR 35:4:213
Gabriella Harvie see John BROCKENBROUGH

RANKIN, Ruth see Walter Lafayette BELL
W R f1865, SC, GA, biog by Starr, bk rev GH 49:5:234

RANSOM, Fletcher m1831, w Elisabeth Noyes, MI, Bible rec KVH 19:9:104

RAPALJE, Annetie Joris see Marten RYERSZEN

RASCH, Christian fc1750, w Wilhelmine Haise, GR, WI, Bible rec MCR 27:1:52

RASIN, William Blackiston b1760, MD, biog & fam hist MD 36:2:299

RATCHFORD, William Preston fc1900, TX, fam & regional hist STK 23:2:75

RATCLIFF, John dc1816, w Elizabeth, LA, fam rec FPG 17:1:5

RAULERSON, John Baggs b1820, w Civility Friar, FL, biog PCQ 14:2:6

RAVENSTEIN, Ernest G b1834, GR, EN, biog sketch PGB 26:5:111

RAWLINS, Elizabeth see Richard B WATTS

RAY, Augusta see Jeter Conley PRITCHARD
Fredrick m1904, w Nora E Barber, KS, Bible rec TOP 25:1:13
Singleton see Singleton RHEA

RAYMOND, Cyrus fc1890, FL, biog sketch PCQ 20:1:6

RAYNOR, Thurston, NY, geneal by Howell, bk rev NYR 126:4:282

REARDON, Priscilla Aylette f1837, AR, recoll & fam hist ARH 33:2:57

RECKARD, Orrill see Elle J ROUNSEVEL

RECKAY, Ed d1895, IL, news abstr re:his death PR 23:1:32

RECORDS, Laban Samuel fc1849, CA, recoll by Wheeler, bk rev RAG 16:4:18

RECTOR, Dianna see John FAUBION
Nancy see Spencer FOLEY

REED, George b1836, ST, geneal by Johnson, bk rev MSG 15:1:55
Jane see John MCDOWELL
OH, fam hist by Hutchinson, bk rev TR 35:4:223
Stanley Forman b1884, KY, biog by Fassett, bk rev REG 93:2:212

REEH, Christian see Karoline ITZ

REEL, Catherine b1818, MD, Bible rec PGB 26:6:126

REEP, William m1875, w Sarah Elizabeth Kunkel, PA, Bible rec PGB 26:5:96

REES, William b1787, WE, geneal by Reese, bk rev RES 26:3:161

REEVES, Charlotte see James ROBERTSON

REID, James Martin b1801, w Emaline Crockett, KY, fam rec FCN 6:4:65
SC, GA, AL, fam hist by Cress, bk rev NC 5:4:180

REIFF, Anna Maria see John George REIFF
Barbara see Peter FEIPEL
John George f1700, w Anna Maria, GR, PA, geneal by Riffe, bk rev TS 37:4:146

REIJER, bc 1574, HO, CN, fam hist by Ryerse/Ryerson, bk rev FAM 34:3:182

RELIGIOUS GENEALOGY, AC, Fortelbach (Fertrupt) Anabaptist burials 1737-1761 MFH 14:1:10
Am religion ency by Gale Research, bk rev ARN 8:2:11
Amish-Mennonite culture of obedience 1693-1993, hist essays by Oyer, bk rev PM 19:1:40
Amish Mennonites in GR, hist by Guth, bk rev GGD 11:4:100 NFB 27:4:74
Anabaptists, 16th cent responses to persecution, hist PM 18:4:2
AR, OK, Quaker hist sketch & sources GSM 12:2:40
Brethren, marr rec abstr from the *Primitive Christian* 1877 NFB 27:2:27
Brethren minister deaths 1928 NFB 27:3:43
Brethren, news abstr from the *Primitive Christian* 1877 cont NFB 27:3:47
Catholic diocesan res guide by Humling, bk rev CSB 30:4:144 FCT 96:124:3 MSG 15:4:225

RELIGIOUS GENEALOGY (continued)
Evangelical Assoc, res bibl TR 35:2:76
Freewill Bapt Publications, marr & div rec 1819-1851 by Young, bk rev NGS 83:1:67 TPI 20:3:160
GA, Bapt ministers & settlers, biog sketches cont SEE 36:153:31
GR, Baden-Durlach, misc Amish-Mennonite fam, geneal corr & add MFH 15:1:40
GR, PA, Pike Mennonite Ch imm fam hist, MFH 14:1:4
Jewish memoirs, misc, bk rev HQ 95:57:54
Luth imm to NY 1843, hist by Camann, bk rev GH 49:3:197
Luth in Am, hist by Nelson, bk rev DPL 17:SPRING:1
Masonic Grand Lodge address list KTP 4:1:3 4:2:28 SCS 32:2:40
Masonic rec address list MCG 18:1/2:82
Masonic res guide by Yates, bk rev ARN 8:2:14 GH 49:4:200 SQ 6:1:44 TTT 20:1:19
MD, Baltimore, Catholic archives, res tips FTR 95:182:7
MD, Quaker rec (early) & hist MD 36:1:3
Mennonite surnames, origin guide by Gratz, bk rev GGD 11:4:100
Mennonites & tent revivals, hist 1951-1962 PM 19:1:9
Mennonites in Belize, 1765 to today, biog sketches MFH 14:1:40
Mennonites in Lithuania, hist MFH 14:2:79
Mennonites, Central Dist Conference 1957-1990, hist by Rich, bk rev PM 18:4:36
MI, Quaker death rec 1861-1862 MI 41:2:64
MN, Luth Synod, hist sketch of the MO Synod in MN CHI 68:1:6
MO, Luth Orphans' home in Des Peres, hist sketch CHI 68:1:34

RELIGIOUS GENEALOGY
(continued)
MO, Luth Synod & GR prisoners of war, WW2 era hist CHI 68:3:120
PA, Cath fam, early settler hist by Adams/O'Keefe, bk rev KTP 9:3:48
PA Dutch, possible Swiss origins, res tips TGC 19:1:3
PA, New Holland Charge hist, repr 1877, bk rev WPG 21:4:54
PA, Quaker Dutch migration hist by Hull, bk rev OK 40:2:46
Psychic geneal essays by Jones, bk rev LC 16:1:15 PM 18:4:37
Puritan anc res tips CC 18:2:1
Quaker geneal ency by Hinshaw, bk rev CTA 37:3:144
Quaker hist sketch CC 17:3:23
Quakers (IR) in PA, imm hist 1682-1750 by Myers, bk rev IS 16:1:11
Quakers, NY yearly meeting hist & rosters by Barbour et al, bk rev RAG 16:4:26
Quakers, VA, Cedar Creek meeting minutes by Bell, bk rev GH 49:4:200
Quakers, VA, hist by Worrall, bk rev AW 21:3:94
Quakers, VA, South River meeting minutes by Bell, bk rev GH 49:4:200
Religious periodicals as a resource, res guide MFH 14:1:35
RU, CN, Mennonites, Odessa Files, hist SGB 26:3:113
Salzburg Luth Expulsion hist, repr 1962, bk rev GR 37:1:50 GH 49:3:196 NCJ 21:1:79 SGS 44:2:90 TRC 10:1:32
Society of Friends rec, res tips CC 17:3:24
South, hist of religion by Boles, bk rev REG 93:4:471
ST, Congregational Ministry hist 1794-1993 by McNaughton, bk rev GWS 95:42:36
VA, Quaker geneal ency vol 6, repr 1950, bk rev QQ 95:25:16
VA, Quaker hist by Worrall, bk rev FCM 7:4:265 WPG 21:4:48

REMY, William b1745, w Eleanor McCarty, VA, KY, geneal EK 31:1:11
RENARD, Catherine see Nicholas DEPUY
RENCUREL, Francisco fc1700, w Mariana Fernandez, SP, Cuba, fam hist CGJ 3:4:36
RENNINGER, Margaret C see Samuel Jared KAUFFMAN
REVE, Robert bc1490, EN, fam hist by Childs, bk rev GH 49:6:210
REVERE, Paul fl775, MA, biog by Fischer, bk rev REG 93:2:218 TEG 15:2:121
REVOLUTIONARY WAR, Black Loyalist direct, bk rev NEH 12:6:200
Bounty land warrant appl files, fed sources, res guide SCH 10:3:83
CN, Am Loyalist geneal, repr 1973, bk rev GJ 22:4:129
Claims & misc rec, repr 1858, bk rev ARN 8:1:8
County lieutenants, state of accts vol 1 1777-1789 by Egle, bk rev WCK 28:2:19
Geneal res guide by Schweitzer, bk rev TTC 21:1:7
Green Mountain heroes & Ethan Allen, hist by DePuy, bk rev BCF 95:Apr/May:8 SLV 12:1:14
Hist 1776 by Edgar, bk rev WPG 22:1:43
Jersey ship prisoner roster OC 31:1:56
Jersey ship, prisoner roster, repr 1888, bk rev RAG 16:2:29
Loyalist geneal res guide AMG 9:6:9
Loyalists in CN, geneal, repr 1973, bk rev GH 49:3:195
MD, muster rolls & other rec 1775-1783 by MHS, bk rev FTR 95:177:3
NC, Loyalists hist, repr 1940, bk rev GH 49:3:213
NJ, bibl by Sinclair, bk rev GSN 8:1:7
Pension rec, lost files, list & res tips AMG 9:6:12 10:2/3:14 10:4:7
Pension rec, res tips RES 26:3:147

REVOLUTIONARY WAR (continued)
  Pensioners 1891, last surviving, roster NGS 83:1:31
  Prison ships (EN), prisoner roster, repr 1888, bk rev GFP 44:4:187 GH 49:5:186 SEE 36:153:52
  VA, MD, PA, SC, KY, patriot geneal by Coulter, bk rev TTT 20:1:19
  VT, soldiers, sailors, & patriots, roster & biog data by Fisher, bk rev AG 70:2:125

REYERSZEN, Marten fl662, w Annetie Joris Rapalje, NL, fam hist by Ryerse/Ryerson, bk rev NYR 126:4:281

REYNOLDS, Alexius see Mary PEASE
  Electious see Alexius REYNOLDS
  James Madison fl1850, AL, Civil War diary NTT 15:1/2:33

RHEA, Singleton bc1800, w Mary Henry, TN, geneal LOB 16:2:39

RHODE ISLAND, Atlas of hist co boundaries by Long, bk rev CTA 37:4:185 FRT 16:3:104 GH 49:4:206 NER 149:594:188 RAG 16:2:30 16:4:25 REG 93:4:511 SEE 36:153:53 TMG 17:2:46
  Bristol, ch rec c1706 cont AG 70:1:55
  Bristol, pass lists 1820-1871 by Taylor, bk rev ACG 21:1:25 GH 49:5:215 GN 13:2:91
  Centredale, hist & biog sketch AGE 24:4:105
  Civil War, soldiers buried in NC (Natl Cem in New Bern) RIR 21:2:41
  Exeter hist cem inscr by Sterling/Good, bk rev NER 149:594:193 RIR 21:1:5
  Factoryville, hist c1914 LWF 15:2:92
  Foster Town council bk personals c1797 RIR 21:4:115
  Geneal dict, repr 1887, bk rev GN 13:3:142 HQ 95:60:91 MN 26:4:185 NHR 12:4:194
  General Assembly pet from the RI State Archives 1743-1748 cont RIR 21:2:44 21:4:118

RHODE ISLAND (continued)
  Multiculturalism in RI, essay RIR 21:1:7
  Name changes 1800-1880 NER 149:595:265
  Narragansett Hist Reg vol 1, repr 1882-1883, bk rev GH 49:3:214 GSM 12:1:16
  Narragansett Hist Reg vol 2, repr 1883-1884, bk rev ACG 21:1:22 GH 49:5:215 RAG 16:2:18 SGS 44:2:83
  Narragansett Hist Reg vol 3, repr 1884-1885, bk rev OK 40:1:7 SGS 44:3:142 TEN 95:16:23
  Narragansett Hist Reg vol 4, repr 1885-1886, bk rev FC 14:1:59 TB 22:1:13
  North Kingstown, cem rec by McAleer et al, bk rev NER 149:594:193
  Pass lists 1798-1872 by Taylor, bk rev ACG 21:1:25 HQ 95:57:83 KA 31:1:44 NGS 83:3:227 NHR 12:2:97 NYR 126:3:219 SGS 44:3:145
  Petitions to General Assembly 1739-1748 cont RIR 21:1:25
  Providence area, British settlement, hist PB 10:2:39
  Providence, pass lists 1798-1808 & 1820-1872 by Taylor, bk rev ACG 21:1:25 GH 49:5:215 GN 13:2:91 TPI 21:1:50
  Providence, runaways, deserters, & villains, news abstr from the *Gazette* by Taylor, bk rev RIR 21:3:68
  Providence, seaman's protection cert reg 1796-1879 by Taylor, bk rev NER 149:596:437
  Residents in NY (Chautauqua Co) census 1855 RIR 21:1:11 21:2:51 21:3:84
  Settlement hist sketch cont PB 10:4:82
  Smithfield, polls & estates list 1778 RIR 21:1:17
  Smithfield, tax list 1778 RIR 21:2:57 21:3:90
  Warren, pass lists 1820-1871 by Taylor, bk rev ACG 21:1:25 GH 49:5:215 GN 13:2:91 TPI 21:1:50

RHODES, Alonzo bc1871, w Letha Ann Watkins, TX, fam rec PWN 2:6:14
  Charles bc1830, w Mary A Franklin, TX, geneal PWN 2:6:9
  Charles Franklin b1893, w Lula May Noyes, TX, fam rec PWN 2:6:15
  Clyde Wendell b1934, w Wilma Jo Mosier, TX, fam rec PWN 2:6:16
  Henry, MA, geneal cont TEG 15:1:31
  John b1705, w Athelred Merriam, w Elizabeth Estes, MA, fam rec TEG 15:2:84
  John b1819, w Dorcas Ann Lamar, TN, MO, biog sketch AUQ 6:4:77
  Margaret see Daniel L BEATY
  Mary Katherine see Daniel BESS
  TX, fam rec PWN 2:6:8
  TX, marr rec, misc co PWN 2:6:17
RIAL, Isaac f1833, OH, pension appl abstr MAG 8:1:13
RICAND, MD, see RICAUD
RICAUD, N fc1660, MD, geneal MD 36:2:280
RICE, George f1920, OK, MT, biog sketch DCH 6:2:10
  William Marsh bc1816, TX, biog sketch STS 35:3:61
RICH, Charles C f1847, roster of his guard GJ 23:1:24
RICHARD, Cleonise see Jean Vileor THERIOT
  Marie-Ann see Francois GIGNAC
  W E f1923, AL, land rec NTT 14:4:142
RICHARDS, Susannah see John WAGGONER
RICHARDSON, John Winn b1897, w Betty Hunt, w Mary Jane Hedrick, MD, TX, biog KTP 6:3:48
  Mary Eliza dc1848, Orangeburg Dist, SC, will SCM 23:2:85
  Roland W f1917, jour & corresp 1917-1919 by Thomas/Becker, bk rev RAG 16:1:20
  William b1829, w Joan Walker Fotheringham, ST, UT, jour by McKinney, bk rev GH 49:3:220

RICHAUX, MD, see RICAUD
RICHELIEU, Charles Francis, CN, NY, fam hist by Richeleu, bk rev GH 49:4:227
RICHHART see Christian RITSCHARD
RICKER, Carrie J see Walter B CROSS
  Samuel b1786, w Sally Knox, NY, Bible rec CDG 15:1:38
RICKERSON, Anna see John MARSHALL
RIDDELL, Hist by Ridlon, bk rev SGS 44:2:85
  John f1865, ST, fam hist sketch ANE 95:56:23
RIDDLE, Hist by Ridlon, bk rev SGS 44:2:85
  John bc1765, NC, geneal FWC 12:2:277 12:4:344
RIDEL, EN, IR, Am, fam hist 860-1884, repr, bk rev GH 49:3:220
RIDGE, Fam hist 1790-1840 by Wilkins, bk rev CN 4:4:64
RIDLON, Hist by Ridlon, bk rev SGS 44:2:85
RIEL, Marie bc1867, h Eusebe Charlebois-Wood, NY, anc ACG 21:2:66
RIEPBERGER, Josef f1841, OH, corresp TPI 20:4:200
RIESEN, David von f1815, PA, biog MFH 14:2:70
RIFE, Tom f1892, TX, biog STS 35:3:40
RIFFE, GR, PA, geneal by Riffe, bk rev TS 37:4:146
RIGGINS, Fannie Jane f1882, h Mann Patterson Riggins, FL, biog sketch PCQ 14:3:5
  Mann Patterson see Fannie Jane RIGGINS
RIGGS, Samuel f1800, TN, pension appl & biog ETR 7:3:124
  Sarah see James ELLIS
RILEY, Am, census 1790 cont IS 16:1:30
RINES, Milton f1873, AR, fam hist by Scott, bk rev ARH 33:3:127

RING, Eliabeth see Ambrose C NEW
RINGER, Louise see Marvin KIEL
RINSHAW, Nannie H see John Martin BROWN
RISLEY, Julia E Smith see Edward Martin AGARD
RITCH, Onie see John William WALTON
RITCHHART, See Christian RITSCHARD
RITCHOT, Jacques b1680, w Elisabeth Dubois, ME, CN, fam hist by Ritchot, bk rev GEN 20:3:32
RITSCHARD, Christian fl750, w Magdalena, SW, PA, fam hist 1500-1993 by Richhart, bk rev EWA 32:1:27 FRT 16:3:100
Elizabeth see Jacob BLESSING
Magdalena see Christian RITSCHARD
RITTER, Eva Rosina see Johan George KISTLER
RIVES, AR, LA, TX, fam rec abstr from *Reliques of the Rives* TJ 7:3:89
EN, Am, fam hist by Childs, bk rev VL 30:1:42
William fc1649, EN, IR, VA, fam hist by Childs, bk rev SGS 44:3:142 TVF 4:3:193
RIVOT, Jean b1734, FR, fam hist sketch ACG 22:1:16
RIZER, Catharine see Rezin BARNES
ROACH, Sara Lee fl946, OH, recoll ACH 16:6:62
ROBBINS, Thomas fl800, CT, rec bk abstr RAG 16:3:12
TX, fam hist by Robbins, bk rev SGS 44:3:146 THT 23:2:91
ROBERSON, Susannah see James KENDRICK
ROBERTS, Elizabeth see Robert HUGHES
Frances Margaret see Arthur Benjamin CANTER
George, w Mary, NH, geneal by Jacobsen, bk rev ACG 21:4:161 SGS 45:1:36 TMG 17:4:138

ROBERTS (continued)
Giles fl658, ME, geneal by Nichols, bk rev AG 70:1:63 NHR 12:1:47 RAG 16:4:25
Harrison Simpson b1847, w Mary Elizabeth Brent, NY, fam hist by Vallentine, bk rev NGS 83:1:61
John b1727, w Susannah Mayhew, VT, fam rec BCF 95:Apr/May:2
John Douglas (Jack), w Peggy Marie Orme, anc by Valentine/Roberts, bk rev GH 49:3:220 49:6:210
John Wesley see Belle Elizabeth HENDERSON
Mary see George ROBERTS
NH, ME, VT, fam hist by Jacobsen, bk rev GH 49:6:210
Rachel see Sharpless MOORE
Rebecca see Thomas ROBERTS
Sherod E b1837, w Keziah Knight, GA, FL, biog PCQ 17:3:6
Thomas, w Rebecca, NH, ME, VT, geneal by Jacobsen, bk rev ACG 21:4:161 SGS 45:1:36 TMG 17:4:138
Wiley Lee fl936, w Letha Williams, TX, fam hist STS 35:3:66
ROBERTSON, James, w Charlotte Reeves, TN, fam hist sketch KA 31:1:14
James b1742, TN, anc by Brayton, bk rev AG 70:4:257 AGS 36:3:102 MTG 9:2:70 NCJ 21:3:308 VAG 39:3:227
John fc1741, w Mary Gower, IR, PA, VA, geneal KTP 8:2:23
Mary Elizabeth b1824, h John Martin Taylor, KY, fam hist sketch KA 31:1:15
Sarah see Robert NICHOLS
ROBEY, EN, Am, fam hist by Robey, bk rev GH 49:3:220
John b1455, EN, NH, MD, fam hist by Robey, bk rev KCG 36:2:103 SGS 44:2:85
ROBIE, EN, Am, fam hist by Robey, bk rev GH 49:3:220
ROBINS, see ROBBINS

ROBINSON, Catherine see Andrew MOORMAN
Elizabeth see W W CARMICAL
Justin T f1863, w Lydia Bagley, VT, corresp abstr BAT 24:2:61
Mary see Jesse PHILLIPS
Rebecca see William EADS
RI, MD, fam hist & corresp by Bunnell, bk rev TFG 8:3/4:27

ROBISON, Chloe Estella see James Smith ABBOTT

ROBSON, Margaret Frances see William Wilbert DRYER

ROBY, John b1455, EN, Am, fam hist by Robey, bk rev GH 49:3:220

ROCKEFELLER, John D (Jr) f1887, NY, corresp by Ernst, bk rev FRT 16:3:107 NYR 126:2:155
John D (Sr) f1887, NY, corresp by Ernst, bk rev FRT 16:3:107 NYR 126:2:155

RODERICK, PA, geneal by Roderick, bk rev WMG 11:2:91

RODES, Charles Greene b1874, w Sadie Mozelle Williams, WV, FL, biog IMP 14:1:21

ROGERS, Bridget see John Milton CONNER
Ebenezer f1820, EN, MO, natu rec MSG 15:1:32
Joseph b1784, w Frances Gardner, TX, Bible rec & fam rec YTD 15:1:16
Joseph b1824, w Ellen Stewart, VA, fam hist by Irwin, bk rev GH 49:5:234

ROGERS, Mollie see William Douglas BROWN
ROGERS, Nancy see George Washington CARLTON
ROGERS, Nathaniel b1745, w Elizabeth Carpenter, NH, fam rec abstr NHR 12:2:65

ROHER, Margaret Ellen see James Weikart

ROLFE, John d1622, w Pocahontas aka Rebecca, w Jane Polthress, EN, VA, fam hist FRT 17:1:18
John see POCAHONTAS

ROLFE (continued)
Rebecca see John ROLFE
Rebecca see POCAHONTAS

ROMANDA, Mary see Christian KLUVER

ROMERO, Joseph f1995, OR, fam hist TFG 8:2:5

ROOD, Azariah b1724, w Desire Prime, w Lydia Drakeley, CT, VT, geneal ANC 30:3:107

ROOSEVELT, Franklin Delano f1933, relationship w/Winston Churchill, hist by Sainsbury, bk rev REG 93:3:365

ROPER, NC, fam hist by McHan et al, bk rev NCJ 21:3:307
Preston Hill b1856, w Rebecca Hennis, FL, biog sketch IMP 14:2:56

ROSE, Charles f1725, ST, VA, biog by Rose, bk rev HQ 95:58:88
David d1845, ON, memorial notice FAM 34:1:14
Robert f1725, ST, VA, biog by Rose, bk rev HQ 95:58:88
William Jefferson b1831, AL, CA, obit NGS 83:1:16

ROSEEN, Sven f1748, PA, diary abstr by Schwarze/Hillman, bk rev DM 58:3:143

ROSENBERRY, Samuel C f1862, OH, corresp abstr KVH 20:4:37

ROSENBURGER, Samuel C see Samuel C ROSENBERRY

ROSS, Clan geneal by Ross, bk rev APR 14:6:3
Shapley Prince f1839, w Catherine Fulkerson, IA, MO, TX, geneal by Daniel, bk rev STS 35:2:74

ROTH, Mary Katherine see Daniel BESS

ROTHRICK, Johannes f1736, PA, geneal by Roderick, bk rev WMG 11:2:91
Ludwig b1723, PA, geneal by Roderick, bk rev WMG 11:2:91
Philip Jacob f1733, PA, geneal by Roderick, bk rev WMG 11:2:91

ROUNSEVEL, Elle J b1801, w Orrill Reckard, NH, fam hist NHR 12:1:1
Elle J b1801, geneal corr NHR 12:2:96
ROUPE, Ernest N f1935, KS, recoll KCG 36:2:84
James Marion dc1932, KS, will abstr KCG 36:2:81
John b1814, w Isabell Davis, KS, Bible rec KCG 36:2:79
John Henry b1851, w Laura E Davis, KS, Bible rec KCG 36:2:78
KS, misc fam rec KCG 36:2:81
ROWAN, Julia Hathaway see William Walker MOORE
ROWAN, MD, TN, MS, fam hist by Linn, bk rev RCR 10:2:2279
ROWE, Alfred d1912, TX, biog STS 35:1:48
ROY, Fam rec by Yelle, bk rev ACG 21:1:23
ROY-DESJARDINS, Antoine bc1635, w Marie Major, CN, FR, fam hist ACG 21:1:10
ROYALL, Joseph bc1600, EN, VA, fam hist by Griner, bk rev NCJ 21:3:305
ROYSTON, Margaret see James R CARR
RUBEL, Jacob f1867, w Margaret, WA, fam hist SGS 44:3:130
Margaret see Jacob RUBEL
RUCKER, Nancy see Warren RUCKER
Susan see Thomas R FREE
Warren b1841, w Nancy, w --- Cannady, w Lucy Blake, NE, biog sketch NW 18:1:21
RUDD, Gordon Arthur, w Alicia Wellwood, IR, Am, fam hist by Rudd, bk rev CI 31:1:22 GEN 20:1:20
RUEGGER, George b1881, IL, biog CRT 16:4:11
RUFF, Johann Friedrich Ferdinand b1858, w Caroline Marotz, PU, MI, biog sketch DM 58:4:172
RUFFIN, Olivia see William BARROW
RUGG, Jerusha see Eliphalet TOWNE

RUGH, Ada Leona, h George Francis Seward, fam hist by Seward, bk rev GH 49:6:210
RUNDELL, Lucinda J see Joel WHITE
RUNNION, Lavenia see Reuben PHILLIPS
RUNYAN, Mary see Abraham ELLIOTT
RUSH, Elizabeth see John IKENBERRY
Joseph f1820, AL, geneal by Horton/Carter, bk rev NTT 15:1/2:5
RUSSELL, A C b1825, w Rebecca C Parks, GA, biog CCM 15:2:4
Andrew bc1763, w Agnes Martin, VA, TN, biog & misc data ETR 7:3:142
Dicey see Barton SCROGGINS
John, IR, OH, fam hist by Deems et al, bk rev TS 37:3:93
RUSSIAN GENEALOGY, Chortitza, settler hist & geneal 1788-1803 cont MFH 14:1:29
GR population hist GL 29:1:20
Kronsweide, Mennonite settlers 1788-1814, hist MFH 14:2:79
NY, pass arrival rec 1875-1886 by Glazier, bk rev HQ 95:59:87 NGS 83:4:310 NYR 126:4:279 TR 35:4:220
Res tips JBC 16:1:6
RUTH, John George f1741, GR, PA, geneal by Allen, bk rev FRT 16:3:106 WPG 21:4:52
Peter f1733, w Sophia Lauer, GR, PA, fam hist sketch JBC 16:1:1
RUTKOWSKI, Bill f1985, MD, fam hist TAC 6:3:17
RUTLEDGE, Edward f1670, MD, fam hist by Clemons, bk rev TOP 25:1:4
Peter f1760, MD, fam hist by Clemons, bk rev TOP 25:1:4
RYALL, Joseph bc1600, EN, fam hist by Griner, bk rev CAL 14:2:28
Fam hist by Griner, bk rev PR 22:4:48
Jesse d1836, SC, AL, geneal by Ryals, bk rev SCM 23:1:60
Agnes b1878, NH, biog HNH 50:3/4:185

RYALL (continued)
Annie Mary see Patrick BANNON
RYEDALE, EN, IR, Am, fam hist, repr 1884, bk rev GH 49:3:220 GN 13:1:20 GR 37:1:49 IS 16:3:79 SGS 44:2:85
RYERSE, Samuel, HO, CN, fam hist by Ryerse/Ryerson, bk rev FAM 34:3:182
RYERSON, Joseph, HO, CN, fam hist by Ryerse/Ryerson, bk rev FAM 34:3:182
RYVE, Robert see Robert REVE
SABIN, William fl643, EN, MA, geneal by Morris et al, bk rev NYR 126:4:284 OC 32:2:53
SAEGER, Elizabeth, h --- Beam, h --- Cox, h Joseph Seager, IL, Bible rec CI 31:3:98
SAGESER, Fam hist by Mattson, bk rev MSG 15:1:57
SALA, Jacob fl798, w Magdalena Mark, PA, biog sketch NFB 27:4:79
SALLEY, Martha Francis see Robert James TURNER
SALLOWS, Elizabeth see Joseph TRASK
SALTER, Mariah J see Henry BRIGHTMAN
SALTS, VA, fam hist BWG 24:1:59
SALZENSTEIN, Albert fl876, IL, biog sketch CR 27:4:92
SAMPSON, --- fc1580, CT, geneal by Ottery, bk rev LL 30:3:85
SAMS, James bc1690, w Katheryne Alden, NC, fam rec LOB 16:1:19
SAMSON, Hannah B see Joshua P LINNEL
SAMUEL, Marion see Asa COBB
William b1770, w Isabella Price, VA, geneal by Samuels, bk rev GH 49:5:234
SAMUELS, Ann see William SAMUELS
William b1770, w Ann, w Isabella Price, KY, geneal by Samuels, bk rev KA 30:3:177

SANBORN, Clara see George Winter SANBORN
George Winter b1881, w Clara, MA, biog sketch LL 31:1:28
SANBORNE, Richard bc1579, EN, geneal 1600-1993 by Sanborn, bk rev FRT 16:3:103
SANDERS, Jared Young b1791, w Rachel Hulick, SC, MS, LA, diary & corresp abstr by Sanders, bk rev AGS 36:3:101 ARH 33:1:33 CSB 30:3:105 GH 49:4:227 GR 37:1:48 HTR 38:4:103 LAB 10:4:134 RCP 17:2:51 SCS 32:11:254 TR 35:4:222 TS 37:3:93
Margaret b1846, IL, obit CI 31:2:49
Ona/Onnica bc1829, h Jacob Elswick, KY, geneal & fam hist PCH 1:1:25
Washington Lafayette, w Nettie Cummins, fam hist by Jones, bk rev GH 49:6:10
SANDERSON, John Gilbert b1878, w Beulah Carden, AL, biog sketch OLR 9:4:143
Susie see Peter KAUFMAN
SASS, Anna Catherine see Adam WERNER
SAUM, Lillian see Jeter Conley PRITCHARD
SAUNDERS, Mary E see M Shelby KENNARD
SAUR, Magdalena see Theo WIEDENFELD
SAUSSER, Gail fl995, ND, recoll NDG 95:65:4
SAYLES, Eunice see Amos WOOLSEY
SCANDINAVIAN GENEALOGY,
Imm & education in Am, hist, bk rev SCN 96:10:4
Mil rec res guide HQ 95:59:58
NW imm to Am, hist speech trans SGS 44:2:65
Res tips HQ 95:58:46
Vr, descr of rec avail HQ 95:57:52
SCARBOROUGH, Fam hist vol 1 by Boone/Morgan, bk rev QQ 95:25:25
Isaac bc1560, EN, fam hist by Boone/Morgan, bk rev GH 49:4:200

SCARLOTT, George m1820, w Nancy Sluts, OH, Bible rec TR 35:3:152

SCHAFFER, Maria Catherina see Heinrich WORSCHLER

SCHALL, Tobias bc1706, w Anna Magdalena Bechtel, PA, geneal by Summerhill, bk rev WPG 21:3:46

SCHANTZ, Catherine see Jacob HAMM

SCHECTER, Joshua b1837, w Mary Jane Swank, w Rosa Pratt, OH, IL, Bible rec IG 31:1:11

SCHEEL, Rupertus b1840, TX, fam cem rec KTP 3:2:19

SCHEID, Fam hist by Miller, bk rev TPI 21:1:47

SCHENCKEL, Philip Jacob b1747, w Juliana Bolender, GR, OH, estate doc TR 35:1:42

SCHILLING, Ernst b1835, w Dorothea Schmidt, GR, TX, biog KTP 6:3:41

SCHINDLER, Peter b1827, w Anna Hagel, GR, TX, fam hist by Arnold, bk rev STS 35:2:71

SCHLATHER, Adam b1827, TX, fam cem rec KTP 3:3:39
George bc1822, TX, fam cem rec KTP 3:4:51

SCHLERTH, Theresia see Walter PARSLEY

SCHLOTTERBECK, John D b1831, GR, NY, recoll TPI 21:1:32

SCHLUPP, Conrad see Conrad SLOOP

SCHMID, Frank b1828, MO, fam hist sketch BGG 3:9:62
Franz Ludwig b1828, MO, fam hist sketch BGG 3:9:62

SCHMIDT, Dorothea see Ernst SCHILLING
Wilhelm fl830, OH, biog by Kohl, bk rev TS 37:3:94

SCHMUCKER, PA, fam cem LM 36:1:199

SCHNEGELBERGER, GR, RU, fam hist by Schnegelberger, bk rev FRT 16:3:108

SCHNEIDER, Arthur J see Clara KLINGEL

SCHOENFELD, Elizabeth see Johan SCHOENFELD
Johan fl733, w Elizabeth, PA, fam hist by Powell, bk rev TR 35:1:52

SCHOENHOLTZER, Johannes fl750, PA, fam hist by Kerns, bk rev WPG 22:2:57
Johannes Henry fl727, GR, PA, VA, fam hist by Kerns, bk rev GFP 45:2:93

SCHONHF, Anna Marie see Bernard BECKMAN

SCHOOLEY, EN, NJ, fam hist by Schooley, bk rev CHG 28:1:34

SCHORR, Gertrude see William HOLZHAUSER

SCHRAG, Andreas D b1821, Ukraine, Dakotas, biog MFH 15:1:28

SCHRAM, William m1895, w Lulu Merriman, OH AH 22:2:173

SCHRAMM, Anna Elizabeth see William George GRAFF

SCHREIDER, August b1834, GR, Am, fam hist by Baxter, bk rev YV 27:4:99

SCHUBDREIN, Johann Nicolaus b1751, AC, GA, land grant JCG 22:1:28

SCHUCK, Conrad fl926, PA, FL, biog & hist of his home PCQ 22:3:1

SCHULMEIER, Roy Richard b1943, TX, anc KTP 12:2:30

SCHULZ, Carl m1868, w Caroline, AA, fam reunion news abstr 1985 KTP 4:4:60
Caroline see Carl SCHULZ

SCHUMACHER, Daniel fl754, PA, rec bk by Weiser, bk rev AG 70:1:58

SCHUYLER, David, NY, fam hist by Christoph, bk rev GH 49:6:210
Philip, NY, fam hist by Christoph, bk rev GH 49:6:210

SCHWAB, Am, geneal 1754-1994 by Swab, bk rev TPI 20:2:89
Catherine see Johannes SCHWAB
Jacob A m1896, w Lura M Cary, IN, Bible rec SBA 20:4:9

SCHWAB (continued)
Johannes b1720, w Catherine, GR, PA, fam hist 1754-1994 by Swab, bk rev CHG 27:3:121 LM 36:2:207 WPG 21:3:49

SCHWEINHARDT, Gabriel m1745, w Esther Neff, PA, fam hist NFB 27:4:61

SCOFIELD, Sarah Youngs see Miles MERWIN

SCOTCH-IRISH GENEALOGY, CN, Christian names, common patterns descr FAM 34:1:38
EN, IR, Am, hist, repr 1902, bk rev DM 58:4:190
PA settler hist by Dunaway, bk rev DM 59:1:45
Tartan guide by Smith, bk rev GN 13:2:90 GSC 17:4:5 IS 16:3:80 RL 30:3:5 SGS 45:1:30

SCOTT, Achsah E see William M BOSWELL
Ann see John SUTHERLAND
Helen C see Frederick C FAIRBANKS
Hiram B b1821, w Elizabeth Gilbert, OH, Bible rec MM 19:6:77
James f1789, IR, PA, apprenticeship doc WPG 22:1:14
Joseph f1831, AL, TX, fam hist THT 23:2:85
Kenneth, res bibl NYR 126:1:46
Mary see Andrew RABB
Robert f1866, KY, corresp abstr LAB 10:4:120
William bc1732, NC, geneal by Scott, bk rev TJ 7:2:76

SCOTTISH GENEALOGY, AA, ST imm roster, 19th cent ANE 95:57:9
Aberdeen Royal Infirmary death rec 1743-1822 by Wilson/Smith, bk rev RAG 16:4:20
Aberdeenshire, biog hist by ANESFHS, bk rev RAG 16:2:29
Aberdeenshire, Kennay Sch hist 1820-1948 by Downie et al, bk rev ANE 95:56:29
Aberdeenshire, poll tax returns 1696, flaws descr ANE 95:57:5

SCOTTISH GENEALOGY (continued)
Accident & disaster timeline, 19th cent GWS 95:42:17
Auchredie, pollable persons, bk rev RAG 16:1:21
Auchterarder, hist sketch BT 26:4:79
Banffshire, census 1851 surname index by Shand, bk rev RAG 16:2:18
Banffshire, census 1851 surname index vol 3 by Shand, bk rev RAG 17:1:15
Banffshire, census abstr ANE 95:57:31
Birth cert res guide ANE 95:56:8
Black Kalendar of crimes 1746-1878 by Ferguson, bk rev ANE 95:57:22
Black watch, hist RL 30:11:5
Brazilian Marine Corps, drums & bugles hist RL 30:5:6
Census rec res guide by Johnson, bk rev GWS 95:42:38 QFH 16:2:66
Ch of ST Kirk Sessions, hist by Gordon, bk rev GWS 95:43:33
Clan Chattan, hist sketch RL 30:11:3
CN, Cape Breton imm hist by Dunn, bk rev GEN 20:1:20
Collins Ency of ST by Keay, bk rev RL 30:2:
Colonial Am, imm 1607-1785 by Dobson, bk rev REG 93:4:507
Commissariot Record of Glasgow, misc rec 1547-1900, repr 1900, bk rev RL 30:9:4
Congregational Ministry hist 1794-1993 by McNaughton, bk rev GWS 95:42:36
Crimond Kirkyard with Rattray, hist by Spiers, bk rev RAG 16:1:21
David Main (ship) disaster 1876, hist ANE 95:56:17
Disasters, hist & names, 19th cent, by Cross, bk rev ANE 95:57:19
Dumfriesshire, hist fam & border wars, hist & geneal, repr 1889, bk rev GH 49:6:179 GR 37:1:49 JCG 22:1:20 LRT 14:2:555 RL 30:7:4
East Kilbride, Moncrieff Par Ch hist GWS 95:42:21

SCOTTISH GENEALOGY
(continued)

Echt, kirkyard cem rec by Spiers, bk rev RAG 17:1:16

Emergency svc rec res tips ANE 95:57:12

Emig to Am 1607-1785, hist by Dobson, bk rev GH 49:5:185 NGS 83:1:62

Emig to Am, rosters 1707-1783 by Graham, bk rev GH 49:5:185

Estate papers, res tips ANE 95:57:15

Fam hist bibl by Ferguson, bk rev FP 38:3:141

Fam hist guide by Stuart, bk rev LRT 14:2:555

First Lanarkshire Engineer Volunteers 1863-1865 GWS 95:43:24

General Reg Ofc index of one-name lists in Lib of Soc of Geneal, bk rev QFH 16:4:140

Glasgow area, local lib microform & publication info GWS 95:44:31

Glasgow Encyclopedia by Fisher, bk rev GWS 95:42:38

Glasgow, commissariot rec 1547-1800, repr 1900, bk rev GH 49:3:198 SGS 44:2:90

Glasgow, Holyrood House burial reg 1706-1900 by Grant, bk rev TTL 23:3:48

Glasgow, Mitchell Lib geneal resources guide GWS 95:42:4

Glossary for res by Burness, bk rev RAG 16:3:18

Govan on the Clyde hist by Donnelly, bk rev GWS 95:42:37

Greening Peerage, repr 1767, bk rev SGS 45:1:30

Highland emig to NC, Canadian Maritimes & Caribbean in 18th cent, hist sketch GWS 95:43:18

Highland Papers of ST Hist Soc, bk rev RL 30:6:3

Highland Papers of ST Hist Soc vol 1, repr 1914, bk rev GH 49:3:198

SCOTTISH GENEALOGY
(continued)

Highland Papers of ST Hist Soc vol 2, repr 1916, bk rev GH 49:4:203 GSC 17:3:10 IMP 14:1:28 SGS 44:2:90

Highland Papers of ST Hist Soc vol 4, repr 1934, bk rev CGJ 3:4:12 OC 32:2:55 SGS 45:1:29 TS 37:4:145

Highlander geneal article compendium vol 2 by Coppage, bk rev GH 49:4:203

Highlanders, hist KTP 9:1:3

Highlands, thatched houses, architectural hist, repr 1952, bk rev GWS 95:42:36

Hist fam geneal, repr 1889, bk rev AB 23:1:11

Hist fam geneal, repr 1889, bk rev GH 49:4:203 GN 13:2:88 GR 37:3:25 GSC 18:1:8 GWS 95:43:33 HQ 95:58:87 IS 16:3:80 JCG 23:2:56 NCJ 21:3:303 NYR 126:3:219 SGS 44:2:90 44:3:144 TFT 6:2:23B TR 35:4:219

Holyroodhouse, Chapel Royal or Abbey burial reg 1706-1900, repr 1900, bk rev GH 49:3:198 SGS 44:2:90

Index of indexes for fam historians by Jones, bk rev GWS 95:43:33

Intl Assoc of Tartan studies, descr TFT 6:2:28A

Kemnay Sch hist 1820-1948 by Downie et al, bk rev RAG 17:1:16

Land rec res tips ANE 95:54:10

Legal terms, glossary by Duncan, bk rev ANE 95:57:19

Living relatives, res tips GWS 95:42:10

Local hist, res guide by Sinclair, bk rev GWS 95:42:36

Marr & illegitimacy, res tips ANE 95:55:32

MD, rebels who arrived 1747, roster AW 21:2:47

Mormon ch resources, res tips ANE 95:54:18

Natl Lib of ST res tips TFT 6:2:19A

SCOTTISH GENEALOGY (continued)

North Am colonists, hist 1707-1783 by Graham, bk rev NCJ 21:2:186

Ordinary of arms in the public reg 1672-1901, repr 1903, bk rev GH 49:3:198

Orkney, Graemsay, census 1851 by Armstrong, bk rev FAM 34:2:117

Orkney, Hoy, census 1851 by Armstrong, bk rev FAM 34:2:117

Orkney, Stromness, census 1821 by Armstrong, bk rev FAM 34:2:117

Paisley, misc fam & technology, 18th & 19th cent hist GWS 95:44:9

Parish reg & registrars, res guide by SAFHS, bk rev RAG 16:2:27

Portlethen, daybk 1840-1869 by Beverly, bk rev RAG 16:1:21

Prince Charles Edward fl745, hist sketch GWS 95:43:21

Res guide by Baxter, bk rev APG 10:4:128 ARH 33:1:34 GFP 44:3:139

Res guide by Goldie, bk rev JCG 22:1:20

Res guide by James, bk rev GWS 95:44:24

Scots overseas, bibl guide by Whyte, bk rev GN 13:2:87 RAG 16:4:20

Seafarers, 17th cent hist by Dobson, bk rev FAM 34:4:251 RAG 16:2:28

Seafaring anc, res tips ANE 95:56:24

Sheriff court rec, res tips ANE 95:57:37

Soldiers who died in India 1930-1936, roster ANE 95:57:28

Statutory rec res guide by Webster, bk rev GWS 95:44:25

Strathclyde res guide by Miller, bk rev GWS 95:44:25

Surname hist by Anderson, bk rev KSL 19:4:154

Surnames & bibl hist, repr 1890, bk rev SGS 45:1:29

Surnames & Highland Clans, hist & geneal by Buchanan, bk rev GH 49:3:198

SCOTTISH GENEALOGY (continued)

Tartan guide by Smith, bk rev GN 13:2:90 GSC 17:4:5 GWS 95:43:35 IS 16:3:80 RL 30:3:5 SGS 45:1:30 TFT 6:2:23B

Trades & professions, bibl & addresses by Torrance, bk rev FAM 34:3:183

TX, migration hist sketch KTP 8:1:6

Whalers, hist ANE 95:56:12

SCRIPTURE, Samuel bc1650, w Elizabeth Knapp, EN, MA, geneal BG 16:1:3

SCROGGINS, Barton fl797, w Dicey Russell, TN, IL, geneal by Dalpozzo, bk rev GH 49:4:227 IGS 27:2:116

Samuel M, MO, TN, biog & identity NGS 83:4:268

SEAGER, Joseph see Elizabeth SEAGER

Richard b1595, RI, geneal by Wright, bk rev STS 35:2:75

SEAGO, Eulene Gentry b1929, TX, obit THT 23:2:87

SEAMAN, Lucy J see David R GILILAND

SEAVEY, Eliakim see Mary BROWN

SECHLER, Abraham b1796, w Mary Freeze AKA Polly, w Catherine Elder, NC, biog sketch RCR 10:2:2254

SEGAR, John, w Elizabeth Moody, RI, geneal by Wright, bk rev STS 35:2:75

SEGOINE, Jesse m1800, w Charlotty Crooker, NY, fam rec NYR 126:3:177

SEGREST, Henry fl784, w Margaret, SC, geneal by Segrest/Tatem, bk rev KCG 36:2:105 TJ 7:2:76

Margaret see Henry SEGREST

SEGURA, SP, fam name hist KTP 7:3:47

SEIBOLD, Baldus Frederick bc1813, w Frederike Neff, GR, IL, fam hist PR 23:1:19

SELF, Frances B see William SELF

SELF (continued)
Tilithia Self b1823, h John Curl, AL, obit AFH 16:4:23
William b1808, w Frances B, AL, Bible rec AFH 16:1:27

SELLERS, Mary f1823, NC, will RAG 16:4:13

SEMINOLE WAR, pension rec, lost files, list & res tips AMG 9:6:12 10:2/3:14 10:4:7

SENEVERS DIT LEMARBRE, Fam bapt & burial rec 1800-1850 MHH 16:2:47

SEQUOYAH, bc1775, OK, biog sketch KTP 7:2:33

SEVIN, Francois see Marie HACHE

SEWARD, Carroll Frances McKay, anc add by Seward, bk rev NCJ 21:4:424 TR 35:3:165
CT, fam hist by Seward, bk rev ARH 33:3:128 BWG 24:2:156 KSL 19:4:155 RCP 17:4:118 RES 27:1:40 TR 35:3:165 TS 37:3:94
George C see Carroll Frances MCKAY
George Francis see Ada Leona RUGH
Obadiah bc1635, w Bethyah Hawes, EN, CT, NY, fam hist by Seward, bk rev CSB 30:4:143 DM 59:1:44 NGS 83:4:303 TOP 25:4:130
William H b1844, gravesite descr cont AW 21:3:103
William H, fam hist by Seward, bk rev SGB 26:3:iii
William Hunter b1844, MA, NH, CA, obit AW 21:2:41

SEXTON, William Free b1814, KY, MO, biog sketch KA 31:2:9

SHACKELFORD, Nancy Ann see Henry GUTHRIE

SHAFFER, Eliza see Levi G HOOVER
Samuel D b1842, w Ellen J Walls, PA, biog sketch BGN 16:4:17

SHAILOR, Elizabeth see Jeremiah SPENCER

SHANAFELT, Elizabeth see John SHANAFELT
John f1773, w Elizabeth, PA, fam hist by Powell, bk rev GH 49:3:221

SHANAFELT (continued)
PA, fam hist by Powell, bk rev TR 35:1:52

SHANDS, Hubert see Laura Francis NOBLES

SHAPLEIGH, Alexander fc1727, ME, geneal by Berry, bk rev NER 149:595:317
Philip fc1727, VA, geneal by Berry, bk rev NER 149:595:317

SHAPLEY, David fc1727, MA, geneal by Berry, bk rev NER 149:595:317
Nicholas fc1727, MA, geneal by Berry, bk rev NER 149:595:317
Reuben fc1727, NH, geneal by Berry, bk rev NER 149:595:317

SHARP, Cornelius b1779, w Abigail Bacon, w Elizabeth Munger, NY, OH, geneal PWN 2:4:7

SHATTUCK, Frances Jane see Louis SURETTE

SHAW, James f1864, OH, biog by McLellon, bk rev QU 12:2:21
Jeremiah f1779, NH, rec of marr he performed SCR 18:4:60 18:5:85

SHEFFIELD, Paul J b1940, w June Campbell, FL, autobiog PCQ 21:1:4

SHEIKS, Deborah see James V PALMER

SHELBY, Catherine see Evan SHELBY
Evan f1735, w Catherine, WE, fam hist by Johnson, bk rev GH 49:4:228
Mary Williams see Joseph Rives DICKENSON

SHELLABARGER, Ephraim f1811, w Elizabeth Sheller, SW, fam hist by Bussard, bk rev GH 49:5:234

SHELLER, Elizabeth see Ephraim SHELLABARGER

SHELLEY, Mennie O see George Washington TURNER

SHELLMAN, Catherine Elizabeth see Solomon Joseph ZIMMERMAN

SHELTON, Ralph f1702, VA, fam hist by Miller, bk rev KCG 36:2:104
Sarah see David NORTON
VA, fam hist by Miller, bk rev TJ 7:2:76

SHEPARD, Dorcas D see David CALLEY
  William fc1677, CT, MA, identity AG 70:2:82
SHEPHERD, Polly see Japer FORBES
SHERMAN, William Tecumseh b1820, New England anc NEH 12:2/3:64
SHERWOOD, William f1870, PA, autobiog abstr LWF 15:2:89
SHETTER, Johann b1761, w Annax Stouffer, PA, geneal by Mast, bk rev GH 49:5:234
SHINN, Ruth f1920, FL, recoll PCQ 10:1:6
SHIPMAN, Richard A m1865, w Otilla M Verhoeff, MI, marr cert DM 58:4:179
SHIRLEY, Myra Belle see Belle STARR
SHMITT, Ludwig m1760, w Anna Gertraud Erfurt, GR, PA, geneal LOB 16:1:11
SHOOK, Jonas b1805, w Polly Ann Land, WI, geneal by Figi, bk rev GH 49:5:235
SHOWMAN, E D d1897, OH, obit TLL 20:4:80
SHREVE, Caleb bc1690, w Mary Hunt, w Mary Atkinson, w Ann Jess, NJ, identity of wives GMN 70:3:97
SHUBDRIEN, Nicholas see Johann Nicolaus SCHUBDREIN
SHUFELT, GR, NY, SC, fam hist by Bergdall, bk rev TPI 21:1:48
SHULTZ, Frances Minerva see Augustus DORSEY
SHUMAKER, Mary see John SMITH
SHUMAN, Catherine see Charles A SMALTZ
SHUMATE, Daniel b1781, w Betty Ellison, WV, fam hist FWC 9:3:252
SHURTLEFF, William b1624, fam hist by Shurtleff, bk rev GH 49:4:228
SIBLEY, George Champlin f1629, MA, biog sketch KCG 36:1:30
SIGERTSON, Bertha see Martein JONSSON
SIMMEN, Louis m1898, w Louisa Opper, AR, surname reç SYH 2:3:20
SIMMONS, Eliza see William DOWNING
  Martin m1823, w Joanna Wilcox, RI, geneal RIR 21:2:37
  Varnum Paine f1885, w Gertrude Burleigh, FL, fam hist PCQ 12:1:6
SIMMONT, David bc1787, MD, fam hist by Orrell, bk rev GH 49:4:228
SIMMS, D M b1853, w Fannie Bayne, AL, Bible rec OLR 9:1:9
SIMONDS, Benjamin f1753, MA, Bible rec BG 16:4:134
SIMPSON, John see Frances DREW
  Mary Sara see John CARNAHAN
  Vincent b1799, w Dicy Cook, NC, geneal by Kallam, bk rev NCJ 21:2:190
SIMS, NC, GA, LA, fam hist by Linn, bk rev RCR 10:2:2279
  Thomas Leroy b1846, w Martha Dean Hallman, NC, GA, fam hist by Linn, bk rev NCJ 21:3:307
SIMSON, Euphemia f1884, h Joseph Kemp, AA, diary by Lipp, bk rev QFH 16:4:139
  SIMSON, Mary see Christopher MERCER
SINCLAIR, Fam rec add by Grigsby, bk rev GH 49:6:210
  Mil rec update 1993 by Grigsby, bk rev GH 49:3:221
SINKLER, Fam rec add by Grigsby, bk rev GH 49:6:210
  Mil rec update 1993 by Grigsby, bk rev GH 49:3:221
SIRWELL, William f1865, PA, biog & hist of his reg by Gancas, bk rev WPG 21:4:53
SISK, Mary Ellen see James Edward MARSDEN
SKAHAN, Mary (Tolmait), WA, descr of grave TRI 35:1:13
SKELDING, James b1775, w Hannah Knapp, CT, Bible rec CTA 37:3:117
SKOLFIELD, Clement see Mary ADAMS

SLAGEL, Arthur b1891, IL, biog & diary abstr MH 22:1:1
Arthur f1923, PA, RU, biog MH 22:4:65
SLAUGHTER, --- see Minnie Hale GORTON
O V, MO, fam hist by Slaughter, bk rev TB 21:3:11
VA, fam hist by Peterson, bk rev APR 14:11:5
SLOAN, Rachel Caroline see William Carrol WILLIAMS
SLOOP, Conrad m1778, w Mary Albright, NC, biog & geneal RCR 10:2:2225
SLOVAKIA, Money, how to send, tips RM 95:10:2
SLUTS, John b1757, w Margreat How, OH, Bible rec TR 35:3:152
Nancy see George SCARLOTT
SMALLEY, Mary see William RABB
SMALLIN, E G b1817, w Jane Stapp, w Elizabeth Horn, TN, MO, geneal OZ 17:4:152
Elbridge Gerry f1852, w Jane Stapp, MO, fam hist OZ 17:3:91
SMALLS, Robert f1862, SC, biog by Miller REG 93:3:359
SMALTZ, Charles A b1833, w Catherine Shuman, PA, biog sketch BGN 16:2:18
SMART, Peter J f1865, w Martha Ann Murphy, TX, Bible rec DG 41:1:108
SMEDLEY, George, w Sarah, PA, geneal by Cope, bk rev QY 22:1:6
James b1804, w Lucy, MA, Bible rec BG 16:4:135
Lucy see James SMEDLEY
Sarah see George SMEDLEY
SMITH, Benjamin f1785, NJ, marr performed by him GMN 70:3:136
Catharine Anna Mongin see William PHILLIPS
Catherine f1900, KS, court case abstr MGR 30:3:69
Henrietta see W D HOLSAPPLE
J D f1936, GA, diary abstr OTC 4:3:6

SMITH (continued)
James f1818, NJ, acct bk abstr MCQ 4:1:1
Jasper K f1905, LA, ledger abstr TJ 7:3:84
John d1877, w Nancy Leonard, MD, OH, obit MM 19:5:60
John m1751, w Mary Shumaker, NJ, marr rec abstr GMN 70:3:117
John Melanchton b1852, NC, jour abstr NCJ 21:3:296
John Melanchton b1852, NC, jour by Smith, bk rev RCR 10:1:2218
LA, AR, misc fam data & corresp FPG 17:1:2
Louisa Myer see Henry Edward BURGER
Louva Marie see Edwin ADDISON
Martha Elizabeth see Richard Roland JACKSON
Martha Gibson see George Washington BROOKS
Mary M see David CALLEY
Mercy see Thomas INGERSOLL
Mordecai f1861, IA, biog VCG 95:MAR:2
Rebecca see Benjamin FESSENDEN
Richard, VA, geneal by Diemer, bk rev BYG 7:1:368
Rutha see Archibald VINSON
Samuel b1765, w Sarah Bishop, OH, fam hist by Fetters, bk rev FRT 16:2:65 QQ 95:25:24
Sarah Evalina see Charles Duval PHILLIPS
Sarah see James Knox Polk BEATY
Sarah see William DAVIS
Silas Hampton b1908, GA, Bible rec SCG 15:1:709
Thomas W b1834, w Emily J Carvey, NY, Bible rec HY 16:2:15
Truman m1832, w Maria Cooke, CT, Bible rec CTA 38:2:59
VA, fam hist cont IMP 14:2:42
VA, KY, fam hist by Smith, bk rev KGF 1:1/2:87
SMOOT, Abraham O f1847, roster of his company GJ 22:4:91

SMYTH, William d1801, IR, PA, geneal by McCable, bk rev WPG 21:3:48

SNEDDEN, ST, CN, fam hist by Snedden, bk rev OBN 28:1:31

SNELL, Calvin dc1849, OH, identity of children NGS 83:1:17

SNELLENBARGER, John b1768, PA, KY, geneal by Davis, bk rev WPG 21:4:51

SNELLING, Josiah fc1820, w Abigail Hunt, MN, fam hist by Luecke, bk rev GH 49:5:235

SNODDY, Samuel, w Elizabeth Sloan, fam hist by Stutesman, bk rev TOP 25:1:5

SNOW, Isaac d1799, w Apphia Atwood, ME, geneal add TMG 17:4:118
   Joshua b1786, w Lucretia McIntire, IN, Bible rec SBA 20:8:13
   Lucinda see Robert POGUE

SNYDER, --- see M F HOUSTON
   Glada see Edward KINTNER
   Rebecca see Meredith E WEBB
   Scharlotte see Daniel J ZIMMERMAN

SOBLETTE, VA, fam hist by Allen/Jackson, bk rev DM 58:4:189

SOLNEKER, Susan Virginia see Jacob Milton MILLER

SOMERS, Jim d1880, SD, biog BHN 28:1:11
   Marvin H see Jim SOMERS

SOMERVILLE, James bc1771, w Mary Ann Linn, IR, OH, biog sketch TLL 20:3:62

SONNANSTINE, Joseph F b1830, w Julia Catherine Hackett, OH, CA, fam hist TR 35:1:16

SOUTH CAROLINA, Abbeville Co, marr rec 1780-1879 by Langdon, bk rev NTT 14:3:82
   Aiken, St Thaddeus Ch hist by McClearen/Sheetz, bk rev SCM 23:1:60
   Berkeley Co, cem inscr by Hood, bk rev GH 49:6:202

SOUTH CAROLINA (continued)
   Bibl of bks on SC & NC fam by Hehir, bk rev AW 21:3:93 CSB 30:4:143 GH 49:4:214 RCR 10:1:2210 SGS 44:2:85
   Camden Dist, coroners inquisitions 1784-1799 cont SCM 23:1:46 23:2:97
   Camden Dist, pet 1793 ODD 7:1:12
   Camden, Historic Camden (bk) index by McKain, bk rev SCM 23:2:120
   Census 1870, CD-ROM rev TEN 95:16:22
   Charleston, Bethany cem inscr by Hood, bk rev HQ 95:58:88
   Charleston, Civil War era hist by Rosen, bk rev REG 93:2:227
   Charleston, marr notices from the *Courier* 1803-1808, repr 1919, bk rev GH 49:5:218
   Charleston, New England Soc hist 1819-1919 by Way, bk rev RAG 16:1:21
   Charleston, pass arrivals 1820-1829 by Holcomb, bk rev GGS 31:1:48 GH 49:5:215 HQ 95:55:92 NCJ 21:1:78 NYR 126:1:87 RCR 10:1:2212 SCS 32:3:64 TPI 21:1:50 TR 35:2:109
   Cheraw Dist, pet 1793 ODD 7:1:12
   Chester Co, Fishing Creek Pres Ch rec 1799-1859 by Holcomb/Parkes, bk rev FGC 95:28:23
   Chester, marr & death notices from the *Palmetto Standard* c1850 SCM 23:4:183
   Chesterfield Dist, census 1839 ODD 7:2:32 7:4:27
   Chesterfield Dist, commissioners of the poor rec 1811 ODD 7:1:31
   Chesterfield Dist, commissioners of the poor rec 1814 ODD 7:2:30
   Chesterfield Dist, commissioners of the poor rec 1819 ODD 7:4:26
   Chesterfield Dist, legal notices c1823 ODD 7:4:31
   Chesterfield Dist, pet roster ODD 7:1:30

SOUTH CAROLINA (continued)
Christian Neighbor news abstr c1869, cont SCM 23:2:108
Civil War rec res guide, SC Dept of Archives & Hist holdings, guide by McCawley, bk rev NGS 83:2:150
Co wills index, repr 1939, bk rev GH 49:3:214
Colonial rec abstr 1663-1721 by Lesser, bk rev ODD 7:4:36 SCM 23:4:210
Darlington Circuit, Meth Epis Ch membership rolls 1840 ODD 7:1:11 7:4:10
Darlington Dist, bastardy rec 1853-1864 ODD 7:4:21
Darlington Dist, soldiers board of relief rec 1863-1864 ODD 7:1:27 7:2:27 7:4:23
Darlington Dist, tax returns 1865 cont ODD 7:4:11
Darlington, House of Representatives pet 1819 ODD 7:2:12
Darlington, Meth Epis Ch membership rolls 1840 ODD 7:2:9
Darlington, tax returns 1865 ODD 7:1:13 7:2:14
Deed abstr 1776-1783 by Holcomb, bk rev RCR 10:1:2219 SCM 23:1:59
Fairfield Co, cem rev vol 1-3 by FGS, bk rev TJ 7:2:73
Florence, Wayside Hospital patient muster roll 1864 ODD 7:2:24
FR naturalization, political hist of THS 95:100:23
Granville Co, general sessions court case rolls 1787-1799 by McCuen at al, bk rev GH 49:4:220
Hartsville, Welsh Neck High Sch & Coker College hist by Simpson, bk rev ODD 7:1:37
Huguenot Soc transactions, index to vol 1-96 by Fischer, bk rev NGS 83:3:228
Lancaster Dist, equity minute bk 1822-1834 cont SCM 23:2:86 23:4:195
Laurens Co, land titles & maps 1749-1775 by Motes, bk rev SCM 23:1:59

SOUTH CAROLINA (continued)
Laurens Co, Polar Springs Bapt Ch hist STS 35:1:17
Legal notice abstr 1824 SCM 23:4:206
Lexington Dist, misc rec abstr, 19th cent SCM 23:2:80
Marr notices from the *Southern Christian Advocate* 1867-1878 by Holcomb, bk rev TFT 6:2:23B
Marr rec 1688-1799 by Holcomb, bk rev NCJ 21:4:421
Marr rec 1688-1820, supp by Holcomb, bk rev NCJ 21:4:422
Marr rec 1787-1875 by Langdon, bk rev SCM 23:2:118 SEE 36:153:23
Marr rec 1800-1820 by Holcomb, bk rev NCJ 21:4:421 RCR 10:4:2377
Misc Rec of the Secretary of the Province (State), abstr 1767-1771 SCM 23:2:63 23:4:191
Muster roll of Capt A McIntosh's company, expedition to Ft Prince George 1759-1760, roster ODD 7:1:29
Muster Roll of Capt R Weaver's Company to Ft Prince George 1759-1760 ODD 7:2:28
Newberry Co, land titles & maps 1749-1775 by Motes, bk rev SCM 23:1:59
News abstr from the *South Carolina Gazette* 1756 ODD 7:1:22
Old Cheraw Dist, hist, repr 1867, bk rev GH 49:5:218
Orangeburgh Co, hist, repr 1898, bk rev GH 49:4:220
Orangeburgh Dist hist & rec 1768-1868 by Culler, bk rev SCM 23:4:211
Orangeburgh, dist rec (pre-1865) abstr, cont SCM 23:1:38
Pendleton Dist, deed bk F cont SCM 23:2:103
Pickens Co, news abstr from the *Pickens Sentinel* 1872-1893 by Rich/Whitehurst, bk rev CSB 30:3:105 NGS 83:4:307
Pres Ch hist index by McKain, bk rev SCM 23:4:211

SOUTH CAROLINA (continued)
Pres Ch hist, repr 1870, bk rev ODD 7:4:6
Prince William Primitive Bapt Ch rec 1812-1912, cont SCM 23:2:112
Residents buried in Georgianna AL, cem rec ODD 7:1:24
Saluda Old Town, land petition abstr 1755 SCM 23:1:13
Settler hist 1768 by Waren, bk rev FP 38:3:142
Spartanburg Co, cem survey vol 2 by PDCSCGS, bk rev GH 49:3:214
Spartanburgh Dist, natu rec c1852-1861 cont SCM 23:1:50 23:2:93 23:4:201
Washington Dist, general sessions court case rolls 1792-1799 by McCuen et al, bk rev GH 49:4:220

SOUTH DAKOTA, Aberdeen Area Geneal Soc charter member roster TTC 21:1:4
Aberdeen Area Geneal Soc hist 1975-1995 TTC 21:1:1
Allen, Inestimable Gift Epis Ch cem rec SD 13:2:50
Brule Co, WW1 servicemen roster SD 13:4:129
Buffalo Co, Civil War vet roster SD 13:2:60
Census 1860 SD 13:2:62 13:4:126 14:1:6
Clay Co, census 1870 SD 14:2:61
Clay Co, deaths 1879-1880 cont BHN 28:2:10
Codington Co, deaths 1879-1880 cont BHN 28:2:11
Custer Co, deaths 1879-1880 cont BHN 28:2:12
Davison Co, census 1890, Civil War vets & widows SD 14:1:23
Davison Co, deaths 1879-1880 cont BHN 28:2:12
Death rec 1879-1880 BHN 28:1:8 28:3:9 28:4:5
Deuel Co, deaths 1879-1880 cont BHN 28:2:12

SOUTH DAKOTA (continued)
East Sioux Falls, hist marker dedication ceremony 1994, descr SVG 21:1:9
Forsythe Co, deaths 1879-1880 cont BHN 28:2:13
Funeral home address list, res aid SVG 21:2:35
Grant Co, deaths 1879-1880 cont BHN 28:2:13
Hamlin Co, deaths 1879-1880 cont BHN 28:2:13
Hutchinson Co, decl of intent c1888-1893 SD 14:2:70
Indian reservation res tips BHN 28:4:15
Java City cem rec SD 14:2:71
Jones Co, res tips SD 14:1:22
Kingsbury Co, atlas 1909 SD 14:1:31 14:2:51
Lyman Co, WW1 servicemen roster SD 13:4:128
Minnehaha Co, biog sketch index SVG 21:2:33
Minnehaha Co, pioneer hist name index abstr SVG 21:3:64
Moody Co, cem & burial site hist & location guide SD 14:2:45
Obits 1994 SVG 21:2:51
Parker, First Meth Ch hist & membership rosters SVG 21:3:66
Rapid City, Behren's burial rec index 1907-1920 cont BHN 28:1:1 28:2:2 28:3:1 28:4:1
Rapid City, public lib res guide BHN 28:4:13
Rapid City, Soc for Geneal Res, microfilm holdings BHN 28:2:14 28:3:15
Roberts Co, Civil War vet & widow census 1890 SD 14:2:59
Sioux Valley Hosp, nursing grad roster 1900-1931 SVG 21:1:6
Spink Co, homestead index cont SD 13:2:69
Stanley Co, res guide SD 13:2:61
Sully Co, res tips SD 14:2:60

SOUTH DAKOTA (continued)
 Swiss RU Mennonite fam before 1874, hist by Krehbiel, bk rev TS 37:4:146
 Vermillion area, Bloomingdale cem rec SVG 21:3:71
 Virginia Twp, Pleasant Valley Cem rec SVG 21:1:12
 Walworth Co, cem rec SD 14:2:71
 Walworth Co, Neuglueckstahl Cem rec SD 14:1:28
 Walworth Co, news abstr re businesses 1907 SD 13:2:45
SPAHR, GR, geneal by Spahr, bk rev TPI 20:2:89
SPAINHOUR, Mary Eve see John DOUB
SPALDING, Charles b1783, w Elizabeth Hampton, MD, KY, MO, geneal by Moore, bk rev GH 49:5:235
SPANGLER, OH, PA, VA, fam hist, 18th & 19th cent, by McKee, bk rev GH 49:3:221
 Rebecca Jane see Harvey NIFONG
SPANISH AMERICAN WAR, Army hist by Cosmas, bk rev RAG 16:1:20
 Santiago Campaign 1898, hist by Feuer, bk rev CGJ 3:4:10
SPANISH GENEALOGY, Arms of Mantegna of Calascibetta & Mendola of Cammarata, hist HER 3:3:30
 Relationship terms, EN trans KTP 5:2:28
SPARKS, Isaac fl832, ME, CA, biog sketch AW 21:3:75
SPARN, GR, geneal by Spahr, bk rev TPI 20:2:89
SPAULDING, Nancy see Willis SPAULDING
 Willis fc1630, w Nancy, New England, identity of wife TR 35:1:27
SPEAKE, Dennis B fl862, AL, corresp abstr OLR 9:4:148
SPEARS, James A see Caledonia G H MOORE
SPEER, Henry fl889, MI, indenture rec FHC 19:1:8
 Mary A W see Patrick CARMICHAEL

SPELLMAN, Richard, w Alcey French, CT, fam hist by Bates, bk rev GH 49:6:209
SPENCER, Elizabeth b1602, m Timothy Tomlins, New England, fam hist CTN 27:4:570
 Fanny see Elijah Stanton FISH
 Jennie N see Joseph D BUDD
 Jeremiah b1723, w Elizabeth Shailor, CT, PA, fam hist by Buffa, bk rev WPG 22:1:48
 New England, fam hist CTN 27:4:570
 Samuel fc1730, CT, PA, fam hist by Buffa, bk rev WPG 22:1:48
SPILLMAN, Mary Louise see George Washington DYE
SPILMAN, Margaret see John THATCHER
SPINK, Eliza b1813, RI(?), Bible rec RIR 21:1:24
SPITZER, Johann Heinrich fl764, GR, PA, geneal by Joyner, bk rev APR 14:12:3 TPI 21:1:42
SPIVEY, Shirley Burrus b1928, w Hellen Donna Butler, IL, Bible rec CI 31:4:140
SPOTSWOOD, Alexander fl711, VA, report abstr BYG 7:5:406
 Alexander fl724, PA, biog sketch & headrights BYG 7:3:382
SPRADLIN, Robert, w Levisa Fitzpatrick, VA, KY, OH, MO, fam hist by Davidson, bk rev MSG 15:3:171
SQUIRE, James J b1836, w Mary Stranathan, MO, biog sketch KCG 36:1:44
 John d1702, NY, geneal by Gardiner, bk rev NYR 126:2:153
SQUIRES, Ellis bc1738, NY, geneal by Gardiner, bk rev NYR 126:2:153
SQUYRES, John W, TX, fam hist vol 2 by Squyres, bk rev FP 38:3:140
ST CLAIR, Mil rec update 1993 by Grigsby, bk rev GH 49:3:221
ST JULIEN, Eli see Eli AUCLAIR

STADIG, Olaf Jonsson b1669, SN, geneal by Larson/Stadig, bk rev GH 49:4:228

STAHL, Lydia b1862, h Josiah C Werner, PA, biog WPG 21:3:46
Lydia b1862, h Josiah C Werner, PA, diary abstr & biog by Woefel, bk rev LM 36:2:207

STAHLMAN, Eleanor see Johannes STAHLMAN
Johannes b1758, w Eleanor, PA, fam hist by Burns/Smith, bk rev WPG 22:2:56

STAMBAUGH, Christena see George HARPST

STAMPER, John fc1660, EN, VA, NC, geneal by Latham, bk rev PR 23:2:66
Marion, KY, fam cem rec KGF 1:1/2:30

STANLEY, Fam hist by Pelcher, bk rev AGS 36:3:100
Liza see Shoto Martin MAYFIELD

STAPP, Jane see Elbridge Gerry SMALLIN

STARBOARD, Eunice B see William H MACGREGOR

STARE, Barbara d1919, IL, will abstr CI 31:2:47

STARK, Clarissa see Walter MCDOUGALL

STARNES, James W fl1861, TN, biog & geneal by Starnes, bk rev GH 49:6:210 SGS 45:1:36

STARR, Belle b1848, MO, biog sketch CN 4:4:55 GSM 12:1:6
John, w Ethel Binns, fam hist 1900-1992 by Starr, bk rev GH 49:3:221

STAUCH, GR, PA, NC, AL, fam hist (multiple vol set) by Huffman, bk rev GH 49:3:221

STAUFFER, Peter m1713, w Barbara Wisler, GR, PA, geneal MHP 22:1:3 22:2:4

STAUGH, GR, PA, NC, AL, fam hist (multiple vol set) by Huffman, bk rev GH 49:3:221

STEELE, Deborah see James LOGAN

STEIGER, John fc1880, w Mary Ann Causer, OH, fam hist corr FTC 17:3:43

STEIN, Daniel F d1898, w Mary Ann Koch, w Elizabeth Conrad, PA, OH, obit FTC 17:3:38

STEPHENS, Elisha bc1803, NC, CA, biog SCC 32:1:1
John b1773, TX, biog sketch STS 35:3:48

STEPHENSON, Elizabeth see William MARES
Henry b1772, w Ruth Ann Graham, TX, biog & geneal MCG 18:1/2:61
John dc1777, VA, brief geneal KA 31:2:37
John fl1873, EN, TX, biog sketch KTP 6:2:27
Kate see George Davis GLASS
Mary see Archibald HUSTON

STERNWEILER, Sara see David ADLER

STEVENS, Elizabeth see William MEARS

STEVENS, Eunice A fl1896, ME, recoll cont AHS 95:14:2 95:15:2
Mary see John BURKE

STEVES, Elizabeth Susan see Louis HEIL

STEWART, Alfred M see Alma STEWART
Alma b1814, h Alfred M, NY, obit GG 7:4:174
Catherine b1784, h William Cooke, VA, WV, biog sketch FWC 9:3:260
Ellen see Joseph ROGERS
James, KY, geneal cont EK 31:1:32
Jasper Byrd, KY, fam cem rec KGF 1:1/2:30
OH, fam hist by Hutchinson, bk rev TR 35:4:223
Walter fl1157, ST, fam hist by Stewart Society, bk rev CHG 28:1:37
William H H b1866, w Martha Victoria Halsey, WV, fam cem rec FWC 9:3:264

STICKEL, Ann Maria see John BRUNNER
Mary Etta see William BROWN
STIENS, GR, LX, IL, fam hist by Stiens, bk rev FRT 16:3:111
STIFF, David f1865, TX, acct paper abstr GR 37:3:34
STIFFLER, Henry, PA, fam reunion news abstr 1912 BGN 16:2:3
STIGGINS, George b1788, w Elizabeth Adcock, AL, biog SEN 3:2:23
Joseph, w Nancy Grey, VA, MS, biog SEN 3:2:22
STILES, Mary Elizabeth b1861, h Henry Hoppe, PA, NB, fam hist by Hoppe, bk rev CSB 30:4:144
STILLGESS, Jane see Joseph STILLGESS
Joseph b1820, w Jane, w Sarah Grimes, fam hist TR 35:2:66
STILLWELL, Martha see Basil HARRISON
STIMPSON, Christian see Moses ABBOTT
STINSON, Sallie see James Stephen HOGG
STIREWALT, Lousina Catherine see James Henry HUBBARD
STOCKTON, Davis, w Sarah, VA, NY, NJ, PA, fam hist by Mitchell, bk rev GH 49:5:235
Sarah see Davis STOCKTON
STODDARD, Gideon f1697, w Olive Curtiss, w Prudence Terrill, w Sarah Hotchkiss Adee, CT, identity of wives CTA 38:2:56
STOKES, Albert Louis b1909, w Dorothy Van Doren, NJ, biog sketch GMN 70:1:1
Chloe see William EDWARDS
STOLTZFUS, Thelma A see Elam GLICK
STONE, Anna see Lewis JONES
Jeff M f1891, OH, corresp TLL 20:3:61
Southern region, fam hist by Stone, bk rev MN 26:3:137

STONE (continued)
WA, NC, KY, fam hist by Stone, bk rev TJ 7:2:77
STONEKING, H L f1884, IA, NE, biog sketch NW 18:1:23
STONER, Marian see Samuel H GARBER
STORDAHL, Ole J b1843, w Brynhil Christenson, MN, SD, biog sketch SVG 21:2:34
STORY, Martha Lucinda see Charles Waters CARTER
STOUFFER, Annax see Johann SHETTER
STOUGH, GR, PA, NC, AL, fam hist (multiple vol set) by Huffman, bk rev GH 49:3:221
Henry b1815, IL, fam hist by Huffman, bk rev GH 49:3:222
STOUT, Philemon b1836, IL, diary abstr cont CR 27:4:94
STOVER, Elijah f1812, AL, vet claim abstr OLR 9:1:10
Sarah see Daniel O KRIST
STOWE, Harriet Beecher b1811, OH, KY, biog by Hedrick, bk rev REG 93:3:350
STRAIN, James f1780, w Nancy Agnes McClintic, PA, VA, biog sketch BWG 24:2:137
STRANATHAN, Mary see James J SQUIRE
STRAND, Allen E m1912, w Mae Allard, MT, marr cert DCH 6:2:2
STRAPPS, Christopher m1829, w Hannah Simpson, EN, QB, fam rec FHC 19:1:3
STREET, Abraham b1829, w Elizabeth Kirby, CN, fam hist NAL 11:2:64
STRICKLAND, Alsey b1800, w Elizabeth Ferrell, NC, GA, biog sketch & geneal OTC 4:3:25
Barnabas see Rachel MACKIE
Mary see Philip WARE
STRICKLER, Barbara see Christian LANDES
STRODE, Elizabeth Hunt see Rees JONES

STROM, Carl Arthur b1901, w Wilhelmina Elmira Dailey, NY, NJ, fam rec AMG 9:6:45

STRONG, Samuel b1789, w Ruth Gage, OH, Bible rec AH 22:4:248

STROUD, Sarah see Baylis MOORE

STUART, Joseph Alonzo b1825, NH, MA, CA, SCS 32:3:56 32:4:82 32:5:107 32:6:130 32:10:230 32:11:246 32:12:272

Mary see William MARTIN

STUCKEY, Amelia Ann see Jeptha BIRD

STUDWELL, Charles E b1838, w Caroline L June, CT, Bible rec CTA 37:4:178

STUHR, Adam b1796, w Margaretha Blocker, GR, fam hist by Stuhr, bk rev EWA 32:1:28 SGS 44:2:91

STULL, Barbara see Jacob ZIMMERMAN

George f1839, w Lucy Mae Coe, IL, fam hist PR 23:2:58

STURGEON, Lucinda see Jacob L SWOPE

STURM, Anna Maria Barbara see Jacob DORNER

SUBLET, VA, fam hist by Allen/Jackson, bk rev DM 58:4:189

SULLIVAN, Nathaniel F f1846, NC, jour of acc FC 13:3:34 13:4:37

SUMMERLIN, Jacob f1883, FL, biog PCQ 20:1:5

SUMMERS, John f1671, w Rebecca, EN, MD, geneal by Dodd/Holweck, bk rev NCJ 21:3:307 PGB 26:9:195 SCM 23:2:120

SUMMERS, Rebecca see John SUMMERS

SUMNER, Zannie see Benjamin Mitchell FORTNER

SURETTE, Louis b1818, w Frances Jane Shattuck, NS, MA, biog sketch AGE 24:2&3:56

SUTHER, Samuel b1722, NC, SC, biog by Scott, bk rev TJ 7:2:76

SUTHERLAND, John m1843, w Ann Scott, CN, fam hist by McWillie, bk rev GEN 20:4:24

William b1690, ST, geneal by Sutherland, bk rev GH 49:3:222

SUTTON, Elizabeth see Marvin HENRY

James T f1853, TN, corresp KTP 3:1:6

SVENSON, Axel b1872, IL, biog & jour abstr CHG 28:1:3

SVERDRUP, Georg f1900, MO, biog & religious views descr CHI 68:4:151

SVOBADA, Mary see John KOUKAL

SWAN, Gustaf N f1900, IA, biog SCN 95:9:5

SWANK, Mary Jane see Joshua SCHECTER

SWEDISH GENEALOGY, Imm in Am, early hist SCN 95:9:1

Imm naming patterns, hist SCN 95:9:4

Jubilees & anniv, hist SCN 96:10:1

Prarieblomman magazine hist SCN 95:9:5

Res tips HQ 95:60:44

Swedish imm in the Civil War, hist SCN 96:10:5

SWEET, Laura M see Edwin GIDDINGS

SWITZER, Daniel f1878, w Esther Burns, CN, fam hist GEN 20:2:11

SWITZERLAND, GR & FR territory, res bibl TGC 19:1:5

RU Mennonite fam in SD & KS before 1874, hist by Krehbiel, bk rev TS 37:4:146

Saanen, marr rec 1563-1751 by Kirchner, bk rev TPI 21:1:51

Saanen, Prot Bapt Reg 1557-1581 by Gibson, bk rev TPI 20:3:170

Surname origin guide by Gratz, bk rev GGD 11:4:100

SWOPE, Jacob L b1831, w Lucinda Sturgeon, OH, biog sketch FTC 17:4:62

SYMONDS, Elizabeth see Nathaniel NEWHALL

Samuel, MA, anc AG 70:2:65

TALBERT, MS, SC, fam hist by Aldridge, bk rev TB 21:3:14

TALLENT, NC, fam hist by McHan et al, bk rev NCJ 21:3:307

TAMM, Ellen see Meredith E WEBB

TANGNEY, Patrick J fl855, IR, WI, geneal by Stafford, bk rev FRT 16:3:102 TR 35:4:221

TAPPER, Mary see Richard FULL

TAYLOE, Sarah see William Augustine WASHINGTON

TAYLOR, AL, chancery court rec 1844 NTT 14:3:113

Frances see Richard BRADFORD

John Barton m1853, w Jane Higginson, IR, fam hist OBN 28:2:55

John Henry b1824, w Mary Ann Elizabeth Jones, EN, NY, corresp & fam hist by Mortensen, bk rev GFP 44:4:192 GH 49:5:235 HQ 95:57:85

John Martin see Mary Elizabeth ROBERTSON

KS, fam hist by Taylor, bk rev MGR 30:3:95

Mary Ann see John Henry TAYLOR

Mary Elizabeth (Molly), h --- Catron, MO, Bible rec MSG 15:1:15

MO, group sheets by Smith, bk rev MSG 15:4:225

Vergil see G W CALROW

WA, fam group sheets by Taylor, bk rev SGS 45:1:38

Walter Herron fl865, VA, corresp by Tower, bk rev REG 93:4:489

TEAG, Katherine see Mark WHITAKER

TEAL, Edward fl806, w Sarah, OH, deed FTC 17:4:61

Sarah see Edward TEAL

TEMPLE, Martha A B see Jesse HICKMAN

TENNESSEE, Bible rec & marr bonds, repr 1933, bk rev PB 11:1:12

Black Patch area, violence hist by Marshall, bk rev REG 93:3:340

TENNESSEE (continued)

Blount Co, chancery court rec 1866-1869 by Dockter, bk rev GH 49:3:214 HPF 95:50:1 NTT 14:4:122 SGS 44:2:87

Blount Co, div rec 1860-1937 by Dockter, bk rev GH 49:3:214 SGS 44:2:87

Blountville hist HPF 14:52:30 95:50:30

Campbell Co, census of manufactures 1820 ETR 7:4:168

Campbell Co, hist by McDonald, bk rev BWG 24:2:156

Carter Co, census 1820 of manufactures ETR 7:3:114

Cem inscr & mass rec, repr 1933, bk rev PB 11:1:12

Census index 1850 by AA, CD-ROM rev TEN 95:16:24

Civil War vet questionnaire 1914-1915, res aid STS 35:3:55

Civil War, 4th TN Calvary Reg hist by Starnes, bk rev SGS 45:1:36

Civil War, 4th TN Vol Infantry Reg hist 1863-1865 by Nikazy, bk rev SGS 45:1:33

Company F, TN Cavalry muster roll 1863 MTG 9:2:82

Confederate pension appl index by Sistler, bk rev BWG 24:1:68 24:2:153 MTG 8:4:165

Cumberland Presbyterian Ch, geneal abstr from by Eddlemon, bk rev APR 14:6:4

Davidson Co, deed bks T & W 1829-1835 by Smith, bk rev ANC 30:2:75 ARN 8:3:9 CCS 16:4:137 GH 49:5:216 GSM 12:2:47 HPF 95:50:1 NTT 15:1/2:4 SGS 44:2:87

Davidson Co, wills 1784-1832 by Marsh, bk rev KTP 11:1:10

Dickson Co, Turnbull Primitive Bapt Ch rec 1805-1806 MTG 9:2:59

Div rec 1797-1857 by Bamman/Spero, bk rev BWG 24:1:65

Early rec, biog & hist, repr 1950, bk rev GH 49:3:214

TENNESSEE (continued)
Fentress Co, entry bk abstr 1824-1901 cont FCN 6:4:75
Fentress Co, hist, repr 1916, bk rev GH 49:4:220
Fentress Co, teacher roster 1939-1940 FCN 7:3:47
Fourth TN Vol Infantry Reg, hist 1863-1865 by Nikazy, bk rev GH 49:6:202 MTG 9:2:70
Franklin Co, pet to the state 1814 MTG 9:2:63
Geneal, misc fam by Alexander, bk rev KA 30:3:175
Giles Co, marr rec by Weddington, bk rev GH 49:5:216
Grainger Co, court minutes 1796-1802 cont ETR 7:3:128
Hardeman Co (east), cem inscr vol 3 by Owens et al, bk rev NTT 14:4:123
Hardeman Co, will abstr 1824-1920 by Davidson et al, bk rev NTT 14:4:123
Hawkins Co, marr rec 1789-1866 by Cook et al, bk rev BWG 24:2:153
Henry Co, wills 1830-1835 by Willis, bk rev GH 49:6:202
Hist, repr 1882, bk rev NTT 15:1/2:7
Jefferson Co, biog hist 1792 to the present by Muncy, bk rev BWG 24:2:154
Jonesboro, Chester Inn, hist add & corr BWG 24:2:118
Knoxville Journal & Tribune news abstr 1900 ETR 7:4:155
Knoxville, news abstr 1816-1830 by Creekmore, bk rev NTT 15:1/2:7
Knoxville, news abstr from the *Knoxville Press* 1816-1830 by Creekmore, bk rev ETR 7:4:184 VAG 39:4:316
Lawrence Co, placenames by Cole, bk rev NTT 15:1/2:5
Middle region, fam hist vol 1 by Tucker/Marsh, bk rev GH 49:5:215
Migration routes, hist MTG 9:2:51
Militiamen court martial 1814, mil report, repr 1823, bk rev NTT 14:4:123

TENNESSEE (continued)
Monroe Co, chancery court rec mentioning Blount Co 1832-1852 by Dockter, bk rev GH 49:3:214 HPF 95:50:1 NTT 14:4:122 SGS 44:2:87
Montgomery Co, wills & admin 1796-1804 by Willis, bk rev GH 49:6:203
Montgomery Co, wills & admin 1805-1814 by Willis, bk rev GH 49:6:203
Nashville, Nashville High Sch grads 1860-1888 MTG 9:2:67
Nashville, Nashville High Sch hist MTG 9:2:66
News abstr 1791-1808 by Eddlemon, bk rev NFB 27:2:34
News abstr 1803-1812 by Eddlemon, bk rev CL 14:1:5 TB 21:3:11
News abstr 1821-1828 by Eddlemon, bk rev EWA 32:1:28
Overton Co, Roaring River cem hist & rec MTG 9:2:71
Paperville Pres Ch rec 1824 HPF 14:52:34 95:50:40
Polk Co, revenue raid 1900, hist ETR 7:3:111
Revolutionary War papers of Capt Joshuway Hadly, abstr BWG 24:1:42
Roane Co, hist 1801-1870, repr 1927, bk rev GH 49:3:215
Rogersville, Harrison Funeral Home death rec by HGHS, bk rev BWG 24:2:153
Scott Co, slave sched 1850 ETR 7:4:173
Settler geneal by TGS, bk rev NTT 15:1/2:3 OLR 9:1:40
Sims Settlement hist 1806-1818 by Dixon & Priest, bk rev NTT 14:3:82
Snow Chapel Bapt Ch, Snow Memorial Bapt Ch minutes BWG 24:1:30
State Lib & Archives, inter-lib loan program, microfilm roster & res tips MTG 8:4:159
Sullivan Co, Cherokee Removal soldier letters 1836 HPF 95:50:32
Sullivan Co, Civil War casualties, biog sketches HPF 14:52:32

TENNESSEE (continued)
 Sullivan Co, death rec 1908-1918 by Nikazy, bk rev AW 21:3:92 BWG 24:1:69 24:2:156 FC 13:2:42 GH 49:4:220 NTT 15:1/2:3 SGS 44:2:87
 Sullivan Co, death rec 1919-1925 by Nikazy, bk rev SGS 45:1:33
 Sullivan Co, deed bk 1 c1782-1783 HPF 14:52:28 95:50:28
 Sullivan Co, marr bk 1 c1871 BWG 24:1:10 24:2:95
 Sumner Co, court minutes 1787-1805 & 1808-1810 by Wells, bk rev APR 14:12:3
 Sumner Co, hist & geneal, repr 1907, bk rev APR 14:2:4
 Supreme Court rec abstr c1868-1875 MTG 8:4:173 9:2:84
 Sweetwater Valley, hist, repr 1916, bk rev GH 49:3:214
 Third TN Infantry, hist 1861-1864 by Barber, bk rev REG 93:2:224
 Warren Co, hist by Wiseman, bk rev BWG 24:2:155 SQ 6:3:53
 Washington Co, court of pleas & quarter sessions minutes 1778-1779 BWG 24:1:14 24:2:88
 Washington Co, death rec abstr 1908-1916 by Nikazy, bk rev BWG 24:1:69 GH 49:5:216 GSM 12:1:17 HPF 95:50:1 MCR 27:1:70 SGS 44:2:87
 Washington Co, Embree house hist BWG 24:1:44
 Washington Co, hist by WAGS, bk rev BWG 24:1:14
 Washington Co, marr rec 1874-1891 BWG 24:2:100
 Washington Co, marr rec c1883 BWG 24:1:15
 Washington Co, taxables, misc rec abstr c1790-1820 BWG 24:1:36
 Wayne Co, chancery court loose rec 1870-1879 by Berry, bk rev NTT 15:1/2:4
 White Co, deed abstr 1801-1820 by Murray, bk rev STS 35:2:73

TENNESSEE (continued)
 White Co, deed abstr 1820-1834 by Murray, bk rev FP 38:3:143 MTG 9:2:70 VL 30:1:44
 White Co, deed abstr, microfiche rev RAG 16:4:19
 Williamson Co, co court minutes 1806-1812 by Wells, bk rev BWG 24:1:66 GH 49:6:203 GSM 12:1:17 HPF 95:50:1 MCR 27:1:70 NTT 15:1/2:3 SGS 44:2:87 TFG 8:2:14
 Williamson Co, co court minutes 1812-1815 by Wells, bk rev BHN 28:2:19 FC 13:2:41 GH 49:6:203
 Williamson Co, co court minutes vol 2 by Wells, bk rev HTR 38:1:8 SGS 44:3:144
 Williamson Co, deed abstr 1799-1811 by Murray, bk rev RAG 16:2:26
 Wilson Co, cem rec MTG 8:4:179
 Wilson Co, Lebanon, misc rec cont RAG 16:3:7
TENNISON, Ignatius fl784, NC, fam hist by Green, bk rev NCJ 21:1:81
TENNISON, John bc1758, MD, NC, fam hist by Green, bk rev NCJ 21:1:81
TERMEER, Beatrix see Johann LUCKEN
TERRELL, Louvisa see James T MAUDLIN
TERRILL, Jerome b1837, w Malinda Campbell, w Mary Elizabeth Trumbull Millins, MI, NY, fam hist by Northuis, bk rev DM 58:4:190 NYR 126:3:216
 Prudence see Gideon STODDARD
TERRY, Census data 1790-1920 by Terry, bk rev OLR 9:3:129
 Fam census rec 1790-1920 by Terry, bk rev RAG 16:4:26
TETREAULT, Henry Joseph b1873, w Delia Girard, CN, MA, fam hist ACG 21:1:27
TEXAS, Alamo, hist of siege, hist critique STS 35:1:4
 Alamo messengers, roster KTP 9:3:49
 Alamo roster KTP 12:1:3

TEXAS (continued)
Amarillo, news abstr from the *Evening News* 1895 REF 37:4:63
Anderson Co Geneal Soc anc charts 1993, bk rev GH 49:3:215
Anderson Co, marr rec 1846-1869 PWN 1:4:8
Anderson Co, tax rec 1890 by ETGS, bk rev NCJ 21:4:422 STS 35:2:15
Anhalt, Germania Farmer Verein charter members 1875 KTP 2:4:41
Athens, muster roll of Capt W H Martin 1861 TJ 7:3:124
Austin Co, marr rec 1824-1858 by Growing Branches, bk rev FP 38:1:13
Austin Colony pioneers, hist 1820s by Ray, bk rev GR 37:4:5 HQ 95:58:89 MT 31:3:113
Austin Colony roster (& hist) KTP 9:3:35 9:4:56 10:1:5 10:2:20
Austin, Convention of the People delegates 1861 GR 37:1:2
Austin, pioneer hist, repr 1949, bk rev AGS 36:3:101 ARH 33:2:82
Bandera Co res tips KTP 3:1:9
Barker TX Hist Center, card catalog guide KTP 10:3:47
Bay City, Cedarvale cem rec by MCGS, bk rev STS 35:2:70
Baylor Co, marr rec c1880-1885 SEE 36:153:1
Baylor Co, settler roster c1874-1888 SEE 36:153:45
Baylor Co, sheriffs, co clerks, & co judges, roster 1879-1897 SEE 36:153:54
Bell Co, hist by Atkinson, bk rev PT 37:1:18
Berlin, GR pioneer fam, surname roster KTP 10:2:30
Bexar Co, Leesch-Uecker cem rec KTP 3:1:11
Bexar Co, Pieper's Settlement hist KTP 2:4:38
Bibl of bks from Southern Hist Press ARN 8:1:10

TEXAS (continued)
Blanco Co, hist by Moursand, bk rev KTP 1:3/4:20
Blanco Co, pet re:co formation 1855 KTP 2:2:19
Block Creek sch #1 census 1896 KTP 14:1:15
Boerne hist KTP 1:2:14
Boerne hist sketch KTP 2:1:8
Boerne, Edith A Gray Lib holdings KTP 2:4:36
Boerne, Hist & Preservation Soc Archives holdings, descr KTP 2:4:42
Boerne, hist, news abstr from the *Texas New Yorker* 1873 KTP 3:2:20
Boerne, Sch roster 1899-1900 KTP 5:4:65 6:3:39
Boerne, Sch #1 roster 1901-1902 KTP 7:4:68 8:2:20
Boerne, Sch #1 roster 1902-1903 KTP 9:1:5 9:4:62 10:1:11
Boerne, Sch #1 roster 1903-1904 KTP 7:3:48 9:3:43
Boerne, Sch #3 roster 1901-1902 KTP 9:2:21
Boerne, settler hist & biog sketches KTP 9:4:51
Brazos Co, marr rec 1873-1887 by TRR, bk rev STS 35:2:74
Brazos Co, marr rec 1887-1895 by TRR, bk rev STS 35:2:74
Brigade companies listed under governor's proclamation GR 37:3:28
Castro colonist hist KTP 4:1:5
Castroville, hist STS 35:2:34
Catholic jurisdictions, descr FRT 16:2:60
Cavalry under General Van Dorn, undated list GR 37:2:30
Census rec abstr 1860-1900, misc co PWN 2:5:19
Census rec owned by San Antonio Public Lib, guide KTP 8:4:54
Cherokee Co, birth & misc rec c1873-1874 PWN 2:1:11
Cibolo Creek area, Voges cem rec KTP 3:1:5
Cibolo Valley hist KTP 1:2:14

TEXAS (continued)
Cistern, hist STS 35:1:9
Civil War, 6th TX Cavalry, news abstr from *Confederate Veteran* mag c1910-1930 DG 41:1:87
Civil War, Confederate Company F muster roll DG 41:1:74
Civil War, Confederate pension appl guide DG 19:2:40
Civil War, Gaines Mill Battle, 5th TX Reg Casualty list 1862 GR 37:1:43
Civil War, soldiers who died in MS (Quitman) 1863 GR 37:1:38
Civil War, Union Army, First TX Cavalry Volunteers 1865 GR 37:1:6
Co map 1850 KTP 9:3:42
Co superintendents sch rec, 19th cent MCG 18:3/4:134
Coletoville cem hist STS 35:3:12
Colin Co, pioneer hist by Hall, bk rev SGS 44:2:85
Collin Co, hist, repr 1975, bk rev IMP 14:1:28
Collin Co, news obit 1920-1929 by Barnes, bk rev GH 49:4:220
Collin Co, news obit 1920-1929 by MMPLV, bk rev FRT 16:2:67
Collin Co, pioneer hist, repr 1975, bk rev GH 49:5:217 KSL 19:2:75 SQ 5:6:43
Comanche Co, marr lic c1900-1915 FP 38:3:144
Comanche Co, Proctor Missionary Bapt Ch member roster 1907 FP 38:3:146 38:4:170
Comfort, Black Sch hist KTP 11:2:25
Comfort, GR freethinkers, hist KTP 7:3:42
Comfort, news abstr 1909 KTP 7:4:63
Concho Co, election returns 1892-1912 cont STK 22:4:155 23:2:59
Confederate deaths at Oxford MS, roster 1862 GR 37:3:26
Confederate pension appl index abstr KTP 1:3/4:20
Confederate pension appl index by Oakley, bk rev KTP 1:2:15

TEXAS (continued)
Confederates buried in McGavock cem (TN) MCG 18:3/4:154
Conroe, hist sketch MCG18:1/2:28
Conroe, news abstr from the *Courier* 1992 MCG 18:1/2:52
Conroe, news abstr from the *Enterprise* 1892 MCG 18:1/2:50
Constitution 1876 GR 37:4:37
Courthouse hist by Kelsey/Dyal, bk rev STS 35:2:71
Dallas, census 1868 DG 41:1:63
Dallas, draft reg polling precincts, locations 1917 DG 41:1:110
Dallas, draft registrants in precinct 15, 1917 DG 41:1:112
Dallas, draft regristrant rosters published in *Daily Times Herald*, list DG 41:1:116
Dallas, Rocker B Ranch hist STK 23:2:83
Dallas Co, census 1880 MT 31:3:102 31:4:122
Dallas Co, heritage & hist by DCPA, bk rev GH 49:3:215
Dallas Co, inquest minute bk 1889-1893 DG 41:1:1
Dallas Co, Union vet burials DG 41:1:98
Dallas Co, voter reg 1867-1869 DG 41:1:15
Dawson Co, marr rec 1905-1928 by LAGS, bk rev GH 49:4:220 STS 35:2:70
Denton Co, wills 1876-1940 by DCGS, bk rev GH 49:4:220
Eastern Eur anc, res tips for TX STS 35:2:21
Falls Co, courthouse marr rec c1889 cont HTR 38:1:19 38:3:70 38:4:108
Frontier Battalion rec 1871-1884 FP 38:1:29
Frontier Regiment monthly returns under Capt. W W Reynolds 1862 GR 37:2:33
Frontier Regiment TST, captain roster 1862 GR 37:1:15

TEXAS (continued)
- *Frontier Times* index by Vandegrift Research, bk rev STS 35:3:69
- GA residents in Austin convention, roster 1861 NC 5:2:74
- Galveston, St Joseph's Cath Ch bapt rec 1860-1952, surname roster KTP 4:4:52 5:1:14
- General Hospital reg 1862 GR 37:3:20
- General Land Ofc res guide KTP 4:3:41
- General Land Ofc res tips STS 35:1:47
- General Order #1 re:frontier regulation 1862 GR 37:4:25
- General Order #25, trans GR 37:4:17
- Ghost towns, missing towns, hist sketches KTP 13:4:59
- Gonzales Co, marr lic 1829-1900 by Parsons, bk rev MCG 18:3/4:166
- Governors, hist & biog by Hendrickson, bk rev STS 35:2:74
- GR imm hist 1847-1861, repr 1970, bk rev GH 49:5:216
- GR settler hist KTP 4:4:56
- Graham, news abstr from the *Leader* 1887 FP 38:1:34 38:3:153 38:4:202
- Granbury, Rock Ch hist HCG 13:3:35
- Hale Co, marr rec 1888-1941 by Evans et al, bk rev GH 49:3:215
- Harris Co, 11th Judicial Dist court minutes 1837-1838 GR 37:3:38
- Harris Co, board of land proceedings 1838 GR 37:3:35 37:4:13
- Harris Co, cem inscr GR 37:1:47 37:3:17
- Harris Co, cem rec abstr 1822-1992 GR 37:2:5
- Harris Co, dist court minutes, 11th dist cont GR 37:4:9
- Harris Co, probate rec 1838-1855 GR 37:3:42
- Harris Co, probate rec 1878-1879 GR 37:4:6
- Harvey Massacre 1836, hist STS 35:1:16
- Hist PWN 2:6:7
- Hist (early) timeline PWN 2:2:3 2:3:2 2:4:3 2:5:4

TEXAS (continued)
- History Center, res guide KTP 1:3/4:26
- Holland Lodge #1 member roster 1926 GR 37:4:39
- Hood Co, Antioch Bapt Ch member roster cont HCG 13:3:42
- Hood Co, death rec index 1941-1945 HCG 13:2:25 13:3:41
- Hood Co, Granbury, geneal abstr 1894 from news HCG 12:4:60
- Hood Co, marr certs 1904 HCG 12:4:51
- Hood Co, marr certs 1907 HCG 13:2:19
- Hood Co, Strouds Creek Cem inscr HCG 12:4:53 13:2:27
- Hopkins Co, anc charts & fam group sheets by Cagle/Elliott, bk rev STS 35:2:69
- Hopkins Co, census 1850 by Price, bk rev STS 35:2:68
- Hopkins Co, census 1910 by Payne, bk rev STS 35:2:69
- Houston, Clayton Libr, descr STS 35:3:33
- Houston, McGee Chapel cem rec GR 37:4:3
- *Houston Morning Star* news abstr c1839-1844 STS 35:4:39
- Houston, Prairie Grove cem rec GR 37:4:4
- Houston, St Martin's Epis Ch Urn Garden cem rec GR 37:4:2
- Indianola hist sketch KTP 9:1:13
- Industry, post ofc hist KTP 10:3:34
- Irion Co, tax rec 1890 STK 22:4:165 23:2:65
- Johnson Co, census 1860 by Basham, bk rev GH 49:6:204
- Kaufman Co, cem inscr vol 1, bk rev NTT 14:4:122
- Kaufman Co, Oakland cem inscr, bk rev NTT 14:4:123
- Kendall Co Geneal Soc, 10 year index to *Keys to the Past* periodical KTP 10:4:54
- Kendall Co, Balcones Sch dist #1 teacher roster 1907 KTP 2:3:33

TEXAS (continued)
Kendall Co, Balcones Sch #1 roster 1895 KTP 11:3:41
Kendall Co, Balcones Sch #1 roster 1900 KTP 11:4:68
Kendall Co, birth rec abstr 1838-1878 KTP 3:1:12 3:2:12 3:3:32
Kendall Co, Boerne cem rec KTP 1:3/4:19
Kendall Co, Brownsboro sch roster 1897 KTP 14:3:43
Kendall Co, census 1870 index KTP 1:2:9
Kendall Co, Confederate muster roll 1864 KTP 1:3/4:24
Kendall Co, Currie's Creek hist KTP 2:3:25
Kendall Co, Curry's Creek sch #1 roster 1896-1898 KTP 13:2:35
Kendall Co, English settlement hist KTP 5:1:6 5:2:25
Kendall Co, Halloween tour ideas (haunted spots) KTP 7:4:54
Kendall Co, hist abstr 1878 KTP 6:2:30
Kendall Co, hist sketch KTP 1:1:1
Kendall Co, hist, news abstr from the *Texas New Yorker* 1873 KTP 3:1:3
Kendall Co, Kreuzberg Sch #1 roster 1897-1898 KTP 12:1:13
Kendall Co, Kreuzberg Sch #1 roster 1899-1900 KTP 12:1:13
Kendall Co, Kreuzberg Sch #1 roster 1900-1902 KTP 12:2:27
Kendall Co, Kreuzberg Sch #1 roster 1902-1904 KTP 13:3:40
Kendall Co, Kreuzberg Sch #1 roster 1905 KTP 14:4:58
Kendall Co, Lindendale sch hist sketch KTP 12:3:39
Kendall Co, Lindendale sch #1 roster 1896-1897 KTP 12:3:39
Kendall Co, Lindendale sch #1 roster 1898-1899 KTP 13:4:68
Kendall Co, marr rec c1862-1889 KTP 11:1:5 11:2:21 11:3:37 11:4:60
Kendall Co, natu rec index abstr KTP 5:1:9 5:2:20 5:3:36 5:4:60

TEXAS (continued)
Kendall Co, officer roster 1862 KTP 3:2:26
Kendall Co, Panther Creek Sch #1 roster 1901-1902 KTP 2:2:16 5:3:47
Kendall Co, Panther Creek Sch #1 roster 1902-1903 KTP 2:3:28 4:4:59
Kendall Co, Panther Creek Sch #1 roster 1904-1905 KTP 2:4:37 5:2:16
Kendall Co, Panther Creek Sch #1 roster 1908-1909 KTP 3:1:5 5:3:42
Kendall Co, Panther Creek Sch #1 roster 1910-1911 KTP 3:2:22 3:3:31 8:3:48
Kendall Co, pet for & against founding of co 1862 KTP 1:1:3
Kendall Co, res tips KTP 6:2:28
Kendall Co, Shepherd's Creek Sch #1 roster 1897 KTP 2:2:22
Kendall Co, Shepherd's Creek Sch #1 roster 1899-1900 KTP 2:2:21
Kendall Co, Shepherd's Creek Sch #1 roster 1905-1906 KTP 2:3:32
Kendall Co, Shepherd's Creek Sch #1 roster 1913-1914 KTP 2:4:43
Kendall Co, Shepherd's Creek Sch #1 roster 1916-1917 KTP 2:4:45
Kendall Co, Simmons Creek Colored Sch #1 roster 1906-1907 KTP 11:2:25
Kendall Co, Sisterdale Sch #1 roster 1897-1898 KTP 6:1:9
Kendall Co, Sisterdale Sch #1 roster 1898-1899 KTP 6:2:22
Kendall Co, Sisterdale Sch #1 roster 1899-1900 KTP 6:3:35
Kendall Co, Sisterdale Sch #1 roster 1904-1905 KTP 3:4:46 5:1:15
Kendall Co, Sisterdale Sch #1 roster 1917-1918 KTP 10:2:23
Kendall Co, Sisterdale Sch #2 roster 1896-1897 KTP 4:1:12
Kendall Co, Sisterdale Sch #2 roster 1899-1900 KTP 4:1:7
Kendall Co, Sisterdale Sch #2 roster 1900-1901 KTP 4:2:27
Kendall Co, Sisterdale Sch #2 roster 1902-1903 KTP 4:3:37

TEXAS (continued)
  Kendall Co, Sisterdale Sch #3 roster 1896-1897 KTP 4:3:39
  Kendall Co, Sisterdale Sch #3 roster 1897-1898 KTP 4:4:59
  Kendall Co, Sisterdale Sch #3 roster 1900-1901 KTP 4:4:61
  Kendall Co, St Helena's Epis Ch centennial hist speech 1981 KTP 6:1:10
  Kendall Co, St Joseph's Cath Ch bapt rec 1860-1952 cont KTP 5:2:29 5:3:43
  Kendall Co, teacher roster 1923-1924 KTP 7:2:23 8:1:15
  Kendall Co, Upper Cibolo Sch #1 roster 1897 KTP 5:2:19
  Kendall Co, Upper Cibolo Sch #1 roster 1899-1900 KTP 5:4:59
  Kendall Co, Upper Cibolo Sch #1 roster 1901-1902 KTP 6:2:25
  Kendall Co, voter reg c1870 KTP 2:3:29
  Kendall Co, Wasp Creek Colored Sch #6 roster 1902 KTP 14:2:24
  Kerr Co, Confederate Army roll 1861-1865 KTP 2:1:5
  Kerr Co, natu rec c1858-1862 KTP 1:3/4:29
  Kerr Co, tax roll 1856 KTP 2:1:4
  Kerr Co, tax roll 1857 KTP 2:2:17
  Kerr Co, Union Army roster 1862-1865 KTP 2:1:7
  King Ranch, hist by Goodwyn, bk rev STS 35:2:72
  KY citizens in early hist, biog sketches KTP 12:3:37
  La Bahia, hist by Roell, bk rev REG 93:4:508
  Lakeview Cem rec 1917-1929 by GCGS, bk rev STS 35:2:67
  Land grant terms, guide NCC 15:2:10
  Limestone Co, Civil War volunteers, roster 1861 HTR 38:3:79
  Lipscomb Co, Lipscomb cem rec cont REF 37:2:31

TEXAS (continued)
  Map, land boundaries under First Republic Congress of TX KTP 9:1:11
  Marr rec, 19th cent PWN 1:2:1
  McLennan Co, Rosemound Cem rec vol 6 by CTGS, bk rev STS 35:3:68
  Mecklenburg Declarartion 1775, hist KTP 14:3:43
  Medical Assoc Jour abstr 1911-1912 FP 38:1:25
  Menard Co, Little Saline cem hist STK 23:2:86
  Menard Co, Little Saline cem rec STK 23:2:53
  Mesquite, Mesquite cem rec, Ebrite addition MT 31:3:91
  Mesquite, news abstr from the *Texas Mesquiter* 1907 MT 31:4:120
  Mexican rule, hist sketch PWN 3:1:4
  Midland, deed bk 1 cont THT 23:2:57
  Midland, div rec 1886-1900 THT 23:2:63
  Mil rec res tips PWN 1:4:5
  Milam Co, Civil War hist by Williams, bk rev STS 35:3:66
  Montague Co, will bk 1 abstr c1878 STS 35:2:60
  Montgomery Co, death rec 1903-1940 MCG 18:1/2:13 18:3/4:115
  Montgomery Co, election returns 1845 MCG 18:1/2:58
  Montgomery Co, natu rec by MCGHS, bk rev TS 37:3:95
  Montgomery Co, sch transfers 1927-1931 MCG18:1/2:8 18:3/4:106
  Montgomery Co, slave owner roster 1850 MCG 18:3/4:132
  Montgomery Co, Treasurer's sch acc reg 1893-1894 MCG 18:3/4:143
  Nacogdoches Co, court rec res guide PWN 1:1:3
  Nacogdoches court rec abstr c1839 GR 37:4:16
  Nacogdoches Masons, biog sketches from question bk 1909-1921 YTD 15:1:29

TEXAS (continued)
 Nacogdoches University, Old Nacogdoches Univ Building hist & roster c1833 YTD 15:1:1
 Natu rec by MCGHS, bk rev TS 37:3:95
 Navy ships, list GR 37:4:36
 Neches Valley, backwoodsmen hist by Sitton, bk rev CN 4:4:64
 News abstr from the *Telegraph & Texas Register* 1835-1841 by Ladd, bk rev GH 49:3:215 SGS 44:2:85
 News abstr from the *Texas Mesquiter* 1907 MT 31:3:90
 News abstr from the *Texas State Journal of Medicine* 1905 FP 38:3:120
 Ordnance officer appointment roster (undated) GR 37:2:17
 Paluxy, Masonic Lodge #393, hist & first members roster HCG 13:3:36
 Panola Co, VA residents in, biog sketches GRI 15:5:130
 Pension files c1837 GR 37:1:12
 Pension files c1874 cont GR 37:3:6
 Pension files c1875 cont GR 37:2:18
 Pension rec res tips PWN 1:4:5
 Peter's Colony, pet MT 31:4:139
 Photographers, 19th cent direct by Haynes, bk rev NGS 83:1:68
 PO imm hist by Hill, bk rev STS 35:2:73
 Postal svc hist sketch KTP 10:3:36
 Power of attorneys to David Stiff 1861-1862, roster of names GR 37:3:34
 Quitman, General Hospital Reg 1862 GR 37:2:35
 Res guide by Ericson, bk rev RAG 16:2:30 WPG 21:4:55
 Revolution hist 1835-1836 by Lack, bk rev STS 35:2:73
 Robertson Colony Collection, res guide KTP 8:1:3
 Round Timber, Round Timber cem rec SEE 36:153:21
 Round Top, hist sketch KTP 11:2:31

TEXAS (continued)
 San Angelo Co, commissioner's court minutes c1878 cont STK 22:4:175
 San Angelo Standard news abstr 1885 STK 22:4:189 23:2:88
 San Antonio, Cath Archives, res tips KTP 6:4:59
 Scurry Co, marr rec 1915-1924 by SCGS, bk rev STS 35:2:68
 Shelby Co, Ramah Bapt Ch cem rec TJ 7:1:21 7:2:48
 Shelby Co, wedding supper poisoning 1847, hist PWN 1:4:6
 Sisterdale, early hist cont KTP 5:1:4
 South Plains Geneal Soc surname res direct, bk rev STS 35:3:68
 Southwestern Stage Company, hist 1850s KTP 11:4:63
 State Archives rec order form explained KTP 1:2:12
 State Lib birth & death indexes, guide KTP 7:2:20
 State Lib Geneal Collect, birth & death index res guide KTP 11:1:15
 State Medical Association Jour 1906 cont FP 38:4:178
 State Troops, brigadier-generals, roster GR 37:1:39
 State Troops, list of companies transferred to Confederate State Service GR 37:2:31
 State Troop returns, cont GR 37:2:26
 Sterling Co, marr lic (unclaimed) 1891-1908 STK 22:4:169
 Sterling Co, marr rec 1891-1920, officials who performed marr STK 22:4:173
 Sulphur Springs, Tapp Funeral Home rec 1944-1991 by Elliott, bk rev STS 35:2:68
 Supreme Court index & docket of causes c1840 GR 37:3:29
 Supreme Court rec c1839 GR 37:1:30
 Supreme Court rec c1849 cont GR 37:3:2
 Supreme Court rec c1850 cont GR 37:2:21

TEXAS (continued)
- Sutton Co, census 1900 index STK 22:4:179
- Tarrant Co, Confederate vets at Lee camp #158, roster FP 38:3:134 38:4:196
- Teachers 1893-1894, co superintendent acc MCG 18:3/4:140
- *Telegraph & TX Register* news abstr c1837 GR 37:2:7
- *Telegraph & TX Register* geneal abstr by Ladd, bk rev OC 31:1:54
- Tenth Congressional Dist, postmasters & post ofcs by Conrad, bk rev KTP 2:2:13
- Thurber, coal mining hist 1888-1926 by Rhinehart, bk rev STS 35:3:70
- Tolar, Antioch Bapt Ch membership roster c1890-1956 HCG 13:2:22
- Tom Green Co, commissioners' court minutes 1877 cont STK 23:2:71
- Travis Co, census 1850 abstr AGS 36:3:106 36:4:120
- Travis Co, Hornsby cem rec STS 35:1:38
- Travis Co, Hornsby cem rec add STS 35:2:18
- Travis Co, pioneer families, misc data AGS 36:4:122
- Treue Der Union organization, hist & roster 1862 KTP 13:2:22
- TST monthly returns c1862 cont GR 37:3:10
- Van Zandt Co, census 1880 by VZCGS, bk rev STS 35:2:69
- Vicksburg Siege, 2nd Reg TX Vol Infantry casualty list 1863 GR 37:2:39
- Victoria, tournament hist c1869 STS 35:2:3
- Voter reg 1867-1869, microfilm by TX State Lib, rev NGS 83:4:308
- Waco, Ch of St Mary of the Assumption bapt rec c1871 cont HTR 38:1:23 38:3:87 38:4:110
- Waco, obits & related items 1874-1908 by CTGS, bk rev STS 35:3:68

TEXAS (continued)
- Waco, obits from the *Times Herald* c1916 HTR 38:1:15 38:3:83 38:4:105
- Walker Co, martial law money disbursements, post Civil War era, roster GR 37:3:32
- Waring, hist KTP 6:3:44
- Washington Co, deed abstr 1834-1841 by Murray, bk rev RAG 16:2:20
- Waverly, Pres hist MCG18:1/2:29
- Wends, hist & descr KTP 10:2:31
- Wilson Guards muster roll 1861 KTP 6:3:42
- Wood Co, news abstr before 1920 by WCGS, bk rev GH 49:6:204 KSL 19:4:153 SGS 45:1:33

THATCHER, John b1809, w Margaret Spilman, KY, Bible rec KA 30:3:126

THERIOT, Jean Vileor f1847, w Cleonise Richard, LA, biog KSL 19:4:129

THIBAULT, Louis m1645, w Renee Gauthier, FR, CN, geneal by Thibault, bk rev AGE 24:4:100

THIBODO, Augustus J f1859, WA, diary abstr TRI 35:1:20

THIER, Bernhard Dietrich b1883, w Lena Miller, GR, IA, fam hist by Niendorf, bk rev GFP 44:3:142
- Dorothea see Heinrich THIER
- Heinrich Friedrich, w Dorothea Christina Hamann, GR, geneal by Niendorf, bk rev FRT 16:3:101 GFP 44:3:142 GH 49:3:222 GJ 23:2/3:143 MN 26:3:138

THOMAS, Christopher bc1614, w Elizabeth Higgins, EN, MD, geneal QY 22:1:1
- Desire f1755, h Carey Clark, RI, identity RIR 21:1:9
- Fam hist, repr 1896, bk rev TTT 19:2:72
- IN, geneal add & corr QY 22:3:2
- Isaac bc1740, w Mary Davies/Davey, SC, geneal QY 21:4:3

THOMAS (continued)
- Isaac f1794, w Elizabeth Isabella Massengill, TN, fam reunion bk, bk rev BWG 24:1:66
- John b1806, w Emmeline Wait, EN, CN, geneal GEN 20:1:19
- Nancy see William KERSEY
- Olive d1886, OH, obit TLL 20:4:80
- Rhyp ap, EN, fam hist, repr 1896, bk rev NYR 126:2:155 RDQ 12:2:29 VL 29:3:145
- Thomas Benjamin f1830, w Margaret Morgan, WE, OH, corresp abstr TR 35:1:22
- WE, EN, geneal by Thomas, bk rev TPI 20:2:95
- Woodson A b1808, VA, fam hist by Morley, bk rev HQ 95:58:90

THOMPSON, Abigail see Stephen LONGFELLOW
- Alexander f1837, SC, corresp abstr SCM 23:1:21
- Charlie see Gerry THOMSPON
- E O b1846, w Mary F Guthrie, IA, Bible rec SEE 36:153:37
- Eleanor see Phllip Schuyler BOARD
- Elizabeth f1885, OH, legal notice TLL 20:3:59
- Gerry, s Charlie, CA, descr of res trip to EN AW 21:2:48
- Jane see Francis Wesley LEWIS
- John f1736, w Mary, VA, KY, IL, geneal by Robertson, bk rev GH 49:4:228
- John, PA, OH, desc by Thompson, bk rev TR 35:1:55
- John, w Sarah Patterson, geneal by Thomspon, bk rev WPG 22:1:49
- Lucinda see Samuel Dabney GROOM
- Mary see John THOMPSON
- Neil fc1760, w Elizabeth Gentry, TN, geneal by Luther, bk rev GH 49:3:222
- R E W, NC, SC, AL, fam hist by Adair, bk rev ARH 33:1:33
- Rachel C see Watson S ALLEN
- Shasta Logan f1913, FL, recoll PCQ 15:1:4

THORNE, Thomas Dresser b1814, ME, list of buildings he built AHS 95:15:2

THORNTON, Billy d1885, KS, obit KK 33:4:75
- J Quinn f1846, w Nancy, OR, biog TFG 8:3/4:4
- James J f1860, w William Ann McCulloch, IN, TX, fam hist STS 35:4:4
- Jonathan b1764, w Freelove Turner, RI, Bible rec RIR 21:3:75
- Joseph F1884, MO, biog sketch CN 4:4:53

THORPE, Martin b1811, NY, OH, obit GG 7:4:175

THRAILKILL, Mary b1874, TN, fam rec ETR 7:4:194

THURBER, Benjamin m1771, w Esther Allen, MA, Bible rec BG 16:3:99

THURLWELL, John b1827, EN, IL, obit MCI 13:2:50

TILLEY, Elizabeth f1620, h John Howland, MA, biog by Shaffer, bk rev WPG 21:3:52

TILLIS, Monte J b1890, FL, biog PCQ 16:4:6
- Willoughby f1856, FL, biog sketch PCQ 6:4:4

TIMBERLAKE, Hannah see John WOODMAN

TIMMONS, John F b1855, w Susan Ann Smith, TX, Bibl rec KTP 6:4:62

TINER, Richard dc1824, GA, will & biog THT 23:2:82

TINKER, John f1638, MA, CT, anc NER 149:596:401
- Robert bc1565, w Agnes/Anne Berrington, w Mary Merwin, EN, geneal NER 149:596:401

TINSLEY, John, IR, SC, biog by Wilkinson, bk rev STS 35:3:67

TIPTON, Joshua bc1775, w Rachel Eagan, MD, TN, biog MTG 9:2:61

TITUS, Elizabeth see Jacob F KLOTZ

TOEPPERWEIN, E A F see Johanna BERGMANN

TOEPPERWEIN (continued)
  Paul b1844, w Kathinka Adam, GR, TX, biog sketch KTP 6:1:7
  Rudolph Herbert b1892, w Alma Pearl Alexander, TX, geneal KTP 6:2:26
TOERKLER, Amelia Von Kettler see Christian Frederick BLAICH
TOMLINS, New England, fam hist CTN 27:4:570
  Timothy see Elizabeth SPENCER
TOMLYNS, Timothy see Timothy TOMLINS
TOMPKINS, Thelma Pearl b1908, h Leroy Wynn, IL, biog sketch LC 16:1:10
TONELLI, Bill f1995, Am, fam hist & stories by Tonelli, bk rev ARN 8:3:4 FAM 34:3:183
TOOL, Barbara see John FUDGE
TOPPERWEIN, Amalia Luckenbach b1843, GR, TX, fam cem rec KTP 4:3:31
  Herman W b1837, PU, TX, fam cem rec KTP 4:3:31
  Lucian Ferdinand f1851, w Marie Elizabeth, TX, fam hist KTP 5:3:48
  Marie Elizabeth see Lucian Ferdinand TOPPERWEIN
  Paul see Katinka ADAM
TOPPING, Thomas b1745, w Naomi Gaylord, NC, fam hist by Topping, bk rev GH 49:5:235
TORREY, Clarence Almon b1869, New England, anc NEH 12:1:22
TOTTEN, Edward bc1615, EN, geneal by Wilcox, bk rev HQ 95:58:91 SGS 44:3:141
TOULOUSE, FR, CN, fam hist sketch ACG 21:2:72
TOWNE, Eliphalet b1752, w Jerusha Rugg, MA, marr data NER 149:596:379
TOWNER, Richard f1686, EN, CT, geneal BGS 27:4:116
TOWNSEND, Robert bc1784, w Deborah Lounsbury, w Ruth Turner, NY, fam hist cont NYR 126:1:25 126:2:108 126:3:192

TOWNSLEY, Alexander m1813, w Margaret Ann Ewing, OH, KS, Bible rec TS 37:4:126
TRAMMEL, Phillip fc1823, AR, TX, fam hist 1807-1850 by Snyder, bk rev GH 49:5:235
TRAMMELL, Nicholas bc1780, TN, AR, fam hist by Snyder, bk rev ARH 33:2:79
TRANTHAM, Anna see Nehemiah POSEY
TRASK, Joseph d1735, w Elizabeth Sallows, MA, geneal TEG 15:1:55
TRAUTVETTER, Franciska b1851, IL, identity of parents IGS 27:2:97
TRAVIS, Allen f1852, IL, biog sketch CI 31:1:28
TREFETHEN, Sebastian J, w Elizabeth Locke, fam hist by Langley, bk rev TS 37:4:147
TRICKEY, Sarah see Samuel WINKLEY
TRIGG, Abram b1690, w Susan Docia Johns, EN, VA, geneal STS 35:4:64
TRIPP, John d1818, GA, estate inv abstr BT 27:2:37
TROUT, PA, Bible rec cont BGN 16:1:13
  William J d1845, PA, Bible rec cont BGN 16:1:13
TRUAX, Samuel Wright b1826, NY, brief fam hist DCG 9:3:11
TRUEMAN, Elizabeth see Richard TRUEMAN
TRUEMAN, Richard f1717, w Elizabeth, VA, fam hist VAG 39:2:83 39:3:181 39:4:295
TRUHITT, Francis see Thomas TRUHITT
  Thomas f1803, w Francis, SC, deed abstr ODD 7:2:28
TRUMAN, Harry S b1884, biog by Ferrell, bk rev REG 93:2:244
TRUMBULL-MULLINS, Mary Elizabeth, MI, fam hist by Northuis, bk rev DM 58:4:190

TRUMMEL, Chrisa f1909, w Pearl Voss, IL, news abstr re:their marriage CI 31:3:96

TUCKER, Barbara Ann see Barbara Ann WRIGHT

Temperance Jane b1804, h James William Brooks, h Alford Ledbetter, NC, will abstr SCG 14:4:693

William f1610, VA, MD, fam hist by Tucker, bk rev APR 14:2:2

TUELL, Ruth see Caleb A W BRIGGS

TUKE, EN, surname hist sketch FWC 9:3:261

TULEY, James f1834, w Martha Folck, IN, geneal by Tuley, bk rev GH 49:5:235

TULIP, Frank f1900, KS, court case abstr MGR 30:3:66

TUMA, Johanna see Wenzl WIDRA

TURNER, Alice P see Leander W TURNER

Bon f1936, KS, news abstr BCS 15:2:12

Carl J b1933, TX, autobiog PWN 1:3:3

Caroline see William Joseph DURRE

Freelove see Jonathan THORNTON

George Washington, b1874, w Mennie O Shelley, VA, Bible rec HPF 14:52:2

J E f1890, TX, fam hist sketch KTP 7:2:22

John Meridy b1747, VA, geneal by Bjorkman, bk rev APR 14:2:3 BHN 28:2:19 VAG 39:2:152

Joseph b1848, w Eliza Newcombe, EN, IL, obit PR 23:1:31

Leander W b1853, w Frances Eugenia Warner Cassel, w Alice P, KS, biog sketch & fam hist KK 33:2:33

Robert James b1857, w Martha Francis Salley, VA, Bible rec HPF 14:52:3

Robert L b1808, w Mary Lee, IL, fam hist sketches MCI 13:1:9

Ruth see Robert TOWNSEND

TUTHILL, John f1635, w Deliverance King, EN, NY, MI, fam hist by LaPorte, GH 49:4:228

TUTTLE, James b1775, w Sarah Clark, w Ruth Atwood, NH, jour abstr NHR 12:3:125

Peter b1660, EN, MD, fam group sheets by Campbell, bk rev GH 49:6:211

TYE, Ann see David BRODHEAD

UECKER, TX, fam cem rec KTP 3:1:11

UKRAINE, Jewish anc towns, res tips HQ 95:55:56

ULSCHI, Jacob b1734, NS, hist of his home GEN 20:3:29

UNITED STATES, Am Canal Soc ency vol 6 by Shank, bk rev WPG 21:4:54

Am character & regional identity, hist essays by Miller/McKivigan, bk rev REG 93:2:219

Anglo-Norman fam geneal, repr 1951, bk rev PR 22:3:8

Anti-Suffragism 1880-1920, hist by Camhi, bk rev REG 93:4:510

Appalachia, census microfilm bks 1850 by SK Publications, bk rev APR 14:2:3

Appalachia, death & dyting, attitudes & practices, hist by Crissman, bk rev REG 92:4:412

Appalachia, folk hist by Higgs et al, bk rev REG 93:4:466

Appalachian migrants in US cities, hist by Borman/Obermiller, bk rev REG 92:4:445

Archives & mss collect guide & bibl by DeWitt, bk rev REG 92:4:454

Army, hist reg & dict, repr 1903, bk rev GJ 23:1:43

Army manual abstr on rifle & light infantry tactics BT 27:1:6

Association of Professional Geneal, hist sketch APG 10:3:100

Battle of Chippawa 1814, hist by Graves, bk rev FAM 34:3:177

Battle of Lake Erie 1813, hist by Altoff, bk rev WPG 21:3:51

Bayou country, Creoles of color, hist by Brasseaux et al, bk rev NGS 83:4:306

Bicycles, hist LM 36:2:212

UNITED STATES (continued)
Biog dict by Bowman, bk rev REG 93:4:512
Cavalry Scouts, geneal res tips GFP 44:4:162
Central America (ship) hist KTP 10:2:18
Children's Aid Soc, hist by Holt, bk rev CHG 27:2:78
Choctaw Nation, whites in Skullyville Co, permit reg 1889-1905 by McKim, bk rev PR 23:2:68
Christmas cards, 19th cent, hist sketch PCQ 6:3:4
Christmas hist PCQ 6:3:2
Church archives & repositories, addresses MCI 13:4:87
Citizen soldiers 1775, hist sketch CTN 27:4:583
Citizens in Cuba 1869-1935, index CGJ 3:3:20
Civil Rights Movement & white Southerners, hist by Chappell, bk rev REG 92:4:438
Co statistics, repr 1960, bk rev RCP 17:3:83
Colonial & Revolutionary pedigrees, surname index to 65 vol, repr 1964, bk rev PB 11:1:12
Colonial Am traveler's guide by Foulke, bk rev WPG 22:2:54
Colonial fam geneal by Mackenzie, bk rev SEE 36:153:41
Colonial fam geneal (misc vol), repr 1907-1920, bk rev TR 35:2:107
Colonial hist, repr 1881, bk rev FC 14:1:58
Colonies, hist ency by Cooke et al, bk rev NYR 126:2:151
Crime & punishment in Am, hist by Freidman, bk rev REG 92:4:441
DAR & WW2, hist DAR 129:8:752
DAR celebration of D-Day anniv, descr DAR 129:1:4
DAR Master Index, repr 1955, bk rev STS 35:4:18
DAR Museum hist rooms, descr DAR 129:3:248

UNITED STATES (continued)
DAR Patriot Index 1994 corr DAR 129:5:501
DAR speech commemorating end of WW2 1995 DAR 129:6:607
Decl of Independence, hist sketch & signers QU 12:4:37
Donner Party, hist, repr c1879, bk rev ANC 30:2:75 IMP 14:2:61 TFG 8:2:13 PR 22:4:47
Eighteenth Amendment, hist by Hamm, bk rev REG 93:4:494
Ellis Island hist & ship manifests GJ 23:2/3:51
Ellis Island myths & misconceptions, hist & res tips GJ 23:2/3:65
English colonies, hist, repr 1881, bk rev SCR 18:6:106
European travel in 19th cent, hist by Stowe, bk rev REG 93:4:477
Federal imm laws, chronology GJ 23:2/3:134
First Americans, origins, hist by Dixon, bk rev REG 92:4:446
First fam geneal by Drake, bk rev NEC 3:3:34 PB 11:1:12
Forts, location guide SEN 2:2:28
Freewill Bapt Publications marr & div rec 1819-1851 by Young, bk rev NGS 83:1:67
Freeze of 1816, hist PV 23:8:1
French & Indian War hist by McAfee, bk rev ACG 21:2:59
Frontier hist essays by Grossman et al, bk rev REG 93:3:343
Gas stations, hist by Jakle/Sculle, bk rev REG 93:3:377
Geneal misc vol 23, repr 1869, bk rev GSM 12:2:48
Geneal soc direct 10th ed by Meyer, bk rev NTT 14:3:83
Genealogical Advertiser compendium, repr 1898-1901, bk rev GH 49:4:201
Gentlemen's Magazine, vr abstr 1731-1868 by Dobson, bk rev PR 22:3:8
Gold rush, 49ers biog sketches, vol 11 by Nelson/Whitworth, bk rev OC 31:1:55

UNITED STATES (continued)
Great Lakes region, lighthouse keepers, hist 1845-1900 TR 35:4:179
Great Plains, CN border emig rec 1896-1918, hist, MN 26:3:100 NDG 95:62:21
Hereditary Soc Blue Bk by Davenport, bk rev AG 70:2:127
Hist (early) by Brown, bk rev TSC 6:2:6
Hist 1776 by Edgar, bk rev WPG 22:1:43
Hist 1809-1860 by Fraysse, bk rev REG 93:2:221
Imm group patterns, hist 1607-1860 FTP 16:4:3
Imm hist & biog 1773-1986 by Dublin, bk rev NER 149:593:77
Imm processing station hist IMP 14:2:47
Indian captives, locating rec of, res tips HQ 95:60:71
Indian territory hist 1866-1906 by Burton, bk rev RAG 17:1:16
Indian Wars, soldier burial guide by Hughes, bk rev GH 49:6:180
Kappa Alpha Order, hist 1865-1897 by Scott, bk rev FGC 95:28:23 PR 22:3:5
Last public execution, hist by Ryan, bk rev REG 92:4:445
Lincoln assassination hist by Mills, bk rev KGF 1:1/2:87 TFT 6:2:23B
Lineages of colonial fam, repr 1912, bk rev NYR 126:3:219
Little Big Horn River battle, participant roster (partial) AW 21:3:84
Local utilities & public works, hist by Keating, bk rev TS 37:4:146
Lotteries, hist & descr LM 36:2:205
Lynching, hist sketch PCQ 6:2:6
Madonna of the Trail monuments, hist KSL 19:4:125
Mann Act 1910, hist by Langum, bk rev REG 93:3:362
Mariners' Museum Res Lib & Archives, geneal res tips GH 49:4:6

UNITED STATES (continued)
Masonic Grand Lodges, addresses SCS 32:2:40
Masonic rec, address list MCG 18:1/2:82
Mayflower Descendant vol 1, repr 1899, bk rev BG 16:1:31 FC 13:2:39 GH 49:6:180
Mayflower Descendant vol 2, repr 1900, bk rev BG 16:1:31 GH 49:6:180
Mayflower Descendant vol 5, repr 1903, bk rev BG 16:2:53 TMG 17:4:136
Mayflower Descendant vol 6, repr 1904, bk rev BG 16:2:53 TMG 17:4:136
Mayflower Descendant vol 7, repr 1905, bk rev NEC 3:3:34
Mayflower Descendant vol 8, repr 1906, bk rev NEC 3:3:34
Mayflower Descendant vol 11, repr 1909, bk rev GG 8:3:112 LWF 15:2:66 SLV 12:3:10
Mayflower Descendant vol 12, repr 1910, bk rev GG 8:3:112 LWF 15:2:66
Mayflower Descendant vol 15, repr 1913, bk rev ACG 22:1:21
Mayflower Descendant vol 16, repr 1914, bk rev ACG 22:1:21
Mayflower Descendant, index of persons in vol 1-34, repr 1959-1962, bk rev KSL 19:2:75
Mayflower descendants, add by Roser, bk rev TR 35:4:218
Mayflower fam deeds & probates by Roser, bk rev CTN 27:4:587 GFP 44:3:140 GH 49:3:199 GJ 22:4:124 MAG 8:2:4 NER 149:594:192 NYR 126:1:87 TR 35:1:54
Mayflower fam geneal by Roser, bk rev ACG 21:4:161 GN 13:3:140 HQ 95:60:93 KA 31:1:44 MN 26:3:136 MN 26:4:184 NHR 12:4:194 NYR 126:4:280 SCS 32:12:285 WPG 22:1:46

UNITED STATES (continued)

Mayflower fam geneal, misc vol by Mayflower Society, bk rev LRT 14:2:555

Mayflower fam geneal vol 8 by Townsend, bk rev AG 70:2:128

Mayflower pass list 1620 AU 19:3:11

Melungeon hist by Kennedy, bk rev SEN 3:2:49

Melungeon hist, repr 1975, bk rev SEN 3:2:48

Memorial Day hist AFH 16:1:4

Migration patterns, descr MM 19:4:47

Migration routes (overland), list FGC 95:28:16

Mil rec see also MILITARY GENEALOGY

Mil res guide by Neagles, bk rev ARH 33:1:34 IGS 27:2:116

Model T Ford car hist PCQ 22:3:6

Mountain culture & movies, hist by Williamson, bk rev REG 93:4:498

Natchez Dist, court rec 1767-1805 by McBee, bk rev GH 49:4:202

National Road, hist, repr 1894, bk rev PR 23:2:65

Nationwide Ellis Island Automation Project, descr GJ 23:2/3:105

Native American regions, tips on locating non-Indian anc HQ 95:59:68

Natl Soc Sons & Daughters of the Pilgrims Lineage Bk 5 by Finnell, bk rev MN 26:2:87

New England, atlas of hist co boundaries by Long, bk rev GH 49:4:206

New England biog dict by Eliot, bk rev CN 4:2:31

New England, communal forests hist by McCullough, bk rev HNH 50:3/4:229

New England, Freewill Bapt marr & div rec 1819-1851 by Young, bk rev BG 16:2:54

New England, geneal handbk by Lindberg, corr & add NEH 12:1:16

New England, geneal notes on misc fam, repr 1883, bk rev GH 49:5:204

UNITED STATES (continued)

New England Hist & Geneal Reg vol 19, repr 1865, bk rev GFP 44:3:141 GH 49:3:201

New England Hist & Geneal Reg vol 20, repr 1866, bk rev GFP 44:3:141 GH 49:3:201

New England Hist & Geneal Reg vol 21, repr 1867, bk rev GH 49:4:202 KA 30:3:177 TMG 17:2:46

New England Hist & Geneal Reg vol 22, repr 1868, bk rev GH 49:4:202 KA 30:3:177 TMG 17:2:46

New England Hist & Geneal Reg vol 23, repr 1869, bk rev ACG 21:1:23 GH 49:6:182 GSM 12:2:48 KSL 19:2:74 MN 26:2:88 SLV 12:1:1

New England Hist & Geneal Reg vol 24, repr 1870, bk rev ACG 21:1:23 BG 16:2:54 CN 4:2:31 GH 49:6:183 GSM 12:2:48 KSL 19:2:74 MN 26:2:88 SLV 12:1:1

New England Hist & Geneal Reg vol 25, repr 1871, bk rev CTA 37:4:183 GG 7:4:156

New England Hist & Geneal Reg vol 26, repr 1872, bk rev GG 7:4:157 GGS 31:2:119

New England Hist & Geneal Reg vol 27, repr 1873, bk rev ACG 21:4:159 KVH 19:10:114

New England Hist & Geneal Reg vol 28, repr 1874, bk rev KSL 19:4:153 MT 31:3:113

New England Hist & Geneal Reg vol 29, repr 1875, bk rev KSL 19:4:153 MT 31:3:113

New England Hist & Geneal Reg vol 30, repr 1876, bk rev GH 49:6:183

New England Hist & Geneal Reg vol 31, repr 1877, bk rev GH 49:6:184

New England Hist & Geneal Reg vol 32, repr 1878, bk rev ACG 21:4:159 MT 31:4:152 WRB 18:1:35

New England Hist & Geneal Reg vol 33, repr 1879, bk rev ACG 21:4:159 MT 31:4:152 WRB 18:1:35

UNITED STATES (continued)
- *New England Hist & Geneal Reg* vol 51-148 index by Fiske, bk rev NYR 126:4:278
- New England, hist dist guide by Richardson, bk rev BCF 95:Apr/May:8
- New England Hist Geneal Soc sesquicentennial hist 1845-1995 by Schutz, bk rev DM 58:3:142 NYR 126:4:278 RAG 16:4:19
- New England hist timeline MCS 15:1:22
- New England inventors, anc NEH 12:4:116 12:5:154
- New England, marr prior to 1700 by Torrey, supp by Sanborn, bk rev GN 13:3:138 HQ 95:59:87 NYR 126:4:279 TR 35:4:220
- New England, Puritan & Indian relations 1620-1675, hist by Vaughan, bk rev RAG 16:4:18
- New England, settler biog dict, repr 1809, bk rev SGS 44:3:140
- New England, settler geneal reg, repr 1829, bk rev LRT 14:2:555
- New England, settlers & kin, fam hist by Burgess, bk rev LL 31:1:11
- New England, surnames, most common, list EWA 32:2:66
- New London Academy hist by Siddons, bk rev TSC 6:1:4
- New York City, pass lists 1715-1844, index by Samuelsen, bk rev GH 49:5:204
- News & politics 1865-1878, hist by Summers, bk rev REG 92:4:426
- News geneal res guide GJ 23:1:3
- Nineteenth amendment & women's rights, hist DAR 129:8:744
- North Am continent settlement hist by Morgan, bk rev REG 92:4:446
- NY, imm rec res strategies GJ 23:2/3:117
- Order of the Founders & Patriots of Am Reg of Lineages of Associates 1896-1993, bk rev TR 35:2:109

UNITED STATES (continued)
- Oregon Trail queries & rev by Terry, bk rev GH 49:4:202
- Orphan train riders, hist sketch KTP 11:1:3
- Orphan trains, hist by Holt, bk rev CHG 27:2:78
- Oxen as westward transport, hist GGP 28:1:18
- Pacific Fur Company employee roster 1813-1814 TRI 35:2:52
- Pacific Northwest, hist by Drawson, bk rev TB 22:1:14
- Pacifist hist essays by Hawkley/Juhnke, bk rev PM 18:4:35
- Panunzio deportation cases 1919-1920, hist & index NGS 83:4:293
- Pass & imm lists index 1991-1995 by Filby/Byers, bk rev RAG 17:1:15
- Pass/emig reg compilation by Ptak, bk rev TVF 4:2:122
- Pass lists for Atlantic & Gulf Coast ports 1820-1873, index vol 4 & 5 by Samuelsen, bk rev GH 49:5:188
- Philosophical questions in Am social hist 1600-1850, hist by Rutman, bk rev REG 93:4:478
- Pioneer frugality, hist sketch PCQ 22:2:7
- Pioneer gourmet foods, hist sketch PCQ 22:1:6
- Pioneer women's hist, repr 1878, bk rev RDQ 12:2:29
- Population before the 1790 census, hist & data by Greene, bk rev FAM 34:1:50
- Post ofcs 1828-1832, guide by TLC Geneal, bk rev VAG 39:2:155
- Presidency, hist by McDonald, bk rev REG 92:4:417
- Presidents, anc by Roberts, bk rev AG 70:4:256 NEH 12:2/3:48 RAG 17:1:14 TTT 20:1:20 WPG 22:2:54
- Presidents, vital statistics RDQ 12:1:5
- Primogeniture law, descr OG 21:1:27
- Progressivism, hist by Eisenach, bk rev REG 93:3:361

UNITED STATES (continued)
- Psychiatry, hist by Lunbeck, bk rev REG 93:2:237
- Puritan Generation, hist SQ 5:5:45
- Race, ethnicity & urbanization, hist essays by Rabinowitz, bk rev REG 92:4:437
- Resort hotels, 19th cent, hist HNH 50:1&2:7
- Rev War, bounty land warrant appl files, fed sources, res guide SCH 10:3:83
- Rev War era Bible, fam & marr rec from pension appl, vol 15 by Edmondson & Sobieski, bk rev GSC 18:1:7 SCM 23:2:119 TJ 7:1:37
- Rev War era Bible, fam & marr rec from pension appl by Edmondson/Sobieski, bk rev GSN 8:1:6
- Rev War era Bible, fam & marr rec index by Edmondson, bk rev TJ 7:1:37
- Rev War, living conditions descr DAR 129:5:488
- Rev War pension list 1813, repr, bk rev APR 14:7:2
- Roads & migration trails, dates used CC 17:3:29
- Royal anc of 500 imm to Am colonies by Roberts, bk rev NCJ 21:2:187
- Settlers prior to 1776, biog sketches, bk rev LRT 14:2:556
- Ship pass list 1861 from New Orleans to Cuba CGJ 3:3:26
- Ships that brought imm to Am, hist & descr by Ptak, bk rev TVF 4:2:122
- Slavery, unpaid & wage, hist essays by Turner, bk rev CGJ 3:4:11
- Social Security death benefit rec 1937-1993 by AGLL, CD-ROM rev TEN 95:16:24
- Social Security Numbers, locality assignments SYH 2:3:26
- South, Cavalier Generation, hist sketch SQ 6:1:46

UNITED STATES (continued)
- South, Kappa Alpha Order fraternity hist 1865-1897 by Scott, bk rev GH 49:5:187 MGR 30:3:67
- South, New London Academy, hist by Siddons, bk rev GH 49:6:180
- South, pre-Civil Rights era, hist by Egerton, bk rev REG 93:4:500
- South, press & editorial spokesmen, 19th cent, hist by Osthaus, bk rev REG 93:3:347
- South, res tips SQ 5:5:7
- South, women & plantations, hist by Clinton, bk rev REG 93:4:480
- South, women's hist by Bernhard et al, bk rev REG 93:2:238
- Southern agriculture, hist 1860-1880 by Otto, bk rev REG 93:2:233
- Southern tradition & conservatism, hist by Genovese, bk rev REG 93:3:375
- Southern women, hist essays by Clinton et al, bk rev REG 93:3:374
- Southwestern Stage Company, hist 1850s KTP 11:4:63
- States, dates they entered the union, res aid WCG 11:5:36
- Suffrage cartoons & political commentary, hist by Sheppard, bk rev REG 92:4:430
- *Sultana* steamship disaster, news abstr HQ 95:57:15
- Supreme Court Bar, hist by McGuire, bk rev REG 93:2:255
- TN Valley Authority, hist 1933-1990 by Hargrove, bk rev REG 93:4:495
- Transportation in 20th cent, vehicle dates BT 27:1:11
- USS Nautilus, hist & crew roster AMG 10:4:5
- V-J Day hist REG 93:3:337
- War of 1812, pension rec, lost files, list & res tips, AMG 9:6:12 10:2/3:14
- War of 1812, preliminary hist, repr 1816, bk rev WPG 22:1:42
- War statistics, Am Rev to Vietnam War AU 19:2:5
- Washboards, hist TPI 21:1:28

UNITED STATES (continued)
West, gunfighter hist by Rosa, bk rev CN 4:3:40
West, Indian Wars, biog ency of soldiers by O'Neal, bk rev RAG 16:3:21
West, women of, hist by Luchetti/Olwell, bk rev PR 22:3:7
West, women's hist by Peavy/Smith, bk rev NGS 83:3:223
Western hist bks, hist by Jacobs, bk rev REG 93:2:245
Western region, hist dist guide by Richardson, bk rev GRC 11:2:28
Western settlement hist by Morgan, bk rev ARN 8:4:16
Wilderness Road & KY settlement hist sketch VCG 95:MAR:15
Women activists, hist essays by Hewitt/Lebsock, bk rev REG 92:4:453
Women imm in Am, hist by Neidle, bk rev NTT 15:1/2:4
Women in the military, memorials, descr DAR 129:3:263
Women on the Western frontier, hist by Fowler, bk rev AMG 10:2/3:7 GH 49:5:186 NC 5:2:72
Women's hist 1945-1960 by Meyerowitz, bk rev REG 93:2:254
WW1 draft reg cards at Natl Archives, res tips NCC 15:1:10
WW2 Pacific remembrances by DAR, descr DAR 129:12:888
UNRUH, Margareta b1926, RU, biog sketch MH 22:1:1
UPDIKE, Susanna m1812, h Robert Long, NJ, fam rec GMN 70:3:107
URQUIDES, Isabel see Cornelio AVILA
USENER, Romilda see Rudolph PETERMAN
UTAH, Charles C Rich Guard, roster 1847 GJ 23:1:24
Geneal Society Irish collection, res guide CTA 37:4:168
Geneal Society res guide CTA 37:4:153

UTAH (continued)
Salt Lake City, res tips TF 23:3:70
VAIL, Jane/t see William STEWART
Jane/t see William Stewart KERR
VALCK, Jonas b1808, w Sarah Wolven, NY, Bible rec UG 24:1:11
VALLI, Lizzie b1852, CN, biog sketch OBN 28:1:26
VANBEBBER, Sarah see Joshua WHEELER
VANBRAMER, NY, fam cem rec GG 8:3:97
VANBREUCKELEN, Gysbert see Gysbert VANDENBERGH
VANBRUGH, Sarah see John JAY
VANCE, Elizabeth dc1781, VA, will abstr BT 27:1:5
LA, fam hist cont TG 29:1:1
Robert Brank bc1730, NC, biog sketch LOB 16:4:92
Zebulon Baird f1863, NC, papers by Mobley, bk rev NCJ 21:3:297
VANCLIEF, Peter, w Mary Ann Dorsey, NJ, OH, geneal by Canfield, bk rev TR 35:2:110
VANDEBURGH, Betsey see Robert ADAMS
VANDEGRIFT, S A f1927, CA, biog GGP 28:1:7
VANDENBERGH, Claas fc1645, HO, NY, fam hist by Grunwell, bk rev GH 49:5:236
Gysbert fc1645, HO, NY, fam hist by Grunwell, bk rev GH 49:5:235
VANDERMARK, Thomas b1643, HO, NY, fam hist by James, bk rev UG 24:1:4
VANDEVENTER, Martha f1915, AR, warranty deed SYH 1:2:25
VANDOREN, Dorothy see Albert Louis STOKES
VANDYCK, Jan Thomaszen, NY, fam rec NYR 126:4:239
VANFLEET, James Alward f1953, NJ, FL, biog PCQ 11:1:6
VANGILDER, Abraham b1805, w Mary Harrison, NJ, Bible rec MAG 8:3:10

VANMATRE, Thomas Jefferson b1834, IL, biog sketch RSQ 17:2:23

VANN, Joseph P bc1832, m Sarah Hogg, AR, fam rec TRC 10:2:51

VARANGUE, Cecile Castel dite, LA, geneal by Mchenry, bk rev NGS 83:3:230

VARCE, Susan see David MOORE

VARNER, Fam hist by Palmer, bk rev KCG 36:1:50

Judea see Isaac HAYES

VARNEY, Mary see Thomas VARNEY
Thomas f1664, w Ann Browne, w Mary, MA, geneal NER 149:593:3 149:594:141 149:595:244

VARNUM, David see Margaret LORD,

VATCHER, Richard m1816, w Martha Cains, EN, NF, fam hist NAL 11:4:142

VENARD-VANASSE, Francois-Noel b1642, w Jeanne Fourrier, FR, geneal ACG 21:4:172

VERHOEFF, Otilla M see Richard A SHIPMAN

VERLY, Jean see Catherine MILLER

VERMONT, Athens, militia rec c1820-1830 BAT 24:2:67

Atlas of hist co boundaries by Long, bk rev AG 70:1:63 NER 149:594:188 NGS 83:3:225 SEE 36:153:53

Bennington Co, Readsboro, sch rosters 1844 BCF 95:Apr/May:5

Bennington Co, Readsboro, tax list 1796 BCF 95:Apr/May:4

Bennington Fam Hist Center res guide BCF 95:FEB:1

Benson, cem inscr by Jenks, bk rev CTN 27:4:590

Benson, cem rec by Griswold, bk rev GFP 44:4:189

Brandon, cem inscr by Jenks, bk rev CTN 27:4:586 GH 49:3:215

Burlington, First Cong Soc bapt, marr & burial rec c1822-1844, repr, bk rev FRT 16:3:110 GH 49:5:217

Cem listings, index by Nichols, bk rev AG 70:4:257

VERMONT (continued)
Census 1771 by Holbrook, bk rev TB 22:1:14

Citizens in MA vr c1850 BAT 24:2:60

Derby, census 1870 cont BAT 24:2:44

Dover, warnings out 1802-1817 NER 149:593:73

Gazetteer, repr 1849, bk rev BCF 95:FEB:6

Georgia, vr by Mallett/GSV, bk rev ACG 21:4:161

Green Mountain heroes & Ethan Allen, hist by DePuy, bk rev BCF 95:Apr/May:8 SLV 12:1:14

Hist to 1830, repr 1830, bk rev GH 49:6:204 NC 5:1:31 TFG 8:2:12

Hubbardton, cem inscr by Jenks, bk rev CTN 27:4:590

Ludlow, deaths 1790-1901, repr 1902, bk rev BG 16:1:32 FRT 16:2:66 GH 49:4:220 RAG 16:2:19 SCS 32:4:87

Putney, cem inscr by Stevens, bk rev GH 49:4:221

Readsboro, Reformed Meth Ch hist BAT 24:2:62

Res tips RAG 16:4:8

Rev War, soldiers, sailors, & patriots, roster & biog data by Fisher, bk rev AG 70:2:125

Stamford, deaths 1879-1880 BCF 95:FEB:4

Sudbury, cem inscr by Jenks, bk rev CTN 27:4:590

Sunderland, res sources BCF 95:Apr/May:1

Wardsborough, warnings out 1802-1817 NER 149:593:73

Windsor, marr rec, 18th & 19th cent BAT 24:2:44

VERNER, Fam hist by Palmer, bk rev KCG 36:1:50

VERTREES, Isaac b1755, w Elizabeth Barkhimer, PA, KY, biog sketch KA 31:1:46

VICKERS, Robert b1828, w Ellen Cook, EN, NY, MI, Bible rec KVH 19:7:81

VIELE, Kathlyne Knickerbacker, NY, fam hist by James, bk rev UG 24:1:3

VIETS, John, female desc by Schell, bk rev CTN 27:4:593

VIEUX, Josette see Solomon JUNEAU

VILLARS, William see Ruth WHITTAKER

VILLWOCK, Edward b1885, GR, IL, fam rec BGS 27:2:38

VINCENT, Sarah see Degory PRIEST

VINES, Jimmy d1875, AL, obit PT 37:3/4:63

VINING, William fl759, NC, fam rec FPG 17:6:43

VINSON, Archibald m1797, w Rutha Smith, NC, Bible rec JC 21:3:58

VIRGINIA, 17th cent social life, hist by Bruce, bk rev CN 4:3:41

Abingdon, news abstr from the *Democrat* 1856 HPF 95:50:26

Accomack Co, cem inscr by Carey et al, bk rev HPF 14:52:1 RCR 10:4:2377 VAG 39:4:318

Accomack Co, marr rec 1776-1854 by Turman, bk rev GH 49:6:206 KSL 19:2:75 TG 29:1:48 TSC 6:2:5 VAG 39:1:77 WPG 21:4:48

Albemarle Co, land entry bk 1744-1749 CVH 12:4:68

Albemarle ship, hist by Elliott, bk rev RAG 16:1:21

Alexandria hist 1820-1830 by Miller, bk rev SGS 45:1:34

Alexandria, death rec 1853-1896 by Pippenger, bk rev GH 49:5:221 TVF 4:1:53

Alexandria, hist 1749-1861 by Powell, bk rev HQ 95:60:92 VAG 39:3:233

Alexandria, hist 1820-1830 by Miller, bk rev GH 49:6:206 HPF 14:52:1 RCR 10:4:2380

Alexandria, legislative pet 1778-1861 by Pippenger, bk rev HQ 95:59:89 95:60:92 TVF 4:3:193 VAG 39:3:231

Alexandria, wills, admin & guard 1786-1800 by Pippenger, bk rev GH 49:5:221 TVF 4:1:54

VIRGINIA (continued)
Alexandria Co, apprenticeship indentures 1808-1817 VAG 39:2:117 39:3:171 39:4:253

Alexandria Co, marr rec 1853-1895 by Pippenger, bk rev MD 36:1:94

Alleghany Co, marr rec 1822-1872 by Nelson, bk rev DM 58:3:142 SGS 44:2:86 TRC 10:1:32

Amelia Co, misc rec 1735-1865 by McConnaughey, bk rev VAG 39:3:227

Arlington Co, death rec 1853-1896 by Pippenger, bk rev GH 49:5:221

Arlington, marr rec 1853-1895 by Pippenger, bk rev MD 36:1:94

Ashland, hist by Shalf, bk rev TVF 4:1:55

Assoc of Westmoreland papers 1766 MCG 18:3/4:171

Augusta Co, St John's Ch Reg 1786-1872 by Joyner, bk rev APR 14:12:3 MGS 13:3:42 TPI 21:1:41 VAG 39:3:237

Back Creek Valley, settler hist 1730-1830 by Kerns, bk rev GFP 45:2:90 TR 35:4:223

Bath Co, slave inv of John Brockenbrough VA 33:2:102

Berkeley Co, deed bk 3 c1774 cont FCM 7:4:223 8:2:103

Bibl 1607-1699, repr 1957, bk rev GH 49:5:219

Biog data 1607-1870 by Wardell, bk rev OC 29:3:130

Border warfare & Indian wars hist, repr 1831, bk rev APR 14:2:3 GH 49:4:221 PR 22:3:6

Bowling Green, death rec from the *Caroline Progress* 1919-1994 by Collins, bk rev HQ 95:60:92

Bristol, news abstr from the *News* 1865 HPF 14:52:20

Buckingham Co, census 1860 by Kidd, bk rev VAG 39:2:153

Buckingham Co, geneal rec, repr 1984, bk rev GH 49:3:216

VIRGINIA (continued)

Buckingham Co, will/deed ledgers 1843-1844 VA 33:4:270

Burned counties, geneal res guide TVF 4:2:71 4:3:139

Campbell Co, fam hist 1782-1926, repr 1927, bk rev GH 49:5:221

Capon Valley, pioneer geneal 1698-1940, repr 1946, bk rev WPG 22:2:51

Caroline Co, cem inscr vol 1 by Collins, bk rev GH 49:5:221 TVF 4:1:53 VAG 39:1:71

Caroline Co, death rec 1919-1994 from the *Caroline Progress* by Collins, bk rev TVF 4:3:192 VAG 39:3:234

Census 1870, CD-ROM rev TEN 95:16:22

Census index 1850, CD-ROM rev APR 14:6:4

Census index 1860, CD-ROM rev APR 14:6:4

Church, minister & fam hist, repr 1857, bk rev TEN 95:16:23 VQ 94:10:26

Charles City Co, civil appointments 1788-1798 TVF 4:1:29

Chiskaike land patents & hist, 17th cent TVF 4:2:76

Chronology 1585-1783, repr 1957, bk rev GH 49:5:219

Civil War, Fredericksburg campaign hist by Gallagher, bk rev REG 93:4:485

Colonial doc & hist 1605-1616, repr 1902, bk rev GSC 17:4:6 GSN 8:1:5

Colonial hist, repr 1890, bk rev AFH 16:2:3 GH 49:6:184

Colonial settlers & their MD relatives, fam hist by Tucker, bk rev APR 14:2:2 GH 49:3:215

Colonial soldier roster, repr 1917, bk rev APR 14:11:5

Company of London rec 1607-1622 by Kingsbury, bk rev EWA 32:4:178

Company of London rec vol 3, repr 1933, bk rev GH 49:6:205 SGS 45:1:34 TSC 6:3:4

VIRGINIA (continued)

Convention of Delegates for the Co & Corporations of VA 1775-1776, proceedings repr 1816, bk rev TJ 7:3:110

Court rec in southwest PA 1775-1780 by Crumrine, bk rev BWG 24:2:153 VAG 39:2:153

Culpeper, Rev war militia hist BYG 7:3:388

Cumberland Parish, hist & vestry bks 1746-1816, repr 1930, bk rev GH 49:5:223

Cumberland Pres Ch, geneal abstr by Eddlemon, bk rev APR 14:6:4

Dickenson Co, hist by DCHBC, bk rev GH 49:4:221

Dinwiddie Co, clerk's fee bk 1763 VAG 39:1:32 39:2:104 39:3:188 39:4:269

Dinwiddie Co, surveyor's platt bk 1755-1796 & court orders 1789-1791, index by TLC Geneal, bk rev VAG 39:3:236

Domestic life, 17th cent, hist, repr 1957, bk rev GH 49:5:219

Dumfries, Payne's store index abstr 1758-1764 cont NPW 14:4:23 14:6:35

Eastern Shore, Rev War soldier & sailor hist by Nottingham, bk rev HQ 95:60:92 MD 36:4:679 VAG 39:3:233

Elizabeth City Co, deed abstr 1787-1800 by Charles, bk rev GH 49:3:216

EN hist chronology FRT 17:1:12

Essex Co, processioner's returns 1796 TVF 4:3:184

Executive Council captain commissions 1781-1783 VA 33:2:109

Explorers & maps, hist by Hammond, bk rev MGS 13:1:12

Fairfax Co, cem inscr vol 1 by FGS, bk rev GH 49:4:221 WPG 21:4:54

Fairfax Co, tithables 1749 TVF 4:1:39 4:2:117

VIRGINIA (continued)
Falls Church hist, repr 1964, bk rev GH 49:6:206 HPF 14:52:1 RCR 10:4:2378 WCK 28:4:44
Fauquier Co, geneal & misc fam rec 1759-1799 by Alcock, bk rev FCM 7:4:266 TVF 4:1:53
Fauquier Co, wills, inv & acc 1759-1800 by Gott, bk rev GH 49:3:216
Frederick Co, Back Creek Valley, settler hist 1730-1830 by Kerns, bk rev MGS 13:3:42
Frederick Co, hist map, repr 1974, bk rev VQ 94:10:25
Frederick Co, Hopewell Friends Hist 1734-1934 by GPC, bk rev QQ 95:25:22
Frederick Co, order bk 1742-1745 FCM 7:4:253 8:2:83
Frederick Co, pioneer hist by ODell, bk rev MGS 13:3:43 WMG 12:1:42
Frederick Co, will bk 1 1743-1751 FCM 7:4:243 8:2:113
Fredericksburg, hist, repr 1937, bk rev GH 49:3:216
Fredericksburg, marr rec 1851-1900 by Fisher, bk rev GH 49:3:217
French & Indian War, land ofc warrants c1764 VA 33:4:260
Galudoghson battle 1742, hist by Draper, bk rev FCM 7:4:267
Galudoghson battle 1742, hist by Lobdell, bk rev DM 59:1:46 WPG 22:1:43
Gate City, tornado casualty roster 1929 HPF 14:52:36
Gazetteer, repr 1904, bk rev GH 49:4:221
Geneal res guide by McGinnis, bk rev NGS 83:1:65
Geneal, misc fam of the Rappahannock River area 1607-1799 by Yurechko, bk rev VAG 39:3:234
Germanna, settler hist BYG 7:6:411 8:1:421
Gloucester Co, civil appointments 1781-1798 TVF 4:1:37

VIRGINIA (continued)
Gloucester Co, colonial rec by Mason, bk rev GH 49:5:222
Goochland Co, fam hist, repr 1974, bk rev GH 49:5:222
Goochland Co, tithable list c1732-1770 VA 33:2:107
Government, 17th cent, hist, repr 1957, bk rev GH 49:5:220
Grayson Co, order bk 1826 by Anderson, bk rev GH 49:4:221 HQ 95:55:91
Greenbrier Co, land entry bk 1780-1786 by Stinson, bk rev MGS 13:1:12
Hampshire Co, co minute bk abstr 1817-1823 by Horton, bk rev FCM 7:4:267
Hampshire Co, deed bk 2 c1768 FCM 7:4:233
Hampshire Co, misc rec 1816-1923 by Horton, bk rev WPG 22:1:46
Hampshire Co, Supreme Court of Appeals misc c1846 FCM 7:4:275
Hampston Co, deed bk 2 cont FCM 8:2:93
Hanover Co, Cedar Creek Quaker Meeting rec, repr 1905, bk rev ARN 8:1:8
Hanover Co, civil appointments & militia fines 1779-1799 cont TVF 4:2:108
Harrisonburg, *Rockingham Register* marr notices 1822-1870 by Boyd-Rush, bk rev TSG 3:2:9
Henrico Co, fam hist, repr 1974, bk rev GH 49:5:222
Henrico Co, rec bk 1678-1693 VA 33:2:119 33:4:277
Henry Co, geneal hist by Parks, bk rev PR 22:3:7
Highland Co, hist, repr 1911, bk rev GH 49:4:222 MGS 13:1:7
Hist by Salmon/Campbell, bk rev MGS 13:1:12
House of Burgesses jour 1727-1734 & 1736-1740, repr 1910, bk rev CI 31:2:68 DM 58:3:142 GH 49:5:220

VIRGINIA (continued)
House of Burgesses jour 1742-1747 & 1748-1749, repr 1910, bk rev DM 59:1:46 WPG 22:2:52
Huguenot ship pass list 1690-1700 SCH 10:3:79
Husbands & wives vol 1, geneal by Wardell, bk rev CCS 17:1:26 CN 4:2:30 DM 59:1:46 GRC 11:2:28 IMP 14:2:62 RCR 10:2:2277 SGS 44:3:140 TFT 6:2:23B WCK 28:3:33 WMG 11:3:140
Imm 1623-1666, rosters, bk rev LL 31:1:10
Indian wars & settlement hist by DeHass, index by Horton, bk rev APR 14:1:3
Isle of Wight Co, marr rec 1628-1800 by GPC, bk rev SEE 36:153:22
James City Co, civil appointments 1782-1789 TVF 4:3:156
James River area, fam hist, repr 1974, bk rev GH 49:5:222
Jamestowne Soc, reg of qualifying anc 1600s, bk rev KA 30:3:177 NCJ 21:3:300 SCM 23:1:60 VAG 39:1:75
Kappa Alpha Order, hist by Scott, bk rev MGR 30:3:67
King & Queen Co, births, marr & deaths 1680-1860 by Fisher, bk rev APR 14:11:4
King & Queen Co, land rec abstr 1719-1858 TVF 4:1:49
King & Queen Co, land rec abstr 1763-1868 TVF 4:2:95
King & Queen Co, Old Ch cem rec TVF 4:3:171
King & Queen Co, Old Ch hist TVF 4:3:168
King & Queen Co, vr 1680-1860 by Fisher, bk rev PR 23:2:64
King George Co, cem inscr by Klein, bk rev GH 49:5:222 TVF 4:2:121
King George Co, death rec 1853-1896 by Lee, bk rev CCS 17:1:28
King George Co, hist 1720-1990 by Harris, bk rev GH 49:5:222 TVF 4:1:55

VIRGINIA (continued)
King William Co, births, marr & deaths 1680-1860 by Fisher, bk rev APR 14:11:4
King William Co, vr 1680-1860 by Fisher, bk rev PR 23:2:64
Lancaster Co, marr bonds 1652-1850, repr 1965, bk rev GH 49:5:223
Lancaster Co, St Mary's Whitechapel Ch hist & cem rec TVF 4:2:101
Lancaster Co, will abstr 1653-1800 by Lee, bk rev TVF 4:3:194
Land patent & grant abstr 1741-1749 by Hudgins, bk rev APR 14:1:2 RCR 10:1:2214 SCM 23:1:59 SGS 44:2:83 TVF 4:2:122
Land patent bk #33 1756-1761 VA 33:2:142
Land patents, hist & res aid TVF 4:3:144
Libby prison, hist, repr 1863, bk rev AW 22:1:8 TVF 4:1:54
Loudoun Co, ch rec 1745-1800 by Hiatt, bk rev HQ 95:59:89 TVF 4:3:193 VAG 39:3:231
Lunenburg Co, census 1810, bk rev TJ 7:3:109
Lunenburg Co, deed bk 1746-1752, bk rev TJ 7:3:110
Lunenburg Co, deed bk 1764-1771 by Evans, bk rev RAG 16:2:26
Lunenburg Co, deed bk 1806-1808 by Evans, bk rev VAG 39:4:317
Lunenburg Co, free negroes & mulattoes 1814 VA 33:4:265
Lunenburg Co, guard acc 1791-1810 by Evans, bk rev TJ 7:3:109 VAG 39:1:72
Lunenburg Co, hist, bk rev TJ 7:3:109
Lunenburg Co, land taxes 1818-1819, bk rev TJ 7:3:109
Lunenburg Co, land taxes 1820-1821 by Evans, bk rev RAG 16:2:26
Lunenburg Co, marr reg 1850-1872 by Evans, bk rev VAG 39:4:317
Lunenburg Co, order bk abstr 1748-1752 by Evans, bk rev VAG 39:2:156

VIRGINIA (continued)
Lunenburg Co, tax list 1783-1784 by Simmons, bk rev RCR 10:1:2211
Lunenburg Co, tax list 1800 VAG 39:1:22
Lunenburg Co, will bk 1800-1802, bk rev TJ 7:3:110
Lunenburg Co, will bk 1810-1818 by Evans, bk rev RAG 16:3:21
Madison Co, hist by Yowell, bk rev HQ 95:59:89
Madison Co, hist, repr 1926, bk rev VAG 39:3:231
Madison Co, tax list 1800 VAG 39:3:213 39:4:305
Maid roster 1621 from the Ferrar Papers VAG 39:4:243
Manassas, City Cem rec by PWCGS, bk rev GH 49:5:224
Mariners' Museum Res Lib & Archives, geneal res tips GH 49:4:6
Marr rec 1607-1800 by Wulfeck, bk rev MGS 13:3:42 TVF 4:3:192
Marr rec vol 1 by Wardell, bk rev GSM 12:2:48
Matadequin, geneal hist by Evans, bk rev TVF 4:2:124
Mecklenburg Co, deeds 1777-1779 by TLC Geneal, bk rev GH 49:4:221
Middlesex Co, militia muster list 1730 TVF 4:1:47
Middlesex Co, Rev War losses 1783 TVF 4:1:51
Middlesex Co, sheriff's receipt bk 1820-1821 TVF 4:2:84 4:3:175
Mil Dist rec at Ohio State Univ, descr TR 35:2:92
Misc rec of emig to & from VA by Hamlin, bk rev GH 49:4:221
Monongalia Co, dist superior & co court rec 1802-1805 by Zinn, bk rev SKC 11:1:5
Montgomery Co, personal property tax list 1806 TJ 7:1:26
New Kent Co, births, marr & deaths 1680-1860 by Fisher, bk rev APR 14:11:4

VIRGINIA (continued)
New Kent Co, Cedar Grove cem inscr TVF 4:1:27
New Kent Co, deed bk 1864-1872 by Evans, bk rev VAG 39:3:232
New Kent Co, Emmaus Bapt Ch hist & cem inscr TVF 4:1:24
New Kent Co, vr 1680-1860 by Fisher, bk rev PR 23:2:64
New London Academy, hist 1795-1995 by Siddons, bk rev TR 35:2:106
APR 14:1:2
BWG 24:2:152
New River area, GR settlement hist c1745-1805, repr 1929, bk rev GH 49:5:220
North Fork Dist, census 1910 HPF 14:52:8 95:50:12
Northampton Co, deeds & wills of emancipation 1782-1864 by Latimer, bk rev CHG 28:1:36 GH 49:3:216 SGS 44:2:86
Northampton Co, marr lic bonds 1706-1854, repr 1929, bk rev GH 49:5:223
Northampton Co, marr rec 1660-1854 by Mihalyka, bk rev APR 14:1:2
Northampton Co, wills & admin abstr by Marshall, bk rev DM 58:3:141
Northern Neck area, warrants & surveys 1653-1781 by Joyner, bk rev MGS 13:3:43 TPI 21:1:40 VAG 39:3:237 WMG 12:1:42
Northern Neck, co boundary corr TVF 4:1:52
Northumberland Co, bks found in estates, listing 1650-1852 by Haynie, bk rev SGS 44:3:143
Northumberland Co, marr lic bonds 1783-1850, repr 1929, bk rev GH 49:5:223
Northumberland Co, rec bk abstr 1647-1652 by Jett, bk rev RSQ 17:2:22
Old Augusta Co, settler hist, repr 1935, bk rev GH 49:3:216
Old Frederick Co, pioneer doc by O'Dell, bk rev NGS 83:4:308 VAG 39:3:236

VIRGINIA (continued)
- Orange Co, court orders 1734-1741, everyname index by TLC Geneal, bk rev GH 49:4:222
- Overwharton Parish, reg 1720-1760, repr 1899, bk rev GH 49:4:222
- Pendleton Co, deeds 1788-1813 by Toothman, bk rev FCM 8:2:139
- Prince Edward Dist, court rec 1789-1809 by Warren/Weeks, bk rev GGS 31:1:48
- Princess Anne Co, land & probate rec from deeds 1691-1783 by Maling, bk rev FCM 7:4:268 HTR 38:3:70 VAG 39:3:229
- Princess Anne Co, probate rec 1783-1871 by Maling, bk rev GSM 12:2:46
- Princess Anne Co, wills 1783-1871 by Maling, bk rev GH 49:3:217 GSM 12:2:46
- Prominent fam geneal, repr 1907, bk rev GH 49:5:219
- Quaker settlers, hist by Worrall, bk rev FCM 7:4:265 WPG 21:4:48
- Railroad, SW region, hist by Noe, bk rev REG 93:3:355
- Rappahannock River area, geneal 1607-1799 by Yurechko, bk rev HQ 95:60:92
- Res guide by Dickinson, bk rev SCS 32:10:232 VAG 39:2:154
- Res tips BT 26:4:75
- Res tips, misc topics OC 31:1:8
- Res trip planning guide by Dickinson, bk rev HQ 95:58:88
- Residents in TX (Panola Co), biog sketches GRI 15:5:130
- Residents mentioned in private mss collect at NC State Archives, geneal gleanings VA 33:4:235
- Rev War pension appl & bounty land warrant rec vol 4 by Wardell, bk rev GJB 20:1:14 GSM 12:2:48 HPF 95:50:1 MGS 13:1:6 SGS 44:3:141

VIRGINIA (continued)
- Rev War rec (misc), repr 1936, bk rev DM 58:4:191 HQ 95:58:89 NCJ 21:3:300 SGS 44:3:145 TR 35:4:220 TVF 4:3:192
- Rev War rec, army & navy bounty land warrants, repr 1936, bk rev WCK 28:2:20
- Richmond Co, male free persons of color roster 1850 TVF 4:3:173
- Richmond, Civil War death rec, repr 1866, bk rev GH 49:6:184
- Richmond, Civil War, Union prisoners, hist by Ryan, bk rev TR 35:4:221
- Richmond, hist by Tyler-McGraw, bk rev REG 93:3:385
- Richmond, Libby prison life, hist, repr 1863, bk rev GH 49:5:224
- Richmond, news abstr from the Independent Chronicle 1788 VAG 39:1:64 39:2:127 39:3:219 39:4:312
- Rockingham Co, atlas 1885, bk rev APR 14:2:2
- Saltville Dist, census 1910 HPF 14:52:8 95:50:14
- Scott Co, hist, repr 1932, bk rev GH 49:5:224
- Scott Co, natu rec abstr HPF 14:52:36
- Shenandoah Co, census 1870 by Vann, bk rev APR 14:2:4 GH 49:4:222 KGF 1:1/2:87 KSL 19:2:73 RCR 10:2:2276 RT 13:1:17
- Shenandoah Co, land tax roll 1815 FCM 8:2:123
- Shenandoah Valley, exploration hist BYG 7:6:413
- Shenandoah Valley, settler hist by Hammond, bk rev MGS 13:3:44
- Silver Mine Patent hist BYG 8:1:423
- Southwest VA & the Valley, gazetteer, repr 1892, bk rev FTR 95:184:5
- Southwest VA hist & biog, repr 1892, bk rev APR 14:4:3 GH 49:6:205
- Spotsylvania Co, proofs of importation of GR 1724-1729 BYG 7:5:401
- St Mark's Parish, hist, repr 1877, bk rev GH 49:3:216

VIRGINIA (continued)
Stafford Co, marr rec 1851-1900 by Fisher, bk rev GH 49:3:217 GSM 12:2:46
State rangers & state line, hist by Osborne/Weaver, bk rev PCH 1:1:35
Stratton Major Parish, Upper Ch hist c1725 TVF 4:3:168
Sussex Co, court rec 1754-1801 by Haun, bk rev TVF 4:2:122
Tax payers 1782-1787 by Fothergill/Nogales, bk rev GH 49:3:215
Tazewell Co, hist essays by Leslie, bk rev MGS 13:1:11
Tazewell Co, marr rec 1800-1853 by Haga, bk rev MGS 13:1:11
Tazewell Co, marr rec 1854-1866 by Haga, bk rev MGS 13:1:11
Thomas (ship), hist & pass list TVF 4:1:12
Tidewater residents in OH wills before 1850, abstr TVF 4:1:32 4:2:106
Unionist societies & Union hole, hist by Turk, bk rev GH 49:6:205 IMP 14:1:29
Upper Accomack Co, cem inscr by Carey, bk rev SGS 45:1:34
Virginia Genealogist vol 15, repr 1971, bk rev JTJ 4:9/10:107 VQ 94:10:26
Virginia Genealogist vol 16, repr 1972, bk rev JTJ 4:9/10:111
Virginia Genealogist vol 19, repr 1975, bk rev GH 49:3:215
Virginia Genealogist vol 20, repr 1976, bk rev GH 49:3:215 LHS 95:2:8 TSG 3:2:9
Virginia Genealogist vol 21, repr 1977, bk rev CI 31:1:22 CN 4:1:16 GH 49:6:204 GSM 12:2:46
Virginia Genealogist vol 22, repr 1978, bk rev CI 31:1:22 CN 4:1:16 GH 49:6:204 GSM 12:2:46 WPG 21:4:48
Virginia Genealogist vol 23, repr 1979, bk rev DM 58:4:189 GH 49:5:220 GSM 12:2:46 NFB 27:2:34

VIRGINIA (continued)
Virginia Genealogist vol 24, repr 1980, bk rev APR 14:4:3 HPF 14:52:1
Virginia Genealogist vol 25, repr 1981, bk rev APR 14:4:3 HPF 14:52:1
Virginia Genealogist vol 26, repr 1982, bk rev APR 14:11:4 FCM 8:2:140
Virginia Genealogist vol 27, repr 1983, bk rev APR 14:11:5 FCM 8:2:140
War of 1812 bounty land & pension appl by Wardell, bk rev WPG 22:1:42
Warren Co, marr rec 1836-1853 by Good/Hackett, bk rev CHG 28:1:32
Washington Co & Southwest, hist by Summers, bk rev VAG 39:2:153
Washington Co, cem rec, misc cem HPF 14:52:26
Washington Co, deed bk 1 c1797 HPF 95:50:10
Washington Co, marr permissions c1890 HPF 14:52:16
Washington Co, marr rec (implied), 19th cent, roster HPF 14:52:18
Washington Co, marr rec 1855-1861 HPF 14:52:14
Washington Co, marr rec 1859-1861 HPF 95:50:20
Washington Co, permissions to marry c1900 HPF 95:50:22
Washington Co, survey bk 1 c1782-1783 HPF 14:52:12 95:50:16
Washington Co, tithables 1797 HPF 95:50:18
Western frontier defense financial rec 1785-1800 VA 33:4:253
Westward Movement hist by Fischer/Kelly, bk rev REG 92:4:413
Women, legal status hist VA 33:2:79
York Co, Burwell residents of King's Creek, hist by John, bk rev TVF 4:2:121

VIRGINIA (continued)
York Co, marr bonds & minister's returns 1769-1853 by Pollock, bk rev VAG 39:2:155
York River area settler hist, bk rev TJ 7:3:109
York River area settler hist by Evans, bk rev TVF 4:3:192

VOELCKER, Eugene fl866, TX, will KTP 2:4:44

VOLKNER, Thorothea see Peter Philip BAKER

VOLLBRECHT, Louis P b1853, w Bertha Luckenbach, GR, TX, fam hist KTP 3:4:45

VONHERFF, Ferdinand b1820, w Mathilde Klingelhoeffer, GR, TX, biog sketch KTP 6:2:31

VONRACKNITZ, Johann b1791, AU, TX, biog sketch AGS 36:3:103

VONWEDEL, Selma see Otto GOERLITZ

VORDEMWALD, Johannes fl817, w Anna Wagler, PA, OH, IA, biog & geneal MFH 14:1:12

VOSBURGH, Abraham Pieterse, NY, MA, fam hist by Stoesser, bk rev NYR 126:4:284

VOSS, Carl Johann Christian Friedrich b1827, GR, IL, fam rec BGS 27:2:38

VOSS, Pearl see Chrisa TRUMMEL

WADE, Lydia Clementine see Frank Dora WILLARD

WAGENKNECHT, Marie Regina Margaretta see Carl HIRDLER

WAGGONER, John b1751, w Margaret Bonnet, w Susannah Richards, PA, VA, geneal by Waggoner, bk rev APR 14:12:3 GH 49:6:211 RCR 10:4:2376 SGS 45:1:36 WMG 12:1:46 WPG 22:1:43

WAGLER, Anna see Johannes VORDEMWALD

WAGNER, Conrad bc1833, RU, fam hist by Baselt, bk rev CCS 16:4:138
Johann Peter fl710, NY, biog by Dixon, bk rev NYR 126:3:214

WAGNER (continued)
Levi m1839, w Mary Davis, KS, Bible rec TS 37:4:129
Peter P b1782, w Catarina Loucks, NY, fam rec TS 37:4:129
RU, GR, NY, fam hist by Baselt, bk rev GH 49:5:236 NYR 126:2:154

WAHRENBERGER, John b1862, TX, obit MCG 18:1/2:70

WAIBEL, Rahel see Martin KERN

WAILES, Benjamin d1719, MD, fam hist MD 36:2:145

WAIT, Emmeline see John THOMAS

WAITE, Marvin E see Jennie YUILL

WAKEFIELD, John see Mary BROWN

WAKEMAN, Lyons see Sarah Rosetta WAKEMAN
Sarah Rosetta (Lyons) d1864, NY, biog sketch CHG 27:2:53

WALDECK, Philipp fl776, GR, diary abstr TPI 21:1:36
Philipp fl776, GR, diary by Burgoyne, bk rev MGS 13:4:61 SGS 45:1:36

WALDESIAN GENEALOGY, NC, Valdese, settler geneal 1893-1900 by HCWPC, bk rev NCJ 21:1:68
NC, Valdese, Waldesian Pres Ch hist 1893-1993 by WPCHC, bk rev NCJ 21:1:68

WALDING, Emma Salilla see James McCager CASEY

WALDREP, George Washington b1848, w Clothida Goodman, w Martha Ann Elender Dillard, VA, GA, fam hist by Waldrep/Mahon, bk rev GGS 31:1:49

WALDRON, John Charles fl942, CA, fam hist corr VCG 95:DEC:3
Joseph fl654, NL, NY, anc NYR 126:1:12 126:2:113 126:3:185
Pamelia M see William PLUMER
Resolved fl654, NL, NY, anc NYR 126:1:12 126:2:113 126:3:185

WALKER, Abraham fl805, MS, will abstr SEN 1:3:19
Ben fl900, Dept of Interior testimony trans SEN 3:2:35

WALKER (continued)
  Dougal fl790, w Mary, ST, PA, fam hist by Walker, bk rev GH 49:4:228
  Ela see Frank JACKSON
  Joel Pickens b1797, KS, VA, biog & fam hist KCG 36:2:61 36:2:67
  Joseph fl790, w Susan Willis, KS, geneal & fam hist KCG 36:2:61
  Joseph R fl820, KS, biog sketch KCG 36:2:67
  Margaret Ann see Alexander HINDMAN
  Martha Frost fl995, TX, fam rec PWN 3:2:6
  Mary see Dougal WALKER
  Sarah fl807, MS, will abstr SEN 1:3:20
  Tandy fc1801, VA, KY, biog SEN 1:2:6
  William, WV, fam cem rec FWC 9:4:287
WALLACE, Elizabeth d1841, SC, estate rec ODD 7:1:32
  George fl970, AL, biog by Lesher, bk rev REG 93:3:384
  M D fl918, TX, WW1 commendation letter THT 23:2:68
  Samuel b1795, desc of by Wallace, bk rev NTT 14:3:82
  Ellen J see Samuel D SHAFFER
WALSH, James m1869, w Catherine Brinan, NS, Bible rec GN 13:3:131
WALTNER, Barbara see John DAGUE
WALTON, John William b1885, w Onie Ritch, FL, biog sketch IMP 14:2:59
WANNEMACHER, C C fl930, OH, corresp TFP 95:12:84
WAR OF 1812, Geneal res guide by Schweitzer, bk rev TTC 21:1:7
  Hist by McAfee, bk rev TPI 20:2:95
  Hist, repr 1816, bk rev GH 49:6:182
  MI, Frenchtown battle, hist by Clift, bk rev HQ 95:58:89
  Niagara campaign, soldier memoirs by Hanks et al, bk rev NYR 126:4:281
  Pension rec, lost files, list & res tips cont AMG 10:4:7

WARD, --- see Annie Louise ALLEN
  Doris Cline fl995, NC, autobiog sketch IFL 6:1:11
  Grace see Joe BALISON
  Huldah see Valentine Rowell PREVATT
  John S b1825, w Anna E Hyer, VT, CA, biog sketch RCP 17:4:138
  KY, fam hist by Wink, bk rev WCK 28:3:34
  N J see O T LOGAN
WARE, Philip fl816, w Mary Strickland, GA, geneal CCM 15:1:5
WARING, Anna see Edmund WARING
  Edmund b1724, w Anna, EN, PA, fam hist by Waring, bk rev WPG 21:3:49
  Laura A see James H KEELING
WARNER, Frances Eugenia see Leander W TURNER
WARTHEN, Albert fl885, OH, legal notice TLL 20:3:56
WASHBURN, Thomas see Mary BROWN
WASHINGTON, Bellingham, public lib geneal collect guide, bk rev TB 22:1:12
  Benton Co, obits c1970s-1990s TRI 35:1:21 35:2:47
  Benton Co, settler biog sketches TRI 35:1:15
  Benton Co, war reg 1917 TRI 35:1:5
  Blaine, hist 1884-1959 by WGS, bk rev TB 22:1:13
  Cashmere, cem rec 1990 cont AB 23:1:24 23:3:23 23:4:23
  Census rec, State Archives res aid EWA 32:4:175
  Chelan Co, Fraternal Cem inscr 1903-1992 by Bradley et al, bk rev GH 49:5:224 TB 21:3:11
  Chelan Co, wills & probates c1908 cont AB 23:1:17
  Clark Co, marr 1920 vol 10 by Matthies et al, bk rev TB 22:1:12
  Clark Co, marr cert of pioneer fam 1864-1912 by Zimmerman, bk rev TB 22:1:13

WASHINGTON (continued)
Clark Co, WW2 deaths, roster TB 21:3:6
Clark Co, WW2 mil deaths, news abstr TB 22:1:6
CN, NW exploration expedition roster 1859 TRI 35:1:20
Colville, cem rec by NWGS, bk rev TB 21:3:10
Colville, census 1860 abstr PB 11:2:30
Colville, high sch grads 1924 PB 10:3:62
Colville, homesteaders 1912 PB 10:2:35
Colville, Marcus cem news abstr PB 10:3:72
Colville, news abstr from the *Examiner* 1917 PB 11:1:11
Douglas Co, teacher roster from news 1925 AB 23:4:10
Elizabeth see John CHAMP
Ellensburgh Localizer abstr 1890 YV 27:1:25 27:4:116
Ferry Co, birth & death rec 1899-1911, bk rev TB 21:3:11
Ferry Co, marr returns index 1900-1932 by NWGS, bk rev TB 21:3:11
Franklin Co facts TRI 35:2:37
George b1732, w Martha, VA, formative years, hist DAR 129:2:144
Jane see William Augustine WASHINGTON
Kennewick, births from the *Courier Reporter* 1921 TRI 35:2:38
King Co, sch census 1901 SGS 45:1:47
Kittitas Co, sch rec, dist 13, 1901 YV 27:4:119
Kittitas Indians, hist sketch YV 27:1:6
Martha f1757, VA, papers by Fields, bk rev REG 93:4:476
Martha see George WASHINGTON
Olympia Co, war vet biog data OG 21:1:19
Oroville, geneal misc 1911 abstr from news BTG 1:2:1
Pacific Fur Company employee roster 1813-1814 TRI 35:2:52

WASHINGTON (continued)
Pen pal list from lonely hearts club 1936 PB 11:2:37
Pend Oreille Co, marr rec 1889-1890 PB 10:4:89
Pierce Co, marks & brands 1886 RES 26:3:127
Pierce Co, probate abstr c1867 cont RES 26:3:131
Pierce Co, probates c1870 RES 27:1:19
Pierce Co, will bk 3 c1880 cont RES 27:1:4
Pierce Co, will bk 3 c1895 cont RES 26:3:152
Pierce Co, WW1 draft numbers, news abstr 1917 RES 26:3:135
Pioneer Assoc members before 1889, roster SGS 45:1:5
San Juan Co, will bk by WGS, bk rev TB 22:1:14
Seattle, census index bk location guide EWA 32:3:111
Skagit Co, census 1885, bk rev TB 22:1:14
Spokane Co, co courthouse res guide EWA 32:2:59
Spokane Co, marr lic to 1903 cont EWA 32:1:15 32:2:69 32:3:139 32:4:191
Spokane, news abstr c1880 EWA 32:3:126
Spokane, news abstr from misc news 1880 EWA 32:1:12
Spokane, news abstr from the *Times* 1881 EWA 32:4:168
Stevens Co, cem rec by NWGS, bk rev TB 21:3:11
Stevens Co, marr rec 1868-1889 EWA 32:3:114
Stevens Co, Polk city direct 1913-1914 cont PB 11:2:31
Stevens Co, post ofc locations (past) PB 10:2:43
Stevens Co, post ofcs & postmasters, roster PB 10:3:67
Stevens Co, R L Polk & Co direct 1913-1914 PB 11:1:13

WASHINGTON (continued)
Stevens Co, road tax list for dist #2 1886 PB 10:3:59 10:4:85
Stevens Co, teacher roster 1907 PB 11:1:9
Tacoma, *Daily Ledger* news abstr c1886 RES 26:3:148 27:1:12
Tacoma, Pacific Meat Company butchers 1893 RES 26:3:155
Tacoma, suffragette hist 1905-1920 RES 27:1:16
Tacoma, WW1 draft numbers, news abstr 1917 RES 26:3:135
Teachers & their districts, roster 1880s-1890s PB 10:4:87
Thurston Co, natu rec index 1850-1974 OG 21:1:15 21:4:100
Thurston Co, war vet biog data OG 21:1:19 21:4:105
U S Army 9th Division roster 1855-1857 cont YV 27:1:17
Union Gap, Emma Street hist sketch YV 27:1:12
Vancouver Register news abstr 1868 cont TB 21:3:22
Vancouver Register abstr 1969 cont TB 22:1:22
Vancouver, Knapp Mortuary Rec 1942 TB 21:3:16 22:1:16
Vancouver, Vancouver High Sch class of 1949 reunion roster, bk rev TB 21:3:14
Wahiakum Co, census rec 1854-1892 by Huerd, bk rev GH 49:3:217
Walla Walla & Ft Benton, mil road workers roster 1859-1862, TRI 35:2:45
Wallula hist TRI 35:2:35
Wenatchee, City Cem 1993 update AB 23:1:21 23:3:18 23:4:20
Whatcom Co, auditor's census 1871, 1885, & 1887, bk rev TB 22:1:14
Whatcom Co, cem rec series 2 vol 1 by WGS, bk rev TB 22:1:12
Whatcom Co, cem rec to 1974 by Christenson, bk rev TB 22:1:12
Whatcom Co, census 1860, 1870 & 1880, bk rev TB 22:1:12

WASHINGTON (continued)
Whatcom Co, census 1889, bk rev TB 22:1:12
Whatcom Co, census 1910, bk rev TB 22:1:14
Whatcom Co, census index 1910, bk rev TB 22:1:14
Whatcom Co, hist, repr 1926, bk rev TB 22:1:14
Whatcom Co, marr rec 1898-1902, bk rev TB 22:1:13
White Bluffs, pioneer hist sketch TRI 35:1:18
Whitman Co, marr rec c1890 WCG 11:9/10:64 11:11:72
Whitman Co, marr rec c1891 WCG 12:1:5 12:3:22
Whitman Co, placenames hist WCG 11:3:22 11:4:31 11:5:37
Whitman Co, probate rec c1891 WCG 12:3:23
Whitman Co, probate rec c1892 WCG 11:6:46
Whitman Co, probate rec c1894 WCG 11:3:23 11:5:39
Whitman Co, probate rec c1895 WCG 11:7/8:56 11:9/10:66
Whitman Co, probate rec c1896 WCG 11:11:74
Whitman Co, probate rec c1896 cont WCG 12:1:7
Whitman Co, vet & widow census rec 1890 WCG 11:4:28 11:5:38 11:6:44 11:7/8:53
Wiley City, Carson ranch hist YV 27:4:102
William Augustine b1757, w Jane w Martha Lee, w Sarah Tayloe, VA, geneal TVF 4:3:181
WSU, Holland Lib res tips EWA 32:1:3
Yakima Valley, Janeck Drug Store acct bk c1894 YV 27:1:15 27:4:106
Yakima Valley, League of Women Voters hist YV 27:4:98
Yakima Valley, Viola Avenue name origins YV 27:4:99

WASHINGTON DC, Cedar Hill, Frederick Douglass Lib bibl by Petrie, bk rev PGB 26:6:123
Census index 1850, CD-ROM rev APR 14:6:4
Census index 1860, CD-ROM rev APR 14:6:4
First landowners, hist & roster HQ 95:55:67
Marr lic reg 1811-1858 by Pippenger, bk rev GH 49:5:191 TVF 4:1:54
WASTLER, Henry see Heinrich WORSCHLER
WATERBURY, Samuel m1817, w Hariette Knapp, CT, Bible rec CTA 37:4:178
WATERMAN, Mary Ann Olin see William PHILLIPS
WATERS, Henry FitzGilbert b1833, New England, anc NEH 12:1:22
Mattie E see Emil C WEHRFRITZ
Nancy Mariah see John Quincy Adams BONEY
WATKINS, Charlotte M see Hiram GOFF
Letha Ann see Alonzo RHODES
WATSON, Abigail see Joshua WATSON
Fanny f1816, SC, pet to state govt ODD 7:4:26
Joshua m1847, w Abigail, NH, Bible rec SCR 18:4:59
Lou Evans f1874, AR, hour abstr FGC 95:28:6
Mary Rutland see Richard B WATTS
WATTS, Mary see Henry MCCARTNEY
Richard B m1810, w Elizabeth Rawlins, w Mary Rutland Watson, MD, geneal MD 36:1:31
WAUGH, James f1858, CN, EN, desertion doc FAM 34:3:173
WAYLAND, Lewis bc1772, w Elizabeth Link, VA, fam hist BYG 7:6:414
WAYMAN, Harmon b1750, VA, pension appl BYG 7:3:389

WEATHERFORD, Charles b1834, autobiog corresp SEN 3:2:26
WEATHERHEAD, John f1887, w Julia, TX, biog sketch KTP 5:4:54
Julia see John WEATHERHEAD
WEAVER, Elias d1805, w Hanna Clore, biog add BYG 8:1:425
George d1897, OH, obit TLL 20:2:36
Robert f1759, SC, muster roll ODD 7:2:28
WEBB, David, OH, fam hist TFP 95:12:15
John bc1754, w Elizabeth Montgomery, OH, fam hist by Fetters, bk rev FRT 16:2:64
Meredith E bc1803, w Charlotte Brown, w Rebecca Snyder, w Caroline McDonald, w Ellen Tamm, NC, TX, geneal PWN 2:1:2
Rachel see Amos MCCURRY
TX, fam hist timeline PWN 2:1:7
WEBBER, Deborah see Andrew WESCOTT
WEBER, Frances f1918, PA, recoll JBC 16:1:10
WEBSTER, Dozier Braswell b1894, GA, fam hist by Farmer, bk rev NGS 83:3:218
Elizabeth Kinloch m1897, h John Smith, ST, TX, fam hist sketch KTP 7:1:14
Frances Lillian see Lafayette Irving FISH
Lydia see John (Samuel) EMERSON
WEED, Abigall see Silvanus KNAPP
WEEKS, Thomas T m1817, w Mary Hoag, OH, biog TFP 95:12:1
WEHRFRITZ, Emil C m1900, w Mattie E Waters, AR, surname rec SYH 2:3:20
WEIKART, James S b1849, w Margaret Ellen Roher, OH, Bibl rec MM 19:6:78
WEILAND, John b1889, HG, fam hist RM 95:10:6
WEINKAUF, Dayle Taylor f1940, FL, recoll PCQ 20:4:1

WEISEL, Charlotte see Lewis Salmon LYON

WELLMAN, EN, fam hist by Hansen, bk rev GH 49:3:218

WELLS, Richard b1777, PA, biog sketch HQ 95:55:18

Rufus b1766, w Prudence Newton, MA, NY, CN, OH, estate rec TR 35:4:215

Thomas, w Frances Albright, CT, geneal corr & add by Deane, bk rev HQ 95:57:84

WELLWOOD, Alicia see Gordon Arthur RUDD

WELSH GENEALOGY, Anc origin res guide by Camp, bk rev FAM 34:3:181

Beginner's geneal res guide by Lloyd, bk rev FRT 16:3:99

Coats of arms guide by Lewis, bk rev GR 37:4:4 RAG 16:3:18 TSC 6:3:5

Congregationalists, hist & res guide by Clifford, bk rev RT 13:1:16

General Reg Ofc index of one-name lists in Lib of Soc of Geneal, bk rev QFH 16:4:140

Naming conventions, guide UG 24:1:5

Pedigrees & geneal vol 3 & 4, repr 1895-1896, bk rev GR 37:4:5

Powys, feudal barons hist & geneal, repr 1868, bk rev CI 31:2:68 GH 49:6:179 TSC 6:2:6

Res guide by Baxter, bk rev APG 10:4:128 ARH 33:1:34 GFP 44:3:139

Res trip planning guide by Lloyd, bk rev GSC 17:4:5 HQ 95:58:87

Visitation of EN & Wales vol 1-4, repr, bk rev SGS 45:1:29

WENDLAND, Elizabeth see George WENDLAND

George fc1890, w Elizabeth, CN, fam hist by Collins, bk rev GEN 20:1:19

WENDLER, Henry August Theodor b1828, w Pauline A Luckenbach, GR, TX, fam hist KTP 4:1:9

Henry b1828, GR, TX, obit KTP 6:4:58

WENGER, Christian b1727, w Eve Greibil, SW, FR, PA, fam hist sketch MFH 15:1:38

Hans b1705, GR, PA, fam hist sketch MFH 15:1:38

WENNER, Fam hist by Miller, bk rev TPI 21:1:47

WENTZ, Louisa see Jonathan WERNER

WERNER, Adam b1800, w Anna Catherine Sass, GR, PA, geneal LM 36:3:222

Fam hist by Palmer, bk rev KCG 36:1:50

Jonathan m1850, w Louisa Wentz, IN, geneal by Stephenson, bk rev FRT 16:3:110

Josiah C see Lydia STAHL,

WESCOTT, Andrew bc1700, w Deborah Webber, ME, fam hist AG 70:4:209

WESSELY, Elenora see George August ZOELLER

WEST, Aaron fl832, w Susannah Kellogg, CT, pension rec HQ 95:60:16

Claiborne see Florinda MCCULLOCH

WEST VIRGINIA, Absentee landowning & exploitation 1760-1920, hist by Rasmussen, bk rev REG 93:4:490

Baileysville Dist, census 1910 index cont FWC 9:3:247

Barbour Co, deaths 1853-1919 by Coffman, bk rev APR 14:2:4 CCK 13:2:13 JCG 23:2:56 OK 40:2:45 SGS 44:3:140

Barbour Co, wills 1839-1889 by Coffman, bk rev APR 14:2:4 CCK 13:2:13 JCG 23:2:56 OK 40:2:45 SGS 44:3:140

Beaver Run Ch cem rec NFB 27:3:41

Berkeley Co, deed bk 3 c1774 cont FCM 7:4:223 8:2:103

Biog data 1607-1870 by Wardell, bk rev OC 29:3:130

Boone Co, Kith & Kin periodical vol 20 by BCGS, bk rev GH 49:5:225

WEST VIRGINIA (continued)
- Capon Valley, pioneer geneal 1698-1940, repr 1946, bk rev GH 49:6:206 GJB 20:2:32 SQ 6:3:54 WPG 22:2:51
- Census 1870, CD-ROM rev TEN 95:16:22
- Census index 1850, CD-ROM rev APR 14:6:4
- Census index 1860, CD-ROM rev APR 14:6:4
- Civil War soldiers residing in WI 1895, roster MTN 1:1:3
- Civil War, Union medals, how to make a claim, res tips PCH 1:4:1
- Cumberland Presbyterian Ch, geneal abstr by Eddlemon, bk rev APR 14:6:4
- Doddridge Co, cem rec vol 3 by Ramage, bk rev GH 49:5:225
- Estate settlements to 1850, index by GPC, bk rev SEE 36:153:22
- Gazetteer, repr 1904, bk rev GH 49:4:221
- Geneal, hist, & preservation soc address list MTN 1:1:4
- Grant Co, census 1910 by Ross, bk rev GH 49:5:225
- Grant Dist, geneal of early fam, repr 1933, bk rev GH 49:5:225
- Greenbrier Co, land entry bk 1780-1786 by Stinson, bk rev MGS 13:1:12
- Hampshire Co, deed bk 2 c1768 FCM 7:4:233
- Hampshire Co, marr 1800s by Horton, bk rev APR 14:1:3
- Hampshire Co, misc rec 1816-1923 by Horton, bk rev WPG 22:1:46
- Hampston Co, deed bk 2 cont FCM 8:2:93
- Harrison Co, deed rec 1785-1810 by Davis, bk rev CHG 28:1:32 VQ 94:10:26

WEST VIRGINIA (continued)
- Husbands & wives vol 1 by Wardell, bk rev CCS 17:1:26 CN 4:2:30 DM 59:1:46 GRC 11:2:28 IMP 14:2:62 RCR 10:2:2277 SGS 44:3:140 TFT 6:2:23B WCK 28:3:33 WMG 11:3:140
- Keyrock, Stewart Cem rec FWC 9:3:264
- Kopperston cem rec FWC 9:3:267
- Land grants c1760-1880, repr 1952, bk rev STS 35:4:20
- Lewis Co, marr bonds & rec 1816-1865 by Smith, bk rev RAG 16:2:27
- Marr vol 1 by Wardell, bk rev GSM 12:2:48
- Monongahela Valley, geneal hist, repr 1912, bk rev GH 49:4:222
- Monongalia Co, court rec 1805-1808 by Zinn, bk rev KA 30:3:177
- Monongalia Co, court rec 1808-1814 by Zinn, bk rev GH 49:5:225 TRC 10:2:74
- Monongalia Co, deeds 1784-1810 by Toothman, bk rev CHG 28:1:35 GH 49:3:217 GSM 12:2:46 PR 22:3:6 WPG 21:3:45
- Monongalia Co, dist, superior & co court rec 1802-1805 by Zinn, bk rev GR 37:1:49 SKC 11:1:5
- Monongalia Co, dist, superior & co court rec 1808-1814 by Zinn, bk rev GJ 23:4:190
- Oceana, cem rec FWC 9:3:267
- Oceana Dist, census 1900 cont FWC 9:3:245 9:4:285
- Oceana, pioneers & builders, hist sketches cont FWC 9:3:242 9:4:290
- Oceana, William Walker Cem inscr FWC 9:4:287
- Pendleton Co, deeds 1788-1813 by Toothman, bk rev FCM 8:2:139
- Pleasant Dist, geneal of early fam, repr 1933, bk rev GH 49:5:225
- Preston Co, geneal of early fam, repr 1933, bk rev GH 49:5:225

WEST VIRGINIA (continued)
Raleigh Co, First United Meth Ch hist 1850-1892 by Wolfe, bk rev TJ 7:2:75
Raleigh Co, hist by Wood, bk rev GH 49:5:226
Regional maps MTN 1:1:18
Rev War pension & bounty land warrant rec abstr vol 4 (Nabors to Rymer) by Wardell, bk rev GJB 20:1:14 GSM 12:2:48 HPF 95:50:1 MGS 13:1:6 SGS 44:3:141
Rockcastle Bapt Ch minutes abstr 1858 cont FWC 9:3:249
Swan Pond, geneal hist by Lowe, bk rev FRT 16:3:112
Upshur Co, death rec 1853-1928 by Hawkins, bk rev SQ 5:4:43
Upshur Co, surname res direct by UCHS, bk rev TR 35:4:218
Webster Co, heritage & hist by WHB, bk rev APR 14:11:5
Wyoming Co, census 1910, index by Cook, bk rev HQ 95:58:89
Wyoming Co, Rev War soldier desc in co FWC 9:4:303
Wyoming Co, Rockcastle Bapt Ch minutes abstr 1858, FWC 9:4:297

WESTMORELAND, EN, fam hist by Mapes, bk rev TPI 21:1:37
James fl652, VA, fam hist by Mapes, bk rev SGS 45:1:36
Thomas fc1650, EN, fam hist by Mapes, bk rev RDQ 12:4A:92

WETHERBEE, John, MA, fam hist by Mazza, bk rev SCR 18:3:52

WETZEL, Hans Martin bc1700, GR, PA, fam hist by Wagoner, bk rev RCR 10:4:2376
John fl747, w Mary Bonnet, HO, SW, PA, repr 1931, bk rev GH 49:6:211
Lewis b1763, KY, PA, WV, OH, biog & fam hist by Allman, bk rev GH 49:6:211 GJB 20:2:32 SGS 45:1:36
Lewis b1763, KY, PA, WV, OH, biog & hist by Lobdell, bk rev AW 22:1:7 GH 49:6:211 GJB 19:3:70 NCJ 21:3:298 QU 12:2:21

WETZEL (continued)
Martin fl747, w --- Bertolet, HO, SW, PA, repr 1931, bk rev GH 49:6:211

WETZLER, Johannes b1750, w Elisabeth Muller, PA, geneal by Hunavy, bk rev WPG 21:3:46

WEYHER, Fam hist supp by Weyher, bk rev GGS 31:2:119

WHATLEY, Robert b1774, w Polley Martin, TX, Bible rec REF 37:2:37

WHEAT, Orvie A fl910, IL, corresp GL 29:4:134
William Buck fl880, w Rebecca, AR, census rec SYH 2:3:17

WHEATCRAFT, Lydia see Josiah GRIMES

WHEATON, Melville b1798, VT, biog sketch BAT 24:2:69

WHEELER, Joseph fl863, w Daniella Jones, AL, hist of home OLR 9:3:111
Joshua m1795, w Sarah Brown, KY, geneal by Wheeler, bk rev GH 49:5:236
Joshua mc1820, w Sarah Vanbebber, KY, IL, geneal by Wheeler, bk rev IGS 27:2:116
Sarah Elizabeth fl907, FL, biog PCQ 10:4:3
TX, fam hist timeline PWN 2:1:7

WHIDDEN, Henry Pasco fl924, FL, biog PCQ 14:4:4
Nancy see William MCCULLOUGH

WHIPPLE, Esther see Asaph PHILLIPS

WHITAKER, Mark bc1670, MD, w Katherine Teag, fam hist by Whitaker-Buck, bk rev DM 59:1:45 MD 36:1:88

WHITE, Daniel bc1845, TN, biog ETR 7:4:171
Elizabeth see William LACKEY
George Avery b1820, w Mary Ann Brown, CN, Bible rec GEN 20:4:17
Isaac bc1775, DE, TN, biog add BWG 24:2:135
Joel m1861, w Lucinda J Rundell, MI, Bible rec FHC 19:1:9

WHITE (continued)
John Edmunda b1834, NY, IL, biog sketch SD 14:1:10
Mahala see Gabriel BELL
Mary see John CAMPBELL
R B b1858, w Susan Bradshaw, w Emma Elizabeth Butler, GA, obit AFH 16:4:11
WHITEHEAD, Isaac see Elizabeth MARTIN
WHITHALL, Frank see Annie GORDON
WHITING, Sarah see Thomas INGERSOLL
WHITNEY, Eli b1765, New England anc NEH 12:4:116
Theodore Roosevelt b1902, w Estelle Davidson, NC, fam hist by Whitney, bk rev EWA 32:4:177 GFP 44:4:191 GH 49:4:228 NCJ 21:4:424
WHITSETT, Henry S fl1874, TN, court doc MTG 8:4:154
William A fl1874, TN, court doc MTG 8:4:154
WHITTAKER, Ruth b1805, h William Villars, NJ, OH, IL, biog & fam hist IG 31:2:49
WHITTEN, John d1830, LA, news abstr FPG 17:3:17
WHITTICK, Jacob fl1842, NJ, biog sketch MCQ 4:1:10
WHITTON, James b1790, w Mary Altman, GA, FL, fam hist PCQ 12:4:4
Thomas Jefferson, w Eudora Virginia Harris, VA, SC, Bible rec ODD 7:4:19
WHITWORTH, Alfred J fl1899, TX, jour KTP 11:4:53
Robert Walton b1830, w Rosa Doherty, EN, TN, IA, biog & recoll KTP 12:1:7 12:2:23 12:3:41 12:4:56 13:1:10
Robert Walton b1830, w Rosa Doherty, EN, TN, IA, fam rec KTP 4:2:29

WHITWORTH (continued)
Robert Walton m1851, w Frances Elizabeth Nickols, EN, TX, biog sketch KTP 6:2:23
Rosa see Robert Walton WHITWORTH
WIDRA, Wenzl, w Johanna Tuma, CZ, geneal by Wangerow, bk rev MI 41:1:2
WIEDENFELD, Theo b1828, w Magdalena Saur, GR, TX, obit KTP 9:2:31
WILCOX, Charles Wesley b1854, w Josephine Esther Henney, IL, MO, Bible rec OZ 17:3:103
Joanna see Martin SIMMONS
Stephen bc1634, w Alice Brownell, RI, identity of wife RIR 21:4:99
WILCOXSON, Horatio m1817, w Cataharine Amelia Williams, MO, Bible rec MSG 15:3:158
WILDER, Fam hist supp by Kuechmann, bk rev TB 22:1:14
WILDS, Nathaniel bc1750, w Cathern Elmore, EN, FL, fam hist TNC 2:2:31
WILHOIT, Abraham b1791, w Martha Ann (Patsy) Mosby, w Francis Powell Mosby, VA, geneal BYG 8:1:425
WILKERSON, W B fl1866, SC, corresp ODD 7:2:10
WILKINS, Daniel b1875, w Rebecca Barnes, WV, OH, biog sketch TLL 20:3:62
Sarah Hortense see Jessie Paul CAPPS
WILKS, Annie fl1935, AA, biog sketch TGO 8:1:24
WILLARD, Elva B b1892, TX, Bible rec KTP 8:3:43
Frank Dora b1870, w Maggie Murphy, w Lydia Clementine Wade, w Rose Ersig Michaels, IL, biog CCS 17:1:20
WILLEMSZE, Maria see Engelbert HUFF

WILLIAMS, Braddock bc1800, w Sarah Deborah, AL, biog sketch & fam hist AGM 27:1/2:2
Catharine Amelia see Horatio WILCOXSON
Eunice Mather f1704, h John Williams, MA, CN, biog by Demos, bk rev ACG 21:1:21 SMN 13:5:80
Grayson Harmon f1990, NC, anc FYC 12:4:352
J B d1911, FL, obit FLG 18:2:46
John d1901, NC, estate abstr FYC 12:4:357
John see Eunice Mather WILLIAMS
Katherine see Abraham GOAD
Letha see Wiley Lee ROBERTS
Maria see Maria WILLEMSZE
Mary Ann see Benajah GRAY
Mary see Henry BURTON
Mavis Holt b1916, LA, fam hist TG 29:1:9
Sadie Mozelle see Charles Greene RODES
Sarah Deborah see Braddock WILLIAMS
Tennessee see Thomas Lanier WILLIAMS
Thomas J m1848, w Francis E Glimp, TN, Bible rec MTG 8:4:167
Thomas Lanier (Tennessee) b1911, MS, TN, anc addendum by Brayton, bk rev AG 70:1:57 AG 70:4:257 GGS 31:2:120 GH 49:5:236 MTG 9:2:70 NCJ 21:3:308 NER 149:596:437 SCM 23:2:119 TVF 4:2:123 VAG 39:1:76
TX, fam rec, PWN 3:1:7
William Carrol m1842, w Rachel Caroline Sloan, TN, Bible rec MTG 8:4:167
WILLIAMSON, Sarah Eveline see William HINNANT
WILLIS, Mary see Lewis BURWELL
WILLIS, Salina Susan see James Harvey EGNOR
WILLIS, Susan see Joseph WALKER
WILLMETTE, Archange Chevalier bc1838, MO, MI, biog sketch MHH 16:1:26
WILLS, Ivah see Charles COBURN
WILMOT, Emily see Harvey NASH
WILSON, Adeline Hendry b1832, h James Thomas Wilson, GA, FL, biog PCQ 11:1:4
AR, probate rec 1916 SYH 3:2:17
David f1881, OH, corresp TLL 20:3:54
Eva m1906, h George Mitchell, FL, wedding hist sketch PCQ 5:1:7
James f1850, NH, fam hist by Heffernan/Stecker, bk rev HNH 49:4:266
James Thomas see Adeline Hendry WILSON
Jerome Robinson see Tillie O BYERS
Milton D b1886, w Daphne Valerie Lewis, FL, biog PCQ 9:4:7
Nancy Eugene see Benjamin MOODY
PA, fam hist by Miller, bk rev WPG 22:2:56
ST, fam hist by Schnegelberger, bk rev FRT 16:3:109
Woodrow b1856, biog by Axson, bk rev REG 92:4:429
WILTROUT, Susanna see Moses GNAGEY
WINKLES, James Thomas b1894, w Georgia Lizzie Camp, GA, fam rec CCM 15:1:16
WINKLEY, John b1795, w Susan Otis, NH, biog sketch SCR 18:6:91
WINKLEY, Samuel bc1666, w Sarah Trickey, w Hannah Adams, w Elizabeth Hunking Fernald, EN, NH, geneal NHR 12:2:49 12:3:107 12:4:164
WINLAND, Albert H m1891, w Martha E Yount, IL, Bible rec IG 31:2:47
WINNER, Fam hist by Miller, bk rev TPI 21:1:47
WINSLOW, Joseph, w Sarah Laurence, NC, fam hist by Herzfeld, bk rev TJ 7:2:77

WINSTON, George fl817, VA, biog sketch TVF 4:2:92
WIRTH, Henrich fl670, GR, PA, geneal by Wert, bk rev TPI 21:1:47
WISCONSIN, Arkansaw, St Joseph's Cath Ch cem rec WI 41:3:169
Blanchardville, Calvary cem rec WI 41:4:219
Civil War hist sketch MCR 26:1:13
Civil War reg muster & descriptive rolls, hist WI 41:4:191
Columbia Co, Otsego cem rec cont WI 41:3:139
Columbia Co, physician direct 1886 WI 41:3:142
Crawford Co, Rising Sun/St James Cath cem rec WI 41:3:143
Dane Co, Springdale Luth Ch cem rec cont WI 41:3:147 41:4:211
Dane Co, Windsor Congregational cem rec WI 42:1:9
Douglas Co, res resource direct MN 26:4:160
Douglas Co, Woodlawn cem rec cont WI 41:3:149 41:4:213
Draper Mss Collect, res guide KTP 8:3:37
Fond du Lac Co, Gudex cem rec WI 41:3:154
Fond du Lac Co, Mitchell cem rec WI 41:3:153
Fond du Lac Co, St James Mission Ch cem rec cont WI 41:3:153
Fox River Valley, biog hist of misc co, repr 1895, bk rev GH 49:6:206 MGR 30:3:69
Ft Winnebago, surgeon's quarters hist MCR 27:1:63
Grant Co, grand & petit juror roster 1859 WI 41:4:218
Grant Co, St Lawrence O'Toole Cath cem rec cont WI 41:3:155 41:4:217
Green Bay, deaths 1888-1889 WI 41:4:210
Green Co, Greenwood cem rec cont WI 41:3:157
Iowa Co, Arena High Sch alumni direct cont WI 41:3:159

WISCONSIN (continued)
Iowa Co, mil Gold Star list 1925 WI 41:3:160
Lafayette Co, Belmont Village cem rec cont WI 41:3:161
Lafayette Co, Cottage Inn cem rec WI 41:4:220
Lafayette Co, Lancaster cem rec WI 42:1:17
Lafayette Co, Mudbranch Sch souvenir 1897-1898 WI 42:1:18
Lafayette Co, Threadgold-Sowl cem rec WI 42:1:18
Lake Geneva, Christmas events from news abstr 1855 & 1860 MCR 26:4:115
Lancaster, letters at post ofc 1859 WI 41:4:218
Langlade Co, Bohemian cem rec WI 42:1:21
Langlade Co, Keaton/Adkins cem rec WI 42:2:73
Langlade Co, St Joseph's Cath cem rec WI 42:2:59
Langlade Co, St Mary Cath cem rec WI 42:2:73
Langlade Co, St Wencel's Cath cem rec WI 42:1:19
Lincoln Co, Chat Community cem rec cont WI 41:3:163
Lincoln Co, Greenwood cem rec WI 42:1:23 42:2:63
Lincoln Co, Our Saviour's Scandinavian Cem rec WI 41:3:164
Lincoln Co, Schneider cem rec WI 41:3:164
Marathon Co, deeds from misc bk 1850-1878 cont WI 41:4:221
Marathon Co, deeds from misc bk 1850-1878, name index WI 41:3:167
Mil Order of the Loyal Legion of the US member reg 1886 MCR 26:1:9
Milwaukee Co, cem burials by Herzfeld, bk rev MGR 30:3:67
Milwaukee Co, mil Gold Star list cont WI 41:3:165
Milwaukee, accident certs 1905-1907 MCR 27:1:47

WISCONSIN (continued)
Milwaukee, Christmas news abstr 1893 MCR 26:4:118
Milwaukee, city health chronology 1834-1848 MCR 27:1:45
Milwaukee, early news hist & abstr MCR 26:1:16
Milwaukee, pensioner roster from the *Sentinel* 1887 MCR 27:1:61
Milwaukee, *Sentinel* news abstr 1838 MCR 26:1:16
Milwaukee, St Hedwig's interment rec 1888-1900 MCR 27:1:54
Milwaukee, Wood National Cem hist MCR 27:1:61
Muster rolls 1866-1885, abbreviations used, list MCR 26:1:14
News abstr from the *Allis Star* 1926 MCR 26:4:121
News index to the *Northern Badger* WI 41:4:217
News index to the *Wisconsin Whig* newspapers WI 41:4:217
News index to the *Wiskonsan Standard* WI 41:4:217
Oconomowoc, news on microfilm, list MCR 26:1:20
Pulaski, incorporation census 1910 cont WI 41:3:137 41:4:209
Racine, city direct 1858 cont WI 41:3:173 41:4:225
Rock Co, Newark cem rec WI 41:3:175
Rusk Co, Holy Trinity cem rec WI 41:3:177
Sauk Co, Black Hawk Village cem rec WI 42:2:73
State Hist Soc Lib collect, res guide CC 17:3:25
Superior, letters at post ofc 1857 WI 41:4:216
US General Land Ofc surveyors' field notes, res guide WI 41:4:193
Vernon Co, Sugar Grove cem rec WI 41:4:229
Waukesha Co, first land grants cont WI 41:3:179 41:4:233 42:1:33 42:2:79

WISCONSIN (continued)
Waukesha Co, physician direct 1886 WI 41:3:180
Waukesha, news abstr from the *Freedman* 1882 MCR 26:4:117
Waushara Co, Brushville cem rec WI 42:2:87
Waushara Co, Grace Evang Luth cem rec WI 42:2:89
Waushara Co, Pine River cem rec WI 41:3:181 41:4:239
Wauwatosa, Civil War Vol roster 1861-1865 MCR 26:1:21
WI, Meth Epis Ch list of appointments 1882 WI 41:3:133
Winnebago Co, Civil War vets (I-T) by Langkau, bk rev GH 49:4:222 SGS 44:2:84
WISE, John B b1837, w M S Price, AR, Bible rec SCH 10:3:90
Marie Norris f1995, LA, anc by Wise, bk rev GH 49:5:234
WISEMAN, James Riley m1867, w Julia Ann Gumm, MO, OR, fam hist sketch SNS 11:1:3
WISLER, Barbara see Peter STAUFFER
WISWELL, EN, MA, ME, fam trivia scrapbk by Wiser, bk rev WPG 21:3:50
WITT, Caroline Rebecca see George BECK
WIUSLER, Barbara see Peter STAUFFER
WOIROL, EN, fam hist by Hansen, bk rev GH 49:3:218
WOLCOTT, Benajah f1796, NY, OH, biog TFP 95:12:29
WOLF, Daniel b1732, w Elizabeth, PA, MD, geneal by Wolf, bk rev MD 36:4:681 NGS 83:4:303
Elizabeth see Daniel WOLF
Fred C f1904, OH, news abstr re:his court case MM 19:2:20
WOLFE, Peter, MA, geneal TEG 15:4:227
Thomas b1900, NC, anc LOB 17:1:19

WOLLSCHLEAGER, Richard d1908, TX, obit abstr KTP 9:3:47

WOLVEN, Sarah see Jonas VALCK

WOLVERTON, Berton m1882, w Lillian Brown, TX, Bible rec GR 37:1:29

WOOD, Clark bc1837, PA, fam hist VCG 95:DEC:21
  Frank, w Ida Ouellet, NY, geneal by Nichols, bk rev ACG 21:1:23
  Martha see Henry JOHNSON
  Susan Glover fl865, TN, biog sketch HPF 95:50:37
  Thomas fl800, SC, deed ODD 7:1:25
  William A fl905, AZ, fam hist sketch SUN 16:4:87

WOODBURY, Helen A see Josiah D PULSIFER

WOODBY, Eppa bc1791, w Mary, TN, NC, fam rec FYC 12:4:368
  Mary see Eppa WOODBY

WOODCOCK, John fl647, MA, geneal by JLW, bk rev TB 21:3:12

WOODHAM, Edward, w Mary, SC, geneal by Richey, bk rev ODD 7:4:37
  Mary see Edward WOODHAM

WOODMAN, John fl663, w Hannah Timberlake, RI, fam hist by Woodman, bk rev TJ 7:1:39

WOODRUFF, Icy Callahan see Thomas R FREE

WOODSON, Carter G fl916, IL, MA, biog by Goggin, bk rev REG 93:2:234

WOODWARD, William bc1774, NC, fam hist sketch LOB 16:4:89

WOOLAM, Absalom fc1805, TX, geneal PWN 2:2:5
  WOOLAM, John C see Missouri M LOCKWOOD

WOOLFOLK, Nancy Ann see Thomas DICKINSON

WOOLSEY, Amos bc1783, w Phoebe Briggs, w Eunice Sayles, NY, biog sketch UG 24:1:12

WORK, TN, KY, fam hist vol 2 by Hamilton, bk rev GH 49:3:222

WORKMAN, Delitha see Thomas COLLINGS
  Fam hist by Terry, bk rev TB 21:3:14
  Margaret see Andrew MCELVAIN

WORLD HISTORY, Columbus ships, pass rosters 1492 OC 29:3:91
  First Americans, origins, hist by Dixon REG 92:4:446
  Food, early plants & gardens, hist PR 22:4:41
  FR migration to North Am, hist 1600-1900 by Houde, bk rev ACG 21:1:23
  Inventions of the 20th cent, list BT 27:2:34
  North Am continent settlement hist by Morgan, bk rev REG 92:4:446
  Passports & travel, hist TGO 8:1:20
  Ship hist TGO 8:1:14
  Situla art, hist ASO 25:1:25
  Viking hist TFG 8:1:3
  Wars prior to 1900, list MCI 13:2:32
  Women's hist, chronology by Olsen, bk rev REG 93:3:381

WORLD WAR II, AR, KS, MO, OK, casualties under Gen Pershing, roster CN 4:4:58
  Battle of the Bulge, hist by Blunt, bk rev REG 93:2:242
  D-Day hist & soldier autobiog by Drez, bk rev REG 92:4:433
  Holocaust, hist by Wolfe, bk rev REG 93:2:254
  Japanese invasion plans & atomic bomb, hist by Skates, bk rev REG 92:4:435
  Malmedy Massacre hist by Bauserman, bk rev RAG 16:2:28
  Manuiwa B-29, hist of her crew FP 38:3:115

WORLEY, Caleb bc1730, VA, KY, geneal AG 70:2:75

WORSCHLER, Heinrich fl752, w Maria Catherina Schaffer, GR, PA, geneal by Wiley, bk rev KCG 36:1:48

WORTENDYKE, Cornelius R b1812, w Ann Berdan, OH, TX, Bible rec KTP 4:1:8

WORTHAM, Gus f1911, UT, TX, biog by Dressman, bk rev STS 35:2:72

WORTHERSPOON, Mary Ruth f1994, autobiog re:her search for her biological parents, bk rev GSC 18:1:7

WORTHINGTON, Saunders bc1800, SC, GA, biog NGS 83:2:96

WRIGHT, Barbara Ann see W T WRIGHT

Catherine see Sebastian HOUPT

Elizabeth B see John W CARTER

Lyman b1796, TX, biog sketch STS 35:4:31

Sarah see Meredith LOONEY

W T d1935, AR, obit SYH 3:3:13

William Francis f1882, EN, NY, TX, biog sketch KTP 6:3:36

Winnie see Meredith LOONEY

WRIGLEY, Elizabeth f1914, RI, recoll LWF 15:2:92

WYLIE, Herbert Eugene b1873, w Emma Hyde, MI, jour abstr, bk rev MI 41:4:123 STS 35:2:66

Herbert Eugene b1873, w Emma Hyde, MI, marr her performed, edited by Wylie, bk rev GH 49:3:211

WYNKOOP, Adaline see John HATTON

WYNN, Leroy see Thelma Pearl TOMPKINS

WYSONG, Fam hist by Liggett, bk rev TOP 25:1:4

YAND, Melchior f1736, BA, PA, fam hist by Yonce, bk rev KCG 36:1:48

YEISLEY, James Walter, geneal by Jones, bk rev TJ 7:1:37

YODER, Catherine see Samuel L PLANK

Stephen see Susan KEIM

YORK, Charity see Robert POWELL

Matilda see James DEALY

YOTT, Madeline see Narcisse JUNEAU

YOUNG, Baltzer b1760, w Mary Elizabeth Buss, OH, geneal by Fetters, bk rev TPI 20:4:192 TR 35:4:223

YOUNG (continued)
GA, reunion news abstr 1909 CCM 14:3:17

James B d1862, AL, Bible rec NTT 14:4:149

Mary see Robert YOUNG

Robert bc1720, w mary, VA, biog HPF 14:52:22

Walter m1920, w Jeannia Desrosiers, MA, fam hist sketch ACG 21:2:62

YOUNGLOVE, Samuel mc1632, w Margaret Legatt, EN, New England, geneal by Butler/Younglove, bk rev GH 49:6:211

YOUNT, Martha E see Albert H WINLAND

YTURRALDE, Carlos M f1995, CA, anc sketch TFT 6:2:17B

YUILL, Jennie b1847, h Marvin E Waite, h Robb McIntyre, CN, recoll OBN 28:1:29

YUNCKER, GR, Am, fam hist by Yuncker, bk rev TPI 21:1:46

ZEHR, John f1841, w Catherine Bachman, OH, fam hist MFH 15:1:15

Michael b1762, w Barbara Bachmann, FR, geneal MFH 15:1:4

Michael f1841, w Elisabeth Ramseyer, OH, IN, fam hist MFH 15:1:15

ZELLER, Grace Irene see Harold Alvin GOFF

ZENNARO, Domenico bc1787, w Marguerite Drapeau, IY, CN, fam hist sketch ACG 21:4:166

ZIEGENFUSS, Freidrich Wilhelm b1845, w Emilie Marx, GR, PA, geneal by Warter, bk rev WPG 21:3:49

ZIMMERMAN, Daniel J m1845, w Scharlotte Snyder, MD, Bible rec WMG 12:1:29

Fam hist by Baty, bk rev GH 49:4:227

Jacob b1801, w Barbara Stull, MD, Bible rec WMG 11:2:87

Johann Jacob f1709, GR, NY, fam hist by Martin, bk rev NYR 126:3:216

ZIMMERMAN (continued)
  John Nicholas b1832, w Julia A S Measell, MD, Bible rec WMG 11:2:87
  Joshua John m1838, w Susan Margarett Beard, MD, Bible rec WMG 11:2:87
  Mary L see Isaac EDGAR
  Solomon Joseph b1822, w Catherine Elizabeth Shellman, MD, Bible rec WMG 11:1:39
ZINK, Matilda see Alfred CLARKE
ZOELLER, George August b1861, w Elenora Wessely, TX, obit KTP 8:4:59
  George d1908, TX, obit KTP 8:3:44

SURNAME PERIODICAL DIRECTORY

The periodicals in this directory are arranged alphabetically in order of the main surnames covered.

Adams Addenda, Adams Addenda Association, 229 S Ridgeland, Oak Park, IL, 60302-3225

Addington Newsletter, Jerry Sue Bowersox, 12407 Millstream Dr, Bowie, MD, 20715

Alger Anchorage, P. C. Alger, 14 Lesley Cir, Derry, NH, 03038

Allen Family Circle, 4906 Ridgeway, Kansas City, MO, 64133

Alton-Allton-Aulton Association Family Newsletter, Cecil C. Alton, 15510 Laurel Ridge Rd, Dumfries, VA, 22026

Appler Family Newsletter, Charles Ross Appler, 10417 New Bedford Ct SE, Lehigh Acres, FL, 33936

Bachiler & Batchelder Buttons, Mary Jane Sanborn Lewis, P O Box 676, Balboa, CA, 92661-0676

Barwick Branches, Laura Tully, P O Box 69, Grandin, FL, 32138

Baxter Family Chronicle, 120 W Boardwalk Place, Park Ridge, IL, 60068

Bear Family Newsletter, Beth Klingensmith, 3765 Windmill Ct, Colorado Springs, CO, 80907

Berry Bulletin, 1232 Carlotta Ave, Berkeley, CA, 94707

Bickford Newsletter, Mahlon Bickford, 27 Aberdeen Ave, Cambridge, MA, 02138

Forge, Bigelow Society Quarterly, P O Box 4115, Flint, MI, 48504

Blackburn Beginnings, Blackburn Family Association, 449 Garfield St, Denver, CO, 80206

Blauvelt News, Association Of Blauvelt Descendants, 7 Maurice Ave, Ossining, NY, 10562

Compass, Boone Society Inc., 23 Nord Circle Rd, North Oaks, MI, 55127

Deanroad, R G Boyd, 12137 Highland Hills Box 539, Mt Morris, MI, 48458

Brake Bugle, Nancy C. Rowe Pope, 1492 Creek Crossing Trail, Wills Point, TX, 75169

Brotherton Family Ties, Brotherton Hunters, 2727 E 53rd Ave #H207, Spokane, WA, 99223

Bryson-Clayton-Synders Family Association Newsletter, P O Box 128, Bethune, SC, 29009

Buck Surname Booklet, Paula P. Mortensen, 363 South Park Victoria Drive, Milpitas, CA, 95035

Burrill News, Burrell/Burrill Family Association, P O Box 31402, Seattle, WA, 98103

Journal Of The Clan Campbell, Clan Campbell Society, P O Box 49398, Denver, CO, 80204

Families: The Casady Newsletter, Imagery Studios, Highway 16 East, Grand Meadow, MN, 55936

Chamberlain Chain, Carolyn Wilson Weidner, 2206 W Borden Rd, Spokane, WA, 99224

Chase Newsletter, 289 Beech Hill Rd, Rockport, ME, 04856

Jacob's Ladder, Christlieb-Chrislip Family Association, 693 Ridge Rd, Queensbury, NY, 12804

Crabb Newsletter, Richard D. Prall, 14104 Piedras Rd Ne, Albuquerque, NM, 87123

Crane Flock, Crane Family Newsletter, 21 Poinsettia Dr, Fort Myers, FL, 33905

Crowl Connections, Gail Komar, 9603 Bel Glade St, Fairfax, VA, 22031

Daniel Family Newsletter, Wayne W. Daniel, 2943 Appling Dr, Chamblee, GA, 30341

Darling Family Of America, Pat Darling, P O Box 32192, Mountain Village, AK, 99632
Daub Digest, Daub Family Reunion, 230 Swatara Cir, Jonestown, PA, 17038
J W Dawes Family Newsletter, Ardath Dawes, 259 East Avenue, Greenville, PA, 16125
Downey Diggins, 5892 Karen Ave, Cypress, CA, 90630
Durkee Family Newsletter, Society Of Genealogists Of Durkee Inc., 3753 E 15th St, Long Beach, CA, 90804
Edsonian, Edson Genealogical Association, 724 S Whitmer St, Richmond, MO, 64085
Eller Chronicles, Eller Association, 500 W Mission St, Crowley, TX, 76036
Elwood Echoes, Beverly Przybylski, 3315 Ford Dr, Medford, OR, 97504
Fifield Flyer, Peter Fifield Wells, P O Box 152, Rindge, NH, 03461
Finley Findings International, Timothy John Kessler, P O Box 314, Wynne, AR, 72396
Frederick Forerunners, Jean Nathan, 3803 Macnicholas Ave, Cincinnati, OH, 45236
Garrett Folklore & Fact, Cathy Wood Osborn, 803 South Buckeye, Abilene, KS, 67410
Garrison Gazette, Edwanna G. Chenault, 5567 Ecton Rd, Winchester, KY, 40391
Geer Family Association Newsletter, Russell Geer, 947 Exeter Road, Lebanon, CT, 06249
Goodwin News, Goodwin Family Organization Newsletter, 39 Lost Trail Rd, Roswell, NM, 88201
Graves Family Newsletter, Graves Family Association, 261 South St, Wrentham, MA, 02093
Hambrook Herald, Boolongie Rd, Mail Service 827, Bundaberg, Queensland, Australia, 4670

Connector, Hamilton National Genealogical Society, 215 SW 20th Terr, Oak Grove, MO, 64075
Hanks Historical Review, P O Box 191, Monroe, OH, 45050
Harris Hunters, P O Box 539, Mt Morris, MI, 48458
Havens Harbor, Jo Ann Havens Wright, 610 North Delaware Ave, Roswell, NM, 88201
Henry Herald, Ancestors In The Attic, 2555 NE 47th St, Lincoln City, OR, 97367
Henson Connection, Ethel Nerim Miner, 14570 N Lost Arrow, Tucson, AZ, 85737
High Family Journal, P O Box 5841, Columbia, SC, 29250
Hinman Heritage, Joan A. Hinman, P O Box 304, Delanson, NY, 12053
Honaker Family Newsletter, P O Box 3636, Alexandria, VA, 22302
Howes Family Association, Nancy S. Howes, P O Box 904, Dennis, MA, 02638
Johnsons & Johnstons Of Alabama, Anita L. McCray, 5821 Satchelford Rd, Columbia, SC, 29206
Kessler Family Newsletter, 3837 Gateway Terr, Burtonsville, MD, 20866
Kinsey/Coskrey Update, Cathy Wood Osborne, 803 South Buckeye, Abilene, KS, 67410
Knight Letter, Don Knight, 811 Longmeadow Dr, Schaumberg, IL, 60193
Kuhn Kuzns, Beverly Przybylski, 3315 Ford Dr, Medford, OR, 97504
Lambert Family Association Newsletter, Randy D. Lambert, P O Box 64007, Sunnyvale, CA, 94088
John Libby Family Association, Libby Homestead Corporation, P O Box 11365, Portland, ME, 04104
Llewellyn Traces, 781 McCarthy Blvd, Pueblo, CO, 81005

Locke Family Association, Donald Hayes, 102 Crooked Spring Rd, Chelmsford, MA, 01863

Luther Family Association, 2531 Lakeview St, Lakeland, FL, 33801

Mason Family Newsletter, Paula P. Mortensen, 363 South Park Victoria Dr, Milpitas, CA, 95035

Communicator, Belva Maybee Perry, 10020 23rd Dr Se, Everett, WA, 98208

Clan Mccullough/McCulloch Newsletter, Betty K. Summers, P O Box 271759, Fort Collins, CO, 80527

MacFaddien News, N J McFaddin Sr., Rr1 Box 28, Sardinia, SC, 29143

Milestones, Miles Merwin Family Association, 1733 Blue Bell Rd, Blue Bell, PA, 19422

Mills Musings, Beverly Przybylski, 3315 Ford Dr, Medford, OR, 97504 or 1730 NE 17th St #2, Lincoln City, OR, 97367-3715

Milton-Melton Pot, Nancy Pratt Melton, 6809 Thunderhead Cir, Orangevale, CA, 95662

Historical Journal Of The More Family, Eric More Marshall, 9831 Sidehill Rd, North East, PA, 16428-4713

Morgan Migrations, Priscilla Kingston, 7315 Colts Neck Rd, Mechanicsville, VA, 23111

Morton Heritage, Janet Margolis Damm, Palouse Publications, 310 SE Camino, Pullman, WA, 99163-2206

Sans Tache, Brig. Gen. John H. Napier III, Kilmahew, Rt 2, Box 614, Ramer, AL, 36069-9245

Nye Family Newsletter, P O Box 134, East Sandwich, MA, 02537

Overholser Family Newsletter, Barbara B. Ford, 313 Henry Lane, Wallingford, PA, 19086

Owsley Family Historical Society, Ronny O. Bodine, 916 Northridge Dr, Columbus, GA, 31904

Parke Society Newsletter, J. Douglas Park, 404 Kenway Dr, Lansing, MI, 48917-3039

Pearce Family Association, Donna Opat, 410 S Chesnut St, Lindsborg, KS, 67456

Perkins Family Newsletter, Paula P. Mortensen, 363 South Park Victoria Drive, Milpitas, CA, 95035

Phelps Family News, Dallas L. Phelps, 1002 Queen St, Camden, SC, 29020

Pilgrims' Progress, Robert F. Huber, 327 Overhill Dr, Lexington, VA, 24450

Polley Pointers, 9146 Winding Way, Ellicott City, MD, 21043

Pollock Potpourri, Lineage Search Associates, 7315 Colts Neck Rd, Mechanicsville, VA, 23111

Prall Newsletter, Richard D. Prall, 14104 Piedras Road NE, Albuquerque, NM, 87123

Radford Ramblings, 5892 Karen Ave, Cypress, CA, 90630

Ransom Researcher, Michael Ransom, P O Box 1754, Albany, OR, 97321

Rawlin(Gs)-Rollin(G)S, Family History Association, 4918 Kenneth Ave, Carmichael, CA, 95608

Rebbecks Reassembled, Rebbeck Worldwide One Name Study Association, P O Box 874, Kenwood, CA, 95452

Kinfolk, Rich Family Association, P O Box 142, Wellfleet, MA, 02667

Rose Family Bulletin, Rose Family Association, 1474 Montelegre Dr, San Jose, CA, 95120

Samuel Searcher, 7805 Linda Lane, Anchorage, AK, 99518

Sanders Siftings, Don E. Schaefer, 1297 Deane St, Fayetteville, AR, 72703-1544

Seeley Genealogical Society, George R. Seeley, 1442 Thousand Acre Rd, Dalanson, NY, 12053

Shackelford Quarterly, Laura Tully, P O Box 69, Grandin, FL, 32138

Shelby Exchange, Judith Trolinger, Hunt Star Rt Box 234, Ingram, TX, 78025
Shively Newsletter, Larry W. Shively, P O Box 25385, Shawnee Mission, KS, 66225
Skinner Kinsmen Update, Gregg Legutki, P O Box 2594, Rancho Cucamonga, CA, 91729
Smithson Family Exchange Newsletter, Addie Dyal Rickey, 235 15th St NE, Salem, OR, 97301-4228
Sparks Quarterly, 155 North Hite Ave, Louisville, KY, 40206
Squires Newsletter, Stanley C. Squires, Rr1 Box 427 Hwy 89, Danbury, NC, 27016
Stanford Sagas, Rod Bush, 5892 Karen Ave, Cypress, CA, 90630
Streeter National Newsletter, Ruth A. Streeter, 512 Stoneridge Dr, East Wenatchee, WA, 98802
Studebaker Family, 6555 S. State Route 202, Tipp City, OH, 45371
Stumme Family Newsletter, 259 Scotts Manor Dr, Glen Burnie, MD, 21061
Tackett Family Journal, James W. Tackitt, 1830 Johnson Dr, Concord, CA, 94520
Taft Talk, Taft Family Association, 175 High St, Uxbridge, MA, 01569
Teeple People, Anne Rahamut, 66 Lawrence Ave East, Toronto, Ontario, Canada, M4N 1S4
Timmons Family Newsletter, Bunnie T. Runman, Box 262, Montrose, MN, 55363
Tolle Family Exchange, Thoren Tolle Meyers, 10351 16th St, Garden Grove, CA, 92843
Tompkins Times, Robert H. Tompkins, 319 Avenue C Suite 2C, New York, NY, 10009
About Towne, 472 Winona Blvd, Rochester, NY, 14617-3437
Vawter-Vauter-Vaughters Newsletter, Bonita Welch, 4145 N 900 W, Scipio, IN, 47273

Venable Letter, Darrell Mcgraw, P O Box 211, Hixson, TN, 37343
Viers-Veirs Family Newsletter, 8720 Petersburg Rd, Evansville, IN, 47711
Whitworth Quarterly, Suzann Peters, HQ USAREUR, CMR 420, Box 502, APO AE 09063
Wolvertons Unlimited, Glenn Gohr, 1040 E Mccanse St, Springfield, MO, 65803
Woodwards Wesearch, Linda W. Geiger, 718 Big Canoe, Jasper, GA, 30143
Wren Kin Newsletter, Ruth Wren, 5809 Tautoga, El Paso, TX, 79924
Yoder Newsletter, P O Box 594, Goshen, IN, 46527
Born Young Newsletter, Vicki Young Albu, 347 12th Ave North, S St Paul, MN, 55075-1957